Ninth Edition

D0148038

CURRICULUM LEADERSHIP

Readings for Developing Quality Educational Programs

Forrest W. Parkay

Washington State University

Eric J. Anctil

University of Portland

Glen Hass

Late, University of Florida

Allyn & Bacon

Boston   New York   San Francisco

Mexico City   Montreal   Toronto   London   Madrid   Munich   Paris

Hong Kong   Singapore   Tokyo   Cape Town   Sydney

Executive Editor and Publisher: Stephen D. Dragin
Series Editorial Assistant: Anne Whittaker
Marketing Manager: Amanda Stedke
Production Editor: Cynthia Parsons
Editorial Production Service: Omegatype Typography, Inc.
Composition Buyer: Linda Cox
Manufacturing Buyer: Megan Cochran
Electronic Composition: Omegatype Typography, Inc.
Interior Design: Omegatype Typography, Inc.
Cover Designer: Elena Sidorova

For related titles and support materials, visit our online catalog at www.pearsonhighered.com.

Between the time website information is gathered and then published, it is not unusual for some sites to have closed. Also, the transcription of URLs can result in typographical errors. The publisher would appreciate notification where these errors occur so that they may be corrected in subsequent editions.

Library of Congress Cataloging-in-Publication Data

Curriculum leadership : readings for developing quality educational programs / [edited by] Forrest W. Parkay, Eric J. Anctil, Glen Hass.— 9th ed.

     p. cm.
  Rev. ed. of: Curriculum planning : a contemporary approach. c2006.
  Includes bibliographical references and index.
  ISBN-13: 978-0-13-715838-6 (pbk.)
  ISBN-10: 0-13-715838-6 (pbk.)
 1. Curriculum planning—United States. 2. Educational leadership—United States. I. Parkay, Forrest W. II. Anctil, Eric J. III. Hass, Glen. IV. Curriculum planning.
  LB2806.15.C6954 2010
  375'.001—dc22

                                2008047848

Printed in the United States of America

Credits appear on pp. 571–574, which constitute an extension of the copyright page.

10 9 8 7 6 5 4 3 2 1   13 12 11 10 09

Allyn & Bacon
is an imprint of

www.pearsonhighered.com

ISBN-10: 0-13-715838-6
ISBN-13: 978-0-13-715838-6

Contents

iii

3 Human Development   127

4 Learning and Learning Styles   189

PART TWO   Developing, Implementing, and Evaluating the Curriculum   249

5   Approaches to Curriculum Development   249

6 Curriculum Implementation, Instruction, and Technology 310

7 Curriculum Evaluation and Assessment of Learning 357

PART THREE The Curriculum in Action 413

Preface

The ninth edition of *Curriculum Leadership: Readings for Developing Quality Educational Programs* (formerly titled *Curriculum Planning: A Contemporary Approach*) presents the knowledge, skills, and understandings needed by curriculum leaders in pre-K through high school settings. This edition of *Curriculum Leadership* has been completely revised and updated; 35 of the 71 articles in the book are new, with most published during the last three years. The book includes a broad spectrum of articles—from historical perspectives on curriculum leadership to contemporary analyses of trends and issues to first-person accounts of curriculum leadership and implementation.

In today's climate of professional accountability, high-stakes testing, and legislation such as No Child Left Behind, providing curriculum leadership is a complex, challenging process. This edition has been thoroughly revised to give readers a realistic picture of curriculum leadership and enhance their continuing professional development. Articles have been carefully selected for insights into the real-world challenges of curriculum leadership and practical solutions to meet those challenges.

Among the features designed to meet the needs of students with wide-ranging interests, learning styles, and leadership experiences, each chapter includes a *Leaders' Voices—Putting Theory into Practice* section that presents an article authored by a curriculum leader. In addition, each chapter in Part III includes a *Case Study in Curriculum Implementation* section that presents a practitioner-authored article illustrating the complexities of providing leadership for curriculum development and implementation at the institutional or systemwide level.

To facilitate instruction and help students study effectively, *Curriculum Leadership* includes focus questions at the beginning of each chapter, abstracts and reflection questions for each article, and end-of-chapter critical thinking questions, application activities, field experiences, and Internet activities. In addition, "Curriculum Leadership Strategies" are included in each chapter to give superintendents, principals, and teacher leaders concrete, practical tips for curriculum leadership.

Part I, "Bases for Curriculum Leadership," examines goals and values and the three bases of the curriculum (social forces, human development, and learning and learning styles). Part II, "Developing and Implementing the Curriculum," has been thoroughly revised and includes two new chapters: Chapter 6, "Curriculum Implementation, Instruction, and Technology," and Chapter 7, "Curriculum Evaluation and Assessment of Learning." Part III, "The Curriculum in Action," emphasizes curriculum leadership at the pre-K, elementary, middle, and high school levels. At each level, current trends, innovations, and issues are examined from both theoretical and practical viewpoints.

The key role of educational philosophy in curriculum leadership is highlighted in the first chapter. Seminal articles by key figures representing each of the four philosophical orientations that had a major influence on curriculum leadership during the twentieth century are presented. These sharply contrasting statements bring contemporary trends and issues into clearer focus, and they highlight how each position will continue to be relevant for curriculum leadership in the future.

Throughout the book, the interrelationships among past, present, and future perspectives on curriculum leadership are stressed. Several articles in this edition address the importance of future planning. Topics covered include curriculum leadership for the future and integrating technology into the curriculum. Other topics that receive increased coverage in this edition are accountability and high-stakes testing, media literacy, inclusion, No Child Left Behind, multicultural education, diversity, curriculum standards, assessment of learning, multiple intelligences, learning styles, commercialism in the schools, and critical perspectives on curriculum leadership.

Curriculum Leadership is designed for upper-level and graduate students in educational leadership, curriculum and instruction, teacher education, foundations of education, and higher education programs. The key principles and concepts discussed throughout apply to educational programs at all levels and, for each chapter, special attention has been paid to identifying commonalities that apply to curriculum leadership in diverse educational settings.

Many members of the Pearson Education team provided expert guidance and support during the preparation of the ninth edition of *Curriculum Leadership*. Clearly, Steve Dragin, executive editor and publisher, and Anne Whittaker, editorial assistant, head this list. From suggestions for revision, feedback on draft manuscripts, and skillful coordination of the revision process, from beginning to end, their hard work is deeply appreciated.

The authors also extend a very special thanks to Paul A. Smith, vice president and editor-in-chief.

Acknowledgment is given to the many authors who have contributed to this book. Their willingness to republish their ideas reflects their dedication to the continuous improvement of curriculum as a field of study. We also wish to thank the following reviewers who provided concise, helpful suggestions for this edition: John Decman, University of Houston, Clear Lake; Kathi H. Gibson, Fayetteville State University; and Donald E. Larsen, Western Washington University.

Forrest W. Parkay gives a sincere thanks to students in his Basic Principles of Curriculum Design classes at Washington State University. Their insightful comments and suggestions have enriched this edition of the book. In addition, Judy N. Mitchell, Dean of the College of Education at Washington State University; Len Foster, Associate Dean; Phyllis Erdman, Chair of the Department of Educational Leadership and Counseling Psychology; and the faculty, teaching assistants, and research assistants in the Department of Educational Leadership and Counseling Psychology gave him much-appreciated encouragement and support. Gail Furman, Professor of Educational Leadership, and Paul Pitre, Assistant Professor of Educational Leadership, also provided invaluable ideas and much-appreciated encouragement and support.

For their patience, encouragement, and understanding while their dad has worked on revisions of this book since the sixth edition in 1993, Forrest W. Parkay gives warm thanks and a hug to each of his wonderful daughters: Anna, Catherine, and Rebecca.

Lastly, he wishes to acknowledge his considerable debt to Glen Hass, who authored the first edition of this book, then titled *Curriculum Planning: A New Approach,* and over the years developed a solid conceptual framework for examining the complexities of curriculum leadership. He was an impressive curriculum scholar, an inspirational mentor, a valued colleague, and a good friend—it is to his memory that this and future editions of *Curriculum Leadership* are dedicated.

Eric J. Anctil would like to thank his partner, Tina, for her patience during the revision process and Jack and Benjamin, his sons, for helping to keep his priorities in order.

F.W.P.
E.J.A.

1

Goals and Values

The ninth edition of *Curriculum Leadership: Readings for Developing Quality Educational Programs* (formerly titled *Curriculum Planning: A Contemporary Approach*) contains the knowledge and resources you will need to provide leadership for developing quality educational programs. Whether you are a superintendent, principal, teacher leader, supervisor, or curriculum coordinator in a K–12 setting, you will make many curriculum-related decisions that will influence student learning. To provide all learners—from those with diverse cultural and linguistic backgrounds and with their variety of needs, abilities, learning styles, and prior educational experiences—meaningful and growth-promoting curricular experiences is not easy. This book is designed to increase your knowledge and skills related to curriculum leadership. In addition, the book emphasizes the critical role that teachers can and should play in curriculum leadership. As Richard Ackerman and Sarah V. Mackenzie point out in "Uncovering Teacher Leadership" in this chapter, "teacher leadership offers a variety of unseen opportunities for forcing schools out of established frames of reference and toward genuine school improvement."

While this book raises many questions about curriculum leadership, its purpose is not to settle these questions, but to help you understand the processes involved in curriculum leadership. For example, if higher standards is currently the public's dominant demand for education (see Kim Marshall's "A Principal Looks Back: Standards Matter" in Chapter 5), then curriculum leaders must raise questions like the following: What is excellence in education? For what purpose is it sought? How can it be achieved? How can it be measured? Which is more important—the pursuit or the achievement of excellence?

If excellence is a major curriculum goal, its attainment will depend primarily on decisions made by curriculum leaders and teachers—those who plan the curriculum. A goal of *Curriculum Leadership: Readings for Developing Quality Educational Programs,* then, is to enable you to be professionally accountable when you make those decisions. Accountability requires that your decisions be informed by an understanding of curriculum goals and values, the bases of the curriculum, and curriculum criteria. In addition, professional accountability requires the ability to apply the knowledge, methods, and skills developed by curriculum theorists, researchers, and practitioners. By studying the processes of curriculum leadership as perceived by the contributing authors of this book, you will continue to develop your own professional competencies.

To become competent in curriculum leadership, you must understand how social factors, stages of human development, and theories of learning and learning styles influence the curriculum. In addition, you must understand the importance of achieving a balance among these three elements as you provide curriculum leadership. At the beginning of this complex process, however, you should be able to answer the following question: What is meant by the term *curriculum*?

DEFINITIONS OF CURRICULUM

Educational practitioners, theorists, and researchers have used the term *curriculum* in various ways, with no definition universally accepted. Among the definitions currently used are the following:

1. A course of study; derived from the Latin *currere,* meaning to run a course
2. Course content, the information or knowledge that students are to learn
3. Planned learning experiences
4. Intended learning outcomes; the *results* of instruction as distinguished from the *means* (activities, materials, etc.) of instruction
5. All the experiences that students have while at school (Parkay & Stanford, 2007, p. 351)

Naturally, no one of these five is the "right" definition. Instead, how we define curriculum reflects our purposes and the educational setting within which we work.

Differences between Curriculum and Instruction

When the term *curriculum* is used to refer to planned learning experiences, it is clear that curriculum and instruction are interdependent, not separate and mutually exclusive. Experiences that are planned for learners, of course, include teachers' planning for instruction and the methods they actually use to teach the material. Thus, curriculum and instruction are part of the same process, a process that consists of planning experiences that lead to students' learning and growth.

While there is some warrant for saying that curriculum refers to the *what* of education and instruction the *how,* each has implications for the other. Chapter 6 is devoted to examining two key points regarding curriculum and instruction: (1) that *curriculum* and *curriculum planning* are partially defined by the *instruction* and *planning for instruction* that are essential elements of effective educational programs, and (2) that effective teachers engage in the full spectrum of curriculum and instruction—from planning the *what* of the curriculum to planning the *how* of instruction.

A Comprehensive Definition of *Curriculum*

None of the preceding views of curriculum are adequate in terms of the needs and trends that will characterize our lives in the future. Though mindful of the previous statement that there is no "right" definition of curriculum, we have found the following definition useful: *The curriculum is all of the educative experiences learners have in an educational program, the purpose of which is to achieve broad goals and related specific objectives that have been developed within a framework of theory and research, past and present professional practice, and the changing needs of society.*

In this definition, the term *educational program* has major significance. It means that the curriculum is a planned program developed by teachers and other professionals. This definition of *curriculum* also incorporates the following points:

1. The curriculum is preplanned. *Curriculum planning* involves gathering, sorting, synthesizing, and selecting relevant information from many sources. This information is then used to design experiences that enable learners to attain the goals of the curriculum.
2. The planned objectives of a curriculum are developed in light of theories and research on social forces, human development, and learning and learning styles.
3. Many decisions must be made while planning a curriculum, and these decisions should be made in light of specific, carefully thought-out criteria.
4. Planning for instruction is a major part of curriculum planning, because instruction often has a greater influence on learners than the preplanned curriculum, which may be partially, even totally, ignored by the teacher. This is as it should be, since the teacher usually has the greatest knowledge of learners and their needs. Nevertheless, when planning for instruction, the teacher, like the curriculum leader, should be guided by theories and research on social forces, human development, and learning and learning styles.
5. The curriculum that each learner comes to know is the result of experiences had while participating in learning opportunities provided by the teacher. Thus, each student plays an important role in determining the *experienced curriculum*.

BASES OF THE CURRICULUM

The three bases of curriculum leadership and planning provide a framework for the organization of much of this book. These bases—*social forces, theories of human development, and the nature of learning and learning styles*—are a major source of guidance for decision making in curriculum leadership and planning for instruction. The next three chapters in Part I are devoted to the study of these curriculum bases.

Social Forces

All civilized societies establish schools and programs of education to induct children and youth into the culture and to transmit the society's way of life. K–12 schools, higher education, and educational programs in nonschool settings operate in the midst of an ever-changing array of social forces and trends. Thus, one of the major areas to be considered in curriculum leadership must be social forces that interact around such factors as social goals, conceptions of culture, tensions between cultural uniformity and diversity, and other social pressures and changes, as well as the influences of futures planning.

Theories of Human Development

K–12 schools emerged in the United States before we knew much about human development and individual differences. However, knowledge of human development and related theories and research expanded significantly during the twentieth century, so that today a vast body of knowledge is available to guide the work of curriculum leaders. We understand, for example, that children are not small adults and that human beings are qualitatively different at the various age levels for which we must target curriculum planning and instruction. Therefore, knowledge of human development is an essential basis of the curriculum because it enables curriculum leaders to provide for age-related and individual differences among learners.

The Nature of Learning and Learning Styles

Knowledge about how human beings learn has also increased significantly during the last century. The complexities of learning and individual differences among learners led to the development of several theories of learning that have been tested and refined through carefully controlled research studies. Today's curriculum leaders are guided by many of these theories, some of which describe different kinds of learning. Other theories describe the "learning styles" that individuals prefer to use when they process information and seek meaning. Since there are many differences among learners, various learning theories can guide curriculum leaders as they address questions such as: How does each learner process information? How does he or she seek meaning? Answers to these questions can guide curriculum leaders as they develop alternative paths for learning that allow for differences in cognitive style.

Emphasizing Curriculum Bases

What degree of emphasis should be placed on each of the three curriculum bases—social forces, human development, and learning and learning styles—when planning the curriculum? While not easily answered, curriculum leaders and teachers should consider this question deliberately and thoughtfully. Therefore, Part I of this book is largely devoted to considering these factors.

   At different intervals during the past, some curriculum leaders placed major emphasis on one of the three bases to the exclusion of the others. Often, the emphasis preferred by a curriculum leader reflected that person's philosophical orientation to education or significant historical developments. Prior to the twentieth century, knowledge in the subject matter disciplines and level of schooling provided the primary foci for curriculum leadership. After 1900, however, theories and research in the new fields of child development, psychology, anthropology, sociology, and learning gave rise to an emphasis on each of these areas as the basis for curriculum planning and instruction. For contemporary curriculum leadership, however, a multidimensional approach must be used, and all three of the bases considered in the quest to improve curriculum and instruction.

CURRICULUM CRITERIA

In addition to the three essential bases of the curriculum, other criteria can guide curriculum leaders. A *criterion* is a standard on which a decision or judgment can be based; it is a basis for discriminating among elements in a complex field of endeavor. Curriculum criteria, then, are guidelines or standards for addressing the central question in the field of curriculum: What knowledge is of most worth? What to exclude from the curriculum is as difficult to determine as what to include.

The articles in Chapter 1 present varying perspectives on the criteria to be followed in answering this central question. In "Perspectives on Four Curriculum Traditions," for example, William H. Schubert suggests that four positions can characterize the approaches curriculum leaders use to answer this question: intellectual traditionalist, social behaviorist, experientialist, and critical reconstructionist.

The goals or purposes of a curriculum are among the most significant criteria for guiding the curriculum planning process. Other frequently suggested curriculum criteria include such values as diversity among learners, continuity, balance, flexibility, self-understanding, relevance to learners, and problem solving. Other leaders emphasize such processes as cooperative planning, student–teacher planning, or systematic planning based on international comparisons of achievement, standards developed by professional organizations, or values to be taught. The importance of these criteria can be derived from the three essential bases of the curriculum. For instance, an understanding of social forces, human development, and learning and learning styles will enhance your ability to develop curricula that allow for diversity among learners.

Similarly, an understanding of all three curriculum bases will help you develop a balanced curriculum. An understanding of social forces will help you provide for relevance and the teaching of values. Knowledge about human development will enable you to provide for continuity in learning and for the development of self-understanding. Lastly, knowledge of learning and learning styles will enable you to plan curricula with learning outcomes that learners find useful and transferable from one situation to another.

The many criteria to guide curriculum-related decision making should suggest the need to develop your own criteria to guide your planning. The ability to articulate how the three curriculum bases and additional curriculum criteria influence your curriculum planning activities should be one of your goals as you study *Curriculum Leadership: Readings for Developing Quality Educational Programs*.

CURRICULUM GOALS

While most people would agree that one goal of a curriculum should be to prepare students for the future, there is often little consensus about what knowledge and skills will be required in the future. Debate over this matter is not new, however; for example, Aristotle expressed the dilemma this way: "The existing practice [of curriculum development] is perplexing; no one knows on what principle we should proceed—should the useful in life, or should virtue, or should the higher knowledge, be the aim of our training; all three opinions have been entertained" (1941, p. 1306).

Curriculum goals provide general guidelines for determining the learning experiences to be included in the curriculum. Unfortunately, schools commonly lack a comprehensive, consistent set of goals on which to base curriculum decisions, and teachers often fail to use these goals to guide their planning for instruction. According to Jacques S. Benninga, Marvin W. Berkowitz, Phyllis Kuehn, and Karen Smith in "Character and Academics: What Good Schools Do," the first reading of this book, "well-conceived programs of character education can and should exist side-by-side with strong academic programs."

Without a set of clearly defined goals in view, curriculum leaders and teachers cannot make sound professional judgments. They cannot use their knowledge of the three curriculum bases to choose content, materials, or methods to facilitate students' learning. To choose among curriculum alternatives or instructional strategies, curriculum leaders must know the goals they seek and the curriculum bases on which they will make their choices. Otherwise, their choices will be little more than random, uninformed by today's knowledge of social forces, human development, and learning and learning styles.

Learners should also be clearly aware of the goals sought by their teachers. In fact, the teacher's instructional strategies should "invite" students to share in clarifying and, if appropriate, modifying the goals. As Glen Hass states in the article, "Who Should Plan the Curriculum?" in Chapter 5, the student is the "major untapped resource in curriculum planning." While the goals the teacher uses to guide planning and those sought by learners need not be identical, they should overlap. The teacher's and learners' goals for a learning experience must be compatible or they are not likely to be achieved. If students are to participate in curriculum planning, teachers must "trust . . . students' innate ability to make good decisions for themselves," as Linda Inlay points out in this chapter's *Leaders' Voices* section ("Values: The Implicit Curriculum").

Broad, general goals are needed to determine the related specific objectives of the curriculum. Once developed, these goals and objectives can be used to identify relevant courses, activities, and other educational experiences. While there is seldom total agreement about what the goals of a curriculum should be, it is useful to think of five broad, general curriculum goals: *citizenship, equal educational opportunity, vocation, self-realization,* and *critical thinking.* In addition, curriculum goals can be clustered into two broad areas, each of which should always be considered in curriculum planning: goals that relate to *society and its values* and goals that relate to the *individual learner's needs, interests, and abilities.*

VALUES IN CURRICULUM PLANNING

Values enter into every curriculum decision. From planning the curriculum to delivering it in the classroom, there is rarely a moment when teachers are not confronted with the influence of values in the choices they make. It is their answers (often covert) to questions such as "What is the good person?" "What is the good society?" "What is the good life?" that determine action. While teachers may not consciously pose these philosophical questions, all their curriculum thinking and work are value-based.

Four philosophical positions have had a major influence on curriculum leaders and teachers since the early twentieth century—*perennialism, essentialism, progressivism,* and *reconstructionism.* The struggle for influence among these philosophical positions remains visible today. Because of the significance of values in formulating curriculum goals and developing learning experiences, and in deciding how to evaluate learning, a statement of each philosophical position by an influential leader in curriculum planning is included in this chapter. Robert M. Hutchins ("The Organization and Subject-Matter of General Education") represents the perennialists, William C. Bagley ("The Case for Essentialism in Education") the essentialists, William Heard Kilpatrick ("The Case for Progressivism in Education") the progressivists, and William E. White, Richard van Scotter, Michael H. Haroonian, and James E. Davis ("Democracy at Risk") the reconstructionists.

That these four positions can lead to heated debate among curriculum leaders even today testifies to the continuing relevance of each position. Thus, today's curriculum leaders might be well advised to pay more attention to areas of agreement among the positions and less to areas of controversy. Toward this end, John Dewey ("Traditional vs. Progressive Education" in this chapter) cautions curriculum leaders against using "either-or" positions to guide their work. His *concept of experience,* for example, includes all the bases of the curriculum—the learner (human development and learning and learning styles) and the society (social forces).

CRITERION QUESTIONS—GOALS AND VALUES

As previously stated, curriculum criteria are guidelines or standards for curriculum decision making. Stating criteria in the form of *criterion questions* is a good way to bring the criteria into clear focus, and we shall use this method in Chapters 1 through 6 of this book. The criterion questions for this chapter on goals and values are as follows:

1. Are the goals of the curriculum clearly stated?
2. To the degree that students' developmental levels will allow, have teachers and students engaged in collaborative planning to define the goals and determine how they will be attained?
3. Do some of the planned goals relate to the society or the community within which the curriculum will be implemented?
4. Do some of the planned goals relate to individual learners and their needs, purposes, interests, and abilities?

5. Are the planned goals used as criteria for selecting and developing learning activities and instructional materials?
6. Are the planned goals used as criteria for assessing students' learning and for further planning of learning subgoals and activities?

The criterion questions bring into clear focus (1) the key role teachers play in curriculum leadership and (2) the fact that curriculum leadership requires interactions with the learners and consideration of the society and community within which the curriculum will be implemented. If all or most of these criterion questions can be answered affirmatively, the goal-setting phase of curriculum leadership has been adequate.

REFERENCES

Aristotle. *Politics* (Book VIII). In *The Basic Works of Aristotle,* edited by Richard McKoen. New York: Random House, 1941.
Parkay, F. W., & B. Stanford. *Becoming a Teacher,* 7th Ed. Boston: Allyn and Bacon, 2007.

Character and Academics: What Good Schools Do

JACQUES S. BENNINGA
MARVIN W. BERKOWITZ
PHYLLIS KUEHN
KAREN SMITH

ABSTRACT: Despite the clear national interest in character education, many schools are hesitant to engage in supplementary initiatives that might detract from their focus on increasing academic performance and satisfying state and federal goals for ongoing academic achievement. In this article, the authors argue that perhaps more schools would accept the challenge of integrating additional character education initiatives into their classrooms if it could be demonstrated that such programs do not detract from efforts to improve school achievement.

The growth of character education programs in the United States has coincided with the rise in high-stakes testing of student achievement. The No Child Left Behind Act asks schools to contribute not only to students' academic performance but also to their character. Both the federal government and the National Education Association (NEA) agree that schools have this dual responsibility. In a statement introducing a new U.S. Department of Education character education website, then Secretary of Education Rod Paige outlined the need for such programs:

> Sadly, we live in a culture without role models, where millions of students are taught the wrong values—or no values at all. This culture of callousness has led to a staggering achievement gap, poor health status, overweight students, crime, violence, teenage pregnancy, and tobacco and alcohol abuse. . . . Good character is the product of good judgments made every day.[1]

And Bob Chase, the former president of the NEA, issued his own forceful call to action:

> We must make an explicit commitment to formal character education. We must integrate character education into the fabric of the curriculum and into extracurricular activities. We must train teachers in character education—both preservice and inservice. And we must consciously set about creating a moral climate within our schools.[2]

Despite the clear national interest in character education, many schools are leery of engaging in supplementary initiatives that, although worthy, might detract from what they see as their primary focus: increasing academic achievement. Moreover, many schools lack the resources to create new curricular initiatives. Yet the enhancement of student character is a bipartisan mandate that derives from the very core of public education. The purpose of public schooling requires that schools seek to improve both academic and character education.

If it could be demonstrated that implementing character education programs is compatible with efforts to improve school achievement, then perhaps more schools would accept the challenge of doing both. But until now there has been little solid evidence of such successful coexistence.

DEFINITIONS AND RESEARCH

Character education is the responsibility of adults. While the term *character education* has historically referred to the duty of the older generation to form the character of the young through experiences affecting their attitudes, knowledge, and behaviors, more recent definitions include such developmental outcomes as a positive perception of school, emotional literacy, and social justice activism.[3]

There are sweeping definitions of character education (e.g., Character Counts' six pillars,

Community of Caring's five values, or the Character Education Partnership's 11 principles) and more narrow ones. Character education can be defined in terms of relationship virtues (e.g., respect, fairness, civility, tolerance), self-oriented virtues (e.g., fortitude, self-discipline, effort, perseverance) or a combination of the two. The state of California has incorporated character education criteria into the application process for its statewide distinguished school recognition program and, in the process, has created its own definition of character education. Each definition directs the practice of character education somewhat differently, so that programs calling themselves "character education" vary in purpose and scope.

There is some research evidence that character education programs enhance academic achievement. For example, an evaluation of the Peaceful Schools Project and research on the Responsive Classroom found that students in schools that implemented these programs had greater gains on standardized test scores than did students in comparison schools.[4] The Child Development Project (CDP) conducted follow-up studies of middle school students (through eighth grade) who had attended CDP elementary schools and found that they had higher course grades and higher achievement test scores than comparison middle school students.[5] Longitudinal studies have reported similar effects for middle school and high school students who had participated as elementary school students in the Seattle Social Development Project.[6]

A growing body of research supports the notion that high-quality character education can promote academic achievement. For example, Marvin Berkowitz and Melinda Bier have identified character education programs for elementary, middle, and high school students that enhance academic achievement.[7] These findings, however, are based on prepackaged curricular programs, and most schools do not rely on such programs. Instead, they create their own customized character education initiatives. It remains to be seen

whether such initiatives also lead to academic gains.

TOWARD AN OPERATIONAL DEFINITION OF CHARACTER EDUCATION

We decided to see if we could determine a relationship between character education and academic achievement across a range of elementary schools. For our sample we used the elementary schools that applied in 2000 to the California Department of Education for recognition as distinguished elementary schools, California's highest level of school attainment. Eligibility to submit an application for the California School Recognition Program (CSRP) in 2000 was based on the previous year's academic performance index (API) results.

However, 1999 was the first year for California's Public School Accountability Act (PSAA), which created the API. Thus, while the state department stated that growth on the API was the central focus of the PSAA, schools applying for the CSRP in 1999–2000 did not receive their 1999 API scores until January 2000, after they had already written and submitted their award applications. Approximately 12.7% of California elementary schools (681 of 5,368 schools) submitted a full application for the award in 2000. The average API of these schools was higher than the average for the schools that did not apply, but both were below the state expectancy score of 800. The mean API for applicant schools was 751; for non-applicant schools, 612. The API range for applicant schools was 365–957; for non-applicant schools, 302–958. Hence the sample for this study is not representative of all California elementary schools. It is a sample of more academically successful schools, but it does represent a broad range of achievement from quite low to very high.

Specific wording related to character education was included for the first time in the CSRP application in 2000. Schools were asked to describe what they were doing to meet a set of nine standards. Of these, the one that most clearly pertained to character education was Standard 1 (Vision and Standards). For this standard, schools were required to include "specific examples and other evidence" of "expectations that promote positive character units in students."[8] Other standards could also be seen as related to character education. For these, schools were asked to document activities and programs that ensured opportunities for students to contribute to the school, to others, and to the community.

We chose for our study a stratified random sample of 120 elementary schools that submitted applications. These 120 schools were not significantly different from the other 561 applicant schools on a variety of academic and demographic indicators. For the schools in our sample, we correlated the extent of their character education implementation with their API and SAT-9 scores—the academic scale and test used by California at that time.[9]

The first problem we needed to grapple with was how to define a character education program. We spent considerable time discussing an operational definition to use for this project. After conferring with experts, we chose our final set of character education criteria, drawn from both the standards used by the California Department of Education and the *Character Education Quality Standards* developed by the Character Education Partnership.[10] Six criteria emerged from this process:

- This school promotes core ethical values as the basis of good character.
- In this school, parents and other community members are active participants in the character education initiative.
- In this school, character education entails intentional promotion of core values in all phases of school life.
- Staff members share responsibility for and attempt to model character education.

- This school fosters an overall caring community.
- This school provides opportunities for most students to practice moral action.

Each of the six criteria addresses one important component of character education. We created a rubric encompassing these six criteria and listing indicators for each, along with a scoring scale.

CHARACTER EDUCATION AND ACADEMIC ACHIEVEMENT

Our study of these high-performing California schools added further evidence of a relationship between academic achievement and the implementation of specific character education programs. In our sample, elementary schools with solid character education programs showed positive relationships between the extent of character education implementation and academic achievement not only in a single year but also across the next two academic years. Over a multi-year period from 1999 to 2002, higher rankings on the API and higher scores on the SAT-9 were significantly and positively correlated with four of our character education indicators: a school's ability to ensure a clean and safe physical environment; evidence that a school's parents and teachers modeled and promoted good character; high-quality opportunities at the school for students to contribute in meaningful ways to the school and its community; and promoting a caring community and positive social relationships.

These are promising results, particularly because the *total character education score* for the year of the school's application was significantly correlated with every language and mathematics achievement score on the SAT-9 for a period of three years. In two of those years, the same was true for reading achievement scores. In other words, good-quality character education was positively associated with academic achievement, both across academic domains and over time.

WHAT GOOD SCHOOLS DO

From our research we derived principles—the four indicators mentioned above—that are common across schools with both thoughtful character education programs and high levels of academic achievement.

• *Good schools ensure a clean and secure physical environment.* Although all schools in our sample fit this description, the higher-scoring character education schools expressed great pride in keeping their buildings and grounds in good shape. This is consistent with what is reported about the virtues of clean and safe learning environments. For example, the Center for Prevention of School Violence notes that "the physical appearance of a school and its campus communicates a lot about the school and its people. Paying attention to appearance so that the facilities are inviting can create a sense of security.[11]

One school in our sample reported that its buildings "are maintained well above district standards. . . . The custodial crew prides themselves in achieving a monthly cleaning score that has exceeded standards in 9 out of 12 months." And another noted, "A daily grounds check is performed to ensure continual safety and cleanliness." Each of the higher-scoring schools in our sample explicitly noted its success in keeping its campus in top shape and mentioned that parents were satisfied that their children were attending school in a physically and psychologically safe environment.

All schools in California are required to have on file a written Safe School Plan, but the emphases in these plans vary. While some schools limited their safety plans to regulations controlling access to the building and defined procedures for violations and intrusions, the schools with better character education programs defined "safety" more broadly and deeply. For example, one school scoring high on our character education rubric explained that the mission of its Safe School Plan was "to provide all students with educational and personal opportunities in a positive and nurturing environment which will enable them to achieve current and future

goals, and for all students to be accepted at their own social, emotional, and academic level of development." Another high-scoring school addressed three concerns in its Safe School Plan: identification of visitors on campus, cultural/ethnic harmony, and safe ingress and egress from school. To support these areas of focus, this school's teachers were all trained to conduct classroom meetings, to implement the Community of Caring core values, and to handle issues related to cultural diversity and communication.

• *Good schools promote and model fairness, equity, caring and respect:* In schools with good character education programs and high academic achievement, adults model and promote the values and attitudes they wish the students to embrace, and they infuse character education throughout the school and across the curriculum. Rick Weissbourd drove home this point in a recent essay: "The moral development of students does not depend primarily on explicit character education efforts but on the maturity and ethical capacities of the adults with whom they interact. . . . Educators influence students' moral development not simply by being good role models—important as that is—but also by what they bring to their relationships with students day to day."[12] The staff of excellent character education schools in our sample tended to see themselves as involved, concerned professional educators, and others see them that way as well.

Thus one school described its teachers as "pivotal in the [curriculum] development process; there is a high level of [teacher] ownership in the curriculum. . . . Fifty percent of our staff currently serves on district curriculum committees." Another school stated that it "fosters the belief that it takes an entire community pulling together to provide the best education for every child; that is best accomplished through communication, trust, and collaboration on ideas that reflect the needs of our school and the community. . . . Teachers are continually empowered and given opportunities to voice their convictions and shape the outcome of what the school represents." A third school described its teachers as "continually encouraged" to grow professionally and to use best practices based on research. In the best character education schools, teachers are recognized by their peers, by district personnel, and by professional organizations for their instructional prowess and their professionalism: They model the academic and prosocial characteristics that show their deep concern for the well-being of children.

• *In good schools students contribute in meaningful ways.* We found that academically excellent character education schools provided opportunities for students to contribute to their school and their community. These schools encouraged students to participate in volunteer activities, such as cross-age tutoring, recycling, fundraising for charities, community cleanup programs, food drives, visitations to local senior centers, and so on.

One elementary school required 20 hours of community service, a program coordinated entirely by parent volunteers. Students in that school volunteered in community gardens and at convalescent hospitals, and they took part in community clean-up days. Such activities, while not directly connected to students' academic programs, were viewed as mechanisms to promote the development of healthy moral character. According to William Damon, a crucial component of moral education is engaging children in positive activities—community service, sports, music, theater, or anything else that inspires them and gives them a sense of purpose.[13]

• *Good schools promote a caring community and positive social relationships.* One school in our sample that exemplified this principle was a school of choice in its community. The district had opened enrollment to students outside district boundaries, and this school not only provided an excellent academic program for its multilingual student population but also worked hard to include parents and community members in significant ways. Its Family Math Night attracted 250 family members, and its Family Literacy Night educated parents about read-aloud

methods. Parents, grandparents, and friends were recruited to become classroom volunteers and donated thousands of hours.

This particular school also rented its classrooms to an after-school Chinese educational program. The two sets of teachers have become professional colleagues, and insights from such cultural interaction have led both groups to a better understanding of the Chinese and American systems of education. One result has been that more English-speaking students are enrolling in the Chinese after-school program. And teachers in both programs now engage in dialogue about the specific needs of children. One parent wrote a letter to the principal that said in part, "It seems you are anxious to build up our young generation more healthy and successful. . . . I am so proud you are not only our children's principal, but also parents' principal."

Other schools with strong social relationship programs provide meaningful opportunities for parent involvement and establish significant partnerships with local businesses. They encourage parents and teachers to work alongside students in service projects, to incorporate diverse communities into the school curriculum, and to partner with high school students who serve as physical education and academic mentors. As one such school put it, all stakeholders "must play an important and active role in the education of the child to ensure the future success of that child."

CONCLUSION

It is clear that well-conceived programs of character education can and should exist side by side with strong academic programs. It is no surprise that students need physically secure and psychologically safe schools, staffed by teachers who model professionalism and caring behaviors and who ask students to demonstrate caring for others. That students who attend such schools achieve academically makes intuitive sense as well. It is in schools with this dual emphasis that adults understand their role in preparing students for future citizenship in a democratic and diverse society. The behaviors and attitudes they model communicate important messages to the young people in their charge.

Future research on the relationship between character education and academic achievement should include a greater representation of schools in the average and below-average achievement categories. In particular, a study of the extent of the implementation of character education in schools that may have test scores at the low end of the spectrum—but are nevertheless performing higher than their socioeconomic characteristics would predict—would be an important contribution to our understanding of the relationship between character education and academic achievement.

While this was our initial attempt to explore the relationship between these two important school purposes, we learned a good deal about what makes up a good character education curriculum in academically strong schools. We know that such a curriculum in such schools is positively related to academic outcomes over time and across content areas. We also know that, to be effective, character education requires adults to act like adults in an environment where children are respected and feel physically and psychologically safe to engage in the academic and social activities that prepare them best for later adult decision making.

At a time when resources are scarce, we see schools cutting programs and narrowing curricula to concentrate on skills measured by standardized tests. Our research suggests that school goals and activities that are associated with good character education programs are also associated with academic achievement. Thus our results argue for maintaining a rich curriculum with support for all aspects of student development and growth.

NOTES

1. U.S. Department of Education, "ED Launches Character Education Web Site," www.thechallenge.org/15-v12no4/v12n4-communitiesandschools.htm.

2. Bob Chase, quoted in "Is Character Education the Answer?," *Education World*, 1999, www.education-world.com/a_admin/admin097.shtml.

3. Marvin W. Berkowitz, "The Science of Character Education," in William Damon, ed., *Bringing in a New Era in Character Education* (Stanford, Calif: Hoover Institution Press, 2002), pp. 43–63.

4. Stuart W. Twemlow et al., "Creating a Peaceful School Learning Environment: A Controlled Study of an Elementary School Intervention to Reduce Violence," *American Journal of Psychiatry*, vol. 158, 2001, pp. 808–10; and Stephen N. Elliott, "Does a Classroom Promoting Social Skills Development Enable Higher Academic Functioning Among Its Students Over Time?," Northeast Foundation for Children, Greenfield, Mass., 1998.

5. Victor Battistich and Sehee Hong, "Enduring Effects of the Child Development Project: Second-Order Latent Linear Growth Modeling of Students' 'Connectedness' to School, Academic Performance, and Social Adjustment During Middle School," unpublished manuscript, Developmental Studies Center, Oakland, Calif., 2003.

6. J. David Hawkins et al., "Long-Term Effects of the Seattle Social Development Intervention on School Bonding Trajectories," *Applied Developmental Science*, vol. 5, 2001, pp. 225–36.

7. Marvin W. Berkowitz and Melinda C. Bier, *What Works in Character Education?* (Washington, D.C.: Character Education Partnership, 2005).

8. "California School Recognition Program, 2000 Elementary Schools Program, Elementary School Rubric," California Department of Education, 2001. (Data are available from Jacques Benninga.)

9. For more detail on the design of the study, see Jacques S. Benninga, Marvin W. Berkowitz, Phyllis Kuehn, and Karen Smith, "The Relationship of Character Education Implementation and Academic Achievement in Elementary Schools," *Journal of Research in Character Education*, vol. 1, 2003, pp. 17–30.

10. *Character Education Quality Standards: A Self-Assessment Tool for Schools and Districts* (Washington, D.C.: Character Education Partnership, 2001).

11. "What Is Character Education?," Center for the Fourth and Fifth Rs, 2003, www.cortland.edu/c4n5rs/ce_iv.asp.

12. Rick Weissbourd, "Moral Teachers, Moral Students," *Educational Leadership*, March 2003, pp. 6–7.

13. Damon is quoted in Susan Gilbert, "Scientists Explore the Molding of Children's Morals." *New York Times*, 18 March 2003.

Jacques S. Benninga is a professor of education and director of the Bonner Center for Character Education, California State University, Fresno. *Marvin W. Berkowitz* is Sanford N. McDonnell Professor of Character Education, University of Missouri, St. Louis. *Phyllis Kuehn* is a professor of educational research, California State University, Fresno. *Karen Smith* is principal of Mark Twain Elementary School, Brentwood, Mo. The research described in this article was funded by a grant from the John Templeton Foundation, but the opinions expressed are those of the authors.

QUESTIONS FOR REFLECTION

1. Do you agree with the authors' premise that well-conceived programs of character education should exist side-by-side with strong academic programs?
2. How might a school district implement such character education programs and how would they defend themselves against critics who would label such programs as "supplements" that schools don't have time for in today's standards-based environment?
3. How early should character education programs be integrated into the curriculum? Who are the school personnel and school leaders most likely to successfully advocate for their adoption?

Uncovering Teacher Leadership

RICHARD ACKERMAN
SARAH V. MACKENZIE

ABSTRACT: *Teacher leaders, Ackerman and Mackenzie argue, are the "pack mules of effective school improvement" because they carry the weight of responsibility for ensuring that reforms take root in the classroom and deepen the learning of all students. As such, teacher leaders contend with several challenges dictated by the status quo, such as antiquated notions of leadership, teacher isolation, and the conservatism that so often reigns in schools. Succeeding as a teacher leader means staying true to one's beliefs, coupling confidence with humility, and being willing to work with colleagues to improve student learning.*

The next generation of teacher leaders is here. They charge ahead with new ideas for improving teaching and learning. Or they resist a change initiative because they believe it would disadvantage certain students. Sometimes teacher leaders voice their colleagues' points of view; sometimes their views merge with those of administrators with whom they lead an effective reform effort. Occasionally, they are lone voices asking hard questions or pushing against what others are willing to let stand.

Teacher leaders carry the weight of responsibility for ensuring that reforms take root in the classroom and deepen the learning of all students.

They are also a school's conscience. They care deeply about students and about the institutions designed to help students learn, and they continually think about the gap between the real and the ideal in schools. The discrepancies they witness compel them to challenge the status quo.

STARTING WITH THE CLASSROOM

In the past, teacher leaders have held formal positions, such as department chair or team leader. They have often moved out of the classroom to take curriculum coordination or consulting teacher roles. In the current wave of teacher leadership, however, teacher leaders derive their authority from their experience in the classroom (Silva, Gimbert, & Nolan, 2000). The formal teacher leader roles still exist, of course, but more teachers lead informally by revealing their classroom practice, sharing their expertise, asking questions of colleagues, mentoring new teachers, and modeling how teachers collaborate on issues of practice. Many principals nurture and support teacher leadership because they know how crucial it is to establish improvements in teaching and learning at the classroom level.

However, teacher leaders still contend with several challenges dictated by the status quo. In many schools, notions of leadership are embedded in hierarchy and role definitions. Moreover, the conservatism of teachers and their isolation in the classroom (Lortie, 1975) frequently frustrate leadership. By surfacing tensions between the school's mission and its actual practices, teacher leaders can also discomfort colleagues and threaten administrators and teachers alike. Nevertheless, teacher leaders, empowered by their confidence in themselves and their colleagues, hold the key to improved learning and offer new contexts and alternatives for genuine school change.

The rub for all teacher leaders? Their strength comes from the classroom, yet unless they venture out of it, connecting and relating to other adults in the school, they do not fulfill the power implicit in their teaching role. One school principal aptly described this broader perspective. When he was teaching full-time, he believed that he needed to be outside the classroom, engaged in school leadership, to effectively fulfill his role. Now that he was a principal, however, he sensed that he needed to spend more time in the classroom to be effective in his job.

Working both inside and outside the classroom toward the ideal of a collective, collaborative enterprise requires a broader perspective. Successful teacher leaders stay true to their beliefs, couple confidence with humility in their practice, and continually work with colleagues to improve student learning.

STAYING TRUE TO ONE'S BELIEFS

Teacher leaders generally are experienced teachers who have tested their beliefs about teaching and learning and codified them into a platform that informs their practice. However, teacher leaders still question those underpinnings and always gauge the extent to which their practices align with their philosophies. This injunction to self-knowledge can be a heavy and demanding challenge.

One teacher leader we know gradually developed a deep understanding of how rewards, punishments, and labels impeded learning in his 4th grade classroom. Like his fellow teachers, he had held reading contests, had given stickers and tickets for homework completion, and had distributed increasingly larger prizes to promote learning and good behavior. He realized, though, that he was promoting compliance, not learning.

When this leader moved to a middle school, he created a classroom free of punishments and rewards. He also made his practice public by discussing it frequently at team meetings and with other faculty members. He started asking questions in a nonthreatening way of both teachers and administrators: Why did they use grades to determine eligibility for cocurricular activities? How did they reward students' behavior or academic performance?

In the spring of that year, the principal brought a related issue to the faculty. He questioned the purpose of the two-hour awards assembly held in front of the entire school. Our teacher leader believed that his questions and modeling played a role in the administrator's and the faculty's willingness to reflect on this method of recognizing students. Small changes were the foundation for larger reforms in the school regarding assessment and motivation for learning.

Another teacher leader was deeply involved in the reform efforts that her high school embraced, framed by the *Breaking Ranks* high school restructuring initiative. She came to grips with her beliefs about rigor and accountability when her school adopted a senior exhibition requirement. She believed that senior exhibitions would add an insurmountable barrier to graduation for those students deemed most at risk. She worried that students from lower socioeconomic backgrounds, faced with so many daunting graduation requirements, would drop out. She thought about her own immigrant family members who had not finished high school. They had left school partly for economic reasons but also because the schools they attended didn't value their needs and learning styles. She also thought of the students whose lives she had tried to improve as she helped them work through their disaffection with school. The new plan made her feel like a traitor to her heritage, her family, and her identity as an educator.

This teacher found that part of leadership is not just voicing beliefs but staying the course and looking for ways to deepen and expand others' understanding of thorny issues. She explained to colleagues how difficult it was to reconcile her personal stance with the direction the school was taking. She wanted to find a way to make school work better for *all* students, but because of her background, she had deep reservations about her ability to be an effective leader in shaping that change. She has let the silent response from faculty members sit for the time being. Knowing the school as she does, however, she is certain that individuals and groups will continue her critique of the senior exhibition requirement.

NUDGING: BEYOND BULLDOZING

A paradox in schools is that teachers—those outstanding facilitators of student learning—are not nearly as effective when it comes to constructively developing their colleagues' learning. The isolation of teaching and the demands on teachers' time are responsible to some degree. To implement reform in schools, however, teachers must break down that isolation. They must reach out, model for others, and help colleagues develop skills and understanding. The way they go about doing so is crucial to any reforms success. As teacher leaders learn some hard lessons about the difficulty of both supporting and critiquing, they develop solid interpersonal skills and overcome inhibitions as they uncover their own and others' leadership.

One teacher leader, fresh out of a graduate school program and with some teaching experience under her belt, plunged into her first day as a new teacher in a charter school where she was eager to be a change agent. She was committed to backward planning and authentic assessment and wanted everyone else in the school to commit to these practices, too. She could see how clarifying what students needed to know and be able to do from 12th grade down to her 6th grade classes would transform teaching and learning.

At the first department meeting of the year, the veteran teachers discussed what they were teaching. When the teacher leader suggested the idea of backward planning, the veteran teachers didn't want to discuss it. Our stalwart teacher leader refused to give up. She broke out chart paper and colored markers, thinking that if she could guide the group with visuals, it would all make sense to them and that backward planning could begin. It didn't.

Reflecting on her method of operating in that school from the vantage point of four more years of experience, she now refers to that mode as the "Bulldozer Effect." She acknowledges that hammering away at her colleagues meant that she failed to recognize the hard work of veteran teachers and too casually dismissed their efforts.

Since then, she has learned to be a better listener, "a nudger," as she described it, and an observer of how colleagues influence one another. She learned to stop blasting others, figured out how to open lines of communication, and developed ways to ensure that all parties listen, hear, trust, and remain open to one another.

A middle school teacher leader needed to surmount his discomfort with true collaboration. He admits that his goal was self-affirmation rather than gaining new perspectives and forging group ownership. He engaged groups in brainstorming and discussion, but all along he waited for the opportunity to push the group in a direction that he had already predetermined. Rather than valuing the input of the group, he valued the *image* of collaboration.

When this teacher participated in collegial collaboration in a graduate program, however, he discovered the give-and-take of shared deliberations and gained a better understanding of collaborative decision making. Over time, this teacher leader learned how to foster his colleagues' capacity for true collaboration. He pushed against their inertia, helping them see that all members' ideas were important. Teacher leaders, in this sense, not only impart knowledge and method but also awaken a sense of collective responsibility.

BEING VULNERABLE

As much of the literature about teacher leadership shows, teachers who step out of the acceptable pattern of quiet acquiescence with the status quo take big risks. When they advocate for what they believe is best for students, colleagues may see them as rude, disloyal, or worse.

For example, one young teacher leader agitated to get a bank of computers for students in his classroom. He also advocated for himself and other teachers who needed more time to read student work before they wrote progress reports. In each instance, he challenged decisions that an administrator had made because he believed that it was in the students' interest.

The assistant principal whom he challenged told him that other teachers thought he was adversely affecting school climate with his "rude" behavior. He was shocked. He had never thought that he would be labeled rude for simply disagreeing with a supervisor. He believed that the concerns he had raised were important for the school, not just for the teachers.

Feeling vulnerable and alone, this teacher leader acknowledged that he now weighs the benefit of speaking out against the cost of being seen as stepping out of bounds. Nevertheless, he points out,

> This is where courage comes in. Leaders are willing to get burned. Leaders are willing to make themselves vulnerable, and do it again and again and again. (West, 2006)

One teacher leader who was a high school English department head dealt with a sticky situation in her school. A portion of the faculty questioned the school leadership team's efforts to promote an interdisciplinary curriculum and personalized student learning. On a feedback form, one teacher filled a page and a half with criticism. Instead of becoming defensive, though, this department head overcame her frustration and sought out the teacher. She listened to her concerns, conceding that she had some valid points.

The critic suggested that the faculty needed time to get some issues out into the open, so the leadership team facilitated a faculty forum to brainstorm ideas. The climate was positive and led to more open meetings and honest communication. Furthermore, it showed the leadership team's willingness to include others in developing goals and plans.

This collegial and collaborative leadership model is the subtle domain of teacher leadership today. Although more swashbuckling sorts of courage are likely to be necessary at times, the quieter bravery of teacher leaders is reflected in new patterns of relating to peers and deeper understanding of fellow teachers, suggesting that teachers themselves are becoming more at ease with the genuine complexities of leadership.

OUR MOST PRECIOUS RESOURCE

Teacher leadership still faces heavy odds. It must compete not only with vested interests in traditional assumptions about leadership, but also with schools that are still uncomfortable with the idea of teacher leaders. Nevertheless, teacher leadership offers a variety of unseen opportunities for forcing schools out of established frames of reference and toward genuine school improvement.

Whether and how teachers decide to lead is determined by what they believe matters in their teaching and, ultimately, by who they are. As Parker Palmer has said,

> In our rush to reform education, we have forgotten a simple truth. Reform will never be achieved by renewing appropriations, rewriting curricula, and revising texts if we continue to demean and dishearten the human resource called the teacher, on whom so much depends. (1998, p. 3)

Teacher leaders struggle for control, not power (Gonzales. 2004), over their work lives. They stand up for what is near and dear to them—improving teaching and learning. Although they may experience conflict with the school culture and within themselves, their goal is to catalyze others to work as hard and care as deeply about what happens in classrooms and schools as they do.

In his recent memoir, *Teacher Man,* Frank McCourt writes,

> You have to make your own way in the classroom. You have to find yourself. You have to develop your own style, your own techniques. You have to tell the truth or you'll be found out. (2005, p. 113)

As students of teacher leadership, we believe that teachers have a profound effect on the quality of schools, influencing the schools themselves and defining innovative leadership in the 21st century. However, this leadership can only come from teachers who "tell the truth" and who accept the vulnerability that results from doing so.

REFERENCES

Gonzales, L. D (2004). *Sustaining teacher leadership: Beyond the boundaries of an enabling school culture.* Lanham, MD: University Press of America.

Lortie, D. (1975). *School-teacher: A sociological study.* Chicago: University of Chicago Press.

McCourt, F. (2005). *Teacher man.* New York: Scribner.

Palmer, P. (1998). *The courage to teach: Exploring the inner landscape of a teacher's life.* San Francisco: Jossey-Bass.

Silva, D. Y., Gimbert, B., & Nolan, J. (2000). Sliding the doors: Locking and unlocking possibilities for teacher leadership. *Teachers College Record, 102*(4), 779–804.

West, T. (2006). The courage to lead. In R. Ackerman & S. Mackenzie (Eds.), *Inside and out: A teacher leader reader.* San Francisco: Corwin Press.

Richard Ackerman is associate professor of educational leadership at the University of Maine; *Sarah V. Mackenzie* is assistant professor of educational leadership, also at the University of Maine. They are editors of *Uncovering Teacher Leadership: Essays and Voices From the Field* (Corwin Press, 2007).

QUESTIONS FOR REFLECTION

1. What do Ackerman and Mackenzie believe are the key ingredients for teacher leaders to be successful?
2. Ackerman and Mackenzie write that "teacher leaders can force schools out of established frames of reference and toward genuine improvement." How does that

occur? What resistance do teacher leaders sometimes face as they push schools toward improvement?

3. A critical component of leadership is the ability to not just voice beliefs, but also to look for ways to deepen others' understanding of "thorny" issues. What kinds of thorny issues are teacher leaders likely to face in schools, and how might they go beyond merely voicing their beliefs?

Perspectives on Four Curriculum Traditions

WILLIAM H. SCHUBERT

ABSTRACT: *The history of curriculum leadership reveals that various theoretical orientations to curriculum have been proposed. By having hypothetical "speakers" address the central curriculum question, "What is worth knowing?" Schubert suggests that there are four theoretical orientations to curriculum thought—intellectual traditionalist, social behaviorist, experientialist, and critical reconstructionist.*

Since the advent of graded textbooks by the mid-1800s, teachers and school administrators have relied on them to such an extent that when many educators and most noneducators hear the term *curriculum,* they think of textbooks. Pioneers in the curriculum field, however (e.g., John Dewey, Franklin Bobbitt, W. W. Charters, Hollis Caswell, Ralph Tyler), argued in the first half of the twentieth century for a much more complex and variegated conceptualization of curriculum. Although these scholars, the array of others who accompanied them, and their more recent descendants have disagreed on many educational issues, they all agreed that curriculum is a great deal more than the textbook.

The most perceptive curriculum scholars throughout history have realized that *curriculum,* at its root, deals with the central question of what is worth knowing; therefore, it deals with what is worth experiencing, doing, and being. Etymologically, *curriculum* is derived from classic meanings associated with the course of a chariot race. Metaphorically, *race course* can be interpreted to mean *journey* or journey of learning, growing,

and becoming. As recent interpretation suggests, the verb form of *curriculum* (the noun) is *currere,* and it can be used to focus attention on the act of running the race or experiencing the journey of becoming who we become in life. Thus, the study of curriculum, taken seriously, invokes questions of the good life for individuals and matters of justice in pursuing life together for societies of human beings.

In several of my surveys of curriculum history, I have identified four recurrent positions on curriculum thought, which I have labeled as *intellectual traditionalist, social behaviorist, experientialist,* and *critical reconstructionist.* Although most curriculum scholars, leaders, and teachers are blends of one or more of these orientations, the pure form of each offers its own unique brand of educational possibility that moves far beyond the curriculum as mere textbook. Instead of writing discursively here *about* each, I will ask each *to speak,* as I have done in several publications and as a pedagogical device that I frequently employ through role-playing in courses or in presentations to groups of teachers, administrators, policy makers, and others interested in education. I have asked the *speakers* to share briefly their basic convictions about the major curriculum question(s) noted above and to augment their responses by explaining how curriculum should be restructured beyond the all-too-pervasive reliance on textbooks.

FOUR CURRICULUM TRADITIONS

Intellectual Traditionalist Speaker

[Appearing somewhat formal, self-assured, and willing to deliver the inspirational lecture or to engage in analytic, Socratic dialogue and debate]

The best answers to the basic curriculum question (What is worth knowing?) are found in the great works and in the organized disciplines of knowledge. The great works are the best expressions of human insight, understanding, and wisdom, and the disciplines are the best organizations of knowledge as created by experts in each field. Most certainly, I am an advocate of what is often called "a liberal education" for all. But why? My rationale for advocating study of the great works (in all fields, e.g., arts, sciences, humanities, social sciences) is that they, more than any other source, stimulate human beings to probe deeply into what Mortimer Adler and Robert M. Hutchins have referred to as the *great ideas,* and more recently what Allan Bloom, E. D. Hirsch, Diane Ravitch, Chester Finn, William Bennett, and others have advocated as necessary and neglected knowledge. Adler, for instance, writes of six great ideas: truth, beauty, goodness, liberty, equality, and justice. These ideas transcend matters of culture, race, gender, class, age, ethnicity, location, health or ableness, national origin, and any other aspects of individual and social life that too many consider reasons for gaining separate or individualized treatment.

This focus on individual differences neglects what all human beings have in common—in fact, it omits what makes them essentially human,

namely, the great ideas. Every human who has ever lived is concerned about these matters in his or her own life and in the social context of that life. The best expressions of insight into the great ideas is found, not in the intellectual pabulum of textbooks, but in the best expressions that human beings have produced, namely the great works of literature, art, music, philosophy, social and psychological theory, mathematics, history, and the natural sciences.

Whenever possible, the primary sources should be read; however, due to barriers of language, cultural frame of reference, and ability, I admit that secondary sources need to be used. These are adequately found in good translations and in the summaries of essential knowledge available in the disciplines of knowledge.

Social Behaviorist Speaker

[Less formal attire, not quite a lab coat—but in that spirit, oozing with the desire to discover and invent, analytically and scientifically, what works for the needs of today's world; a little rough around the edges]

Basically, I am a grubby empiricist *[with a gleam of eye that shows great respect for scientific investigation, with the "grubby" merely being a way of asking listeners to put more stock in results than in appearances].* I don't ask for too much, only that one have evidence for one's advocacy. The Intellectual Traditionalist seems to think that just because a content area has stood the test of time, so to speak, it is valuable for what students need today.

Textbooks of today carry little more than redigested relics of past textbooks, and the same unquestioned curriculum is passed from generation to generation. These textbooks rarely even get to the level of "great ideas" that the Intellectual Traditionalist promotes. Even those ideas, however, need to be looked at for their relevance to today's students. Taking a cue from one of the greatest Intellectual Traditionalists of all (though I disagree with much that he promotes), I recall that Socrates warned that the unexamined life is not worth living. I want to add that the unexamined curriculum is not worth offering.

To that end I want to tell you a little story from a curriculum classic called *The Saber-Tooth Curriculum*, written by Harold Benjamin in 1939. (By the way, intellectual traditionalists were so powerful in education at the time that Benjamin had to write under a pseudonym, J. Abner Peddiwell.) Being an advocate of economy of time (an earlier version of "time on task"), I am pleased to tell you that the book is short and to the point, even if it is literary and one of the only funny curriculum books in existence!

The story line has a young man who just graduated from college, planning to be a teacher, on a celebratory vacation seated at the longest bar in the world in Tijuana. He sees his old professor from an introduction to education course, strikes up a conversation, and learns that the professor has been on sabbatical studying the educational system of prehistoric peoples.

The conversations are about what he learned. He learned, for example, that prehistoric education classes bore such titles as "Fish Grabbing with the Bare Hands" and "Saber-tooth Tiger Chasing with Fire." The practical value of these courses for prehistoric life is obvious. However, as time went on and as the climate became intensely colder (glaciers arrived), the streams froze up and the saber-tooth tigers migrated to warmer parts of the world. Nevertheless, even then, there were Intellectual Traditionalist educators who argued that the *great ideas* embedded in fish grabbing and tiger chasing would build the mind and must be preserved for all generations. The absurdity of this hardly needs to be noted . . . (or does it, given contemporary intellectual traditionalists?).

With this in mind, I want to say that I am a *behaviorist* in the sense that we need to identify the kinds of behaviors that help students become successful in today's world (as well as the behaviors of teachers that lead to achievement of the desired behaviors in students). I am *social* in the sense that I think that such behaviors should not be taken mindlessly from traditional curriculum values and practices, but rather from systematic investigation of what it takes to be successful in society today.

Experientialist Speaker

[Very casual, trying to "tune in" to the audience, obviously desirous of engaging them in an interpersonal fashion, rather than by lecture or by precept]

Sometimes we think of curriculum as a configuration of experiences that leads to the acquisition of skills, bodies of knowledge, and values or beliefs. I am not altogether happy with this three-part separation, and see skill, knowledge, and value as part of a seamless fabric; nevertheless, each of these categories has a heuristic value for my present purposes.

I want you to think of a skill you have that helps you frequently. I want you to think of a body of knowledge that you are glad you have. Similarly, I want you to think of a value or belief that guides your life and helps you deal with difficult circumstances.

Take some time to ponder. *[pause]* Then ask yourself how and where you acquired the skill, or body of knowledge, or guiding value. Tell someone else stories about getting to the place that you now are regarding this skill, knowledge, or value. Try to understand the conditions under which you gained these capacities. If these are powerful learnings, then understanding more about the conditions under which they occurred (in your own life and the lives of others with whom you exchange) will help you to understand powerful learning for your students. Are the conditions of powerful learning in your life, and in the lives of others you know, present in the lives of your students in your school?

What I am trying to convey here is a natural way of learning and teaching, one that we all experience outside of formal learning contexts. Learning, teaching, and curriculum of formal learning contexts, however, are often contrived. My position is that we learn best when learning springs from our genuine interests and concerns.

John Dewey argued this in his many writings. He referred to a progressive curriculum organization centered not in authority outside of the learner, but derived from each learner's experience. He referred to this organization as movement from *the psychological* to *the logical*. By *psychological* he meant concerns and interests of learners and by *logical* he meant the disciplines or funds of knowledge accumulated by the human race. He said that we need to move back and forth on a continuum between the psychological and the logical as we learn and grow.

In other words, Dewey's view is that the usual way of teaching (whether textbook-based, or even as either the Intellectual Traditionalist or the Social Behaviorist recommends) is the antithesis of the natural way of teaching. It is artificial and contrived, and needs to be turned on its head. The *logical* organization of the disciplines of knowledge is fine for encyclopedias and computer banks, but it is not pedagogically sound. The *logical*, however, has the power to inform and illuminate the *psychological*. The reverse is also true.

Critical Reconstructionist Speaker

[Starkly serious, upset with injustice and the complicity of the status quo about it; suspicious of conspiracies—intentional and unintentional—restless about the lack of time to right wrongs before injustice reigns supreme]

Although I do agree, in principle, with my Experientialist colleague, I think he is a bit too hopeful—maybe even naive. I am convinced that schools are "sorting machines" for society, as Joel Spring has put it so well. Thus, students are accorded different opportunities to grow and learn, depending on different dimensions of their lives or contexts. I guess that the Social Behaviorist would refer to them as "variables." In any case these dimensions include socioeconomic class, gender, race, ethnicity, health, ableness, appearance, place of living or location, marital status, religion or beliefs, age, nationality, and more.

Much has been written about most of these aspects of life and their impact on providing differential treatment of students, giving them a great disparity of kinds and qualities of educational experiences. For instance, students of a particular race, or ethnicity, or social class background, or status of health, ableness/disableness, and so on may not be given equal access to certain kinds of textbooks, instructional materials, and teaching-learning environments. The variables are often covert sources of tracking students, and it is well-known that students in different tracks are taught in different and unequal ways with materials of unequal quality.

All of this is part of a process that the critical theory literature refers to as *hegemony*. *Hegemony* is the process whereby a society or culture reproduces patterns of inequity. Each institution of a society, school being a prominent one, passes along the hierarchies of the society at large. Students of a given race or social class or gender, for instance, are given messages in schools similar to what they receive from the society at large or from other institutions within the society.

CONCLUSION

The speakers portrayed here represent four quite different curriculum positions. They might be considered akin to archetypes of curriculum that re-emerge in different incarnations and under different labels in each generation all around our globe. Intellectual Traditionalists call for realization of the power of the classics and the great ideas embedded in them (and the accompanying disciplines of knowledge) to overcome the problems of any day. Social Behaviorists, in contrast, call for a new look at what knowledges, skills, and values lead to success in each generation. Experientialists and Critical Reconstructionists decry what they consider to be the authoritarianism of Social Behaviorists and Intellectual Traditionalists, and call for greater grassroots participation. This means that students themselves and the concerns, interests, and injustices they feel deeply must be the starting point for meaningful and worthwhile learning.

What does this all mean? Must the reader (any educator or policymaker, teacher, parent, or student) choose one side or another? In the heat of an earlier battle in the progressive era, John Dewey argued that choosing either progressive or traditional education as superficially practiced was not the main point. In *Experience and Education,* one of Dewey's last books on education, he said prophetically, in the preface, "It is the business of an intelligent theory of education to ascertain the causes for the conflicts that exist and then, instead of taking one side or the other, to indicate a plan of operations proceeding from a level deeper and more inclusive than is represented by the practices and ideas of the contending parties." Dewey's admonition makes it necessary not to become a card-carrying Experientialist, Critical Reconstructionist, Social Behaviorist, or Intellectual Traditionalist, but instead to remember and develop relevant aspects of all of these positions as possibilities for each educational situation encountered.

The fundamental question is not merely whether to have textbooks, but to ask continuously what should be done and why it should be done—with or without textbooks. Each of the curriculum positions offers an avenue to curriculum that transcends most textbooks available, enabling teachers to meet student needs, concerns, and interests more fully. This, however, does not mean that textbooks and other more interactive instructional materials are irrelevant. In fact, rather than rejecting textbooks and related instructional materials, it would be better to ask how instructional media (teacher made, commercially prepared, or student generated) can be created to deeply capture the essence of the Social Behaviorist, Intellectual Traditionalist, Critical Reconstructionist, and Experientialist, alike. Surely, these positions do contradict one another at many points, and practices that bespeak mindless contradiction should be avoided at all costs. However, it is also possible to see each position as complementary to one another, speaking at once to different needs in any complex educational context.

Thus, the great curriculum development task before us is to draw upon all curriculum traditions for the insights and understandings that best fit situations at hand. This means that no text or policy or written curriculum is the final answer. Good answers lie in continuously asking what knowledge and experiences are most worthwhile now, and now, and now . . . throughout the whole panoply of situations that lie ahead. Moreover, such asking must be done by all who are affected by the consequences of that asking, including students who have the greatest vested interest, yet are too often left out of the process of considering matters of purpose that affect them so dearly.

William H. Schubert is professor of education and coordinator of graduate curriculum studies at the University of Illinois at Chicago.

QUESTIONS FOR REFLECTION

1. Is the intellectual traditionalist orientation elitist? How might Schubert's intellectual traditionalist speaker respond to this criticism?
2. The social behaviorist speaker states that "we need to identify the kinds of behaviors that help students become successful in today's world." How would this person determine what will make students "successful"? How would this contrast with the approach used by the other three speakers?
3. If, as the experientialist speaker suggests, the curriculum should be based on students' "genuine interests and concerns," will students acquire the knowledge and skills they will need to function effectively in our society?
4. At this point in your study of curriculum leadership, which curriculum orientation is most compatible with your views? Least compatible?

Democracy at Risk

WILLIAM E. WHITE
RICHARD VAN SCOTTER
MICHAEL H. HAROONIAN
JAMES E. DAVIS

ABSTRACT: According to the authors, civic responsibility has been reduced to the act of voting, although voting is only a small part of civic engagement. Developing appropriate skills is a requirement of useful employment, but increasingly, schools, colleges, and universities focus on skills and information students will need to acquire a job, status, and money at the expense of educating students about civic participation and responsibilities. A successful curriculum, the authors maintain, should emphasize how past generations of American citizens have engaged in civic debate in their communities, states, and nation while helping students acquire (1) the ability to challenge opinions and value statements and (2) the skills needed to debate current issues in their communities.

The future of the American experiment, and the life of the democratic republic that is the United States, is at risk. American citizens have endangered the republic by failing to educate new generations of citizens about civic responsibility. Elders have told new generations that they have rights and freedoms but have done little to help them understand what is required to protect those liberties, both for themselves and for future citizens. Civic responsibility has been reduced to the act of voting, but voting is only a small part of the civic engagement that every citizen must contribute to secure the future of the American republic.

To understand their responsibility, citizens must first embrace the idea that the legitimacy of government is found in the individual. The founders of the American republic endorsed Enlightenment thinkers such as John Locke and Montesquieu, who emphasized individual rights and personal virtue. The founders of the new republic understood that each person living under a monarchy was a dutiful subject. However, the republic required citizens of character—informed, engaged, and caring critics of the republic.

Even today, the belief that people can govern themselves is not generally accepted. A quick survey of world governments demonstrates the predominance of monarchy, dictatorship, aristocracy, and theocracy. Many governments grant a grudging nod to the people by allowing them to vote, but that is a far cry from the principles on which the American republic was founded. The people of the United States are not subjects. Understanding that American citizens must live in common society together, individuals grant rights and privileges to their government.

When the republic began, moving from subject to citizen required a fundamental transformation of personal identity and a change in obligations and duties. However, this new identity was not activated by birth or immigration. The individual had to learn to be a citizen. Not only schools but also other institutions of society and within communities taught civility, courage, integrity, concern, and curiosity—in short, virtue or character appropriate for daily participation in democratic principles and republican responsibility.

LOSS OF COMMUNITY AND CONNECTION

America is an ideal expressed in the Declaration of Independence and implemented through the U.S. Constitution. Some people argue that the nation continually strives for but never achieves that ideal of a democratic republic anchored in character and virtue. Ralph Waldo Emerson

(1844/1937) worried about the breakdown of communities and loss of dependable morality. He wrote that the state of society "is one in which the members have suffered amputation from the trunk, and strut about so many walking monsters—a good finger, a neck, a stomach, an elbow, but never a man" (419).

As early as the nineteenth century, the tension between individualism and American republican principles was evident. Americans often act out of self-interest without regard for community interests. Economic and technological advancements have increased social fragmentation, segmented communities, dispersed families, and left individuals increasingly isolated. Twenty-first-century technology such as television, the Internet, and electronic headsets may heighten this isolation. Engaging in civic discourse is hard work and is more difficult when means for opting out are easily available. With a population of more than three hundred million people (Phillips 2002), the United States has an increasing number of citizens who have little or no tradition in understanding democracy.

Thomas Jefferson's republican ideal of engaged citizenry in small rural communities gave way to increasingly larger urban areas. By the mid-twentieth century, more people struggled to remain connected and maintain community in sprawling suburban settlements and enclaves (Morison 1965). Some small villages and towns still exist in many regions of the nation. Also, within larger cities or urban centers, small neighborhoods bring people together socially, culturally, and politically. However, there are also people such as airline pilots who live in the United States but consider their communities to be New York, Paris, Amsterdam, Hong Kong, and Tokyo, where their jobs take them regularly. Such individuals may have homes in America, but they otherwise have little connection with the community and civic life. This condition is not unique; people increasingly work for multinational companies in the global economy.

In modern corporate America, large organizations—businesses, the government, the news media, and foundations—play a powerful role in making economic and political decisions that often transcend national borders. Although people often are aware of the situation, they choose to allow these entities to make decisions. When people do this, they act as subjects, not citizens. Individuals normally do not like to engage in argument and debate on complex issues. This type of debate requires considerable effort, time, and courage. Too often, it is easier to go along with the will of experts or specialists.

Unchecked, the state or government tends to take on a life of its own and act individually. This personification of a political entity can be a direct and serious affront to the individual's freedom to act as a citizen. When this occurs, democracy is gradually diminished, and it becomes more important for citizens to assume a watchdog responsibility and challenge the actions of the state.

WORKING TOGETHER

In a democratic society, the individual is extremely important. Foremost, citizens serve as a countervailing force to inform or check on the state. The role of a citizen is simultaneously to be loyal to the state and to criticize its actions—to both love and discipline government—because the people are both the government and the governed. Most citizens do not understand this dual role, but it is critical. The ability to exercise these two responsibilities is an essential characteristic of the democratic citizen.

Maintaining the office of citizen requires energy, intellect, and a keen awareness of mutual interests. The work of democracy cannot he done alone; democracy involves continuous debate. Civil and respectful debate is often the most productive, but even when debates become rancorous, citizens must remain engaged. Democracy requires that citizens constantly monitor the progress of debate and engage it to represent their interests and opinions. It is easy to revert to the role of a subject. Serving as a vigilant citizen requires effort and is even risky when it places the individual in a political spotlight.

Citizens also abdicate their responsibilities when self-interest trumps public interest. Plato and Aristotle concluded that democracy is corrupt (Held 1996), and they believed that ordinary humans are incapable of the discipline required of a democratic citizen. Many American founders held similar doubts (Morison 1965). George Washington referred to commoners as "the grazing multitude," John Adams referred to them as the "common herd of mankind," and Alexander Hamilton doubted people's moral capacities (Wood 2002, 101). However, these students of the Enlightenment also believed in the power of learning and education. This belief created in them a more optimistic attitude toward human potential.

Some pundits argue that the American public today lacks a sense of civic responsibility. Cultural observers throughout American history have similarly questioned whether their generation or the next generation was capable of bearing their civic responsibility (Lasch 1995). For example, the nation's physical infrastructure is in need of repair, as evidenced by bridges collapsing, steam pipes exploding, and schools deteriorating. Rather than cope with the civic issues many U.S. cities face, many citizens have abandoned them for new facilities in suburban communities (Lasch). However, because the nation has prevailed and advanced, there is hope. Experience suggests that current and future generations can meet social, economic, and political challenges. However, with each new era, people face new cultural conditions. Today's Americans face an ever-increasing organizational or institutional society whose goals can conflict with the welfare of the individual.

CHANGING EDUCATION

The key to reactivating American civic life lies in education. This has long been the view of learned people, including many who laid the political foundation of the United States (Jefferson 1816). Early Americans faced a profound challenge: how to create and preserve community, morality, and social order without destroying individual liberty. The nation's founders knew that the aim of education in a republic was to give people purpose by providing them with the opportunity to understand the cultural heritage and possess the knowledge that would make it possible to act rightly and lead happy lives. Educated citizens are engaged citizens.

We believe that only enlightened individuals are capable of carrying out the duties of a citizen. This ability is acquired through an education based on powerful ideas that, in a democracy, must be accessible to all on equitable terms. What people want for the best and brightest should be provided for all children. This is the responsibility of adults to the youths in society; it is the essential passing on of cultural heritage. For the most part, this heritage can be conveyed by a critical study of history, the humanities, literature, art, and natural and social science. History, and in particular American history, plays an important role in the education of democratic citizens. The ideal is an educated society in which all institutions and individuals understand that it is their responsibility to serve as teachers.

The condition Americans find today differs from this perennial purpose of education. Today's educational system focuses almost completely on workforce preparation. Work has an important, even central, place in the education of older students. Developing appropriate skills is a requirement of useful employment, but increasingly, schools, colleges, and universities focus on skills and information students will need to acquire a job, status, and money at the expense of educating students about civic participation and responsibilities. When the purpose of schooling is primarily for skill building, information acquisition, and job preparation, civic education has been replaced with job training.

Citizens must understand that there is only one purpose for education in the republic: to educate citizens to know about and participate in issues important to the flourishing of the republic. Everything else flows from this core purpose. Without qualified citizens, there are no individual freedoms, accumulations of private wealth, or innovators creating economic opportunity, and there is not a capable workforce to support businesses and institutions.

THE CHALLENGE OF DEMOCRACY

Contemporary America faces significant challenges, and the only way to meet those challenges is to have an informed and engaged citizenry. The best way to ensure that is through education, and particularly American history education with a focus on civic engagement. U.S. history has long been a mainstay in the curriculum of American schools. Throughout much of the nation, students study the subject in grades five, eight, and eleven. However, the emphasis is often on facts, events, dates, and personalities and is based on standards set by curriculum authorities, including corporate publishers of textbooks. The approach taken by these authorities is largely based on didactic historical chronology. In the quest to cover all events in American history, historical themes and trends are neglected and critical thought is minimized.

A successful curriculum should emphasize how past generations of American citizens have engaged civic debate in their communities, states, and nation while helping students acquire (a) the ability to challenge opinions and value statements and (b) the skills needed to debate current issues in their communities. A successful curriculum should engender affection for the nation's history and the civic responsibilities of individual citizens.

For many people, the study of history ends with high school education. College students in many fields never return to an investigation and understanding of deeper lessons in history. Also, continuing education in history is rare for adults, except for those who pursue this subject through reading and civic engagement. If Americans are to meet the challenges of modern society, citizens must recommit themselves to the historic reality that the United States is an idea sustained through an enduring debate of the issues, challenges, and opportunities that face its citizens.

REFERENCES

Emerson, R. W. 1937. Politics. In *The Harvard classics: Essays and English traits by Ralph Waldo Emerson*, ed. C. W. Eliot, 248. New York: Collier. (Orig. pub. 1844.)

Held, D. 1996. *Models of democracy*. Stanford, CA: Stanford University Press.

Jefferson, T. 1816, April 24. "Constitutionally and conscientiously democrats." [Letter to P. S. Dupont de Nemours.] Electronic Text Center, University of Virginia Library. http://etext.lib.virginia.edu/etcbin/ot2www-singleauthor?specfile=/web/data/jefferson/texts/jefall.o2w&act=text&offset=6825783&textreg=1&query=nemours (accessed August 23, 2007).

Lasch, C. 1995. *Revolt of the elites and betrayal of democracy*. New York: Norton.

Morison, S. E. 1965. *The Oxford history of the American people*. New York: Oxford University Press.

Phillips, K. 2002. *Wealth and democracy*. New York: Broadway.

Wood, G. S. 2002. *The American Revolution: A history*. New York: Modern Library Chronicles.

William E. White is the executive producer and director of educational program development at the Colonial Williamsburg Foundation and is responsible for the foundation's Teacher Institute Programs and Electronic Field Trip Series. *Richard van Scotter* is an educator and writer who lives in Colorado Springs, Colorado, and is a contributor to the media on cultural issues. *Michael H. Haroonian* is a professor emeritus at the University of Minnesota and past president of the National Council for the Social Studies. *James E. Davis* is the executive director of the Social Science Educational Consortium in Boulder, Colorado. He is also a civics textbook author.

QUESTIONS FOR REFLECTION

1. According to the authors, how is democracy at risk in the U.S. curriculum? Do you accept their basic premise for making such a claim?
2. The authors assert that "successful curriculum should engender affection for the nation's history and the civic responsibilities of individual citizens," but they do not say how this affection should be engendered. What do you think are the necessary steps to provoke more interest in U.S. history and the shared civic responsibilities of citizens?
3. It could be argued that the decline in teaching about history and civic responsibilities stems from those topics being left off national standards testing. Should history, social studies, and civic responsibilities curricula be included on state standards tests? If so, how might one accomplish this?

The Organization and Subject-Matter of General Education

ROBERT M. HUTCHINS
(1899–1977)

ABSTRACT: As president of the University of Chicago, Hutchins developed an undergraduate curriculum based on the Great Books. A well-known advocate for using perennialist philosophy to guide curriculum planning, he championed the need to preserve the intellectual traditions of Western culture. This article reflects the key elements of perennialist educational philosophy: education should (1) promote humankind's continuing search for truth, which is universal and timeless; (2) focus on ideas and the cultivation of human rationality and the intellect; and (3) stimulate students to think thoughtfully and critically about significant ideas.

I assume that we are all agreed on the purpose of general education and that we want to confine our discussion to its organization and subject-matter. I believe that general education should be given as soon as possible, that is, as soon as the student has the tools and the maturity it requires. I think that the program I favor can be experienced with profit by juniors in high school. I therefore propose beginning general education at about the beginning of the junior year in high school. Since I abhor the credit system and wish to mark intellectual progress by examinations taken when the student is ready to take them, I shall have no difficulty in admitting younger students to the program if they are ready for it and excluding juniors if they are not.

The course of study that I shall propose is rigorous and prolonged. I think, however, that the ordinary student can complete it in four years. By the ingenious device I have already suggested I shall be able to graduate some students earlier and some later, depending on the ability and industry that they display.

General education should, then, absorb the attention of students between the ages of fifteen or sixteen and nineteen or twenty. This is the case in every country of the world but this. It is the case in some eight or nine places in the United States.

If general education is to be given between the beginning of the junior year in high school and the end of the sophomore year in college and if a bachelor's degree is to signify the completion of it, the next question is what is the subject-matter that we should expect the student to master in this period to qualify for this degree.

I do not hold that general education should be limited to the classics of Greece and Rome. I do not believe that it is possible or desirable to insist that all students who should have a general education must study Greek and Latin. I do hold that tradition is important in education; that its primary purpose, indeed, is to help the student understand the intellectual tradition in which he lives. I do not see how he can reach this understanding unless he understands the great books of the western world, beginning with Homer and coming down to our own day. If anybody can suggest a better method of accomplishing the purpose, I shall gladly embrace him and it.

Nor do I hold that the spirit, the philosophy, the technology, or the theology of the Middle Ages is important in general education. I have no desire to return to this period any more than I wish to revert to antiquity. Some books written in the Middle Ages seem to me of some consequence to mankind. Most Ph.D.'s have never heard of them. I should like to have all students read some of them. Moreover, medieval scholars did have one insight; they saw that in order to read books you had to know how to do it. They developed the techniques of grammar, rhetoric, and logic as methods of reading, understanding and talking about things intelligently and intelligibly. I think it can not be denied that our students in the highest reaches of the university are woefully deficient in all these abilities today. They cannot read, write, speak, or think. Most of the great books of the western world were written for laymen. Many of them were written for very young laymen. Nothing reveals so clearly the indolence and inertia into which we have fallen as the steady decline in the number of these books read in our schools and colleges and the steady elimination of instruction in the disciplines through which they

may be understood. And all this has gone on in the sacred name of liberalizing the curriculum.

The curriculum I favor is not too difficult even for ordinary American students. It is difficult for the professors, but not for the students. And the younger the students are the better they like the books, because they are not old enough to know that the books are too hard for them to read.

Those who think that this is a barren, arid program, remote from real life and devoid of contemporary interest, have either never read the books or do not know how to teach. Or perhaps they have merely forgotten their youth. These books contain what the race regards as the permanent, abiding contributions its intellect and imagination have made. They deal with fundamental questions. It is a mistake to suppose that young people are interested only in football, the dramatic association, and the student newspaper. I think it could be proved that these activities have grown to their present overwhelming importance in proportion as the curriculum has been denatured. Students resort to the extracurriculum because the curriculum is stupid. Young people are interested in fundamental questions. They are interested in great minds and great works of art. They are, of course, interested in the bearing of these works on the problems of the world today. It is, therefore, impossible to keep out of the discussion, even if the teacher were so fossilized as to want to, the consideration of current events. But these events then take on meaning; the points of difference and the points of similarity between then and now can be presented. Think what a mine of references to what is now going on in the world is Plato's "Republic" or Mill's "Essay on Liberty." If I had to prescribe an exclusive diet for young Americans, I should rather have them read books like these than gain their political, economic, and social orientation by listening to the best radio commentators or absorbing the *New York Times*. Fortunately, we do not have to make the choice; they can read the books and listen to the commentators and absorb the *New York Times*, too. I repeat: these important agencies of instruction—the radio and the newspaper—and all other experiences of life, as a matter of fact—take on intelligibility as the student comes to understand the tradition in which he lives. Though we have made great advances in technology, so that the steam turbine of last year may not be of much value in understanding the steam turbine of 1938, we must remember that the fundamental questions today are the same with which the Greeks were concerned; and the reason is that human nature has not changed. The answers that the Greeks gave are still the answers with which we must begin if we hope to give the right answer today.

Do not suppose that in thus including the ancients in my course of study I am excluding the moderns. I do not need to make a case for the moderns. I do apparently need to remind you that the ancients may have some value, too.

Do not suppose, either, that because I have used as examples the great books in literature, philosophy and the social sciences, I am ignoring natural science. The great works in natural science and the great experiments must be a part and an important part of general education.

Another problem that has disturbed those who have discussed this issue is what books I am going to select to cram down the throats of the young. The answer is that if any reasonably intelligent person will conscientiously try to list the one hundred most important books that have ever been written I will accept his list. I feel safe in doing this because (a) the books would all be worth reading, and (b) his list would be almost the same as mine. There is, in fact, startling unanimity about what the good books are. The real question is whether they have any place in education. The suggestion that nobody knows what books to select is put forward as an alibi by those who have never read any that would be on anybody's list.

Only one criticism of this program has been made which has seemed to me on the level. That is that students who can not learn through books will not be able to learn through the course of study that I propose. This, of course, is true. It is what might be called a self-evident proposition. I suggest, however, that we employ this curriculum for students who can be taught to read and that we continue our efforts to discover methods of teaching the rest of the youthful population how to do it. The undisputed fact that some students can not read any books should not prevent us from giving those who can read some the chance to read the best there are.

I could go on here indefinitely discussing the details of this program and the details of the attacks that have been made upon it. But these would be details. The real question is which side are you on? If you believe that the aim of general education is to teach students to make money; if you believe that the educational system should mirror the chaos of the world; if you think that we have nothing to learn from the past; if you think that the way to prepare students for life is to put them through little fake experiences inside or outside the classroom; if you think that education is information; if you believe that the whims of children should determine what they should study—then I am afraid we can never agree. If, however, you believe that education should train students to think so that they may act intelligently when they face new situations; if you regard it as important for them to understand the tradition in which they live; if you feel that the present educational program leaves something to be desired because of its "progressivism," utilitarianism, and diffusion; if you want to open up to the youth of America the treasures of the thought, imagination, and accomplishment of the past—then we can agree, for I shall gladly accept any course of study that will take us even a little way along this road.

Robert M. Hutchins was both president of the University of Chicago and head of the Center for the Study of Democratic Institutions.

QUESTIONS FOR REFLECTION

1. What is the current "status" of the perennialist orientation to the curriculum? In other words, how widespread is this approach to curriculum leadership at the elementary, middle, and secondary levels?
2. What are the strengths and weaknesses of a perennialist curriculum?
3. Hutchins states that he "wish[es] to mark intellectual progress by examinations." What additional strategies can educators use to assess students' "intellectual progress"?
4. What does Hutchins mean when he says "The curriculum I favor is not too difficult even for ordinary American students. It is difficult for the professors [and teachers], but not for the students"?

The Case for Essentialism in Education

WILLIAM C. BAGLEY
(1874–1946)

ABSTRACT: *Founder of the Essentialistic Education Society and author of* Education and Emergent Man *(1934), Bagley was critical of progressive education, which he believed damaged the intellectual and moral standards of students. This article reflects the essentialist belief that our culture has a core of common knowledge that should be transmitted to students in a systematic, disciplined manner. Though similar to perennialism, essentialism stresses the "essential" knowledge and skills that productive citizens should have, rather than a set of external truths.*

What kind of education do we want for our children? Essentialism and Progressivism are terms currently used to represent two schools of educational theory that have been in conflict over a long period of time—centuries in fact. The conflict may be indicated by pairing such opposites as: effort vs. interest; discipline vs. freedom; race experience vs. individual experience; teacher-initiative vs. learner-initiative; logical organization vs. psychological organization; subjects vs. activities; remote goals vs. immediate goals; and the like.

Thus baldly stated, these pairings of assumed opposites are misleading, for every member of every pair represents a legitimate—indeed a needed—factor in the educative process. The two schools of educational theory differ primarily in the relative emphasis given to each term as compared with its mate, for what both schools attempt is an integration of the dualisms which are brought so sharply into focus when the opposites are set off against one another.

The fundamental dualism suggested by these terms has persisted over the centuries. It appeared in the seventeenth century in a school of educational theory the adherents of which styled themselves the "Progressives." It was explicit in reforms proposed by Rousseau, Pestalozzi, Froebel, and Herbart. It was reflected in the work of Bronson Alcott, Horace Mann, and later of E. A. Sheldon and Francis W. Parker; while the present outstanding leader, John Dewey, first came into prominence during the 1890s in an effort to resolve the dualism in his classic essay, now called "Interest and Effort in Education."

PROBLEMS OF AMERICAN EDUCATION

The upward expansion of mass education, first to the secondary and now to the college level, has been an outcome not alone of a pervasive faith in education, but also of economic factors. Power-driven machinery, while reducing occupations on routine levels, opened new opportunities in work for which general and technical training was essential. That young people should seek extended education has been inevitable. In opening high schools and colleges to ever-increasing numbers, it was just as inevitable that scholastic standards should be reduced. Theories that emphasized freedom, immediate needs, personal interest, and which in so doing tended to discredit their opposites—effort, discipline, remote goals—naturally made a powerful appeal. Let us consider, in a few examples, these differences in emphasis.

1. *Effort against Interest*—Progressives have given the primary emphasis to interest, and have maintained that interest in solving a problem or in realizing a purpose generates effort. The Essentialists would recognize clearly enough the motivating force of interest, but would maintain that many interests, and practically all the higher and more nearly permanent interests grow out of efforts to learn that are not at the outset interesting or appealing in themselves. If higher interests can grow out of initial interests that are intrinsically pleasing and attractive, well and good; but if this is not the case, the Essentialists provide a solution for the problem (at least, with some learners) by their recognition of discipline and duty—two concepts which the Progressives are disposed to reject unless discipline is self-discipline and duty self-recognized duty.

2. *Teacher against Learner Initiative*—Progressive theory tends to regard teacher-initiative as at best a necessary evil. The Essentialist

holds that adult responsibility for the guidance and direction of the immature is inherent in human nature—that it is, indeed, the real meaning of the prolonged period of necessary dependence upon the part of the human offspring for adult care and support. It is the biological condition of human progress, as John Fiske so clearly pointed out in his essay, "The Meaning of Infancy." The Essentialists would have the teachers responsible for a systematic program of studies and activities to develop the recognized essentials. Informal learning through experiences initiated by the learners is important, and abundant opportunities for such experiences should be provided; but informal learning should be regarded as supplementary rather than central.

3. *Race against Individual Experience*—It is this plastic period of necessary dependence that has furnished the opportunities for inducting each generation into its heritage of culture. The cultures of primitive people are relatively simple and can be transmitted by imitation or by coming-of-age ceremonies. More highly organized systems of education, however, become necessary with the development of more complicated cultures. The need of a firmer control of the young came with this development. Primitive peoples pamper and indulge their offspring. They do not sense a responsibility to provide for their own future, much less for the future of their children. This responsibility, with its correlative duty of discipline, is distinctly a product of civilization. The Progressives imply that the "child-freedom" they advocate is new, whereas in a real sense it is a return to the conditions of primitive social life.

4. *Subjects against Activities*—The Essentialists have always emphasized the prime significance of race-experience and especially of organized experience or culture—in common parlance, *subject-matter*. They have recognized, of course, the importance of individual or personal experience as an indispensable basis for interpreting organized race-experience, but the former is a means to an end rather than an educational end in itself. The Progressives, on the other hand, have tended to set the "living present" against what they often call the "dead past." There has been an element of value in this position of the Progressives, as in many other of their teachings. Throughout the centuries they have been protestants against formalism, and especially against the verbalism into which bookish instruction is so likely to degenerate. Present day Essentialists clearly recognize these dangers.

5. *Logical against Psychological Organization—* The Essentialists recognize, too, that the organization of experience in the form of subjects involves the use of large-scale concepts and meanings, and that a certain proportion of the members of each generation are unable to master these abstract concepts. For immature learners and for those who never grow up mentally, a relatively simple educational program limited in the earliest years of childhood to the most simple and concrete problems must suffice. This the Essentialists (who do not quarrel with facts) readily admit. The tendency throughout the long history of Progressivism, however, has been to discredit formal, organized, and abstract learnings *in toto,* thus in effect throwing the baby out with the bath, and in effect discouraging even competent learners from attempting studies that are "exact and exacting."

WHAT ABOUT FAILURE?

The Essentialists recognize that failure in school is unpleasant and that repetition of a grade is costly and often not effective. On the other hand, lack of a stimulus that will keep the learner to his task is a serious injustice to him and to the democratic group which has a stake in his education. Too severe a stigma has undoubtedly been placed upon school failure by implying that it is symptomatic of permanent weakness. By no means is this always the case. No less a genius than Pasteur did so poorly in his efforts to enter

the Higher Normal School of Paris that he had to go home for further preparation. One of the outstanding scientists of the present century had a hard time in meeting the requirements of the secondary school, failing in elementary work of the field in which he later became world-famous.

WHAT ARE THE ESSENTIALS?

There can be little question as to the essentials. It is no accident that the arts of recording, computing, and measuring have been among the first concerns of organized education. Every civilized society has been founded upon these arts, and when they have been lost, civilization has invariably collapsed. Nor is it accidental that a knowledge of the world that lies beyond one's immediate experience has been among the recognized essentials of universal education, and that at least a speaking acquaintance with man's past and especially with the story of one's country was early provided for in the program of the universal school. Investigation, invention, and creative art have added to our heritage. Health instruction is a basic phase of the work of the lower schools. The elements of natural science have their place. Neither the fine arts nor the industrial arts should be neglected.

ESSENTIALISTS ON DEMOCRACY

The Essentialists are sure that if our democratic society is to meet the conflict with totalitarian states, there must be a discipline that will give strength to the democratic purpose and ideal. If the theory of democracy finds no place for discipline, then before long the theory will have only historical significance. The Essentialists stand for a literate electorate. That such an electorate is indispensable to its survival is demonstrated by the fate that overtook every unschooled democracy founded as a result of the war that was "to make the world safe for democracy." And literacy means the development and expansion of ideas; it means the basis for the collective thought and judgment which are the essence of democratic institutions. These needs are so fundamental that it would be folly to leave them to the whim or caprice of either learner or teacher.

SUMMARY OF THE CASE FOR ESSENTIALISM

To summarize briefly the principal tenets of the present-day Essentialists:

1. Gripping and enduring interests frequently, and in respect of the higher interests almost always, grow out of initial learning efforts that are not intrinsically appealing or attractive. Man is the only animal that can sustain effort in the face of immediate desire. To deny to the young the benefits that may be theirs by the exercise of this unique human prerogative would be a gross injustice.

2. The control, direction, and guidance of the immature by the mature is inherent in the prolonged period of infancy or necessary dependence peculiar to the human species.

3. While the capacity for self-discipline should be the goal, imposed discipline is a necessary means to this end. Among individuals, as among nations, true freedom is always a conquest, never a gift.

4. The freedom of the immature learner to choose what he shall learn is not at all to be compared with his later freedom from want, fraud, fear, superstition, error, and oppression—and the price of this latter freedom is the effortful and systematic mastery of what has been winnowed and refined through the long struggle of mankind upward from the savage—and a mastery that, for most learners, must be under guidance of competent and sympathetic but firm and exacting teachers.

5. Essentialism provides a strong theory of education; its competing school offers a weak theory. If there has been a question in the past as to the kind of educational theory that the few remaining democracies of the world need, there can be no question today.

William C. Bagley was professor of education, Teachers College, Columbia University.

QUESTIONS FOR REFLECTION

1. What is the current "status" of the essentialist orientation to the curriculum? How widespread is this approach to curriculum leadership at the elementary, middle, and secondary levels?
2. What are the strengths and weaknesses of an essentialist curriculum?
3. How might Bagley respond to critics who charge that a tradition-bound essentialist curriculum indoctrinates students and makes it more difficult to bring about desired changes in society?
4. Bagley states: "There can be little question as to the essentials. It is no accident that the arts of recording, computing, and measuring have been among the first concerns of organized education." Do you agree with his view? What "basics" might be overlooked in an essentialist curriculum?

The Case for Progressivism in Education

**WILLIAM HEARD
KILPATRICK (1871–1965)**

ABSTRACT: Often called "the father of progressive education," Kilpatrick believed that the curriculum should be based on "actual living." In this article, Kilpatrick sets forth the key tenets of a progressive curriculum: (1) the curriculum, which begins with children's natural interests, gradually prepares them to assume more socially responsible roles; (2) learning is most effective if it addresses students' purposes and concerns; (3) students learn to become worthy members of society by actively participating in socially useful work; (4) the curriculum should teach students to think intelligently and independently; (5) the curriculum should be planned jointly by teachers and students; and (6) students learn best what they practice and live.

The title of this article is the editor's. The writer himself questions whether labels as applied to a living and growing outlook may not do more harm than good. Still, for certain purposes, a name is desirable. In what follows the writer tries to state his own position in a way to seem fair and true to that growing number who approve the same general outlook.

1. The center and nub of what is here advocated is that we start with the child as a growing and developing person and help him live and grow best; live now as a child, live richly, live well; and thus living, to increase his effective participation in surrounding social life so as to grow steadily into an ever more adequate member of the social whole.

Among the signs that this desirable living and consequent growth are being achieved, two seem especially significant. One is child happiness—for best work is interested work, and to be zestfully interested and reasonably successful is to be happy. The other, less obvious, but highly desirable is that what is done now shall of itself continually sprout more of life, deeper insights bringing new suggestions with new desires to pursue them.

2. The second main point has to do with learning and how this best goes on so as most surely to come back helpfully into life. For the test of learning is whether it so builds mind and character as to enhance life.

Two types of learning must here be opposed, differing so much in degree as to amount to a difference in kind. In one the learner faces a situation of his own, such that he himself feels inwardly called upon to face it; his own interests are inherently at stake. And his response thereto is also his own; it comes out of his own mind and heart, out of his own very self. He may, to be sure, have had help from teacher or book, but the response when it comes is his.

With the other kind of learning, the situation is set by the school in examination or recitation demands. This accordingly seems to the typical learner as more or less artificial and arbitrary; it does not arise out of his own felt needs. Except for the school demands there would be no situation to him. His response to this hardly felt situation is itself hardly felt, coming mainly out of words and ideas furnished by the textbook or, with older students, by the professor's lectures.

This second, the formal school kind of learning, we all know. Most of us were brought up on it. Except for those more capable in abstract ideas, the learning thus got tends to be wordy and shallow. It does little for mind or heart, and possibly even less for character, for it hardly gets into life.

The first kind has great possibilities. We may call it life's kind. It furnishes the foundation for the type of school herein advocated. Since what is learned is the pupil's own response to a situation felt to be his own, it is at once both heartfelt and mind-created. It is learned as it is lived; in fact, it is learned because it is lived. And the more one's heart is in what he does, the more important (short of too painful solicitude) it is to him, the more impelling will be the situation he faces; and the stronger accordingly will be his response and in consequence the stronger the learning. Such learning comes from deeper down in the soul and carries with it a wider range of connection both in its backward and in its forward look.

If we take the verb "to live" in a full enough sense, we may then say that, by definition, *learning has taken place when any part or phase of experience, once it has been lived, stays on with one to affect pertinently his further experience.* And we assert that *we learn what we live and in the degree that we live it.*

A further word about the school use of this life-kind of learning may help. Suppose a class is studying Whittier's "Barefoot Boy." I as teacher cannot hand over appreciation to John, nor tell it to him, nor can I compel him to get it. He must in his own mind and heart see something in the poem that calls out in him approval and appreciation. He must first respond that way before he can learn appreciation. Learning here is, in fact, the felt appreciation so staying with John as to get into his mind and character and thence come out appropriately into his subsequent life.

It is the same way with any genuinely moral response attitude. I cannot compel it. John must first feel that way in his own heart and accept it as his way of responding. Such an acceptance on John's part fixes what is thus learned in his character there to stay till the right occasion shall bring it forth again in his life. As it is accepted, so is it learned.

It is the same with ideas. These can be learned only as they are first lived. I cannot simply give John an idea, no matter how skillful I am with words. He may read and I may talk, but he has to respond *out of his own mind* with the appropriate idea as his own personal insight. He has to *see it* himself; something has to *click* inside him; the idea has to come from within, with a certain degree of personal creative insight, as his response to the problematic situation. Otherwise he hasn't it even though he may fool himself and us by using the appropriate words. I as teacher may help John to see better than otherwise he would, and his fellow pupils and I may help him make up his own mind and heart more surely to the good, but he learns only and exactly his own response as he himself accepts this as his way of behaving.

We may sum all this up in the following words: *I learn my responses, only my responses, and all my responses, each as I accept it to act on. I learn each response in the degree that I feel it or count it important, and also in the degree that it interrelates itself with what I already know. All that I thus learn I build at once into character.*

The foregoing discussion makes plain once more how the presence of interest or purpose constitutes a favorable condition for learning. Interest and felt purpose mean that the learner faces a situation in which he is concerned. The purpose as aim guides his thought and effort. Because of his interest and concern he gets more wholeheartedly into action; he puts forth more effort; what he learns has accordingly more importance to him and probably more meaningful connections. From both counts it is better learned.

3. Each learner should grow up to be a worthy member of the social whole. Thus to grow up means to enter more fully and responsibly into the society of which one is a member and in so doing to acquire ever more adequately the culture in terms of which the group lives.

The school exists primarily to foster both these aspects of growing up. The older type school, holding itself relatively secluded within its own four walls, shut its pupils off from significant contact with actual surrounding life and instead had them learn words about life and about the actual culture. The newer school aims explicitly to have its pupils engage actively in life, especially in socially useful work within the community, thus learning to manage life by participation in life, and acquiring the culture in life's varied settings where alone the culture is actually at work.

4. The world in which we live is changing at so rapid a rate that past-founded knowledge no longer suffices. Intelligent thinking and not mere habit must henceforth rule. Youth must learn better to think for themselves. They must understand the why of our institutions, of our system of legal rights, of moral right and wrong—because only then can they use these essential things adequately or change them intelligently. The newer school thus adds to its learning by living the further fact of pervasive change and undertakes to upbuild its pupils to the kind of thoughtful character and citizenship necessary for adequate living in such a changing social world. The older school cared little either for living or for change. Stressing book study and formal information and minimizing present-day problems, it failed to build the mind or character needed in modern life.

5. The curriculum, where pupil and teacher meet, is of necessity the vital focus of all educational theory.

The older curriculum was made in advance and given to the teacher who in turn assigned it as lessons to the pupils. It was a bookish content divided into separate subjects, in result remote from life. The pupils in their turn "learned" the lessons thus assigned and gave them back to the teacher in recitation or examination, the test being (in the main) whether what was given back was the same as what had been given out. Even the few who "succeeded" on this basis tended to get at best a pedantic learning. The many suffered, being denied the favorable opportunity for living sketched above. The lowest third suffered worst; such a curriculum clearly did not fit them, as becomes now more obvious with each advance of school leaving age.

The newer curriculum here advocated is first of all actual living—all the living of the child for which the school accepts responsibility. As we saw earlier, the child learns what he actually lives and this he builds at once into character. The quality of this living becomes then of supreme importance. The school, as we say, exists precisely to foster good living in the children, the kind of living fit to be built into character. The teacher's work is to help develop and steer this desirable living. This kind of curriculum, being real child living, cannot be made in advance and handed down either to teachers or to pupils. Living at the external command of another ceases by that much to be living for the person himself and so fails to meet desirable learning conditions.

The curriculum here sought is, then, built jointly by pupils and teacher, the teacher remaining in charge, but the pupils doing as much as they can. For these learn by their thinking and their decisions. The teacher helps at each stage to steer the process so as to get as rich living and, in the long run, as all-round living as possible. The richness of living sought includes specifically as much of meaning as the children can, with help from teacher and books, put into their living, meanings as distinctions made, knowledge used, considerations for others sensed, responsibilities accepted. The all-roundedness refers to all sides and aspects of life, immediately practical, social-moral, vocational, esthetic, intellectual. To base a curriculum on a scheme of set subjects is for most children to feed them on husks; the plan here advocated is devised to bring life to our youth and bring it more abundantly.

6. Are we losing anything in this new type school?

a. Do the children learn? Yes. Read the scientific studies (Wrightstone's, for example, and Aikin's report on the Thirty Schools) and see that the evidence is overwhelming. The "tool subjects" are learned at least as well, while the others depending on initiative and creative thinking are learned better. Honesty is much better built.

b. Does the new plan mean pupils will not use books? Exactly no; they do now show far more actual use of books. Textbooks as such will decrease perhaps to nothing, but the use of other books will appreciably increase, as experience already well shows.

c. Will children be "spoiled" by such a regime? Exactly no. For character building, this kind of school far surpasses the old sit-quietly-at-your-desk type of school. Modern psychology is well agreed that one cannot learn what one does not practice or live. The school here advocated offers abundant opportunity to associate on living terms with others and to consider them as persons. The schoolroom of the older school, in the degree that it succeeded with its rules, allowed no communication or other association except through the teacher. Accordingly, except for a kind of negative morality, it gave next to no chance to practice regard for others. The discipline of the school here advocated is positive and inclusive, consciously provided by the school, steered by the teacher, and lived by the pupils. Prejudiced journalists have caricatured the liberty as license; intelligent observation of any reasonably well run school shows exactly the contrary. This discipline is emphatically the constructive kind.

William Heard Kilpatrick was professor of education, Teachers College, Columbia University.

QUESTIONS FOR REFLECTION

1. What is the current "status" of the progressive orientation to the curriculum? How widespread is this approach to curriculum leadership at the elementary, middle, and secondary levels?
2. What are the strengths and weaknesses of a progressive curriculum?
3. What does Kilpatrick mean when he says, *"we learn what we live and in the degree that we live it"*? What learning experiences from your own life support Kilpatrick's view?
4. What is Kilpatrick's view of *discipline* as reflected in the following: "The discipline of the school here advocated is positive and inclusive, consciously provided by the school, steered by the teacher, and lived by the pupils"? How does this view differ from that usually associated with the term *discipline*?

Traditional vs. Progressive Education

JOHN DEWEY (1859–1952)

ABSTRACT: The most influential thinker of his time, John Dewey had a profound influence on educational theory and practice, philosophy, psychology, law, and political science. He was an eloquent spokesperson for progressive education; however, his ideas were adopted and often distorted by other educators. He protested these distortions in Experience and Education *(1938), the book from which this article was taken. In what follows, he expresses concern about how some progressive schools of the day were focusing on the learner while giving little or no attention to organized subject matter and the need for adults to provide guidance to learners.*

Mankind likes to think in terms of extreme opposites. It is given to formulating its beliefs in terms of *Either-Ors,* between which it recognizes no intermediate possibilities. When forced to recognize that the extremes cannot be acted upon, it is still inclined to hold that they are all right in theory but that when it comes to practical matters circumstances compel us to compromise. Educational philosophy is no exception. The history of educational theory is marked by opposition between the idea that education is development from within and that it is formation from without; that it is based upon natural endowments and that education is a process of overcoming natural inclination and substituting in its place habits acquired under external pressure.

At present, the opposition, so far as practical affairs of the school are concerned, tends to take the form of contrast between traditional and progressive education. If the underlying ideas of the former are formulated broadly, without the qualifications required for accurate statement, they are found to be about as follows: The subject-matter of education consists of bodies of information and of skills that have been worked out in the past; therefore, the chief business of the school is to transmit them to the new generation. In the past, there have also been developed standards and rules of conduct; moral training consists in forming habits of action in conformity with these rules and standards. Finally, the general pattern of school organization (by which I mean the relations of pupils to one another and to the teachers) constitutes the school a kind of institution sharply marked off from other social institutions. Call up in imagination the ordinary schoolroom, its time-schedules, schemes of classification, of examination and promotion, of rules of order, and I think you will grasp what is meant by "pattern of organization." If then you contrast this scene with what goes on in the family for example, you will appreciate what is meant by the school being a kind of institution sharply marked off from any other form of social organization.

The three characteristics just mentioned fix the aims and methods of instruction and discipline. The main purpose or objective is to prepare the young for future responsibilities and for success in life, by means of acquisition of the organized bodies of information and prepared forms of skill which comprehend the material of instruction. Since the subject-matter as well as standards of proper conduct are handed down from the past, the attitude of pupils must, upon the whole, be one of docility, receptivity, and obedience. Books, especially textbooks, are the chief representatives of the lore and wisdom of the past, while teachers are the organs through which pupils are brought into effective connection with the material. Teachers are the agents through which knowledge and skills are communicated and rules of conduct enforced.

I have not made this brief summary for the purpose of criticizing the underlying philosophy. The rise of what is called new education and progressive schools is of itself a product of discontent with traditional education. In effect it is a criticism of the latter. When the implied criticism is made explicit it reads somewhat as follows: The traditional scheme is, in essence, one of imposition from above and from outside. It imposes adult standards, subject-matter, and methods upon those who are only growing slowly toward maturity. The gap is so great that the required subject-matter, the methods of learning and of behaving are foreign to the existing capacities of the young. They are beyond the reach of the experience the young learners already possess. Consequently, they must be imposed; even though good teachers will use devices of art to cover up the imposition so as to relieve it of obviously brutal features.

But the gulf between the mature or adult products and the experience and abilities of the young is so wide that the very situation forbids much active participation by pupils in the development of what is taught. Theirs is to do—and learn, as it was the part of the six hundred to do and die. Learning here means acquisition of what already is incorporated in books and in the heads of the elders. Moreover, that which is taught is thought of as essentially static. It is taught as a finished product, with little regard either to the ways in which it was originally built up or to changes that will surely occur in the future. It is to a large extent the cultural product of societies that assumed the future would be much like the past, and yet it is used as educational food in a society where change is the rule, not the exception.

If one attempts to formulate the philosophy of education implicit in the practices of the newer education, we may, I think, discover certain common principles amid the variety of progressive schools now existing. To imposition from above is opposed expression and cultivation of individuality; to external discipline is opposed free activity; to learning from texts and teachers, learning through experience; to acquisition of isolated skills and techniques by drill, is opposed acquisition of them as means of attaining ends which make direct vital appeal; to preparation for a more or less remote future is opposed making the most of the opportunities of present life; to static aims and materials is opposed acquaintance with a changing world.

Now, all principles by themselves are abstract. They become concrete only in the consequences which result from their application. Just because the principles set forth are so fundamental and far-reaching, everything depends upon the interpretation given them as they are put into practice in the school and the home. It is at this point that the reference made earlier to *Either-Or* philosophies becomes peculiarly pertinent. The general philosophy of the new education may be sound, and yet the difference in abstract principles will not decide the way in which the moral and intellectual preference involved shall be worked out in practice. There is always the danger in a new movement that in rejecting the aims and methods of that which it would supplant, it may develop its principles negatively rather than positively and constructively. Then it takes its clue in practice from that which is rejected instead of from the constructive development of its own philosophy.

I take it that the fundamental unity of the newer philosophy is found in the idea that there is an intimate and necessary relation between the processes of actual experience and education. If this be true, then a positive and constructive development of its own basic idea depends upon having a correct idea of experience. Take, for example, the question of organized subject-matter—which will be discussed in detail later. The problem for progressive education is: What is the place and meaning of subject-matter and of organization *within* experience? How does subject-matter function? Is there anything inherent in experience which tends towards progressive organization of its contents? What results follow when the materials of experience are not progressively organized? A philosophy which proceeds on the basis of rejection, of sheer opposition, will neglect these questions. It will tend to suppose that because the old education was based on ready-made organization, therefore it suffices to reject the principle of organization *in toto*, instead of striving to discover what it means and how it is to be attained on the basis of experience. We might go through all the points of difference between the new and the old education and reach similar conclusions. When external control is rejected, the problem becomes that of finding the factors of control that are inherent within experience. When external authority is rejected, it does not follow that all authority should be rejected, but rather that there is need to search for a more effective source of authority. Because the older education imposed the knowledge, methods, and the rules of conduct of the mature person upon the young, it does not follow, except upon the basis of the extreme *Either-Or* philosophy, that the knowledge and skill of the mature person has no directive value for the experience of the immature. On the contrary, basing education upon personal experience may mean more multiplied and more intimate contacts between the mature and the immature than ever existed in the traditional school, and consequently more, rather than less, guidance by others. The problem, then, is how these contacts can be established without violating the principle of learning through personal experience. The solution of this problem requires a well thought-out philosophy of the social factors that operate in the constitution of individual experience.

What is indicated in the foregoing remarks is that the general principles of the new education do not of themselves solve any of the problems of the actual or practical conduct and management of progressive schools. Rather, they set new problems which have to be worked out on the basis of a new philosophy of experience. The problems are not even recognized, to say nothing of being solved, when it is assumed that it suffices to reject the ideas and practices of the old education and then go to the opposite extreme. Yet I am sure that you will appreciate what is meant when I say that many of the newer schools tend to make little or nothing of organized subject-matter of study; to proceed as if any form of direction and guidance by adults were an invasion of individual freedom, and as if the idea that education should be concerned with the present and future meant that acquaintance with the past has little or no role to play in education. Without pressing these defects to the point of exaggeration, they at least illustrate what is meant by a theory and practice of education which proceeds negatively or by reaction against what has been current in education rather than by a positive and constructive development of purposes, methods, and subject-matter on the foundation of a theory of experience and its educational potentialities.

John Dewey was, at various times during his career, professor of philosophy, Columbia University; head of the Department of Philosophy and director of the School of Education at the University of Chicago; and professor of philosophy at the University of Michigan.

QUESTIONS FOR REFLECTION

1. Using Dewey's concept of *Either-Or* thinking, can you identify other current examples of such thinking in education?
2. A key tenet of progressive education is that there is a close, vital relationship between actual experience and education. What is the nature of this relationship?
3. What does Dewey mean in the following: "When external control is rejected, the problem becomes that of finding the factors of control that are inherent within experience"? In regard to the curricular area with which you are most familiar, what are some examples of how "control" might reside within the experiences students have while they are learning?

Leaders' Voices— Putting Theory into Practice

Values: The Implicit Curriculum

LINDA INLAY

ABSTRACT: *The "implicit curriculum" of a school teaches values; however, there is often a gap between the values a school espouses and the values students experience. The author describes the development of a charter middle school culture that teaches character through the explicit curriculum of reading, writing, and arithmetic and through an implicit curriculum of values.*

Whether teachers intend to or not, they teach values. Teachers' behaviors are, in fact, moral practices that are deeply embedded in the day-to-day functioning of the classroom (Jackson, Boostrom, & Hansen, 1993). Likewise, a school's culture communicates values through the ways in which faculty, parents, and students treat one another and through school policies on such issues as discipline and decision making.

In his eight-year study of more than 1,000 classrooms, Goodlad found a "great hypocrisy" (1984, p. 241) in the differences between what schools espouse as values and what students experience. This disparity produces cynical students who don't take seriously what schools say about character (Postman & Weingartner, 1969).

At River School, a charter middle school of approximately 160 students, we work hard to develop an entire school culture that teaches character through the explicit curriculum of reading, writing, and arithmetic and through an implicit curriculum of values—what Adlerian psychologist Raymond Corsini called the implicit four *R*s: responsibility, respect, resourcefulness, and responsiveness (Adler, 1927/1992; Ignas & Corsini, 1979). My introduction to this school-wide approach to character education began 30 years ago when school director and Catholic nun Sr. Joan Madden, who was

collaborating with Corsini in implementing what they called Individual Education, hired me as a teacher. She told me, "You are not teaching subjects. You are teaching who you are."

At River School, we rarely talk about character—nor do we have posters or pencils that trumpet values—because we know that the most effective character education is to model the values that we want to see in our students. We attempt to align every part of our school—from assessment to awards, from decision making to discipline—to encourage and foster students' character development. Our mission is to help students cultivate a strong sense of self through demonstrations of personal and social responsibility.

FOSTERING PERSONAL RESPONSIBILITY

We have barely spent a month in our school's new location when the fire alarm goes off. We have not yet established our safety protocols, and two of our students have pulled the fire alarm while horsing around, a typical middle school antic. Before I even get back to my office, the two students who pulled the alarm have voluntarily acknowledged the mistake that they made. They decide to "clean up their mistake" by apologizing to the affected people on campus, from the caretakers in the toddler program to the senior citizens in the Alzheimer's Center. One student voluntarily talks with the fire chief about her error. The mistake becomes an important lesson, as all mistakes should be.

These students are willing to be accountable for their actions. We view negative behavior as a sign of neediness, and we respond with positive contact, not just discipline of the behavior. Humans resist the diminution of spirit that comes with typical messages implying that they are "bad" or "wrong." These students have instead heard a call to responsibility:

You made a mistake. To be human means making mistakes and learning from them.

What do you think you should do to clean up this mistake?

Teachers focus on creating an atmosphere in which it is emotionally safe to make mistakes. We acknowledge when we have made a mistake and work hard not to get angry at students' mistakes. Within this emotionally safe terrain, we hold students accountable for their actions, allowing them to experience appropriate and natural consequences. Parents know, for example, that they are not responsible for bringing their children's forgotten homework to school.

The view of responsibility is the essential notion of our systems approach to character and relates to our underlying assumption about human beings. Humans are self-determining creatures; we have free will to make choices. Because of our ability to think, discern, and reflect, we want to make our own choices.

If humans have free will and the capacity to choose, then experiencing the consequences of "good" or "poor" choices is how humans learn to make choices. At the River School, we organize our school's curriculum and culture to provide many age-appropriate choices so that students learn, through trial and error, what works and what doesn't work for growing as independent learners and human beings.

The middle school years are about testing limits and shedding the old skin of the elementary school years, and we expect our students to cross

boundaries as a way to learn about choice, consequences, freedom, and responsibility. Students say that they notice that our discipline system is different because we treat them like adults, even when they don't act like adults. We trust in our students' innate ability to make good decisions for themselves—with practice over time.

We define responsibility as an attitude that reflects a willingness to see oneself as cause, instead of victim. Students who see themselves as active rather than passive don't blame others. They see the mistake or the situation as the result of the choices that they have made. If the situation is out of their control, they see their responses to the situation as their own choice to be positive or to be negative.

This approach lessens extrinsic control, nurtures our students' intrinsic motivation to learn, and increases their self-confidence to meet and overcome challenges.

FOSTERING SOCIAL RESPONSIBILITY

Self-determination is one side of human need; a sense of community and belonging is the other. Our vision of students developing fully as individuals cannot occur without the community being a safe place that accepts the different qualities of each individual. Particularly in middle school, we see students struggling to meet these two needs. They desperately want to belong, so they assume the external trappings and mannerisms of their peer group. At the same time, they try to break away from traditions and develop their individual identities.

To grow as individuals, students must believe that the school community accepts individual differences. One test of a school's effectiveness in teaching social responsibility is how well students treat those who are socially inept on the playground. Most of the time, our students respect one another. When they do not, the school community has opportunities to learn about making our school safe for everyone.

Last year, for example, students were picking on a classmate who we suspected had a mild form of autism. With the student's consent, we devoted several team meetings to helping the school community understand why he sometimes stared at others or made odd noises. As a result of these conversations, students began to include him at lunch tables, lessened the teasing considerably, and defended him when teasing occasionally occurred. Such open conversations help each student become aware of how he or she makes a difference to every other student in school.

How do we teach *responsiveness,* this value of being responsible for one another? We begin with the recognition that we need to fulfill our students' needs for significance ("I matter") and for belonging (being part of a community) by structuring the school's culture so that we listen to students, take their concerns seriously, and depend on them.

We organize students into homeroom advisories in which the homeroom teacher is their advocate. The homeroom groups further divide into smaller "listening groups" that meet every other week with their teachers to share concerns and acknowledge successes. These meetings provide one of the ways in which we allow students to participate in solving problems in the school.

In one case, for example, someone was trashing the boys' bathroom. Student advisories discussed the problem, and one homeroom class volunteered to monitor the bathrooms throughout the day. Instead of the unspoken code of silence often practiced by middle schoolers, students reported the boy involved because they trusted that he would be treated with respect in the discipline process. In another case, students disliked some features of the dress code that had been developed by the student council and teachers. Students presented a proposal for changes at a staff meeting and did such an outstanding job of responding to the purposes of the dress code that the changes were approved.

We also take time to listen to students' ideas and questions as we develop the school's curriculum, modeling responsiveness by taking their concerns seriously. We follow the approach of the National Middle School Association (2002) to curriculum integration by asking students to develop their own questions for dealing with particular standards. The student question "What do you wish you could say but don't have the courage to say?" was the impetus for a unit last year that studied the First Amendment; various positions on evolution; and Galileo, Gandhi, Susan B. Anthony, and other figures who dared to take an unpopular stand.

If a student has problems with a teacher, he or she can call on a facilitator to mediate a conference. The purpose of a facilitating conference with a teacher is not to question his or her authority or to find out who is wrong and who is right. The goal of the conference is common understanding; the teacher works to understand the student's point of view and the student works to understand the teacher's point of view. Earlier this year, for example, a student felt picked on by his teacher and asked for a conference. Following the protocol of the facilitating conference, the teacher began with an "invitation" and asked, "What do you want to say to me?" After the student spoke, the teacher rephrased what the student said, and after the teacher spoke, the student rephrased what the teacher said. Through this active listening format, each came to a better understanding of the reasons for the other's behavior, and their relationship and classroom interactions improved.

We use this same conference format with students, faculty, and parents. Facilitators for conflicts are usually the advisors or the principal, with new teachers learning these communication skills primarily through observation and special training during faculty meetings. In some situations, students facilitate their own conflicts in listening groups, or they ask teachers to allow them time to do so. Last year, for example, two students began harassing each other on Halloween, when one laughed at the other's costume. When their conflict came to a head four months later, a facilitating conference helped them come to a resolution. They apologized to each other without being asked to and were friendly for the rest of the year.

Once understanding occurs, both sides can reach a solution together. Conflicts in the community become opportunities to learn how to deal with differences, to learn how to listen and solve problems. In this way, we empower our students to voice their beliefs and opinions more effectively. Whether expressing their beliefs and opinions about personal relationships, the dress code, or the

First Amendment, students have to think through the logic and rationale of their position. This active engagement results in improved critical thinking skills, and the students develop a sense of responsibility for their community and their learning.

Students also learn that the community depends on them as they perform community chores, offer community service, and plan school meetings and events. When the school's environment meets students' needs for significance and belonging, students are more likely to cooperate with others and look toward the common good.

Throughout our school, the implicit message is clear: We deeply respect our students, not just because they are our students, but because all human beings have the right to be respected in these ways. The seminal ideas of our program are not new. We have simply translated them into practical, day-to-day applications embedded in the school setting so that the entire school's culture becomes our implicit curriculum. Everything that we do and say teaches character.

REFERENCES

Adler, A. (1927/1992). (Trans. C. Brett.) *Understanding human nature*. Oxford, UK: One World Publications.

Goodlad, J. (1984). *A place called school*. New York: McGraw-Hill.

Ignas, E., & Corsini, R. J. (1979). *Alternative educational systems*. Itasca, IL: F. E. Peacock Publisher.

Jackson, P., Boostrom, R., & Hansen, D. (1993). *The moral life of schools*. San Francisco: Jossey-Bass.

National Middle School Association. (2002). NMSA position statement on curriculum integration [Online]. Available: www.nmsa.org/cnews/positionpapers/integrativecurriculum.htm

Postman, N., & Weingartner, C. (1969). *Teaching as a subversive activity*. New York: Delacourt Press.

Linda Inlay is director of the River School in Napa, California.

QUESTIONS FOR REFLECTION

1. With reference to the grade level and subject area with which you are most familiar, what examples can you cite to support Inlay's assertion that "whether teachers intend to or not, they teach values"?
2. Inlay suggests that "we need to fulfill our students' needs for significance ('I matter') and for belonging (being part of a community)." To what extent do you agree (or disagree) with Inlay's position?
3. According to Inlay, the culture at River School has become part of the school's "implicit curriculum." Reflect on the schools you have attended and describe the implicit curricula you have experienced.

LEARNING ACTIVITIES

Critical Thinking

1. Imagine that Dewey was alive today, teaching in the subject area and at the level with which you are most familiar. Describe the curricular experiences students would have in his classes. Develop similar hypothetical scenarios for the other influential

historical curriculum theorists whose work appears in this chapter: Robert M. Hutchins, William C. Bagley, and William Heard Kilpatrick.

2. Think back to the teachers you had during your K–12 and undergraduate years in school. Which ones would you classify as being predominantly perennialist? Essentialist? Progressive? Reconstructionist?

3. How do you imagine teachers at the elementary, middle/junior, and senior high levels differ in regard to their preferred philosophical orientation to curriculum?

4. Of the four philosophical orientations to curriculum covered in this chapter, which one do you prefer? Least prefer? If you look ahead ten years, do you anticipate any shift in your preference?

5. Study the goals of a curriculum plan of your choice and try to determine whether they are "subject-centered," "society-centered," or "learner-centered." Which do you think they should be? Which of the four philosophical orientations covered in this chapter is closest to each of these three approaches to curriculum goals? Share your findings with other students in your class.

6. There were many important statements about the goals of education during the 1900s, each of which has influenced the processes of curriculum planning. One of the best-known statements of broad goals is known as the "Seven Cardinal Principles of Education," issued in 1918 by the Commission on Reorganization of Secondary Education. The seven goals in *Cardinal Principles of Secondary Education* included the following: health, command of fundamental processes (reading, writing, and computation), worthy home membership, vocation, citizenship, worthy use of leisure time, and ethical character. More recently, the U.S. Department of Education, under the Clinton Administration, developed Goals 2000, which called for the attainment of goals in the following eight areas: school readiness; school completion; student achievement and citizenship; mathematics and science; adult literacy and lifelong learning; safe, disciplined, and alcohol- and drug-free schools; teacher education and professional development; and parental participation. How have the goals changed? In what respects have they remained the same?

Application Activities

1. What specific steps will you take throughout the remainder of your professional career to ensure that your philosophical orientation to curriculum remains dynamic, growing, and open to new perspectives rather than becoming static and limited?

2. Conduct a survey of current journals in education and try to locate articles that reflect the four philosophical orientations to curriculum that are covered in this chapter: perennialism, essentialism, progressivism, and reconstructionism.

3. Help your instructor set up a group activity wherein four to six students role-play teachers who are meeting for the purpose of determining broad, general goals for a curriculum. (The students should focus on a level and subject with which they are most familiar.) The rest of the class should observe and take notes on the curricular orientations expressed by the role-players. After the role-play (about 15–20 minutes), the entire class should discuss the curriculum planning process it has just observed.

4. For a one-month period, keep a tally of all the comments that are made in the mass media regarding what is (or should be) taught in schools. Compare your list with

those of other students and identify the philosophical orientations to curriculum that are reflected in the comments.

Field Experiences

1. Visit a school and interview the principal or other member of the administrative team about the broad goals of the school's curriculum. Which of the following educational philosophies are reflected in his or her comments: perennialism, essentialism, progressivism, or reconstructionism?
2. Observe the classes of two different teachers at the level with which you are most familiar. Which *one* of the four philosophical orientations to curriculum most characterizes each teacher?
3. Ask your instructor to arrange for a curriculum coordinator from the local school district to visit your class. In addition to finding out about this individual's work, ask him or her to describe the curriculum planning process in the district.

Internet Activities

The Internet Activities for each chapter of *Curriculum Leadership: Readings for Developing Quality Educational Programs* are designed to help you use the Internet to further your study of curriculum leadership. Use key words related to curriculum leadership and your favorite search engine to gather the latest information and resources.

1. Visit the following three sites on the Internet and begin a search for materials of interest on philosophical orientations to curriculum: the home page of the American Philosophical Association (APA) "WWW Philosophy Sites" maintained by the University of Waterloo, and "Philosophy in Cyberspace."
2. Visit the Center for Dewey Studies maintained by Southern Illinois University at Carbondale and compile a list of online publications, associations, and reference materials related to the influence of Dewey's work on education.
3. Subscribe to the John Dewey Discussion Group ("open to anyone with an interest in any facet of Dewey's philosophy") on the Internet. Then participate in discussions, seminars, and other online activities of interest.
4. Numerous organizations influence the development of curriculum goals in the United States. Visit the websites of two or more of the following organizations and compare the curriculum goals reflected in their position statements and political activities with regard to education.

Alternative Public Schools Inc. (APS)
American Federation of Teachers (AFT)
National Education Association (NEA)
Chicago Teachers Union (or other municipal teachers' organization)
National Congress of Parents and Teachers (PTA)
Parents as Teachers (PAT)
Texas State Teachers Association (or other state teachers' organization)

2

Social Forces: Present and Future

FOCUS QUESTIONS

1. What are ten contemporary social forces that influence the curriculum?

2. What are three developmental tasks that effective curricula help learners accomplish?

3. What are three levels of social forces, and how do they influence the curriculum?

4. Which concepts from the social sciences can help curriculum leaders understand the social forces that influence the curriculum?

5. What is the role of futures planning in developing a curriculum that prepares students for an unknown future?

Just as education plays an important role in shaping the world of tomorrow, it is in turn shaped by current and future economic, political, social, demographic, and technological forces. Since education reflects the goals and values of a society, schools must harmonize with the lives and ideas of people in a particular time and place. Curriculum leaders, therefore, must understand how schools and school systems mirror the surrounding societal milieu.

Since social environments are dynamic rather than static, descriptions of a society must be modified continually. A critical dimension of curriculum leadership, then, is the continuous reconsideration of present social forces and future trends. Though no one can foretell the future, it has a profound effect on curriculum leadership. As Alvin Toffler (1970, p. 363) stated in *Future Shock*, a book that captured the nation's attention four decades ago, "All education springs from some image of the future. If the image of the future held by a society is grossly inaccurate, its educational system will betray its youth." Thus, current social forces and future trends should be examined regularly in an effort to understand their significance for curricula from kindergarten through high school.

Today, we are faced with an array of challenges and opportunities unimagined at the start of the previous century. Though we don't know what the future holds, we do know that there will be a vital link between education and the quality of that future. Now, more than ever, we are aware of the role education can play in shaping a desired future—virtually every country in the world realizes that education is essential to the individual and collective well-being of its citizens in the future.

CURRICULUM AND THE FUTURE

For curriculum leaders, the key question becomes "How do I incorporate an unknown future into the curriculum?"

Lined up behind this question, like so many airplanes on a runway, are major trends and issues that will have a profound influence on education at all levels in the future: increasing ethnic and cultural diversity; the environment; changing values and morality; the family; the technological revolution; the changing world of work; equal rights; crime and violence; lack of purpose and meaning; and global interdependence. Each of these trends and issues has profound implications for the processes of curriculum leadership.

Curriculum Leadership Strategy

Identify a group of teacher leaders to develop an analysis of how the trends and issues discussed in this chapter specifically impact schools within a district. What commonalities and differences are there across grade levels?

---

1. *Increasing Ethnic and Cultural Diversity.* The percentage of ethnic minorities in the United States has been growing steadily since the end of World War II. In 2007, 37.9 million immigrants lived in the United States. According to the Center for Immigration Studies (2007) immigrants account for one in eight U.S. residents, and between 1.5 and 1.6 million immigrants arrive in the United States each year. The center (2007) describes the challenge of providing equal educational opportunity to America's growing immigrant population:

> Immigrants and their young children (under 18) now account for one-fifth of the school-age population, one-fourth of those in poverty, and nearly one-third of those without health insurance, creating enormous challenges for the nation's schools. . . . The low educational attainment of many immigrants, 31 percent of whom have not completed high school, is the primary reason so many live in poverty, use welfare programs, or lack health insurance, not their legal status or an unwillingness to work.

In addition, the Census Bureau estimates that by 2025, half of U.S. youth will be white and half "minority," and by 2050, no one group will be a majority among adults.

Increasing diversity in the United States is reflected, of course, in the nation's schools. In 2007, 41.3 percent of public school students were considered to be part of a minority group, an increase of more than 19 percentage points from 1972 (National Center for Education Statistics, 2007). This increase was largely due to the growth in the proportion of Latino students. In 2007, Latino students accounted for 19.2 percent of the public school enrollment, up by more than 13 percentage points from 1972. African Americans were 17.3 percent of the public school enrollment in 2000, up by more than 2 percentage points from 1972. The percentage of students from other racial and ethnic minority groups also increased, from 1 percent in 1972 to 5.7 percent in 2007 (National Center for Education Statistics, 2007).

Changes in the racial and ethnic composition of student enrollments are expanding the array of languages and cultures found in the nation's public schools. Differences in student backgrounds offer opportunities to enhance the learning environment; however, these differences also raise challenges for schools. There is, for example, an increased demand for bilingual programs and teachers in many parts of the country. All but a few school districts face a critical shortage of minority teachers. And there is a need to develop curricula that address the needs and backgrounds of all students—regardless of their social class, gender, sexual orientation, or ethnic, racial, or cultural identity. In "The Dimensions of Multicultural Education" in this chapter, James A. Banks outlines five dimensions of comprehensive multicultural education to meet the needs of all students.

Though at one time it was believed that the United States was a "melting pot" in which ethnic cultures would melt into one, ethnic and cultural differences have remained very much a part of life in the United States. A "salad-bowl" analogy captures more accurately the cultural pluralism of U.S. society. That is, the distinguishing characteristics of cultures are to be preserved rather than blended into a single culture. Or, as one columnist observed regarding the continuing increase in people of mixed race identity in the United States: "America's melting pot isn't going to create a bland, homogenous porridge so much as a deeply flavored, spicy stew" (Stuckey, 2008). The United States has always derived strength from the diversity of its people, and all students should receive a high-quality education so that they may make their unique contributions to society.

2. *The Environment.* People have become increasingly proficient in their efforts to control and use nature to increase their safety, comfort, and convenience. Scientific and technological advances and the increased industrialization of the United States led many to believe that people could indeed control and use nature as they pleased. We now realize that is not the case. Sophisticated computer simulations and ecological experts, as well as such events as the break-up of Arctic ice, warn us that we must become careful stewards of the planet. Some people believe that we have already passed the point of no return—that we have so polluted our air and water and plundered our natural resources that it is only a matter of time before we perish, regardless of what corrective measures we now take. The number of species that have become extinct or been placed on the endangered species list during our lifetimes indicates that the worldwide ecosystem is in peril. Clearly, problems such as overpopulation, global warming, pollution, depletion of the ozone layer, and the grim possibility of other environmental disasters should be addressed by curricula at all levels.

3. *Changing Values and Morality.* For some time, we have been losing faith in many of our institutions, including government, schools, religion, and the professions. The dizzying pace of events around the globe pushes aside values almost as rapidly as styles come and go in the fashion world. For example, in a short period of time we have undergone a shift in values ranging from frugality to conspicuous consumption to ecologically oriented frugality to renewed conspicuous consumption and currently, questions of an economic meltdown. There is much unrest in today's middle-aged generation because of its inability to pass its values on to the young. Our fluctuating moral standards contribute to adult and child drug abuse, teen alcoholism, and the divorce rate. Our private lives are played out in a world where much of the landscape seems threatening and constantly changing.

There is an increasing belief on the part of many educators that curricula should include experiences in the process of valuing and values clarification. One approach to teaching values and moral reasoning is known as *character education.* The need for character education is reflected in the *2004 Report Card: The Ethics of American Youth,* based on a national survey of nearly 25,000 high school students conducted by the Josephson Institute of Ethics, a nonprofit, nonsectarian corporation. The survey revealed that nearly two-thirds (62 percent) cheated on exams and more than one in four (27 percent) stole from a store within the past 12 months. Additionally, 40 percent admitted they "sometimes lie to save money."

Some educators, who support their positions with extensive research, assert that the processes of moral judgment should be taught at all school levels to help students develop so that they live according to principles of equity, justice, caring, and empathy (see, for example, Lawrence Kohlberg's "The Cognitive-Developmental Approach to Moral Education" in Chapter 3). Many parents and teachers oppose the inclusion of values and morals as part of the curriculum. They believe this is an area of instruction that should be reserved for the home and church or synagogue. At the very least, our various social institutions—the schools, the media, the government, organized religion, the family—must redefine and clarify their responsibilities for instruction in values and morality.

4. *Family.* The family has traditionally been one of the most important institutions in American society. In many cases today, however, the family no longer functions as a closely knit unit. There is great mobility among a large segment of the population—the family is not tied closely to the community, and family members are spread out over a wide geographical area. The roles of father and mother have undergone change, and more and more children are raised without benefit of their natural father's or mother's presence. In "Dialogue across Cultures: Communicating with Diverse Families" in this chapter, Arti Joshi, Jody Eberly, and Jean Konzal stress the importance of communicating with today's diverse families.

The stress placed on families in a complex society is extensive and not easily handled. For some families, such stress can be overwhelming. The structure of families who are experiencing the effects of financial problems, substance abuse, or violence, for example, can easily begin to crumble. Children in these families are more likely to experience health and emotional problems as well as difficulties at school.

With the high rise in divorce and women's entry into the workforce, family constellations have changed dramatically. No longer is a working father, a mother who stays at home, and two or three children the only kind of family in the United States. The number of single-parent families, stepparent families, blended families, and extended families has increased dramatically during the last decade. Three million children are now being raised by their grandparents, and an equal number are raised by same-sex parents (Hodgkinson, 2002). Twenty-eight percent of families with children were headed by a single parent in 2000. Of these children, 20 percent lived with only their mothers, about 4 percent lived with only their fathers, and 4 percent with neither parent (Federal Interagency Forum on Child and Family Statistics, 2003).

5. *Technological Revolution.* Learners in the future will need to attain extensive skills in computer-based technologies; they will use computers to communicate worldwide and to generate creative solutions to complex problems. To equip students to access vast stores of information available on the Internet, on CD-ROMs and DVDs, and in countless data banks, schools, colleges, and universities will need to become more technologically rich and teachers more technologically sophisticated. No longer able to resist the "irresistible force" of Information Age technology (Mehlinger, 1996), they will need to understand that computers are not merely tools—their expanding capabilities and interactivity now provide students with structured learning environments with complex, comprehensive capabilities to access and manipulate information.

Clearly, the Internet, the World Wide Web, and related telecommunications technologies have transformed the world in which we live. This includes the times and places where work is done; the range of products and services available; and how, when, and where we learn. Computers, interactive multimedia, and communication devices that employ the awesome power of tiny silicon microchips are having a profound effect on curriculum and instruction at all levels. Within the context of expanding telecommunications technologies, Cynthia L. Scheibe stresses the importance of "A Deeper Sense of (Media) Literacy," to use the title of her article in this chapter. Similarly, Kevin Maness suggests that teachers should "protect" children from a "bombardment of media exposure" by providing them with critical media literacy skills (see "Teaching Media-Savvy Students about the Popular Media" in this chapter).

6. *Changing World of Work.* The technological revolution is radically changing work and the workplace. Clearly, we are in the midst of a revolution that will leave virtually no form of work unchanged.

A key aim that should guide curriculum leaders is to develop educational experiences that create within students the ability and the desire to continue self-directed learning over a lifetime. In a rapidly changing job market, career changes will be the norm, and the ability to continue learning throughout one's career a necessity.

7. *Equal Rights.* Women and minority groups in America have become more vocal and more active in demanding equal rights. African Americans, Latino and Hispanic Americans, Asian Americans and Pacific Islanders, and Native Americans and Alaskan natives often do not agree among themselves about how to proceed, but they share in a common cause of fighting back against years of inequality, inferior status, marginalization, and often inhumane treatment. In addition, those who know poverty, regardless of ethnicity or race, also struggle for a better life. In response, however, some members of the historically dominant Anglo-European American culture believe that their rights are now being violated in favor of other groups.

Though much has been accomplished to provide equal educational opportunity to all students, regardless of social class, abilities or disabilities, gender, sexual orientation, ethnicity, or race, much remains to be done. According to Raymond V. Padilla's article in this chapter, "High-Stakes Testing and Accountability as Social Constructs across Cultures," legislation such as No Child Left Behind (NCLB) can lead to curricula that result in "the isolation of people and schools."

In spite of legislation such as NCLB, the curricular and instructional experiences provided to students are not always appropriate. Many students who have no disabilities now end up in special education classes because of a lack of adequate education options designed to meet the needs of children and youth with diverse learning styles. With the continuing emphasis on higher standards, there is the risk that many low-achieving students will be inappropriately labeled as having a disability. In "The 'Three A's' of Creating an Inclusive Curriculum and Classroom" in this chapter, Tina M. Anctil provides guidelines for teachers to follow as they meet the needs of students with differing abilities.

In spite of a general consensus that schools should promote social change and equal opportunity, some individuals believe that educational practices reproduce the existing social order by providing qualitatively different curricular and instructional experiences to children from different socioeconomic classes. In effect, schools help to maintain the existing stratification in society and the differences between the "haves" and the "have-nots." As Joel Spring (1999, pp. 290–291) asserts: "the affluent members of U.S. society can protect the educational advantages and, consequently, economic advantages, of their children by living in affluent school districts or by using private schools. [T]heir children will attend the elite institutions of higher education, and their privileged educational backgrounds will make it easy for them to follow in the footsteps of their parents' financial success." Similarly, in "Remembering Capital: On the Connections between French Fries and Education" in this chapter, Michael W. Apple maintains that a conservative power bloc in the United States "has integrated education into a wider set of ideological commitments [and] one of its major achievements has been to shift the blame for unemployment and underemployment, for the loss of economic competitiveness, and for the supposed breakdown of 'traditional' values and standards in the family, education, and paid and unpaid workplaces *from* the economic, cultural, and social policies and effects of dominant groups *to* the school and other public agencies."

Curriculum Leadership Strategy

Develop several in-depth case studies of students with diverse cultural and linguistic backgrounds in the school district or school with which you are most familiar. To what extent are the curricula these students experience meeting their needs? Not meeting their needs? As a curriculum leader, what steps should you take as a result of your conclusions?

---

8. *Crime and Violence.* Ours is a violent, crime-ridden world, as terrorism, street crime, family violence, gang violence, hate crimes, and organized crime attest. Repeated investigations into crime and dishonesty at the highest levels of government, welfare and tax fraud, corruption in business, television and movie violence, and drug abuse have contributed to an alarming erosion of concern for the rights and property of others.

The impact of crime on education is staggering; more than $600 million is spent annually on school vandalism, a figure the National Parent Teacher Association points out exceeds the amount spent on textbooks for our nation's schools. The National Association of School Security Directors gives the following estimates of school-based crimes committed each year:

- 12,000 armed robberies
- 270,000 burglaries
- 204,000 aggravated assaults
- 9,000 rapes (Rich, 1992)

The rate of victimization in U.S. schools has decreased since 1992, according to *Indicators of School Crime and Safety, 2003,* jointly published by the Bureau of Justice Statistics and the National Center for Education Statistics. However, students ages 12–18 were victims of about 764,000 violent crimes and 1.2 million crimes of theft at school in 2001 (Bureau of Justice Statistics and the National Center for Education Statistics, 2003). Seventy-one percent of public schools experienced one or more violent incidents, while 36 percent reported one or more such incidents to the police.

In addition, the U.S. Department of Justice estimates that there are more than 30,500 gangs and approximately 816,000 gang members (Moore and Terrett, 1999). According to *Indicators of School Crime and Safety, 2003,* 22 percent of students in public schools reported that there were street gangs in their schools, compared with 5 percent in private schools. Urban students were more likely to report street gangs at their schools (29 percent) than were suburban and rural students (18 percent and 13 percent, respectively).

Since 1996, the nation's concern about school crime and safety heightened as a result of a string of school shootings. Among the communities that had to cope with such tragic incidents were Moses Lake, Washington (1996); Pearl, Mississippi (1997); West Paducah, Kentucky (1997); Jonesboro, Arkansas (1998); Springfield, Oregon (1998); Littleton, Colorado (1999); Conyers, Georgia (1999); and Santee and El Cajon, California (2001). Since the recurring question after each instance of horrific school violence was "Why?" there was a renewed effort to understand the origins of youth violence.

9. *Lack of Purpose and Meaning.* The inability of many individuals to develop and pursue goals they consider worthwhile has led to a lack of purpose and meaning in their lives. Fragmented communities, changes in family structure, the seeming immorality of many leaders, injustice, income disparities, the dizzying pace of technological changes, sharp fluctuations in the global economy, our loss of faith in science and the "experts"— all make it difficult to establish a sense of purpose and meaning. An alarming number of people feel disconnected from the larger society, their families, and themselves.

An increasing number of children and youth live in situations characterized by extreme stress, family violence, grinding poverty, crime, and lack of adult guidance. Searching for purpose and meaning in their lives, they may escape into music, video games, movies, sex, cruising shopping malls, or hanging out with friends on the street. The vulnerability of today's adolescents was vividly portrayed in *Great Transitions: Preparing Adolescents for a New Century,* a report by the Carnegie Council on Adolescent Development: "Altogether, nearly half of American adolescents are at high or moderate risk of seriously damaging their life chances. The damage may be near-term and vivid, or it may be delayed, like a time bomb set in youth" (Carnegie Council on Adolescent Development, 1995). The list of alarming concerns among children and youth is sobering: academic failure, retention, and dropping out; accidents; anorexia; violent behavior; criminal activity; cultism; depression; drug abuse; suicide; teenage pregnancy; and sexually transmitted diseases.

10. *Global Interdependence.* The relationships among the nations of the world can have a significant impact on curriculum development at all levels. It is crucial that education help us understand our interconnectedness with all countries and all people and become more sensitive to our own and other's motives and needs. Our future well-being depends on being able to participate intelligently and empathetically in the global community. Curricula of the future must emphasize global interdependence, respect for the views and values of others, and an orientation toward international cooperation for resolving global threats to security, health, the environment, and human rights.

Our fate is inextricably bound up with that of the rest of the world. For example, the horrific events of September 11, 2001, were felt around the world. Thus, an important aim of the curriculum at all levels is to cultivate an understanding of the social, psychological, and historical settings that cause others to think and act as they do.

Social Forces and the Individual

The close relationship between the social environment and the development of curricula is evident if we consider three developmental tasks that citizens in a democratic society must accomplish. First, each person must select an occupation. With the exception of the family, the work environment is the setting for most individuals' day-to-day experiences. Second, a democratic society requires citizens who are prepared to deal with the current issues of government. Finally, each person faces the challenge of achieving self-fulfillment and self-development. Thus, from the learner's standpoint, an appropriate school program—from preschool through the graduate level—must enhance his or her ability to accomplish developmental tasks in three areas: *vocation, citizenship,* and *self-fulfillment.* In every society the nature of these developmental tasks is different. In industrialized societies such as ours, for example, rapid change is the norm; thus pathways for accomplishing life's developmental tasks are continually changing.

Since social forces are constantly changing, educational programs should change with them. Moreover, few social forces exist independent of each other. They are interrelated, and each individual in the society experiences the influence of most, if not all, of them at the same time. This point is illustrated by the following hypothetical situation.

Liza is an African American who lives in the ghetto of a large city. She is fourteen years old, the oldest of a family of nine children. Her father left the family five years ago because he could not find employment and knew that his children could receive more financial support from the government if he left home. Liza's mother works during the evening, so Liza is expected to care for the apartment and children when she gets home from school. The apartment has only two rooms and is infested with rats. It has poor plumbing and toilet facilities, and the heating system works only occasionally. The children get only one real meal a day and have no money to spend at school. Their clothing is old and worn.

Kevin is a white boy who lives in a middle-class suburb. He is fourteen years old, and has a seventeen-year-old sister. His father is a lawyer who works downtown and commutes daily, often arriving home very late in the evening. Kevin's mother attends many social functions and has a serious drinking problem. His parents often have loud arguments and are openly talking about divorce. Kevin's sister uses cocaine. She often spends the weekend with her boyfriend. Kevin is well fed, lives in an attractive home with a good-sized yard, and is given a generous allowance.

Roy is a white boy who lives near a factory on the outer fringe of the city. He is fourteen years old, and he has one older brother and one older sister. His father is employed at the nearby factory as a blue collar worker. Roy lives in a small but comfortable house. His family does not have many luxuries, but their needs are well satisfied. His parents are deeply religious and take Roy to church with them twice on Sunday and again on Wednesday evening. His father is a veteran and proudly displays several medals. He also belongs to the local VFW. Roy's parents spend much time with their children. He often hears them talk about how radicals and the minority groups are taking over the country.

All three of these young people attend the same school and most of the same classes. Roy walks three blocks to school, but both Liza and Kevin ride the bus. Consider these questions and try to formulate some answers to them in your own mind.

1. How are all three of these young people alike?
2. How are they different?
3. What social forces have played a significant part in their lives?
4. How can the school curriculum plan for meeting the needs of these students, considering the social setting from which they come?
5. How would you, as the teacher of these three students, deal with the similarities and differences they bring from diverse social backgrounds?

It is obvious that each person is unique in the way that social forces have affected his or her life, and the school curriculum is challenged to deal with that individuality. But the curriculum is also asked to meet the needs of the total society. This problem can be seen as you consider the following questions:

1. How actively involved should the school become in dealing with social forces? (Should the faculty lead the students in picket lines?)
2. What percentage of the curriculum should be devoted to learning about social issues?
3. How should the school respond to parents who feel that the curriculum is either overemphasizing or underemphasizing particular social issues?

Levels of Social Forces

Curriculum leaders should consider three levels of social forces that influence the curriculum (see Figure 2.1). First, there is the *national and international level* where concerns such as the preceding ten trends and issues should be identified and utilized in planning.

There is also the level of social forces found in the *local community*, including family structure; class structure; the ethnic, racial, and religious backgrounds of students; and the values of the community in which the curriculum will be implemented. Social forces at the community level significantly affect learners and decidedly influence their perceptions regarding the appropriateness of the curriculum they experience.

Curriculum Leadership Strategy

With respect to Figure 2.1, develop a report that describes how the local community influences curricula in the school district or school with which you are most familiar. What implications do your findings have for your role as a curriculum leader?

Finally, there is the *culture* of the educational setting within which the curriculum is implemented—the social forces that determine the quality of life at the school. The many social forces at this level include the individual learner's social status, the teacher's role in the school, the teacher's role in relation to other professional staff, and the degree of harmony or discord that characterizes school–community relationships.

FIGURE 2.1

Levels of Social Forces that Influence the Curriculum

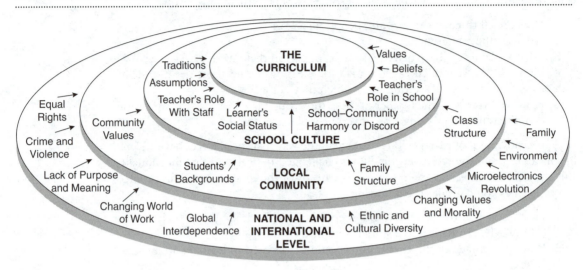

On one level, schools are much alike; on another, they are very unique. Each has a distinctive culture—a set of guiding beliefs, assumptions, values, and traditions that distinguish it from other educational settings at the same level. Some may be characterized as communal places where there is a shared sense of purpose and a commitment to providing students with meaningful, carefully thought out curricular experiences. Others lack a unified sense of purpose or direction, and they drift, rudderless, from year to year. Still others may be characterized by internal discord, conflict, and divisiveness. Regardless of how they become manifest in a school's culture, social forces at this level are of major significance in curriculum planning and instruction.

Concepts from the Social Sciences

Several concepts from sociology, anthropology, and social psychology are very useful in defining and describing the social forces to be considered in curriculum leadership. Among these concepts are *humanity, culture, enculturation* or *socialization, subculture,* and *cultural pluralism*. This list of relevant concepts could be extended greatly, but these are among the most salient when considering the influence of social forces on contemporary curriculum leadership.

The concept of *humanity* can be a significant organizing element in curriculum leadership, and it is one that is particularly needed as the nations of the world become more interdependent and together address problems of pollution, energy and food shortages, and terrorism. In addition to trying to understand the social forces that affect society in the United States or Canada, curriculum leaders should consider forces that affect humanity as a whole. The issues and information to be considered and the curricular approaches developed should go well beyond national borders. These "cultural universals" would be a major guiding focus in curriculum leadership. For example, an increased global perspective on the arts could enlarge students' understanding in many areas of the curriculum.

The concept of culture has been defined in many ways. Simply put, *culture* is the way of life common to a group of people; it represents their way of looking at the world. It also consists of the values, attitudes, and beliefs that influence their behavior. There are hundreds of different cultures, and no one can hope to learn about all of them. In spite of their specific differences, however, all cultures are alike in that they serve important functions within the group. For example, a group's culture may prescribe certain ways of obtaining food, clothing, and shelter. It may also indicate how work is divided up and how relationships among men, women, and children, and between the old and the young, are patterned. Within the United States, we find cultural groups that differ according to language, ethnicity, religion, politics, economics, and region of the country. The regional culture of the South, for example, is quite different from that of New England. North Dakotans are different from Californians, and so on. Socioeconomic factors, such as income and occupation, also contribute to the culture of communities. Recall, for instance, the hypothetical scenario earlier in this chapter—Liza, Kevin, and Roy had very different cultural backgrounds.

From birth to death, each person is immersed in a culture or cultures. Early in life, each person learns the patterns of behavior supported by the culture into which he or she was born. Learning this first culture is called *enculturation* or *socialization*. As our society becomes more complex and places ever-increasing demands and stresses on parents, various agencies assume more responsibility for enculturating and socializing children and youth.

A *subculture* is a division of a cultural group consisting of persons who have certain characteristics in common while they share some of the major characteristics of the larger culture. For example, our society consists of varied subcultures, and many children from these subcultures come to school with life experiences that differ significantly from those of children the schools and teachers are used to encountering. Therefore, curriculum leaders should understand the differences and similarities among the subcultures in a community, as well as those within the national culture.

An additional critical point is that the individual learner should have positive feelings about his or her culture. This is possible only if curriculum leaders understand that the behaviors, attitudes, and beliefs that children from nonmainstream cultures bring to school are just *different,* not wrong—a point Shirley Brice Heath (1996) brings out in *Ways with Words,* an insightful analysis of how children from two subcultures, "Roadville" and "Trackton," come to school possessing "ways with words" that are incongruent with the "school's ways":

> Roadville and Trackton residents have a variety of literate traditions, and in each community these are interwoven in different ways with oral uses of language, ways of negotiating meaning, deciding on action, and achieving status. . . . Roadville parents believe it their task to praise and practice reading with their young children; Trackton adults believe the young have to learn to be and do, and if reading is necessary for this learning, that will come. . . . In Trackton, the written word is for negotiation and manipulation—both serious and playful. Changing and changeable, words are the tools performers use to

create images of themselves and the world they see. For Roadville, the written word limits alternatives of expression; in Trackton, it opens alternatives. Neither community's ways with the written word prepares it for the school's ways. (pp. 234–235)

Cultural pluralism refers to a comingling of a variety of ethnic and generational lifestyles, each grounded in a complexity of values, linguistic variations, skin hues, and perhaps even cognitive world views. The term *pluralism* implies that, theoretically at least, no one culture takes precedence over any other. Cultural pluralism means that each person, regardless of self- or group-identification, is entitled to the respect, dignity, freedom, and citizen rights promised by law and tradition.

Cultural pluralism requires that curriculum leaders develop learning experiences and environments in which each group's contribution to the richness of the entire society is genuinely validated and reflected to the extent possible in the curriculum. Schools that facilitate understanding of cultural pluralism radiate a tone of inclusiveness in policies, practices, and programs. So significant are the implications of cultural pluralism for contemporary curriculum leadership that the concept is discussed in several articles throughout this book.

Futures Planning

What curricula will best prepare learners to meet the challenges of the future? Of course, no one has *the* answer to this question. Nevertheless, it is important for curriculum leaders to think carefully about the future. *Futures planning* is the process of conceptualizing the future as a set of possibilities and then taking steps to create the future we want. As Alvin Toffler (1970, p. 460) pointed out in *Future Shock,* we must choose wisely from among several courses of action: "Every society faces not merely a succession of *probable* futures, but an array of *possible* futures, and a conflict over *preferable* futures. The management of change is the effort to convert certain possibles into probables, in pursuit of agreed-on preferables. Determining the probable calls for a science of futurism. Delineating the possible calls for an art of futurism. Defining the preferable calls for a politics of futurism."

Futures planners project current social forces into the future with the hope of identifying and developing ways to meet the challenges associated with those forces. Unlike past futurists, today's futures planners seldom predict a single future; to use Toffler's term, they develop a set of *possible* futures.

In using the processes of futures planning, curriculum leaders work with students, parents, and other members of the community in identifying and discussing present trends, and forecasting and projecting the effects of one trend compared to another. Alternative scenarios are developed based on efforts to "change" the future, either by taking action or by doing nothing.

For example, the Internet, the World Wide Web, and related telecommunications technologies illustrate how planning for the future in light of present social forces influences the curriculum. For more than thirty years, there have been continued improvements in technology. Computers have moved from the laboratories, universities, and big companies into the mainstream of everyday life. They are at the grocery checkout counter, the neighborhood service station, and in our homes. Each day, millions of people around the world spend countless hours in cyberspace where they visit chat rooms, make business transactions, participate in distance learning programs, and receive instantaneous reports on newsworthy events. In light of the continued dazzling pace of developments in technology, what are the implications for today's curriculum leaders? Clearly, a critical form of literacy for the future is the ability to use computers for learning and solving problems.

The rapid pace of change demands that the curriculum prepare children, youth, and adults for the present as well as the future. Learning to look ahead—to see local, national, and global forces and trends in terms of alternative futures and consequences—must be part of the curriculum. Today, the curriculum should help learners participate in the development of the future through their involvement in meaningful, authentic learning experiences in the present.

CRITERION QUESTIONS—SOCIAL FORCES

What criterion questions may be derived from the social forces discussed in this chapter? Providing for individual differences among learners, the teaching of values, the development of self-understanding, and the development of problem-solving skills are four important curriculum planning criteria that illustrate how social forces influence the curriculum.

First, individual differences among learners are related to family and home background, subculture, and community background. The descriptions of Liza, Kevin, and Roy earlier in this chapter illustrate how social forces provide a key to understanding individual differences which should be provided for in the curriculum. In light of individual differences among learners, then, the criterion questions for curriculum leaders are as follows:

1. What social or cultural factors contribute to individual differences among learners?
2. How can the curriculum provide for these differences?

Second, all curricula are implemented within a social climate that teaches values that may or may not be clearly stated, or about which curriculum planners and teachers may be unaware. This "hidden curriculum," as it is commonly termed, also refers to the attitudes and knowledge the culture of a school unintentionally teaches students. The discussion of cultural pluralism earlier in this chapter illustrates the relationship between social forces and the teaching of values. Thus, the criterion questions in regard to teaching values are as follows:

3. What values *are* we teaching?
4. What values do we *wish* to teach?

Third, self-understanding as a curriculum criterion is related to cultural pluralism and to various social forces such as changing values and changes in family life. Effective educational programs help students—regardless of cultural background, family situation, or challenging life circumstances—to understand themselves more fully. Thus, a salient criterion question in regard to facilitating self-understanding is:

5. How can the school program assist learners in achieving their goals of self-understanding and self-realization?

Finally, problem solving as a curriculum criterion asks whether the curriculum and the teaching of that curriculum help learners to clarify problems and develop appropriate problem-solving strategies. Three criterion questions to gauge the effectiveness of a curriculum at promoting problem-solving skills are as follows:

6. Has the curriculum been planned and organized to assist learners in identifying and clarifying personal and social problems?
7. Does the curriculum help learners acquire the problem-solving skills they will need now and in the future?
8. Does the curriculum include the development of skills in futures planning?

REFERENCES

Annie E. Casey Foundation. *Kids Count Data Book 1998.* Baltimore, MD: Author, 1998.

Bureau of Justice Statistics and National Center for Education Statistics. *Indicators of School Crime and Safety, 2003.* Washington, DC: Authors, 2003.

Carnegie Council on Adolescent Development. *Great Transitions: Preparing Adolescents for a New Century.* New York: Carnegie Corporation of New York, 1995.

Center for Immigration Studies. *Immigrants in the United States, 2007: A Profile of America's Foreign-Born Population.* Washington, DC: Author, 2007.

Heath, Shirley Brice. *Ways with Words: Language, Life and Work in Communities and Classrooms.* Cambridge, UK: Cambridge University Press, 1996.

Hodgkinson, H. "Changing demographics: A call for leadership." In W. Owens & L. Kaplan, eds., *Best practices, best thinking, and emerging issues in school leadership,* pp. 3–14. Thousand Oaks, CA: Sage, 2002.

Josephson Institute: Center for Youth Ethics. *2004 Report Card: The Ethics of American Youth.* Los Angeles, CA: Joseph Institute, 2004.

Mehlinger, Howard D. "School Reform in the Information Age." *Phi Delta Kappan* 77, no. 6 (February 1996): 400–407.

Moore, J. P., & C. P. Terrett. *Highlights of the 1997 National Youth Gang Survey. Fact Sheet.* Washington, DC: U.S. Department of Justice, Office of Justice Programs, Office of Juvenile Justice and Delinquency Prevention, 1999.

National Center for Education Statistics. *Status and Trends in The Education of Racial and Ethnic Minorities.* Washington, DC: Author, September, 2007.

Rich, J. M. "Predicting and confronting violence." *Contemporary Education,* 64 (1992): 35–9.

Spring, Joel. *American Education,* 8th Ed. New York: McGraw-Hill, Inc., 1999.

Stuckey, M. "Multiracial Americans Surge in Numbers, Voice: Obama Candidacy Focuses New Attention on Their Quest for Understanding." MSNBC Interactive. Retrieved May 28, 2008, from www.msnbc.msn.com/id/24542138.

Toffler, Alvin. *Future Shock.* New York: Random House, 1970.

U.S. Department of Justice, Office of Justice Programs. *2003 America's Children in Brief: Key National Indicators of Well-Being.* Federal Interagency Forum on Child and Family Statistics, 2003.

Dialogue across Cultures: Communicating with Diverse Families

ARTI JOSHI
JODY EBERLY
JEAN KONZAL

ABSTRACT: It is well accepted in the field of home-school relations and child development that parents and teachers must work together to build common expectations and to support student learning. In this article, the authors assess teachers' perceptions about communication with diverse families as they seek to learn more about how teachers currently understand their students' family cultures, how they come to these understandings, and how this understanding influences how they reach out to parents.

INTRODUCTION

It is well accepted in the field of home-school relations and child development that parents and teachers must work together to build common expectations and to support student learning (Bronfenbrenner, 1986, 1979; Coleman & Hoffer, 1987; Epstein, 2001; Henderson & Berla, 1994). It follows, therefore, that the teacher must establish good relations and open communication with parents.[1] Building strong, trusting, and mutually respectful relationships between parents and teachers who share similar cultural backgrounds is difficult enough. Doing so between parents and teachers who come from different backgrounds is even more difficult.

New Jersey, like many other states, is experiencing a significant influx of new immigrants—from countries such as India, Pakistan, China, Russia, Poland, Nigeria, Liberia, Mexico, Dominican Republic, and Haiti. In addition, New Jersey remains one of the most segregated states in the country, educating the majority of its African-American families in the inner city and first-ring communities that surround the cities. Our teaching profession consists primarily of European-American women who are, in Lisa Delpit's words, teaching "other people's children" and who need help in doing so (1995).

Given this diversity in New Jersey classrooms, we conceptualized a multiphase research project with the ultimate goal of helping teachers understand family values, beliefs, and practices in order to create a learning environment at school that acknowledges and builds upon these. Simultaneously, the project aims to facilitate parents' understanding of the school's values, beliefs, and practices so they can create a congruent learning environment at home.

It is the first goal that this study seeks to address. We need to learn more about how teachers currently understand their students' family cultures, how they come to these understandings, and how this understanding influences how they reach out to parents. Little has been written about this "missing link" in our knowledge base related to parent involvement (Caspe, 2003, p. 128).

Towards this end, we designed a survey to assess New Jersey teachers' current knowledge and practices. Therefore the following questions are addressed in the article:

1. How do teachers define parent involvement; how do they define culture?
2. What practices do teachers use in working with families in general and, more specifically, with families from cultures different from their own?

3. What is the extent and nature of awareness of teachers with respect to the cultural beliefs and practices of the families in their classrooms?
4. What aspects of culture do teachers identify as important influences on children's education?
5. In what ways do teachers currently make use of what they know about their students' cultural backgrounds when planning instruction?

THE IMPACT OF CULTURE ON CHILD DEVELOPMENT AND LEARNING

Bronfenbrenner's ecological theory of development (1979, 1986) and Super and Harkness's developmental niche theory (1997) argue that a child's development is influenced not only by their parents, but by other systems as well, including the family's culture, the caregivers' "ethno-theories" related to child development, and school and community values and beliefs.

Related to this, Gutierrez and Rogoff's (2003) definition of culture as a dynamic, situational, and historic construct stresses that a person's culture is not solely influenced by their ethnicity or race, but rather by a number of additional variables as well: i.e., historical context, geographic location, gender, generation, age, religion, group memberships, and level of education. Gutierrez and Rogoff (2003) argue that the way one approaches learning is influenced by the practices inherent within the individual's cultural community characterized by all of the variables mentioned above—not solely a person's ethnicity.

Even Patricia Greenfield (1994), whose theory of cultural differences based on child-rearing goals towards either independence or interdependence, warns against jumping to conclusions that a person is automatically inclined towards either one or the other solely based on their ethnicity. Therefore, this study raises questions of how to translate understandings of a child's multifaceted culture into classroom practices that open communication with parents and engage the child in a culturally responsive way.

THE IMPORTANCE OF PARENT/ SCHOOL COMMUNICATION

Since it is acknowledged that both parents and teachers are responsible for educating our children, it would seem that it would be in the child's best interest for us all to be working towards the same goals. This common-sense notion is also supported by research. For example, studies into the impact of facilitating ongoing interactions with parents in order to help parents reinforce the school's goals and objectives at home (Berger, 1996; Epstein, 1990), the impact of parental interest in and encouragement of school activities on positive attitudes towards school and learning (Epstein, 2001), and finally the impact of communication and cooperation between home and school on children's learning (Epstein, 1990) all point to the critical importance of this relationship.

When dealing with parents from cultures different from their own, open lines of communication with parents are even more essential. If teachers are to create learning environments conducive to learning for children from different cultures, they need insight into the values, beliefs, and practices of those cultures (Bensman, 2000; Trumbull, Rothstein-Fisch, Greenfield, & Quiroz, 2001; Delpit, 1995; Lee, Spencer, & Harpalani, 2003).

Bensman (2000) argues that cultural interchange, the process by which teachers learn about cultures that their students bring to class and parents learn about the school/classroom culture, is the way to facilitate student success. Delpit (1995), Lee et al. (2003), and Trumbull (2001) argue that this knowledge can then be translated into classroom activities that honor and incorporate culturally-based knowledge.

Unfortunately such open communication between parents and teachers is not common place. The dynamics of the parent-teacher relationship create communication problems that under the best of circumstances can be problematic. However, teachers and parents carry many preconceived notions about each other that make communication even more difficult.

BARRIERS TO GOOD PARENT/ SCHOOL RELATIONS

Researchers have identified a variety of factors that inhibit open communication between parents and teachers regardless of cultural backgrounds (Epstein & Becker, 1982; Dodd & Konzal, 1999, 2001). These include different knowledge bases of teachers and parents, different perspectives in relation to "my" child versus "all children," use of jargon or "educator-speak"[2] when communicating with parents (Dodd & Konzal, 1999, 2001), lack of time for informal opportunities to get to know each other in non-stressful, non-bureaucratic encounters (Henry, 1996), and, finally, different understandings of the "proper" roles for teachers and parents (Greenwood & Hickman, 1991; Hughes & MacNaughton, 2000; Joshi, 2002).

Unfortunately, when parents and teachers come from different backgrounds, the barriers listed above are exacerbated and further barriers are introduced. Reviewing the literature, Bermudez and Marquez (1996) identified the following additional barriers that prevent parents and teachers from communicating openly and honestly, ". . . lack of English language skills, lack of understanding of the home-school partnership, lack of understanding of the school system, lack of confidence, work interference, negative past experiences with schools, and insensitivity or hostility on the part of the school personnel" (p. 3). These (and other) teacher attitudes towards parents many times lead to what parents perceive as insensitivity and even hostility (Bermudez & Marquez, 1996). Many times these negative and/or stereotypical teacher attitudes towards parents derive from cultural blinders.

Trumbull et al. (2001) argue that the major barrier to parent-school communication is the lack of understanding of the very different beliefs that parents and educators may hold in relation to the purposes, goals, and outcomes of schooling. They argue ". . . it, is rare that schools (or those in charge of them) get below the surface to understand how those differences can lead not only to different goals but also completely different views of schooling and, hence, parent involvement" (p. 31).

This lack of understanding of the underlying beliefs about the parents' goals for child-rearing and education may lead to an unarticulated clash with educators' values and beliefs. In such cases, parents and educators are each pulling in different directions without necessarily being aware of what is happening. The child, of course, is in the middle, receiving one set of messages at home and another set at school. Surfacing these unarticulated different belief systems is in the best interests of the children—but it is not easy.

TRANSLATING CROSS-CULTURAL UNDERSTANDINGS INTO PRACTICE

For communication between parents and teachers to be meaningful and responsive, it is necessary to understand the cultural frameworks within which parents' function, since parental attitudes are influenced by cultural and economic factors (Greenfield, 1994; Trumbull et al., 2001). Parents foster the development of children through developmental pathways which are couched within a given culture (Weisner, 1998). Aspects of culture like communication, education, dress, religion, and values for socialization and interactions influence an individual's behavior, values, and attitudes.

"The schools then become the agents who help children build bridges between the cultures of the family and other communities, by means of practices that respect and respond to the diversity of families" (Wright & Stegelin, 2003). In order to do this, is important for teachers to understand the cultural frameworks from which they function (Caspe, 2003).

Unfortunately, more often than not, teachers don't have deep understandings of either their own or their students' family cultural pathways and do not know how to build these bridges (e.g., see Gonzalez-Mena, 2000). There has been significant work in identifying the need for and developing strategies for culturally responsive teaching (Caspe, 2003; Delpit, 1995; Ladson-Billings, 1991; Marion, 1980; Trumbull et al., 2001; Voltz, 1994). However, in the schools we visit we see little evidence that teachers are familiar with these practices.

Being able to build bridges for families and teachers so that they have insight into each other's worlds is essential for the well being of the children we hold in common. As a first step towards helping teachers understand how culture influences beliefs, values, and practices related to education and to connecting this understanding to their professional practice, we conducted a survey in order to find out (1) what teachers currently know and believe about the influence of culture on learning and (2) the practices they currently use to interact with parents and to design instructional activities for children from cultures different from their own.

Method

Participants were practicing teachers, specialists, and administrators in public and private central New Jersey schools serving children from preschool to 5th grade. One of the local elementary schools was approached and permission of the principal was obtained. The purpose of the survey was explained to the teachers and other faculty members in a faculty meeting. Subsequently, at a second faculty meeting, surveys were distributed and completed by all teachers, administrators, and other faculty members.

The total number of the respondents from this school was 25. The remaining respondents were working in preschools that were state funded and were enrolled in a graduate class at a local college. The purpose of the research was explained. All the students agreed to participate in the research. Informed consent was received from all of the participants. The final sample consisted of 40 respondents.

A majority of the respondents were females (92%) and PK–3 classroom teachers (82%). Of the respondents who reported their teaching experience, 42% (14) had 3 years or less teaching experience, while 30% (10) had more than 14 years of teaching experience. Ninety percent of the respondents identified their ethnicity, out of which 83% (30) were European American, 11% (4) were African American, 3% (1 each) were Hispanic-Latino and Middle Eastern. In terms of the demographic composition of the children, many of the classrooms had approximately half European American, while the remaining were African American, Hispanic, or Asian.

In order to design the questionnaire for this study an extensive review of literature on parent involvement and culture was undertaken. Based on the literature, common practices of parent involvement and components of culture were identified and a draft of the questions was developed (Bennett, 2003; Shade, Kelly, & Oberg, 1997; Wright & Stegelin, 2003). The questionnaire was refined from feedback from a focus group of practicing teachers and parents who had similar demographics as the final sample. To further refine the questionnaire, it was piloted with a group of central and southern New Jersey teachers enrolled in a graduate class at a local college.

The final questionnaire was comprised of three types of questions: open ended, ranking, and Likert type rating questions. The survey had two main sections: (1) parental involvement and (2) knowledge of culture and its impact upon a child's education. The first section of the survey consisted of questions where participants were asked to define parental involvement and to address means and challenges of involving parents.

In the second section, participants were first asked to define culture and then rank the most important components of understanding culture. The components of culture consisted of six different categories: communication patterns, social values, ways of learning, child rearing, outward displays, and religious practices (See Benett, 2003; Shade, Kelly, & Oberg, 1997; Wright & Stegelin, 2003).

Other questions asked participants to rate, on a 4-point scale, their awareness of cultural components and the components of culture that they felt most influenced a child's academic success. Open ended questions were used to seek the participants' definitions of parent involvement and culture along with their own practices regarding the same.

Likert type and ranking scales were used for all other questions. After the data were collected, the open ended questions were read by each of the researchers and emergent themes were identified. Consensus was reached amongst the researchers on the themes that emerged.

FINDINGS ABOUT PARENT INVOLVEMENT

When asked to define parent involvement, the most common response was participation in school activities. Other common responses included communicating with school, demonstrating interest in school, and supporting children at home. Respondents were then asked to identify the important ways in which parents should be involved in their child(ren)'s education. The parent involvement practices most frequently rated as being important were communicating with teachers (38%), teaching children family values and beliefs (28%), and attending parent conferences/meetings (23%).

When asked to describe how parents are currently involved in their classrooms, the most common themes were participating in the classroom, attending special events and parties, chaperoning field trips, and attending parent-teacher conferences. Teachers also reported that written communication and conferences were the strategies that they most often employed in their efforts to involve parents and less frequently responded that home reading logs, telephone calls home, and class presentations were also effective strategies for including parents in their child's education.

The survey also sought to investigate the teachers' perceptions about the reasons for lack of parental involvement in their child(ren)'s education. About half of the teachers identified parents' other time commitments as being the number one reason for lack of involvement (53%). Parents' struggle to provide basic needs of the families emerged as the second reason by about one third of the respondents (35%). Other reasons for lack of parental involvement were difficulty in comprehending language (18%), educational constraints of the parents (18%), and parental difficulty in understanding the school culture (18%). An open-ended question about the challenges of involving parents revealed similar findings: parents' lack of time and language barriers. A third theme, though, also emerged: parents' lack of interest in their child's education.

FINDINGS ABOUT CULTURE

The second section of the survey focused on identifying the respondents' beliefs and knowledge related to developing an understanding of cultures of families in their classrooms. Respondents were first asked to define culture. An overwhelming number of them defined culture as a set of beliefs and values. The next most frequently used definition of culture was customs and traditions, followed by religion and language.

In a second open-ended question, respondents were asked to explain whether or not they felt it was important to understand the different cultures of the families of the children in their classroom. Although all of the respondents answered in the affirmative, they gave varying reasons for doing so. The most common theme was to understand their students' backgrounds, followed by the effect it has on children's education and learning, and that it aids in communicating with parents.

With respect to how teachers acknowledge culture in their curriculum, the most common responses included reading multicultural books, celebrating holidays, implementing cultural heritage units, and inviting parents to participate in the classroom. In their interactions with families, teachers stated that they addressed culture through their own awareness of holidays and celebrations, through discussion of culture, and by translating communication into the families' preferred language.

For the purposes of this study, culture was conceptualized as having six main components: patterns of communication (body language, personal space, comfort with touching, talking and listening); social values (do's and don'ts of behavior, determination of status, and definitions of achievement); preferred ways of learning and knowledge most valued in a given culture; ideas about raising children (child rearing patterns and goals, family structure, adult-child interactions, discipline, dependence-independence orientation); outward displays of culture (celebrations, artifacts, food, art, literature, and music); and religious values practiced in any given culture.

Table 1 reports on teacher responses to the following survey questions: To what degree are you aware of these cultural components of the families in your classroom? Which of these components of culture do you think most influence a child's academic learning/performance? On which of these areas have you sought information from parents?

David Bensman (2000) defines cultural interchange as "the process by which members of groups with different traditions, values, beliefs, and experiences gained a greater degree of mutual understanding" (p. iii). It is our contention that this "cultural interchange" is essential if teachers are to design culturally responsive instruction. In order for teachers to develop this knowledge-base and to translate it into practice, it is first important to surface their current and often unarticulated knowledge and beliefs about how cultural traditions, values, and beliefs influence learning and how teachers card take an active role in promoting open communication that leads to mutual understandings. Our findings suggest that the teachers we surveyed may have conflicting beliefs and practices in both of these areas.

Parent Involvement

The findings indicated that the common understanding of parent involvement was having the parents participate in the school. However, whether or not these practices actually lead to cultural interchange is not known.

Are teachers and parents getting to know each other during these activities in ways that lead to building trusting relationships? (Bensman, 2000; Dodd & Konzal, 2001). During these activities, are teachers communicating in ways that encourage parents to share their cultural beliefs and values? Are teachers able to observe how parents interact with their children and other children in order to gain cultural insights (Caspe, 2003; Trumbull et al., 2001)? This will be investigated in future research subsequent to the current study.

TABLE 1

Dissonance between Teacher Beliefs and Practice in Teacher Responses to Survey Questions

	Percentages			
	High Awareness	Little Awareness	High Influence on Learning	Seeks Information About
Patterns of Communication	66	34	95	63
Social Value	60	40	92	54
Ways of Learning	49	51	97	57
Child Rearing Practices	43	57	79	63
Outward Displays	50	50	41	66
Religious Values	15	85	44	37

When asked about their most effective strategies for involving parents, teachers responded that written communication and conferences were most effective. The teachers in our study recognized what the researchers tell us about the importance of communicating with parents, but it is unclear of the actual usage of these parent/teacher conferences. Researchers tell us that two-way communication is essential for building mutual trust and respect between parents and teachers; that two-way communication invites parents to tell teachers what they know about their children, their community, and their culture (Bensman, 2000; Dodd & Konzal, 2001; Edwards, 1999; Atkin & Bastiani, 1988).

Written communication is clearly one-way communication either from the parent or the teacher. It serves to maintain the social distance of teachers from parents (Powell, 1978). Parent-teacher conferences, on the other hand, are a perfect opportunity for parents and teachers to have two-way communication. However, many times these conferences, rather than promoting cultural interchange, revert to another form of one-way communication—teachers telling parents (Lawrence-Lightfoot, 2003; Trumbull et al., 2001).

Therefore, concluding the findings about parent involvement, it is unclear whether or not the teachers use the parent/teacher conference as a means of promoting two-way communication and cultural interchange (Bensman, 2000) or use it more as a unidirectional way of passing information.

Cultural Knowledge

One of the most interesting findings is that at times there appears to be a disparity between what teachers report about their awareness of culture, what they say about how culture influences learning, their actual practice in the classroom, and the topics about which they seek information. While we did expect some disparity between teacher beliefs and practices (Lee et al., 2003; Trumbull et al., 2001), we did find it surprising that the information that teachers seek about culture was also a part of this disparity. (See Table 1.)

One possible reason for this disparity could be that teachers [who] on a conceptual level understand the importance and influence of culture, however might be ill-equipped to translate it into actual practice. It might reflect the teachers' narrow view of culture (e.g., emphasis on overt aspects like food, celebrations, dress). They might also lack skills or training in integrating other more or less tangible aspects of culture into the curriculum and classroom practice.

Teachers overwhelmingly felt that patterns of communication, social values, preferred ways of learning and knowledge, and child raising patterns had a strong influence on students' learning. However, with respect to the outward displays of culture (dress, celebrations, food, art, literature, etc.) and religious values, less than half of the respondents felt that these had an influence on students' learning.

Yet, when asked how they acknowledge culture in their classrooms, the most common themes that emerged were books, holidays, and cultural heritage units, all of which fall under the category of outward displays of culture. Likewise, when asked how they affirm culture in their interactions with families, they reported that they demonstrate their own awareness of the culture's holidays.

Therefore, there seems to be a discrepancy between the fact that teachers feel that outward displays of culture do not have an important influence in learning and the fact that that is exactly what they choose to incorporate in their curriculum and interactions with families and what they mostly seek information about from parents.

Another interesting finding related to religious values. While 44% felt that religious values have some influence on learning, only a little over one-third of the respondents seek information on these values. It appears that teachers are uncomfortable with discussions related to religious values, especially in public school settings.

This is understandable given the confusion in schools about what is allowed and what is not allowed in relation to talking about and teaching about religion. We find it a problem since it is generally acknowledged that religious values significantly influence parents' beliefs about child rearing and education.

LIMITATIONS AND IMPLICATIONS

This study is comprised of a small sample of preschool through third grade teachers in one state. These participants were volunteers and a sample of convenience. This leads to limitations of generalizability of the findings of the study. However, this study is a pilot for subsequent research that will be more extensive in its outreach as well as its depth. Additionally, this study was specifically implemented to provide data for the design and formulation of a in-service professional development program for schools.

This study reveals that the New Jersey teachers who responded to this survey have a rhetorical understanding of the important aspects of culture, but lack the ability to interpret that knowledge into practices. It leaves us wondering what they mean when they say that culture is the beliefs and values people hold. How do they operationalize this concept?

The same is true for their understanding of parent involvement practices. They identify communication and parent/teacher conferences as important, but we are left wondering about the specific strategies they use and if they use them for the purpose of cultural interchange. Future research will be designed to further probe these questions.

NOTES

1. We use the term parents to include all family members who act as caregivers.
2. Parent term for educational jargon from Konzal, 1996.

REFERENCES

Atkin, J., & Bastiani, J. (1988). *Listening to parents: An approach to the improvement of home/school relations.* London, UK: Crown Helm.

Bensman, D. (2000). *Building school-family partnerships in a South Bronx classroom.* New York: NCREST.

Bennett, C. L. (2003). *Comprehensive multicultural education: Theory and practice.* Boston: Allyn & Bacon.

Berger, E. H. (1996). Working with families. Communication: Key to parent involvement. *Early Childhood Journal, 23*(3), 179–183.

Bermudez, A. B., & Marquez, J. A. (1996). An examination of a four-way collaborative to increase parental involvement in schools. *The Journal of Educational Issues of Language Minority Students, 16*(6), 1–16.

Bronfenbrenner, U. (1979). *The ecology of human development: Experiments by nature and design.* Cambridge, MA: Harvard University Press.

Bronfenbrenner, U. (1986). Ecology of the family as a context for human development: Research perspectives. *Developmental Psychology, 22*(6), 723–742.

Caspe, M. S. (2003). How teachers come to understand families. *The School Community Journal, 13*(1), 115–131.

Coleman, J. S., & Hoffer, T. (1987). *Public and private high schools.* New York: Basic Books.

Delpit, L. (1995). *Other people's children: Cultural conflict in the classroom.* New York: New Press. ED 387274.

Dodd, A. W., & Konzal, J. L. (2002). *How communities build stronger schools: Stories, strategies and promising practices for educating every child.* New York: Palgrave Macmillan.

Dodd, A. W., & Konzal, J. L. (1999). *Making our high schools better: How parents and teachers can work together.* New York: St. Martin's Press.

Edwards, P. A. (1999). *A path to follow: Learning to listen to parents.* Portsmouth, NH: Heinemann.

Epstein, J. L. (1990). School and family connections: Theory, research and implications for integrating sociologies of education and family. *Marriage and Family Review, 15*(1), 99–126.

Epstein, J. L. (2001). *School, family, and community partnerships: Preparing educators and improving schools.* Boulder, CO: Westview Press.

Epstein, J. L., & Becker, H. J. (1982). Teachers' reported practices of parent involvement: Problems and possibilities. *The Elementary School Journal, 83*(2), 103–113.

Gonzalez-Mena, J. (2000). High-maintenance parent or cultural differences? *Child Care Information Exchange, 134,* 40–42.

Greenfield, P. M. (1994). Independence and interdependence as developmental scripts: Implications for theory, research, and practice. In Greenfield, P. M., & Cocking, R. R. (Eds.), *Cross-cultural roots of minority child development.* Hillsdale, NJ: Lawrence Erlbaum Associates.

Greenwood, G. E., & Hickman, C. W. (1991). Research and practice in parent involvement: Implications for teacher education. *Elementary School Journal, 91*(3), 279–288.

Gutierrez, K. D., & Rogoff, B. (2003). Cultural ways of learning: Individual traits or repertoires of practice. *Educational Researcher, 32*(5), 19–25.

Henderson, A. T., & Berla, N. (1994). A *new generation of evidence: The family* is *critical to student achievement.* Washington, DC: National Committee for Citizens in Education, ERIC [Online]. Available: Doc. No. 375968.

Henry, M. E. (1996). *Parent-school collaboration: Feminist organizational structure and school leadership.* New York: State University of New York Press.

Hughes, P., & MacNaughton, G. (2000). Building equitable staff parent communication in early childhood settings: An Australian case study. Paper presented at the Annual Conference and Exhibition of the Association for Childhood Education International, Baltimore, MD. ERIC (Online). Available: Doc. No. 444647.

Joshi, A. (2002). Effectiveness of early childhood teachers in the Indian context. Unpublished Doctoral Dissertation. Syracuse University.

Ladson-Billings, G. (1991). *The dreamkeepers: Successful teachers of African American children.* San Francisco: Jossey-Bass.

Lasky, S. (2000). The cultural and emotional politics of teacher-parent interactions. *Teaching and Teacher Education, 16,* 843–860.

Lawrence-Lightfoot, S. (2003). *The essential conversation: What parents and teachers can learn from each other.* New York: Random House.

Lee, C. K., Spencer, M. B., & Harpalani, V. (2003). "Every shut eye ain't sleep": Studying how people live culturally. *Educational Researcher, 32*(5), 6–13.

Marion, R. L. (1980). Communicating with parents of culturally diverse exceptional children. *Exceptional Children, 46*(8), 616–623.

Powell, D. R. (1978). Correlates of parent-teacher communication frequency and diversity, *The Journal of Educational Research, 71,* 333–341.

Shade, B. J., Kelly, C., & Oberg, M. (1997). *Creating culturally responsive classrooms.* Washington, D.C.: American Psychological Association.

Super, C. M., & Harkness, S. (1997). The cultural structuring of child development. In J. Berry, P. Dasen, & T. Saraswathi (Eds.), *Handbook of cross-cultural psychology: Basic processes & human development* (pp. 1–39). Boston: Allyn & Bacon.

Trumbull, E., Rothstein-Fisch, C., Greenfield, P. M., & Quiroz, B. (2001). *Bridging cultures between home and school: A guide for teachers.* Mahwah, NJ: Lawrence Erlbaum Associates.

Voltz, D. L. (1994). Developing collaborative parent-teacher relationships with culturally diverse parents. *Intervention in School and Clinic, 29*(5), 288–291.

Weisner, T. S. (1998). Human development, child well-being, and the cultural project of development. *New Directions for Child Development, 81,* 69–147.

Wright, K., & Stegelin, D. A. (2003). *Building school and community partnerships through parent involvement.* Upper Saddle River, NJ: Merrill Prentice Hall.

Arti Joshi, Jody Eberly, and *Jean Konzal* are professors in the Department of Elementary and Early Childhood Education at The College of New Jersey, Ewing, New Jersey.

QUESTIONS FOR REFLECTION

1. What barriers that inhibit good parent/school relations do the authors identify? Do you think their solutions to these barriers are realistic? Explain.
2. How critical a role do cultural differences play in parent/school relations in your school and/or district? Who works hardest to bridge the cultural differences that

exist? Could more be done in your current setting to better bridge the differences? If so, what could be done?

3. This article points out that teachers have a "rhetorical understanding" of the important aspects of culture but lack the ability to put that knowledge into practice. How might teachers better "operationalize" the important value of culture and cultural awareness in their classrooms?

High-Stakes Testing and Accountability as Social Constructs across Cultures

RAYMOND V. PADILLA

ABSTRACT: Padilla explores the idea that notions such as "high-stakes testing" and "educational accountability," which are the hallmarks of some educational reform efforts, are social constructions that can lead to the organization of schooling within very specific and narrow sociocultural frameworks. Although such sociocultural frameworks can go largely unacknowledged, their effects are significant. Padilla discusses three major topics: (1) testing in relation to the culture of measurement; (2) the reductionist view of accountability and the need to counteract it; and (3) alternative social constructions of educational reform that provide a higher degree of sociocultural contextualization for diverse groups of students and the schools that serve them.

THE CULTURE OF MEASUREMENT VERSUS THE CULTURE OF ENGAGEMENT

Although high-stakes testing, such as the Texas Assessment of Academic Skills (TAAS) and the Arizona Instrument to Measure Standards (AIMS) has been critiqued from various perspectives (Haney, 2000; Hilliard, 1990; Klein, Hamilton, McCaffrey, & Stecher, 2000; McNeil, 2000; McNeil & Valenzuela, 2000; Mitchell, Robinson, Plake, & Knowles, 2001; President's Advisory Commission on Educational Excellence for Hispanic Americans, 2000; Spring, 1998), little has been said thus far about the *cultural presuppositions* that undergird these testing practices. A culturally-based critique reveals that state-sponsored testing instruments and practices are part of a specific social construction of schooling, one that can lead to different consequences for various groups of students in terms of

their schooling experiences and outcomes. Drawing (and perhaps even overdrawing) distinctions between the *culture of measurement* (which occasionally turns into the "cult of measurement") and an alternative *culture of engagement* helps clarify the ways in which schooling practices are socially constructed across cultures. Each of these cultural frameworks has its own set of deeply rooted assumptions about fundamental aspects of existence such as the nature of knowing, being, valuing, and purpose. Each also has its own fundamental goals, worldview, and influence on schooling practices.

High-stakes testing and educational accountability, two anchor points of recent educational reform efforts, so far are strictly framed within the culture of measurement. The chief goals here are the identification of merit and the distribution of material and social rewards based on that merit. Students are defined in terms of parameters whose values can be precisely measured. Using instruments developed under the sway of psychologism, beginning with Binet's intelligence test, assessment efforts have continued unbroken for almost one hundred years. The current reliance on high-stakes tests—measurement instruments that often are developed, tested, and administered by corporate interests (Spring, 1998)—is part of this tradition. The epistemological perspective of the culture of measurement is objectivist knowing, or what is called *saber* in Spanish (Padilla, 2000). Such knowledge is presumed to be universally valid and free from "subjectivist" influences or local perturbations. Under these conditions, a "norm" can be objectively set to any scale and various comparisons then can be made against that norm.

With respect to schooling practices, the culture of measurement strongly influences at least two important areas: teaching and curriculum. Teaching becomes highly decontextualized from larger pedagogical concerns. This can be seen in schooling practices such as teaching to the test (McNeil & Valenzuela, 2000) and in the overemphasis on process, credentialism, and test-taking competence. The abstract student becomes a reality and the real student becomes an abstraction whose learning and development can be determined only with the aid of a paper-and-pencil test and a presumed universal norm as a reference point.

With respect to curriculum, the culture of measurement leads to the isolation of people and schools. This isolation is driven by the evaluation of individual teachers, students, and schools through test taking, ratings, rankings, grading, and so on. Such individualistic evaluation is premised on a narrow range of curricular offerings, often limited to low-level, monolingual reading and writing skills and the rudiments of arithmetic and science (McNeil & Valenzuela, 2000; Ruiz de Velasco & Fix, 2000).

An alternative to the culture of measurement is the *culture of engagement*. The chief goal of this social construction is inclusion and human development in pursuit of democratic participation and *justicia* (justice). This goal is embedded within a worldview that values and fosters a culture of caring and inclusion (Freire, 2001; Reyes, Scribner, & Paredes Scribner, 1999; Trueba, 1999; Valenzuela, 1999). The epistemological foundation of the culture of engagement is local "relational knowing," or what is called *conocer* in Spanish (Padilla, 2000). Relational knowing has no universalistic or objectivist pretensions. It relies instead on local knowledge that is interactively acquired and validated. The norm is always locally contextualized and socially negotiated.

The influence of the culture of engagement on teaching and curriculum is quite different from that of the culture of measurement. With respect to teaching, the culture of engagement accepts students as they are and values their sociocultural context (Trueba, Spindler, & Spindler, 1989). It promotes student development by providing relevant learning, enhancing social competence, and engendering a sense of rootedness (García, 2001). Regarding curriculum, the culture of engagement emphasizes teaching teams, which develop and deliver curriculum as a group (Romo & Falbo, 1996), and studying integrated themes in the context of the daily life of the student and the community in which the student lives (González, Huerta-Macías, & Tinajero, 1998).

In theory, schooling practices can come under the sway of either the culture of measurement or the culture of engagement. In practice, differential political power privileges the culture of measurement. The consequences of this social choice are evident today in the profound teacher and student alienation (Romo & Falbo, 1996) that has led to teacher burnout, student violence, deteriorating schools, and widespread discontent with public education (Datnow, 2000). These conditions underscore the need for alternative social constructions of schooling practices.

THE PRACTICE OF ASSIMILATION VERSUS THE PRACTICE OF DIVERSITY

At the ontological (being) level, the culture of measurement is premised on an absolutist view of being. Thus, much as Shakespeare put it, "to be" has only one ontological alternative, "not to be." This cultural view contrasts with Spanish, which makes a distinction between absolute being, *ser,* and temporary or conditional being, *estar.* The absolutist view of being leads logically to the practice (some would say the malpractice) of assimilation. The goal of assimilation is to absorb all languages, cultures, and peoples into a melting pot of Eurocentric peoples and culture, and to destroy, enslave, or erase those not susceptible to such assimilation (Menchaca, 1997). The worldview of assimilation, based on absolutist ontology, presumes the superiority of Anglo-European peoples and culture. This presumption, in turn, supports the righteous imposition of this culture on all foreign peoples and the simultaneous elimination of all foreign languages and cultures (De León, 1998). The absolutist ontology holds that to be (in the sense of *ser)* is to exist in an evolutionarily determined hierarchy of human groups and their associated languages and cultures. These rankings are understood to be immutable, and those at the upper end of the hierarchy are to be preferred to those at the bottom.

The practice of assimilation has consequences for both teaching and curriculum. Its influence on teaching can be seen in the school practice of subtracting from students all foreign languages and cultural elements and replacing them with "superior" Eurocentric and Anglo-American ones (García, 2001; Valenzuela, 1999). Often, this cultural displacement is championed as being for the good of the student. The practice of assimilation shapes curriculum by emphasizing Anglo-American history and culture and attempting to erase the histories, languages, and cultures of all other groups. The English-only movement is an example of a particularly virulent version of this linguistic and cultural erasure (Hakuta, 1986; Krashen, 1996; Schmidt, 2000).

In contrast to the practice of assimilation is the practice of diversity, which fits well within the culture of engagement. The goal of diversity is to recognize, embrace, and celebrate the world's variety of languages, cultures, and peoples. Diversity is accepting of those who are different. It promotes the idea of *convivencia,* or getting along (literally, "living together"). The worldview of diversity is that all languages and cultures have inherent value and all need resources to thrive. Ontologically, diversity is based on *estar,* conditional or time-sensitive being. To be, in the sense of *estar,* is to exist in a historical and changing set of relationships across groups and cultures. Hence, all social and cultural hierarchies are historically conditioned, transient, and mutable (Freire, 1995).

The practice of diversity influences both teaching and curriculum. Because different languages and cultures are appreciated and shared, teaching becomes an additive practice (Valenzuela, 1999): New language and cultural elements are added to what the student already possesses. The curriculum emphasizes multiple languages, cultures, and histories, encouraging students from diverse backgrounds to see themselves positively.

Despite the affirming and inclusive nature of the practice of diversity, it is not the dominant framework. Instead, differential political power has led to the privileging of assimilation practices. The negative effects of this social choice include the following:

- The perpetuation of "White privilege" as a foundation for social relationships (McIntosh, 1989; Padilla & Chávez Chávez, 1995);
- The alienation of students and communities as a result of subtractive schooling practices aimed at removing foreign languages and cultural elements (Valenzuela, 1999);
- The loss of educational equity brought about by high student dropout rates and chronically low academic achievement among those who stay in school (Romo & Falbo, 1996; Trueba, Spindler, & Spindler, 1989);
- The perpetuation of impoverished communities.

As this list shows, social constructions of schooling practices can exact extremely high costs. Alternatives to the current culture of measurement need to be seriously considered.

THINKING DEFICITS VERSUS ASSETS

The culture of measurement often includes cultural deficit thinking (Trueba, Spindler, & Spindler, 1989; Valencia, 1997). The worldview of cultural deficit thinking, like that of assimilation, assumes the superiority of Eurocentered, Anglo-American language and culture (De León, 1998). All other languages and cultures are seen as deficient by comparison and, therefore, all must give way. Such views can strongly influence teaching. Students are seen as needing to be cleansed of their foreign languages and cultures; more wholesome Anglo-American language and culture can then be substituted for their home counterparts (Valenzuela, 1999). At the curriculum level, cultural deficit thinking emphasizes English-only instruction, teaching Anglo-American history exclusively, and inculcating Anglo-American values.

By contrast, the culture of engagement includes the thinking and rethinking of cultural assets. The goal is to accept all languages and cultures as valuable. The underlying worldview perceives all languages and cultures as having both assets and liabilities and seeks to use cultural assets to enhance schooling outcomes (García, 2001; Trueba, Spindler, & Spindler, 1989). No language or culture is assumed to be inherently superior to any other language or culture. Teachers working within this perspective value students from diverse language and cultural backgrounds. They also use language and cultural differences to enhance their teaching and their students' learning. At the curriculum level, an additive model of schooling is followed (Valenzuela, 1999). Students are given the opportunity to learn in more than one language, diverse languages and cultures are studied, and different values are acknowledged and examined. Most important, culture is defined as problematic and is critically examined (Freire, 1995) so that students can develop a global perspective and a secure sense of personal and cultural identity.

Unfortunately, it is cultural deficit thinking that currently holds sway, and it will continue to do so as long as those who hold cultural deficit thinking views also wield the most political power. But the consequences of cultural deficit thinking are serious. These include the demise of diverse languages and cultures [Fishman, 1966], the entrenchment of subtractive schooling (Valenzuela, 1999) and its attendant failure to provide all students with a comprehensive, relevant education (Romo & Falbo, 1996), and the continued impoverishment of diverse language and cultural communities. In a world that is becoming ever more interdependent and interconnected (Figueroa, Wilkie, & Arroyo Alejandre, 1996), the value of cultural deficit thinking seems increasingly questionable.

SELF INTEREST VERSUS THE PUBLIC INTEREST

The culture of measurement often supports an extreme focus on self interest. The goal of this self(ish) interest is the pursuit of individual gain or benefit by virtually any means, with little or no regard for the common good or the condition of the physical environment. The worldview emphasizes the individual over the group and private gain over public good. Self(ish) interest is supported by a teleological perspective that holds that the purpose of human life is to achieve personal gain in a competitive social environment. Winners achieve their position as the result of their superior individual effort (variously augmented by government action). Losers have only themselves to blame for their failure (and thus should not complain).

This teleological perspective shapes teaching by casting students as individual, competitive learners. Students are individually tested, graded, and sorted as a basis for distributing rewards such as who goes to college and who gets into which occupations and positions of power (Spring, 1998). At the curriculum level, a focus on self(ish) interest promotes competition among students and supports academic tracking (Oakes, 1985; Romo & Falbo, 1996; Solomon, 1992) whereby students are sorted into different curricular strands according to their tested "ability," resulting in different outcomes for further study and narrowed career opportunities.

The culture of engagement, in contrast, shows greater concern for the public interest. The goal is to moderate the pursuit of individual gain by taking into account the common good and the condition of the physical environment. The worldview is that individual gain is subordinate to the common good and the preservation of a healthy environment. The role of government is primarily to promote the common good rather than to help individuals achieve private gain. The teleological perspective of the culture of engagement is that the purpose of human life is to promote community and a healthy environment. These views influence teaching in that students are seen as capable of learning through cooperation and collaboration. Rewards are provided for group as well as for individual effort. At the curriculum level, students of varying ability are grouped together and individual performance within group effort is rewarded. Democratic participation and democratic values are promoted (Freire, 2001).

Currently, self(ish) interest is privileged over the common good, with notable consequences: Schools reproduce existing social hierarchies (Bourdieu & Passeron, 1990; McNeil, 2000), stifle the upward mobility of students, retard the economic development of certain communities, and contribute to the degradation of the physical environment.

Social constructions of schooling significantly influence the goals educational reformers seek to implement (Berliner & Biddle, 1995). They also shape the set of probable educational outcomes that students are likely to experience. Given the likelihood that within a set of educational outcomes not all will be equally desirable, social constructions of schooling can have a powerful impact on students' life chances. Educational outcomes are determined not only on the basis of ability differentials in students, but also by differences in background characteristics over which students have little or no control (such as culture,

language, gender, and social class) and by the quality of the schools the students attend (Romo & Falbo, 1996). When narrowly framed, social constructions of schooling can serve to severely decontextualize the learning process for certain students, putting them at a disadvantage compared to students for whom the social construction of schooling offers a more congenial and coherent connection to home and community (Trueba, Spindler, & Spindler, 1989).

A CULTURALLY-BASED ACCOUNT OF ACCOUNTABILITY

The problem of severe decontextualization of schooling can be seen not only in high-stakes testing but also in the socially constructed idea of accountability with which testing is frequently paired. Within the culture of measurement, accountability, like testing, becomes a narrowly defined program that can have a differential impact on educational outcomes and students' educational experiences. Students who fare the best under current accountability programs are those whose home and community most closely adhere to the underlying assumptions of the prevailing social construction of accountability. Students who come from homes and communities where these assumptions are different tend to do less well in school (McNeil & Valenzuela, 2000).

The decontextualization of accountability promoted by the culture of measurement occurs on several levels, not the least of which is the reduction of the semantic space related to the word "accountability" (see Haney & Raczek, 1994). Adherents of the culture of measurement assume that accountability is mostly about numbers and measurements based on numbers. However, both the English word *accountability* and its Spanish equivalent, *contabilidad,* share the same Latin root, *putare,* which means "to think." In Spanish, the verb *contar* means both "to count" and "to recount" in the sense of "to tell." Thus, in Spanish, accountability can be reported either by counting or by recounting, by numbers or by narratives. In its broader linguistic context, the English word accountability also includes as part of its semantic space the idea of an account, such as a story or narrative. However, the adherents of the culture of measurement tend to downplay the narrative part and limit accountability mostly to "the bottom line," a number or statistic that presumably tells the whole story about a student's learning and schooling.

The bottom-line approach to educational accountability can lead to severe decontextualization of the learning process and learning outcomes. Under numbers-based accountability programs, high scores on state or nationally sponsored tests become the educational goal for schools. To achieve this goal, students are required to master both substantive content and the heuristics of test taking. Thus, teachers shift instructional time from substantive content to drills designed to help students learn how to take tests. At the same time, the focus of the curriculum is redirected to cover whatever appears on the test (Spring, 1998). State-sponsored high-stakes testing displaces assessments of student learning that are based on a well-balanced local curriculum.

To be accountable is to be responsible for something, and the discharge of that responsibility is typically recounted through a narrative that presents facts, opinions, actions taken, and results achieved. Numbers may be an important element in the narrative report, but they are never the whole story, and they certainly do not speak for themselves. In other words, numbers, like all other kinds of information, must be provided some interpretive context before they make any sense (Lincoln & Guba, 1985). But the adherents of the culture of measurement rely on numbers for the whole story. Where policies require individuals to pass a test before they can be promoted to the next grade, otherwise knowledgeable students who simply do not perform well on tests can be retained in grade.

The classroom teacher may be well aware that a low-scoring student works at grade level on a daily basis, but if this competency is not proven by an acceptable score on a high-stakes test, the student must be retained. . . . Ironically, high-stakes testing often is promoted as a strategy for decreasing the incidence of social promotion. Yet, these tests themselves can produce social demotion, an outcome that goes unnoticed by the adherents of the culture of measurement.

The blind eye numbers-based accountability that turns toward the social demotion of students is both an example and a telltale sign of how numbers-based accountability reflects a specific social construction of schooling. How a student performs in school is based on many factors that interact in complex ways. For example, school finance, the quality of teachers and teaching materials, students' level of health and nutrition, their family background, their home language, and a host of other factors influence school performance. Yet, the most noticeable consequences of high-stakes testing are those the individual student bears: promotion in grade or lack thereof; graduation from high school, or failure to graduate; acceptance to college or denial of admittance; and similar lifelong effects (Ruiz de Velasco & Fix, 2000; Solomon, 1992; Spring, 1998). High-stakes testing coupled with accountability makes individual students responsible for their own test performance as if none of the many factors other than individual effort and native talent, such as poor schools (Romo & Falbo, 1996), contribute to and shape performance. In numbers-based accountability, the state decontextualizes test performance and certifies the test taker as either competent or incompetent, worthy or unworthy of gaining access to community resources in pursuit of further education and advancement.

Under such circumstances, accountability unfairly punishes students and gives the state unwarranted power to label students in permanent and harmful ways (for a historic case of state centralism in pursuit of cultural hegemony, see Getz, 1997). As nearly all teachers agree, a student whose language background differs from the language of the test and who lacks English fluency will be disadvantaged in taking such a test. Test scores for these students need to be carefully interpreted to avoid inappropriate retention of students in grade level (Ovando & Collier, 1998). Yet, thousands of students with limited English proficiency are routinely subjected to high-stakes testing without taking into account their unique linguistic situation, let alone the quality and appropriateness of the instruction that they are receiving. . . . The result is the mislabeling and excessive grade retention of students with limited English proficiency under the guise of numbers-based accountability programs. The culture of measurement sidetracks the thinking part of accountability and brings the full force of the state apparatus to bear on individual students and their school performance. With schools acting as handmaidens of the state's numbers-driven certification machinery, accountability becomes a means for maintaining existing social hierarchies on a broad scale and for exerting tighter control across large populations to determine who has access to public resources.

An alternative social construction of accountability can be formulated based on the culture of engagement (for other alternatives, see Valenzuela, 2002). *Engaged accountability* emphasizes through narratives the local, contextualized aspects of student learning. It fosters effective local decision making about student evaluation and proper placement in differentiated learning environments. Most importantly, rather than holding students solely responsible for school performance, it sees schools and communities as equally responsible for the academic achievement of their students (Reyes, Scribner, & Paredes Scribner, 1999).

Under engaged accountability, the thinking part of accountability is brought to the forefront. Teachers are empowered to make important decisions about how to teach and evaluate students under the guidance of local boards of education, whose members, in turn, are responsive to the wishes of local constituencies. Centralized state machinery plays no role in certifying which students may be promoted to the next grade level and which may not. Given that context is crucial to teaching and learning, evaluation of student performance should include multiple indicators of learning and a rich understanding of the circumstances under which the student is attempting to learn and the teacher is attempting to teach (Ovando & Collier, 1998). Reliance on abstract numbers or on a single test score is viewed as misguided and not likely to enhance student learning.

The idea of localism is an important aspect of engaged accountability. Emphasizing the local permits and promotes great diversity. Fostering diversity does not mean abandoning standards or quality. Rather, it means rejecting the universalist pretensions of the positivist culture of measurement; the culture of engagement challenges the supposition that all evaluations of learning are reducible to a single, one-size-fits-all package. Instead of supporting tests and assessment instruments that turn students into abstractions and subject content into disconnected bits of information that do not make sense in any particular place, engaged accountability programs would foster student learning within the context of students' everyday lives—incorporating family and community, for example (Chavkin, 1993; Torres-Guzmán, Mercado, Quintero, & Viera, 1994)—and within the context of positive, useful learning that can lead to social and economic advancement (Romo & Falbo, 1996). Engaged accountability programs would provide a thoughtful basis for the assessment of student progress, the effectiveness of schools, and the identification of community goals and priorities. . . .

REFERENCES

Berger, P. L., & Luckmann, T. (1966). *The social construction of reality: A treatise in the sociology of knowledge.* New York: Anchor Books.

Berliner, D. C., & Biddle, B. J. (1995). *The manufactured crisis: Myths, fraud, and the attack on America's public schools.* New York: Addison-Wesley.

Bourdieu, P., & Passeron, J. C. (1990). *Reproduction in education, society, and culture* (Richard Nice, Trans.). Newbury Park, CA: Sage Publications. (Original work published 1970.)

Chavkin, N. D. (Ed.). (1993). *Families and schools in a pluralistic society*. Albany: State University of New York Press.

Datnow, A. (2000). Power politics in the adoption of school reform models. *Educational Evaluation and Policy Analysis, 22*(4), 357–374.

De León, A. (1998). Initial contacts: Niggers, redskins and greasers. In R. Delgado & J. Stafancic (Eds.), *The Latino condition: A critical reader* (pp. 158–164). New York: New York University Press.

Figueroa, C. P., Wilkie, J. W., & Arroyo Alejandre, J. (Eds.). (1996). *Mexico and the Americas*. VIII PROFMEX-ANUIES Conference proceedings. Mexico City: Asociación National de Universidades y Instituciones de Educación Superior.

Fishman, J. A. (1966). *Language loyalty in the United States*. The Hague: Mouton.

Freire, P. (1995). *Pedagogy of the oppressed*. New revised 20th anniversary edition. New York: Continuum.

Freire, P. (2001). *Pedagogy of freedom: Ethics, democracy, and civic courage*. New York: Rowman & Littlefield.

García, E. (2001). *Hispanic education in the United States: Raíces y alas*. New York: Rowman & Littlefield.

Getz, L. M. (1997). Schools *of their own: The education of Hispanos in New Mexico, 1850–1940*. Albuquerque, NM: University of New Mexico Press.

González, M. L., Huerta-Macías, A., & Villamil Tinajero, J. (Eds.). (1998). *Educating Latino students: A guide to successful practice*. Lancaster, PA: Technomic Publishing.

Hakuta, K. (1986). *Mirror of language: The debate on bilingualism*. New York: Basic Books.

Haney, W. (2000). The myth of the Texas miracle in education. *Education Policy Analysis Archives, 8*(41). Retrieved March 1, 2001, from http://epaa.asu.edu/epaa/v8n41.partl.htm

Haney, W., & Raczek, A. (1994). *Surmounting outcomes accountability in education: Paper prepared for the U.S. Congress Office of Technology Assessment*. Boston: Boston College, Center for the Study of Testing, Evaluation and Educational Policy.

Hilliard, A. G., III. (1990). Limitations of current academic achievement measures. In K. Lomotey (Ed.), *Going to school: The African-American experience* (pp. 135–142). Albany: State University of New York Press.

Klein, S. P., Hamilton, L. S., McCaffrey, D. F., & Stecher, B. M. (2000). What do test scores in Texas tell us? *Education Policy Analysis Archives, 8(49)*.

Krashen, S. D. (1996). *Under attack: The case against bilingual education*. Culver City, CA: Language Education Associates.

Lincoln, Y., & Guba, E. (1985). *Naturalistic inquiry*. Beverly Hills, CA: Sage Publications.

McIntosh, P. (1989, July/August). White privilege: Unpacking the invisible knapsack. *Peace and Freedom*, 10–12.

McNeil, L., & Valenzuela, A. (2000). *The harmful impact of the TAAS system of testing in Texas: Beneath the accountability rhetoric*. In M. Kornhaber & G. Orfield (Eds.), *Raising standards or raising barriers: Inequality and high-stakes testing in public education* (pp. 127–150).

McNeil, L. M. (2000). *Contradictions of school reform: Educational costs of standardized testing*. New York: Routledge.

Menchaca, M. (1997). Early racist discourses: The roots of deficit thinking. In R. Valencia (Ed.), *The evolution of deficit thinking: Educational thought and practice* (pp.13–40). Washington, DC: Falmer Press.

Mitchell, K. J., Robinson, D. Z., Plake, B. S., & Knowles, K. T. (Eds.). (2001). *Testing teacher candidates: The role of licensure tests in improving teacher quality*. Washington, DC: Committee on Assessment and Teacher Quality, National Research Council. National Academy Press.

Oakes, J. (1985). *Keeping track: How schools structure inequality*. New Haven, CT: Yale University Press.

Ovando, C. J., & Collier, V. P. (1998). *Bilingual and ESL classrooms: Teaching in multicultural contexts* (2nd ed.). New York: McGraw-Hill.

Padilla, R. V. (2000). *Sabiduría in the Chican@ context: Some epistemological notes*. Paper presented at the XXVII Conférence of the National Association for Chicana and Chicano Studies (NACCS), Portland, OR, March 22–25, 2000. Retrieved April 6, 2001. Available at: http://coehd.utsa.edu/users/rpadilla

Padilla, R. V., & Chávez Chávez, R. (Eds.). (1995). *The leaning ivory tower: Latino Professors in American universities*. Albany: State University of New York Press.

President's Advisory Commission on Educational Excellence for Hispanic Americans. (2000). *Testing Hispanic students in the United States: Technical and policy issues*. [Prepared by Richard A. Figueroa & Sonia Hernández]. Washington, DC: Author.

Reyes, P., Scribner, J. D., & Paredes Scribner, A. (1999). *Lessons from high-performing Hispanic schools*. New York: Teachers College Press.

Romo, H. D., & Falbo, T. (1996). *Latino high school graduation: Defying the odds.* Austin: University of Texas Press.

Ruiz de Velasco, J., & Fix, M. (2000). *Overlooked & underserved: Immigrant students in U.S. secondary schools.* Washington, DC: Urban Institute.

Schmidt, R., Sr. (2000). *Language policy and identity politics in the United States.* Philadelphia: Temple University Press.

Solomon, R. P. (1992). *Black resistance in high school: Forging a separatist culture.* Albany: State University of New York Press.

Spring, J. (1998). *Conflict of interests: The politics of American education* (3rd ed.). Boston: McGraw-Hill.

Torres-Guzmán, M. E., Mercado, C. I., Quintero, A. H., & Viera, D. R. (1994). Teaching and learning in Puerto Rican/Latino collaboratives: Implications for teacher education. In E. R. Hollins, J. E. King, & W. C. Hayman (Eds.), *Teaching diverse populations: Formulating a knowledge base* (pp.105–127). Albany: State University of New York Press.

Trueba, H. T. (1999). *Latinos unidos: From cultural diversity to the politics of solidarity.* New York: Roman & Littlefield.

Trueba, H. T., Spindler, G., & Spindler, L. (Eds.). (1989). *What do anthropologists have to say about dropouts?* New York: Falmer Press.

Valencia, R. (Ed.). (1997). *The evolution of deficit thinking: Educational thought and practice.* Washington, DC: Falmer Press.

Valenzuela, A. (2002). High-stakes testing and U.S.-Mexican youth in Texas: The case for multiple compensatory criteria in assessment. *Harvard Journal of Hispanic Policy, 14,* 97–116.

Valenzuela, A. (1999). *Subtractive schooling: U.S.-Mexican youth and the politics of caring.* Albany: State University of New York Press.

Raymond V. Padilla is a professor in the College of Education and Human Development at the University of Texas at San Antonio.

QUESTIONS FOR REFLECTION

1. Padilla writes that "high-stakes testing" and "educational accountability" can lead to the organization of schooling within very specific and narrow sociocultural frameworks. What are these sociocultural frameworks and what are the effects of organizing schools based on these frameworks?

2. How does Padilla differentiate between the practice of "assimilation" and the practice of "diversity," and which does he advocate for greater use as a framework? What evidence does he present to support his ideas?

3. How might the current organization of schooling be transformed into the "culture of engagement" that Padilla says will promote a more democratic community and greater equity in accessing resources and which offers an alternative to the "culture of measurement" we currently have?

The "Three A's" of Creating an Inclusive Curriculum and Classroom

TINA M. ANCTIL

ABSTRACT: Tina Anctil provides an overview of inclusive teaching practices for regular education teachers. The legal basis for inclusion, disability prevalence, and curricular and assessment strategies for teaching students with disabilities are also discussed. Anctil provides information all teachers need to know as they confront students of differing abilities in today's classroom.

Since the landmark passage of P.L. 94-142, the Education of All Handicapped Children Act (1975), which guaranteed all children with disabilities a free, appropriate public education (FAPE), children with disabilities have been attending public schools. Prior to this legislation, children with disabilities were largely uneducated, residing in institutions or with family members. Today, the inclusion of students with disabilities in the "regular" education classroom has been coined a revolution. This recent excerpt from *The New York Times Magazine* captures the experience of one classroom.

> Thomas, one of two motor impaired, nonverbal children, was in a custom built wheelchair, his blue eyes wide, his gentle face animated, watching from on high as the others drew and chattered and explored. [The parents] noticed that while the class list, posted by the cubbies, had barely a dozen names, a small army of teachers—including an occupational therapist, a speech therapist, an augmentative communication expert and several other aids—had greeted them at the door. Even those who were arriving as kindergarten parents for the first time could sense that this class was different. 'Inclusion', said Suzanne Blake, the head teacher. (Belkin, 2001)

While this example may not be typical of students with disabilities in today's classrooms—as most students with more significant physical disabilities are still not fully included in the regular

classroom—95% of students with disabilities are served in regular school buildings (U.S. Department of Education, 2002). In the 2001–2002 school year, over 5 million school aged children, or 9% of the U.S. resident population, had been identified as requiring special education services due to specific disabilities. The most common disabilities represented in U.S. schools are specific learning disabilities, speech or language impairments, mental retardation, and emotional disturbance. Of those students, white students made up 62.3% of the students served; 19.8% were African American; 14.5% were Hispanic; 1.9% were Asian/Pacific Islander; and 1.5% were American Indian/Alaska Native (U.S. Department of Education, 2002). There continues to be overrepresentation of disabilities in some racial/ethnic groups according to specific disability categories, as well as under representation of certain disabilities in some racial/ethnic groups, when compared with the special education student population as a whole (U.S. Department of Education, 2002). Table 1 provides more details about the special education population according to disability type and race/ethnicity.

The Phi Delta Kappa Center for Evaluation, Development and Research (Rogers, 1993) provided a summary of the various terms used to describe the inclusion of students with disabilities in regular classrooms as these terms are often used incorrectly and interchangeably in practice:

TABLE 1

Percentage of Students Ages 6 through 21 Served Under IDEA During 2000–2001

Disability	American Indian/ Alaska Native	Asian/ Pacific Islander	Black (non-Hispanic)	Hispanic	White (non-Hispanic)	All Students Served
Specific learning disabilities	56.3	43.2	45.2	60.3	48.9	50.0
Speech or language impairments	17.1	25.2	15.1	17.3	20.8	18.9
Mental retardation	8.5	10.1	18.9	8.6	9.3	10.6
Emotional disturbance	7.5	5.3	10.7	4.5	8.0	8.2
Multiple disabilities	2.5	2.3	1.9	1.8	1.8	2.1
Hearing impairments	1.1	2.9	1.0	1.5	1.2	1.2
Orthopedic impairments	0.8	2.0	0.9	1.4	1.1	1.3
Other health impairments	4.1	3.9	3.7	2.8	5.9	5.1
Visual impairments	0.4	0.8	0.4	0.5	0.5	0.4
Autism	0.6	3.4	1.2	0.9	1.4	1.4
Deaf-blindness	0.0	0.0	0.0	0.0	0.0	0.0
Traumatic brain injury	0.3	0.3	0.2	0.2	0.3	0.3
Developmental delay	0.7	0.6	0.7	0.2	0.6	0.5
All disabilities	100.00	100.00	100.00	100.00	100.00	100.00

Note: Does not include New York State
Source: U.S. Department of Education, Office of Special Education Programs, Data Analysis System (DANS)

• *Mainstreaming* generally refers to selectively placing a student with a disability into one or more regular education classrooms. There is often the assumption that mainstreamed students will need to "keep up" with the other students through the same instructional strategies (Rogers, 1993).

• *Inclusion* is a more global term referring to a commitment to educate each child in the same classroom or school as his or her peers. The assumption is that the necessary "supports will be brought to the child (rather than moving the child to the services) and requires only that the child will benefit from being in the class (rather than keeping up with the other students)" (Rogers, 1993, p. 2).

• *Full inclusion* indicates that a school has the instructional capacity available to "accommodate all students in the schools and classrooms they would normally attend if not disabled" (Rogers, 1993, p. 2). Many proponents of full inclusion view the role of the special education teacher to be that of a trainer and technical assistance provider to the regular education teachers.

LEGAL BASIS FOR INCLUSION

Today, P.L. 94-142 has been amended five times and has evolved into the Individualized Disability Education Act (IDEA), with the most recent amendments passed in 2004. The amendments of 1997 were particularly significant in creating a renewed focus requiring children with disabilities be guaranteed the "least restrictive environment" for learning while also addressing the importance of a thorough evaluation for services (including diagnosis by qualified professionals), individualized education programs for each student, student and parent participation in decision making, and the procedural safeguards to insure that the regulations and the rights of students with disabilities are being followed (Individuals with Disabilities Act Amendments of 1997). The recent passage of the 2004 amendments address discipline, paperwork, overrepresentation of minorities in certain special education categories, hiring highly qualified teachers, litigation, and other issues.

Also important to curricular planning is Section 504 of the Rehabilitation Act, originally passed in 1973, as the first civil rights law that prohibited discrimination on the basis of disability. Specifically, this law required that all federally funded entities (e.g., schools, libraries, universities, local and state government agencies) provide physical as well as programmatic accommodations for people with disabilities of all ages. Many students with health impairments, such as juvenile diabetes, that do not interfere with classroom learning receive 504 accommodations instead of IDEA related services. For example, if a seventh grade student with diabetes needs regular breaks throughout the day to administer and monitor his insulin, the school will establish a 504 plan, rather than an individualized education plan (IEP) in order to assure that this student has the necessary accommodations to do so.

The latest flagship regular education law, No Child Left Behind (NCLB), was authorized in 2002, replacing the Elementary and Secondary Education Act (ESEA) and bringing broad changes to U.S. educational systems. Although not a special education law in particular, NCLB does have significant impact on students with disabilities, especially in the terms of assessment. Building on IDEA, NCLB requires schools to measure how well students with disabilities have learned reading and mathematics curriculum. The law includes provisions for students with the most significant cognitive disabilities, allowing for designed alternate assessments when appropriate. Since the majority of students with disabilities are

required to meet the academic achievement goals of their schools, they must also have access to the general education curriculum. Shrag (2003) contends that, "Clearly, students with disabilities cannot demonstrate knowledge about content that they have not been taught. Our current challenge is to ensure this access to these students" (p. 10). Furthermore, Shrag warns that with the emphasis on high stakes testing and academic achievement success, some schools may be tempted to place more students in more restrictive environments, which only distances them from the general curriculum and their peers (2003).

Other indirect effects of NCLB for students with disabilities may be that schools will be less welcoming of students with special learning needs because they may threaten the schools' assessment results. Finally, because NCLB includes this assessment mandate of students with disabilities—*without* adequate funding to implement the mandate—it may be very difficult for schools to "provide the appropriate remediation or special education services that many students with disabilities may need if they are going to reach the levels of proficiency on statewide assessments that NCLB requires" (Shrag, 2003, p. 10).

In summary, classroom teachers need to understand that these laws mandate the education of students with disabilities with the expectation that both regular education and special education teachers provide instruction for students with disabilities. Understanding how one's teaching practices fit into the national legal mandates provides a framework for implementing best practices in the classroom, including designing educational tasks and providing assessment accommodations.

THE THREE A'S OF CREATING AN INCLUSIVE CURRICULUM AND CURRICULUM

To many teachers, meeting the educational needs of students with disabilities can be both overwhelming and frightening. Fortunately, the regular education teacher is not alone in this endeavor. Special education teachers, school counselors, school psychologists, nurses, speech pathologists, occupational therapists, educational assistants, and educational administrators all play a unique role in supporting the regular education teacher to educate students with disabilities. However, it is absolutely necessary for the regular education teacher to be proactive and knowledgeable regarding inclusion.

How can a regular education teacher ensure he or she is practicing effective instructional techniques that meet the educational needs of all students in the classroom? Practicing the three A's of creating an inclusive curriculum (aware, active, and achieve) is an excellent place to begin.

Consider the three A's of creating an inclusive curriculum to be like a garden, with each component necessary for growth. In gardens some plants are hardier than others—many need special attention, accommodations, and pruning before they can flourish. Teachers tend to the needs of the classroom and the students in the same way a gardener tends to the individual plants in the garden.

Aware Think of awareness as the soil of the garden. Effective gardeners understand the unique needs of each plant and make certain the soil is formulated to maximize the success of all plants in the garden.

An aware teacher can articulate the individual needs to various students in the classroom. The aware teacher not only knows which students are on IEPs and/or 504 plans, but also knows the content of the plans.

Active Effective gardeners must tend to the plants in the garden on a regular basis—some plants require daily watering, others are drought resistant, and still others require regular pruning. If the soil nutrients are perfectly balanced but the plants are not maintained properly, many will not survive or thrive.

Similarly, successful inclusionary practices require the teacher to be constantly active and engaged in the students' learning. Beyond knowing what the students need, the curriculum should be designed and frequently modified with these diverse learning styles in mind. The teacher must reach out to the students rather than expect the student to reach out to him or her. Students with disabilities may have become academically disengaged by other teachers who have not met their needs and may need to be "nurtured" back to learning. Many *active* teachers attend and participate in IEP meetings, with the goal of learning more about students' strengths and weaknesses to better accommodate their learning and curricular needs.

Achieve Now that the garden is filled with rich soil, and a variety of plants with unique needs that are carefully tended to, the gardener expects the plants to grow, thrive, and bloom. However, despite these perfect conditions for growth, not all plants may mature: perhaps environmental conditions have become challenging, such as extreme weather or an insect infestation; or maybe some other *unseen* threat to plant health and vitality. Does the gardener give up on the deteriorating plant or stay the course and continue to try and address the plant's needs?

In the same manner, a successful inclusive teacher provides all students with a rich, engaging curriculum, and expects all students will succeed. However, when a student does not achieve adequately, effective inclusionary practices require the teacher to assess why. Why was the student not able to achieve the learning objectives with the current curriculum and what must be addressed, adapted, or changed for the student to succeed? Many times environmental factors impede a student's ability to learn. For example, a student with a behavioral disorder whose parents are divorcing may require intervention from the school counselor, rather than a modification of the curriculum. Regardless, the teacher must assess the reasons for academic failure and be prepared to address them.

AUTHENTIC PEDAGOGY AND INCLUSION

Beyond practicing the *Three A's of Inclusion*, NCLB emphasizes the importance of implementing research-based practices for schools to meet state educational standards. Braden, Schroeder, and Buckley (2001) note the importance of high quality inclusionary practices across the curriculum:

> A commitment to educational equity demands inclusion. Students cannot learn what they have not been taught; educators must include students with disabilities in opportunities to learn, and they must provide the supports those students need to gain access to general education. (Braden, Schroeder, & Buckley, 2001)

Authentic pedagogy is an outstanding example of a research based practice that has emerged from the education reform movement, and has been shown to increase the learning of students with disabilities educated in inclusive classrooms, (King, Schroeder, & Chawszczewski, 2001; [Newmann], Marks, & Garmoran, 1996).

Authenticity is defined as the extent to which a lesson, assessment task, or sample of student performance represents construction of new knowledge, through the use of disciplined inquiry, which has some value or meaning beyond success in school (Newmann, Secada, & Wehlage, 1995). According to [Newmann] et al. (1995) the three primary components of authentic intellectual work include *higher order thinking, depth of knowledge and understanding, and connectedness to the real world.*

Higher order thinking requires that students manipulate information and ideas in ways that transfer their meaning and their implications, rather than rote memorization, for example. Depth of knowledge and student understanding in authentic schools and classrooms requires that students successfully produce new knowledge by discovering relationships, solving problems, constructing explanations, and drawing conclusions. The final key component of authentic education—connectedness to the real world—implies that there is a connection to the larger social context within which students live. For example, a science experiment that relates to the environment or a history assignment that relates an historical event to a current event.

When curriculum is designed with authentic tasks that include the above components, all students achieve; however, students with disabilities achieve at a higher rate. According to a study by King, Schroeder, and Chawszczewski (2001) there is a significant relationship between authentic tasks and student learning. In other words, when teachers assigned authentic tasks, students produced authentic work. Furthermore, in their study, "sixty-two percent of the students with disabilities produced work that was the same, or higher, in authenticity than that produced by their nondisabled peers" (p. 12).

Finally, learning how to design authentic tasks requires practice and skill; however, once mastered can transform a teacher's pedagogical practice. For more information and examples of highly authentic tasks, see the Research Institute on Secondary Education Reform at the University of Wisconsin–Madison: http://www.wcer.wisc.edu/riser.

ASSESSMENT ACCOMMODATIONS AND STUDENTS WITH DISABILITIES

Another issue essential for inclusionary practice is that of assessment accommodations for students with disabilities. Assessment accommodations is a hotly contested topic within education, especially as it pertains to large scale standardized tests such as the SAT or state-wide high stakes tests. For the purposes of this article, only classroom assessment will be addressed.

The classroom teacher must always address each assessment accommodation separately as each student and each assessment task vary. What is a necessary accommodation for one student with a learning disability may not be necessary for another. The I.E.P. and any supporting medical or psychological documentation are important foundational data to consider when making assessment decisions. For example, does the psychological evaluation indicate that the student requires a distraction free environment for test taking?

It is also important to distinguish assessment accommodations from assessment modifications and instructional supports. Accommodations do not change the assessment content but may change the assessment process components, such as setting, time, administration, or response format. Conversely, the nature of the assessment is changed with assessment modifications which alter assessment content. Meanwhile, instructional supports help students gain access to the general education curriculum (Braden et al., 2001).

With those distinctions in mind, Braden, Schroeder, and Buckley have suggested an assessment accommodations framework, along with principles for implementation of accommodations for students with disabilities (2001). This framework will allow teachers to make more informed assessment accommodation decisions. Referring to Table 2, the guiding framework includes the following provisions: students should not receive accommodations unless they are needed; accommodations decisions presume target and access skills are clearly identified; accommodations should address access, not target, or skills; target skill complexity should be modified when access is insufficient to allow for reasonable assessment of skills; and assessments should retain authenticity, even if they are modified to a simpler skill level.

The principles further assist the teacher with assessment accommodation decision making. Teachers should encourage risk taking by allowing the student to try the task without accommodations. The option for later accommodations without penalty should always be offered. Teachers should know what knowledge and skills the assessment intends to measure and what skills are required to respond to the assignment. An accommodation should allow access to the task, but not if it changes the skill targeted by the assessment. An accommodation may be appropriate in one circumstance but not

TABLE 2

Assessment Accommodations Framework: Principles for Implementation

Accommodations Framework	Implementation
Students should not receive accommodations unless they are needed.	Encourage risk taking by allowing the student to try to task without accommodations. Offer the option for later accommodations without penalty.
Accommodations decisions presume target and access skills are clearly identified.	Know what knowledge and skills the assessment intends to measure and what skills are required to respond to the assignment.
Accommodations should address access, not target, skills.	An accommodation should allow access to the task, but not if it changes the skill targeted by the assessment. An accommodation may be appropriate in one circumstance but not another.
Target skill complexity should be modified when access is insufficient to allow for reasonable assessment of skills.	Some skills levels are so far below the level targeted, even with successful access, the task is of no educational value. One should always seek to eliminate barriers posed by access skills. However, with some target skills, the task demands are so different from the test taker's current skill that the assessment is meaningless.
Assessments should retain authenticity, even if they are modified to a simpler skill level.	The teacher should not substitute an assessment with limited authenticity (e.g., labeling the parts of a rocket diagram rather than producing an experiment).

Source: Braden, J., Schroeder, J., & Buckley, J. (2001). *Secondary school reform, inclusion, and authentic assessment.* Madison, WI: Research Institute on Secondary School Reform. Reprinted with permission.

another. Some skill levels are so different from the level targeted, even with successful access, the task is of no educational value. In these cases, teachers should consider modifying the assessment to assess a less complex level of targeted skills. Lastly, the teacher should not substitute an assessment with limited authenticity (e.g., labeling the parts of a rocket diagram rather than producing an experiment) (Braden et al., 2001).

For teachers to practice effective inclusive education, teachers must have an awareness of who the students with disabilities are in the classroom, as well as the unique educational needs of each of those students. Having a solid appreciation of the legal mandates of education for students with disabilities provides a framework for understanding the teacher's role in providing an education to this population.

REFERENCES

Belkin, L. (2004, September 4). The lessons of classroom 506. *The New York Times Magazine*, 40–49.

Braden, J., Schroeder, J., & Buckley, J. (2001). *Secondary school reform, inclusion, and authentic assessment*. Madison, WI: Research Institute on Secondary Education Reform (Author).

Individuals with Disabilities Act Amendments of 1997.

King, M. B., Schroeder, J., & Chawszczewski, D. (2001). *Authentic assessment and student performance in inclusive schools*. Madison, WI: Research Institute on Secondary Education Reform (Author).

Newmann, F. M., Marks, H. M., & Garmoran, A. (1996). Authentic pedagogy and student performance. *American Journal of Education, 104,* 208–312.

Newmann, F. M., Secada, W. G., & Wehlage, G. G. (1995). *A guide to authentic instruction and assessment: Vision, standards and scoring*. Madison, WI: University of Wisconsin-Madison, Wisconsin Center for Education Research.

Rogers, J. (1993). *The inclusion revolution*. Bloomington, IN: Phi Delta Kappa Center for Evaluation, Development, and Research (Author).

Shrag, J. A. (2003). No Child Left Behind and its implications for students with disabilities. *The Special Edge, 16*(2), 1–12.

U.S. Department of Education. (2002). *Twenty-fourth annual report to Congress on the implementation of the Individuals with Disabilities Education Act*. Washington, DC.

Tina M. Anctil is an assistant professor in the Department of Counselor Education at Portland State University.

QUESTIONS FOR REFLECTION

1. Did this article challenge any stereotypes you may have about people with disabilities? Did the statistical data on the number and type of students with disabilities in the classroom surprise you?
2. The author explained how some disabilities are "over-diagnosed" for some ethnicities. How might this happen and what might be done to prevent this practice? How does this over-diagnosis harm children?
3. When thinking about applying the three A's of inclusive curriculum to your role as a curriculum leader, which "A" is most challenging for you to consider doing? Why? What might you need to do to successfully integrate all three A's in your curriculum leadership activities?

The Dimensions of Multicultural Education

JAMES A. BANKS

ABSTRACT: The author describes the goals of multicultural education and its five dimensions. The dimensions are designed to help practicing educators understand the different aspects of multicultural education and to enable them to implement it comprehensively. The dimensions help educators understand, for example, that content integration is only one important part of comprehensive multicultural education. Another important dimension of multicultural education is a school culture and social structure that promotes gender, racial, and social-class equity.

THE AIMS AND GOALS OF MULTICULTURAL EDUCATION

The heated discourse on multicultural education, especially in the popular press and among writers outside the field (Fullinwider, 1996; Graff, 1992; Sleeter, 2001; Taylor, 1994), often obscures the theory, research, and consensus among multicultural education scholars and researchers about the nature, aims, and scope of the field (Banks, 2004b; Gay, 2004). A major goal of multicultural education—as stated by specialists in the field—is to reform schools, colleges, and universities so that students from diverse racial, ethnic, and social-class groups will experience educational equality.

Another important goal of multicultural education is to give both male and female students an equal chance to experience educational success and mobility (Sadker & Sadker, 2004). Multicultural education theorists are increasingly interested in how the interaction of race, class, and gender influences education (Banks, 1997; Cyrus, 1999). However, the emphasis that different theorists give to each of these variables varies considerably. Although there is an emerging consensus about the aims and scope of multicultural education, the variety of typologies, conceptual schemes, and perspectives within the field reflects its emergent status and the fact that complete agreement about its aims and boundaries has not been attained (Banks, 2003; Garcia, 2005; Gay, 2000; Nieto, 1999).

There is general agreement among most scholars and researchers in multicultural education that, for it to be implemented successfully, institutional changes must be made, including changes in the curriculum; the teaching materials; teaching and learning styles; the attitudes, perceptions, and behaviors of teachers and administrators; and in the goals, norms, and culture of the school (Banks & Banks, 2004). However, many school and university practitioners have a limited conception of multicultural education; they view it primarily as curriculum reform that involves changing or restructuring the curriculum to include content about ethnic groups, women, and other cultural groups. This conception of multicultural education is widespread because curriculum reform was the main focus when the movement first emerged in the 1960s and 1970s and because the multiculturalism discourse in the popular media has focused on curriculum reform and has largely ignored other dimensions and components of multicultural education (Hughes, 1993).

THE DIMENSIONS AND THEIR IMPORTANCE

If multicultural education is to become better understood and implemented in ways more consistent with theory, its various dimensions must be more clearly described, conceptualized, and researched. Multicultural education is conceptualized in this chapter as a field that consists of five dimensions I have formulated (Banks, 2004b):

1. Content integration,
2. The knowledge construction process,
3. Prejudice reduction,
4. An equity pedagogy, and
5. An empowering school culture and social structure (see Figure 1).

Each of the five dimensions is defined and illustrated later in this chapter.

Educators need to be able to identify, to differentiate, and to understand the meanings of each dimension of multicultural education. They also need to understand that multicultural education includes but is much more than content integration. Part of the controversy in multicultural education results from the fact that many writers in the popular press see it only as content integration and as an educational movement that benefits only people of color. When multicultural education is conceptualized broadly, it becomes clear that it is for all students, and not just for low-income students and students of color (Banks, 2004a;

FIGURE 1
The Dimensions of Multicultural Education

Content Integration

Content integration deals with the extent to which teachers use examples and content from a variety of cultures and groups to illustrate key concepts, principles, generalizations, and theories in their subject area or discipline.

The Knowledge Construction Process

The knowledge construction process relates to the extent to which teachers help students to understand, investigate, and determine how the implicit cultural assumptions, frames of references, perspectives, and biases within a discipline influence the ways in which knowledge is constructed within it.

Prejudice Reduction

This dimension focuses on the characteristics of students' racial attitudes and how they can be modified by teaching methods and materials.

An Equity Pedagogy

An equity pedagogy exists when teachers modify their teaching in ways that will facilitate the academic achievement of students from diverse racial, cultural, and social-class groups. This includes using a variety of teaching styles that are consistent with the wide range of learning styles within various cultural and ethnic groups.

Multicultural Education

An Empowering School Culture and Social Structure

Grouping and labeling practices, sports participation, disproportionality in achievement, and the interaction of the staff and the students across ethnic and racial lines are among the components of the school culture that empowers students from diverse racial, ethnic, and cultural groups.

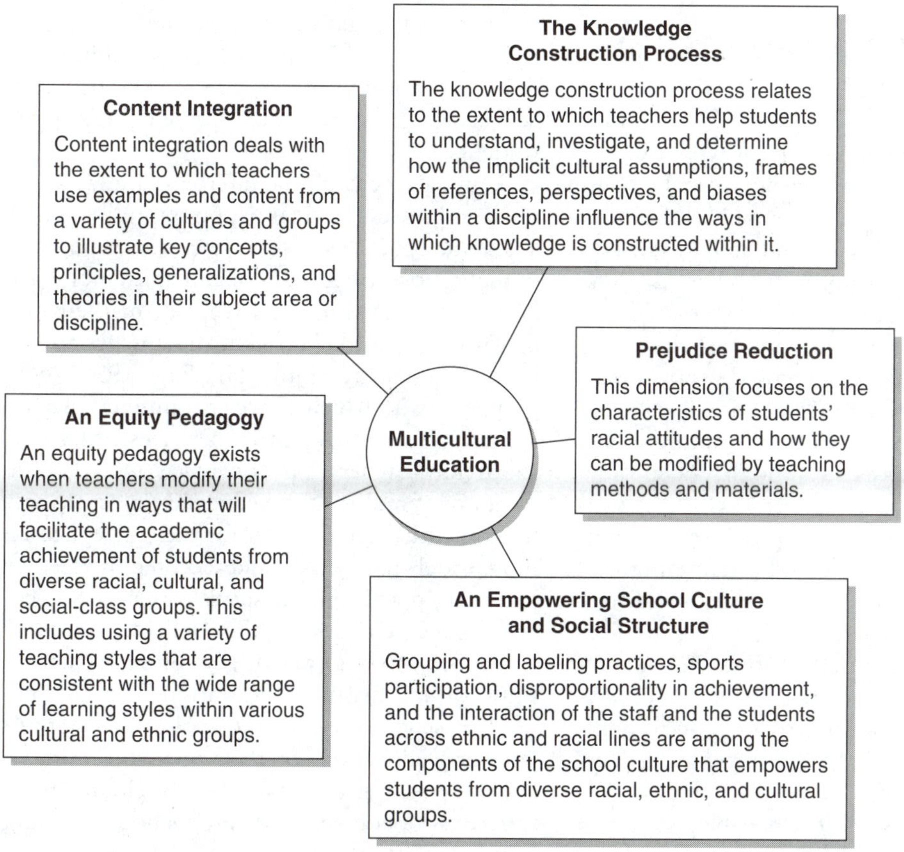

May, 1999; Nieto, 1999). Research and practice will also improve if we more clearly delineate the boundaries and dimensions of multicultural education.

This chapter defines and describes each of the five dimensions of multicultural education. The knowledge construction process is discussed more extensively than the other four dimensions. The kind of knowledge that teachers examine and master will have a powerful influence on the teaching methods they create, on their interpretations of school knowledge, and on how they use student cultural knowledge. The knowledge construction process is fundamental in the implementation of multicultural education. It has implications for each of the other four dimensions—for example, for the construction of knowledge about pedagogy.

LIMITATIONS AND INTERRELATIONSHIP OF THE DIMENSIONS

The dimensions typology is an ideal-type conception. It approximates but does not describe reality in its total complexity. Like all classification schema, it has both strengths and limitations. Typologies are helpful conceptual tools because they provide a way to organize and make sense of complex and distinct data and observations. However, their categories are interrelated and overlapping, not mutually exclusive. Typologies rarely encompass the total universe of existing or future cases. Consequently, some cases can he described only by using several of the categories.

The dimensions typology provides a useful framework for categorizing and interpreting the extensive and myriad literature on cultural diversity, ethnicity, and education. However, the five dimensions are conceptually distinct but highly interrelated. Content integration, for example, describes any approach used to integrate content about racial and cultural groups into the curriculum. The knowledge construction process describes a method in which teachers help students to understand how knowledge is created and how

it reflects the experiences of various ethnic, racial, cultural, and language groups.

THE MEANING OF MULTICULTURAL EDUCATION TO TEACHERS

A widely held and discussed idea among theorists is that, in order for multicultural education to be effectively implemented within a school, changes must be made in the total school culture as well as within all subject areas, including mathematics and science (Moses & Cobb, 2001). Despite the wide acceptance of this basic tenet by theorists, it confuses many teachers, especially those in subject areas such as science and mathematics. This confusion often takes the form of resistance to multicultural education. Many teachers have told me after a conference presentation on the characteristics and goals of multicultural education: "These ideas are fine for the social studies, but they have nothing to do with science or math. Science is science, regardless of the culture of the students."

This statement can be interpreted in a variety of ways. However, one way of interpreting it is as a genuine belief held by a teacher who is unaware of higher-level philosophical and epistemological knowledge and issues in science or mathematics or who does not believe that these issues are related to school teaching (Harding, 1998). The frequency with which I have encountered this belief in staff development conferences and workshops for teachers has convinced me that the meaning of multicultural education must be better contextualized in order for the concept to be more widely understood and accepted by teachers and other practitioners, especially in such subject areas as mathematics and the sciences.

We need to better clarify the different dimensions of multicultural education and to help teachers see more clearly the implications of multicultural education for their own subject areas and teaching situations. The development of active, cooperative, and motivating teaching strategies that makes physics more interesting for students of color might be a more important goal for a physics teacher of a course in which few African American students are enrolling or successfully completing than is a search for ways to infuse African contributions to physics into the course. Of course, in the best possible world both goals would be attained. However, given the real world of the schools, we might experience more success in multicultural teaching if we set limited but essential goals for teachers, especially in the early phases of multicultural educational reform.

The development of a phase conceptualization for the implementation of multicultural educational reform would be useful. During the first or early phases, all teachers would be encouraged to determine ways in which they could adapt or modify their teaching for a multicultural population with diverse abilities, learning characteristics, and motivational styles. A second or later phase would focus on curriculum content integration. One phase would not end when another began. Rather, the goal would be to reach a phase in which all aspects of multicultural educational reform would be implemented simultaneously. In multicultural educational reform, the first focus is often on content integration rather than on knowledge construction or pedagogy. A content-integration focus often results in many mathematics and science teachers believing that multicultural education has little or no meaning for them. The remainder of this chapter describes the dimensions of multicultural education with the hope that this discussion will help teachers and other practitioners determine how they can implement multicultural education in powerful and effective ways.

CONTEXTUALIZING MULTICULTURAL EDUCATION

We need to do a better job of contextualizing the concept of multicultural education. When we tell practitioners that multicultural education implies reform in a discipline or subject area without specifying in detail the nature of that reform, we risk frustrating motivated and committed teachers because they do not have the knowledge and skills to act on their beliefs. Educators who reject multicultural education will use the "irrelevance of multicultural education" argument as a convenient and publicly sanctioned form of resistance and as a justification for inaction.

Many of us who are active in multicultural education have backgrounds in the social sciences and humanities. Consequently, we understand the content and process implications of multicultural education in these disciplines. A variety of programs, units, and lessons have been developed illustrating how the curriculum can be reformed and infused with multicultural perspectives, issues, and points of view from the social sciences and the humanities (Banks, 2003; Derman-Sparks, 2004). As students of society and of the sociology of knowledge, we also understand, in general ways, how mathematics and science are cultural systems that developed within social and political contexts (Harding, 1998).

Most mathematics and science teachers do not have the kind of knowledge and understanding of their disciplines that enables them to construct and formulate lessons, units, and examples that deal with the cultural assumptions, frames of references, and perspectives within their disciplines. Few teachers seem able to identify and describe the assumptions and paradigms that underlie science and mathematics (Kuhn, 1970). They often make such statements as, "Math and science have no cultural contexts and assumptions. These disciplines are universal across cultures." Knowledge about the philosophical and epistemological issues and problems in science and mathematics, and the philosophy of science, is often limited to graduate seminars and academic specialists in these disciplines (Harding, 1998; Powell & Frankenstein, 1997).

Specialists and leaders in multicultural education, because of their academic backgrounds, have been able to identify the basic issues and problems in mathematics and science but have not, in my view, provided the field with the clarity, curriculum work, and examples of lessons that mathematics and science teachers need in order to view the content within their disciplines from multicultural perspectives. Some promising attempts have been made to develop multicultural materials for mathematics and science teachers (Moses & Cobb, 2001; Powell & Frankenstein, 1997). However, more work must be done in this area before most mathematics and science teachers can develop and implement a curriculum-content approach to multicultural education.

Multicultural education is a way of viewing reality and a way of thinking, and not just content about various ethnic, racial, and cultural groups. Much more important work needs to be done in order to provide teachers with the examples and specifics they need. In the meantime, we can help all teachers, including mathematics and science teachers, to conceptualize and develop an equity pedagogy (Banks, 2003), a way of teaching that is not discipline-specific but that has implications for all subject areas and for teaching in general.

THE DIMENSIONS OF MULTICULTURAL EDUCATION

Teachers can examine five dimensions of the school when trying to implement multicultural education. These dimensions, identified above, are summarized in Figure 1. They are defined and illustrated below.

Content Integration

Content integration deals with the extent to which teachers use examples and content from a variety of cultures and groups to illustrate key concepts, principles, generalizations, and theories in their subject area or discipline. The infusion of ethnic and cultural content into the subject area should be logical, not contrived. The widespread belief that content integration constitutes the whole of multicultural education might be an important factor that causes many teachers of subjects such as mathematics and science to view multicultural education as an endeavor primarily for social studies and language arts teachers.

More opportunities exist for the integration of ethnic and cultural content in some subject areas than in others. In the social studies, the language arts, music, and family and consumer sciences, there are frequent and ample opportunities for teachers to use ethnic and cultural content to illustrate concepts, themes, and principles. There are also opportunities to integrate the math and science curriculum with ethnic and cultural content (Addison-Wesley, 1992). However, these opportunities are not as apparent or as easy to identify as they are in subject areas such as the social studies and the language arts.

In the language arts, for example, students can examine the ways in which Ebonics (Black English) is both similar to and different from mainstream U.S. English (Delpit & Dowdy, 2002). The students can also study how African American oratory is used to engage the audience with the speaker. They can read and listen to speeches by such African Americans as Martin Luther King, Jr., Congresswoman Maxine Waters of California, Marian Wright Edelman, Al Sharpton, and Senator Barack Obama from Illinois when studying Ebonics and African American oratory (Foner & Branham, 1998). The importance of oral traditions in Native American cultures can also be examined. Personal accounts by Native Americans can he studied and read aloud (Hirschfelder, 1995).

The scientific explanation of skin color differences, the biological kinship of the human species, and the frequency of certain diseases among specific human groups are also content issues that can be investigated in science. The contributions to science made by cultures such as the Aztecs, the Egyptians, and the Native Americans are other possibilities for content integration in science (Bernal, 1987, 1991; Weatherford, 1988).

The Knowledge Construction Process

The knowledge construction process consists of the methods, activities, and questions teachers use to help students to understand, investigate, and determine how implicit cultural assumptions, frames of reference, perspectives, and biases within a discipline influence the ways in which knowledge is constructed. When the knowledge construction process is implemented in the classroom, teachers help students to understand how knowledge is created and how it is influenced by the racial, ethnic, and social-class positions of individuals and groups (Code, 1991; Harding, 1991). *Positionality* is the term used to describe the ways in which race, social class, gender, and other personal and cultural characteristics of knowers influence the knowledge they construct or produce.

In the Western empirical tradition, the ideal within each academic discipline is the formulation of knowledge without the influence of the researchers' personal or cultural characteristics (Myrdal, 1969). However, as critical theorists, scholars of color, and feminist scholars have pointed out, personal, cultural, and social factors influence the formulation of knowledge even when objective knowledge is the ideal within a discipline (Banks, 1996; Code, 1991; Collins, 1998). Often the researchers themselves are unaware of how their personal experiences and positions within society influence the knowledge they produce. Most mainstream U.S. historians were unaware of how their regional and cultural biases influenced their interpretation of the Reconstruction period until W. E. B. Du Bois (1935) published a study that challenged the accepted and established interpretations of that period.

It is important for teachers as well as students to understand how knowledge is constructed within all disciplines, including mathematics and science. Social scientists, as well as physical and biological scientists on the cutting edges of their disciplines, understand the nature and limitations of their fields. However, the disciplines are often taught to students as a body of truth not to be questioned or critically analyzed. Students need to understand, even in the sciences, how cultural assumptions, perspectives, and frames of reference influence the questions that researchers ask and the conclusions, generalizations, and principles they formulate.

Students can analyze the knowledge construction process in science by studying how racism has been perpetuated in science by genetic theories of intelligence, Darwinism, and eugenics (Gould, 1996; Harding, 1998). Scientists developed theories such as polygeny and craniometry that supported and reinforced racist assumptions and beliefs in the eighteenth and nineteenth centuries (Gould, 1996; Hannaford, 1996). Although science has supported and reinforced institutionalized racism at various times and places, it has also contributed to the eradication of racist beliefs and practices. Biological theories and data that revealed the characteristics that different racial and ethnic groups share, and anthropological theory and research about the universals in human cultures, have contributed greatly to the erosion of racist beliefs and practices (Benedict, 1940; Boas, 1940).

Knowledge Construction and the Transformative Curriculum. The curriculum in the schools must be transformed in order to help students develop the skills needed to participate in the knowledge construction process. The transformative curriculum changes the basic assumptions of the curriculum and enables students to view concepts, issues, themes, and problems from diverse ethnic and cultural perspectives (Banks, 1996). The transformative curriculum can teach students to think by encouraging them, when they are reading or listening to resources, to consider the author's purposes for writing or speaking, his or her basic assumptions, and how the author's perspective or point of view compares with that of other authors and resources. Students can develop the skills to analyze critically historical and contemporary resources by being given several accounts of the same event or situation that present different perspectives and points of view.

Teaching about Knowledge Construction and Production. Teachers can use two important concepts in U.S. history to help students to better understand the ways in which knowledge is constructed and to participate in rethinking, reconceptualizing, and constructing knowledge. "The New World" and "The European Discovery of America" are two central ideas that are pervasive in the school and university curriculum as well as within popular culture. The teacher can begin a unit focused on these concepts with readings, discussions, and visual presentations that describe the archaeological theories about the peopling of the Americas nearly 40,000 years ago by groups that crossed the Bering Strait while hunting for animals and plants to eat. The students can then study about the Aztecs, the Incas, and the Iroquois and other highly developed civilizations that developed in the Americas prior to the arrival of Europeans in the fifteenth century.

After the study of the Native American cultures and civilizations, the teacher can provide the students with brief accounts of some of the earliest Europeans, such as Columbus and Cortés, who came to America. The teacher can then ask the students what they think the phrase "The New World" means, whose point of view it reflects, and to list other and more neutral words to describe the Americas (Bigelow & Peterson, 1998). The students could then be asked to describe "The European Discovery of America" from two different perspectives: (1) from the point of view of a Taino or Arawak Indian (Rouse, 1992; the Tainos were living in the Caribbean when Columbus arrived there in 1492); and (2) from the point of view of an objective or neutral historian who has no particular attachment to either American Indian or European society.

The major objective of this lesson is to help students to understand knowledge as a social construction and to understand how concepts such as The New World and The European Discovery of America are not only ethnocentric and Eurocentric terms, but are also normative concepts that serve latent but important political purposes, such as justifying the destruction of Native American peoples and civilizations by Europeans such as Columbus and those who came after him (Stannard, 1992; Todorov, 1992; Zinn & Kirschner, 1995). The New World is a concept that subtly denies the political existence of Native Americans and their nations prior to the coming of the Europeans.

The goal of teaching knowledge as a social construction is neither to make students cynics nor to encourage them to desecrate European heroes such as Columbus and Cortés. Rather, the aim is to help students to understand the nature of knowledge and the complexity of the development of U.S. society and how the history that becomes institutionalized within a society reflects the perspectives and points of views of the victors rather than those of the vanquished. When viewed within a global context, the students will be able to understand how the creation of historical knowledge in the United States parallels the creation of knowledge in other democratic societies and is a much more open and democratic process than in totalitarian nation-states.

Another important goal of teaching knowledge as a construction process is to help students to develop higher-level thinking skills and empathy for the peoples who have been victimized by the expansion and growth of the United States. When diverse and conflicting perspectives are juxtaposed, students are required to compare, contrast, weigh evidence, and make reflective decisions. They are also able to develop empathy and an understanding of each group's perspective and point of view. The creation of their own versions of events and situations, and new concepts and terms, also requires students to reason at high levels and to think critically about data and information.

Prejudice Reduction

The prejudice reduction dimension of multicultural education describes the characteristics of students' racial attitudes and strategies that can be used to help them develop more democratic attitudes and values. Researchers have been investigating the characteristics of children's racial attitudes since the 1920s (Lasker, 1929). This research indicates that most voting children enter school with negative racial attitudes that mirror those of adults (Aboud, 1988; Stephan & Stephan, 2004). Research also indicates that effective curricular interventions can help students develop more positive racial and gender attitudes (Banks, 2001; Stephan & Stephan, 2004). Since the intergroup education movement of the 1940s and 1950s (Trager & Yarrow, 1952), a number of investigators have designed interventions to help students develop more positive racial attitudes and values (Slavin, 2001).

Since the 1940s, a number of curriculum intervention studies have been conducted to determine the effects of teaching units and lessons, multiethnic materials, role playing, and other kinds of simulated experiences on the racial attitudes and perceptions of students. These studies, which have some important limitations and findings that are not always consistent, indicate that under certain conditions curriculum interventions can help students develop more positive racial and ethnic attitudes (Stephan & Vogt, 2004).

Despite the limitations of these studies, they provide guidelines that can help teachers improve intergroup relations in their classrooms and schools. Trager and Yarrow (1952) conducted one of the earliest curriculum studies. They examined the effects of a curriculum intervention on the racial attitudes of children in the first and second grades. In one experimental condition, the children experienced a democratic curriculum; in the other, non-democratic values were taught and perpetuated. No experimental condition was created in the control group. The democratic curriculum had a positive effect on the attitudes of both students and teachers.

White, second-grade children developed more positive racial attitudes after using multiethnic readers in a study conducted by Litcher and Johnson (1969). However, when Litcher, Johnson, and Ryan (1973) replicated this study using photographs instead of readers, the children's racial attitudes were not significantly changed. The investigators stated that the shorter length of the later study (one month compared to four), and

the different racial compositions of the two communities in which the studies were conducted, may help to explain why no significant effects were produced on the children's racial attitudes in the second study. The community in which the second study was conducted had a much higher percentage of African American residents than did the community in which the first was conducted.

The longitudinal evaluation of the television program, *Sesame Street,* by Bogatz and Ball (1971) supports the hypothesis that multiethnic simulated materials and interventions can have a positive effect on the racial attitudes of young children. These investigators found that children who had watched the program for long periods had more positive racial attitudes toward outgroups than did children who had watched the show for shorter periods.

Weiner and Wright (1973) examined the effects of a simulation on the racial attitudes of third-grade children. They divided a class into Orange and Green people. The children wore colored armbands that designated their group status. On one day of the intervention the students who wore Orange armbands experienced discrimination. On the other day, the children who wrote Green armbands were the victims. On the third day and again two weeks later, the children expressed less prejudiced beliefs and attitudes.

In an intervention that has now attained the status of a classic, Jane Elliot (cited in Peters, 1987) used simulation to teach her students the pain of discrimination. One day she discriminated against the blue-eyed children in her third-grade class; the next day she discriminated against the brown-eyed children. Elliot's intervention is described in the award-winning documentary, *The Eye of the Storm.* Eleven of Elliot's former students returned to Riceville, Iowa fourteen years later and shared their powerful memories of the simulation with their former teacher. This reunion is described in *A Class Divided,* a revealing and important documentary film.

Byrnes and Kiger (1990) conducted an experimental study to determine the effects of the kind of simulation for which Elliot had attained fame. They found that no experimental data existed on the effects of the blue-eyes–brown-eyes simulation, and that all of the evidence on the effects of the intervention were anecdotal. The subjects in their study were university students preparing to become elementary teachers. Their simulation had positive effects on the attitudes of non-Black students toward Blacks, but had no effects on the subjects' "stated level of comfort with Blacks in various social situations, as measured by the Social Distance scale" (p. 351).

Yawkey and Blackwell (1974) examined the effects of multiethnic social studies materials and related experiences on the racial attitudes of Black four-year-old children. The children were divided into three groups. The students in Group One read and discussed the materials. The Group Two students read and discussed the materials as well as took a related field trip. The students in Group 3 experienced the traditional preschool curriculum. The interventions in Groups 1 and 2 had a significant, positive effect on the students' racial attitudes toward African Americans and Whites.

Research indicates that curriculum interventions such as plays, folk dances, music, role playing, exclusion from a group, discussion in dyads, and interracial contact can also have positive effects on the racial attitudes of students. A curriculum intervention that consisted of folk dances, music, crafts, and role playing had a positive effect on the racial attitudes of elementary students in a study conducted by Ijaz and Ijaz (1981) in Canada. Four plays about African Americans, Chinese Americans, Jews, and Puerto Ricans increased racial acceptance and cultural knowledge among fourth-, fifth-, and sixth-grade students in the New York City schools in a study conducted by Gimmestad and DeChiara (1982).

Ciullo and Troiani (1988) found that children who were excluded from a group exercise became more sensitive to the feelings of children from other ethnic groups. McGregor (1993) used meta-analysis to integrate findings and to examine the effects of role playing and antiracist teaching on reducing prejudice in students. Twenty-six studies were located and examined. McGregor concluded that role playing and antiracist teaching "significantly reduce racial prejudice, and do not differ from each other in their effectiveness" (p. 215).

Aboud and Doyle (1996) designed a study to determine how children's racial evaluations were affected by talking about racial issues with a friend who had a different level of prejudice than their own. The researchers found that "high-prejudice children became significantly less prejudiced in their evaluations after the discussion. Changes were greater in children whose low-prejudice partner made more statements about cross-racial similarity, along with more positive Black and negative White evaluations" (p. 161). A study by Wood and Sonleitner (1996) indicates that childhood interracial contact has a positive, long-term influence on the racial attitudes and behavior of adults. They found that interracial contact in schools and neighborhoods has a direct and significant positive influence on adult racial attitudes toward African Americans.

Creating Cross-Cutting Superordinate Groups. Research indicates that creating or making salient superordinate and cross-cutting group memberships improve intergroup relations (Banks et al., 2001; Stephan & Stephan, 2004). Write Banks et al. (2001): "When membership in superordinate groups is salient, other group differences become less important. Creating superordinate groups stimulates cohesion, which can mitigate preexisting animosities" (p. 9).

Members of a sports team, Future Farmers of America, Girl Scouts, and Campfire are examples of cross-cutting or superordinate groups. Research and theory indicate that, when students from diverse cultural, racial, and language groups share a superordinate identity such as Girl Scouts, cultural boundaries weaken. Students are consequently able to form friendships and to have positive interactions and relationships with students from different racial, cultural, language, and religious groups. Extra- and co-curriculum activities, such as the drama club, the debating club, the basketball team, and the school chorus, create rich possibilities for structuring superordinate groups and cross-cutting group memberships.

When teachers create cross-cutting or super-ordinate groups, they should make sure that the integrity of different cultures represented in the classroom is respected and given legitimacy within the framework of the superordinate group that is created. Superordinate groups that only reflect the norms and values of dominant and powerful groups within the school are not likely to improve intergroup relations among different groups in the school. If they are not carefully structured and monitored, cross-cutting groups can reproduce the dominant power relationships that exist within the school and the larger society.

The Effects of Cooperation Learning on Academic Achievement and Racial Attitudes. Within the last three decades a number of researchers have studied the effects of cooperative learning on the academic achievement and racial attitudes of students from different racial and ethnic groups (Aronson & Gonzalez, 1988; Cohen, 1972; Cohen & Lotan, 2004; Slavin, 1979, 2001). This research has been, heavily influenced by the theory developed by Allport (1954). Allport hypothesized that prejudice would be reduced if interracial contact situations have the following characteristics:

1. They are cooperative rather than competitive.
2. The individuals experience equal status.
3. The individuals have shared goals.
4. The contact is sanctioned by authorities such as parents, the principal, and the teacher.

The research on cooperative learning activities indicates that African American, Mexican American, and White students develop more positive racial attitudes and choose more friends from outside racial groups when they participate in group activities that have the conditions identified by Allport. Cooperative learning activities also have a positive effect on the academic achievement of students of color (Slavin, 2001).

Equity Pedagogy

An equity pedagogy exists when teachers modify their teaching in ways that will facilitate the academic achievement of students from diverse racial, cultural, ethnic, language, and gender groups (Banks, 2004b). Research indicates that teachers can increase the classroom participation and academic achievement of students from different ethnic and cultural groups by modifying their instruction so that it draws on their cultural and language strengths. In a study by Philips (1993), American Indian students participated more actively in class discussions when teachers used group-oriented participation structures that were consistent with their community cultures. Au (1980) and Tharp (1989), working in the Kamehameha Early Education Program (KEEP), found that both student participation and standardized achievement test scores increased when they incorporated teaching strategies consistent with the cultures of Native Hawaiian students and used the children's experiences in reading instruction.

Studies summarized by Darling-Hammond (1995) indicate that the academic achievement of students of color and low-income students increases when they have high-quality teachers who are experts in their content specialization, pedagogy, and child development. She reports a significant study by Dreeben and Gamoran (1986), who found that, when African American students received high-quality instruction, their reading achievement was as high as that of White students. The quality of instruction, not the race of the students, was the significant variable.

Research and theories developed by Ladson-Billings (1994), Delpit (1995), and Heath (1983) indicate that teachers can improve the school success of students if they are knowledgeable about the cultures, values, language, and learning characteristics of their students. Research indicates that cooperative—rather than competitive—teaching strategies help African American and Mexican American students to increase their academic achievement as well as help all students, including White mainstream students, to develop more positive racial attitudes and values (Aronson & Gonzalez, 1988).

An Empowering School Culture and Social Structure

This dimension of multicultural education involves restructuring the culture and organization of the school so that students from diverse racial, ethnic, and gender groups will experience equality. This variable must be examined and addressed by the entire school staff including the principal and support staff. It involves an examination of the latent and manifest culture and organization of the school to determine the extent to which it fosters or hinders educational equity.

The four dimensions of multicultural education discussed above, content integration, the knowledge construction process, prejudice reduction, and an equity pedagogy—each deals with an aspect of a cultural or social system, the school. However, the school can also be conceptualized as one social system, which is larger than its interrelated parts, such as its formal and informal curriculum, teaching materials, counseling program, and teaching strategies. When conceptualized as a social system, the school is viewed as an institution that "includes a social structure of interrelated statuses and roles and the functioning of that structure in terms of patterns of actions and interactions" (Theodorson & Theodorson, 1969, p. 395). The school can also be conceptualized as a cultural system with a specific set of values, norms, shared meanings, and an identifiable ethos.

Among the variables that need to be examined in order to create a school culture that empowers students from diverse cultural groups are grouping practices (Wheelock, 1992), labeling practices, sports participation, and whether there are ethnic turfs that exist in the cafeteria or in other parts of the school (Tatum, 1997). The behavior of the school staff must also be examined in order to determine the subtle messages it gives the students about racial, ethnic, cultural, and social-class diversity. Testing practices, grouping practices, tracking, and gifted programs often contribute to ethnic and racial inequality within the school (Sapon-Shevin, 1994).

A number of school reformers have used a systems approach to reform the school in order to increase the academic achievement of low-income students and students of color. There are a number of advantages to approaching school reform from a holistic perspective. To implement any reform in a school effectively, such as effective prejudice reduction teaching, changes are required in a number of other school variables. Teachers, for example, need more knowledge and need to examine their racial and ethnic attitudes; consequently, they need more time as well as a variety of instructional materials. Many school reform efforts fail because the roles, norms, and ethos of the school do not change in ways that will make the institutionalization of the reforms possible.

The effective school reformers are one group of change agents that has approached school reform from a systems perspective. Brookover and Erickson (1975) developed a social-psychological theory of learning, which states that students internalize the conceptions of themselves that are institutionalized within the ethos and structures of the school. Related to Merton's (1968) self-fulfilling prophecy, this theory states that student academic achievement will increase if the adults within the school have high expectations for students, clearly identify the skills they wish them to learn, and teach those skills to them.

Research by Brookover and his colleagues (Brookover & Lezotte, 1979; Brookover, Beady, Flood, [Schweitzer] & Wisenbaker, 1979) indicates that schools populated by low-income students within the same school district vary greatly in student achievement levels. Consequently, Brookover attributes the differences to variations in the schools' social structures. He calls the schools in low-income areas that have high academic achievement improving schools. Other researchers, such as Edmonds (1986) and Lezotte (1993), call them effective schools (Levine & Lezotte, 1995).

Comer and his colleagues (Comer, Haynes, Joyner, & Ben-Avie, 1996) have developed a structural intervention model that involves changes in the social-psychological climate of the school. The teachers, principal, and other school professionals make collaborative decisions about the school. The parents also participate in the decision-making process. The data collected by Comer and his colleagues indicate that this approach has been successful in increasing the academic achievement of low-income, inner-city African American students.

REFERENCES

Aboud, F. E. (1988). *Children and prejudice.* New York: Basil Blackwell.

Aboud, F. E., & Doyle, A. B. (1996). Does talk foster prejudice or tolerance in children? *Canadian Journal of Behavioural Science, 28*(3), 161–171.

Addison-Wesley Publishing Company. (1992). *Multiculturalism in mathematics, science, and technology: Readings and activities.* Menlo Park, CA: Author.

Allport, G. W. (1954). *The nature of prejudice.* Cambridge, MA: Addison-Wesley.

Aronson, E., & Gonzalez, A. (1988). Desegregation, jigsaw, and the Mexican-American experience. In P. A. Katz & D. A. Taylor (Eds.), *Eliminating racism: Profiles in controversy* (pp. 301–314). New York: Plenum.

Au, K. (1980). Participation structures in a reading lesson with Hawaiian children. *Anthropology and Education Quarterly, 11*(2), 91–115,

Banks, J. A. (1993). Multicultural education for young children: Racial and ethnic attitudes and their modification. In B. Spodek (Ed.), *Handbook of research on the education of young children* (pp. 236–230). New York: Macmillan.

Banks, J. A. (Ed.). (1996). *Multicultural education, transformational knowledge and action: Historical and contemporary perspectives.* New York: Teachers College Press.

Banks, J. A. (1997). *Educating citizens in a multicultural society.* New York: Teachers College Press.

Banks, J. A. (2001). Multicultural education: Its effects on students' ethnic and gender role attitudes. In J. A. Banks & C. A. M. Banks (Eds.), *Handbook of research on multicultural education* (pp. 617–627). San Francisco: Jossey-Bass.

Banks, J. A. (2003). *Teaching strategies for ethnic studies* (7th ed.). Boston: Allyn and Bacon.

Banks, J. A. (2004a). Multicultural education: Characteristics and goals. In J. A. Banks & C. A. M. Banks (Eds.), *Multicultural education: Issues and perspectives* (5th ed., pp. 3–30). Hoboken, NJ: Wiley.

Banks, J. A. (2004b). Multicultural education: Historical development, dimensions, and practice. In J. A. Banks & C. A. M. Banks (Eds.), *Handbook of research on multicultural education* (2nd ed., pp. 3–29). San Francisco: Jossey-Bass.

Banks, J. A., & Banks, C. A. M. (Eds.). (2004). *Handbook of research on multicultural education* (2nd ed.). San Francisco: Jossey-Bass.

Banks, J. A., Cookson, P., Gay, G., Hawley, W. D., Irvine, J. J., Nieto, S., Schofield, J. W., & Stephan, W. G. (2001). *Diversity within unity: Essential principles for teaching and learning in a multicultural society.* Seattle: Center for Multicultural Education, University of Washington.

Benedict. R. (1940). *Race, science, and politics.* New York: Modern Age.

Bernal, M. (1987, 1991). *Black Athena: The Afro-Asiatic roots of classical civilization,* (Vols. 1–2). New Brunswick, NJ: Rutgers University Press.

Bigelow, B., & Peterson, B. (Eds.). (1998). *Rethinking Columbus: The next 500 years.* Milwaukee: Rethinking Schools.

Boas, F. (1940). *Race, language, and culture.* New York: Macmillan.

Bogatz, G. A., & Ball, S. (1971). *The second year of Sesame Street: A continuing evaluation.* Princeton, NJ: Educational Testing Service.

Brookover, W. B., Beady, C., Flood, P., Schweitzer, J., & Wisenbaker, J. (1979). *School social systems and strident achievement: Schools can make a difference.* New York: Praeger.

Brookover, W. B., & Erickson, E. (1975). *Sociology of education.* Homewood, IL: Dorset.

Brookover, W. B., & Lezotte, L. W. (1979). *Changes in school characteristics coincident with changes in student achievement.* East Lansing: Institute for Research on Teaching, College of Education, Michigan State University.

Byrnes, D. A., & Kiger, G. (1990). The effect of prejudice-reduction simulation on attitude change. *Journal of Applied Social Psychology, 20*(4), 341–356.

Ciullo, R., & Troiani, M. Y. (1988). Resolution of prejudice: Small group interaction and behavior of latency-age children. *Small Group Behavior, 19*(3), 386–394.

Code, L. (1991). *What can she know? Feminist theory and the construction of knowledge.* Ithaca, NY: Cornell University Press.

Cohen, E. G. (1972). Interracial interaction disability. *Human Relations, 25,* 9–24.

Cohen, E. G., & Lotan, R. (2004). Equity in heterogeneous classrooms. In J. A. Banks & C. A. M. Banks (Eds.). *Handbook of research on multicultural education* (2nd ed., pp. 736–750). San Francisco: Jossey-Bass.

Collins, P. H. (1998). *Fighting words: Black women and fire march for justice.* Minneapolis: University of Minnesota Press.

Comer, J. P, Haynes, N. M., Joyner, E. T., & Ben-Avie, M. (Eds.). (1996). *Rallying the whole village: The Comer process for reforming education.* New York: Teachers College Press.

Cyrus, V. (Ed.). (1999). *Experiencing race, class, and gender in the United* States (3rd ed.). New York: McGraw-Hill.

Darling-Hammond, L. (1995). Inequality and access to knowledge. In J. A. Banks & C. A. M. Banks (Eds.), *Handbook of research on multicultural education* (pp. 465–483). New York: Macmillan.

Delpit, L. (1995). *Other people's children: Cultural conflict in the classroom.* New York: New Press.

Delpit, L., & Dowdy, J. K. (Eds.). (2002). *The skin that we speak: Thoughts on language and culture in the classroom.* New York: New Press.

Derman-Sparks, L. (2004). Culturally relevant antibias education with young children. In W. G. Stephan & W. P. Vogt (Eds.), *Education programs for improving intergroup relations* (pp. 19–36). New York: Teachers College Press.

Dreeben, R., & Gamoran, A. (1986). Race, instruction, and learning. *American Sociological Review, 57*(5), 660–669.

Du Bois, W. E. B. (1935). *Black reconstruction.* New York: Harcourt, Brace.

Edmonds, R. (1986). Characteristics of effective schools. In U. Neisser (Ed.), *The school achievement of minority children* (pp. 93–104). Hillsdale, NJ: Erlbaum.

Foner, P. S., & Branham, R. J. (Eds.). (1998). *Lift every voice: African American oratory 1787–1900.* Tuscaloosa: University of Alabama Press.

Fullinwider, R. K. (Ed.). (1996). *Public education in a multicultural society: Policy, theory, critique.* New York: Cambridge University Press.

Garcia, E. (2005). *Teaching and learning in two languages: Bilingualism and schooling in the United States.* New York: Teachers College Press.

Gay, G. (2000). *Culturally responsive teaching: Theory, research, and practice.* New York: Teachers College Press.

Gay, G. (2004). Curriculum theory and multicultural education. In J. A. Banks & C. A. M. Banks (Eds.), *Handbook of research on multicultural education* (2nd ed., pp. 30–49). San Francisco: Jossey-Bass.

Gimmestad, B. J., & DeChiara, E. (1982). Dramatic plays: A vehicle for prejudice reduction in the elementary school. *Journal of Educational Research, 76*(1), 43–49.

Gould, S. J. (1996). *The mismeasure of man* (Rev. & expanded ed.). New York: Norton.

Graff, G. (1992). *Beyond the culture wars: How teaching the conflicts can revitalize American education.* New York: Norton.

Hannaford, I. (1996). *Race: The history of an idea in the West.* Baltimore: Johns Hopkins University Press.

Harding, S. (1991). *Whose science? Whose knowledge? Thinking from women's lives.* Ithaca, NY: Cornell University Press.

Harding, S. (1998). *Is science multicultural? Postcolonialisms, feminisms, and epistemologies.* Bloomington: Indiana University Press.

Heath, S. B. (1983). *Ways with words: language, life, and work in communities and classrooms,* New York: Cambridge University Press.

Hirschfelder, A. (Ed.). (1995). *Native heritage: Personal accounts by American Indians 1790 to the present.* New York: Macmillan.

Hughes, R. (1993). *Culture of complaint: The fraying of America.* New York: Oxford University Press.

Ijaz, M. A., & Ijaz, I. H. (1981). A cultural program for changing racial attitudes. *History and Social Science Teacher, 17*(1), 17–20.

Kuhn, T. S. (1970). *The structure of scientific revolutions* (2nd ed., enlarged). Chicago: University of Chicago Press.

Ladson-Billings, G. (1994). *The dreamkeepers: Successful teachers of African American children.* New York: Jossey-Bass.

Lasker, B. (1929). *Race attitudes in children.* New York: Holt, Rinehart & Winston.

Levine, D. U., & Lezotte, L. W. (1995). Effective schools research. In J. A. Banks & C. A. M. Banks

(Eds.), *Handbook of research on multicultural education* (pp. 525–547). New York: Macmillan.

Lezotte, L. W. (1993). Effective schools: A framework for increasing student achievement. In J. A. Banks & C. A. M. Banks (Eds.), *Multicultural education: Issues and perspectives* (2nd ed., pp. 303–316). Boston: Allyn and Bacon.

Litcher, J. H., & Johnson, D. W. (1969). Changes in attitudes toward Negroes of white elementary school students after use of multiethnic readers. *Journal of Educational Psychology, 60,* 148–152.

Litcher, J. H., Johnson, D. W., & Ryan, E. L. (1973). Use of pictures of multiethnic interaction to change attitudes of White elementary school students toward Blacks. *Psychological Reports, 33,* 367–372.

May, S. (Ed.). (1999). *Critical multiculturalism: Rethinking multicultural and antiracist education.* Philadelphia:Falmer.

McGregor, J. (1993). Effectiveness of role playing and antiracist teaching in reducing student prejudice. *Journal of Educational Research, 86*(4), 215–226.

Merton, R. K. (1968). *Social theory and social structure,* (1968 enlarged ed.) New York: Free Press.

Moses, R. P., & Cobb, C. E., Jr. (2001). *Radical equations: Math literacy and civil rights.* Boston: Beacon.

Myrdal, G. (1969). *Objectivity in social research.* Middletown, CT: Wesleyan University Press.

Nieto, S. (1999). *The light in their eyes: Creating multicultural learning communities.* New York: Teachers College Press.

Peters, W. (1987). *A class divided: Then and now* (Expanded ed.). New Haven, CT: Yale University Press.

Philips, S. U. (1993). *The invisible culture: Communication in classroom and community on the Warren Springs Indian Reservation.* Prospect Heights, IL: Waveland. (originally published 1983)

Powell, A. B., & Frankenstein, M. (Eds.). (1997). *Ethnomathematics: Challenging Eurocentrism in mathematics education.* Albany: State University of New York Press.

Rouse, I. (1992). *The Tainos: Rise and decline of the people who greeted Columbus.* New Haven: Yale University Press.

Sadker, M. P., & Sadker, D. M. (2004): Gender bias: Prom colonial America to today's classrooms. In J. A. Banks & C. A. M. Banks (Eds.), *Multicultural education: Issues and perspectives* (5th ed., pp. 135–163). Hoboken, NJ: Wiley.

Sapon-Shevin, M. (1994). *Playing favorites: Gifted education and the disruption of community.* Albany: State University of New York Press.

Slavin, R. E. (1979). Effects of biracial learning teams on cross-racial friendships. *Journal of Educational Psychology, 71,* 381–387.

Slavin, R. E. (2001). Cooperative learning and intergroup relations. In J. A. Banks & C. A. M. Banks (Eds.), *Handbook of research on multicultural education* (pp. 628–634). San Francisco: Jossey-Bass.

Sleeter, C. E. (2001). An analysis of the critiques of multicultural education. In J. A. Banks & C. A. M. Banks (Eds.), *Handbook of research on multicultural education* (pp. 81–94). San Francisco: Jossey-Bass.

Stannard, D. E. (1992). *American holocaust: Columbus and the conquest of the New World.* New York: Oxford University Press.

Stephan, W. G., & Stephan, C. W. (2004). Intergroup relations in multicultural education programs. In J. A. Banks & C. A. M. Banks (Eds.), *Handbook of research on multicultural education* (2nd ed., pp. 782–798). San Francisco: Jossey-Bass.

Stephan, W. G., & Vogt, W. P. (Eds.). (2004). *Education programs for improving intergroup relations.* New York: Teachers College Press.

Tajfel, H. (1970). Experiments in intergroup discrimination. *Scientific American, 223*(5), 96–102.

Tatum, B. U. (1997). *"Why are all the black kids sitting together in the cafeteria?" and other conversations about race.* New York: Basic Books.

Taylor, C. (1994). *Multiculturalism: Examining the politics of recognition.* (Edited and introduced by A. Gutmann) Princeton, NJ: Princeton University Press.

Tharp, R. G. (1989). Culturally compatible education: A formula for designing effective classrooms. In H. T. Trueba, G. Spindler, & L. Spindler (Eds.), *What do anthropologists have to say about dropouts?* (pp. 51–66). New York: Palmer.

Theodorson, G. A., & Theodorson, A. G. (1969). *A modern dictionary of sociology.* New York: Barnes & Noble.

Todorov, T. (1992). *The conquest of America: The question of the other.* New York: Harper.

Trager, H. G., & Yarrow, M. R. (1952). *They learn what they live: Prejudice in young children.* New York: Harper & Brothers.

Weatherford, J. (1988). *Indian givers: How the Indians of the Americas transformed the world.* New York: Fawcett Columbine.

Weiner, M. J., & Wright, F. E. (1973). Effects of undergoing arbitrary discrimination upon subsequent attitudes toward a minority group. *Journal of Applied Social Psychology, 3,* 94–102.

Wheelock, A. (1992). *Crossing the tracks: How "untracking" can save America's schools.* New York: New Press.

Williams, J. E., & Edwards, C. U. (1969). An exploratory study of the modification of color and racial concept attitudes in preschool children. *Child Development, 40,* 737–750.

Williams, J. E., & Morland, J. K. (1976). *Race, color, and the young child.* Chapel Hill: University of North Carolina Press.

Wood, P. B., & Sonleitner, N. (1996). The effect of childhood interracial contact on adult antiBlack prejudice. *International Journal of Intercultural Relations, 20*(1), 1–17.

Yawkey, T. D., & Blackwell, J. (1974). Attitudes of 4-year-old urban Black children toward themselves and Whites based upon multiethnic social studies materials and experiences. *Journal of Educational Research, 67,* 373–377.

Zinn, H., & Kirschner, G. (1995). *A people's history of the United States: The wall charts.* New York: New Press.

James A. Banks is Russell R. Stark University Professor and Director of the Center for Multicultural Education at the University of Washington, Seattle.

QUESTIONS FOR REFLECTION

1. What are the five dimensions of multicultural education that Banks writes about? Which one resonates with you most? Why?

2. Banks focuses on the knowledge construction process to illustrate how mainstream scholars and researchers influence the ways in which they construct academic knowledge to legitimize institutionalized inequity. What is it about the knowledge construction process that allows this institutionalized inequity to occur? What could be done to change this practice? Can it be changed?

3. In your own educational experience, what kinds of multicultural experiences helped you frame how you see the pluralistic, democratic society we live in? Is there any one event that had a bigger impact on you than others? If so, what was it, and what made it so significant for you?

A Deeper Sense of (Media) Literacy

CYNTHIA L. SCHEIBE

ABSTRACT: Media literacy can be used effectively as a pedagogical approach for teaching core content across the K–12 curriculum, thus meeting the needs of both teachers and students by promoting critical thinking, communication, and technology skills. This article focuses on the work of Project Look Sharp at Ithaca College, a media literacy initiative working primarily with school districts in upstate New York. Basic principles and best practices for using a curriculum-driven approach are described, with specific examples from social studies, English/language arts, math, science, health, and art, along with methods of assessment used to address effectiveness in the classroom.

One hundred elementary school students are chattering loudly as they walk back up the snowy hill to their school, coming from the local movie theater where they have just been treated to a special holiday showing of the movie *Antz*. The children are not just excited about seeing the movie; they have spent the past 2 weeks in their science class learning about ants and other insects, and now they are calling out examples of ways in which the movie misrepresented true ants. "Ants don't have teeth!" calls one boy. "Who were all those boy ants?" a girl asks. "I thought almost all ants were girls!" Her teacher nods and confirms that nearly all soldier and worker ants are sterile females.

Back in their classrooms, the students and teachers list the ways in which the ants were portrayed correctly (with six legs, three body segments, living in tunneled communities, carrying large loads) and incorrectly (talking, wearing clothes, with white eyes, etc.). The teachers take time to correct any misperceptions and to reinforce accurate information and then lead a discussion about why the moviemakers showed ants in ways that were not true. "Because they didn't know any better?" proposes one girl. "Because they wanted them to look like people!" suggests another. "It would be boring if they couldn't talk and just ran around like ants!"

This type of curriculum-driven approach to media literacy is at the heart of our work with

K–12 teachers at Project Look Sharp, a collaborative initiative of the teacher education, psychology, and communications programs at Ithaca College. As many theorists have noted (e.g., Hobbs, 1997), media literacy is a logical extension of traditional literacy: learning to "read" visual and audiovisual messages as well as text-based ones, recognizing the basic "language" used in each media form, being able to judge the credibility and accuracy of information presented in different formats, evaluating the "author's" intent and meaning, appreciating the techniques used to persuade and convey emotion, and being able to communicate effectively through different media forms. Media literacy, then, incorporates many elements from multiple literacies that are already central to today's education, including information literacy, computer literacy, scientific literacy, and cultural literacy. In addition, media literacy builds critical-thinking, communication, and technology skills and is an effective way to address different learning styles and an appreciation for multiple perspectives.

Before building media literacy into a curriculum unit, it is essential for teachers to have some basic training in media literacy theory and analysis (through staff development workshops and trainings). Project Look Sharp encourages teachers to weave the core elements of media literacy into their teaching practice early in the school year (see Best Practices [on p. 105]). We then work directly with individual teachers (or teams of teachers) to develop unique media literacy lessons that will help teach core content required by their districts and the state. We always start with core content (rather than the media literacy aspects), keeping in mind the teacher's own goals and needs, with a focus on basic learning standards for their grade and curriculum area.

Sometimes we are asked by school administrators to develop a series of lessons or resources to address a particular issue or need. For example, the second-grade social studies curriculum in New York State includes teaching about rural, urban, and suburban communities, and teachers were having a hard time conveying those concepts to 7- and 8-year-old children. Working with the teachers, we developed a series of lessons based on collective reading of historical pictures and short clips from television shows reflecting the three types of communities. Students from rural, urban, and suburban elementary schools then produced digital videos about their own communities and shared them with classes from the other schools. Students were surprised to find that there were many similarities in their videos (they all included fire stations, for example), and that some of the stereotypes they held about different types of communities were not true. Although this was a great deal of work, the unit went far beyond simply teaching the desired social studies and media literacy lessons by building (or reinforcing) a host of other social and organizational skills.

This approach has been surprisingly effective, not just in increasing the students' interest in a particular topic but also in deepening their understanding of the information itself. Teachers who gave a test about insects following the *Antz* movie found that students performed best on questions that related to the discussion of accuracy in the movie (e.g., the physical characteristics of insects), and that even 6 months later—at the end of the school year—most students remembered that information accurately.

By emphasizing media literacy as a pedagogical approach rather than a separate content or skill

area, we have been able to help teachers multi-task. We have also found that once teachers have developed an awareness themselves of the basic concepts and practices of media literacy, they begin to see opportunities for incorporating media literacy into their classrooms on an ongoing basis. For example, teachers whose classes were going to see *Antz* took a few minutes to explain the concept of "product placements" and told the students that they would be seeing some product placements in the film. When the first bottle of Pepsi appeared in the scene of Insectopia, there was a shout from the children in the audience— "Product placement!"—and students continued to identify product placements in videos and other media for the remainder of the school year.

In using a curriculum-driven approach, teachers sometimes take a narrow focus for a particular topic or lesson (e.g., linking current advertising appeals to a sixth-grade unit on Greek myths) or weave media literacy into ongoing activities in their classrooms (e.g., in a weekly discussion of current events). Sometimes media literacy is used to link several different parts of the curriculum together (e.g., investigating local history and literature through examining original documents at a local museum). And sometimes the production aspect of media literacy is used creatively to convey information to parents and administrators (e.g., fourth-grade students' producing a video to illustrate a typical school day for their parents to watch at open house).

This, of course, is not the only way to approach media literacy education. Students benefit greatly from specific lessons or courses focusing solely on media literacy, media production, and other media-related issues. But our experience has shown that this is rarely possible in the public school system, especially with the increasing focus on tests and a "back to basics" approach. For many teachers, finding even a few days to devote to media literacy is problematic; they are already swamped with core-content requirements they must teach. Even with a growing emphasis on technology skills and critical thinking, there are still only seven states that mandate media literacy as a separate strand in their state standards (Baker, 2004), and even those states have had difficulty grappling with how to assess media literacy as part of standardized state testing.

Kubey and Baker (2000) have noted, however, that nearly all states do refer to aspects of media literacy education as part of the mandated state standards, although they do not typically use the phrase *media literacy.* In New York, for example, media literacy is clearly reflected in requirements that students "evaluate importance, reliability and credibility of evidence" (Social Studies Standard 1, No. 4) and "comprehend, interpret and critique texts in every medium" (English Standard 2, No. 1). In California, social studies standards for Grades 9 through 12 specifically refer to evaluating "the role of electronic, broadcast, print media, and the Internet as means of communication in American politics" and "how public officials use the media to communicate with the citizenry and to shape public opinion" (Kubey & Baker, 2000, p. 9). Many states include specific references to media issues in their health standards, especially related to tobacco and alcohol use, nutrition, and body image.

In taking a curriculum-driven approach to media literacy integration, it is crucial to explicitly lay out these connections between media literacy and state or district learning standards. Teachers then feel more comfortable about taking class time to teach the basics of media literacy and to weave a media literacy approach into their overall teaching practice. Media literacy can also be used to develop "parallel tasks" for students to build and practice their skills in analyzing information from different sources, listening and taking notes, and supporting their opinions with evidence in written essays—all of which are key components in standardized testing.

BEST PRACTICES FOR USING MEDIA LITERACY IN THE K–12 CLASSROOM

Various writers have described key concepts of media literacy (e.g., Hobbs, 1997) and basic questions to ask about any media message (e.g.,

Thoman, 1999). We have found the following set of questions to work well with students from elementary school through college:

1. Who made—and who sponsored—this message, and what is their purpose?
2. Who is the target audience and how is the message specifically tailored to that audience?
3. What are the different techniques used to inform, persuade, entertain, and attract attention?
4. What messages arc communicated (and/or implied) about certain people, places, events, behaviors, lifestyles, and so forth?
5. How current, accurate, and credible is the information in this message?
6. What is left out of this message that might be important to know?

Introducing these questions at the beginning of the school year as standard practice for evaluating any information or image that is part of the classroom experience promotes general critical-thinking and analysis skills. Other best practices include the following:

• Beginning the school year or the exploration of a new unit by developing an *information plan* in consultation with the students. What types of media and other information sources will the class be using? Where could students go for information on a particular topic, and what might be the strengths and weaknesses of each source? This overlays media literacy questions on the typical K-W-L pedagogical approach to teaching a new topic: What do you already *know* about this topic and where did you learn about it? What do you *want* to know, and where could you find it?

• For any media source (including textbooks, videos, and Web sites), making sure the students know who wrote or produced it and when it was produced or published. If appropriate, discuss the implications for its usefulness in your current exploration. (What perspectives might be included or left out? What information might be out of date?)

• Training students to learn from videos (and other traditionally entertaining forms of media) in the same way that they learn from teachers, books, and other sources. When showing videos or films in the classroom, show only short segments at a time rather than the full film without interruption, leaving the lights on—if possible—to facilitate active viewing and discussion. Before showing a video, let the students know what things they should be looking and listening for. If appropriate, encourage students to take notes and to raise their hands during a video if they do not understand something they saw or heard.

• Building elements of media production into the classroom experience by

encouraging students to scan or download images into reports and term papers, making sure that they use images as part of the research process by including captions and citing the appropriate sources.

providing options for individual or small group presentations such as using PowerPoint, audio or videotape, or desktop publishing.

emphasizing an awareness of the six media literacy questions as part of the production process (e.g., What is *your* purpose? Who is *your* target audience? What information will *you* leave out, and how will that bias *your* message?).

BASIC PRINCIPLES FOR CURRICULUM INTEGRATION

In working with a range of teachers and curriculum areas, we have also developed 12 basic principles for integrating media literacy and critical thinking into the K–12 curriculum (Scheibe & Rogow, 2004). Discussions of 4 of these principles follow.

Identify erroneous beliefs about a topic fostered by media content. This is particularly relevant to curricular areas that emphasize "facts," such as science and social studies. Even young students bring existing assumptions and expectations to the classroom situation, and it is critical to examine those

assumptions with the students to correct misperceptions and identify the media sources involved. Many adults, for example, believe that tarantulas are deadly or that lemmings follow each other blindly and commit mass suicide by jumping off cliffs into the sea. Both of these erroneous beliefs have been reinforced by the media, such as the 1957 Disney movie *White Wilderness* that showed lemmings falling off cliffs into the sea (they were actually herded off the cliffs by the production crew off camera; see http://www.snopes.com/disney/films/lemmings.htm).

Develop an awareness of issues of credibility and bias in the media. This is critical in evaluating how any information is presented and has increased in importance with the rise of the Internet as the dominant source of information students now use in preparing papers and reports. It also applies to math, especially with respect to media reports of statistics (particularly in misleading graphs in advertisements). Although math teachers already emphasize the importance of having both the x-axis and y-axis correctly labeled, for example, a media literacy approach would go beyond that to ask why those producing the graph (or reporting the statistics) would leave out such important information.

Compare the ways different media present information about a topic. Many English/language arts teachers have students compare the same story or play when presented in different media formats or by different directors. Approaching this from a media literacy perspective, the teacher might ask the basic six questions about each presentation, comparing the purposes and target audiences of each and identifying what is left out—and what is added—in each case and why. The same principle can be applied easily to the study of current events at nearly any grade level. Instead of having students cut out newspaper articles reporting three different events, for example, a teacher could have students identify *one* event that is reported in three different sources (e.g., English language versions of newspapers from different countries). The resulting report about the event would then draw from all three sources and could include an analysis of how the three sources differed and why.

Use media as an assessment tool. There are a number of ways to use media as part of authentic assessment at the end of a curriculum unit. For example, students can be shown an advertisement, a news article, or a short video clip and asked to identify information that is accurate (or inaccurate) in what they see (e.g., showing a clip from the movie *Twister* following a unit on tornadoes or a news report on the results of a political poll following a unit on statistics). Students can also work in small groups to produce their own media messages (e.g., a newspaper article, an advertisement, a digital video) illustrating their knowledge and/or opinion on a topic.

RESOURCES AND CURRICULUM MATERIALS

There are many excellent media literacy resources and materials that can be used within the context of teaching core content in K–12 education. Some media literacy curricula are designed with clear links to many subject areas, such as *Assignment: Media Literacy*, which was developed in line with Maryland state learning standards and features connections to language arts, social studies, math, health, and the arts (Hobbs, 2000). Other materials are excellent resources when using a media literacy approach to a specific subject area, such as *Past Imperfect: History According to the Movies* (Carnes, 1995). There are several good Web analysis resources. The two we have found most useful for teachers and librarians are both online: Canada's Web-awareness site (http://www.mediaawareness.ca/english/ special initiatives/web_awareness/) and Alan November's site (http://www.anovember.com/ infolit/index.html). One outstanding resource for curriculum-driven media literacy lesson plans and ideas is Frank Baker's *Media Literacy Clearinghouse* Web site (http://www.med.sc.edu:1081/).

Project Look Sharp has recently begun developing a series of media literacy kits that take a curriculum-driven approach. The first of these kits, *Media Construction of War: A Critical Reading of History* (Sperry, 2003), uses slides, print, and video materials to teach core historical information about the Vietnam War, the Gulf War of 1991, and the War in Afghanistan following Sept. 11, 2001. . . . After students read short histories of each war, teachers lead collective readings of each image, discussing the overt and implied messages in each and relating the images back to core content that is part of their history curriculum. Among the multiple assessments included in the kit, students are asked to compare these three images of the opposition leaders during each war, discussing who each figure was and how each is portrayed by *Newsweek*.

EVALUATION AND ASSESSMENT

Project Look Sharp has begun conducting empirical studies of the effectiveness of media literacy integration using this type of curriculum-driven approach (reported elsewhere). Some of these studies involve pretest/posttest designs collecting data directly from the students, and some involve assessments of student-produced work. From a program evaluation standpoint, however, we have found it most useful to solicit qualitative feedback from the teachers themselves. They repeatedly say that media literacy lessons evoke active participation on the part of students, especially students who are nontraditional learners or disenfranchised for other reasons. Teachers also report that after adopting a media literacy approach to teach specific core content, they gradually find themselves weaving media literacy into other aspects of their pedagogy. As one teacher put it, "Oh, I see. You're trying to get us to change teaching practice!"

We also sometimes send home questionnaires to parents of students who have participated in a media literacy lesson or unit to assess what we call the "trickle up" effect—when students come home and talk about what they have learned and even change their behaviors related to media issues.

Some parents have said that the "media literacy stuff" is the only thing their child has talked about related to school all year; many say their children raise media literacy questions when they are watching television or reading newspapers at home.

We believe that it is this ability for media literacy to empower students in so many ways that, in the end, will lead to its growth and stability in K–12 education. By meeting the needs of teachers and administrators, of parents, and of the students themselves, we can indeed foster a deeper sense of literacy in our children.

REFERENCES

Baker, F. (2004). State standards. *Media literacy clearinghouse*. Retrieved February 24, 2004, from www.med.sc.edu:1081/statelit.htm

Carves, M. C. (Ed.). (1995). *Past imperfect: History according to the movies*. New York: Henry Holt.

Hobbs, R. (1997). Expanding the concept of literacy. In R. Kubey (Ed.), *Media literacy in the information age* (pp. 163–183). New Brunswick, NJ: Transaction.

Hobbs, R. (2000). *Assignment: Media literacy*. Bethesda, MD: Discovery Communications.

Kubey, R., & Baker. F. (2000, Spring). Has media literacy found a curricular foothold? *Telemedium, The Journal of Media Literacy, 46*, 8–9, 30.

Scheibe, C., & Rogow, F. (2004). *12 basic principles for incorporating media literacy and critical thinking into any curriculum* (2nd ed.). Ithaca, NY: Project Look Sharp—Ithaca College.

Sperry, C. (2003). *Media construction of war: A critical reading of history*. Ithaca. NY: Project Look Sharp—Ithaca College.

Thoman, E. (1999, February). Skills and strategies for media education. *Educational Leadership, 46*, 50–54.

Cynthia L. Scheibe, Ph.D., is an associate professor in developmental psychology at Ithaca College. She is the director of the Center for Research on the Effects of Television, which she founded with *John Condry* at Cornell University in 1983. She is also the executive director of Project Look Sharp, a media literacy initiative of Ithaca College, providing support, resources, and training for K–12 teachers and support staff to integrate media literacy and critical thinking across the curriculum.

QUESTIONS FOR REFLECTION

1. What is media literacy and why is it important to the curriculum today? What features distinguish a media literate person from someone who is media illiterate?
2. What are some of the potential assessments of outcomes seen as critical to the widespread adoption of media literacy in the curriculum?
3. With all of the media images that we see on a daily basis, why do you think media literacy has been slow to catch on as a main curriculum topic? What needs to change within education to make media literacy a basic requirement of classroom learning?

Remembering Capital: On the Connections between French Fries and Education

MICHAEL W. APPLE

ABSTRACT: Education in the United States is experiencing the effects of a "tense alliance" between neoconservatism and neoliberalism. Neoconservative educational policies and proposals are evidenced by choice plans, the standards movement, increasing attacks on the school curriculum for its failure to promote conservative values, and pressure to make the needs of business and industry the primary goals of education. Neoliberalism, which claims that a democratic society should be founded on a free market perspective, is seen as complementing efforts to implement a neoconservative educational agenda. Thus, schooling should be seen as fundamentally connected to patterns of domination and exploitation in the larger society.

Everyone stared at the department chair in amazement. Jaws simply dropped. Soon the room was filled with a nearly chaotic mixture of sounds of anger and disbelief. It wasn't the first time she had informed us about what was "coming down from on high." Similar things had occurred before. After all, this was just another brick that was being removed. Yet, to each and every one of us in that room it was clear from that moment on that for all of our struggles to protect education from being totally integrated into the rightist project of economic competitiveness and rationalization, we were losing.

It was hard to bring order to the meeting. But, slowly, we got our emotions under control long enough to hear what the State Department of Public Instruction and the Legislature had determined was best for all of the students in Wisconsin—from kindergarten to the university. Starting the next year, all undergraduate students who wished to become teachers would have to take a course on Education for Employment, in essence a course on the "benefits of the free enterprise system." At the same time, all school curricula at the elementary and secondary levels—from five year olds on up—would have to integrate within their teaching a coherent program of education for employment as well. After all, you can't start too young, can you? Education was simply the supplier of "human capital" for the private sector, after all.

I begin with this story because I think it is often better to start in our guts so to speak, to start with our experiences as teachers and students in this time of conservatism. I begin here as well because, even though the administration in Washington may attempt to rein in some of the excesses of the rightist social agenda—in largely ineffectual ways—the terms of debate and the existing economic and social conditions have been transformed remarkably in a conservative direction (Apple 1993). We should not be romantic about what will happen at our schools and universities, especially given the fiscal crisis of the state and the acceptance of major aspects of the conservative social and economic agenda within both political parties. The story I told a moment ago can serve as a metaphor for what is happening to so much of educational life at universities and elsewhere.

Let me situate this story within the larger transformations in education and the wider society that the conservative alliance has attempted. Because of space limitations in an article of this size, my discussion here will by necessity be brief. A much more detailed analysis can be found in my newest book, *Cultural Politics and Education* (Apple 1996).

BETWEEN NEO-CONSERVATISM AND NEO-LIBERALISM

Conservatism by its very name announces one interpretation of its agenda. It conserves. Other interpretations are possible of course. One could say, something more wryly, that conservatism believes that nothing should be done for the first time (Honderich 1990, 1). Yet in many ways, in the current situation this is deceptive. For with the Right now in ascendancy in many nations, we are witnessing a much more activist project. Conservative politics now are very much the politics of alteration—not always, but clearly the idea of "Do nothing for the first time" is not a sufficient explanation of what is going on either in education or elsewhere (Honderich 1990, 4).

Conservatism has in fact meant different things at different times and places. At times, it will involve defensive actions; at other times, it will involve taking initiative against the status quo (Honderich 1990, 15). Today, we are witnessing both.

Because of this, it is important that I set out the larger social context in which the current politics of official knowledge operates. There has been a breakdown in the accord that guided a good deal of educational policy since World War II. Powerful groups within government and the economy, and within "authoritarian populist" social movements, have been able to redefine—often in very retrogressive ways—the terms of debate in education, social welfare, and other areas of the common good. What education is for is being transformed (Apple 1993). No longer is education seen as part of a social alliance which combined many "minority" groups, women, teachers, community activists, progressive legislators and government officials, and others who acted together to propose (limited)

social democratic policies for schools (e.g., expanding educational opportunities, limited attempts at equalizing outcomes, developing special programs in bilingual and multicultural education, and so on).[1] A new alliance has been formed, one that has increasing power in educational and social policy. This power bloc combines business with the New Right and with neo-conservative intellectuals. Its interests are less in increasing the life chances of women, people of color, or labor. (These groups are obviously not mutually exclusive.) Rather it aims at providing the educational conditions believed necessary both for increasing international competitiveness, profit, and discipline and for returning us to a romanticized past of the "ideal" home, family, and school (Apple 1993). There is no need to control the White House for this agenda to continue to have a major effect.

The power of this alliance can be seen in a number of educational policies and proposals. These include: 1) programs for "choice" such as voucher plans and tax credits to make schools like the thoroughly idealized free-market economy; 2) the movement at national and state levels throughout the country to "raise standards" and mandate both teacher and student "competencies" and basic curricular goals and knowledge increasingly now through the implementation of statewide and national testing; 3) the increasingly effective attacks on the school curriculum for its anti-family and anti-free enterprise "bias," its secular humanism, its lack of patriotism, and its supposed neglect of the knowledge and values of the "western tradition" and of "real knowledge"; and 4) the growing pressure to make the perceived needs of business and industry into the primary goals of education at all levels (Apple 1988; Apple 1993; Apple 1996). The effects of all this—the culture wars, the immensity of the fiscal crisis in education, the attacks on "political correctness," and so on—are being painfully felt in the university as well.

In essence, the new alliance in favor of the conservative restoration has integrated education into a wider set of ideological commitments. The objectives in education are the same as those which serve as a guide to its economic and social welfare goals. These include the expansion of the "free market," the drastic reduction of government responsibility for social needs (though the Clinton Administration will mediate this in not very extensive—and not very expensive—ways), the reinforcement of intensely competitive structures of mobility, the lowering of people's expectations for economic security, and the popularization of what is clearly a form of Social Darwinist thinking (Bastian, Fruchter, Gittell, Greer, & Haskins 1986).

As I have argued at length elsewhere, the political right in the United States has been very successful in mobilizing support *against* the educational system and its employees, often exporting the crisis in the economy onto the schools. Thus, one of its major achievements has been to shift the blame for unemployment and underemployment, for the loss of economic competitiveness, and for the supposed breakdown of "traditional" values and standards in the family, education, and paid and unpaid workplaces *from* the economic, cultural, and social policies and effects of dominant groups *to* the school and other public agencies. "Public" now is the center of all evil; "private" is the center of all that is good (Apple 1995).

In essence, then, four trends have characterized the conservative restoration both in the United States and Britain—privatization, centralization, vocationalization, and differentiation (Green 1991, 27). These are actually largely the results of differences within the most powerful wings of this tense alliance—neo-liberalism and neo-conservatism.

Neo-liberalism has a vision of the weak state. A society that lets the "invisible hand" of the free market guide *all* aspects of its forms of social interaction is seen as both efficient and democratic. On the other hand, neo-conservatism is guided by a vision of the strong state in certain areas, especially over the politics of the body and gender and race relations, over standards, values, and conduct, and over what knowledge should be passed on to future generations (Hunter 1988).[2]

While these are no more than ideal types, those two positions do not easily sit side by side in the conservative coalition.

Thus the rightist movement is contradictory. Is there not something paradoxical about linking all of the feelings of loss and nostalgia to the unpredictability of the market, "in replacing loss by sheer flux"? (Johnson 1991, 40).

At the elementary and secondary school level, the contradictions between neo-conservative and neo-liberal elements in the rightist coalition are "solved" through a policy of what Roger Dale has called *conservative modernization* (Dale quoted in Edwards, Gewirtz, & Whitty in press, 22). Such a policy is engaged in:

> simultaneously "freeing" individuals for economic purposes while controlling them for social purposes; indeed, in so far as economic "freedom" increases inequalities, it is likely to increase the need for social control. A "small, strong state" limits the range of its activities by transferring to the market, which it defends and legitimizes, as much welfare [and other activities] as possible. In education, the new reliance on competition and choice is not all pervasive; instead, "what is intended is a dual system, polarized between . . . market schools and minimum schools." (Dale quoted in Edwards, Gewirtz, & Whitty in press, 22)

That is, there will be a relatively less regulated and increasingly privatized sector for the children of the better off. For the rest—and the economic status and racial composition in, say, our urban areas of the people who attend these minimum schools will be thoroughly predictable—the schools will be tightly controlled and policed and will continue to be underfunded and unlinked to decent paid employment.

One of the major effects of the combination of marketization and strong state is "to remove educational policies from public debate." That is, the choice is left up to individual parents and "the hidden hand of unintended consequences does the rest." In the process, the very idea of education being part of a *public* political sphere in which its means and ends are publicly debated atrophies (Education Group II 1991, 268).

There are major differences between democratic attempts at enhancing people's rights over the policies and practices of schooling and the neo-liberal emphasis on marketization and privatization. The goal of the former is to *extend politics,* to "revivify democratic practice by devising ways of enhancing public discussion, debate, and negotiation." It is inherently based on a vision of democracy that sees it as an educative practice. The latter, on the other hand, seeks to *contain politics.* It wants to *reduce all politics to economics,* to an ethic of "choice" and "consumption" (Johnson 1991, 68). The world, in essence, becomes a vast supermarket (Apple 1993).

Enlarging the private sector so that buying and selling—in a word competition—is the dominant ethic of society involves a set of closely related propositions. It assumes that more individuals are motivated to work harder under these conditions. After all, we "already know" that public servants are inefficient and slothful while private enterprises are efficient and energetic. It assumes that self-interest and competitiveness are the engines of creativity. More knowledge, more experimentation, is created and used to alter what we have now. In the process, less waste is created. Supply and demand stay in a kind of equilibrium. A more efficient machine is thus created, one which minimizes administrative costs and ultimately distributes resources more widely (Honderich 1990, 104).

This is of course not meant simply to privilege the few. However, it is the equivalent of saying that everyone has the right to climb the north face of the Eiger or scale Mount Everest without exception, providing of course that you are very good at mountain climbing and have the institutional and financial resources to do it (Honderich 1990, 99–100).

Thus, in a conservative society, access to a society's private resources (and, remember, the attempt is to make nearly *all* of society's resources private) is largely dependent on one's ability to pay. And this is dependent on one's being a person of an *entrepreneurial or efficiently acquisitive class type.* On the other hand, society's public resources (that rapidly decreasing segment) are dependent on need (Honderich 1990, 89). In a conservative society, the former is to be maximized, the latter is to be minimized.

However, most forms of conservatism do not merely depend in a large portion of their arguments and policies on a particular view of human nature—a view of human nature as primarily self-interested. They have gone further, they have set out to degrade that human nature, to force all people to conform to what at first could only be pretended to be true. Unfortunately, in no small measure they have succeeded. Perhaps blinded by their own absolutist and reductive vision of what it means to be human, many of our political "leaders" do not seem to be capable of recognizing what they have done. They have set out, aggressively, to drag down the character of a people (Honderich 1991, 81), while at the same time attacking the poor and the disenfranchised for their supposed lack of values and character.

But I digress here and some of my anger begins to show. You will forgive me I trust; but if we cannot allow ourselves to be angry about the lives of our children, what can we be angry about?

Unfortunately, major elements of this restructuring are hardly on the agenda of discussions of some of the groups within the critical and "progressive" communities within education itself, especially by *some* (not all) of those people who have turned uncritically to postmodernism.

LOSING MEMORY

What I shall say here is still rather tentative, but it responds to some of my intuitions that a good deal of the storm and fury over the politics of one form of textual analysis over another or even over whether we should see the world as a text, as discursively constructed, for example, is at least partly beside the point and that "we" may be losing some of the most important insights generated by, say, the neo-marxist tradition in education and elsewhere.

In what I say here, I hope I do not sound like an unreconstructed Stalinist (after all I've spent all too much of my life writing and speaking about the reductive tendencies within the marxist traditions). I simply want us to remember the utterly essential—not essentialist—understandings of the relationships (admittedly very complex) between education and some of the relations of power we need to consider but seem to have forgotten a bit too readily.

The growth of the multiple positions associated with postmodernism and poststructuralism is indicative of the transformation of our discourse and understandings of the relationship between culture and power. The rejection of the comforting illusion that there can (and must) be one grand narrative under which all relations of domination can be subsumed, the focus on the "micro-level" as a site of the political, the illumination of the utter complexity of the power-knowledge nexus, the extension of our political concerns well beyond the "holy trinity" of class, gender, and race, the idea of the decentered subject where identity is both non-fixed and a site of political struggle, the focus on the politics and practices of consumption, not only production— all of this has been important, though not totally unproblematic to say the least (Clarke 1991; Best & Kellner 1991).

With the growth of postmodern and post-structural literature in critical educational and cultural studies, however, we have tended to move too quickly away from traditions that continue to be filled with vitality and provide essential insights into the nature of the curriculum and pedagogy that dominate schools at all levels. Thus, for example, the mere fact that class does not explain all can be used as an excuse to deny its power. This would be a serious error. Class is of course an analytic construct as well as a set of relations that have an existence outside of our minds. Thus, what we mean by it and how it is mobilized as a category needs to be continually deconstructed and rethought. Thus, we must be very careful when and how it is used, with due recognition of the multiple ways in which people are formed. Even given this, however, it would be wrong to assume that, since many people do not identify

with or act on what we might expect from theories that link, say, identity and ideology with one's class position, this means that class has gone away (Apple 1992).

The same must be said about the economy. Capitalism may be being transformed, but it still exists as a massive structuring force. Many people may not think and act in ways predicted by class essentializing theories, but this does *not* mean the racial, sexual, and class divisions of paid and unpaid labor have disappeared; nor does it mean that relations of production (both economic *and* cultural, since how we think about these two may be different) can be ignored if we do it in non-essentializing ways (Apple 1992).

I say all this because of very real dangers that now exist in critical educational studies. One is our loss of collective memory. While there is currently great and necessary vitality at the "level" of theory, a considerable portion of critical research has often been faddish. It moves from theory to theory rapidly, often seemingly assuming that the harder something is to understand or the more it rests on European cultural theory (preferably French) the better it is. The rapidity of its movement and its partial capture by an upwardly mobile function of the new middle class within the academy—so intent on mobilizing its cultural resources within the status hierarchies of the university that it has often lost any but the most rhetorical connections with the multiple struggles against domination and subordination at the university and elsewhere— has as one of its effects the denial of gains that have been made in other traditions or restating them in new garb (Apple 1992). Or it may actually move backwards, as in the reappropriation of, say, Foucault into just another (but somewhat more elegant) theorist of social control, a discredited and a-historical concept that denies the power of social movements and historical agents. In our rush toward poststructuralism, we may have forgotten how very powerful the structural dynamics are in which we participate. In the process, we seem to be losing our capacity to be angry.

One of the major issues here is the tendency of all too many critical and oppositional educators to become overly theoretical. Sometimes, in this process, we fail to see things that are actually not that hard to understand. I want to tell a story here that I hope makes my arguments clear. It is a story that perhaps will be all too familiar to those of you who have opposed the North American Free Trade Agreement (NAFTA).

EATING FRENCH FRIES

The sun glared off of the hood of the small car as we made our way along the two lane road. The heat and humidity made me wonder if I'd have any liquid left in my body at the end of the trip and led me to appreciate Wisconsin winters a bit more than one might expect. The idea of winter seemed more than a little remote in this Asian country for which I have a good deal of fondness. But the topic at hand was not the weather; rather, it was the struggles of educators and social activists to build an education that was considerably more democratic than what was in place in that country now. This was a dangerous topic. Discussing it in philosophical and formalistically academic terms was tolerated. Openly calling for it and situating it within a serious analysis of the economic, political, and military power structures that now exerted control over so much of this nation's daily life was another matter.

As we traveled along that rural road in the midst of one of the best conversations I had engaged in about the possibilities of educational transformations and the realities of the oppressive conditions so many people were facing in that land, my gaze somehow was drawn to the side of the road. In one of those nearly accidental happenings that clarify and crystallize what reality is *really* like, my gaze fell upon a seemingly inconsequential object. At regular intervals, there were small signs planted in the dirt a few yards from where the road met the fields. The sign was more than a little familiar. It bore the insignia of one of the most famous fast food restaurants in the United States. We drove for miles past seemingly deserted fields along a flat hot plain, passing sign

after sign, each a replica of the previous one, each less than a foot high. These were not billboards. Such things hardly existed in this poor rural region. Rather, they looked exactly—exactly—like the small signs one finds next to farms in the American mid-west that signify the kinds of seed corn that each farmer had planted in her or his fields. This was a good guess it turned out.

I asked the driver—a close friend and former student of mine who had returned to this country to work for the social and educational reforms that were so necessary—what turned out to be a naive but ultimately crucial question in my own education. "Why are those signs for ***** there? Is there a ***** restaurant nearby?" My friend looked at me in amazement. "Michael, don't you know what these signs signify? There's no western restaurant within fifty miles of where we are. These signs represent exactly what is wrong with education in this nation. Listen to this." And I listened.

The story is one that has left an indelible mark on me, for it condenses in one powerful set of historical experiences the connections between our struggles as educators and activists in so many countries and the ways differential power works in ordinary life. I cannot match the tensions and passions in my friend's voice as this story was told; nor can I convey exactly the almost eerie feelings one gets when looking at that vast, sometimes beautiful, sometimes scarred, and increasingly depopulated plain. Yet the story is crucial to hear. Listen to this.

The government of the nation has decided that the importation of foreign capital is critical to its own survival. Bringing in American, German, British, Japanese, and other investors and factories will ostensibly create jobs, will create capital for investment, and will enable the nation to speed into the 21st century. (This is of course elite group talk, but let us assume that all of this is indeed truly believed by dominant groups.) One of the ways the military dominated government has planned to do this is to focus part of its recruitment efforts on agri-business. In pursuit of this aim, it has offered vast tracts of land to international agri-business concerns at very low cost.

Of particular importance to the plain we are driving through is the fact that much of this land has been given over to a large American fast food restaurant corporation for the growing of potatoes for the restaurant's french fries, one of the trademarks of its extensive success throughout the world.

The corporation was eager to jump at the opportunity to shift a good deal of its potato production from the U.S. to Asia. Since many of the farm workers in the United States were now unionized and were (correctly) asking for a livable wage, and since the government of that Asian nation officially frowned on unions of any kind, the cost of growing potatoes would be lower. Further, the land on that plain was perfect for the use of newly developed technology to plant and harvest the crop with considerably fewer workers. Machines would replace living human beings. Finally, the government was much less concerned about environmental regulations. All in all, this was a fine bargain for capital.

Of course, *people* lived on some of this land and farmed it for their own food and to sell what might be left over after their own—relatively minimal—needs were met. This deterred neither agri-business nor the government. After all, people could be moved to make way for "progress." And after all, the villagers along that plain did not actually have deeds to the land. (They had lived there for perhaps hundreds of years, well before the invention of banks, and mortgages, and deeds—no paper, no ownership). It would not be too hard to move the people off of the plain to other areas to "free" it for intensive potato production and to "create jobs" by taking away the livelihood of thousands upon thousands of small scale farmers in the region.

I listened with rapt attention as the rest of the story unfolded and as we passed by the fields with their miniature corporate signs and the abandoned villages. The people whose land had been taken for so little moved, of course. As in so many other similar places throughout what dominant groups call the Third World, they trekked to the city. They took their meager possessions and moved into the ever expanding slums within and surrounding the one place that held out some hope of finding enough paid work (if *everyone*—including children—labored) so that they could survive.

The government and major segments of the business elite officially discouraged this, sometimes by hiring thugs to burn the shanty towns, other times by keeping conditions so horrible that no one would "want" to live there. But still the dispossessed came, by the tens of thousands. Poor people are not irrational, after all. The loss of arable land had to be compensated for somehow and if it took cramming into places that were deadly at times, well what were the other choices? There *were* factories being built in and around the cities which paid incredibly low wages—sometimes less than enough money to buy sufficient food to replace the calories expended by workers in the production process—but at least there might be paid work if one was lucky.

So the giant machines harvested the potatoes and the people poured into the cities and international capital was happy. It's not a nice story, but what does it have to do with *education*? My friend continued my education.

The military dominated government had given all of these large international businesses twenty years of tax breaks to sweeten the conditions for their coming to that country. Thus, there was now very little money to supply the health care facilities, housing, running water, electricity, sewage disposal, and schools for the thousands upon thousands of people who had sought their future in or had literally been driven into the city. The mechanism for not building these necessities was quite clever. Take the lack of any formal educational institutions as a case in point. In order for the government to build schools it had to be shown that there was a "legitimate" need for such expenditure. Statistics had to be produced in a form that was *officially* accepted. This could only be done through the official determination of numbers of registered births. Yet, the very process of official registration made it impossible for thousands of children to be recognized as actually existing.

In order to register for school, a parent had to register the birth of the child at the local hospital or government office—none of which existed in these slum areas. And even if you could somehow find such an office, the government officially discouraged people who had originally come from outside the region of the city from moving there. It often refused to recognize the legitimacy of the move as a way of keeping displaced farmers from coming into the urban areas and thereby increasing the population. Births from people who had no "legitimate" right to be there did not count as births at all. It is a brilliant strategy in which the state creates categories of legitimacy that define social problems in quite interesting ways. (See, e.g., Curtis 1992 and Fraser 1989.) Foucault would have been proud, I am certain.

Thus, there are no schools, no teachers, no hospitals, no infrastructure. The root causes of this situation rest not in the immediate situation. They can only be illuminated if we focus on the chain of capital formation internationally and nationally, on the contradictory needs of the state, on the class relations and the relations between country and city that organize and disorganize that country.

My friend and I had been driving for quite a while now. I had forgotten about the heat. The ending sentence of the story pulled no punches. It was said slowly and quietly, said in a way that made it even more compelling. "Michael, these fields are the reason there's no schools in my city. There's no schools because so many folks like cheap french fries."

I tell this story about the story told to me for a number of reasons. First, it is simply one of the most powerful ways I know of reminding myself and all of us of the utter importance of seeing schooling relationally, of seeing it as connected—fundamentally—to the relations of domination and exploitation of the larger society. Second, and equally as importantly, I tell this story to make a crucial theoretical and political point. Relations of power are indeed complex and we do need to take very seriously the postmodern focus on the local and on the multiplicity of the forms of struggle that need to be engaged in. It is important as well

to recognize the changes that are occurring in many societies and to see the complexity of the "power/knowledge" nexus. Yet in our attempts to avoid the dangers that accompanied some aspects of previous "grand narratives," let us *not* act as if capitalism has somehow disappeared. Let us not act as if class relations don't count. Let us not act as if all of the things we learned about how the world might be understood politically have been somehow overthrown because our theories are now more complex.

The denial of basic human rights, the destruction of the environment, the deadly conditions under which people (barely) survive, the lack of a meaningful future for the thousands of children I noted in my story—all of this is not only or even primarily a "text" to be deciphered in our academic volumes as we pursue our postmodern themes. It is a reality that millions of people experience in their very bodies everyday. Educational work that is not connected deeply to a powerful understanding of these realities (and this understanding cannot evacuate a serious analysis of political economy and class relations without losing much of its power) is in danger of losing its soul. The lives of our children demand no less.

NOTES

1. I put the word "minority" in inverted commas here to remind us that the vast majority of the world's population is composed of persons of color. It would be wholly salutary for our ideas about culture and education to remember this fact.
2. Neo-liberalism doesn't ignore the idea of a strong state, but it wants to limit it to specific areas (e.g., defense of markets).

REFERENCES

Apple, Michael W. *Teachers and Texts: A Political Economy of Class and Gender Relations in Education.* New York: Routledge, 1988.

Apple, Michael W. "Education, Culture and Class Power." *Educational Theory* 42 (Spring 1992): 127–145.

Apple, Michael W. *Official Knowledge: Democratic Education in a Conservative Age*. New York: Routledge, 1993.

Apple, Michael W. *Education and Power*, second edition. New York: Routledge, 1995.

Apple, Michael W. *Cultural Politics and Education*. New York: Teachers College Press, 1996.

Bastian, Ann, Fruchter, Norm, Gittell, Marilyn, Greer, Colin, & Haskins, Kenneth. *Choosing Equality*. Philadelphia: Temple University Press, 1986.

Best, Steven, & Kellner, Douglas. *Postmodern Theory*. London: Macmillan, 1991.

Clarke, John. *New Times and Old Enemies*. London: HarperCollins, 1991.

Curtis, Bruce. *True Government By Choice Men?* Toronto: University of Toronto Press, 1992.

Education Group II, eds. *Education Limited*. London: Unwin Hyman, 1991.

Edwards, Tony, Gewirtz, Sharon, & Whitty, Geoff. "Whose Choice of Schools." *Sociological Perspectives on Contemporary Educational Reforms*. Edited by Madeleine Arnot and Len Barton. London: Triangle Books, in press.

Fraser, Nancy. *Unruly Practices*. Minneapolis: University of Minnesota Press, 1989.

Green, Andy. "The Peculiarities of English Education." *Education Limited*. Edited by Education Group II. London: Unwin Hyman, 1991.

Honderich, Ted. *Conservatism*. Boulder, CO: Westview Press, 1990.

Hunter, Allen. *Children in the Service of Conservatism*. Madison, WI: University of Wisconsin Law School, Institute for Legal Studies, 1988.

Johnson, Richard. "A New Road to Serfdom." *Education Limited*. Edited by Education Group II. London: Unwin Hyman, 1991.

Michael W. Apple is professor of curriculum and instruction and educational policy studies at the University of Wisconsin-Madison.

QUESTIONS FOR REFLECTION

1. What evidence can you cite to illustrate the influence of conservatism on curricula at the K–12 level?

2. Do you agree with Apple's assertion that "'Public' now is the center of all evil; 'private' is the center of all that is good"?

3. How might issues of domination and exploitation be incorporated into the curriculum with which you are most familiar?

Leaders' Voices—
Putting Theory into Practice

Teaching Media-Savvy Students about the Popular Media

KEVIN MANESS

ABSTRACT: It seems natural that teachers should wish to protect children from what seems to be a bombardment of media exposure by providing them with critical media literacy skills. Kevin Maness offers a framework for media education that helps students enhance their understanding of the media and use their knowledge to influence individual and community action.

When I began teaching about the media in my high school English classes, it was with the best sense of crusading zeal. I wanted to save students from all manner of societal ills, foremost among them the scourge of consumerism. I think my experience is common—many media teachers are initially moved by alarm about what the media are doing to our children. One teacher in the January 1998 *English Journal,* an issue dedicated to media literacy, begins her article by reciting a litany of disturbing statistics: 162 million TV sets viewed by American families seven hours a day; 260,000 billboards; 23,076 magazines and newspapers; and "between 350,000 and 640,000 TV commercials" seen by students by the time they graduate from high school (Curry-Tash 43). It seems natural that teachers should wish to protect children from what seems to be a bombardment of media exposure by providing them with critical media literacy skills.

COMMON ASSUMPTIONS

The problem with educating children *against,* rather than *about,* the media is the assumption that students are passive audiences of the media, lacking the critical, analytical skills necessary to resist media manipulation. Although holding this assumption is now unfashionable, evidence of its existence persists in the ways that some teachers talk about media literacy education. I often see an implicit distinction made between the "bad" viewing *habits* of young people and the "good" critical-viewing *skills* held by adults. When media teachers assume that students are passive, disengaged viewers, they risk designing media curricula that fail to acknowledge students' fluency in the languages of the mass media. Students' media savvy, gained through years of informal media literacy training before they reach high school, poses a dilemma for English teachers designing media literacy programs.

My own sense—based on years of teaching media in a high school English classroom and, now, on substantial research about media education—is that media literacy education cannot be effective until teachers find out what students already understand about the popular media (see Fisherkeller, "Learning from"; Shor, esp. chs. 1–2). When media education is not based on students' prior experience, it often deteriorates into "teaching" students media literacy skills that they already possess or into futile attempts to impose new, "good" media habits on students who have no interest in relinquishing their old, "bad" habits. Understanding students' media literacy is the important and often-overlooked first step in making them more media literate.

CHALLENGING OUR PRECONCEPTIONS: HOW MEDIA LITERATE ARE OUR STUDENTS?

Young people do, in fact, bring considerable expertise to their use of mass media products. In the last twenty-five years or so, the research on children's media experience has drawn from a new set of perspectives in psychology, sociology, semiotics, and cultural studies (Buckingham 106–11). Instead of focusing on the ways that mass media use and manipulate audiences, contemporary audience research emphasizes the many ways young people use the media, as well as the sophisticated (if often implicit) media skills and media knowledge that they employ in their everyday media experiences.

Media Uses

Jeanne R. Steele and Jane D. Brown observe that adolescents, like adults, use media for a variety of purposes: to enhance their mood, to sort through cultural norms and values, to make statements about their identity, to emulate desired behaviors (e.g., imitating role models), and to fantasize about a possible (alternative) self (565–69). The writers describe a circular process in which teenagers draw from their lived experience to *select* particular media products; *interact* with those media in an interpretive and evaluative process; and then *apply* aspects of the media product to their lives, appropriating them as part of their lived experience, which then serves to motivate new selections of media and continue the process (556).

David Buckingham and Julian Sefton-Green insist that the media are not all-powerful conditioning forces in the lives of young people; rather, media provide "symbolic resources" that young audiences use "to define and to resist the various social identities that are available to them." While that freedom is limited by numerous factors, it is difficult to know or guess, without asking, how students experience and use the media (30).

Junior high school girls were the subjects of a study by Margaret Finders, who states that students' use of media serves powerful social functions involving belonging, membership, status, and power (*Just Girls* 32). Of particular interest is her inquiry into the use of teen magazines by a group of girls who used the magazines to mark their womanhood and distinguish themselves from other girls ("Queens" 74). The magazines served important purposes within the group as well—the girls read the magazines together, negotiating for consensus on which models and celebrities were cool, pretty, or otherwise desirable. In addition to creating and maintaining intragroup norms, these group readings served as rehearsals where the girls could practice adolescent roles with the magazines as scripts; the magazines, therefore, provided a stable set of roles at a time when the girls' identities were particularly shifting and fluid (78–79). Clearly, these young women were engaged in a markedly critical, evaluative activity.

At the heart of JoEllen Fisherkeller's work with young people in New York City is the question of how they use television. A young male student who had recently moved to New York City found assurance in televised basketball, not only for the pleasure of watching, but also explicitly to learn techniques and styles that would allow him to enter into schoolyard basketball games; moreover, watching the games gave him something he could talk about with the other boys, whom he wanted to befriend. This young man used television for individual identity development and coping as well as to foster his entry into the social interactions of his school and neighborhood environment ("It's Just Like" 158).

There are two important insights that may be gained from this partial account of the purposes for which young people use the media. First, adolescents' uses of media are as wide-ranging and complex as adults' uses of media. Second, young people use media to achieve goals that are intimately connected with their identity and their social interaction. These media uses are neither good nor bad, healthy nor unhealthy. These uses are significant in the lives of young people, necessitating considerable awareness and sensitivity on the part of the critical media teacher. Fisherkeller asks an important question: How often are we expecting—implicitly or explicitly—students to reject the very media stories that provide them with a sense of who they are and of how to achieve empowerment and mainstream acceptance? Surely media representations of power, success, beauty, and belonging demand critical scrutiny, but teachers must remain mindful of what is at stake for their students ("Learning about" 207).

Media Skills

To accomplish their purposes, young people must use a substantial array of critical media skills. Although these skills may be used unconsciously, they are effective and often sophisticated.

Young people may be quite critical of the media they use. Fisherkeller reminds us that we should not let students' enjoyment of the media suggest that they are not also critical of media products. She points out that young viewers evaluate television as a storytelling medium (focusing on narrative quality and plausibility), as "an organizer of stories" (focusing on narrative structure and patterns), and as "an industry" ("Writers" 596).

Before beginning critical media study in class, therefore, teachers should take stock of the critical media skills their students already have, so that they can encourage students to use them more consciously, more effectively, and in new ways for different purposes.

Media Knowledge

Youth also possess considerable media knowledge that they can apply to their media experiences. Fisherkeller compares students' everyday media knowledge to the information objectives that generally characterize media education curricula, finding that the children in her study already understood a great deal about media agencies, categories, technologies, languages, and representations, but that they were not as knowledgeable about media audiences ("Learning from" 158–61). This does not suggest

that all students enter the classroom with knowledge about these aspects, but the fact that they already have some command of the information generally taught in media education classes reinforces the need for a careful assessment of what students actually know about media.

A MODEL FOR MEDIA TEACHING: LISTEN, ACTIVATE, EXTEND

I offer a framework that can help media educators conceptualize their media teaching and design instruction more effectively. The model I propose is based predominantly on the work of Buckingham and Sefton-Green (who draw from the theories of Lev Vygotsky) and Fisherkeller.

For Buckingham and Sefton-Green, a Vygotskian approach to media education consists of teachers helping students make their existing knowledge explicit and more deliberately organized. This more systematic and generalized knowledge can then be used to help students move beyond their original, self-taught knowledge (148). The purpose of media education is not primarily to teach new knowledge—although this does happen—but to "encourage students to make explicit, to reformulate and to question the knowledge which they already possess" (163–64). Reflection is the vital element—students must be given the opportunity and encouragement not just to make meaning out of media texts or to produce their own but to reflect on and understand the processes of "reading" and "writing" media texts (148).

Fisherkeller agrees. She introduces what, for me, becomes a three-stage model for media education when she lists three major insights that can be drawn from her audience research:

> It shows how researchers and educators can: (a) recognize the integrity of young people's "informal" media knowledge and experience, (b) categorize their current understandings according to media educational objectives, and (c) make meaningful connections with their actual cultural experiences. ("Learning from" 164)

In formulating my proposed model for media education, I distill the essence of the research of Fisherkeller and Buckingham and Sefton-Green into three stages. The stages are not steps to be followed sequentially; they will often occur simultaneously and repeatedly in the course of a class period, unit, semester, or school year. However, by presenting three distinct stages, I hope that this model can serve as a framework for planning media instruction. The three stages are Listen, Activate, and Extend.

Listen

The first stage in any media education practice should be listening to students to determine their prior understanding and their needs for further understanding. I know that I often placed my own intentions, assumptions, and agendas first, failing to hear the voices of my students. Consequently, although students in my media education classes were generally engaged and motivated, I am not confident that instruction was truly based on the students' needs and experiences.

Listening for students' prior understanding leads directly to the second stage—Activate—while listening for students' needs helps to inform the third stage—Extend.

Activate

Teachers must help students to make their media expertise explicit and to see it as socially and academically valuable. Although students possess a great deal of media skill and knowledge, they are often unaware of it as skill and knowledge, and they are sometimes unaware of how it might benefit them in school or in life beyond the classroom.

Deconstructing advertisements, producing spoof ads, analyzing film, comparing television news to print journalism, analyzing pop music lyrics, and even comparing popular texts to canonical literary ones make use of critical media skills and knowledge that students generally possess when they walk into the classroom. Ending the unit with an oral presentation, a video, or an essay can limit media education to activating students' spontaneous concepts without really encouraging students to understand them, question them, or to change their media behavior as needed.

Students must do more. Encouraging students to reflect on their media writing and reading process—both during and after the process is complete—helps them to develop the metalinguistic and metacognitive skills that Máire Messenger Davies describes as crucial to students' media understanding (Davies 16–17).

Extend

When media teachers listen to their students, we may discover not only areas of media expertise but also needs. Students may need specific kinds of media skills and knowledge, or they may need to understand relationships between themselves, the media, and society. For instance, the girls in Finders' study may need specific instruction to enable them to perceive the difference between advertisements and the editorial content of magazines, as well as an understanding of the constraints on media industries that create an increasingly thin line between editorial content and advertising.

Fisherkeller, believing strongly that one of the imperatives of school is to help students achieve power and success in society, stresses the importance of linking students' media experience to their goals and dreams, their "sense of possibility and purpose" ("Learning from" 163). Extensions of students' media understanding may lead into "political" regions, which may trouble some teachers. But Curry-Tash reminds us that ignoring the social and political implications of media "is itself a political act" (48). If the goal of media education is to enable students to become critically autonomous, then it is vital that we help them extend their media skills and knowledge beyond self-contained textual deconstruction exercises and classroom oral reports to the larger society beyond the classroom walls.

SUGGESTIONS FOR THE MEDIA EDUCATION CLASSROOM

Many of the media education activities that I have read about, in *English Journal* and in other teacher resources both in print and online, can be easily adapted to include all three stages of the model I suggest here. Media literacy activities could be enhanced by (1) determining students' prior media expertise and their educational needs, (2) incorporating more teacher-assisted reflection on the process of media writing and reading, (3) treating the "final product" as a further opportunity for reflective discussion rather than the end of a teaching unit, and (4) extending the "final product" into the world outside the classroom where it can influence the actions of students and other community members.

When I taught high school, I emphasized learning about the media industries themselves since industry constraints (economics, politics, and so forth) have such a significant influence on media experience. This can be difficult because it involves a considerable amount of information that can seem dry and overwhelming. In addition to traditional textbook readings and photocopied articles, I also found videos helpful in teaching about industry dynamics. PBS–Frontline's *The Merchants of Cool* and the Media Education Foundation's *Advertising and the End of the World* stimulated discussion of the advertising industry and, specifically, marketing to young audiences. I learned that it is very important to present these films as texts to be interpreted and questioned rather than as straightforward, authoritative information about other media products. I showed approximately ten minutes of the video at a time, while students watched and reflected in journals; then we discussed the viewpoints represented and the issues raised. This allowed students to draw from their media experience to raise questions and make comparisons and judgments, while also urging them to consider information and opinions that were new to them.

Suggestions from Fisherkeller

My teaching could have benefited from additional recommendations based on current research, but when I was teaching, I did not really know where to look. This year, as a student myself, I have found a lot of value in the work of Fisherkeller, who provides numerous suggestions for media educators. The ideas that follow reflect her influence on my thinking.

Media education can and should address students' hopes for the future. Teachers can listen to students discuss the careers they want to pursue (and why) and explore media models of "success," evaluate their strengths and weaknesses, and look for alternative models. This can help students refine their aims and seek creative ways of accomplishing them, while at the same time scrutinizing media representations and asking critical questions about them ("Learning from" 163; "Learning about" 208).

Teachers can encourage comparisons between mainstream media and alternative media, asking critical questions to account for the similarities and differences. Students can experiment with producing media texts that both emulate conventional media and explore alternatives ("Writers" 603).

Media educators should be wary of overemphasizing deconstructive exercises at the expense of production because media education that relies more on direct structural analysis and criticism often seems to encourage students to reject commercial media products that, as I discuss above, are sometimes very dear to them.

A strength of production-oriented media activities is that they can support community action. Students can make short documentary features about their neighborhoods and screen the films for an audience that includes members of the community. Such a project allows students to "correct" the omissions of the popular media and to tell their stories using their own voices. Students simultaneously learn about the intricacies of media production and draw attention to their daily realities.

Educators can encourage students to compare "adult-sanctioned" media with the students' favorites. How are the symbolic worlds different, especially in terms of identity and social power ("Learning about" 206)? This can help students develop important metacognitive understanding of how value judgments are made regarding media and can lead to inquiry about where the values come from.

THE NEED FOR EDUCATION

If students are so media savvy, why bother to teach them about media at all? There are many important reasons for engaging in critical media education in our classrooms.

Although it may be true that the media are serving students by providing symbolic resources for identity formation, it is also true that those resources are terribly constrained by the commercial nature of media industries. Even the most critical adolescent will find only a limited range of identity resources from which to choose (Steele and Brown 553). Communications researcher Paul Willis cites the need for a greater "range of usable symbolic resources available" for the identity work of youth, and he suggests that media critics—and I think the suggestion applies to media educators as well—focus on what is missing or disappearing from programming, rather than simply on what is there (37).

At the same time, many researchers are careful to demarcate the limits on young people's media savvy. Finders, in particular, is alarmed by some of the blind spots in the media literacy of the girls she studied. She finds that the young girls in her research lacked critical distance from the magazines they enjoyed ("Queens" 81). Many of the girls believed that the articles and advice columns in teen magazines were authored by the teen models pictured (75), and one girl she interviewed saw the ads as informational pieces providing her with facts and advice about products she might purchase (82–83). There is considerable need for instruction about popular media, despite students' significant media uses, skills, and knowledge.

Chances are that listening, activating, and extending are already part of most teachers' media education curricula. My hope is that this model can help media teachers incorporate these three vital elements more consciously. Doing so would have increased my effectiveness.

I started teaching about the popular media because there is a freshness and currency about today's popular media that energized my teaching and because study of the media appealed to the students. I think that there is great activist potential in studying the media—it is my hope that by encouraging students to become more independent, critical agents, they will question the relationship between the media, their identities, their dreams for future success, and the society in which they live. Media teachers who can master the art of listening to students' experiences and needs, activating their prior knowledge, and extending that knowledge to new territory are enabling and empowering students to become active, informed, thoughtful, and intentional participants in all aspects of American society.

WORKS CITED

Advertising and the End of the World. Written, edited, and produced by Sut Jhally. Media Education Foundation, 1997.

Buckingham, David. *After the Death of Childhood: Growing Up in the Age of Electronic Media*. Cambridge: Polity, 2000.

Buckingham, David, and Julian Sefton-Green. *Cultural Studies Goes to School: Reading and Teaching Popular Media*. London: Taylor, 1994.

Curry-Tash, Marnie W. "The Politics of Teleliteracy and Adbusting in the Classroom." *English Journal* 87.1 (1998): 43–48.

Davies, Máire Messenger. *Fake, Fact, and Fantasy: Children's Interpretations of Television Reality*. Mahwah: Erlbaum, 1997.

Finders, Margaret J. *Just Girls: Hidden Literacies and Life in Junior High*. New York: Teachers College, 1997.

———. "Queens and Teen Zines: Early Adolescent Females Reading Their Way toward Adulthood." *Anthropology and Education Quarterly* 27.1 (1996): 71–89.

Fisherkeller, JoEllen. "It's Just Like Teaching People 'Do the Right Things'": Using TV to Become a Good and Powerful Man. *Say It Loud! African-American Audiences, Media, and Identity.* Ed. Robin R. Means Coleman. New York: Routledge, 2002. 147–85.

———. "Learning about Power and Success: Young Urban Adolescents Interpret TV Culture." *The Communication Review* 3.3 (1999): 187–212.

———. "Learning from Young Adolescent Television Viewers." *The New Jersey Journal of Communication* 6.2 (1998): 149–69.

———. " 'The Writers Are Getting Kind of Desperate': Young Adolescents, Television, and Literacy." *Journal of Adolescent and Adult Literacy* 43.7 (2000): 596–606.

The Merchants of Cool. Dir. Barak Goodman. PBS–Frontline, 2001.

Shor, Ira. *Empowering Education: Critical Teaching for Social Change.* Chicago: U of Chicago P, 1992.

Steele, Jeanne R., and Jane D. Brown. "Adolescent Room Culture: Studying Media in the Context of Everyday Life." *Journal of Youth and Adolescence* 24.5 (1995): 551–76.

Willis, Paul. *Common Culture: Symbolic Work at Play in the Everyday Cultures of the Young.* Boulder: Westview, 1990.

Kevin Maness is a Ph.D. student in media ecology at New York University. Before going back to school as a student, he taught English at Penncrest High School in Media, Pennsylvania.

QUESTIONS FOR REFLECTION

1. Why does Maness believe students today are media-savvy in a way that no generation has been before? What makes the students of today so media-savvy and why could this be a problem? What are they *lacking* in their savvy approach to media?
2. Maness claims that media literacy cannot be effective until teachers find out what students already understand about the popular media. Why does he make this claim? What do teachers risk doing when they don't survey the experiences their students have with media?
3. What is the "listen, activate, extend" model for media teaching that Maness proposes? Do you think it is a model that most, if not all, teachers can teach? What would be some barriers for getting teachers to adopt such a model?

LEARNING ACTIVITIES

Critical Thinking

1. Have your personal beliefs and attitudes about social forces changed as a result of reading this chapter? If so, how?
2. With respect to a school with which you are familiar, describe the social forces that *are* reflected in the curriculum and compare these with the social forces that *should be* reflected in the curriculum. To what extent is there a lack of fit between the two sets of social forces?

3. Some people have suggested that emphasizing our nation's multicultural heritage exalts racial and ethnic pride at the expense of social cohesion. How might a curriculum that emphasizes multicultural diversity also *contribute* to social cohesion?
4. To what extent do you believe that schools in the United States reproduce the existing class and social structure—that curricula tend not to prepare students from the lower socioeconomic classes for upward social mobility?

Application Activities

1. Review the section on futures planning in this chapter and then identify several objectives and some appropriate learning activities for a futures-oriented curriculum at the level of education with which you are most familiar.
2. Herbert A. Thelen has developed a model for teaching called *group investigation*. The model combines the democratic process and the processes of problem solving. (You can read about this model of teaching in Bruce Joyce and Marsha Weil's *Models of Teaching,* seventh edition [Allyn and Bacon, 2004, pp. 214–227]). Describe how you might use this approach to address a social force that influences the curriculum with which you are most familiar.
3. Examine several recent curriculum guides to determine what, if any, provisions have been made to consider changing social forces in the curriculum (e.g., changes in values, work, the environment, family). In light of the material presented in this chapter, what changes or additions would you suggest in these curriculum guides?
4. In this chapter's discussion of concepts from the social sciences, it was pointed out that "the concept of *humanity* can be a significant organizing element in curriculum planning." To gain further understanding of how this concept might be applied to curriculum planning, look at the 503 photographs from 68 countries that Edward Steichen presents in *The Family of Man* (New York: Museum of Modern Art, 2002). What does one learn about humanity by viewing these photographs, often referred to as the "greatest photographic exhibition of all time"? How might this learning be applied to curriculum leadership?

Field Experiences

1. Visit a local school and then develop a case study of that school's culture. Organize your case in terms of the following: (1) *Environment:* Describe the school facility in regard to material and human resources. Describe the climate of the school. To what extent is the surrounding social milieu reflected in the school's curriculum? (2) *Formal practices:* What grades are included at the school? What are the goals of the curriculum? (3) *Traditions:* What events, activities, and rituals are important to students, teachers, administrators, and parents? How do community members describe the school?
2. Visit a local school and gather information on activities, programs, and services the school has developed to meet the needs of students placed at risk by social problems and their families.

Internet Activities

1. Visit the Equity Online home page funded by the Women's Educational Equity Act and compile a list of gender-fair curriculum materials related to the level and subject area with which you are most familiar.
2. Go to the "Futures-Related Links and World-Wide Resources" home page and gather resources you could use to incorporate a futures-oriented perspective into your curriculum planning activities.
3. Explore the U.S. government's Children, Youth and Families Education and Research Network (CYFERNet) and gather information and resources related to several of the social forces discussed in this chapter.
4. Conduct an online keyword search for sources of information on one or more of the ten social forces discussed in this chapter. Share your findings with others in your class.

3

FOCUS QUESTIONS

1. How do learners differ in their stages of development?
2. What are five aspects of human development that should guide curriculum leaders?
3. What is the "problem of the match," and how does it influence curriculum leadership?
4. What are the salient characteristics of learners' cognitive, psychosocial, and moral development?

Human Development

Human development throughout the life span is a significant basis of the curriculum. For decades, the study of child and adolescent development has been regarded as an important part of the knowledge base for K–12 education. Now, with the increasing significance of lifelong learning, curriculum leaders must also focus attention on human development during adulthood.

The generally accepted stages of human development include infancy, childhood, early adolescence, middle adolescence, late adolescence, and adulthood. The elementary school years correspond roughly to the stage known as childhood. Early, middle, and late adolescence correspond roughly to the middle school, high school, and community college levels of education.

Knowledge of human development enables curriculum leaders to design curricula that are shaped, in part, by the nature and needs of individual learners. Articles that focus on various aspects of human development are included in this chapter. For example, in "Schools That Develop Children," James P. Comer discusses how to design school programs around students' developmental needs in several areas. David A. Hamburg's "Toward a Strategy for Healthy Adolescent Development" examines the biological, physical, behavioral, and social transformations that characterize adolescence. These and other articles in this chapter illustrate the need for curriculum planning to be guided by the five aspects of human development presented in Figure 3.1: the biological basis of individual differences, physical maturation, intellectual development and achievement, emotional growth and development, and cultural and social development. In "What Ever Happened to Kick the Can? Wellness in School and Community" in this chapter, Tom Burton reminds us that physical wellness is often overlooked in favor of curriculum goals that emphasize academic achievement.

The concept of stages of human development is a useful tool for understanding the needs of learners at various

FIGURE 3.1

Five Aspects of Human Development to Guide Curriculum Planning and Planning for Instruction

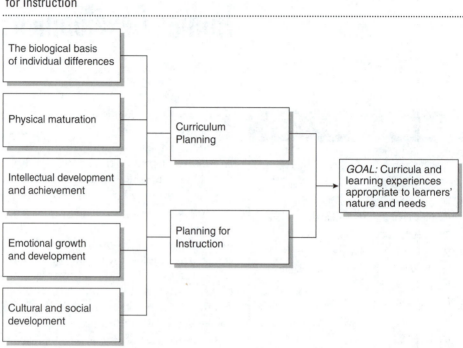

levels of education, but it cannot define the development of any one learner at a particular age. Each learner is innately unique, and this inborn individuality indicates the importance of providing many alternatives in educational programs. Nevertheless, humans as learners have much in common.

Maturation and change in human development occur over the entire life span, providing one of the bases for curriculum planning at all age levels, including higher and adult education. Maturation follows different courses of development for different individuals. One of the guidelines for curriculum leadership derived from the study of human development, then, is the *problem of the match*. In other words, there must be a match between the learner's developmental stage and the explicit curriculum. There should also be a match between the learner's developmental stage and the informal, "hidden" curriculum. For example, the informal curriculum often forces students to develop their identity within a school climate that communicates rejection and intolerance. In addition, some students must work through their developmental challenges in over-crowded, under-funded schools situated in impoverished communities and neighborhoods. In "The Biology of Risk Taking" in this chapter, Lisa F. Price suggests that findings from the fields of neuroscience and developmental psychology are useful to educators as they help adolescents cope with these challenges in difficult settings. And, in "Family and School Spillover in Adolescents' Daily Lives" in this chapter, Lisa Flook and Andrew J. Fuligni point out that family stressors experienced by adolescents "spill over" into the school and impact their academic achievement and general well-being.

Curriculum Leadership Strategy

Effective curriculum leaders strive for a deep understanding of how the informal, or hidden, curriculum at the district and/or school levels impacts the growth and development of students.

Research on brain growth periodization has significance for curriculum planning and the problem of the match at various age levels, suggesting that there are five periods of growth spurt, which alternate with intervals of growth lag, in the development of the human brain from birth to about the age of seventeen. Herman Epstein (1978, 1990), a biologist, reports that growth spurts occur at 3–10 months, 2–4 years, 6–8 years, 10–12 or 13 years, and 14–16 or 17 years. He suggests that "intensive intellectual input should be situated at the spurt ages" (Epstein, 1978, p. 362) and that too much input during the plateau periods may reduce the learner's ability to absorb information at a later, more appropriate age. The challenge for curriculum leaders, then, is to make the timing and content of learning experiences fit these known patterns of brain growth.

THEORIES OF HUMAN DEVELOPMENT

Several theorists' and researchers' ideas about human development have significantly influenced curriculum leadership, including Jean Piaget's theory of cognitive development, Erik Erikson's developmental outline for stages of "growth toward a mature personality," and Lawrence Kohlberg's cognitive-developmental view of moral development. These three human development theorists maintain that the developmental stages they describe have a fixed order, and that each person passes through these stages in this order. Sufficient resolution of the challenges and developmental tasks associated with each stage is necessary for the individual to proceed with vigor and confidence to the next stage, and there is a "teachable moment" or opportune time for this development to occur.

Piaget's Model of Cognitive Development

Piaget's theory maintains that children learn through interacting with their environments, much as scientists do, and that a child's thinking progresses through a sequence of four cognitive stages. At the sensorimotor intelligence stage (birth to 2 years), behavior is largely sensory and motor, and, while cognitive development is occurring, the child does not yet "think" conceptually. At the preoperational thought stage (2–7 years), the development of language occurs, and the child can think of objects and people beyond the immediate environment. At the concrete operations stage

(7–11 years), the child explores and masters basic concepts of objects, numbers, time, space, and causality and can use logical thought to solve problems. Finally, at the formal operations stage (11–15 years), the child can make predictions, think hypothetically, and reason abstractly about language.

Erikson's Model of Psychosocial Development

Erik Erikson's model is based on eight stages of growth—from infancy to old age. Each stage is characterized by a psychosocial crisis for the individual's emotional and social growth. These crises are expressed in polar terms; for example, in infancy, the psychosocial crisis is trust versus mistrust. The infant must come to trust the world sufficiently in order to move on to the next stage, autonomy versus shame and doubt. Shortly before his death in 1994, Erikson postulated a ninth stage in the human life cycle, *gerotranscendence,* during which humans must confront—and, if possible, transcend—the reality of their deteriorating bodies and faculties. In the final chapter of an extended version of Erikson's *The Life Cycle Completed,* first published in 1982, his wife and lifelong colleague, Joan M. Erikson, describes the challenges of moving into gerotranscendence:

> Old age in one's eighties and nineties brings with it new demands, reevaluations, and daily difficulties. . . . Even the best cared-for bodies begin to weaken and do not function as they once did. In spite of every effort to maintain strength and control, the body continues to lose its autonomy. Despair, which haunts the eighth stage, is a close companion in the ninth, because it is almost impossible to know what emergencies and losses of physical ability are imminent. As independence and control are challenged, self-esteem and confidence weaken. Hope and trust, which once provided firm support, are no longer the sturdy props of former days. To face down despair with faith and appropriate humility is perhaps the wisest course. (Erikson, 1997, pp. 105–106)

Kohlberg's and Gilligan's Models for Moral Development

Among the many perspectives on the moral development of human beings, Kohlberg's cognitive-developmental approach to moral education, based on Piaget's stages of cognitive development and John Dewey's levels of moral development, has had perhaps the greatest influence on curriculum leadership. However, one might ask: Should moral education be an aspect of human development that is considered by curriculum leaders? Perhaps the question is moot, since education is not value-free—it is a moral enterprise whether we wish it to be or not. Students' curricular experiences, including countless hours observing their teachers as moral models, have a profound influence on how they think and behave regarding moral issues.

In "The Cognitive-Developmental Approach to Moral Education" in this chapter, Kohlberg states that moral principals are ultimately "principles of justice," and that at each stage of moral development the concept of justice is reorganized. However, Carol Gilligan, at one point a colleague of Kohlberg, believes that his research depends too heavily on studies of men and that women's moral judgments are more likely to reflect care and concern for others. In "Woman's Place in Man's Life Cycle" in this chapter, Gilligan examines these two perspectives and suggests that the female perspective on morality is based on the understanding of responsibility and relationships, while the male perspective is based on rights and rules.

Curriculum Leadership Strategy

Effective curriculum leaders base their professional decisions on comprehensive, detailed information about the stressors students confront in their homes and communities.

CRITERION QUESTIONS—HUMAN DEVELOPMENT

Although stages of human development can be identified, no two individuals of the same age are alike in physical, emotional, intellectual, or social development. Knowing how development occurs in each of these areas helps curriculum leaders identify two important curriculum criteria that should be reflected in the curriculum: individual differences and continuity in learning (i.e., the curriculum and teaching begin "where the learner is").

The following are among the criterion questions that can be derived from the theories of human development discussed in this chapter.

1. Does the curriculum reflect the inborn individuality and innate uniqueness of each learner?
2. Does the curriculum provide for developmental differences among the learners being taught?
3. Does the curriculum provide for continuity of learning?
4. Have the significance of developmental tasks, stages of growth toward a mature personality, and the development of morality been considered when planning the curriculum?
5. Does the curriculum attempt to provide for earlier tasks inadequately achieved, and for their maintenance when successfully achieved?
6. Does the curriculum reflect social and cultural changes that have occurred in recent years at each stage of human development?

REFERENCES

Epstein, Herman T. "Stages in Human Mental Growth." *Journal of Educational Psychology* 82, no. 4 (December 1990): 876–880.

———. "Growth Spurts During Brain Development: Implications for Educational Policy and Practice." In Jeanne S. Chall and Allan F. Mirsky, eds., *Education and the Brain, The 77th Yearbook of the National Society for the Study of Education, Part II.* Chicago: University of Chicago Press, 1978.

Erikson, Erik H. *The Life Cycle Completed: Extended Version with New Chapters on the Ninth Stage of Development by Joan M. Erikson.* New York: W. W. Norton & Company, 1997.

Schools That Develop Children

JAMES P. COMER

ABSTRACT: *Schools everywhere are said to be failing, Comer writes, and everyone seems to have a solution. To address the perceived problems in U.S. schools, various policy changes that are being suggested to reform them. However, most of these cures, traditional and reform, are based on flawed models and at best will have only limited effectiveness. Comer maintains that America will be able to create a successful system of education nationwide only when education is based on what is known about how children and youths develop and learn.*

American schools are said to be failing. Like nineteenth-century medicine men, everybody is promoting everything, whether there is any evidence that it works or not. Over here we have vouchers, charters, privatization, longer school days, summer school, and merit pay. Over there we have the frequent testing of students, the testing of teachers, smaller class size, report cards on schools, and high-stakes accountability. And over here, a very special offer: student uniforms, flag-raising ceremonies every morning, the posting of the Ten Commandments on schoolhouse walls, and sophisticated diagnostic instruments to identify children at risk for acting violently—when many administrators and teachers can't even identify children who need glasses.

Most of these "cures"—traditional and reform—can't work or, at best, will have limited effectiveness. They all are based on flawed models. We will be able to create a successful system of education nationwide only when we base everything we do on what is known about how children and youths develop and learn. And this knowledge must be applied throughout the enterprise of education—in child rearing before school age, in schools and school districts, in schools of education, in state education departments, in legislatures, and everywhere else that personnel preparation takes place and school policy is made.

Given the purpose of education—to prepare students to become successful workers, family members, and citizens in a democratic society—even many "good" traditional schools, as measured by high test scores, are not doing their job adequately. But test scores alone are too narrow a measure. A good education should help students to solve problems encountered at work and in personal relationships, to take on the responsibility of caring for themselves and their families, to get along well in a variety of life settings, and to be motivated, contributing members of a democratic society. Such learning requires conditions that promote positive child-and-youth development.

Children begin to develop and learn through their first interactions with their consistent caretakers. And the eventual learning of basic academic skills—reading, writing, mathematics—and development are inextricably linked. Indeed, learning is an aspect of development and simultaneously facilitates it. Basic academic skills grow out of the fertile soil of overall development; they provide the platform for higher-order learning.

Through the early interactions, a bond is established that enables the child to imitate, identify with, and internalize the attitudes, values, and ways of their caretakers, and then those of other people around them. These people become important because they mediate (help make sense of and manage) a child's experiences and protect the child and help him or her to grow along the important developmental pathways—physical, social-interactive, psycho-emotional, ethical, linguistic, intellectual-cognitive, and eventually academic. The more mature thus help the less mature to channel potentially harmful aggressive energy into the energy of constructive learning, work, and play. But good early development is not a kind of inoculation that will protect a child for life. Future good development builds on the past and is mediated continuously by more mature people, step by step.

Understanding this process is no longer a matter of conjecture or the whining of "fuzzy-headed" social scientists or, as in my case, psychiatrists. Hard science—brain research—has confirmed the nature and critical importance of this interactive process. Without it children can lose the "sense"—the intelligence potential—they were born with. Children who have had positive developmental experiences before starting school acquire a set of beliefs, attitudes, and values—as well as social, verbal, and problem-solving skills, connections, and power—that they can use to succeed in school. They are the ones best able to elicit a positive response from people at school and to bond with them.

People at school can then influence children's development in ways similar to competent parents. To be successful, schools must create the conditions that make good development and learning possible: positive and powerful social and academic interactions between students and staff. When this happens, students gain social and academic competence, confidence, and comfort. Also, when parents and their social networks value school success and school experiences are positive and powerful, students are likely to acquire an internal desire to be successful in school and in life, and to gain and express the skills and behavior necessary to do so.

In order to realize the full potential of schools and students, we must create—and adequately support—a wide and deep pool of teachers and administrators who, in addition to having thorough knowledge of their disciplines, know how children develop generally and academically and how to support that development. They must be able to engage the families of students and the institutions and people in communities in a way that benefits student growth in school and society.

Vouchers and similar reforms currently being touted do not address these standards. They are simply changes in infrastructure, curriculum, and service delivery. They do not offer the potential for a nationwide transformation that a developmental focus does. And vouchers can reduce funds needed to improve the schools that must educate the majority of American children.

The Challenge of Change

The function of promoting good child-and-youth development and achievement was once served in our society through families and their social networks and through community life in small towns and rural areas. If students did not do well in school, they could leave, earn a living, still take care of themselves and their families, and become positive, contributing members of their communities. Despite massive and rapid scientific, technological, and social change, children have the same needs they always did: They must be protected and their development must be guided and supported by the people around them. They cannot rear themselves.

High mobility and modern communication created by technological change have undermined supports for child-and-youth development. Children experience many stimulating models of potentially troublesome behaviors—often in the absence of emotionally meaningful, influential adults. As a result, too many young people receive too little help in learning to manage feelings and act appropriately on the increased and more stimulating information they receive. This makes adequate social, psychological, and ethical development difficult.

Meanwhile, the new economy has made a high level of development and education a necessity for 90 percent of the population instead of the 20 percent we got by with half a century ago. Yet the rise of technology has led to an overvaluation of measured intelligence rather than an appreciation of overall development and the kind of intellectual growth that promotes strong problem-solving capacities.

Many successful people are inclined to attribute their situations to their own ability and effort—making them, in their minds, more deserving than less successful people. They ignore the support they received from families, networks of friends and kin, schools, and powerful others. They see no need for improved support of youth development. These misperceptions influence many education policies and practices.

Adequate support for development must be restored. And school is the first place this can happen. It is the common pathway for all children—the only place where a significant number of adults are working with young people in a way that enables them to call on family and community resources to support growth systematically and continually. And school is one of the few places where students, staff, and community can create environments in which to help young people achieve the necessary levels of maturity.

In the early 1980s, James Coleman, the late and respected University of Chicago sociologist, called what children gain from their parents and their networks "social capital." I do not like this term in discussing humans, but it is much used. Many poor children grow up in primary social networks that are marginal to mainstream institutions and transmit social capital that is different from that needed for school success. School requires mainstream social capital. In a January 2000 *New York Times Magazine* article, James Traub said that "Coleman consistently pointed out that we now expect the school to provide all the child's human and social capital—an impossibility."

I agree that the school can't do it alone. But schools can do much more than what they now do. Most students, even those from very difficult social conditions, enter school with the potential needed to gain mainstream social capital. But traditional schools—and most reforms—fail such students.

Not long ago I asked approximately 300 experienced teachers and administrators from across the country if they'd taken a child development course; about half had. But when I asked how many had taken a school-based, supervised course in applied child development, only seven hands remained up. This lack of training is why many educators can't discuss the underlying factors involved in a playground fight or how to create social and academic experiences that motivate learning by tapping into the developmental needs and information level of today's students. Even fewer could construct environments conducive to overcoming racial, ethnic, income, and gender barriers.

But schools can succeed if they are prepared to embrace poor or marginalized families and to provide their children with conditions that promote mainstream skills. And when these conditions are continued throughout the school years, children from low-income backgrounds can do well in school; they will have better life chances. I was first convinced that this was the case for very personal reasons.

My mother was born into the family of a sharecropper in rural Mississippi in 1904. Her father was a good man, but he was killed by lightning when she was six years old. There were no family assistance programs, and a cruel, abusive stepfather came into their lives. He would not allow the children to go to school, and they lived under conditions of extreme poverty. At about eight years of age, as a barefoot child in the cotton fields, my mother realized that education was the way to a better life. When she was 16, she ran away to live with a sister in East Chicago, Indiana, with the hope of getting an education. But that was not possible.

When she had to leave school, my mother declared that if she ever had children, she would make certain they all got a good education. And then she set out—very, very, very carefully—to find my father, a person of like mind and purpose. Her caution paid off. My father, with six or seven years of education, worked as a steel mill laborer; and my mother, with no education, worked as a domestic. The two of them eventually sent the five of us to college, where we earned a total of 13 degrees.

Our family was enmeshed in an African-American church culture that provided the necessary social, ethical, and emotional context. My parents took us to everything educational they could afford; they talked and interacted with us in a way that encouraged learning and promoted overall development. Working for and respected by some of the most powerful people in our community, my mother observed and acquired mainstream success skills and made useful social contacts. Most of the summer jobs that helped us pay our way through college came from those contacts. And I enjoyed caviar brought home after parties before my working-class friends knew that it existed. Indeed, many European, black, and brown immigrants "made it" through similar experiences.

My three best friends were as intelligent as anybody in our family and in the predominantly white working- and middle-class school we attended. On the playground and the street corner, they could think as fast and as well as students who were more successful in school. But all three went on a downhill course: one died early from alcoholism, one spent time in jail, and one was in and out of mental institutions until he died recently. My parents had the same kind of jobs as their parents did, and we all attended the same school. Why the difference? It was the more useful developmental experience we were provided.

This notion was confirmed a few years ago when I visited my mother in the hospital. My spry, 80-plus-year-old first-grade teacher, Ms. Walsh, was a hospital volunteer. When she saw me, she threw her arms around me and said, "Oh, my little James." I was 55 years old going on six. She stepped back and said, "We just loved the Comer children. You came to school with those bright, eager eyes, and you got along so well with the other children, and you all were so smart," and more. She was describing the outcome of a home and community experience that provided adequate development and school readiness—social capital, if I must use the term.

I acknowledge that my parents, perhaps even my community and school, were not and are not typical. And again, the community conditions that supported family functioning, child rearing, and development to a much greater degree in the past are weaker today. The positive connections that the poor previously had with the more privileged in American society have decreased.

A few scattered programs make good education and life opportunities possible for poor and working-class children. Prep for Prep lays the groundwork for students to attend elite private schools; A Better Chance places students in good suburban schools; the Summer Study Skills Program prepares students for challenging academic courses, these "pull-out" programs provide the social capital, knowledge, and skills needed for mainstream participation. But they do not serve that large body of able young people, like my childhood friends, who are lost in elementary schools. Prepared and supported differently, such children could succeed.

Models of Development

The Yale Child Study Center's School Development Program has been working with schools for the past 32 years. The outcomes suggest that by basing what we do in schools (and in the education enterprise beyond schools) on what we know about how children develop and learn, we can provide most children with what they need to succeed in school and in life.

I recently visited the Samuel Gompers Elementary School in one of the poorest neighborhoods in Detroit, a school with 97 percent student poverty. The Yale program has been used in this school for the past six years. The neighborhood was a disaster; the school was a pearl. The students were lively, spontaneous, and engaged in their work at appropriate times, yet quiet and attentive when they were supposed to be. They got along well with one another and were eager to demonstrate their skills to their parents and teachers. Eighty percent of the students passed the 1999 fourth-grade Michigan Educational Assessment Program (MEAP) test in reading and science, and 100 percent passed in mathematics. In 2000 they achieved the highest MEAP test scores among elementary schools in their size category in the state. Why here? It is not a mystery.

The Gompers School's success is related as much to the conditions that promote development and learning as it is to curriculum and instruction. How did it create these conditions and achieve good academic outcomes? The Yale program provided the conceptual and operational framework, child development–centered training for staff and parents, and very limited field support. The Skillman Foundation in Detroit, the Detroit Public Schools, Eastern Michigan University College of Education staff members, and parents (key members of the education enterprise) all came together to help the Gompers School and others provide the social capital the students need. The philosophy of the principal, Marilee Bylsma, is an important underpinning: "The school should be a safe haven for children, someplace that inspires learning." The staff, parents, and students did the work.

Committees, operations, and guidelines help schools create a culture of mutual respect and collaboration as well as social and academic programs that enable them to support students' development and learning. The transformation is gradual but frequent in schools that work to form good adult relationships. Good student relationships can follow.

At Gompers there is a 15-minute assembly every morning in which the students say the Pledge of Allegiance and make a school pledge. They sing a patriotic song and the school song. The custodian recognizes the "birthday boys and girls." (Message: It's everybody's school; we all play important roles.) The class with the best previous-day behavior gets "Gator points." Other recognitions take place. During the announcements, the students often discuss what's going on in their lives—the unexpected death of a teacher, problems in the neighborhood, and so on—and the adults help them learn to manage related feelings.

When the school basketball team lost a tournament they had expected to win, the principal gave much thought to how to help the players manage

their disappointment and grow from the experience. The next morning, she talked about how important it is to try to be number one in all you do. But the team members should celebrate their effort, she explained—they came in third in a large field—and look forward to the next opportunity. The students can tell you that they participate in extracurricular activities to create a good community, a condition that they value.

Activities and interactions like those at Gompers can't be carried out very long, if at all, in a school where the staff members don't like, trust, or respect one another or the parents. And you can't just mandate these conditions. Child development–oriented structures and processes must operate in a way that brings about these conditions.

Initially, the Yale program's work was just in elementary schools, but it is now being carried out in many middle schools and high schools. Admittedly, middle school is difficult, and high school is even more so. That's when teens are "placing" themselves in the world and establishing their identity. Young people who place themselves and their futures in family and social networks that are dysfunctional are likely to perform in school in ways that lead to similar poor or marginal outcomes for themselves. Additionally, they are physically able to engage in adult behaviors. Only a half-century ago, many teens were married, working, and raising families; but in these more complex times, they often lack the experiences and resultant judgment, personal control, discipline, and problem solving skills needed to manage adult living.

In traditional high schools, teachers are often much more anchored in subject matter than in student development. Peer groups provide belonging and therefore become very powerful. They are sometimes positive, but too often are troublesome—it's the inexperienced and immature leading the inexperienced and immature. Aside from athletic coaches and teachers in the arts and other special areas, too few mature adults can interact with students in sustained and meaningful ways. These are powder keg conditions. And in communities where there are too few constructive supports for good development both inside and outside school, bad things happen—among staff, students, and parents.

In all schools—but particularly in low-income and nonmainstream communities—it is important for the staff to expose students to mainstream work as well as civic activities so that the connection between learning and later expectations is clear. School should help young people to learn what is needed for life success. Social and academic skills, attitudes, management of feelings, and other attributes needed to participate successfully in the mainstream can then be developed.

West Mecklenberg High School in Charlotte, North Carolina, received an additional 222 students in 1992 from a competing high school; its enrollment went from 1,144 to 1,366, precipitating a crisis. The school was almost evenly divided between whites and African Americans. Most of the students were children of blue-collar workers. Fourteen guns and many knives were confiscated during the first year, and parents, teachers, and students were concerned about their safety. Dennis Williams was assigned to the school as principal; Haywood Homsley, then the guidance counselor and coach, became the Yale-program facilitator. Williams and Homsley began to focus on reducing intergroup tensions and creating a climate that enabled staff members to consider and respond to the developmental needs of the students.

The transformation was dramatic. On April 28, 1995, *The Leader,* Charlotte's major newspaper, highlighted the gains seen at West Mecklenberg since the Yale program was introduced: Scholastic Assessment Test (SAT) scores rose by an average of 16 points; the number of students who made the honor roll jumped 75 percent; the number of students enrolled in advanced courses increased 25 percent; and the average daily attendance rate for the year went from 89 percent to almost 94 percent. The process of change at West Mecklenberg was essentially the same as in elementary schools like Gompers except that the students themselves were more involved in the thinking and planning of the programs.

In the 1994–1995 academic year, West Mecklenberg was designated a "school of excellence" by the state of North Carolina for the high level at which it reached its benchmark goals, and it was the only high school of 11 in its district to attain this status. Despite the fact that there have been three principals since 1992, the school has held the "excellence" rating for three of the past five years.

Sustaining Gains

Are the academic gains large enough? Can they be sustained? What about the schools that do not improve? And what about middle- and upper-income young people, who face a more complex world? Even with developmentally based programs and other reform models, it's true that academic gains in schools serving students who are most in need do not quickly and routinely match those of more privileged students. Sometimes they can't be sustained; and sometimes there is no improvement at all. But when the process is well implemented, large gains have been achieved and sustained.

For example, the Norman Weir K–8 school in Paterson, New Jersey, went from 34th to first in academic achievement among eighth-graders in 1995. They equaled or surpassed suburban schools for four consecutive years. A school in Virginia went from 24th to first but fell apart the next year because the principal and several key senior staff members were removed or left and were replaced by untrained staff. Weir escaped the same fate because a group of staff members went to the superintendent and asked for and were assigned a good principal whose educational philosophy was grounded in child development.

Before a school can experience large, widespread, sustained achievement-test gains and adequately prepare students for adult life, it must be able to promote student development and manage its way to success, as Gompers, West Mecklenberg, and others have done. For this to be possible, we must produce large numbers of adequately prepared and supported staff. The policies and practices of the major players in the education enterprise nationwide—schools of education, legislators at all levels, state and federal departments of education, school districts, businesses—must be coherent by virtue of being based in child-and-youth development.

There are many obstacles to significant school improvement. Five in particular are very troublesome yet more accessible than the seemingly intransigent issues of race, class, and financial equity. These five are the ones that prevent the education enterprise as a whole from empowering school staffs, as in the case of the Gompers School. If these were addressed all at once, the United States could begin to foster widespread, sustained, high-level school improvement—and perhaps, eventually, could even address the most resistant issues.

First, frequent changes in personnel—particularly in districts and schools faced with great challenges— is a major problem. Child development–based strategies require continuity, training, and support of school staff. Frequent changes in administrators or governance at the district or building level, or in teachers—without careful selection and training of new people—can undo in several months or less a school culture that took three to five years to create. Understanding student and organization needs, developing resources and staff, and building community support isn't possible in the two-year tenure of most school superintendents.

Second, education policy is often fragmented rather than prioritized. This is because it is made everywhere—legislatures, state departments, districts, unions, city councils, businesses, and more. Many policy makers have no expertise in child development, teaching, and learning. And when crafting policy, most do not talk to one another, to students, or to school staff. Rarely are these policies guided by what we know about child growth and development and its relationship to learning.

And legislators, businesspeople, state departments, and others are—like school administrators— under great pressure to "Do something!" Because

they widely believe that test scores alone can measure school effectiveness, that is what they focus on most. And without well-considered, evidence-based, coherent education policies, equitable funding will be impossible. In one city, eight of the 10 schools listed as "failing" had made the greatest gains in the system over the previous two years. The listing was demoralizing and led to harmful staff turnover and achievement setbacks, but it was the only way to get funds to help those schools.

Third, most schools of education do not provide future teachers or administrators with adequate knowledge or skills to promote a culture supportive of overall student development. Most focus— and in the college classroom, particularly—on curriculum, instruction, assessment, administration, and, sometimes, use of technology.

Sound knowledge of academic disciplines is important but not sufficient. Many schools of education provide courses in abnormal child development but no study of normal development. And the preparation to teach reading is often limited. Yet a child who has difficulty learning to read—the academic task that serves as a foundation for all future learning—is likely to experience feelings that limit emotional, psychological, ethical, and social developmental growth, or that promote troublesome growth.

Fourth, schools of education are seldom involved with other departments of the university in mutually enriching ways. Meaningful interaction between colleges of education and other university departments would be beneficial also to the institutions and the communities around them.

And fifth, there is no vehicle in universities or among research-and-development groups that will enable working educators to update their skills regularly and learn best practices. Also, there is no existing way to address these five most troublesome obstacles simultaneously so that synergy results.

Agricultural extension provides a useful model for educators. The Smith-Lever Act of 1914 created the Agricultural Extension Service to transmit knowledge to a large number of farmers through federal, state, and county partnerships. Farm agents, in addition to changing farmer practice, changed policy makers' and the public's understanding of best practice, as well as the policies needed to promote it. Improved agriculture enriched the economy and made America the breadbasket of the world.

Education is to the information-age economy of today what agriculture was to the economy at the turn of the twentieth century. Schools of education could create centers designed to overcome major obstacles in the education enterprise. Such centers would provide education agents. Schools of education will need to incorporate and institutionalize child development knowledge and expertise. But once this is done, education scholars and agents will be well positioned to share with and learn from colleagues at universities, to help future and current teachers and administrators become more effective practitioners, and to help policy makers and the public better understand and support good schooling.

Few schools of education or university programs are presently prepared to work in this way. We should not rush into such programs without sound pilot and infrastructure work. But knowledge, organization, and support can be acquired. The states—who are legally responsible for educating America's children—should support such efforts. Most, largely through their departments of education, have been involved in standard-setting as well as in regulatory and oversight activities. They are involved in takeovers of failing districts. Yet they have little experience in—and no mechanisms for—correcting the complex problems involved in school improvement.

The decisions we make in the next few years will involve significant amounts of money and will lock us into helpful or harmful directions. A miracle quick fix is not possible. But if we today begin to mount programs that connect to practice and to policy what we know about how children develop and learn, we could soon be well on our way to having better-functioning systems of education in five years and good ones in a decade. If we continue to be guided by tradition, ideology, and power, however, we will reach a point of no return—one where too many young people are undereducated, acting out, and gradually undermining our economy and our democracy.

James P. Comer, M.D., is the Maurice Falk Professor of Child Psychiatry at the Yale University Child Study Center. He is the founder of the center's School Development Program, which started in 1968.

QUESTIONS FOR REFLECTION

1. Comer states that most curricula are not informed by an understanding of child development. What do you think might account for the fact that this important basis of the curriculum is often overlooked?
2. What objections might some teachers, parents, and community members raise about Comer's criticisms and solutions to school reform? As an educational leader, how would you respond to those objections?
3. Comer argues that "most schools of education do not provide future teachers or administrators with adequate knowledge or skills to promote a culture supportive of overall student development." Has this been your experience? What would you recommend colleges and universities do to address this shortcoming?

Toward a Strategy for Healthy Adolescent Development

DAVID A. HAMBURG

ABSTRACT: Adolescence is a critical transition period for young people. Contemporary society confronts adolescents with formidable stresses and risks that, for some youth, impair physical and mental health, erode motivation for success in school and workplace, and damage their relationships with others. With support from families, schools, health care professionals, and the community, however, adolescents can grow up to assume the responsibilities of democratic citizenship. For example, schools can promote healthy development by emphasizing a life sciences curriculum, life skills training, and social support.

Adolescence is one of the most complex transitions in the lifespan—a time of metamorphosis from childhood to adulthood. Its beginning is associated with biological, physical, behavioral, and social transformations that roughly correspond with the move from elementary school to middle or junior high school. The events of this crucially formative phase can shape an individual's entire lifespan.

Many adolescents manage to negotiate their way through this critical transition. With caring families, good schools, preventive health care, and supportive community institutions, they grow up healthy and vigorous, reasonably well educated, committed to families and friends, and prepared for the workplace and the responsibilities of democratic citizenship. For many others, however, the obstacles in their path can impair their physical and emotional health, erode their motivation and ability to succeed in school and the workplace, and damage their human relationships.

Adolescents from the ages of 10 to 15 are being confronted with pressures to use legal and illegal drugs and weapons and to engage in premature, unprotected sexual behavior. Many are depressed, and one-third report that they have contemplated suicide. Others lack the competence to handle interpersonal conflict without resorting to violence. By age 17, about one-quarter of all adolescents have engaged in behaviors that are harmful to themselves and others, such as

getting pregnant, using drugs, taking part in antisocial activity, and failing in school. Altogether, nearly half of American adolescents are at high or moderate risk of seriously damaging their life chances.

The technological and social changes of recent decades have provided many young people with remarkable material benefits and opportunities but have also brought formidable stresses and risks into the adolescent experience. These changes are most striking in relation to their effect on family configurations: high divorce rates, both parents working full time outside the home, and the growth of single-parent families. Indeed, about half of all young Americans will spend part or all of their childhood and adolescence living with only one parent. These problems are exacerbated by the erosion of neighborhood networks and other traditional social support systems. Children now spend less time in the company of adults than a few decades ago; more of their time is spent either watching television or on the street, generally with peers in age-segregated, largely unsupervised environments.

Such conditions are common among families of all economic strata, social backgrounds, and geographic areas. But these conditions are especially prevalent in neighborhoods of concentrated poverty, where young adolescents so often lack two crucial prerequisites for their healthy growth and development: a close relationship with at least one dependable adult and the perception that meaningful opportunities exist in the adult life course.

What are fundamental requirements for healthy adolescent development? Adolescents must 1) find a valued place in a constructive group; 2) learn how to form close, durable human relationships; 3) feel a sense of worth as individuals; 4) achieve a reliable basis for making informed choices; 5) know how to use the support systems available to them; 6) express constructive curiosity and exploratory behavior; 7) believe in a promising future with real opportunities; 8) find ways of being useful to others; 9) learn to live respectfully with others in circumstances of democratic pluralism; and 10) cultivate the inquiring and problem-solving skills that serve lifelong learning and adaptability.

Early adolescence—the phase during which young people are just beginning to engage in very risky behaviors but before damaging patterns have become firmly established—offers an excellent opportunity for intervention to prevent later casualties and promote successful adult lives. Over a 10-year span in which several major reports were published, the Carnegie Council on Adolescent Development recommended ways in which pivotal institutions can adapt to contemporary circumstances so as to meet the requirements for healthy adolescent development. These institutions are the family, schools, health care systems, community organizations, and the media.

Many current interventions on behalf of young adolescents are targeted to one problem behavior, such as drug abuse or teenage pregnancy. While targeted approaches are useful, they often do not take adequate account of two important findings from research: 1) serious problem behaviors tend to cluster in the same individual and reinforce one another, and 2) such behaviors often have common antecedents in childhood experience.

Therefore, generic approaches that address the fundamental requirements in a comprehensive way—a youth development strategy—are attractive. The pivotal, frontline institutions that have a daily impact on adolescent experience have a special opportunity and obligation to foster healthy lifestyles in childhood and adolescence, while taking into consideration the underlying factors that promote either positive or negative outcomes. For better and worse, these institutions have powerful effects on adolescent development.

DISEASE PREVENTION IN ADOLESCENCE

Over the past few decades, the burden of adolescent illness has shifted from traditional causes of disease toward the "new morbidities" associated with health-damaging behaviors such as depression, suicide, substance use (alcohol, tobacco, and drugs), sexually transmitted diseases—including HIV and AIDS—and gun-related homicides.

Early adolescence is characterized by exploratory behavior in which the individual seeks adult-like roles and status. This is developmentally appropriate and socially adaptive, even though it involves some high-risk behavior. Yet such behavior can readily become dangerous and inflict damage, such as sexually transmitted diseases, death or trauma from violence, and disabling accidents related to alcohol. In addition, long-term consequences include cancer and cardiovascular disease, which are made more likely by high-calorie, high-fat dietary patterns, inadequate exercise, and heavy smoking. Destructive behaviors may constrict life options. For example, a teenage mother who drops out of junior or senior high school diminishes her prospects for lifetime employment and increases the risk of living in poverty, with the associated risks to her own health and the health of her child.

Early adolescence is a time of opportunity for the formation of healthy practices that have both short-term and long-term effects. Research of recent years has shown how the frontline institutions can provide accurate and personally meaningful information about health risks as well as foster the skills and motivation to avoid these risks and adopt healthy practices.

The health-related perceptions of adolescents can be helpful in motivating them to adopt healthy behavior. Their health concerns vary according to their gender, ethnicity, and socioeconomic status. Still, most are preoccupied with how they look, how they feel about themselves, their relationships to their peers, and educational pressures. Many adolescents are similarly concerned about substance abuse, sexuality, nutrition, and exercise. They tend wishfully to minimize the potentially damaging effects of high-risk behavior, in effect saying, "It can't happen to me." Such views are relevant to the design of social supports to adolescents, including clinical contacts. If health services are not user-friendly, they are not likely to be used by the individuals who need them most. By responding in meaningful ways to the interests, concerns, and perceptions of adolescents, health professionals can be helpful in ways that may have enduring value.

EDUCATION FOR HEALTH IN EARLY ADOLESCENCE

There is an inextricable link between education and health. Adolescents in poor health have difficulty learning (e.g., substance abuse destroys attention to instruction). Conversely, young people fully engaged in learning tend to form health-promoting habits. Many adolescents arrive at middle school with inadequate skills to cope with their great transition to adulthood. Much of what they need goes beyond the traditional curriculum offered by the public school system.

Middle schools can play a crucial role in fostering health among young adolescents through the curriculum, school policy, and clear examples of health-promoting behavior. A substantial approach to education for health includes 1) teaching adequate nutrition in the classroom and offering a corresponding diet in the cafeteria; 2) smoke-free buildings and programs to help students and staff avoid tobacco; 3) education on the effects of alcohol and illicit drugs on the brain and other organs; 4) opportunities for exercise not just for students in varsity competition but for

all in the school community; and 5) emphasis on safety and the prevention of violence, including violence inherently associated with drug dealing and the carrying of weapons.

In 1989, the Carnegie Council on Adolescent Development published an interdisciplinary analysis of middle-grade education entitled *Turning Points*. This task force recommended reforms that were aimed at creating health-promoting, developmentally appropriate middle schools. For example, by organizing smaller units out of large schools, these new units can function on a human scale and provide sustained individual attention to students in a supportive group setting. A mutual aid ethic can be fostered among teachers and students, e.g., through interdisciplinary team teaching, cooperative learning, and academically supervised community service. These units can stimulate thinking skills, especially through a substantial life sciences curriculum, and can offer life skills training, especially in decision making, constructive interpersonal relations, nonviolent problem solving, and the ability to take advantage of opportunities. Since three approaches (life skills curriculum, life skills training, and social supports) offer sufficient potential for healthy development, some further words are in order.

Life sciences curriculum. The life sciences tap into the natural curiosity that surges in early adolescence. Students are intensely interested in the changes taking place in their own bodies. The life sciences clarify growth and development and specifically address adolescent development. The study of human biology includes the scientific study of behavior and illuminates ways in which high-risk behavior, especially in adolescence, bears on health throughout the lifespan.

Life skills training. The vital knowledge obtained from the life sciences curriculum is crucial but needs augmentation to be effective in shaping behavior. Such information becomes more useful when combined with training in interpersonal and decision-making skills. These skills can be useful in a variety of ways, such as helping students to 1) resist pressure from peers or from the media to engage in high-risk behaviors, 2) increase their self-control, 3) acquire ways to reduce stress without engaging in dangerous activity, 4) learn how to make friends and overcome isolation, and 5) learn how to avoid violence. Research shows that such skills can be effectively taught by using systematic instruction and practice through role playing.

Social supports. Research evidence shows that social supports that involve dependable relationships and shared values can provide leverage in the promotion of adolescent health. Schools, community organizations, and health care providers can supplement the family by arranging constructive social support programs.

Taken together, the life sciences curriculum, life skills training, and social supports constitute effective facilitators of healthy adolescent development.

Categorical or targeted approaches are complementary to the generic comprehensive approach of educating youth for lifelong health. Four issues are selected for brief illustration here: responsible sexuality, preparation for parenthood, prevention of youth violence, and prevention of drug abuse. Clearly, other problems also deserve attention and none more so than mental health, particularly depression.

RESPONSIBLE SEXUALITY

Early adolescence is not a time to become seriously engaged in sexual activity, yet adolescents are sorely tempted to do so. They get conflicting messages about desirable body image and appropriate sexual behavior, especially from the media and from peers. They badly need to understand sexuality, including the dynamics of intimate relationships, when to become sexually active, the biological process of conception, and the risks of contracting sexually transmitted diseases, including HIV infection.

Young adolescents get their information about sexuality primarily from peers but also from family, school, television, and movies. Peer information is often inaccurate; for example, the assumption is widespread that "everybody does it." This assumption applies to a variety of risky behaviors such as smoking and alcohol use. Families and schools are in a better position to provide accurate information and health-protective choices. Adolescents who rate communication with their parents as poor are likely to initiate sex, smoking, and drinking earlier than peers who rate communication with their parents as good. However, parents need help in becoming well informed about reproductive health and in overcoming embarrassment about discussing sex with their children.

Adolescents need information about human sexuality and reproduction before they become sexually active. Organized efforts to meet these needs should begin not later than early adolescence in middle schools and in community organizations. Information about preventing the transmission of the AIDS virus is now a crucial although controversial part of health education for young adolescents. Adolescents typically do not know that the incubation period for AIDS can be a decade and that mothers can transmit the virus to their offspring. Interventions should identify the emotionally charged situations that adolescents are likely to encounter and provide life skills training on how to manage or avoid those situations of high risk. Schools, families, and the media, through health-promoting knowledge and skills, can contribute to this effort.

Even so, good information and skills may not be enough; motivation for constructive choices is crucial. Determining how to bring this about remains a formidable task. A recent Institute of Medicine study concluded that fewer than 25 programs to reduce unintended pregnancy have been carefully evaluated; of these programs, about half were found to be effective in the short term. This is one of the many indications that research in this field has not been given adequate priority.

The vast majority of adolescent pregnancies are unintended. Education for health must make it clear that to be sufficiently mature to raise a family, an individual not only must be knowledgeable about reproductive information, birth control, and the prevention of unwanted pregnancies but also must be aware that raising a family brings responsibilities as well as joys and that it takes a lot of learning and coping to become a reliable, competent parent.

PREPARATION FOR PARENTHOOD

Preparing adolescents for the time when they form families of their own is a neglected aspect of healthy development. All too many adolescents become pregnant only to find later that they are poorly prepared for the challenge of raising a child. The fulfillment of each child's potential requires a profound parental investment of time, energy, caregiving, resources, persistence, and resilience in coping with adversity.

The 1994 Carnegie report, *Starting Points: Meeting the Needs of Our Youngest Children,* emphasized the importance of preparing adolescents for responsible parenthood. When people make an informed, thoughtful commitment to have children, they are more likely to be good parents, and their children are more likely to develop in healthy ways. By the same token, when young parents are unprepared for the opportunities and responsibilities of parenthood, the risks to their children are formidable.

Therefore, *Starting Points* recommended a substantial expansion of efforts to educate young people about parenthood. Families are the first source of such education, but schools, places of worship, and community organizations can also be useful. Performing community service in child care centers can provide a valuable learning experience for adolescents about what is required to raise young children. Age-appropriate education about parenthood should begin in late elementary school but no later than early adolescence. It can be a part of either a life sciences curriculum or health education. In either case, it must be substantial and meaningful to adolescents.

PREVENTION OF YOUTH VIOLENCE

Nearly one million adolescents between the ages of 12 and 19 are victims of violent crimes each year. This problem has been accelerating, yet evidence is emerging on ways to prevent adolescent violence. To be effective, prevention requires a comprehensive approach that addresses both individual and social factors. Optimally, this would build on generic approaches that meet essential requirements for healthy adolescent development through developmentally appropriate schools, supportive families, and youth-oriented community organizations. In addition, specific interventions that target youth violence can enhance adolescents' ability to deal with conflict in nonviolent ways. Policy changes, such as implementing stronger measures to restrict the availability of guns, are urgently needed, especially in light of the growing propensity of juveniles to use guns, even semiautomatic weapons.

One promising strategy for preventing youth violence is the teaching of conflict resolution skills as part of health education in elementary and middle schools. Research indicates that conflict resolution programs can reduce violence; best results are achieved if these skills are embedded in long-term, comprehensive programs that address the multiple risk factors that lead to empty, shattered lives, which offer little recourse except violence. Serious, in-depth conflict resolution training over extended periods is increasingly important in a culture that is saturated with media and street violence. Supervised practice of conflict-resolution skills is important. Assertiveness, taught as a social skill, helps young people learn how to resist unwanted pressures and intimidation, resolve conflicts nonviolently, and make sound decisions about the use of weapons.

High-risk youth in impoverished communities urgently need social support networks and life skills training. Both can be provided in schools and school-related health centers as well as in community organizations, including church-related youth activities and sports programs. These programs work best by building enduring relationships with adults as well as with constructive peers. Such an approach offers alternatives to violent groups by providing a sense of belonging, a source of enjoyable activity, a perception of opportunity, a basis for mentoring, and a chance to prepare for social roles that earn respect.

PREVENTION OF DRUG ABUSE

Drugs are cheaper and more plentiful today than they were a decade ago. The United States has the highest addiction rates in its history, and the judicial system is clogged with drug-related cases. Adolescents consider alcohol and other drugs less harmful today than they did a few years ago. For many, the use of drugs, even the sale of drugs, constitutes an attractive path to what they perceive as adult status. Society has been searching desperately for answers. Meanwhile, serious research efforts oriented to prevention have gone through several "generations" of insight, and some promising evidence is at hand.

Community-wide preventive interventions in a few places have substantially diminished the use of "gateway" substances (tobacco, alcohol, and marijuana) in early adolescence, concomitantly enhancing personal and social competence. These efforts have used rigorous research designs on a long-term basis. Several preventive programs for young adolescents have been shown to reduce drug use. The learning of life skills has been effective in the prevention of cigarette smoking and alcohol and marijuana use if applied with sufficient intensity and duration. The systematic, explicit teaching of these skills can contribute to personal competence and provide constructive alternatives to health-damaging behavior.

When booster sessions are provided in high school, the preventive effects of early interventions are sustained through the senior year. The prevention of cigarette smoking is very important, both because of its "gateway" function and the many pathologies throughout the lifespan that flow from this addiction in early adolescence. The well-designed, community-wide interventions are encouraging in this respect. Their success suggests that social norms on cigarette use can be changed by systematic, intensive, and long-term efforts. A striking example is the recent decline in smoking reported by African American adolescents.

Beyond the targeted approach to substance abuse, parents, teachers, and health professionals should understand that adolescent immersion in high-risk behavior is exacerbated by developmental problems such as low self-esteem, poor performance in school, depression, or inability to make deliberate, informed decisions. Using drugs may be a way of feeling mature, courageous, sophisticated, or otherwise grown-up. Disadvantaged youth need to be shown how individuals from comparable backgrounds have done well in the mainstream economy—in contrast to the putatively successful drug dealers who are involved in crime and violence. The fostering of family-augmenting functions by community organizations and health-social services can provide accurate, pertinent information and supportive human relationships that facilitate healthy development even in circumstances of adversity.

STRENGTHENING HEALTH SERVICES FOR ADOLESCENTS

A comprehensive study of adolescent health, conducted by the U.S. Office of Technology Assessment in 1991, pointed to serious barriers to establishing developmentally appropriate health services for adolescents. Current services are particularly lacking in disease prevention and health-promotion services. Recent studies and innovations show what can be done, but there is a long way to go.

One in seven American adolescents has no health insurance coverage; many more have very little. Within the Medicaid population, only one-third of eligible adolescents are currently covered because of funding constraints. Health insurance, even when provided by employers for working families, often excludes their adolescent children.

As managed care spreads rapidly throughout the United States, it is essential to include explicit provisions for coverage of adolescents. This will be especially important to monitor as states increasingly enroll their Medicaid population in managed care plans. Managed care organizations can contract with school-based health centers that serve adolescents. Some community health and school-based adolescent health centers have shown how various barriers can be overcome so that adolescents can get adequate care during these years that are crucially formative for healthy lifestyles.

At present, there is a shortage of experienced and well-trained health providers who can sensitively treat the health problems of adolescents. The conjunction of psychiatry with pediatrics and internal medicine is important in this context.

One promising approach to filling the service gap for adolescents is manifested in school-related health facilities, either at or near the school, and functionally integrated with respect to curriculum and accessibility. Such facilities have demonstrated their ability to deal with acute medical problems, including mental health. They have strong potential for disease prevention and health promotion.

Since students often request help with feelings of depression, loneliness, and anxiety, these centers must provide mental health services. Treatment of depression can represent an important opportunity to prevent further problems, for example, self-medication that leads to substance abuse and addiction.

CONCLUSIONS

The early adolescent years have become the starting point for an upsurge of health-compromising behaviors that have lifelong consequences. Yet early adolescence presents a neglected and overlooked opportunity for health promotion. The interest of adolescents in their own developing bodies can be a potent force for building healthy lifestyles of enduring significance. The best chance to fulfill this promise lies in enhancing understanding of adolescent development among health care professionals, schools, community organizations, families, and media.

A crucial ingredient is the guiding and motivating influence of caring adults. Information and skills are necessary but not sufficient to shape the behavior of adolescents unless they are motivated to put them to use in the service of their own health. This requires the protection and support of families and health professionals who are trained to work effectively with adolescents as distinctive individuals. Health policy makers must find ways to improve adolescents' access to health care through dependable primary care providers and school-linked preventive services, including services for mental health.

A comprehensive health-promotion strategy would optimally involve a community-wide commitment from the full range of institutions with which adolescents are involved. Such a commitment to adolescents is potentially a powerful means of shaping young lives in healthy, constructive patterns of lifelong learning and adaptation. This approach is highly congruent with Mel Sabshin's career-long vision of research, education, and care for healthy development and social responsibility.

David A. Hamburg is president emeritus of the Carnegie Corporation of New York and former chair of psychiatry at Stanford University School of Medicine. In 1996, he received the Presidential Medal of Freedom, the nation's highest civilian honor, and in 1998, he received the Public Welfare Medal from the National Academy of Sciences.

QUESTIONS FOR REFLECTION

1. Reflect on your experiences as an adolescent. In what ways did your school experiences help you to cope with the stresses associated with this transition period?
2. What concerns might some teachers, parents, and community members raise about Hamburg's call for schools to emphasize a life sciences curriculum, life skills training, and social support? How might Hamburg respond to these concerns?
3. What evidence indicates that some adolescents in your local community may not be on the path toward healthy adult development?

The Cognitive-Developmental Approach to Moral Education

LAWRENCE KOHLBERG
(1927–1987)

ABSTRACT: Building on Dewey's and Piaget's ideas about moral development, Kohlberg suggests that the reasoning processes people use to differentiate between right and wrong progress through three levels of development. At the preconventional level, people decide what is right on the basis of personal needs and rules developed by others; at the conventional level, moral decisions reflect a desire for others' approval and a willingness to conform to expectations of family, community, and country; and at the postconventional level, decisions are based on rational, personal choices that can be separated from conventional values.

In this article, I present an overview of the cognitive-developmental approach to moral education and its research foundations, compare it with other approaches, and report the experimental work my colleagues and I are doing to apply the approach.

I. MORAL STAGES

The cognitive-developmental approach was fully stated for the first time by John Dewey. The approach is called *cognitive* because it recognizes that moral education, like intellectual education, has its basis in stimulating the *active thinking* of the child about moral issues and decisions. It is called developmental because it sees the aims of moral education as movement through moral stages. According to Dewey:

> The aim of education is growth or *development,* both intellectual and moral. Ethical and psychological

principles can aid the school in the *greatest of all the constructions—the building of a free and powerful character.* Only knowledge of the *order and connection of the stages in psychological development can insure this.* Education is the work of *supplying the conditions* which will enable the psychological functions to mature in the freest and fullest manner.[1]

Dewey postulated three levels of moral development: (1) the *pre-moral* or *preconventional* level "of behavior motivated by biological and social impulses with results for morals," (2) the *conventional* level of behavior "in which the individual accepts with little critical reflection the standards of his group," and (3) the *autonomous* level of behavior in which "conduct is guided by the individual thinking and judging for himself whether a purpose is good, and does not accept the standard of his group without reflection."[2]

Dewey's thinking about moral stages was theoretical. Building upon his prior studies of cognitive stages, Jean Piaget made the first effort to define stages of moral reasoning in children through actual interviews and through observations of children (in games with rules).[3] Using this interview material, Piaget defined the premoral, the conventional, and the autonomous levels as follows: (1) the *premoral stage*, where there was no sense of obligation to rules; (2) the *heteronomous stage*, where the right was literal obedience to rules and an equation of obligation with submission to power and punishment (roughly ages four to eight); and (3) the *autonomous stage*, where the purpose and consequences of following rules are considered and obligation is based on reciprocity and exchange (roughly ages eight to twelve).[4]

In 1955 I started to redefine and validate (through longitudinal and cross-cultural study) the Dewey-Piaget levels and stages. The resulting stages are presented in Table 1.

We claim to have validated the stages defined in Table 1. The notion that stages can be *validated* by longitudinal study implies that stages have definite empirical characteristics.[5] The concept of stages (as used by Piaget and myself) implies the following characteristics:

1. Stages are "structured wholes," or organized systems of thought. Individuals are *consistent* in level of moral judgment.
2. Stages form an *invariant sequence*. Under all conditions except extreme trauma, movement is always forward, never backward. Individuals never skip stages; movement is always to the next stage up.
3. Stages are "hierarchical integrations." Thinking at a higher stage includes or comprehends within it lower-stage thinking. There is a tendency to function at or prefer the highest stage available.

Each of these characteristics has been demonstrated for moral stages. Stages are defined by responses to a set of verbal moral dilemmas classified according to an elaborate scoring scheme. Validating studies include:

1. A twenty-year study of fifty Chicago-area boys, middle- and working-class. Initially interviewed at ages ten to sixteen, they have been reinterviewed at three-year intervals thereafter.
2. A small, six-year longitudinal study of a Turkish village and city boys of the same age.
3. A variety of other cross-sectional studies in Canada, Britain, Israel, Taiwan, Yucatan, Honduras, and India.

With regard to the structured whole or consistency criterion, we have found that more than 50 percent of an individual's thinking is always at one stage, with the remainder at the next adjacent stage (which he is leaving or which he is moving into).

With regard to invariant sequence, our longitudinal results have been presented in the *American Journal of Orthopsychiatry* (see note 12), and indicate that on every retest individuals were either at the same stage as three years earlier or had moved up. This was true in Turkey as well as in the United States.

With regard to the hierarchical integration criterion, it has been demonstrated that adolescents exposed to written statements at each of the six stages comprehend or correctly put in their own words all statements at or below their own stage but fail to comprehend any statements more than one stage above their own.[6] Some individuals comprehend the next stage above their own; some do not. Adolescents prefer (or rank as best) the highest stage they can comprehend.

To understand moral stages, it is important to clarify their relations to stage of logic or intelligence, on the one hand, and to moral behavior on the other. Maturity of moral judgment is not highly correlated with IQ or verbal intelligence (correlations are only in the 30s, accounting for 10 percent of the variance). Cognitive development, in the stage sense, however, is more important for moral development than such correlations suggest. Piaget has found that after the child learns to speak there are three major stages of reasoning: the intuitive, the concrete operational, and the formal operational. At around age seven, the child enters the stage of concrete logical thought: He can make logical inferences, classify, and handle quantitative relations about

TABLE 1

Definition of Moral Stages

I. Preconventional level

At this level, the child is responsive to cultural rules and labels of good and bad, right or wrong, but interprets these labels either in terms of the physical or the hedonistic consequences of action (punishment, reward, exchange of favors) or in terms of the physical power of those who enunciate the rules and labels. The level is divided into the following two stages:

Stage 1: *The punishment-and-obedience orientation.* The physical consequences of action determine its goodness or badness, regardless of the human meaning or value of these consequences. Avoidance of punishment and unquestioning deference to power are valued in their own right, not in terms of respect for an underlying moral order supported by punishment and authority (the latter being Stage 4).

Stage 2: *The instrumental-relativist orientation.* Right action consists of that which instrumentally satisfies one's own needs and occasionally the needs of others. Human relations are viewed in terms like those of the marketplace. Elements of fairness, of reciprocity, and of equal sharing are present, but they are always interpreted in a physical, pragmatic way. Reciprocity is a matter of "You scratch my back and I'll scratch yours," not of loyalty, gratitude, or justice.

II. Conventional level

At this level, maintaining the expectations of the individual's family, group, or nation is perceived as valuable in its own right, regardless of immediate and obvious consequences. The attitude is not only one of *conformity* to personal expectations and social order, but of loyalty to it, of actively *maintaining,* supporting, and justifying the order, and of identifying with the persons or group involved in it. At this level, there are the following two stages:

Stage 3: *The interpersonal concordance or "good boy-nice girl" orientation.* Good behavior is that which pleases or helps others and is approved by them. There is much conformity to stereotypical images of what is majority or "natural" behavior. Behavior is frequently judged by intention—"he means well" becomes important for the first time. One earns approval by being "nice."

Stage 4: *The "law and order" orientation.* There is orientation toward authority, fixed rules, and the maintenance of the social order. Right behavior consists of doing one's duty, showing respect for authority, and maintaining the given social order for its own sake.

III. Postconventional, autonomous, or principled level

At this level, there is a clear effort to define moral values and principles that have validity and application apart from the authority of the groups or persons holding these principles and apart from the individual's own identification with these groups. This level also has two stages:

Stage 5: *The social-contract, legalistic orientation,* generally with utilitarian overtones. Right action tends to be defined in terms of general individual rights and standards which have been critically examined and agreed upon by the whole society. There is a clear awareness of the relativism of personal values and opinions and a corresponding emphasis upon procedural rules for reaching consensus. Aside from what is constitutionally and democratically agreed upon, the right is a matter of personal "values"; and "opinion." The result is an emphasis upon the "legal point of view," but with an emphasis upon the possibility of changing law in terms of rational considerations of social utility (rather than freezing it in terms of Stage 4 "law and order"). Outside the legal realm, free agreement and contract is the binding element of obligation. This is the "official" morality of the American government and constitution.

Stage 6: *The universal-ethical-principle orientation.* Right is defined by the decision of conscience in accord with self-chosen *ethical principles* appealing to logical comprehensiveness, universality, and consistency. These principles are abstract and ethical (the Golden Rule, the categorical imperative); they are not concrete moral rules like the Ten Commandments. At heart, these are universal principles of *justice,* of the *reciprocity* and *equality* of human *rights,* and of respect for the dignity of human beings as *individual persons* ("From Is to Ought," pp. 164, 165).

From *Journal of Philosophy* 70, no. 18 (October 25, 1973): 631–632. Reprinted by permission.

concrete things. In adolescence individuals usually enter the stage of formal operations. At this stage they can reason abstractly, i.e., consider all possibilities, form hypotheses, deduce implications from hypotheses, and test them against reality.[7]

Since moral reasoning clearly is reasoning, advanced moral reasoning depends upon advanced logical reasoning; a person's logical stage puts a certain ceiling on the moral stage he can attain. A person whose logical stage is only concrete operational is limited to the preconventional moral stages (Stages 1 and 2). A person whose logical stage is only partially formal operational is limited to the conventional moral stages (Stages 3 and 4). While logical development is necessary for moral development and sets limits to it, most individuals are higher in logical stage than they are in moral stage. As an example, over 50 percent of late adolescents and adults are capable of full formal reasoning, but only 10 percent of these adults (all formal operational) display principled (Stages 5 and 6) moral reasoning.

The moral stages are *structures of moral judgment* or *moral reasoning. Structures* of moral judgment must be distinguished from the *content* of moral judgment. As an example, we cite responses to a dilemma used in our various studies to identify moral stage. The dilemma raises the issue of stealing a drug to save a dying woman. The inventor of the drug is selling it for ten times what it costs him to make it. The woman's husband cannot raise the money, and the seller refuses to lower the price or wait for payment. What should the husband do?

The choice endorsed by a subject (steal, don't steal) is called the *content* of his moral judgment in the situation. His reasoning about the choice defines the structure of his moral judgment. This reasoning centers on the following ten universal moral values or issues of concern to persons in these moral dilemmas:

1. Punishment
2. Property
3. Roles and concerns of affection
4. Roles and concerns of authority
5. Law
6. Life
7. Liberty
8. Distributive justice
9. Truth
10. Sex

A moral choice involves choosing between two (or more) of these values as they *conflict* in concrete situations of choice.

The stage or structure of a person's moral judgment defines: (1) *what* he finds valuable in each of these moral issues (life, law), i.e., how he defines the value, and (2) *why* he finds it valuable, i.e., the reasons he gives for valuing it. As an example, at Stage 1 life is valued in terms of the power or possessions of the person involved; at Stage 2, for its usefulness in satisfying the needs of the individual in question or others; at Stage 3, in terms of the individual's relations with others and their valuation of him; at Stage 4, in terms of social or religious law. Only at Stages 5 and 6 is each life seen as inherently worthwhile, aside from other considerations.

Moral Judgment vs. Moral Action

Having clarified the nature of stages of moral *judgment,* we must consider the relation of moral judgment to moral *action.* If logical reasoning is a necessary but not sufficient condition for mature moral judgment, mature moral judgment is a necessary but not sufficient condition for mature moral action. One cannot follow moral principles if one does not understand (or believe in) moral principles. However, one can reason in terms of principles and not live up to these principles. As an example, Richard Krebs and I found that only 15 percent of students showing some principled thinking cheated as compared to 55 percent of conventional subjects and 70 percent of preconventional subjects.[8] Nevertheless, 15 percent of the principled subjects did cheat, suggesting that factors additional to moral judgment are necessary for principled moral reasoning to be translated into "moral action." Partly, these factors include the situation and its pressures. Partly, what happens depends upon the individual's motives and emotions. Partly, what the individual does depends upon a general sense of will, purpose, or "ego strength." As an example of the role of will or ego strength in moral behavior, we may cite the study by Krebs: Slightly more than half of his conventional subjects cheated. These subjects were also divided by a measure of attention/will. Only 26 percent of the "strong-willed" conventional subjects cheated; however, 74 percent of the "weak-willed" subjects cheated.

If maturity of moral reasoning is only one factor in moral behavior, why does the cognitive-developmental approach to moral education focus so heavily upon moral reasoning? For the following reasons:

1. Moral judgment, while only one factor in moral behavior, is the single most important or influential factor yet discovered in moral behavior.
2. While other factors influence moral behavior, moral judgment is the only distinctively *moral* factor in moral behavior. To illustrate, we noted that the Krebs study indicated that "strong-willed" conventional stage subjects resisted cheating more than "weak-willed" subjects. For those at a preconventional level of moral reasoning, however, "will" had an opposite effect. "Strong-willed" Stages 1 and 2 subjects cheated more, not less, than "weak-willed" subjects, i.e., they had the "courage of their (amoral) convictions" that it was worthwhile to cheat. "Will," then, is an important factor in moral behavior, but it is not distinctively moral; it becomes moral only when informed by mature moral judgment.
3. Moral judgment change is long-range or irreversible; a higher stage is never lost. Moral behavior as such is largely situational and reversible or "losable" in new situations.

II. AIMS OF MORAL AND CIVIC EDUCATION

Moral psychology describes what moral development is, as studied empirically. Moral education must also consider moral philosophy, which strives to tell us what moral development ideally *ought to be*. Psychology finds an invariant sequence of moral stages; moral philosophy must be invoked to answer whether a later stage is a better stage. The "stage" of senescence and death follows the "stage" of adulthood, but that does not mean that senescence and death are better. Our claim that the latest or principled stages of moral reasoning are morally better stages, then, must rest on considerations of moral philosophy.

The tradition of moral philosophy to which we appeal is the liberal or rational tradition, in particular the "formalistic" or "deontological" tradition running from Immanuel Kant to John Rawls.[9] Central to this tradition is the claim that an adequate morality is *principled*, i.e., that it makes judgments in terms of *universal* principles applicable to all mankind. *Principles* are to be distinguished from *rules*. Conventional morality is grounded on rules, primarily "thou shalt nots" such as are represented by the Ten Commandments, prescriptions of kinds of actions. Principles are, rather, universal guides to making a moral decision. An example is Kant's "categorical imperative," formulated in two ways. The first is the maxim of respect for human personality "Act always toward the other as an end, not as a means." The second is the maxim of universalization, "Choose only as you would be willing to have everyone choose in your situation." Principles like that of Kant's state the formal conditions of a moral choice or action. In the dilemma in which a woman is dying because a druggist refuses to release his drug for less than the stated price, the druggist is not acting morally, though he is not violating the ordinary moral rules (he is not actually stealing or murdering). But he is violating principles: He is treating the woman simply as a means to his ends of profit, and he is not choosing as he would wish anyone to choose (if the druggist were in the dying woman's place, he would not want a druggist to choose as he is choosing). Under most circumstances, choice in terms of conventional moral rules and choice in terms of principles coincide. Ordinarily, principles dictate not stealing (avoiding stealing is implied by acting in terms of a regard for others as ends and in terms of what one would want everyone to do). In a situation where stealing is the only means to save a life, however, principles contradict the ordinary rules and would dictate stealing. Unlike rules which are supported by social authority, principles are freely chosen by the individual because of their intrinsic moral validity.[10]

The conception that a moral choice is a choice made in terms of moral principles is related to the claim of liberal moral philosophy that moral principles are ultimately principles of justice. In essence, moral conflicts are conflicts between the claims of persons, and principles for resolving these claims are principles of justice, "for giving each his due." Central to justice are the demands of *liberty, equality,* and *reciprocity.* At every moral stage, there is a concern for justice. The most damning statement a school child can make about a teacher is that "he's not fair." At each higher stage, however, the conception of justice is reorganized. At Stage 1, justice is punishing the bad in terms of "an eye for an eye and a tooth for a tooth." At Stage 2, it is exchanging favors and goods in an equal manner. At Stages 3 and 4, it is treating people as they desire in terms of the conventional rules. At Stage 5, it is recognized that all rules and laws flow from justice, from a social contract between the governors and the governed designed to protect the equal rights of all. At Stage 6, personally chosen moral principles are also principles of justice, the principles any member of a society would choose for that society if he did not know what his position was to be in the society and in which he might be the least advantaged.[11] Principles chosen from this point of view are, first, the maximum liberty compatible with the like liberty of others and, second, no inequalities of goods and respect which are not to the benefit of all, including the least advantaged.

As an example of stage progression in the orientation to justice, we may take judgments about capital punishment.[12] Capital punishment is only firmly rejected at the two principled stages, when the notion of justice as vengeance or retribution is abandoned. At the sixth stage, capital punishment is not condoned even if it may have some useful deterrent effect in promoting law and order. This is because it is not a punishment we would choose for a society if we assumed we had as much chance of being born into the position of a criminal or murderer as being born into the position of a law abider.

Why are decisions based on universal principles of justice better decisions? Because they are decisions on which all moral men could agree. When decisions are based on conventional moral rules, men will disagree, since they adhere to conflicting systems of rules dependent on culture and social position. Throughout history men have killed one another in the name of conflicting moral rules and values, most recently in Vietnam and the Middle East. Truly moral or just resolutions of conflicts require principles which are, or can be, universalizable.

Alternative Approaches

We have given a philosophic rationale for stage advance as the aim of moral education. Given this rationale, the developmental approach to moral education can avoid the problems inherent in the other two major approaches to moral education. The first alternative approach is that of indoctrinative moral education, the preaching and imposition of the rules and values of the teacher and his culture on the child. In America, when this indoctrinative approach has been developed in a systematic manner, it has usually been termed "character education."

Moral values, in the character education approach, are preached or taught in terms of what may be called the "bag of virtues." In the classic studies of character by Hugh Hartshorne and Mark May, the virtues chosen were honesty, services and self-control.[13] It is easy to get superficial consensus on such a bag of virtues—until one examines in detail the list of virtues involved and the details of their definition. Is the Hartshorne and May bag more adequate than the Boy Scout bag (a Scout should be honest, loyal, reverent, clean, brave, etc.)? When one turns to the details of defining each virtue, one finds equal uncertainty or difficulty in reaching consensus. Does honesty mean one should not steal to save a life? Does it mean that a student should not help another student with his homework?

Character education and other forms of indoctrinative moral education have aimed at teaching universal values (it is assumed that honesty or service is a desirable trait for all men in all societies), but the detailed definitions used are relative; they are defined by the opinions of the teacher and the conventional culture and rest on the authority of the teacher for their justification. In this sense character education is close to the unreflective valuings by teachers which constitute the hidden curriculum of the school.[14] Because of the current unpopularity of indoctrinative approaches to moral education, a family of approaches called "values clarification" has become appealing to teachers. Values clarification takes the first step implied by a rational approach to moral education: the eliciting of the child's own judgment or opinion about issues or situations in which values conflict, rather than imposing the teacher's opinion on him. Values clarification, however, does not attempt to go further than eliciting awareness of values; it is assumed that becoming more self-aware about one's values is an end in itself. Fundamentally, the definition of the end of values education as self-awareness derives from a belief in ethical relativity held by many value-clarifiers. As stated by Peter Engel, "One must contrast value clarification and value inculcation. Value clarification implies the principle that in the consideration of values there is no single correct answer." Within these premises of "no correct answer," children are to discuss moral dilemmas in such a way as to reveal different values and discuss their value differences with each other. The teacher is to stress that "our values are different," not that one value is more adequate than others. If this program is systematically followed, students will themselves become relativists, believing there is no "right" moral answer. For instance, a student caught cheating might argue that he did nothing wrong, since his own

hierarchy of values, which may be different from that of the teacher, made it right for him to cheat.

Like values clarification, the cognitive-developmental approach to moral education stresses open or Socratic peer discussion of value dilemmas. Such discussion, however, has an aim: stimulation of movement to the next stage of moral reasoning. Like values clarification, the developmental approach opposes indoctrination. Stimulation of movement to the next stage of reasoning is not indoctrinative, for the following reasons:

1. Change is in the way of reasoning rather than in the particular beliefs involved.
2. Students in a class are at different stages; the aim is to aid movement of each to the next stage, not convergence on a common pattern.
3. The teacher's own opinion is neither stressed nor invoked as authoritative. It enters in only as one of many opinions, hopefully one of those at a next higher stage.
4. The notion that some judgments are more adequate than others is communicated. Fundamentally, however, this means that the student is encouraged to articulate a position which seems most adequate to him and to judge the adequacy of the reasoning of others.

In addition to having more definite aims than values clarification, the moral development approach restricts value education to that which is moral or, more specifically, to justice. This is for two reasons. First, it is not clear that the whole realm of personal, political, and religious values is a realm which is nonrelative, i.e., in which there are universals and a direction of development. Second, it is not clear that the public school has a right or mandate to develop values in general.[15] In our view, value education in the public schools should be restricted to that which the school has the right and mandate to develop: an awareness of justice, or of the rights of others in our Constitutional system. While the Bill of Rights prohibits the teaching of religious beliefs, or of specific value systems, it does not prohibit the teaching of the awareness of rights and principles of justice fundamental to the Constitution itself.

When moral education is recognized as centered in justice and differentiated from value education or affective education, it becomes apparent that moral and civic education are much the same thing. This equation, taken for granted by the classic philosophers of education from Plato and Aristotle to Dewey, is basic to our claim that a concern for moral education is central to the educational objectives of social studies.

The term *civic education* is used to refer to social studies as more than the study of the facts and concepts of social science, history, and civics. It is education for the analytic understanding, value principles, and motivation necessary for a citizen in a democracy if democracy is to be an effective process. It is political education. Civic or political education means the stimulation of development of more advanced patterns of reasoning about political and social decisions and their implementation directly derivative of broader patterns of moral reasoning. Our studies show that reasoning and decision making about political decisions are directly derivative of broader patterns of moral reasoning and decision making. We have interviewed high school and college students about concrete political situations involving laws to govern open housing, civil disobedience for peace in Vietnam, free press rights to publish what might disturb national order, and distribution of income through taxation. We find that reasoning on these political decisions can be classified according to moral stage and that an individual's stage on political dilemmas is at the same level as on nonpolitical moral dilemmas (euthanasia, violating authority to maintain trust in a family, stealing a drug to save one's dying wife). Turning from reasoning to action, similar findings are obtained. In 1963 a study was made of those who sat in at the University of California, Berkeley, administration building and those who did not in the Free Speech Movement crisis. Of those at Stage 6, 80 percent sat in, believing that principles of free speech were being compromised, and that all efforts to compromise and negotiate with the administration had failed. In contrast, only 15 percent of the conventional (Stage 3 or Stage 4)

subjects sat in. (Stage 5 subjects were in between.)[16]

From a psychological side, then, political development is part of moral development. The same is true from the philosophic side. In the *Republic,* Plato sees political education as part of a broader education for moral justice and finds a rationale for such education in terms of universal philosophic principles rather than the demands of a particular society. More recently, Dewey claims the same.

In historical perspective, America was the first nation whose government was publicly founded on postconventional principles of justice, rather than upon the authority central to conventional moral reasoning. At the time of our founding, postconventional or principled moral and political reasoning was the possession of the minority, as it still is. Today, as in the time of our founding, the majority of our adults are at the conventional level, particularly the "law and order" (fourth) moral stage. (Every few years the Gallup Poll circulates the Bill of Rights unidentified, and every year it is turned down.) The Founding Fathers intuitively understood this without benefit of our elaborate social science research; they constructed a document designing a government which would maintain principles of justice and the rights of man even though principled men were not the men in power. The machinery included checks and balances, the independent judiciary, and freedom of the press. Most recently, this machinery found its use at Watergate. The tragedy of Richard Nixon, as Harry Truman said long ago, was that he never understood the Constitution (a Stage 5 document), but the Constitution understood Richard Nixon.[17]

Watergate, then, is not some sign of moral decay of the nation, but rather of the fact that understanding and action in support of justice principles are still the possession of a minority of our society. Insofar as there is moral decay, it represents the weakening of conventional morality in the face of social and value conflict today. This can lead the less fortunate adolescent to fixation at the preconventional level, the more fortunate to movement to principles. We find a larger proportion of youths at the principled level today than was the case in their fathers' day, but also a larger proportion at the preconventional level.

Given this state, moral and civic education in the schools becomes a more urgent task. In the high school today, one often hears both preconventional adolescents and those beginning to move beyond convention sounding the same note of disaffection for the school. While our political institutions are in principle Stage 5 (i.e., vehicles for maintaining universal rights through the democratic process), our schools have traditionally been Stage 4 institutions of convention and authority. Today more than ever, democratic schools systematically engaged in civic education are required.

Our approach to moral and civic education relates the study of law and government to the actual creation of a democratic school in which moral dilemmas are discussed and resolved in a manner which will stimulate moral development.

Planned Moral Education

For many years, moral development was held by psychologists to be primarily a result of family upbringing and family conditions. In particular, conditions of affection and authority in the home were believed to be critical, some balance of warmth and firmness being optimal for moral development. This view arises if morality is conceived as an internalization of the arbitrary rules of parents and culture, since such acceptance must be based on affection and respect for parents as authorities rather than on the rational nature of the rules involved.

Studies of family correlates of moral stage development do not support this internalization view of the conditions for moral development. Instead, they suggest that the conditions for moral development in homes and schools are similar and that the conditions are consistent with cognitive-developmental theory. In the cognitive-developmental view, morality is a natural product of a universal human tendency toward empathy or role taking, toward putting oneself in the shoes of other conscious beings. It is also a product of a universal human concern for justice, for reciprocity or equality in the relation of one person to another. As an example, when my son was four, he became a morally principled vegetarian and refused to eat meat, resisting all parental persuasion to increase his protein intake. His reason was, "It's bad to kill animals." His moral commitment to vegetarianism was not taught or acquired from parental authority; it was the result of the universal tendency of the young self to project its consciousness and values into other living things, other selves. My son's vegetarianism also involved a sense of justice, revealed when I read him a book about Eskimos in which a seal hunting expedition was described. His response was to say, "Daddy, there is one kind of meat I would eat—Eskimo meat. It's all right to eat Eskimos because they eat animals." This natural sense of justice or reciprocity was Stage 1—an eye for an eye, a tooth for a tooth. My son's sense of the value of life was also Stage 1 and involved no differentiation between human personality and physical life. His morality, though Stage 1, was, however, natural and internal. Moral development past Stage 1, then, is not an internalization but the reconstruction of role taking and conceptions of justice toward greater adequacy. These reconstructions occur in order to achieve a better match between the child's own moral structures and the structures of the social and moral situations he confronts. We divide these conditions of match into two kinds: those dealing with moral discussions and communication and those dealing with the total moral environment or atmosphere in which the child lives.

In terms of moral discussion, the important conditions appear to be:

1. Exposure to the next higher stage of reasoning
2. Exposure to situations posing problems and contradictions for the child's current moral structure, leading to dissatisfaction with his current level
3. An atmosphere of interchange and dialogue combining the first two conditions, in which

conflicting moral views are compared in an open manner.

Studies of families in India and America suggest that morally advanced children have parents at higher stages. Parents expose children to the next higher stage, raising moral issues and engaging in open dialogue or interchange about such issues.[18]

Drawing on this notion of the discussion conditions stimulating advance, Moshe Blatt conducted classroom discussions of conflict-laden hypothetical moral dilemmas with four classes of junior high and high school students for a semester.[19] In each of these classes, students were to be found at three stages. Since the children were not all responding at the same stage, the arguments they used with each other were at different levels. In the course of these discussions among the students, the teacher first supported and clarified those arguments that were one stage above the lowest stage among the children; for example, the teacher supported Stage 3 rather than Stage 2. When it seemed that these arguments were understood by the students, the teacher then challenged that stage, using new situations, and clarified the arguments one stage above the previous one: Stage 4 rather than Stage 3. At the end of the semester, all the students were retested; they showed significant upward change when compared to the controls, and they maintained the change one year later. In the experimental classrooms, from one-fourth to one-half of the students moved up a stage, while there was essentially no change during the course of the experiment in the control group.

Given the Blatt studies showing that moral discussion could raise moral stage, we undertook the next step: to see if teachers could conduct moral discussions in the course of teaching high school social studies with the same results. This step we took in cooperation with Edwin Fenton, who introduced moral dilemmas in his ninth- and eleventh-grade social studies texts. Twenty-four teachers in the Boston and Pittsburgh areas were given some instruction in conducting moral discussions around the dilemmas in the text. About

half of the teachers stimulated significant developmental change in their classrooms—upward stage movement of one-quarter to one-half a stage. In control classes using the text but no moral dilemma discussions, the same teachers failed to stimulate any moral change in the students. Moral discussion, then, can be a usable and effective part of the curriculum at any grade level. Working with filmstrip dilemmas produced in cooperation with Guidance Association, second-grade teachers conducted moral discussions yielding a similar amount of moral stage movement.

Moral discussion and curriculum, however, constitute only one portion of the conditions stimulating moral growth. When we turn to analyzing the broader life environment, we turn to a consideration of the *moral atmosphere* of the home, the school, and the broader society. The first basic dimension of social atmosphere is the role-taking opportunities it provides, the extent to which it encourages the child to take the point of view of others. Role taking is related to the amount of social interaction and social communication in which the child engages, as well as to his sense of efficacy in influencing attitudes of others. The second dimension of social atmosphere, more strictly moral, is the level of justice of the environment or institution. The justice structure of an institution refers to the perceived rules or principles for distributing rewards, punishments, responsibilities, and privileges among institutional members. This structure may exist or be perceived at any of our moral stages. As an example, a study of a traditional prison revealed that inmates perceived it as Stage 1, regardless of their own level.[20] Obedience to arbitrary command by power figures and punishment for disobedience were seen as the governing justice norms of the prison. A behavior-modification prison using point rewards for conformity was perceived as a Stage 2 system of instrumental exchange. Inmates at Stage 3 or 4 perceived this institution as more fair than the traditional prison, but not as fair in their own terms.

These and other studies suggest that a higher level of institutional justice is a condition for individual development of a higher sense of justice. Working on these premises, Joseph Hickey, Peter Scharf, and I worked with guards and inmates in a women's prison to create a more just community.[21] A social contract was set up in which guards and inmates each had a vote of one and in which rules were made and conflicts resolved through discussions of fairness and a democratic vote in a community meeting. The program has been operating four years and has stimulated moral stage advance in inmates, though it is still too early to draw conclusions as to its overall long-range effectiveness for rehabilitation.

One year ago, Fenton, Ralph Mosher, and I received a grant from the Danforth Foundation (with additional support from the Kennedy Foundation) to make moral education a living matter in two high schools in the Boston area (Cambridge and Brookline) and two in Pittsburgh. The plan had two components. The first was training counselors and social studies and English teachers in conducting moral discussions and making moral discussion an integral part of the curriculum. The second was establishing a just community school within a public high school.

We have stated the theory of the just community high school, postulating that discussing real-life moral situations and actions as issues of fairness and as matters for democratic decision would stimulate advance in both moral reasoning and moral action. A participatory democracy provides more extensive opportunities for role taking and a higher level of perceived institutional justice than does any other social arrangement. Most alternative schools strive to establish a democratic governance, but none we have observed has achieved a vital or viable participatory democracy. Our theory suggested reasons why we might succeed where others failed. First, we felt that democracy had to be a central commitment of a school, rather than a humanitarian frill. Democracy as moral education provides that commitment. Second, democracy in alternative schools often fails because it bores the students. Students prefer to let teachers make decisions about staff,

courses, and schedules, rather than to attend lengthy, complicated meetings. Our theory said that the issues a democracy should focus on are issues of morality and fairness. Real issues concerning drugs, stealing, disruptions, and grading are never boring if handled as issues of fairness. Third, our theory told us that if large democratic community meetings were preceded by small-group moral discussion, higher-stage thinking by students would win out in later decisions, avoiding the disasters of mob rule.[22]

Currently, we can report that the school based on our theory makes democracy work or function where other schools have failed. It is too early to make any claims for its effectiveness in causing moral development, however.

Our Cambridge just community school within the public high school was started after a small summer planning session of volunteer teachers, students, and parents. At the time the school opened in the fall, only a commitment to democracy and a skeleton program of English and social studies had been decided on. The school started with six teachers from the regular school and sixty students, twenty from academic professional homes and twenty from working-class homes. The other twenty were dropouts and troublemakers or petty delinquents in terms of previous record. The usual mistakes and usual chaos of a beginning alternative school ensued. Within a few weeks, however, a successful democratic community process had been established. Rules were made around pressing issues: disturbances, drugs, hooking. A student discipline committee or jury was formed. The resulting rules and enforcement have been relatively effective and reasonable. We do not see reasonable rules as ends in themselves, however, but as vehicles for moral discussion and an emerging sense of community. This sense of community and a resulting morale are perhaps the most immediate signs of success. This sense of community seems to lead to behavior change of a positive sort. An example is a fifteen-year-old student who started as one of the greatest combinations of humor, aggression, light-fingeredness, and hyperactivity I have ever known. From being the principal disturber of all community meetings, he has become an excellent community meeting participant and occasional chairman. He is still more ready to enforce rules for others than to observe them himself, yet his commitment to the school has led to a steady decrease in exotic behavior. In addition, he has become more involved in classes and projects and has begun to listen and ask questions in order to pursue a line of interest.

We attribute such behavior change not only to peer pressure and moral discussion but to the sense of community which has emerged from the democratic process in which angry conflicts are resolved through fairness and community decision. This sense of community is reflected in statements of the students to us that there are no cliques—that the blacks and the whites, the professors' sons and the project students, are friends. These statements are supported by observation. Such a sense of community is needed where students in a given classroom range in reading level from fifth-grade to college.

Fenton, Mosher, the Cambridge and Brookline teachers, and I are now planning a four-year curriculum in English and social studies centering on moral discussion, on role taking and communication, and on relating the government, laws, and justice system of the school to that of the American society and other world societies. This will integrate an intellectual curriculum for a higher level of understanding of society with the experiential components of school democracy and moral decision.

There is very little new in this—or in anything else we are doing. Dewey wanted democratic experimental schools for moral and intellectual development seventy years ago. Perhaps Dewey's time has come.

NOTES

1. John Dewey, "What Psychology Can Do for the Teacher," in Reginald Archambault, ed., *John Dewey on Education: Selected Writings* (New York: Random House, 1964).

2. These levels correspond roughly to our three major levels: the preconventional, the conventional, and the principled. Similar levels were propounded by William McDougall, Leonard Hobhouse, and James Mark Baldwin.

3. Jean Piaget, *The Moral Judgment of the Child*, 2nd ed. (Glencoe, Ill.: Free Press, 1948).

4. Piaget's stages correspond to our first three stages: Stage 0 (premoral), Stage 1 (heteronomous), and Stage 2 (instrumental reciprocity).

5. Lawrence Kohlberg, "Moral Stages and Moralization: The Cognitive-Developmental Approach," in Thomas Lickona, ed., *Man, Morality, and Society* (New York: Holt, Rinehart and Winston, in press).

6. James Rest, Elliott Turiel, and Lawrence Kohlberg, "Relations Between Level of Moral Judgment and Preference and Comprehension of the Moral Judgment of Others," *Journal of Personality*, vol. 37, 1969, pp. 225–52, and James Rest, "Comprehension, Preference, and Spontaneous Usage in Moral Judgment," in Lawrence Kohlberg, ed., *Recent Research in Moral Development* (New York: Holt, Rinehart and Winston, in preparation).

7. Many adolescents and adults only partially attain the stage of formal operations. They do consider all the actual relations of one thing to another at the same time, but they do not consider all possibilities and form abstract hypotheses. A few do not advance this far, remaining "concrete operational."

8. Richard Krebs and Lawrence Kohlberg, "Moral Judgment and Ego Controls as Determinants of Resistance to Cheating," in Lawrence Kohlberg, ed., *Recent Research*.

9. John Rawls, *A Theory of Justice* (Cambridge, Mass.: Harvard University Press, 1971).

10. Not all freely chosen values or rules are principles, however. Hitler chose the "rule," "exterminate the enemies of the Aryan race," but such a rule is not a universalizable principle.

11. Rawls, *A Theory of Justice*.

12. Lawrence Kohlberg and Donald Elfenbein, "Development of Moral Reasoning and Attitudes Toward Capital Punishment," *American Journal of Orthopsychiatry*, Summer, 1975.

13. Hugh Hartshorne and Mark May, *Studies in the Nature of Character: Studies in Deceit*, vol. 1; *Studies in Service and Self-Control*, vol. 2; *Studies*

in Organization of Character, vol. 3 (New York: Macmillan, 1928–30).

14. As an example of the "hidden curriculum," we may cite a second-grade classroom. My son came home from this classroom one day saying he did not want to be "one of the bad boys." Asked "Who are the bad boys?" he replied, "The ones who don't put their books back and get yelled at."

15. Restriction of deliberate value education to the moral may be clarified by our example of the second-grade teacher who made tidying up of books a matter of moral indoctrination. Tidiness is a value, but it is not a moral value. Cheating is a moral issue, intrinsically one of fairness. It involves issues of violation of trust and taking advantage. Failing to tidy the room may under certain conditions be an issue of fairness, when it puts an undue burden on others. If it is handled by the teacher as a matter of cooperation among the group in this sense, it is a legitimate focus of deliberate moral education. If it is not, it simply represents the arbitrary imposition of the teacher's values on the child.

16. The differential action of the principled subjects was determined by two things. First, they were more likely to judge it right to violate authority by sitting in. But second, they were also in general more consistent in engaging in political action according to their judgment. Ninety percent of all Stage 6 subjects thought it right to sit in, and all 90 percent lived up to this belief. Among the Stage 4 subjects, 45 percent thought it right to sit in, but only 33 percent lived up to this belief by acting.

17. No public or private word or deed of Nixon ever rose above Stage 4, the "law and order" stage. His last comments in the White House were of wonderment that the Republican Congress could turn on him after so many Stage 2 exchanges of favors in getting them elected.

18. Bindu Parilch, "A Cross-Cultural Study of Parent-Child Moral Judgment," unpublished doctoral dissertation, Harvard University, 1975.

19. Moshe Blatt and Lawrence Kohlberg, "Effects of Classroom Discussions upon Children's Level of Moral Judgment," in Lawrence Kohlberg, ed., *Recent Research.*

20. Lawrence Kohlberg, Peter Scharf, and Joseph Hickey, "The Justice Structure of the Prison: A Theory and an Intervention," *The Prison Journal,* Autumn-Winter, 1972.

21. Lawrence Kohlberg, Kelsey Kauffman, Peter Scharf, and Joseph Hickey, *The Just Community Approach to Corrections: A Manual, Part I* (Cambridge, Mass.: Education Research Foundation, 1973).

22. An example of the need for small-group discussion comes from an alternative school community meeting called because a pair of the students had stolen the school's video-recorder. The resulting majority decision was that the school should buy back the recorder from the culprits through a fence. The teachers could not accept this decision and returned to a more authoritative approach. I believe if the moral reasoning of students urging this solution had been confronted by students at a higher stage, a different decision would have emerged.

Lawrence Kohlberg was professor of education and psychology and director of the Center for Moral Education, Graduate School of Education, Harvard University.

QUESTIONS FOR REFLECTION

1. Are there universal moral values that educators, parents, and community members—regardless of philosophical, political, or religious beliefs—would include in the school curriculum? What are these values?

2. What does Kohlberg mean when he makes a distinction between the *structures* of moral judgment and the *content* of moral judgment? Give an example of a moral dilemma to illustrate this point.

3. What is the relationship between moral *judgment* and moral *action*? What factors determine whether an individual's moral judgment will be translated into moral action?

Woman's Place in Man's Life Cycle

CAROL GILLIGAN

ABSTRACT: Arguing that Kohlberg's model of moral reasoning is based on a male perspective and addresses the rights of the individual, Gilligan suggests that moral reasoning from a female perspective stresses the individual's responsibility to other people. Life-cycle theories, she concludes, should encompass the experiences of both sexes.

. . . Relationships, and particularly issues of dependency, are experienced differently by women and men. For boys and men, separation and individuation are critically tied to gender identity since separation from the mother is essential for the development of masculinity. For girls and women, issues of femininity or feminine identity do not depend on the achievement of separation from the mother or on the progress of individuation. Since masculinity is defined through separation while femininity is defined through attachment, male gender identity is threatened by intimacy while female gender identity is threatened by separation. Thus males tend to have difficulty with relationships, while females tend to have problems with individuation. The quality of embeddedness in social interaction and personal relationships that characterizes women's lives in contrast to men's, however, becomes not only a descriptive difference but also a developmental liability when the milestones of childhood and adolescent development in the psychological literature are markers of increasing separation. Women's failure to separate then becomes by definition a failure to develop.

When one begins with the study of women and derives developmental constructs from their lives, the outline of a moral conception different from that described by Freud, Piaget, or Kohlberg begins to emerge and informs a different description of development. In this conception, the moral problem arises from conflicting responsibilities rather than from competing rights and requires for its resolution a mode of thinking that is contextual and narrative rather than formal and abstract. This conception of morality as concerned with the activity of care centers moral development around the understanding of responsibility and relationships, just as the conception of morality as fairness ties moral development to the understanding of rights and rules.

This different construction of the moral problem by women may be seen as the critical reason for their failure to develop within the constraints of Kohlberg's system. Regarding all constructions of responsibility as evidence of a conventional moral understanding, Kohlberg defines the highest stages of moral development as deriving from a reflective understanding of human rights. That the morality of rights differs from the morality of responsibility in its emphasis on separation rather than connection, in its consideration of the individual rather than the relationship as primary, is illustrated by two responses to interview questions about the nature of morality. The first comes from a twenty-five-year-old man, one of the participants in Kohlberg's study:

[*What does the word morality mean to you?*] Nobody in the world knows the answer. I think it is recognizing the right of the individual, the rights of other individuals, not interfering with those rights. Act as fairly as you would have them treat you. I think it is basically to preserve the human being's right to existence. I think that is the most important. Secondly, the human being's right to do as he pleases, again without interfering with somebody else's rights.

[*How have your views on morality changed since the last interview?*] I think I am more aware of an individual's rights now. I used to be looking at it strictly from my point of view, just for me. Now I think I am more aware of what the individual has a right to.

Kohlberg (1973) cites this man's response as illustrative of the principled conception of human rights that exemplifies his fifth and sixth stages. Commenting on the response, Kohlberg says: "Moving to a perspective outside of that of his society, he identifies morality with justice (fairness, rights, the Golden Rule), with recognition of the rights of others as these are defined naturally or intrinsically. The human being's right to do as he pleases without interfering with somebody else's rights is a formula defining rights prior to social legislation" (pp. 29–30).

The second response comes from a woman who participated in the rights and responsibilities study. She also was twenty-five and, at the time, a third-year law student:

[*Is there really some correct solution to moral problems, or is everybody's opinion equally right?*] No, I don't think everybody's opinion is equally right. I think that in some situations there may be opinions that are equally valid, and one could conscientiously adopt one of several courses of action. But there are other situations in which I think there are right and wrong answers, that sort of inhere in the nature of existence, of all individuals here who need to live with each other to live. We need to depend on each other, and hopefully it is not only a physical need but a need of fulfillment in ourselves, that a person's life is enriched by cooperating with other people and striving to live in harmony with everybody else, and to that end, there are right and wrong, there are things which promote that end and that move away from it, and in that way it is possible to choose in certain cases among different courses of action that obviously promote or harm that goal.

[*Is there a time in the past when you would have thought about these things differently?*] Oh, yeah, I think that I went through a time when I thought that things were pretty relative, that I can't tell you what to do and you can't tell me what to do, because you've got your conscience and I've got mine.

[*When was that?*] When I was in high school. I guess that it just sort of dawned on me that my own ideas changed, and because my own judgment changed, I felt I couldn't judge another person's judgment. But now I think even when it is only the person himself who is going to be affected I say it is wrong to the extent it doesn't cohere with what I know about human nature and what I know about you, and just from what I think is true about the operation of the universe, I could say I think you are making a mistake.

[*What led you to change, do you think?*] Just seeing more of life, just recognizing that there are an awful lot of things that are common among people. There are certain things that you come to learn promote a better life and better relationships and more personal fulfillment than other things that in general tend to do the opposite, and the things that promote these things, you would call morally right.

This response also represents a personal reconstruction of morality following a period of questioning and doubt, but the reconstruction of moral understanding is based not on the primacy and universality of individual rights, but rather on what she describes as a "very strong sense of being responsible to the world." Within this construction, the moral dilemma changes from how to exercise one's rights without interfering with the rights of others to how "to lead a moral life which includes obligations to myself and my family and people in general." The problem then becomes one of limiting responsibilities without abandoning moral concern. When asked to describe herself, this woman says that she values "having other people that I am tied to, and also having people that I am responsible to. I have a very strong sense of being responsible to the world, that I can't just live for my enjoyment, but just the fact of being in the world gives me an obligation to do what I can to make the world a better place to live in, no matter how small a scale that may be on." Thus while Kohlberg's subject worries about people interfering with each other's rights, this woman worries about "the possibility of omission, of your not helping others when you could help them."

The issue that this woman raises is addressed by Jane Loevinger's fifth "autonomous" stage of ego development, where autonomy, placed in a context of relationships, is defined as modulating an excessive sense of responsibility through the recognition that other people have responsibility for their own destiny. The autonomous stage in Loevinger's account (1970) witnesses a relinquishing of moral dichotomies and their replacement with "a feeling for the complexity and multifaceted character of real people and real situations" (p. 6). Whereas the rights conception of morality that informs Kohlberg's principled level (stages five and six) is geared to arriving at an objectively fair or just resolution to moral dilemmas upon which all rational persons could agree, the responsibility conception focuses instead on the limitations of any particular resolution and describes the conflicts that remain.

Thus it becomes clear why a morality of rights and noninterference may appear frightening to women in its potential justification of indifference and unconcern. At the same time, it becomes clear why, from a male perspective, a morality of responsibility appears inconclusive and diffuse, given its insistent contextual relativism. Women's moral judgments thus elucidate the pattern observed in the description of the developmental differences between the sexes, but they also provide an alternative conception of maturity by which these differences can be assessed and their implications traced. The psychology of women that has consistently been described as distinctive in its greater orientation toward relationships and interdependence implies a more contextual mode of judgment and a different moral understanding. Given the differences in women's conceptions of self and morality, women bring to the life cycle a different point of view and order human experience in terms of different priorities.

The myth of Demeter and Persephone, which McClelland (1975) cites as exemplifying the feminine attitude toward power, was associated with the Eleusinian Mysteries celebrated in ancient Greece for over two thousand years. As told in the Homeric *Hymn to Demeter,* the story of Persephone indicates the strengths of interdependence, building up resources and giving, that McClelland found in his research on power

motivation to characterize the mature feminine style. Although, McClelland says, "it is fashionable to conclude that no one knows what went on in the Mysteries, it is known that they were probably the most important religious ceremonies, even partly on the historical record, which were organized by and for women, especially at the onset before men by means of the cult of Dionysos began to take them over." Thus McClelland regards the myth as "a special presentation of feminine psychology" (p. 96). It is, as well, a life-cycle story par excellence.

Persephone, the daughter of Demeter, while playing in a meadow with her girlfriends, sees a beautiful narcissus which she runs to pick. As she does so, the earth opens and she is snatched away by Hades, who takes her to his underworld kingdom. Demeter, goddess of the earth, so mourns the loss of her daughter that she refuses to allow anything to grow. The crops that sustain life on earth shrivel up, killing men and animals alike, until Zeus takes pity on man's suffering and persuades his brother to return Persephone to her mother. But before she leaves, Persephone eats some pomegranate seeds, which ensures that she will spend part of every year with Hades in the underworld.

The elusive mystery of women's development lies in its recognition of the continuing importance of attachment in the human life cycle. Woman's place in man's life cycle is to protect this recognition while the developmental litany intones the celebration of separation, autonomy, individuation, and natural rights. The myth of Persephone speaks directly to the distortion in this view by reminding us that narcissism leads to death, that the fertility of the earth is in some mysterious way tied to the continuation of the mother-daughter relationship, and that the life cycle itself arises from an alternation between the world of women and that of men. Only when life-cycle theorists divide their attention and begin to live with women as they have lived with men will their vision encompass the experience of both sexes and their theories become correspondingly more fertile.

REFERENCES

Kohlberg, L. (1973). "Continuities and Discontinuities in Childhood and Adult Moral Development Revisited." In *Collected Papers on Moral Development and Moral Education*. Moral Education Research Foundation, Harvard University.

Lovinger, J., and Wessler, R. (1970). *Measuring Ego Development*. San Francisco: Jossey-Bass.

McClelland, D. C. (1975). *Power: The Inner Experience*. New York: Irvington.

Carol Gilligan is professor at New York University and professor in the Human Development and Psychology Program at the Graduate School of Education, Harvard University.

QUESTIONS FOR REFLECTION

1. What does the word *morality* mean to you? With whose view of morality is your answer most congruent—Kohlberg's or Gilligan's?
2. Do you agree with Gilligan's statement that "masculinity is defined through separation while femininity is defined through attachment, [and] male gender identity is threatened by intimacy while female gender identity is threatened by separation"? According to Gilligan, how are these gender differences reflected in moral reasoning?
3. What are the implications for the curriculum of Gilligan's view of male and female moral reasoning?

The Biology of Risk Taking

LISA F. PRICE

ABSTRACT: *Price writes that educators can look to new findings in the fields of neuroscience and developmental psychology for help in guiding adolescents into healthy adulthood. She explains the reasons that many adolescents engage in risk taking behavior and discusses risk taking in relationship to hormonal changes and the stages and ages of puberty. Teenagers generally thrive in reasonable, supportive environments that have a predictive, enforced structure. Price recommends educators provide adolescents with vital supports and reduce risk with firm structure.*

I celebrate myself,
And what I assume you shall assume,
For every atom belonging to me as good
  belongs to you.

                    —Walt Whitman, *Leaves of Grass*

Adolescence is a time of excitement, growth, and change. Whitman's words capture the enthusiasm and passion with which teenagers approach the world. Sometimes adolescents direct this passion toward a positive goal, such as a creative essay, an art project, after-school sports, or a healthy romance. At other times, they divert their passions to problematic activities, such as drug experimentation, reckless driving, shoplifting, fights, or school truancy.

Why do adolescents take risks? Why are teens so passionate? Are adolescents just young adults, or are they fundamentally different? Advances in developmental psychology and neuroscience have provided us with some answers. We now understand that adolescent turmoil, which we used to view as an expression of raging hormones, is actually the result of a complex interplay of body chemistry, brain development, and cognitive growth (Buchanan, Eccles, & Becker, 1992). Moreover, the changes that teenagers experience occur in the context of multiple systems—such as individual relationships, family, school, and community—that support and influence change.

Educators are in a pivotal position to promote healthy adolescent growth. Understanding the biological changes that adolescents undergo and the behaviors that result can provide the foundation for realistic expectations and effective interventions.

THE IMPACT OF PUBERTY

The hormonal changes of adolescence are often considered synonymous with puberty. The word *puberty* comes from the Latin term *pubertas,* meaning "age of maturity." As implied by the word's etymology, the changes of puberty have long been understood to usher in adulthood; in many cultures, puberty and the capacity to conceive continue to mark entry into adulthood. In contrast, puberty in modern Western culture has become a multistep entry process into a much longer period of adolescence (King, 2002).

Hormonal changes of adolescence include adrenarche, gonadarche, and menarche (Dahl, 2004; King, 2002). Adrenarche refers to the increased production of adrenal hormones and occurs as early as age 6–8. These hormones influence skeletal growth, hair production, and skin changes. Gonadarche refers to the pulsatile production of a cascade of hormones and contributes to driving the growth spurt and genital, breast, and pubic hair development. Menarche refers to the beginning of girls' menses, which generally occurs late in girls' pubertal development.

THE STAGES AND AGES OF PUBERTY

The clinician J. M. Tanner developed a system for classifying male and female pubertal growth into five stages (Tanner I–V). In the 1960s, he identified a trend of progressively earlier age at menarche across cultures (1968). Since then, investigators have identified similar trends of earlier arrival of other markers of puberty, such as breast and pubic hair development (Herman-Giddens et al., 1997). These trends have diverged across race in the United States, with proportionately more African American girls experiencing earlier-onset puberty than white girls. The implications of these trends have ranged from debates over the threshold for premature puberty to investigations into factors that contribute to earlier-onset puberty (Kaplowitz & Oberfield, 1999).

Boys who enter puberty at an earlier age experience certain advantages, including higher self-esteem, greater popularity, and some advances in cognitive capabilities (King, 2002). These same boys may also be more likely to engage in risk-taking behavior, possibly because they often socialize with older boys (Steinberg & Morris, 2001). Girls, on the other hand, often have more problems associated with earlier entry into puberty, including lower self-esteem and elevated risk for anxiety, depression, and eating disorders. These girls are also more likely to engage in risk-taking behaviors, including earlier sexual intercourse.

DON'T BLAME IT ON HORMONES

In the past, hormones were believed to be in a state of great flux, which presumably caused adolescents to be dramatic, erratic, intense, and risk-prone. Evidence suggests, however, that only minimal association exists between adolescent hormone levels and emotional/behavioral problems (Buchanan et al., 1992; King, 2002). Youth with higher levels of hormones do not appear to be at higher risk for emotional or behavioral problems (Dahl, 2004).

Today, adolescent specialists view emotional intensity and sensation-seeking as normative behaviors of adolescence that are more broadly linked to pubertal maturation than to hormone levels. Pubertal stage rather than chronological age is linked to romantic and sexual pursuits, increased appetite, changes in sleep patterns, and risk for emotional disorders in girls. One group of investigators studying teen smoking and substance use found that increased age had no correlation with increased sensation-seeking or risky behavior (Martin et al., 2002). Instead, they determined that pubertal maturation was correlated with sensation-seeking in boys and girls, which, in turn, led to a greater likelihood of cigarette smoking and substance use.

Pubertal stage was clearly linked to difficulties that Derek began experiencing in school. He had been a solid student in 6th grade who scored in the average range and generally turned his homework in on time. He socialized with a group of same-age friends and was teased occasionally because he was skinnier and shorter than his peers. By 7th grade, however, he had begun his growth spurt. He was now a few inches taller and had developed facial hair. Although he appeared more confident, he also seemed more aggressive and was involved in several fights at school. He began to spend part of his time with a few 8th grade boys who were suspected of writing graffiti on a school wall.

A teacher who had a good relationship with Derek took him aside and spoke with him about the change in his behavior from 6th to 7th grade. Derek was able to talk about his own surprise at the changes, his wish for more respect, and his ambivalence about entering high school—he was worried about what teachers would expect of him. Derek and the teacher agreed to talk periodically, and the teacher arranged for Derek to meet with the school counselor.

THE ADOLESCENT BRAIN

Neuroscientists used to believe that by the time they reached puberty, youth had undergone the crucial transformations in brain development and circuitry. Data obtained through available technology supported this view, identifying similar brain structures in children and adults. The adolescent brain seemed entirely comparable to the adult brain.

This view of adolescent brain development has undergone a radical shift during the last decade, with the identification of ongoing brain changes throughout adolescence, such as synaptic pruning and myelination. People have the mature capacity to consistently control behavior in both low-stress and high-stress environments only after these neurobiological developments are complete. This maturation does not take place until the early 20s.

Synaptic pruning refers to the elimination of connections between neurons in the brain's cortex, or gray matter. In the 1990s, researchers determined that during adolescence, up to 30,000 synapses are eliminated each second (Bourgeois & Rakic, 1993; Rakic, Bourgeois, & Goldman-Rakic, 1994). The removal of these redundant synaptic links increases the computational ability of brain circuits, which, in turn, enhances a function intricately connected to risk taking: the capacity to regulate and rapidly stop activity. Myelination, which refers to the wrapping of glial cell membranes around the axon of neurons, results in increased speed of signal transmission along the axon (Luna & Sweeney, 2004). This facilitates more rapid and integrated communication among diverse brain regions.

Synaptic pruning and myelination, along with other neurobiological changes, facilitate enhanced cognitive capacity as well as behavioral control, also known as executive function. Executive function is the ability to interact in a self-directed, appropriate, organized, and purposeful manner. The prefrontal cortex plays a vital role in guiding executive function, which is also influenced by such areas of the brain as the hippocampus (which coordinates memory), the amygdala (which coordinates emotional processing), and the ventral striatum (which coordinates reward-processing). The prefrontal cortex is less mature, however, in young adolescents than in adults.

Given these three factors—an inability to completely regulate and refrain from certain activities, an absence of fully integrated communication among the various regions of the brain, and a less developed prefrontal cortex—it is not surprising that adolescents biologically do not have the same capacities as adults to inhibit their impulses in a timely manner.

BIOLOGY AND THRILL-SEEKING

By their mid-teens, adolescents appear to have achieved many decision-making abilities seen in adults (Steinberg & Cauffman, 1996). In fact, studies have found that teens can identify the same degree of danger in risky activities that adults can—driving while intoxicated, for example (Cauffman, Steinberg, & Woolard, 2002). However, certain methodological flaws in studies of adolescents may have prevented investigators from accurately assessing adolescent risk taking (Steinberg, 2004). These flaws include evaluating teens individually rather than in the context of a group, within which most risk-taking behavior occurs; asking teens to evaluate theoretical situations, which may not sufficiently represent the challenges of actual situations; and evaluating teens in settings that reduce the influence of emotion or induce anxiety rather than generate the exhilaration associated with risk taking.

One result of these flaws may be that measures of adolescents' cognitive abilities—particularly their evaluation of risk—do not adequately reflect their actual cognitive and emotional processes in real time. Consequently, teens appear to have the cognitive capacities of adults yet continue to engage in more risky behaviors.

The emotional lives of adolescents also appear to shift during these years. Adolescents seek more intense emotional experiences than children and adults do. They appear to need higher degrees of stimulation to obtain the same experience of pleasure (Steinberg, 2004). Developments in an area of the brain called the limbic system may explain this shift in pursuit and experience of pleasure (Spear, 2000).

Ongoing cognitive development and emotional shifts result in a biologically based drive for thrill-seeking, which may account for adolescents' continued risk taking despite knowledge of the accompanying hazards. Some interventions attempt to reduce the potential for risky behavior through external means—laws and rules, for example—rather than placing sole emphasis on the practice of educating teens in risk assessment (Steinberg, 2004). Others have considered teens' ability to reason well in "cool" circumstances but their failure to do so when in "hot" situations that arouse the emotions. Providing adolescents with sufficient scaffolding, or a good balance of support and autonomy, may be particularly important (Dahl, 2004).

This kind of scaffolding would be especially effective with a student like Shauna. Shauna raised the concerns of school faculty soon after she started 9th grade. Her attendance, class participation, and assignment completion were erratic. She had also run away from home during the summer and received a warning for shoplifting. The school counselor learned that Shauna's parents had separated over the summer and that her mother was struggling to set limits in the absence of Shauna's father. The school counselor, several teachers, and the vice principal decided to meet with both of Shauna's parents.

Although tension between the parents was evident, both parents agreed that Shauna should come home immediately after school instead of going to the mall, which she had recently started to do. Both parents also felt strongly that she needed to regularly attend school and complete assignments. The parents arranged to meet with Shauna together to discuss their shared expectations for her. The parents and teachers agreed to stay in contact with one another regarding Shauna's attendance and homework. The group also decided that a home-based reward system might encourage Shauna's success at school. The reward system would involve outings to the mall and to friends' homes, with incrementally less adult supervision and more autonomy as she continued to succeed.

THE ROLE OF EDUCATORS

These new findings suggest some beneficial approaches that educators might follow to guide adolescents into healthy adulthood.

• Ensure that schools provide adolescents with vital support. School bonding provides a protective influence for youth. The mentorship of a teacher can make the difference in a teen's course.

• Keep a long view. Researchers have found that the benefits of successful interventions may disappear for a few years in adolescence to reappear in later adolescence (Masten, 2004). Other teens are late bloomers whose troubled earlier years are followed by success.

• Prioritize your concern. The junior who has never been a problem and gets into trouble once is at a different level of risk than the 7th grader who has a long history of worrisome behaviors, such as fights, school truancy, mental illness, exposure to trauma, loss of important adult figures, or absence of stable supports. Act early for adolescents with long histories of risk taking.

• Remember that puberty is not the same for all teens. Some adolescents enter puberty earlier than others, giving them a perceived social advantage as well as possible disadvantages. There may be a biological drive to risk taking in teens, which is expressed by individual teens at different ages.

• Remember that teens are not adults. Having the scientific evidence to support the view that teens are not adults can be helpful to educators working with families, adolescents, or other professionals who may have unrealistic expectations for adolescents.

• Take advantage of adolescent passion. Direct adolescents' enthusiasm toward productive ends. A teen's passion can become a bridge to learning about such topics as music theory, history, politics, race relations, or marketing.

• Reduce risk with firm structure. Although teenagers dislike rules, they generally thrive in reasonable, supportive environments that have a predictable, enforced structure. For example, an authoritative stance in parenting—which reflects firmness coupled with caring—has repeatedly been found to be the most effective parenting strategy. Continue to maintain school rules and expectations, even when an adolescent continues to break the rules.

• Collaborate to solve problems. Working with risk-taking adolescents can be demanding, taxing, and worrisome. Talk regularly with colleagues for support. Contact appropriate consultants when your concern grows. Teens who see teachers collaborate with other adults benefit from these healthy models of problem solving.

It's important for educators to keep in mind that up to 80 percent of adolescents have few or no major problems during this period (Dahl, 2004). Remembering that most adolescents do well can encourage the positive outlook that educators need to effectively work with youth during this exciting and challenging time in their lives.

REFERENCES

Bourgeois, J-P., & Rakic, P. (1993). Changes of synaptic density in the primary visual cortex of the macaque monkey from fetal to adult stage. *Journal of Neuroscience, 13,* 2801–2820.

Buchanan, C. M., Eccles, J. S., & Becket, J. B. (1992). Are adolescents the victims of raging hormones? *Psychological Bulletin, 111,* 62–107.

Cauffman, E., Steinberg, L., & Woolard, J. (2002, April 13). Age differences in capacities underlying competence to stand trial. Presentation at the Biennial Meeting of the Society for Research for Adolescence, New Orleans, Louisiana.

Dahl, R. E. (2004). Adolescent brain development: A period of vulnerabilities and opportunities. *Annals of the New York Academy of Science, 1021,* 1–22.

Herman-Giddens, M. E., Slora, E. J., Wasserman, R. C., Bourdony, C. J., Bhapkar, M. V., Koch, G. G., et al. (1997). Secondary sexual characteristics and menses in young girls seen in office practice. *Pediatrics, 99,* 505–512.

Kaplowitz, P. B., & Oberfield, S. E. (1999). Reexamination of the age limit for defining when puberty is precocious in girls in the United States. *Pediatrics, 104,* 936–941.

King, R. A. (2002). Adolescence. In M. Lewis (Ed.), *Child and adolescent psychiatry* (pp. 332–342). Philadelphia: Lippincott Williams & Wilkins.

Luna, B., & Sweeney, J. A. (2004). The emergence of collaborative brain function: fMRI studies of the development of response inhibition. *Annals of the New York Academy of Science, 1021,* 296–309.

Martin, C. A., Kelly, T. H., Rayens, M. K., Brogli, B. R., Brenzel, A., Smith, W. J., et al. (2002). Sensation seeking, puberty, and nicotine, alcohol, and marijuana use in adolescence. *Journal of the American Academy of Child and Adolescent Psychiatry, 41,* 1495–1502.

Masten, A. S. (2004). Regulatory processes, risk, and resilience in adolescent development. *Annals of the New York Academy of Science, 1021,* 310–319.

Rakic, P., Bourgeois, J-P., & Goldman-Rakic, P. S. (1994). Synaptic development of the cerebral cortex. *Progress in Brain Research, 102,* 227–243.

Spear, P. (2000). The adolescent brain and age-related behavioral manifestations. *Neuroscience and Biobehavioral Reviews, 24,* 417–463.

Steinberg, L. (2004). Risk taking in adolescence: What changes, and why? *Annals of the New York Academy of Science, 1021,* 51–58.

Steinberg, L., & Cauffman, E. (1996). Maturity of judgment in adolescence. *Law and Human Behavior, 20,* 249–272.

Steinberg, L., & Morris, A. S. (2001). Adolescent development. *Annual Review of Psychology, 52,* 83–110.

Tanner, J. M. (1968). Early maturation in man. *Scientific American, 218,* 21–27.

Lisa F. Price, M.D., is the assistant director of the School Psychiatry Program in the Department of Psychiatry at Massachusetts General Hospital, Boston. She is also an instructor in psychiatry at Harvard Medical School.

QUESTIONS FOR REFLECTION

1. What are the reasons Price cites for increased risk taking behavior during adolescence, and how does the "context of multiple systems" play a role in adolescent choices and behavior?
2. What does brain research tell us about adolescent brain development, and how might we use this information to inform educational programs and practices?
3. Price gives several recommendations for educators to help guide adolescents into healthy adulthood. What are they, and do you think they are practical? Is there anything missing from her list that you would add?

Family and School Spillover in Adolescents' Daily Lives

LISA FLOOK
ANDREW J. FULIGNI

ABSTRACT: Family and school substantially shape adolescents' lives as they provide the two primary contexts for adolescent development. In this study, Flook and Fuligni examined spillover between daily family stressors and school problems among 589 ninth-grade students from Mexican, Chinese, and European backgrounds. Adolescents reported on their school and family experiences each day for two weeks. Analyses revealed that reciprocal spillover occurred between adolescents' daily functioning in the family and school domains that spanned over several days. According to the findings, spillover between family stressors and school problems also occurs across the high school years, from 9th to 12th grade, which is predictive of poorer academic performance in 12th grade. Flook and Fuligni discuss the practical implications for adolescents' academic achievement trajectories and general well-being.

As two of the primary contexts for development, family and school substantially shape adolescents' lives. In addition to directly informing adolescents' experiences, events in each setting can also affect what happens in the other setting. This sphere of influence, referred to as the mesosystem, occurs as a transaction between primary developmental contexts (Bronfenbrenner, 1986). The centrality of family and school to adolescent development is reflected in the wealth of research that has examined the role of family resources and parenting in the school adjustment of teenagers (e.g., Steinberg, Lamborn, Dornbusch, & Darling, 1992). However, these studies have focused primarily on more global measures of family resources and practices, such as parental education and parenting style, as opposed to a more microlevel approach that examines the daily experiences of adolescents in families and schools. The primary goal of the current study was to provide a twofold view of how the family may shape school adjustment and vice versa. We examine this both in the short term, by focusing on the daily transaction between experiences at home and at school, and over the long term, by considering the implications for adjust-

ment and achievement across the years of high school.

Spillover in Adolescents' Daily Lives

The process by which experiences in one context influence the experiences in another context is often referred to as spillover (Almeida, Wethington, & Chandler, 1999). The concept of spillover has been used primarily in studies of adult stress and coping, such as research that has focused on the linkages between work stress and family experience. These studies have found that stressful experiences at the workplace can lead to greater conflict and emotional distress between family members (e.g., Repetti, 1989; Schulz, Cowan, Pape Cowan, & Brennan, 2004). The concept of spillover offers a useful framework with which to examine the linkages between family and school experiences among children and adolescents. Such an approach was taken by Repetti and colleagues in their study of the connections between the family and school settings among elementary school children. Children's daily social and academic failure experiences at school increased the likelihood of subsequent aversive interactions with parents at home (Repetti,

1996). Parents' aversive behavior, on the other hand, was not associated with problems at school the following day. Furthermore, negative mood was found to mediate the association between school failure and aversive parent–child interactions (Lehman & Repetti, 2007).

Although comparable studies have not been done among older children, there are several reasons to believe that the years of adolescence would be a particularly fruitful time to examine spillover processes between experiences at home and at school. Adolescence represents a period of significant changes in the family and school contexts. The move into the teenage years is accompanied by greater academic and family demands, such as more homework and responsibilities at home (Isakson & Jarvis, 1999). As parental monitoring of children's school behaviors decreases during secondary school, school responsibilities, such as completing homework and attending classes, increasingly fall upon the adolescents themselves (Spera, 2005). In terms of family relationships, disagreements and conflicts with parents become more intense and less easily resolved (Laursen, Coy, & Collins, 1998; Smetana & Asquith, 1994). As a result of the need to negotiate changes in these settings in their lives, adolescents frequently identify school and family as sources of stress and concern (de Anda et al., 2000; Phelan, Yu, & Davidson, 1994).

Along with the increased demands and pressures that they experience at home and school, adolescents undergo cognitive and emotional changes. As a result of their increased cognitive skills, adolescents have a greater propensity for rumination. Stressful experiences may be more likely to carry across settings as teenagers mull over and hold on to negative events for a longer period of time (Muris, Roelofs, Meesters, & Boomsma, 2004). Adolescents also exhibit a decline in positive emotion and an increase in intensity of negative emotion (Larson, Moneta, Richards, & Wilson, 2002). Such a tendency toward experiencing stronger negative emotion may enhance the likelihood of spillover. Finally, compared to adults, adolescents' sense of self tends to be less well developed (Harter, 1999). Because their concept of themselves in different roles, such as family members and students, is less differentiated, events that happen in one area may be more likely to impact their functioning and experiences in other areas (Harter, Bresnick, Bouchey, & Whitesell, 1997).

Increased stress in the family and school contexts accompanied by cognitive and emotional changes, therefore, makes adolescence a developmental period during which spillover effects may be particularly prominent. The preceding discussion suggests that key events to examine within the family include experiences of conflict and too many demands, as these are experiences that have been shown to be particularly salient and stressful for adolescents (de Anda et al., 2000; Phelan et al., 1994). At school, experiences relevant to adolescents' achievement and motivation, such as their effort and learning difficulties, would be important to examine given that school is a setting that requires a level of attention and performance that may be hard for students to muster if they have had trying experiences in the home. It is also possible that diminished effort or learning difficulties at school, in turn, could carry over into the home environment and create higher levels of parent–child conflict and parental discipline, as was observed in prior research with elementary school-age children (Lehman & Repetti, 2007; Repetti, 1996).

A Daily Diary Approach to Spillover

Daily diary methods are ideal techniques for observing spillover processes because they capture naturally occurring events as they unfold over time (Bolger, Davis, & Rafaeli, 2003). In the daily diary approach, study participants are asked to complete diary checklists each day for a short period of time, often ranging from several days to several weeks. This method allows researchers to estimate whether specific events, behaviors, and feelings co-occur with one another on a daily basis. For example, Repetti (1996) documented spillover between elementary school-age children's academic functioning and interactions with their parents by having children first report on their academic experiences during the day and then, later, on interactions with their parents in the evening for two consecutive weekdays. The temporal sequencing of reports made it possible to more strongly infer that children's academic failure experiences at school were associated with aversive interactions with parents at home. In another example, Almeida et al. (1999) examined spillover of emotions emanating from the marital dyad and flowing to the parent–child dyad. Tension in parent–child dyads was observed on days following tense marital interactions, with controls for parent–child tension from the prior day.

The daily diary method possesses other strengths suitable for the examination of family and school spillover among adolescents. By assessing experiences on a daily basis, this method reduces potential biases associated with extended recall. In addition, although causality cannot be determined because of the nonexperimental nature of the data, the ability to establish a temporal sequence while also controlling for prior levels of the dependent variable allows for stronger inferences about the linkages between experiences in the different settings of adolescents' daily lives (Bolger et al., 2003). In the current study, adolescents reported on family and school experiences once each day over a 2-week period. The daily diary checklists that adolescents completed included items that assessed experiences such as parental conflict and discipline, family demands, learning difficulties, and school attendance. Using the daily diary method allowed us to examine the daily associations between family and school experiences, controlling for prior levels of the outcome variable. We conducted tests of spillover in each direction to compare how family stressors impacted school functioning and, conversely, how school events influenced subsequent family functioning. The design of this study also allowed us to examine lagged effects of spillover in both directions. For example, we explored the possibility that effects of heightened levels of family stress would continue to linger and be associated with poorer academic adjustment for multiple days after the

initial stress. In addition, by aggregating the daily diary data, we were able to examine long-term patterns of spillover and implications for academic achievement over the course of high school, thus gaining a macroscopic view while taking advantage of the daily diary design. This longitudinal approach also complements the microscopic perspective afforded by daily-level analyses.

Group Differences in Spillover

In the current study, we examined whether spillover between family and school varied according to adolescents' gender and ethnic background. Although we did not expect there to be large gender differences, we hypothesized that differences would reflect greater spillover among girls. Females have been shown to report more daily stress and greater emotional reactivity than males (Almeida & Kessler, 1998; Kearney, Drabman, & Beasley, 1993). In particular, events that involve family members have been found to have a greater impact on girls than boys (Larson & Asmussen, 1991). In addition, research with adults has found gender differences in work–home spillover, with females subject to greater spillover effects in both directions (Keene & Reynolds, 2005; Schulz et al., 2004). Therefore, although under some conditions boys have shown a greater susceptibility to major family changes such as divorce (Hetherington & Stanley-Hagan, 1999), prior research on daily stress and reactivity would seem to suggest that any gender differences observed in the present study would be in the direction of greater spillover from family to school on the part of girls.

Predictions about potential ethnic differences are tentative given the paucity of research on any kind of spillover among ethnically diverse populations. Yet, it is possible that spillover in either direction would be greater for adolescents from Mexican and Chinese backgrounds. Adolescents from both these groups come from traditions that place great importance upon the family in children's lives (Chao & Tseng, 2002; Fuligni & Hardway, 2006; García-Coil & Vázquez García, 1995), such that adolescents may show greater reactivity to negative family experiences that would spill over into their school experiences. Adolescents from Chinese backgrounds may experience greater spillover from school to family because of the strong emphasis placed upon high levels of academic success among their families (Chao & Tseng, 2002; Fuligni, 1997). Finally, socioeconomic differences among adolescents could produce ethnic differences in spillover. Prior research has shown that lower socioeconomic status (SES) is a risk factor for increased vulnerability to stress in children (Wadsworth, Raviv, Compas, & Connor-Smith, 2005) and higher reactivity to stress among adults (Grzywacz, Almeida, Neupert, & Ettner, 2004).

Long-Term Consequences of Stress

Effects of such daily stress may accumulate over time and have negative long-term consequences. The toll of chronic stress on mental and physical health outcomes is well documented. Certain groups are disproportionately subject to stressful experiences, such as individuals from low-SES backgrounds (Almeida, Neupert, Banks, & Serido, 2005; Grzywacz et al., 2004). Therefore, examining the effect of high levels of daily stress on adolescents' long term functioning would be informative. Examining how stress in the family and school domains predicts one another at a between-subjects level, over the long term, complements the within-subjects, daily-level perspective. Additionally, academic performance is an important indicator of current functioning and a prognosticator of advancement and future opportunities. Therefore, it is relevant to examine the predictive association between high levels of family stress and school problems at the beginning of high school and academic achievement by the end of high school.

Primary Research Questions

The present study addressed the following key questions about family and school spillover among adolescents from Latin American, Asian,

and European backgrounds who are in their 1st year of high school: (a) Are daily family conflict and demands associated with attendance and learning problems at school the following day? (b) Does spillover also occur in the reverse direction, with daily academic problems predicting increased difficulties at home on the following day? (c) Are spillover effects pervasive, persisting for up to 2 days following the occurrence of the initial stressor? (d) Are there gender, ethnic, or socioeconomic differences in the extent of spillover between home and school? (e) What are the long-term implications of heightened levels of daily family stress and school problems?

METHOD

Participants

Students in the 9th grade from three high schools in the greater Los Angeles metropolitan area were invited to participate in the study. Approximately 65% of adolescents agreed to participate and returned a signed parent consent form. Of the 783 ninth-grade students who participated, 589 adolescents of Chinese ($n = 174$), Mexican ($n = 241$), and European American ($n = 174$) descent comprised the target sample for this study (mean age of students = 14.86 years, $SD = 0.38$). The 194 participants from ethnic minority groups that comprised too small a number for meaningful comparisons in our sample (e.g., other Latino, other Asian, Middle Eastern, and African American backgrounds) were excluded from these analyses. The sample was relatively evenly split between boys (48%) and girls (52%). Longitudinal analyses, across the high school years, were conducted on data from a subset of 503 adolescents who participated in both 9th and 12th grades.

The three schools represented a diverse cross-section of Los Angeles in terms of ethnic composition, SES, and levels of overall academic achievement. Enrollment at the first school consisted of primarily Asian American and Latino students with academic achievement in the lower-middle to middle range, based on state-mandated standardized achievement tests, and from working to lower-middle socioeconomic backgrounds. The student body at the second school was predominantly European American and Latino from families in the lower-middle- to middle-class spectrum of parental education, occupation, and income. The third school enrolled primarily European American and Asian American students from middle- to upper-middle-class socioeconomic backgrounds. Schools 2 and 3 were characterized by average to above-average levels of academic achievement, respectively. The two largest ethnic groups at each school comprised approximately 30%–50% of the total population of students at each school; however, no single ethnic group predominated.

Adolescents indicated the highest level of education attained by each parent on the following scale: *1 = elementary/junior high school, 2 = some high school, 3 = graduated from high school, 4 = some college, 5 = graduated from college,* and *6 = law, medical, or graduate school.* Mothers' and fathers' levels of education were highly significantly correlated ($r = .71$, $p < .001$); therefore, an index was created based on parents' average education level. Parents of students from Mexican backgrounds had lower levels of education than those from Chinese backgrounds, whose education level was lower than that of those from European American backgrounds, $F(2, 505) = 85.14$, $p < .001$, $\eta^2 = 0.25$. On average, Mexican parents had attained approximately a high school education ($M = 3.09$, $SD = 1.27$), Chinese parents had between a high school education and some college ($M = 3.79$, $SD = 1.52$), and European American parents had between some college and graduated from college ($M = 4.85$, $SD = 1.00$).

A similar pattern of ethnic group differences emerged for parent occupation. Parent occupation was classified into standard categories: *1 = unskilled, 2 = semiskilled, 3 = skilled, 4 = semiprofessional,* and *5 = professional.* Parents of students from Mexican American backgrounds had lower occupational status jobs as compared to Chinese parents, who had lower occupational

status jobs relative to European American parents, $F(2,468) = 54.80$, $p < .001$, $\eta^2 = 0.19$. On average, Mexican parents were employed in semiskilled to skilled jobs ($M = 2.92$, $SD = 0.92$), Chinese parents held skilled to semiprofessional jobs ($M = 3.39$, $SD = 0.97$), and European American parents were in semiprofessional jobs ($M = 3.96$, $SD = 0.81$).

Procedure

Participants were recruited from spring semester classes which all ninth-grade students were required to take regardless of their academic ability (e.g., social studies, physical education). At two of the three high schools, the entire ninth-grade student body was invited to participate. At the third high school, approximately half of the ninth graders were invited to participate because the large size of the school did not make it feasible to recruit all the students. Consent forms and study materials were available to students and their parents in English, Chinese, and Spanish. Eight participants chose to complete the questionnaires in a language other than English (4 in Chinese and 4 in Spanish).

Students who returned signed parent consent forms and provided their own assent to participate completed an initial background questionnaire during a 50-min class period. In the background questionnaire, adolescents reported on their family, peer, and academic values in addition to demographic variables. After completing the background questionnaire, adolescents were provided with a 14-day supply of diary checklists to complete at home each night before going to bed. The three-page diary checklists, which consisted of daily family-, peer-, and school-related experiences, took approximately 5–10 min to complete. Adolescents were instructed to seal the diary sheets in individual envelopes each night and to stamp the seal of the envelope with a pre-programmed electronic time stamper to record the date and time of completion. The electronic time stamper was programmed such that adolescents could not alter the date and time.

Adolescents were contacted by phone during the 2-week period to answer questions about the procedures and to monitor the status of their diary completion. Adolescents received $30 for participating in the study after returning their questionnaires at the end of the 2nd week. In addition, they were offered two movie passes for accurately and fully completing all materials. The time stamper method of monitoring daily diary completion and incentives resulted in a high rate of compliance. Approximately 95% of daily diaries were completed, and 86% of these were completed on time, either that night or before noon the following day. All analyses were conducted using only those diaries completed on time to reduce possible biases associated with late diaries.

Measures

Adolescents reported on their experiences and events in the school and family domains each day. Adolescents provided these reports at the end of each day over the course of the 2-week study period. The items comprising each scale were designed for use in this study and were selected based upon their relevance to adolescents' daily lives. Spillover effects involving experiences between home and school were examined on both a daily and a longitudinal basis. Daily analyses were conducted using ninth-grade daily diary reports. Longitudinal analyses were conducted using aggregated data from 9th-grade and 12th-grade diaries and 12th-grade grade point average (GPA) as an outcome variable. Analyses of attrition compared the initial 9th-grade sample and final 12th-grade sample to the longitudinal sample ($N = 503$), with significant differences noted below.

Family Stress

Daily family conflict and demands. Five items presented in a checklist format tapped into stressful experiences related to the family. Each day for 2 weeks, adolescents indicated whether any of the following had occurred: (a) punished or disciplined by parents, (b) argued with your mother

about something, (c) argued with your father about something, (d) argued with another family member about something, and (e) had a lot of demands made by your family. The total number of items endorsed each day was summed to create an index of daily family stress ($M = 0.46$, $SD = 0.83$, range $= 0–5$). Daily family stress was examined in conjunction with school stress to observe within-person, daily and lagged spillover effects. For between-person, individual-level analyses, assessing change across the high school years, family conflict, and demands were summed over the 2-week study period, in each year of the study, to form an overall estimate of family stress (9th grade: $M = 6.22$, $SD = 6.95$; 12th grade: $M = 4.70$, $SD = 5.22$). No differences in daily family stress emerged between adolescents who participated in the study in both 9th and 12th grades (i.e., the longitudinal sample) as compared with those who only participated in 9th grade.

School Problems

Daily attendance and learning problems. Seven items presented in a checklist format assessed problems related to attendance and learning at school. Each day, adolescents indicated whether they had experienced any of the following: (a) had difficulty getting to school on time; (b) were late for class; (c) skipped or cut a class; (d) skipped school; (e) did not understand something taught in class; (f) did poorly on a test, quiz, or homework; and (g) did not turn in homework that was due. Total attendance and learning problems were summed each day as an indicator of academic adjustment ($M = 0.74$, $SD = 1.01$, range $= 0–7$). The association between daily school stress and family stress was used to examine within-person, daily and lagged spillover effects. Between-person, individual-level analyses were conducted across the high school years by summing the number of attendance and learning problems over the 2-week study period, separately for each year of the study (9th grade: $M = 7.13$, $SD = 6.60$; 12th grade: $M = 8.80$, $SD = 7.11$). Adolescents in the longitudinal sample had lower average levels of attendance and learning problems ($M = 6.56$, $SD = 6.02$) as compared with students who participated only in 9th grade ($M = 8.23$, $SD = 7.47$), $t(439.40) = 3.12$, $p < .01$.

GPA

GPA, on a 4-point scale, was obtained from school records at the end of the 9th- ($M = 3.00$, $SD = 0.72$) and 12th-grade ($M = 3.00$, $SD = 0.69$) school years. GPA at both time points was obtained for 460 students ($N = 479$ in 9th grade, $N = 481$ in 12th grade). The longitudinal sample had higher 9th-grade GPAs ($M = 3.00$, $SD = 0.72$) than students who only participated in 9th grade ($M = 2.47$, $SD = 0.94$), $t(386.46) = -7.71$, $p < .001$.

RESULTS

Analysis Plan

The nested design of this daily diary study, in which daily reports were nested within individuals, made multilevel modeling appropriate for statistical analysis (Raudenbush & Bryk, 2002). Daily-level analyses examined spillover effects within and between subjects. Daily- and individual-level equations were estimated simultaneously using hierarchical linear modeling (HLM) statistical software. Hierarchical generalized linear modeling (HGLM), a nonlinear analysis, was applied to count variable outcomes by specifying a Poisson model with equal exposure. A similar pattern of results emerged from HGLM and standard HLM analyses; therefore, for ease of interpretation, results of standard HLM models are presented. Daily-level equations allowed for the estimation of associations between prior-day family stressors and next-day school adjustment and vice versa. Individual-level equations allowed for estimating whether group characteristics according to gender and ethnicity moderated those daily-level associations.

The following analyses are based on data from diary sheets that were completed on time. Late diaries were excluded from these analyses in order to reduce biases resulting from inaccurate reporting. First, the proposed home-to-school spillover hypothesis was tested, followed by 2-day lagged spillover analyses. Second, gender and ethnicity were examined as potential moderators of family-to-school spillover, and the interactions between ethnicity and gender were examined. Whenever significant effects of ethnicity were observed, follow-up analyses were conducted in order to examine whether the effects of ethnicity could be explained by differences in parental education. The same plan of analysis was followed in order to examine spillover in the opposite direction. School-to-family spillover and 2-day lagged spillover were first examined, followed by tests of the effects of gender, ethnicity, Ethnicity × Gender interactions, and when applicable, SES. Next, we examined between-subjects effects of high levels of stress over time, from 9th to 12th grade, using regression analyses.

Spillover from Family to School

The following daily-level equations show the basic model for academic adjustment predicted by prior-day family stress while controlling for academic adjustment the prior day:

$$\text{School problems}_{ij} = b_{0j} + b_{1j}(\text{family stress}_{t-1})$$
$$+ b_{2j}(\text{school problems}_{t-1})$$
$$+ b_{3j}(\text{week of study}) + e_{ij} \quad (1)$$

Academic adjustment on a given day (i) for a particular adolescent (j) was modeled as a function of each individual's intercept (b_{0j}) and family stress experienced the previous day (b_{1j}). Prior-day academic adjustment (b_{2j}) was included to control for prior-day effects and to capture the spillover across days resulting from events in the family domain carrying over to influence changes in experiences in the school domain the next day. In order to reduce possible confounds resulting from effects of the repeated-measures diary method, the week of the study (effect coded -1 for Week 1, Days 1–7, and 1 for Week 2, Days 8–14) was entered as a control variable in all equations (b_{3j}). The error term in the equation represents unexplained variance (e_{ij}).

Two-day lagged spillover was modeled according to the following equation:

$$\text{School problems}_{ij} = b_{0j} + b_{1j}(\text{family stress}_{t-2})$$
$$+ b_{2j}(\text{family stress}_{t-1})$$
$$+ b_{3j}(\text{school problems}_{t-1})$$
$$+ b_{4j}(\text{school problems}_{t-2})$$
$$+ b_{5j}(\text{week of study}) + e_{ij}. \quad (2)$$

Academic adjustment on a given day (i) for a particular adolescent (j) was modeled as a function of each individual's intercept (b_{0j}) and family stress experienced 2 days earlier (b_{1j}). Prior-day family stress (b_{2j}) and academic adjustment from the previous day (b_{3j}) and 2 days before (b_{4j}) were included as control variables to isolate the spillover resulting from events in the family domain carrying over to experiences in the school domain across a 3-day span.

As shown in Table 1, family stressors from the prior day significantly predicted more problems with attendance and learning the next day, even after controlling for school adjustment the prior day. Spillover effects continued to persist 2 days after the occurrence of the initial stressor, controlling for subsequent levels of stress. That is, family stress uniquely predicted school adjustment problems not only the next day but also 2 days later.

Gender and Ethnicity

In order to examine whether the spillover of family stress onto academic adjustment varied by gender or ethnicity, the following individual-level equations were mapped onto the daily-level equations from above:

$$(\text{Intercept})\, b_{0j} = c_{00} + c_{01}(\text{gender}) + c_{02}(\text{Mexican})$$
$$+ c_{03}(\text{Chinese}) + u_{0j}. \quad (3)$$
$$(\text{Slope})\, b_{1j} = c_{10} + c_{11}(\text{gender}) + c_{12}(\text{Mexican})$$
$$+ c_{13}(\text{Chinese}) + u_{1j}. \quad (4)$$

The intercept Equation 3 tested whether there are gender or ethnic differences in the average levels of academic adjustment. The slope Equation 4 examined gender and ethnicity as moderators of spillover effects from home to school. Gender was effect coded, with −1 for boys and 1 for girls. Ethnicity was dummy coded, with adolescents from European backgrounds designated as the baseline group for comparison with adolescents from Mexican and Chinese backgrounds. Comparisons between adolescents from Mexican and Chinese backgrounds were made by changing the baseline group in Equations 3 and 4 to Mexican American adolescents. Error terms contributing to unexplained variance are represented by u_{0j} and u_{1j}. Error terms were specified

TABLE 1

Predicting Daily School Problems From Family Stress 1 and 2 Days Prior

1 day prior		2 days prior	
Daily level	**School problems, b (SE)**	**Daily level**	**School problems, b (SE)**
Intercept	.34 (.02)**	Intercept	.25 (.01)**
Family stress$_{(t-1)}$	.10 (.02)**	Family stress$_{(t-1)}$	.05 (.01)**
School problems$_{(t-1)}$	.46 (.02)**	Family stress$_{(t-2)}$	.05 (.01)**
Week of study	−.01 (.00)	School problems$_{(t-1)}$	.32 (.01)**
		School problems$_{(t-2)}$	.26 (.01)**
		Week of study	.00 (.00)

Note: Subscripts: $(t-1) = 1$ day prior; $(t-2) = 2$ days prior. Gender coded: $-1 =$ boy; $1 =$ girl. Week of study coded: $-1 =$ Week 1 (Days 1–7); $1 =$ Week 2 (Days 8–14).
**$p < .01$.

as random or fixed according to the significance of variance estimates. Data for 9 days of the 14-day study period permitted examination of academic adjustment as the outcome, predicted by family stress on the prior day. The first day of the study was excluded because there was no information about prior-day family stressors before the study began. In addition, Saturdays and Sundays were excluded from analyses because students did not attend school on these days and academic adjustment could not be predicted on weekends.

In terms of gender, no differences emerged in the average level of daily academic adjustment. Likewise, gender did not moderate the spillover of prior-day academic adjustment onto family stressors the following day. However, ethnic group differences emerged in the average daily level of academic adjustment. Adolescents with Chinese backgrounds reported fewer problems with attendance and learning as compared to those with European and Mexican backgrounds (b_{CA} = .44, b_{EA} = .63, b_{MA} = .70, p < .01). Results also showed that spillover from family stress to attendance and learning problems the next day was stronger among adolescents from Chinese backgrounds (between-group difference, p < .05; slope intercepts and significance level by ethnicity: b_{CA} = .08, p < .01; b_{EA} = .02, ns; b_{MA} = .04, p < .05). That is, family stress predicted significantly more attendance and learning problems the following day for students from Chinese backgrounds as compared to those with European backgrounds. There was no substantial variability in 2-day lagged spillover, as indicated by the nonsignificant variance component for family stress predicting school problems 2 days later; therefore, individual-level moderators were not examined for this association.

To test for interactions between gender and ethnicity, an interaction term was added as an additional individual-level predictor to Equations 3 and 4. No significant Gender × Ethnicity interactions emerged.

Parental Education

In order to determine whether observed ethnic differences were due to variations in socioeconomic background, the analyses involving ethnicity described above were conducted again, this time adding parental education as an additional individual-level predictor in Equations 3 and 4. Parental education did not independently predict average daily academic adjustment (b = .02, ns). Ethnic differences in the average level of daily academic adjustment remained significant.

In terms of spillover from family stressors to school adjustment, parental education again was not a significant independent predictor of spillover (b = .00, ns). The difference in spillover to attendance and learning problems between students from Chinese and European backgrounds remained significant controlling for parent education (b_{CA} = .07, p < .05).

Spillover from School to Family

The same plan of analysis was followed in order to examine spillover from school adjustment to family stressors and demands on the following day. The following daily-level equation is the basic model used to predict family stressors from academic adjustment, controlling for family stressors on the prior day:

$$\text{Family stress}_{ij} = b_{0j} + b_{1j}(\text{school problems}_{t-1})$$
$$+ b_{2j}(\text{family stress}_{t-1})$$
$$+ b_{3j}(\text{week of study}) + e_{ij}. \qquad (5)$$

This model is similar to the model testing spillover in the reverse direction, except here the variables are reversed, with family stressors as the outcome and academic adjustment as the predictor. Family stressors on a given day (i) for a particular adolescent (j) were modeled as a function of each individual's intercept (b_{0j}) and academic adjustment experienced the previous day (b_{1j}). Prior-day family stressors (b_{2j}) were included to control for any prior-day effects and thereby capture the spillover across days resulting from events in the academic domain carrying over to influence changes in family stress on the following day. The week of the study (b_{3j}) was entered as a control variable. The error term in the equation represents unexplained variance (e_{ij}). Data for 9 days of the 14-day study period permitted examination of family stressors as the outcome, predicted by academic adjustment on the prior day. The first day of the study was excluded because there was no information about prior-day academic adjustment before Day 1. In addition, Sundays and Mondays were excluded from analyses because no school data were available from the prior day (i.e., Saturdays and Sundays) to predict family stressors.

Two-day lagged spillover was modeled according to the following equation:

$$\text{Family stress}_{ij} = b_{0j} + b_{1j}(\text{school problems}_{t-2})$$
$$+ b_{2j}(\text{school problems}_{t-1})$$
$$+ b_{3j}(\text{family stress}_{t-1})$$
$$+ b_{4j}(\text{family stress}_{t-2})$$
$$+ b_{5j}(\text{week of study}) + e_{ij}. \quad (6)$$

Family stress on a given day (i) for a particular adolescent (j) was modeled as a function of each individual's intercept (b_{0j}) and academic adjustment 2 days earlier (b_{1j}). Prior-day academic adjustment (b_{2j}), prior-day family stress (b_{3j}), and family stress 2 days earlier (b_{4j}) were included as controls to capture spillover of experiences from the school domain to the family domain over a span of 3 days.

At the individual level, the same equations, as described in Equations 3 and 4 above, were used to examine differences in daily family stressors

and the spillover from school to family according gender, ethnicity, and parental education.

Results

As shown in Table 2, problems with attendance and learning modestly but significantly predicted an increase in family stressors on the following day. Additional lagged spillover analyses indicated that academic adjustment problems continued to independently predict family stress 2 days later. These associations remained significant when controlling for academic adjustment and family stress from the prior day.

Gender and Ethnicity

In terms of gender differences, girls reported experiencing a higher average level of daily family stressors as compared to boys ($b_{\text{girl}} = .36$, $b_{\text{boy}} = .28$, $p < .01$). Gender, however, did not moderate the spillover of prior-day academic adjustment onto family stressors the following day. In terms of ethnic differences, adolescents from Chinese backgrounds generally reported fewer average daily family stressors than adolescents from European and Mexican backgrounds ($b_{\text{CA}} = .24$, $b_{\text{EA}} = .35$, $b_{\text{MA}} = .35$, $p < .01$). There were

TABLE 2

Predicting Daily Family Stress From School Problems 1 and 2 Days Prior

1 day prior		2 days prior	
Daily level	Family stress, *b (SE)*	Daily level	Family stress, *b (SE)*
Intercept	.21 (.01)**	Intercept	.14 (.01)**
School problems$_{(t-1)}$	.08 (.01)**	School problems$_{(t-1)}$	.04 (.01)**
Family stress$_{(t-1)}$	.40 (.02)**	School problems$_{(t-2)}$	.03 (.01)**
Week of study	−.02 (.01)	Family stress$_{(t-1)}$	.30 (.02)**
		Family stress$_{(t-2)}$	.25 (.02)**
		Week of study	.01 (.01)*

Note: Subscripts: $(t-1) = 1$ day prior; $(t-2) = 2$ days prior. Gender coded: $-1 =$ boy; $1 =$ girl. Week of study coded: $-1 =$ Week 1 (Days 1–7); $1 =$ Week 2 (Days 8–14).
*$p < .05$. **$p < .01$.

no significant ethnic differences in the spillover of attendance and learning problems onto family stressors the next day. As indicated by the nonsignificant variance component for academic adjustment, there was no substantial variability in 2-day lagged spillover predicting family stress as the outcome; therefore, individual-level moderators were not examined for this association.

Analyses examining the interaction between gender and ethnicity indicated significant differences in spillover from attendance and learning problems to family stressors the next day. This difference emerged among adolescents from Chinese and Mexican backgrounds as compared to European backgrounds. Girls from Chinese and Mexican backgrounds experienced greater spillover than boys from their respective backgrounds as compared to girls from European American backgrounds, who experienced less spillover than European American boys (interaction terms, $p < .01$; gender differences for each ethnic group with significance levels: $b_{CAgirl} = .06$, $b_{CAboy} = -.01$, $p < .05$; $b_{MAgirl} = .06$, $b_{MAboy} = .02$, *ns*; $b_{EAgirl} = -.01$, $b_{EAboy} = .09$, $p < .01$).

Parental Education

Parental education was associated with higher average daily levels of family stress ($b = .03$, $p < .05$) but was not independently associated with the spillover from school to family ($b = .00$, *ns*). All the previously reported ethnic differences remained significant.

Long-Term Consequences of Stress

Longitudinal spillover between family stress and academic adjustment was examined between 9th and 12th grades using multiple regression. Average family stress in 9th grade was used to predict average academic adjustment in 12th grade while controlling for average academic adjustment in 9th grade. Similarly, average academic adjustment in 9th grade was examined as a predictor of average family stress in 12th grade while controlling for average family stress in 9th grade. As shown in

Table 3, more family stress in 9th grade predicted more academic adjustment problems 4 years later. Likewise, a higher level of academic problems in 9th grade predicted more family stress at the end of high school.

Next, the consequences of high levels of family stress and academic adjustment problems at the beginning of high school, for GPA by the end of high school, were examined. As shown in Table 3, higher average levels of family stress in 9th grade predicted lower 12th-grade GPA, controlling for earlier GPA. Additionally, more academic adjustment problems in 9th grade predicted lower GPA in 12th grade, controlling for GPA in 9th grade. These longitudinal associations did not vary by gender or ethnicity.

DISCUSSION

The findings from this study highlight the interconnectivity between school and family functioning in adolescents' daily lives. Even controlling for the recurring nature of daily stressors, family and school experiences are found to reciprocally predict adolescents' functioning across domains. Specifically, family stress predicts more problems with attendance and learning at school the next day, and the effect is still observed 2 days later. Likewise, problems with attendance and learning are related to increased family stress the following day and 2 days later. Thus, family stress and attendance and learning problems are linked to one another, forming a spillover loop that carries across time and settings. Global patterns of spillover were detected across the span of high school, with higher average levels of daily family stress in 9th grade predicting more school problems 4 years later and, conversely, more school problems in 9th grade predicting higher levels of family stress in 12th grade. Furthermore, higher levels of family stress and school problems at the beginning of high school were associated with declines in academic achievement by the end of high school.

Overall, there were remarkable similarities among adolescents, across ethnicity and gender,

TABLE 3

Longitudinal Associations between Family Stress, School Problems, and GPA from 9th to 12th Grades

Predictor variables	Outcome variables				
	12th-grade school problems ($N = 501$)				
	B	*SE B*	*β*	*t*	*ΔR²*
9th-grade family stress	.11	0.051	.10	2.19*	.07
9th-grade school problems	.45	0.055	.37	8.31**	.11
	12th-grade family stress ($N = 501$)				
	B	*SE B*	*β*	*t*	*ΔR²*
9th-grade school problems	.10	0.041	.12	2.53*	.06
9th-grade family stress	.24	0.038	.30	6.40**	.07
	12th-grade GPA ($N = 458$)				
	B	*SE B*	*β*	*t*	*ΔR²*
9th-grade family stress	−.013	0.004	−.13	−3.63**	.04
9th-grade GPA	.640	0.035	.64	18.30**	.41
	12th-grade GPA ($N = 458$)				
	B	*SE B*	*β*	*t*	*ΔR²*
9th-grade school problems	−.012	0.004	−.11	−2.90**	.06
9th-grade GPA	.626	0.036	.63	17.29**	.13

$p < .05.$ **$p < .01.$

in patterns of spillover between family and school problems. The modest variation that was evidenced in spillover, however, may shed light onto the adaptation of adolescents from diverse backgrounds. With regard to ethnicity, family stressors predicted more school adjustment problems for Chinese American adolescents even after controlling for parental education. On average, Chinese Americans reported fewer daily family stressors, but the effect of such stressors was stronger in terms of being associated with more attendance and learning problems the following school day. Perhaps for Chinese Americans, because they tended to experience fewer family stressors, their

occurrence was particularly disruptive. Another possible explanation is that a threshold effect is operating, such that Chinese Americans report stressors that are more severe and not readily resolvable. Consequently, they might weigh adolescents down and, thus, be related to more problems with school adjustment. Another possibility is that because Chinese Americans reported far fewer problems with attendance and learning at school than other ethnic groups, this indicator of academic adjustment was more subject to deviation. Although spillover effects are more pronounced among Chinese American adolescents, on average these adolescents experienced less stress on a daily basis; therefore, the stronger propensity for spillover may be offset by the lower average levels of family and school stress reported by Chinese Americans.

Patterns of spillover were consistent across boys and girls in this study and thus did not reflect the pattern of gender differences previously documented in work–family spillover among adults. Prior studies have assessed spillover of mood, whereas the current study emphasizes family and school behaviors. Perhaps gender differences are more likely to be observed in terms of spillover of emotions. Girls maybe more inclined to express or endorse emotions such as sadness or anxiety than boys (Brody, 1985). If adjustment were measured in terms of emotions (e.g., depressed and anxious feelings), a different pattern of gender differences might emerge. Exploring such a possibility could uncover potential differences in spillover processes across gender.

A strength of this study is its focus on adolescence, a developmental period for which remarkably little is known about spillover. The findings from this study demonstrate how spillover operates in adolescents' daily home and school lives. Rather than directly asking adolescents about how events in different domains are related, using spillover methods enables detecting associations that adolescents may not recognize exist. This is powerful because adolescents may not be fully aware of how they are affected by stressful experiences. Stressful events may manifest across domains and carry across time, even if adolescents themselves are not aware of how stress at home and school is affecting them. Whether or not the relative impact of stressors is discernible on a daily basis, the accumulation of daily stress is perpetuated by the pervasive and cyclical nature of spillover. This may eventually result in even more serious problems, as suggested by the longitudinal findings concerning increases in stress and decrements in academic achievement over time. Overlooking the subtle, yet real, impact that stressful family experiences and academic adjustment problems have on adolescents in their daily lives could be detrimental in the long term. Al-

though these findings highlight possible negative short- and long-term consequences of daily stress, by the same token, they also point to the potential for improvement in adjustment across domains and over time by bolstering adolescents' ability to manage stress in their daily lives.

A limitation and important distinction to make in this study is that although temporal sequencing indicates directionality, it does not determine causality. Therefore, although we can draw conclusions about the timing and order of events, in terms of which preceded and which followed, we cannot infer that an earlier event caused a later event to occur. Other moderators that may alter spillover such as individual coping style should be explored. There are also likely to be other factors at the individual, family, community and societal levels that influence spillover processes, as these stressors do not exist in isolation but, rather, are embedded within a broader context (Allison et al., 1999). Given that chronic stressors or minor hassles, such as those studied here in the context of daily life, are associated with poorer physical and mental health outcomes (DeLongis, Folkman, & Lazarus, 1988; Larson & Ham, 1993), it will be important to explore whether continuous transmission of stress over time and across domains increases adolescents' vulnerability to negative health outcomes.

This study contributed to the extant literature by focusing on spillover relevant to the daily family and school lives of adolescents. Although some stressful experience may be inevitable in daily life, these findings document the concerning potential for stressors to become compounded as they carry over across time and domains of functioning. In order to attenuate some of the negative effects associated with the spillover of stress, identifying and understanding how stressful experiences are transmitted are important. The bidirectional process of spillover between family and school identified here suggests that reducing stress in the family may have benefits for adolescents' school adjustment and vice versa. Adolescents' lives are embedded within multiple contexts such that capturing the interactions between them furthers our understanding of processes relevant to adolescents' behavior and adjustment, which may in turn encourage and promote healthy development.

REFERENCES

Allison, K. W., Burton, L., Marshall, S., Perez-Febles, A., Yarrington, J., Kirsh, L. B., et al. (1999). Life experiences among urban adolescents: Examining the role of context. *Child Development, 70,* 1017–1029.

Almeida, D. M., & Kessler, R. C. (1998). Everyday stressors and gender differences in daily distress. *Journal of Personality and Social Psychology, 75,* 670–680.

Almeida, D. M., Neupert, S. D., Banks, S. R., & Serido, J. (2005). Do daily stress processes account for socioeconomic health disparities? *Journals of Gerontology, Series B, Psychological Sciences and Social Sciences, 60,* 34–39.

Almeida, D. M., Wethington, E., & Chandler, A. L. (1999). Daily transmission of tensions between marital dyads and parent-child dyads. *Journal of Marriage and the Family, 61,* 49–61.

Bolger, N., Davis, A., & Rafaeli, E. (2003). Diary methods: Capturing life as it is lived. *Annual Review of Psychology, 54,* 579–616.

Brody, L. R. (1985). Gender differences in emotional development: A review of theories and research. *Journal of Personality. Special Issue: Conceptualizing Gender* in *Personality Theory and Research, 53,* 102–149.

Chao, R., & Tseng, V. (2002). Parenting of Asians. In M. H. Bornstein (Ed.), *Handbook of parenting: Vol. 4. Social conditions and applied parenting* (2nd ed., pp. 59–93). Mahwah, NJ: Erlbaum.

de Anda, D., Baroni, S., Buskin, L., Buchwald, L., Morgan, J., Ow, J., et al. (2000). Stress, stressors and coping among high school students. *Children and Youth Services Review, 22,* 441–463.

DeLongis, A., Folkman, S., & Lazarus, R. S. (1988). The impact of daily stress on health and mood: Psychological and social resources as mediators. *Journal of Personality and Social Psychology, 54,* 486–496.

Fuligni, A. J. (1997). The academic achievement of adolescents from immigrant families: The roles of family background, attitudes, and behavior. *Child Development, 68, 351–363.*

Fuligni, A. J., & Hardway, C. (2006). Dimensions of family connectedness among adolescents from Mexican, Chinese, and European backgrounds. *Developmental Psychology, 42,* 1246–1258.

García-Coll, C., & Vázquez García, H. A. (1995). Hispanic children and their families: On a different track from the very beginning. In H. E. Fitzgerald, B. M. Lester, et al. (Eds.), *Children of poverty: Research, health, and policy issues. Reference books on family issues, Vol. 23 and Garland reference library of social science.* (Vol. 968, pp. 57–83). New York: Garland.

Grzywacz, J. G., Almeida, D. M., Neupert, S. D., & Ettner, S. L. (2004). Socioeconomic status and health: A microlevel analysis of exposure and vulnerability to daily stressors. *Journal of Health and Social Behavior, 45,* 1–16.

Harter, S. (1999). *The construction of the self: A developmental perspective.* New York: Guilford.

Harter, S., Bresnick, S., Bouchey, H. A., & Whitesell, N. R. (1997). The development of multiple role-related selves during adolescence. *Development and Psychopathology, 9,* 835–853.

Hetherington, E. M., & Stanley-Hagan, M. (1999). The adjustment of children with divorced parents: A risk and resiliency perspective. *Journal of Child Psychology and Psychiatry, 40,* 129–140.

Isakson, K., & Jarvis, P. (1999). The adjustment of adolescents during the transition into high school: A short term longitudinal study. *Journal of Youth and Adolescence, 28,* 1–26.

Kearney, C. A., Drabman, R. S., & Beasley, J. F. (1993). The trials of childhood: The development, reliability, and validity of the Daily Life Stressors Scale. *Journal of Child and Family Studies, 2,* 371–388.

Keene, J. R., & Reynolds, J. R. (2005). The job costs of family demands: Gender differences in negative family-to-work spillover. *Journal of Family Issues, 26,* 275–299.

Larson, R., & Asmussen, L. (Eds.). (1991). *Anger, worry, and hurt in early adolescence: An enlarging world of negative emotions.* Hawthorne, NY: Aldine de Gruyter.

Larson, R., & Ham, M. (1993). Stress and "storm and stress" in early adolescence: The relationship of negative events with dysphoric affect. *Developmental Psychology, 29,* 130–140.

Larson, R. W., Moneta, G., Richards, M. H., & Wilson, S. (2002). Continuity, stability, and change in daily emotional experience across adolescence. *Child Development, 73,* 1151–1165.

Laursen, B., Coy, K. C., & Collins, W. A. (1998). Reconsidering changes in parent-child conflict across adolescence: A meta-analysis. *Child Development, 69,* 817–832.

Lehman, B. J., & Repetti, R. L. (2007). Bad days don't end when the school bell rings: The lingering effects of negative school events on children's mood, self-esteem, and perceptions of parent-child interaction. *Social Development, 16*(3), 1–23.

Muris, P., Roelofs, J., Meesters, C., & Boomsma, P. (2004). Rumination and worry in non-clinical adolescents. *Cognitive Therapy and Research, 28,* 539–554.

Phelan, P., Yu, C. H., & Davidson, A. L. (1994). Navigating the psychosocial pressures of adolescence: The voices and experiences of high school youth. *American Educational Research Journal, 31,* 415–447.

Raudenbush, S. W., & Bryk, A. S. (2002). *Hierarchical linear models applications and data analysis methods.* Thousand Oaks, CA: Sage.

Repetti, R. L. (1989). Effects of daily workload on subsequent behavior during marital interaction: The roles of social withdrawal and spouse support. *Journal of Personality and Social Psychology, 57,* 651–659.

Repetti, R. L. (1996). The effects of perceived daily social and academic failure experiences on school-age children's subsequent interactions with parents. *Child Development, 67,* 1467–1482.

Schulz, M. S., Cowan, P. A., Pape Cowan, C., & Brennan, R. T. (2004). Coming home upset: Gender, marital satisfaction, and the daily spillover of workday experience into couple interactions. *Journal of Family Psychology, 18,* 250–263.

Smetana, J. G., & Asquith, P. (1994). Adolescents' and parents' conceptions of parental authority and personal autonomy. *Child Development, 65,* 1147–1162.

Spera, C. (2005). A review of the relationship among parenting practices, parenting styles, and adolescent school achievement. *Educational Psychology Review, 17,* 125–146.

Steinberg, L., Lamborn, S. D., Dornbusch, S. M., & Darling, N. (1992). Impact of parenting practices on adolescent achievement: Authoritative parenting, school involvement, and encouragement to succeed. *Child Development, 63,* 1266–1281.

Wadsworth, M. E., Raviv, T., Compas, B. E., & Connor-Smith, J. K. (2005). Parent and adolescent responses to poverty-related stress: Tests of mediated and moderated coping models. *Journal of Child and Family Studies, 14,* 283–298.

Lisa Flook is a postdoctoral fellow at the University of California, Los Angeles; and *Andrew J. Fuligni* is a professor of psychiatry and biobehavioral sciences in the David Geffen School of Medicine at UCLA.

QUESTIONS FOR REFLECTION

1. Do you see school and family spillover like that cited by Flook and Fuligni in your educational setting? If it looks different, how is it different?

2. According to the research in this article, how does family stress at home affect academic life at school? Conversely, how does academic stress at school affect family life at home?

3. How might you take the findings from this study and apply them to your educational setting? What are the practical applications of Flook and Fuligni's research and findings?

Leaders' Voices—
Putting Theory into Practice

What Ever Happened to Kick the Can? Wellness in School and Community

TOM BURTON

ABSTRACT: *In conversations about healthy student development and the curriculum, wellness is often overlooked in favor of learning goals and outcomes. In this article, Burton addresses the fact that young people today are inside more than ever and it shows too often in increased obesity rates and poorer overall health. He points out that the responsibility to help children become more physically fit has shifted from the family to schools, which creates an opportunity to establish new wellness policies in schools. Burton discusses how parents, teachers, administrators, and support staff joined with the Cuyahoga Heights School District to establish an ongoing committee to address physical fitness concerns, and he documents the changes which occurred as he offers suggestions to educators to promote wellness in support of human development.*

On most summer days in my youth, the warmth of the sun streaming through my open bedroom window woke me up. As I shook off the cobwebs of sleep, I could hear the sounds of children bolting out of their houses, hollering a quick good-bye to their mothers and fathers over their shoulders, eager to play until dark. I would join them, sprinting down my driveway, barely hearing my mother's admonition to be home for supper, hoping that the other neighborhood kids would agree to play my favorite game, Kick the Can.

It seemed like we played this game forever, sprinting, jogging, setting boundaries, establishing rules, honing our ability to kick that can. When we were done playing, we laughed and shared stories, rehashing the game. We got an incredible workout without making a conscious decision to exercise. Imagine that: kids running around all day long and enjoying the workout.

Ok, times are different now. We do need to be careful and watch our children. We can't let them play outside unsupervised in the same manner that my parents did. However, we also need to find a way to allow them to run and play—critical activities that are being neglected in our increasingly technological society.

The current generation is inside too much, playing on the computer or playing one of the many game systems that have captivated our society. In short, kids today are inside more than ever and it shows too often in their waistlines. While the increase in childhood obesity can be attributed to a variety of factors, more running and playing would almost certainly result in fewer obese children, especially when paired with better nutritional information and a better understanding of fitness in general.

Not surprisingly, the responsibility to help children become more physically fit has shifted from the family to schools. The federal Child Nutrition and WIC Reauthorization Act of 2004 (Public Law 108-265) required each local school district participating in the National School Lunch and/or Breakfast Program to establish a local wellness policy.

Long before mandated by PL 108-265, parents, teachers, administrators, and support staff joined forces in the Cuyahoga Heights School District (located just outside of Cleveland, Ohio) to establish an ongoing committee to address nutrition and physical fitness concerns. For the past several years, the committee has investigated cafeteria selections, physical education and health curricula, wellness fairs, and intramural schedules.

We realized that even though we initially felt that we were doing our best to keep our students active and healthy, we could and should do more for our students, staff, and community. We also realized the importance of approaching wellness through a systemic plan and allowing others a chance to give authentic input into the decisions that we made.

STUDENTS ON THE MOVE

Our first step was to promote the activities we already had in place, such as our existing sports teams. Teachers, parents, and staff members always encourage our students to get involved in school cocurricular activities, and approximately 75% of the students participate on athletic teams during the year. While that percentage is something to be proud of, we believed we needed to offer activities during the day as often as possible. Here are some of the activities and programs that we have implemented to encourage students to become more aware of the importance of their overall health.

Walking Club

As with many middle schools, it's hard to add an activity to our limited schedule without giving up anything in the exchange. The only flexibility in our schedule was at lunchtime, where we had 15 available minutes. We decided to use this time to start a walking club, held outside during good weather and in the gymnasium during inclement days. We rotate the grade levels each day and focus on 100% participation.

Intramurals

Also during this 15-minute block of time, we created an intramural schedule that affords opportunity for team play. Schedules are posted on an intramural bulletin board in the cafeteria to give the students plenty of notice. Before we knew it, we had games in the cafeteria, students walking around while watching the games, and others outside walking around the track.

Pedometers

Our physical education teachers use pedometers to keep the students moving throughout class. Each student receives a pedometer at the beginning of class. Once set, the students begin the activity for the day. At the end of class, all the students record their steps. On Friday, the steps are totaled and small rewards presented to the students for hitting a goal or new step level.

Students love seeing how many steps they are taking during class. Eventually, those students who are waiting to participate in a game or activities are walking around instead of sitting. It is clear to Tricia Broski, physical education teacher, that "the pedometers helped motivate students to move throughout class."

Fitness Day

This year we implemented a Fitness Day in all of our PE classes. Students divide into several groups and participate in different activities focused solely on developing their cardiovascular stamina and muscular strength.

Stations are set up around the gymnasium. Each station has a card with a team name on one side and a letter on the other. The object is to complete the station assignment and then turn over a card. If a team member finds her team's logo on the first try, she can take the card back to the team. Once the team has accumulated all the cards, the letters on the backside of the cards form a word. The first team to figure out the word wins; however, every team must finish.

Other Fitness Day activities involve the use of our fitness center, which includes treadmills, stationary bikes, and Nautilus machines.

VENDING MACHINES AND CAFETERIA OFFERINGS

While only a small percentage of meals are served in school in comparison to home, it is critical that we evaluate our selections. After all, for some of our students, the best meal they get is at school.

Director of Food Service Kim Schoeffler says that "since our state review in 2003, we have continued to cut the fat in our lunch program. Our menu is at a week's average of 30% or below total fat, with our saturated fat below 10%. Our chips are all baked and contain no trans fat. We continue to meet these requirements."

During the past three years, we have removed many of the unhealthy snacks from the vending machines, including soda pop and high sugar content drinks, and replaced them with healthier selections. Since many of our students stay after school to participate in cocurricular activities, it was paramount that we remove those items that provided no nutritional value.

STAFF AND COMMUNITY WELLNESS

While student wellness is a clear priority for us, it was also necessary to address staff wellness, not only to maintain a healthy staff, but also to provide our students with wellness role models.

To encourage staff members to get up and move, our superintendent, Peter Guerrera, offered

a 10,000-step challenge. Any staff member wishing to participate could sign up to receive a free pedometer. At the end of each week, staff members totaled their step totals and the superintendent posted the results. The goal was to have each participant reach at least 10,000 steps.

Another way to promote wellness is through staff meetings. Bill Porter, middle school principal at Willoughby Middle School, says that these meetings should include some healthy food and drink choices for attendees. "Several years ago, I tried to appeal to the sweet tastes of my staff members with pop and candy. Most recently, I have been serving bottled water and pretzels. If your budget allows, a faculty will really enjoy a fruit or vegetable tray. Some PTOs can help make that happen. Also, no matter what topic I'm covering at a given meeting, to promote mental health, I always open or close with something motivational, uplifting, interesting, or humorous."

In discussing what our committee can offer for our staff and community, we evaluated the possibility of hosting a Wellness Fair. While several area organizations have offered similar fairs, we want to make it as convenient as possible for the community to attend.

We will offer several health screenings (cholesterol, blood pressure, etc.) free of charge, provide information regarding health and fitness for all ages, showcase healthy cooking demonstrations, and so forth.

GET MOVING

We've heard a lot lately about the research on obesity and the unhealthy lifestyle of young adolescents. The data trends are not encouraging, as our youth are less healthy and becoming further detached from a healthy lifestyle. To put it bluntly, it is time we start getting off of our can and start kicking it!

Tom Burton is in his fourteenth year in administration and his eighth year as principal of Cuyahoga Heights Middle School in Cuyahoga Heights, Ohio. He is the president of the Ohio Middle School Association, serves on the Affiliate Task Force for the National Middle School Association, and has presented across the state of Ohio on a variety of topics.

QUESTIONS FOR REFLECTION

1. What do you think are the major contributing factors that have led to a decrease in physical activity for children both in and out of school? How might this trend be reversed?
2. Of all the new activities and programs that the Cuyahoga Heights School District introduced as part of its wellness plan, which do you think would be easiest to implement in your educational setting? Which would be the most difficult?
3. Do you consider health and wellness a major component of human development? How might learning be impacted by one's physical activities, both positively and negatively?

LEARNING ACTIVITIES

Critical Thinking

1. With respect to a school with which you are familiar, describe the curriculum as it relates to human development. To what extent are the theories of human development presented in this chapter reflected in the curriculum?
2. In *All Grown Up and No Place to Go: Teenagers in Crisis* (Addison-Wesley, 1998), David Elkind suggests that adolescents behave according to an "imaginary audience" (the belief that others are preoccupied with one's appearance and behavior) and the "personal fable" (the belief that one is immortal and not subject to the limitations that affect other human beings). How might the school curriculum help students to become more realistic in both of these areas?
3. In *Blackberry Winter: My Earlier Years* (Kodansha, 1995), noted anthropologist Margaret Mead expresses the view that the lack of a close relationship between grandparents and grandchildren in today's society is a serious loss to society and the child. She states that children need to grow up with three generations. Do you agree? Why? Will "adopt a grandparent" programs which many communities have implemented help this developmental need of children?
4. Studies by the Center on Organization and Restructuring of Schools at the University of Wisconsin-Madison have found that students at "successfully restructured" schools are more likely to conform to their school's expectations if they believe the school "cares" about students. How can teachers convey this attitude toward their students?
5. Piaget's theory of cognitive development has been criticized for having only four discrete stages tied to chronological age and for underestimating the cognitive abilities and competence of young children. To what extent do you agree with these

criticisms? (For more information see Gelman, R., and Baillargeon, R. (1983). "A Review of Some Piagetian Concepts." In P. Mussen, ed., *Carmichael's Manual of Child Psychology, Vol. 3: Cognitive Development* (E. Markman and J. Flavel, volume eds.). New York: Wiley, 1983; Woolfolk, A. *Educational Psychology*, 6th Ed. Boston: Allyn and Bacon, 1995, pp. 44–46; and Lourenco, Orlando, and Machado, Armando. "In Defense of Piaget's Theory: A Reply to 10 Common Criticisms." *Psychological Review* 103 (January 1996): 143–164.).

6. What are some developmental challenges that today's children and youth must confront that were unknown or little known to their parents or grandparents?

Application Activities

1. Ask your instructor to invite a counselor from the K–12 levels to your class. Ask this individual to discuss the most frequent developmental needs they encounter among students and to suggest ways that the curriculum can address those needs.

2. The March 2003 issue of *Educational Leadership* is devoted to the theme of creating caring schools. Read the articles in this journal and make a list of learning experiences that, with appropriate modification, could be incorporated into the curriculum with which you are most familiar.

Field Experiences

1. Visit a classroom at the level with which you are most familiar. What differences do you note among learners that are related to their stages of development? How might these differences affect their learning?

2. At the level with which you are most familiar, interview a student and, if possible, observe his or her classroom behavior. Then write a brief case study that focuses on common developmental tasks of learners in that age group. As appropriate, make references to the articles on human development included in this chapter.

Internet Activities

1. Go to the home page for James P. Comer's School Development Program and gather information on the structure and "operational expectations" of the three "teams" that make up the School Development Program.

2. Visit a few of the following web sites for K–12 students and determine to what extent each site reflects the developmental needs of children and youth:

The Awesome Lists
Berit's Best Sites for Children
Canada's SchoolNet
Discovery Channel School
KidLink
Kid's Web
Newton's Apple
Online Educator
Young Person's Guide to the Internet

4

Learning and Learning Styles

FOCUS QUESTIONS

1. What are the key principles of behavioral learning theories?

2. What role does socialization play in learning?

3. What are the key principles of cognitive learning theories?

4. What is the constructivist view of learning?

5. How do learning styles influence learning?

6. What are multiple intelligences?

The third basis of the curriculum is the nature of learning and learning styles. An understanding of how human beings learn is obviously of central importance for curriculum leaders. Learning theorists and researchers have not arrived at a universally accepted, precise definition of *learning;* however, most agree that learning is a change in an individual's knowledge or behavior that results from experience (Mazur, 1997; Slavin, 2003; Woolfolk, 2005). It is generally acknowledged that there are two families of learning theories—*behavioral* and *cognitive*—and that many subgroups exist within these two families. At the very least, curriculum leaders should understand the distinguishing features of each family, because each defines the curriculum differently, and each leads to or supports different instructional strategies. In addition, curricula and teaching practices are usually based on both families of theories to allow for the diverse needs of learners or different types of knowledge to be learned.

BEHAVIORAL LEARNING THEORIES

Behavioral learning theories emphasize observable changes in behavior that result from stimulus-response associations made by the learner. Thinking is part of a stimulus-response (S-R) sequence that begins and ends outside the individual learner, and learning is the product of design rather than accident. Learning is a conditioning process by which a person acquires a new response; and motivation is the urge to act, which results from a stimulus. Behavior is directed by stimuli from the environment, and a person selects one response instead of another because of the particular combination of prior conditioning and physiological drives operating at the moment of action. A person does not have to want to learn something in order to learn it. People can learn anything of which they are capable if they are willing to go through the pattern of activity necessary for conditioning to take place.

A major construct of S-R behavioral learning theories is the *rewarded response*. A response must be rewarded for learning to take place. What counts as a "reward" varies from learner to learner; although the reward must be important to the learner in some way. Rewards are often effective for certain types of learners: slow learners, those less prepared for the learning task, and those in need of step-by-step learning. Some teachers set up a system of rewards in their classrooms based on the concept of the rewarded response.

John B. Watson (1878–1958) and B. F. Skinner (1904–1990) are the two principal originators of behaviorist approaches to learning. Watson asserted that human behavior was the result of specific stimuli that elicited certain responses. Watson's view of learning was based partially on experiments conducted by Russian psychologist Ivan Pavlov (1849–1936), who noticed that a dog he was working with salivated shortly before he was given food. Pavlov discovered that by ringing a bell when food was given and repeating this several times, the sound of the bell alone (a conditioned stimulus) would make the dog salivate (a conditioned response). Watson believed that all learning conformed to the Pavlovian S-R model, which has become known as *classical* or *type S conditioning*.

Expanding on Watson's basic S-R model, Skinner developed a more comprehensive view of conditioning known as *operant* (or *type R*) *conditioning*. His model was based on the premise that satisfying responses are conditioned, unsatisfying ones are not; as he put it: "the things we call pleasant have an energizing or strengthening effect on our behaviour" (Skinner, 1972, p. 74).

Skinner believed that a "scientific" S-R approach to learning could serve humanitarian aims and help to create a better world. He maintained that notions about human free will based on an eighteenth-century political philosophy should not be allowed to interfere with the application of scientific methods to human affairs. In his novel *Walden Two* (1962), Skinner describes how a utopian society could be created through "behavioral engineering." By focusing on external conditions that shape and maintain human behavior, educators could turn their attention from ill-defined inner qualities and faculties to the observable and manipulable.

Social Learning Theories

While social learning theories reflect many of the principles of behavioral learning theories, they place greater emphasis on the influence of external cues on behavior and on how thinking influences action and vice versa. Social learning theories— which are widely endorsed by sociologists, anthropologists, and social psychologists— maintain that human beings have an unlimited capacity to learn. This capacity, however, *is* limited by social expectations and by constraints on behavior patterns that the immediate social environment considers appropriate. According to this view, the learning process is primarily social, and learning occurs through socialization. Socialization occurs in a variety of social settings, including the family, the peer group, the school, and the job, and it continues throughout life. According to Albert Bandura (1977, p. 12), the originator of social learning theory, "virtually all learning phenomena resulting from direct experience occur on a vicarious basis by observing other people's behavior and its consequences for them." Bandura's view of learning is often referred to as *modeling* or *observational learning.*

COGNITIVE LEARNING THEORIES

Cognitive learning theories focus on the mental processes people use as they acquire new knowledge and skills. Unlike behavioral learning theories, which focus on observable behavior, cognitive theories focus on the unobservable processing, storage, and retrieval of information from the brain. According to cognitive learning theories, the individual acts, originates, and thinks, and this is the important source of learning; according to behavioral learning theory, however, the individual learns by reacting to external forces.

Cognitive learning theories emphasize personal meaning, generalizations, principles, advance organizers, discovery learning, coding, and superordinate categories. In "Structures in Learning" in Chapter 6, Jerome Bruner, a leading cognitive learning theorist, applies generalizations concerning the following to curriculum planning: structure, organization, discovery learning, the "connectedness" of knowledge, meaningfulness, and the "problems approach."

Cognitive views of learning provide the theoretical basis for current approaches to "authentic" pedagogy and assessment of learning. As M. Bruce King, Jennifer Schroeder, and David Chawszczewski point out in "Authentic Assessment and Student Performance in Inclusive Secondary Schools" in this chapter: "teaching and learning of high intellectual quality and teaching for understanding offer compelling alternatives to more traditional forms of instruction focused on basic skills and content." Moreover, such approaches increase the learning of students with and without disabilities.

Cognitive Science

By adding to our understanding of how people think and learn, research in the field of cognitive science has contributed to the development of cognitive learning theories. Drawing from research in linguistics, psychology, anthropology, and computer science, cognitive scientists study the mental processes learners use as they acquire new knowledge. Often, cognitive scientists develop computer flow charts to illustrate how learners use their short- and long-term memory to manipulate symbols and process information. In "We Feel, Therefore We Learn: The Relevance of Affective and Social Neuroscience to Education" in this chapter, Mary Helen Immordinao-Yang and António Damásio explain how "emotional thought" influences the aspects of cognition that are most heavily emphasized in schools.

Curriculum Leadership Strategy

Periodically review the curriculum to ensure that it addresses not just the cognitive realm, but also the affective and psychomotor realms.

Gestalt-Field Views of Learning

During the first few decades of the twentieth century, several psychologists in Germany—and later in the United States—began to look at how learners organize information into patterns and wholes. *Gestalt* is a German term meaning "configuration" or "pattern," and Gestalt theorists maintain that "wholeness" is primary; one should start with the total aspects of a learning situation and then move to particulars in light of the whole. Thus, obtaining an "overview" is often an important step in learning, for without it we may be, as the popular saying goes, "unable to see the forest for the trees."

Another major element of the Gestalt view of learning is that the whole is always greater than the sum of its parts. Experiencing a moving symphony is more than hearing individual musical notes; watching a movie is more than looking at the thousands of individual still pictures that make up the movie. The nature of the whole determines the meaning of its parts, and individual perceptions determine meaning.

Constructivist Learning Theories

Since the mid-1980s, several educational researchers have attempted to identify how learners *construct* understanding of new material. Constructivist views of learning, therefore, focus on how learners make sense of new information—how they construct meaning based on what they already know. In part, the roots of constructivism can be traced back to Gestalt views of learning in that learners seek to organize new information into meaningful wholes.

According to constructivism, "*students develop new knowledge through a process of active construction.* They do not merely passively receive or copy input from teachers or textbooks. Instead, they actively mediate it by trying to make sense of it and relate it to what they already know (or think they know) about the topic" (Good & Brophy, 2003, p. 398). Constructivist-oriented curricula and instructional strategies focus on students' thinking about the material to be learned and, through carefully thought out prompts and questions, enable students to arrive at a deeper understanding of new material. Among the common elements of constructivist approaches to curriculum and teaching, research has identified the following effective practices:

1. The curriculum is designed to equip students with knowledge, skills, values, and dispositions that they will find useful both inside and outside of school.
2. Instructional goals emphasize developing student expertise within an application context and with emphasis on conceptual understanding of knowledge and self-regulated application of skills.
3. The curriculum balances breadth with depth by addressing limited content but developing this content sufficiently to foster conceptual understanding.
4. The content is organized around a limited set of powerful ideas (basic understandings and principles).
5. The teacher's role is not just to present information but also to scaffold and respond to students' learning efforts.

6. The students' role is not just to absorb or copy input but also to actively make sense and construct meaning.

7. Students' prior knowledge about the topic is elicited and used as a starting place for instruction, which builds on accurate prior knowledge and stimulates conceptual change if necessary (Good & Brophy, 2003, pp. 420–421).

A common element of constructivist approaches to curriculum planning and teaching is known as *scaffolding*—that is, providing learners with greater support during the early phases of learning and then gradually reducing support as their competence and ability to assume responsibility increase. The concept of scaffolding is based on the work of Lev Semenovich Vygotsky (1896–1934), a well-known Russian psychologist. Vygotsky coined the phrase *zone of proximal development* to refer to the point at which the learner needs assistance to continue learning. According to this view, effective instruction neither exceeds the learner's current level of understanding nor underestimates the learner's ability to learn independent of the teacher. The effective teacher varies the amount of help given to learners

> on the basis of their moment-to-moment understanding. If they do not understand an instruction given at one level, then more help is forthcoming. When they do understand, the teacher steps back and gives the child more room for initiative. In this way, the child is never left alone when he [or she] is in difficulty nor is he [or she] "held back" by teaching that is too directive and intrusive. (Wood, 1988, p. 81)

LEARNING STYLES

Much of the recent research on learning focuses on students' learning styles—that is, the approaches to learning that work best for them. Put differently, *learning styles* refers to individual typical ways of processing information and seeking meaning. These differences have also been called *learning modes, learning style preferences,* or *cognitive styles.* In "How Boys Learn" in this chapter, Michael Gurian and Kathy Stevens explore the "mismatch" between boys and conventional education, and they call for greater support for the ways boys learn. However, in "Where the Girls Are: The Facts about Gender Equity in Education" in this chapter, Christianne Corbett, Catherine Hill, and Andresse St. Rose maintain that there is no "crisis" in the education of boys. Their conclusions are based on the American Association of University Women's landmark study that summarizes decades of research on the relationship between gender and academic achievement.

Students' preferred learning styles are determined by a combination of hereditary and environmental factors. Some learners rapidly acquire new knowledge that they encounter; others learn best when they are independent and can shape their own learning. Some learn best in formal academic settings, while others learn best in informal, relaxed settings. Some learners require almost total silence, while others learn well in noisy, busy environments. Some learn intuitively, while others learn best in a step-by-step, linear, concrete fashion.

Learning style is an emerging concept, and there is no single "correct" view of learning styles to guide curriculum planners. In this chapter's *Leaders' Voices* section,

Elsa C. Bro chronicles how she used ethnographic research methods to identify the preferred learning style of a high school sophomore with learning difficulties. However, cultural differences in learning styles are subtle and difficult to identify. In "Culturally Relevant Pedagogy: Ingredients for Critical Reflection" in this chapter, Tyrone C. Howard presents five recommendations for developing culturally relevant teaching.

Within the last decade, much research has been conducted on students' preferred learning styles, and scores of conceptual models and accompanying learning-style assessment instruments have been developed. While critics have pointed out flaws in many learning-style schemes and maintain that there is little evidence to support their validity (Snider, 1990, 1992), curriculum leaders should be aware of the concept of learning styles and realize that some curricula may be more effective for some students than for others. In addition, though preferences for learning styles can be strong, they can also change as a person matures.

Multiple Intelligences

While many learning theorists believe that intelligence is the general ability to learn—to acquire and use new knowledge—others believe that "the weight of the evidence at the present time is that intelligence is multidimensional, and that the full range of these dimensions is not completely captured by any single general ability" (Sternberg, 1996, p. 11). For example, in response to cognitive theories of learning, which he believed were limited to logical-mathematical or scientific forms of intelligence valued in the West, Howard Gardner proposed in *Frames of Mind: The Theory of Multiple Intelligences* (1983, 1993a, p. 8) that "there is persuasive evidence for the existence of several relatively autonomous human intellectual competencies, [referred to] as 'human intelligences.' . . . [The] exact nature and breadth of each has not so far been satisfactorily established, nor has the precise number of intelligences been fixed." Gardner suggested that there were at least seven human intelligences: logical-mathematical, linguistic, musical, spatial, bodily-kinesthetic, intrapersonal, and interpersonal (in the mid-1990s, he identified an eighth intelligence, that of the naturalist).

The concept of multiple intelligences is clearly useful in curriculum planning and teaching. However, in his reflections twelve years after the publication of *Frames of Mind* (Gardner, 1995, p. 206), Gardner asserted that "MI [multiple intelligences] theory is in no way an educational prescription. [E]ducators are in the best position to determine the uses to which MI theory should be put. . . ." And, in "Probing More Deeply into the Theory of Multiple Intelligences" in this chapter, Gardner states that "educators should be cautious about characterizing the intellectual profiles of students."

Curriculum Leadership Strategy

Periodically review the curriculum to ensure that it addresses students' multiple intelligences and varied learning styles.

CRITERION QUESTIONS—LEARNING AND LEARNING STYLES

In light of individual differences among learners, curriculum planners and teachers need many ways to encourage learning. Knowledge and use of theories about learning and learning styles offer important guidelines in providing for individual differences and instructional alternatives. The following are among the criterion questions that can be derived from the theories of learning and learning styles discussed in this chapter.

1. Have both behavioral and cognitive views of learning been considered in planning the curriculum?
2. Has the significance of individual learning styles and how learners construct meaning been considered in planning the curriculum?
3. Does the curriculum include diverse activities for learning?
4. Does the curriculum allow learners to exhibit and develop different forms of intelligence?
5. Is the significance of learning theory concepts such as the following reflected in the curriculum: rewarded response, socialization, modeling, scaffolding, and zones of proximal development?

REFERENCES

Bandura, Albert. *Social Learning Theory.* Englewood Cliffs, NJ: Prentice-Hall, 1977.

Gardner, Howard. *Frames of Mind: The Theory of Multiple Intelligences.* New York: Basic Books, 1983. (A tenth-anniversary edition with a new introduction was published in 1993.)

———. "Reflections on Multiple Intelligences: Myths and Messages." *Phi Delta Kappan* 77, no. 3 (November 1995): 200–203, 206–209.

Good, Thomas E., & Brophy, Jere E. *Looking in Classrooms,* 9th Ed. Boston: Allyn and Bacon, 2003.

Mazur, J. *Learning and Behavior,* 4th Ed. Englewood Cliffs, NJ: Prentice-Hall, 1997.

Skinner, B. F. "Utopia through the Control of Human Behavior." In John Martin Rich, ed., *Readings in the Philosophy of Education.* Belmont, CA: Wadsworth, 1972.

Slavin, Robert. *Educational Psychology: Theory and Practice,* 7th Ed. Boston: Allyn and Bacon, 2003.

Snider, Vicki E. "Learning Styles and Learning to Read: A Critique." *Remedial and Special Education (RASE)* 13, no. 1 (January–February 1992): 6–18.

———. "What We Know about Learning Styles from Research in Special Education." *Educational Leadership* 48, no. 2 (October 1990): 53.

Sternberg, Robert J. "Myths, Countermyths, and Truths about Intelligence." *Educational Researcher* 25, no. 2 (March 1996): 11–16.

Wood, David. *How Children Think and Learn.* New York: Basil Blackwell, 1988.

Woolfolk, Anita. *Educational Psychology,* 9th Ed. Boston: Allyn and Bacon, 2005.

We Feel, Therefore We Learn: The Relevance of Affective and Social Neuroscience to Education

MARY HELEN
IMMORDINO-YANG
ANTÓNIO DAMÁSIO

ABSTRACT: *Recent advances in neuroscience are highlighting connections between emotion, social functioning, and decision making that have the potential to revolutionize understanding of the role of affect in education. In particular, the neurobiological evidence suggests that the aspects of cognition that we recruit most heavily in schools—namely learning, attention, memory, decision making, and social functioning—are both profoundly affected by and subsumed within the processes of emotion; we call these aspects emotional thought. The authors present evidence that sketches an account of the neurobiological underpinnings of morality, creativity, and culture, all topics of critical importance to education. The hope is that a better understanding of the neurobiological relationships between these constructs will provide a new basis for innovation in the design of learning environments.*

Recent advances in the neuroscience of emotions are highlighting connections between cognitive and emotional functions that have the potential to revolutionize our understanding of learning in the context of schools. In particular, connections between decision making, social functioning, and moral reasoning hold new promise for breakthroughs in understanding the role of emotion in decision making, the relationship between learning and emotion, how culture shapes learning, and ultimately the development of morality and human ethics. These are all topics of eminent importance to educators as they work to prepare skilled, informed, and ethical students who can navigate the world's social, moral, and cognitive challenges as citizens. In this article, we sketch a biological and evolutionary account of the relationship between emotion and rational thought, with the purpose of highlighting new connections between emotional, cognitive, and social functioning, and presenting a framework that we hope will inspire further work on the critical role of emotion in education.

Modern biology reveals humans to be fundamentally emotional and social creatures. And yet those of us in the field of education often fail to consider that the high-level cognitive skills taught in schools, including reasoning, decision making, and processes related to language, reading, and mathematics, do not function as rational, disembodied systems, somehow influenced by but detached from emotion and the body. Instead, these crowning evolutionary achievements are grounded in a long history of emotional functions, themselves deeply grounded in humble homeostatic beginnings. Any competent teacher recognizes that emotions and feelings affect students' performance and learning, as does the state of the body, such as how well students have slept and eaten or whether they are feeling sick or well. We contend, however, that the relationship between learning, emotion and body state runs much deeper than many educators realize and is interwoven with the notion of learning itself. It is not that emotions rule our cognition, nor that rational thought does not exist. It is, rather, that the original purpose for which our brains evolved was to manage our physiology, to optimize our survival, and to allow us to flourish. When one considers that this purpose inherently involves monitoring and altering the state of the body and mind in increasingly complex ways, one can appreciate that emotions, which play out in the body and mind, are profoundly intertwined with thought. And after all, this should not be surprising. Complex brains could not have evolved separately from the organisms they were meant to regulate.

But there is another layer to the problem of surviving and flourishing, which probably evolved as a specialized aspect of the relationship between emotion and learning. As brains and the minds they support became more complex, the problem became not only dealing with one's own self but managing social interactions and relationships. The evolution of human societies has produced an amazingly complex social and cultural context, and flourishing within this context means that only our most trivial, routine decisions and actions, and perhaps not even these, occur outside of our socially and culturally constructed reality. Why does a high school student solve a math problem, for example? The reasons range from the intrinsic reward of having found the solution, to getting a good grade, to avoiding punishment, to helping tutor a friend, to getting into a good college, to pleasing his/her parents or the teacher. All of these reasons have a powerful emotional component and relate both to pleasurable sensations and to survival within our culture. Although the notion of surviving and flourishing is interpreted in a cultural and social framework at this late stage in evolution, our brains still bear evidence of their original purpose: to manage our bodies and minds in the service of living, and living happily, in the world with other people.

This realization has several important implications for research at the nexus of education and neuroscience. It points to new directions for understanding the interface of biology, learning, and culture, a critical topic in education that has proven difficult to investigate systematically (Davis, 2003; Rueda, 2006; Rueda, August, & Goldenberg, 2006). It promises to shed light on the elusive link between body and mind, for it describes how the health and sickness of the brain and body can influence each other. And importantly, it underscores our fundamentally social

nature, making clear that the very neurobiological systems that support our social interactions and relationships are recruited for the often covert and private decision making that underlies much of our thought. In brief, learning, in the complex sense in which it happens in schools or the real world, is not a rational or disembodied process; neither is it a lonely one.

REASONING, DECISION MAKING, AND EMOTION: EVIDENCE FROM PATIENTS WITH BRAIN DAMAGE

To understand why this is so, we begin with some history, and a problem. Well into the 1980s, the study of brain systems underlying behavior and cognition was heavily dominated by a top-down approach in which the processes of learning, language, and reasoning were understood as high-order systems that imposed themselves upon an obedient body. It is not that emotions were completely ignored or that they were not viewed by some as having a brain basis. Rather, their critical role in governing behavior, and in particular rational thought, was overlooked (Damasio, 1994). Emotions were like a toddler in a china shop, interfering with the orderly rows of stemware on the shelves.

And then an interesting problem emerged. In a research atmosphere in which cognition ruled supreme, it became apparent that the irrational behavior of neurological patients who had sustained lesions to a particular sector of the frontal lobe could not be adequately accounted for by invoking cognitive mechanisms alone. After sustaining damage to the ventromedial prefrontal cortex, these patients' social behavior was compromised, making them oblivious to the consequences of their actions, insensitive to others' emotions, and unable to learn from their mistakes. In some instances, these patients violated social convention and even ethical rules, failing to show embarrassment when it was due and failing to provide appropriate sympathetic support to those who expected it and had received it in the past.

These patients' ability to make advantageous decisions became compromised in ways that it had not been before. In fact, there was a complete separation between the period that anteceded the onset of the lesion, when these patients had been upstanding, reliable, and foresightful citizens, and the period thereafter, when they would make decisions that were often disadvantageous to themselves and their families. They would not perform adequately in their jobs, in spite of having the required skills; they would make poor business deals in spite of knowing the risks involved; they would lose their savings and choose the wrong partners in all sorts of relationships. Why would patients suffering from compromised social conduct also make poor decisions about apparently rational matters, such as business investments?

The traditional way to explain these patients' symptoms had been that something had gone wrong with their logical abilities or their knowledge base, such that they could no longer make decisions in a rational way. But, in fact, with further testing, it became apparent that these patients did not have a primary problem with knowledge, knowledge access, or logical reasoning, as had previously been assumed. To the contrary, they could explain cogently the conventional social and logical rules that ought to guide one's behavior and future planning. They had no loss of knowledge or lowering of IQ in the traditional sense. Instead, it gradually became clear that disturbances in the realm of emotion, which had been viewed as a secondary consequence of their brain damage, could provide a better account of their poor decision making. Those emotional aspects included a diminished resonance of emotional reactions generally as well as a specific compromise of social emotions, such as compassion, embarrassment, and guilt. By compromising the possibility of evoking emotions associated with certain past situations, decision options, and outcomes, the patients became unable to select the most appropriate response based on their past experience. Their logic and knowledge could be intact, but they failed to use past emotional knowledge to guide the reasoning process. Furthermore, they

could no longer learn from the emotional repercussions of their decisions or respond emotionally to the reactions of their social partners. Their reasoning was flawed because the emotions and social considerations that underlie good reasoning were compromised (Damasio, Grabowski, Frank, Galaburda, & Damasio, 1994; Damasio, Tranel, & Damasio, 1990, 1991).

In retrospect, these patients provided a first glimpse into the fundamental role of emotion in reasoning and decision making. Missing a brain region that is now understood as needed to trigger a cascade of neurological and somatic events that together comprise a social emotion, such as embarrassment, compassion, envy, or admiration, their social behavior suffered. This is significant in itself, but even more intriguing was the realization that, without the ability to adequately access the guiding intuitions that accrue through emotional learning and social feedback, decision making and rational thought became compromised, as did learning from their mistakes and successes. While these patients can reason logically and ethically about standard cognitive and social problems in a laboratory setting (Saver & Damasio, 1991), out in the real world and in real time, they cannot use emotional information to decide between alternative courses of action. They can no longer adequately consider previous rewards and punishments or successes and failures, nor do they notice others' praise or disapproval. These patients have lost their ability to analyze events for their emotional consequences and to tag memories of these events accordingly. Their emotions are dissociated from their rational thought, resulting in compromised reason, decision making, and learning.

What does this mean for our argument about relevance to education? In addition to these patients, further evidence from psychophysiological and other studies of brain-damaged and normal people has allowed us to propose specific neural mechanisms underlying the role and operation of emotional signaling in normal and abnormal decision making (Bechara, 2005; Bechara & Damasio, 1997; Damasio, 1996). While the details of these neural mechanisms and evidence are beyond the scope of this article, taken as a whole, they show that emotions are not just messy toddlers in a china shop, running around breaking and obscuring delicate cognitive glassware. Instead, they are more like the shelves underlying the glassware; without them cognition has less support.

To recap, the prefrontal patients we have described have social deficits. We have argued that these are fundamentally problems of emotion and therefore manifest as well in the realm of decision making. The relationship between these symptoms is very informative, in that it suggests that hidden emotional processes underlie our apparently rational real-world decision making and learning. Furthermore, this relationship underscores the importance of the ability to perceive and incorporate social feedback in learning.

While the relevance of these insights to educational contexts has not yet been empirically tested, they lead us to formulate two important hypotheses. First, because these findings underscore the critical role of emotion in bringing previously acquired knowledge to inform real-world decision making in social contexts, they suggest the intriguing possibility that emotional processes are required for the skills and knowledge acquired in school to transfer to novel situations and to real life. That is, emotion may play a vital role in helping children decide when and how to apply what they have teamed in school to the rest of their lives. Second, the close ties between these patients' decision making, emotion, and social functioning may provide a new take on the relationship between biology and culture. Specifically, it may be via an emotional route that the social influences of culture come to shape learning, thought, and behavior.

While more work on the educational and cultural implications of these findings is warranted, interestingly, and sadly, some further insights into the biological connections between learning, emotion, and social functioning, especially as they relate to our hypothesis about culture, can be gleaned from another group of patients that has been discovered over the past few years. In this group, patients sustained comparable prefrontal damage in early childhood, rather than as adults. As they developed, these children were cognitively normal in the traditional IQ sense, able to use logical reasoning and factual knowledge to solve the kinds of academic problems expected of students. However, while smart in the everyday sense of the word, these children slowly revealed themselves as having varying degrees of psychopathic and antisocial tendencies. They were insensitive to punishment and reward and did not seek approval or social acceptance as typical children do. As adults, they were unable to competently manage their lives, wasting time and squandering resources and engaging in dangerous, antisocial, and aggressive behaviors. By outward appearances, these patients behaved in most ways similarly to the patients described above, who sustained prefrontal damage as adults (Anderson, Bechara, Damasio, Tranel, & Damasio, 1999; Damasio, 2005).

Additional investigation of adult patients with childhood onset of brain damage, though, revealed an intriguing difference between childhood and adult-onset prefrontal brain damage. While both groups can reason about traditional cognitive problems in the structure of the laboratory setting and both have normal IQs in the traditional sense, unlike patients with adult-onset prefrontal damage, childhood-onset patients appear never to have learned the rules that govern social and moral behavior. While adult-onset patients know right from wrong in the lab but are unable to use this information to guide their behavior, childhood-onset patients have apparently not learned right from wrong or the proper rules of social conduct. They do not know the social and ethical rules that they are breaking.

What is happening with these patients and how is it relevant to the argument at hand? Unlike the often remarkable compensation for linguistic and other capacities after early childhood brain damage, so far the system for social conduct and ethical behavior does not show this kind of compensation. It is not that access in an abstract sense to the rules of social conduct requires intact frontal cortices, as the adult-onset patients show, and it is not that a social or moral conduct center in the brain has been irreparably damaged, as this scenario would not explain changes in general decision making. Instead, the situation is both simpler and more grave. These early-onset prefrontal patients may be suffering from the loss of what we might term the *emotional rudder.* Without the ability to manipulate situations and to mark those situations as positive or negative from an affective point of view, these children fail to learn normal social behavior. In turn, they lose the commensurate decision-making abilities described earlier. Insensitive to others' responses to their actions, these children fail to respond to educators' and others' attempts to teach them normal behavior.

But there is another intriguing piece to be learned from these children regarding the relationship between cognition and emotion and the role of the emotional rudder in learning. As in the adult-onset patients, it is still possible for these patients to have an operating cognitive system that allows them to be smart on certain measures and in certain contexts, solving standard cognitive tasks in a laboratory or structured educational setting without difficulty. In these contexts, their lack of knowledge is confined to the social and moral domains.

And yet, once outside of the structured school setting, their social deficits manifest as a much broader problem. They have the nonsocial knowledge they need, but without the guiding effects of the emotional rudder, they cannot use this information to guide their everyday living, even in nonsocial contexts. What these patients confirm is that the very neurobiological systems that support emotional functioning in social interactions also support decision making generally. Without adequate access to social and cultural knowledge, these children cannot use their knowledge efficaciously. As Vygotsky posited more than three quarters of a century ago, social and cultural functioning actually does underlie much of our nonsocial decision making and reasoning. Or, more precisely, social behavior turns out to be a special case of decision making and morality to be a special case of social behavior (see Damasio, 2005, for

a more complete treatment of this argument). The neurological systems that support decision making generally are the same systems that support social and moral behavior. Without adequate access to emotional, social, and moral feedback, in effect the important elements of culture, learning cannot inform real-world functioning as effectively.

A PHYSIOLOGICAL AND EVOLUTIONARY ACCOUNT OF EMOTION AND COGNITION: FROM AUTOMATIC RESPONSES TO MORALITY, CREATIVITY, HIGH REASON, AND CULTURE

In the perspective of the insights described earlier, and of much research in neurobiology and general biology in the two intervening decades, the connection between emotion and cognition is being seen in a very different light. To outline the current position, we shall present a simple scenario. Think of an ant crawling along a sidewalk, carrying a piece of food back to its nest. The ant scurries into a sidewalk crack to avoid being stepped on, then continues industriously on its way. What motivates this ant to preserve its own life? How did it decide, albeit nonconsciously and automatically, to carry the piece of food and to turn toward its nest? Clearly, the decisions to hide to avoid being crushed, to carry the food, and to continue in the direction of the nest are primitive instances of cognition, composed of complex packages of innate responses that enable the ant to react advantageously to particular classes of situations. But what is essential to understand is that these and myriads of other primitive examples of cognition, even in the lowly ant, act together in the service of an emotional goal: to maintain and promote homeostasis and thus fitness. In short, the ant behaves the way it does because those behaviors promote its survival and efficiency. (Humans, as conscious beings, perceive that efficiency as well-being and pleasure.) Every action the ant takes is inherently biased toward helping the ant, or its group, do well.

Taking an evolutionary perspective, even the simplest unicellular organism has within the nucleus of its cell a master controller that permits that living organism to maintain itself for a certain span of life and to seek during that period the conditions that will allow it to thrive. Emotions and the mechanisms that constitute them as behaviors, which humans experience as resulting in punishment or reward, pain or pleasure, are, in essence, nature's answer to one central problem, that of surviving and flourishing in an ambivalent world. Put simply, the brain has evolved under numerous pressures and oppressions precisely to cope with the problem of reading the body's condition and responding accordingly and begins doing so via the machinery of emotion. This coping shows up in simple ways in simple organisms and in remarkably rich ways as brains get more complex. In the brains of higher animals and people, the richness is such that they can perceive the world through sensory processing and control their behavior in a way that includes what is traditionally called the mind. Out of the basic need to survive and flourish derives a way of dealing with thoughts, with ideas, and eventually with making plans, using imagination, and creating. At their core, all of these complex and artful human behaviors, the sorts of behaviors fostered in education, are carried out in the service of managing life within a culture and as such, use emotional strategies (Damasio, 1999).

Emotion, then, is a basic form of decision making, a repertoire of know-how and actions that allows people to respond appropriately in different situations. The more advanced cognition becomes, the more high-level reasoning supports the customization of these responses, both in thought and in action. With evolution and development, the specifications of conditions to which people respond, and the modes of response at their disposal, become increasingly nuanced. The more people develop and educate themselves, the more they refine their behavioral and cognitive options. In fact, one could argue that the chief purpose of education is to cultivate children's building of repertoires of cognitive and behavioral strategies and options, helping them to recognize the complexity of situations and to respond in increasingly flexible, sophisticated, and creative ways. In our view, out of these processes of recognizing and responding, the very processes that form the interface between cognition and emotion, emerge the origins of creativity—the artistic, scientific, and technological innovations that are unique to our species. Further, out of these same kinds of processing emerges a special kind of human innovation: the social creativity that we call morality and ethical thought.

As the childhood-onset prefrontal patients show, morality and ethical decision making are special cases of social and emotional functioning. While the beginnings of altruism, compassion, and other notions of social equity exist in simpler forms in the nonhuman primates (Damasio, 2003; Hauser, 2006), human cognitive and emotional abilities far outpace those of the other animals. Our collective accomplishments range from the elevating and awe inspiring to the evil and grotesque. Human ethics and morality are direct evidence that we are able to move beyond the opportunistic ambivalence of nature; indeed, the hallmark of ethical action is the inhibition of immediately advantageous or profitable solutions in the favor of what is good or right within our cultural frame of reference. In this way, ethical decision making represents a pinnacle cognitive and emotional achievement of humans. At its best, ethical decision making weaves together emotion, high reasoning, creativity, and social functioning, all in a cultural context (Gardner, Csikszentmihaly, & Damon, 2001).

Returning to the example of the ant, our purpose in including this example was not to suggest that human emotions are equivalent to those of the ant or that human behavior can be reduced to simple, nonspecific packages that unfold purely nonconsciously in response to particular situations. Although some aspects of human behavior and emotion could be characterized in this way, such reductionism would be grossly misplaced, especially in an essay about connections to education.

Instead, we aimed to illustrate that most, if not all, human decisions, behaviors, thoughts, and creations, no matter how far removed from survival in the homeostatic sense, bear the shadow of their emotive start.

In addition, as the prefrontal patients show, the processes of recognizing and responding to complex situations, which we suggest hold the origins of creativity, are fundamentally emotional and social. As such, they are shaped by and evaluated within a cultural context and, as we described in the previous section, are based upon emotional processing. No matter how complex and esoteric they become, our repertoire of behavioral and cognitive options continues to exist in the service of emotional goals. Neurobiologically and evolutionarily speaking, creativity is a means to survive and flourish in a social and cultural context, a statement that appears to apply from the relatively banal circumstances of daily living to the complex arena of ethical thought and behavior. In beginning to elucidate the neurobiological interdependencies between high reasoning, ethics, and creativity, all of which are fundamentally tied to emotion and critically relevant to education, we hope to provide a new vantage point from which to investigate the development and nurturance of these processes in schools.

EMOTIONAL THOUGHT: TOWARD AN EVIDENCE-BASED FRAMEWORK

In general, cognition and emotion are regarded as two interrelated aspects of human functioning. However, while it is perfectly reasonable and in fact necessary to distinguish between these two aspects in studying learning and development (Fischer & Bidell, 1998), the overly stringent preservation of this dichotomy may actually obscure the fact that emotions comprise cognitive as well as sensory processes. Furthermore, the aspects of cognition that are recruited most heavily in education, including learning, attention, memory, decision making motivation, and social functioning, are both profoundly affected by emotion and

in fact subsumed within the processes of emotion. Emotions entail the perception of an emotionally competent trigger, a situation either real or imagined that has the power to induce an emotion, as well as a chain of physiological events that will enable changes in both the body and mind (Damasio, 1994). These changes in the mind, involving focusing of attention, calling up of relevant memories, and learning the associations between events and their outcomes, among other things, are the processes with which education is most concerned. Yes, rational thought and logical reasoning do exist, although hardly ever truly devoid of emotion, but they cannot be recruited appropriately and usefully in the real world without emotion. Emotions help to direct our reasoning into the sector of knowledge that is relevant to the current situation or problem.

In Figure 1, we provide a graphical depiction of the neurological relationship between cognition and emotion. In the diagram, we have used the term emotional thought to refer to the large overlap between cognition and emotion. Emotional thought encompasses processes of learning, memory, and decision making, in both social and nonsocial contexts. It is within the domain of emotional thought that creativity plays out, through increasingly nuanced recognition of complex dilemmas and situations and through the invention of correspondingly flexible and innovative responses. Both the recognition and response aspects of creativity can be informed by rational thought and high reason. In our model, recognition and response processes are much like the concepts of assimilation and accommodation proposed by Piaget (1952, 1954). However, Piaget focused almost exclusively on cognition and the development of logic, and although he recognized a role for emotion in child development (Piaget, 1981), he did not fully appreciate the fundamentally emotional nature of the processes he described.

In the diagram, high reason and rational thought also contribute to high-level social and moral emotions to form the specialized branch of decision making that is ethics. Motivated reasoning works in a similar manner and refers to the

FIGURE 1

The evolutionary shadow cast by emotion over cognition influences the modern mind. In the diagram, the solid ellipse represents emotion; the dashed ellipse represents cognition. The extensive overlap between the two ellipses represents the domain of emotional thought. Emotional thought can be conscious or nonconscious and is the means by which bodily sensations come into our conscious awareness. High reason is a small section of the diagram and requires consciousness.

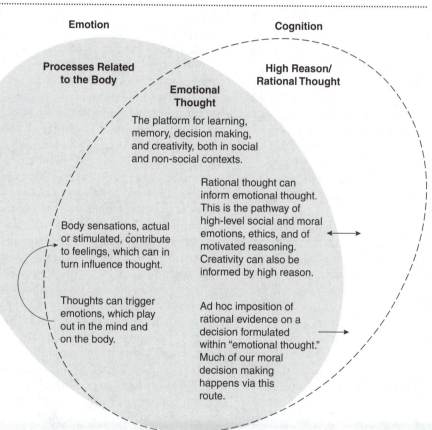

Emotion   **Cognition**

Processes Related   **High Reason/**
to the Body   **Rational Thought**

Emotional
Thought

The platform for learning, memory, decision making, and creativity, both in social and non-social contexts.

Rational thought can inform emotional thought. This is the pathway of high-level social and moral emotions, ethics, and of motivated reasoning. Creativity can also be informed by high reason.

Body sensations, actual or stimulated, contribute to feelings, which can in turn influence thought.

Thoughts can trigger emotions, which play out in the mind and on the body.

Ad hoc imposition of rational evidence on a decision formulated within "emotional thought." Much of our moral decision making happens via this route.

process by which emotional thoughts gain additional significance through the application of rational evidence and knowledge. In the other direction, rational evidence can be imposed upon certain kinds of emotional thought to produce the sort of automatic moral decision making that underlies intuitive notions of good and evil (Greene, Nystrom, Engell, Darley, & Cohen, 2004; Greene, Sommerville, Nystrom, Darley, & Cohen, 2001; Haidt, 2001). For example, in evaluating the morality of incest, experimental evidence suggests

that people decide quickly at the subconscious and intuitive level and later impose ad hoc rational evidence on their decision (Haidt, 2001). Conversely, complex moral dilemmas such as whether to send a nation to war are (one hopes) informed by an abundance of rational evidence.

On the left side of the diagram, the bodily aspects of emotion are represented as a loop from emotional thought to the body and back. Here, emotional thoughts, either conscious or nonconscious, can alter the state of the body in characteristic ways, such as by tensing or relaxing the skeletal muscles or by changing the heart rate. In turn, the bodily sensations of these changes, either actual or simulated, contribute either consciously or nonconsciously to feelings, which can then influence thought. (Simulated body sensation refers to the fact that sometimes imagining bodily changes is sufficient; actually tensing the fists, for example, is not necessary.) This is the route by which rational deliberations over, say, a nation's wartime decisions can produce high-level social emotions such as indignation, as well as the bodily manifestations of these emotions, such as tensed fists, increased heart rate, or loss of appetite. The feeling of these bodily sensations, either consciously or not, can then bias cognitive processes such as attention and memory toward, in this case, aggression. The end result may be an unprovoked argument with one's friend over a topic totally unrelated to the war, the creation of a bleak and angry abstract painting, or a generally tense mood.

In addition to the evidence discussed above, support for these relationships between the body, emotion, and cognition comes mainly from neurobiological and psychophysiological research, in which the induction of emotion, either directly by a stimulus in the environment or indirectly via thoughts or memories, causes mental changes as well as physiological effects on the body. In turn, feelings of emotion rely on the somatosensory systems of the brain. That is, the brain areas associated with interoception (the sensing of body states) are particularly active as people feel emotions such as happiness, fear, anger, or sadness (Damasio et al., 2000).

To conclude, in presenting this model, our goal is not to devalue established notions of cognition and emotion but to provide a biologically based account of this relationship and to begin to specify the nature of the overlap between cognition and emotion in a way that highlights processes relevant to education. These processes include learning, memory, decision making, and creativity, as well as high reason and rational thinking. They also include the influence of the mind on the body and of the body on the mind.

EDUCATIONAL IMPLICATIONS: A CALL FOR FURTHER RESEARCH

In teaching children, the focus is often on the logical reasoning skills and factual knowledge that are the most direct indicators of educational success. But there are two problems with this approach. First, neither learning nor recall happen in a purely rational domain, divorced from emotion, even though some of our knowledge will eventually distill into a moderately rational, unemotional form. Second, in teaching students to minimize the emotional aspects of their academic curriculum and function as much as possible in the rational domain, educators may be encouraging students to develop the sorts of knowledge that inherently do not transfer well to real-world situations. As both the early- and late-acquired prefrontal damage patients show, knowledge and reasoning divorced from emotional implications and learning lack meaning and motivation and are of little use in the real world. Simply having the knowledge does not imply that a student will be able to use it advantageously outside of school.

As recent advances in the neurobiology of emotions reveal, in the real world, cognition functions in the service of life regulating goals, implemented by emotional machinery. Moreover, people's thoughts and feelings are evaluated within a sociocultural context and serve to help them survive and flourish in a social, rather than simply opportunistic, world. While the idea that learning happens in a cultural context is far from new (Tomasello, Carpenter, Call, Behne, & Moll, 2005), we hope that these new insights from neurobiology, which shed light on the nested relationships between emotion, cognition, decision making, and social functioning, will provide a jumping-off point for new thinking on the role of emotion in education. As educators have long known, it is simply not enough for students to master knowledge and logical reasoning skills in the traditional academic sense. They must be able to choose among and recruit these skills and knowledge usefully outside of the structured context of a school or laboratory. Because these choices are grounded in emotion and emotional thought, the physiology of emotion and its consequent process of feeling have enormous repercussions for the way we learn and for the way we consolidate and access knowledge. The more educators come to understand the nature of the relationship between emotion and cognition, the better they may be able to leverage this relationship in the design of learning environments.

In conclusion, new neurobiological evidence regarding the fundamental role of emotion in cognition holds the potential for important innovations in the science of learning and the practice of teaching. As researchers struggle with new directions and techniques for learning about these connections, a biological framework may help to constrain possibilities and generate new hypotheses and research directions. Just as neuroscience is coming to inform other education-related topics and problems (Goswami, 2006), the study of emotions, creativity, and culture is ripe for interdisciplinary collaborations among neuroscientists, psychologists, and educators. After all, we humans cannot divorce ourselves from our biology, nor can we ignore the high-level sociocultural and cognitive forces that make us special within the animal kingdom. When we educators fail to appreciate the importance of students' emotions, we fail to appreciate a critical force in students' learning. One could argue, in fact, that we fail to appreciate the very reason that students learn at all.

Acknowledgments—This work was supported by a grant from the Annenberg Center for Communication at the University of Southern California and by a grant from the Mathers Foundation.

REFERENCES

Anderson, S. W., Bechara, A., Damasio, H., Tranel, D., & Damasio, A. R. (1999). Impairment of social and moral behavior related to early damage in human prefrontal cortex. *Nature Neuroscience, 2,* 1032–1037.

Bechara, A. (2005). Decision making, impulse control and loss of willpower to resist drugs: A neurocognitive perspective. *Nature Neuroscience, 8,* 1458–1463.

Bechara, A., & Damasio, H. (1997). Deciding advantageously before knowing the advantageous strategy. *Science, 275,* 1293–1295.

Damasio, A. R. (1994). *Descartes' error: Emotion, reason and the human brain.* New York: Avon Books.

Damasio, A. R. (1996). The somatic marker hypothesis and the possible functions of the prefrontal cortex. *Transactions of the Royal Society (London), 351,* 1413–1420.

Damasio, A. R. (1999). *The feeling of what happens.* New York: Harcourt Brace.

Damasio, A. R. (2003). *Looking for Spinoza: Joy, sorrow and the feeling brain.* Orlando, FL: Harcourt.

Damasio, A. R. (2005). The neurobiological grounding of human values. In J. P. Changeux, A. R. Damasio, W. Singer, & Y. Christen (Eds.), *Neurobiology of human values* (pp. 47–56). London: Springer Verlag.

Damasio, A. R., Grabowski, T. J., Bechara, A., Damasio, H., Ponto, L. L. B., Parvizi, J., & Hichwa, R. D. (2000). Subcortical and cortical brain activity during the feeling of self-generated emotions. *Nature Neuroscience, 3,* 1049–1056.

Damasio, A. R., Tranel, D., & Damasio, H. (1990). Individuals with sociopathic behavior caused by frontal damage fail to respond autonomically to social stimuli. *Behavioral Brain Research, 41,* 81–94.

Damasio, A. R., Tranel, D., & Damasio, H. (1991). Somatic markers and the guidance of behavior. Theory and preliminary testing. In H. S. Levin, H. M. Eisenberg, & A. L. Benton (Eds.), *Frontal lobe function and dysfunction* (pp. 217–229). New York: Oxford University Press.

Damasio, H. (2005). Disorders of social conduct following damage to prefrontal cortices. In J. P. Changeux, A. R. Damasio, W. Singer, & Y. Christen (Eds.), *Neurobiology of human values* (pp. 37–46). London: Springer Verlag.

Damasio, H., Grabowski, T., Frank, R., Galaburda, A. M., & Damasio, A. R. (1994). The return of Phineas Gage: Clues about the brain from the skull of a famous patient. *Science, 264,* 1102–1105.

Davis, H. A. (2003). Conceptualizing the role and influence of student-teacher relationships on children's social and cognitive development. *Educational Psychologist, 38,* 207–234.

Fischer, K. W., & Bidell, T. R. (1998). Dynamic development of psychological structures in action and thought. In R. M. Lerner (Ed.), *Handbook of child psychology: Theoretical models of human development* (5th ed., Vol. 1, pp. 467–561). New York: Wiley.

Gardner, H., Csikszentmihaly, M., & Damon, W. (2001). *Good work: When excellence and ethics meet.* New York: Basic Books.

Goswami, U. (2006). Neuroscience and education: From research to practice? *Nature Reviews Neuroscience, 7, 406–411.*

Greene, J. D., Nystrom, L. E., Engell, A. D., Darley, J. M., & Cohen, J. D. (2004). The neural bases of cognitive conflict and control in moral judgment. *Neuron, 44,* 389–400.

Greene, J. D., Sommerville, R. B., Nystrom, L. E., Darley, J. M., & Cohen, J. D. (2001). An fMRI investigation of emotional engagement in moral judgment. *Science, 293,* 2105–2108.

Haidt, J. (2001). The emotional dog and its rational tail: A social intuitionist approach to moral judgment. *Psychological Review, 108,* 814–834.

Hauser, M. (2006). *Moral minds: How nature designed our universal sense of right and wrong.* New York: Harper Collins.

Piaget, J. (1952). *The origins of intelligence in children* (M. Cook, Trans.). New York: International Universities Press. (Original work published 1936)

Piaget, J. (1954). *The construction of reality in the child* (M. Cook, Trans.). New York: Basic Books. (Original work published 1937)

Piaget, J. (1981). *Intelligence and affectivity: Their relationship during child development* (T. A. Brown & C. E. Kaegi, Eds./Trans.). Palo Alto, CA: Annual Reviews Monograph. (Originally presented as lectures, 1953–1954)

Rueda, R. (2006). Motivational and cognitive aspects of culturally accommodated instruction: The case of reading comprehension. In D. M. McInerney, M. Dowson, & S. V. Etten (Eds.), *Effective schools: Vol. 6: Research on sociocultural influences on motivation and learning* (pp. 135–158). Greenwich, CT: Information Age Publishing.

Rueda, R., August, D., & Goldenberg, C. (2006). The sociocultural context in which children acquire literacy. In D. August & T. Shanahan (Eds.), *Developing literacy in second-language learners: Report of the National Literary Panel on language-minority children and youth* (pp. 319–340). Mahwah, NJ: Erlbaum.

Saver, J. L., & Damasio, A. R. (1991). Preserved access and processing of social knowledge in a patient with acquired sociopathy due to ventromedial frontal damage. *Neuropsychologia, 29,* 1241–1249.

Tomasello, M., Carpenter, M., Call, J., Behne, T., & Moll, H. (2005). Understanding and sharing of intentions: The origins of cultural cognition. *Behavioral and Brain Sciences, 28,* 675–735.

Mary Helen Immordino-Yang holds a postdoctoral appointment at the USC Brain and Creativity Institute and the USC Rossier School of Education; and *António Damásio* is David Dornsife Professor of Neuroscience at the University of Southern California, where he heads USC's Brain and Creativity Institute.

QUESTIONS FOR REFLECTION

1. What does the research on patients with brain damage tell researchers about reasoning, decision making, and emotion, especially as it relates to education?
2. The authors write that "knowledge and reasoning divorced from emotional implications and learning lack meaning and motivation and are of little use in the real world." What does this statement suggest about the importance of emotional learning in schools and how might educators better support emotional learning in the acquisition of knowledge and reasoning skills?
3. How should educators initiate interdisciplinary collaboration with neuroscientists and psychologists as the authors recommend? Is it possible for collaborative relationships such as those between educators and neuroscientists and psychologists to develop, or is that goal unrealistic?

How Boys Learn

MICHAEL GURIAN
KATHY STEVENS

ABSTRACT: *Gurian and Stevens explore the ways in which boys learn as they discuss a mismatch between boys and conventional education. They discuss gender and the brain and call for an end to the gender plasticity myth. Furthermore, the authors call for greater support and research into the ways that boys learn. They conclude by presenting a model they believe will "help protect the minds of boys."*

To respect that fury or those giddy high spirits or a body that seems perpetually mobile is to respect nature, much as one respects the strength of a hurricane, the rush of a waterfall.

—Sara Ruddick, author and mother

I. THE MISMATCH BETWEEN BOYS AND CONVENTIONAL EDUCATION

The image of a schoolchild as someone sitting and reading has become the poster image for education, especially in the past fifty years. This is not a bad image, but it is an incomplete match with the way the minds of many of our boys work. Perhaps you have seen the mismatch in your own homes and schools: boys struggling to learn in the ways provided for them, teachers and families becoming frustrated, boys being labeled "difficult" or "failures" and becoming morose with self-doubt.

In a recent Gurian Institute workshop, material on "boy energy" and the male brain led to a spirited discussion about the issues our sons face. A teacher raised a key question—a question that is raised in nearly every setting in which the nature-based material is presented: "Should we keep trying to change the boys and their energy, or should we change the educational system they find themselves in?" Another teacher asked, "Is this just a pedagogical issue, or are we now facing a moral one?"

Those are questions each of us must now answer, armed as we are with scientific information about the nature of our sons. The authors believe that every time a teacher wonders why boys are "trouble in the classroom," he or she is asking a moral question. Every time the faculty lounge becomes a place of conversation about why boys are bringing down standardized test scores, the teachers are asking the same question. When a mother and father agonize over whether to put their son on medication, they are asking the question. Among our children themselves, the question is silently resounding as the kids who are having trouble learning their lessons look at others who learn so very well.

Should we keep trying to change our boys, or should we change the educational system in which they are now taught? The answer to that question will require parents, teachers, and schools to decide what parts of nature, nurture, and culture can and should be changed, and what parts can't and shouldn't. It tacitly—directly—raises these questions:

- Is male nature—the male brain—plastic enough to be changed to fit today's classrooms?
- If it is, how do we better effect change than we are now doing, so that boys no longer get most of the failing grades?
- If it is not, how can our educational system change to accommodate the male brain so that we can gain the positive results we all want for our sons?

II. HOW GENDER *REALLY* HAPPENS IN THE BRAIN

Human nature hardwires gender into our brains in three biological stages. The first stage has been clarified by genetics research, the second by endocrinological research, and the third by psychosocial research.[1]

Stage 1. Chromosome markers for gender are included in the genomes of girls and boys at the time of conception. Researchers at UCLA have identified chromosome markers—built into the fetal brain—for the development of a male and female.

Stage 2. Those chromosome markers compel surges of male and female hormones in the womb that format XX brains to be female and XY brains to be male. In-utero bombardment of hormones into the brain occurs with intense frequency between the second and fifth months of gestation. Researchers at various universities around the world, including the University of London, McMaster University in Canada, UCLA, and the University of Pennsylvania, can now trace the development of gender in the fetal brain via bombardments of testosterone and other hormones.

Stage 3. The child is born a boy or girl, sending nonverbal and then verbal cues to parents, the nurturing community, and the larger culture. These cues are biological—based in the child's genetics and hardwiring. Mom, Dad, and extended family, then teachers, schools, and community members like you, like us, read the male and female signals, cues, and characteristics. These signals and readings are now being visually traced through SPECT and PET scan research in attachment theory, conducted in many parts of the world, including the University of Denver and Harvard University.

It's important to remember that none of these researchers is involved in a nature-*versus*-nurture framework. All this research recognizes the *vast*

interplay between genetic, hormonal, neural, and social forces. All the researchers also recognize that maleness and femaleness are things we start out with: we are born with them. Although it was popular thirty years ago to believe otherwise, scientific research in our era has put to rest the idea that gender is completely a matter of nurture. Gender is inborn and then it becomes socialized by cultures.

Why is the human genome, brain, and bonding system set up to be male and female by nature? No

---

DID YOU KNOW?

- As of four days of age, girls tend to spend twice as much time as boys maintaining eye contact with adults. Bonding chemistry and the visual cortex of boys and girls already differ at four days old.

- By four months of age, boys are less likely than girls to distinguish between a known individual and a stranger. Memory centers as well as spatial-mechanical pathways already work differently in boys and girls. Male babies are in general more inclined than female babies to spend more time during a day looking at objects moving in space—for instance, mobiles hung from a ceiling. Girls, in contrast, are more likely to turn their gaze immediately to their caregivers.

- Infant girls also pay closer attention to the words of caregivers. Verbal centers are developing in the female brain more quickly than in the male.

- Little boys, when given dolls to play with, more often than girls pull the heads off, hit them against a table, throw them in the air, or generally engage in some kind of physical, kinesthetic, or spatial play with the dolls. Girls, in contrast, from very early in life, begin to use words with the doll. Given how much earlier the female centers for verbal communication develop in the brain, this comes as no surprise. Because of higher levels of oxytocin, girls form bonds with objects that boys merely use as physical learning tools.[2]

researcher can be completely sure. People with a religious base for understanding human nature say, "This is how God created us." The more science-based work in evolutionary biology suggests that the most probable cause for our male-female brain difference lies in the millions of years of human evolution, during which humans primarily hunted and gathered.

Because males mainly hunted, they needed to develop a more spatial-mechanical brain. They needed to see well, but did not need fine detail sensory awareness as much as did females, who cared far offspring. The male brain was wired, therefore, for more physical movement—with more blood flow in the brain stem than the female brain has—but for less verbal input and output. (Words weren't needed much during the hunt.)

Whether you choose a religious or scientific explanation, the new brain technologies allow us to see the differences for ourselves between male and female in the brain. And even if you don't have PET scan equipment in your living room—none of us does! —you can still see what the geneticists, biologists, and sociologists are getting at.

III. ENDING THE MYTH OF GENDER PLASTICITY AND SUPPORTING THE WAY BOYS *ACTUALLY* LEARN

Given the biological and social evidence of male-female brain difference, can a nurturing community, a school, a family, a culture make a boy change the gender of his brain? Can a typical mom, by just talking to or reading to an average little boy, force his verbal centers to be like an average girl's? Should a school compel a boy to become the kind of learner it has decided will be "easiest to teach"?

The new sciences now challenge all of us—moms, dads, grandparents, teachers, policymakers—to come to an informed conclusion about the relationship between a boy's nature, his nurtured life, and his cultural experience. We spend only a few years in a close, day—today supervisory relationship with our children: how do we want to spend those years? What kind of care do we want to give to their very human nature, their wonderful minds?

The new scientific research merits concluding that although all children are unique and individual, and although everyone is constantly learning new skills and developing new modes of communication, *the gender of the human brain is not plastic, not a new skill to be learned, not a new mode of communication*. It is as hardwired into the brain as a person's genetic personality. In the same way that you cannot change a shy person into an extrovert, you cannot change the brain of a boy into the brain of a girl.

The idea that not all elements of the brain—especially not gender—are plastic is very important to our dialogue about the state of boyhood in education. Our educational system has bought into the idea of "overall neural plasticity." Because of this mythical concept of the brain as a magical, changing device, very few academic institutions train teachers in the neural sciences of gender. This aspect of human development is ignored, and young teachers, like young parents, are taught that being a "boy" or a "girl" is culturally insignificant in education, that basically all kids learn the same way and can be educated in a way that ensures gender-exclusive, predictable results.

Research from the new gender and brain sciences begs us to move beyond this myth. The move constitutes a second major step toward solving the crisis of male education. As step two finds its way into schools of education, young teachers will be shown PET scans, SPECT scans, and MRIs of the male and female brain and be trained to understand the gender reality we all experience.

You as an individual—and your school as a collective—can become a leader in making this happen. Because our biological sciences are now able to use PET scans, MRIs, and other tests, we can now discern how gender is marked into our genomes from millions of years of human development and still lights up the individual brains of boys and girls. You can bring this information to homes, schools, social policies, and universities and colleges. You can help your community notice how tough the myth of gender plasticity is making life for our sons. When you notice males in educational distress, you can point out that we are creating for our sons an educational system not well suited to certain aspects of their brains; a system that claims they are defective, disordered, or incorrigible because they can't learn; a system that insists that they should be able to change— even further, that their inability to change is yet another flaw in their character as males, one that supposedly requires medication.

If our civilization continues to buy into the myth of gender plasticity, larger numbers of our sons will continue to do poorly in school. They will emerge from years of waste and failure without the normal development and skills we've all assumed for years that they would acquire, and, during this entire struggle and conflict, *they* will continue to frustrate us by "not changing."

IV. A BOY-FRIENDLY MODEL FOR PROTECTING THE MINDS OF BOYS

If you agree with our argument that the current educational system often fails to accommodate the hardwiring of boys' brains and does not provide them with an appropriate system of learning, and if you agree that our homes and schools should do less to try to change our boys and more to help them learn naturally, then you can become an ambassador for boys, a protector of their minds. As an ambassador you'll join us, not in trying to alter the nature of boys or girls, but instead in working toward two goals:

1. *Expression and development of the natural self of the child.* The child's genetic self is most important to his or her learning, and those who aid the child are charged with helping that self become fully expressive and developed within the frameworks of a humane society.

2. *Compensation for areas of inherent disadvantage or fragility.* These areas of disadvantage emerge for any child because of particular genetic or environmentally caused weaknesses in his or her learning brain or because the child as an individual carries learning characteristics that don't fit the mass.

Our suggestions detailed in other sections of *The Minds of Boys* avoid joining with any ideologies that measure success of the child's education by *measuring significant alteration* of the child's mind, whatever part of the gender-brain continuum the child is on. We believe that to base a child's education on the hope of altering a brain's inherent method of self-development is an affront to freedom and ultimately leads to suppression or disengagement of the child's true self and potential for success.

A child who expresses himself and learns to compensate for weaknesses is following one of the most natural instincts of our species: to *adapt*. We as adults protect the minds of children when we help the children adapt, using their own natural skills and talents, to the needs of a society. We don't protect their minds by putting a generation of schoolboys on drugs or watching them gradually fail.

Breaking down the myth of gender plasticity is not necessarily a simple thing to accomplish. But our culture has, in a few decades, successfully confronted a great deal of the patriarchal, sexist, and industrial system that was hurting girls, and improved the lives of girls and women. There's still a way to go, but there has been substantial change. And in this process, our culture did not force girls' brains or nature to change in order for them to succeed in our educational system. All of us came together to change the system in order to fit girls.

Specifically, we brought more verbal functioning to our math and science classes, trained teachers to use more writing and group conversation in teaching those subjects, changed our testing of those subjects to include more explanative and discursive essay answers, and developed new ways to encourage our girls at home that fit their natural need for verbal encouragement.

The proof of our success with girls is measurable today: the industrialized world has closed the female-to-male math and science gaps in our schools. Girls now receive grades as good as and better than boys in these classes. In California, girls are now actually outperforming boys in math and science. As we noted earlier, girls are no longer shortchanged in many schools—they are high performers. The changes we made to our educational system worked!

Changing our educational system to help boys will admittedly be harder, because the changes that have been made to help our daughters will actually make boys' education more problematic. Furthermore, in our consideration of girls' needs, we never had to fight the myth of gender plasticity—we never said, "Our girls are defective." We always said, "The system is defective." Changing the system for our boys can be also accomplished—without hurting our girls—and it must be.

NOTES

1 Dewing, Phoebe, Tao Shi, Steve Horvath, and Eric Vilain. 2003. "Sexually Dimorphic Gene Expression in Mouse Brain Precedes Gonadal Differentiation." *Molecular Brain Research* 118 (1–2): 82–90; Schore, Allan N. 2001. "Effects of a Secure Attachment Relationship on Right Brain Development, Affect Regulation, and Infant Mental Health." *Infant Mental Health* 22 (1–2): 7–66.
2 Rhoades, Steven E. 2004. *Taking Sex Differences Seriously.* San Francisco: Encounter Books.

Michael Gurian is the author of twenty books, among them *The Wonder of Boys* and *The Wonder of Girls.* He is the cofounder of the Gurian Institute in Colorado Springs, Colorado. *Kathy Stevens* is the training director of the Gurian Institute.

QUESTIONS FOR REFLECTION

1. Gurian and Stevens ask if we should "keep trying to change our boys" or do we need to instead "change the educational system in which they are now taught." How do they address this question and do you agree or disagree with their position?
2. Does the information provided in the article about boys and learning match your experiences working with boys in schools? If not, what is different about boys you have worked with?
3. The authors conclude by offering a model designed to "protect the minds of boys." What does their model call for educators (and others) to do, and do you think what they are suggesting is realistic? How might you bring this model to your current educational setting?

Where the Girls Are:
The Facts about Gender Equity in Education

CHRISTIANNE CORBETT
CATHERINE HILL
ANDRESSE ST. ROSE

ABSTRACT: Women and girls have made remarkable gains in education during the past 100 years, disrupting the belief—now largely unspoken—that boys and men are better "suited" to intellectual work. Today, few journalists or policymakers would publicly admit to such a prejudice. Since 1881, the American Association of University Women has helped make this progress possible. AAUW released its landmark study, The AAUW Report: How Schools Shortchange Girls, *in 1992, sparking a national debate on gender equity in education. Building on the success of that report, AAUW developed a multiyear research agenda on gender equity in education. Research reports released since 1992 have focused on school climate and sexual harassment, girls in science and technology, race and gender on campus, and other topics. This substantial body of research established AAUW as a leader on the issue of educational equity. This article is excerpted from* Where the Girls Are: The Facts about Gender Equity in Education, *which is the most recent research agenda report from AAUW. This report illustrates that, while educational trends for both girls and boys are generally positive, disparities by race/ethnicity and family income level exist and are critical to understanding the landscape of education in America today.*

Women and girls have made tremendous progress in education during the past 100 years. Throughout the first part of the 20th century, colleges could—and did—openly exclude or limit the number of female students. The passage of Title IX of the Education Amendments of 1972 marked the recognition by Congress that girls and boys hold the right to equal educational opportunities and put an end to overt displays of gender bias. In the ensuing decades, women and girls have made progress at every level of education. Today, women make up a majority of undergraduates on college campuses. Women also have made rapid progress in some historically male fields, such as biology, chemistry, and mathematics, and are nearly as likely as men to pursue advanced degrees in medicine, law, and business.

Yet many people remain uncomfortable with the educational and professional advances of girls and women, especially when they threaten to outdistance their male peers. *The AAUW Report: How Schools Shortchange Girls,* published in 1992, set off a stormy public debate fueled, at least in part, by this discomfort. The report found that girls received less attention in the classroom than boys did and girls were not well represented in math-related fields. As the "girls' crisis" received increasing attention, critics countered that boys were the new disadvantaged group, facing discrimination in schools now designed to favor girls. From the incendiary book *The War Against Boys: How Misguided Feminism Is Harming Our Young Men* (Sommers, 2000) to more subtle insinuations such as the *New York Times* headline "At Colleges, Women Are Leaving Men in the Dust" (Lewin, 2006), a backlash against the achievements of girls and women emerged.

Building on work by Mead (2006), Susan S. Klein et al. (2007), and others, *Where the Girls Are: The Facts About Gender Equity in Education* refutes the notion of a "boys' crisis" in education today. The report provides information on trends in educational achievement based on data from the National Assessment of Educational Progress (NAEP), college entrance examinations, and other educational indicators, such as high school and college graduation rates. Information on educational achievement is examined by gender, race/ethnicity, and family income level. Using both published and unpublished sources, the report presents a comprehensive picture of recent achievements by girls and boys in the U.S. educational system.

Where the Girls Are considers gender differences in educational achievement with attention to race/ethnicity and family income level. Despite the vast literature on education, analysis of gender differences *within* racial/ethnic and income groups is surprisingly uncommon. For example, Lubienski's review of mathematics education research from 1982 to 1998 revealed that "only 3 of the 3,011 articles considered ethnicity, class and gender together" (2001, p. 3). Even the U.S. Department of Education's latest reports of the NAEP long-term trend assessment and other key indicators of educational achievement do not disaggregate scores by gender within family income levels or racial/ethnic groups (U.S. Department of Education, National Center for Education Statistics, 2004, 2005a). Standardized test scores and graduation rates are not the only measures of educational progress, but they are widely acknowledged to be valid measures of achievement.

Taken together, these analyses support three overarching conclusions:

1. Girls' successes don't come at boys' expense. Girls' educational successes have not—and should not—come at the expense of boys. If girls' achievements come at the expense of boys, one would expect to see boys' scores decline as girls' scores rise, but boys' average test scores have improved alongside girls' scores in recent decades. For example, girls' average scores on the NAEP mathematics test have risen during the past three decades—as have boys' scores (indeed, older boys retain a small lead in math). Girls tend to earn

higher average scores on the NAEP reading assessments, but this lead has narrowed or remained the same during the past three decades.

Geographical patterns further demonstrate the positive connection between girls' and boys' educational achievement. In states where girls do well on tests, boys also do well, and states with low average test scores among boys tend to have low scores among girls. For example, test scores on the 2007 main NAEP fourth-grade math assessment by state show that the five highest-scoring states for boys—Massachusetts, New Jersey, New Hampshire, Kansas, and Minnesota—were also the highest-scoring states for girls. Similarly, three of the four states with the lowest scores for boys—Mississippi, New Mexico, and Alabama—were also three of the lowest-scoring states for girls (U.S. Department of Education, National Center for Education Statistics, 2007g).

On both college entrance exams, boys retain a small, consistent lead. On the SAT, the largest gender gap occurs on the math exam in favor of boys. In contrast to the NAEP exam, boys maintain an advantage on the SAT verbal exam as well. Boys also have slightly higher average ACT composite scores. Boys perform better on the ACT mathematics and science sections, and girls perform better on the English and reading sections.

High school graduation rates and college attendance present a similar story. Women are attending and graduating from high school and college at a higher rate than are their male peers, but these gains have not come at men's expense. Indeed, the proportion of young men graduating from high school and earning college degrees today is at an all-time high. Women have made more rapid gains in earning college degrees, but both women and men are more likely to graduate from college today than ever before, and among traditional-age (under age 24) undergraduates from high-income families, men are still more likely than women to attend college.

Perhaps the most compelling evidence against the existence of a boys' crisis is that men continue to outearn women in the workplace. Among all women and men working full time, year round, women's median annual earnings were 77 percent of men's earnings in 2005 (Institute for Women's Policy Research, 2007). Looking at the college-educated, full-time work force one year out of college, women earned 80 percent of men's earnings on average in 2001, and 10 years out of college, women earned only 69 percent of men's earnings in 2003 (AAUW Educational Foundation, 2007). After controlling for factors known to affect earnings, regression analyses demonstrate that a portion of these pay gaps remains unexplained (ibid.).

2. On average, girls' and boys' educational performance has improved. From standardized tests in elementary and secondary school to college entrance examinations, average test scores have risen or remained stable for both girls and boys in recent decades. This rise reflects gains among both low- and high-achieving students. A larger proportion of fourth and eighth graders in all racial/ethnic groups scored at or above a basic level on the main NAEP math and reading assessments in 2007 compared to 1992. Likewise, overall scores on college entrance examinations have risen since the mid-1990s for both girls and boys. Average ACT scores for both girls and boys rose between 1995 and 2007 in both English and math, and between 1994 and 2004, average SAT math and verbal scores also rose for both girls and boys. While the number of girls taking these exams has risen, so too has the number of boys. Girls taking the tests outnumber boys taking the tests, just as women outnumber men on college campuses. Yet the rising number of girls taking these exams has not deterred boys, and the number of boys taking the SAT and ACT is higher today than ever before.

On average, girls' and boys' performance in high school and college has also improved. Girls' and boys' grades in high school are higher today than in 1990, and despite a lack of consensus on the actual number of dropouts, researchers agree that overall graduation rates for boys have improved (Greene & Winters, 2005; Mishel & Roy, 2006). The number and percentage of both women and men attending and graduating from college are higher than ever before and continue to rise.

3. Understanding disparities by race/ethnicity and family level is critical to understanding girls' and boys' achievement. Family income level and race/ethnicity are closely associated with academic performance. On standardized tests such as the NAEP, SAT, and ACT, children from the lowest-income families have the lowest average test scores, with an incremental rise in family income associated with a rise in test scores. Race/ethnicity is also strongly associated with test scores, with African American and Hispanic children scoring lower on average than white and Asian American children. African American and Hispanic students and students from low-income families also have lower high school and college graduation rates than do Asian American and white students and students from higher-income families.

African American and Hispanic girls have a great deal in common with African American and Hispanic boys in terms of educational performance. For example, while average ACT English scores improved from 1995 to 2007 for Asian American and white girls and boys, scores for African American and Hispanic girls and boys either stayed the same or declined. As another example, the U.S. Census Bureau reported in 2006 that, overall, approximately 4 percent more women than men ages 25 to 29 had completed high school. But while 95 percent of white women had completed high school, only 67 percent of Hispanic women and 61 percent of Hispanic men had done so, resulting in a gap of 28 percentage points between white and Hispanic women and a much smaller gap of 6 percentage points between Hispanic women and men.

Gender differences in educational achievement vary by race/ethnicity and family income level as well. The 2007 main NAEP math assessment for the eighth grade is a good example of this variation. Among students who took this exam, boys outperformed girls by two points. When broken down by race/ethnicity, however, a three-point gap favored males among white students, no significant gender gap appeared among Hispanic students, and among African American students, girls outscored boys by an average of one point.

Similarly, boys outperformed girls on average on both the math and verbal portions of the SAT. Disaggregated by race/ethnicity and family income level, however, the male advantage on the verbal portion of the SAT is consistently seen only among students from low-income families and is not seen among African Americans. Gender differences cannot be fully understood without attention to race/ethnicity and family income level.

The decade following *The AAUW Report: How Schools Shortchange Girls* saw rapid gains for girls and women across many measures of educational achievement. Today, much of the popular discourse on gender and education reflects a shift in focus from girls to boys, implying that issues of equity for girls have been addressed and now it is time to focus on boys. As this report demonstrates, however, neither girls nor boys are unilaterally succeeding or failing. The true crisis is that American schoolchildren are deeply divided across race/ethnicity and family income level, and improvement has been too slow and unsteady.

REFERENCES

AAUW Educational Foundation. (1992). *The AAUW report: How schools shortchange girls.* Washington, DC: Author.

———. (1996). *Girls in the middle: Working to succeed in school.* Washington, DC: Author.

———. (2001). *Beyond the "gender wars": A conversation about girls, boys, and education.* Washington, DC: Author.

———. (2007). *Behind the pay gap,* by Judy Goldberg Dey & Catherine Hill. Washington, DC: Author.

Greene, Jay P., & Marcus A. Winters. (2002, November). *Public school graduation rates in the United States* (Civic Report No. 31). New York: Manhattan Institute for Policy Research. Retrieved October 17, 2007, from http://www.manhattan-institute.org/pdf/cr_31.pdf.

———. (2005, February). *Public high school graduation and college-readiness rates. 1991–2002* (Education Working Paper 8). New York: Manhattan Institute for Policy Research. Retrieved October 17, 2007, from http://www.manhattan-institute.org/pdf/ewp_08.pdf.

———. (2006, April). *Leaving boys behind: Public high school graduation rates* (Civic Report No. 48). New York: Manhattan Institute for Policy Research. Retrieved October 17, 2007, from http://www.manhattan-institute.org/pdf/cr_48.pdf.

Institute for Women's Policy Research. (2007, April). *The gender wage ratio: Women's and men's earnings* (IWPR Fact Sheet #C350). Retrieved July 10, 2007, from http://www.iwpr.org/pdf/C350.pdf.

Klein, Joseph. (2004). Who is most responsible for gender differences in scholastic achievements: Pupils or teachers? *Educational Research, 46*(2), 183–193.

Klein, Susan S., Barbara Richardson, Dolores A. Grayson, Lynn H. Fox, Cheris Kramarae, Diane S. Pollard, & Carol Anne Dwyer (Eds.). (2007). *Handbook for achieving gender equity through education* (2nd ed.). Mahwah, NJ: Lawrence Erlbaum Associates.

Leonard, David K., & Jiming Jiang. (1999). Gender bias and the college predictions of the SATs: A cry of despair. *Research in Higher Education, 40*(4), 375–407.

Lewin, Tamar. (2006, July 9). At colleges, women are leaving men in the dust. *The New York Times.*

Lubienski, Sarah T. (2001, April). *A second look at mathematics achievement gaps: Intersections of race, class, and gender in NAEP data.* Paper presented at the annual meeting of the American Educational Research Association, Seattle, WA. (ERIC Document Reproduction Service No. ED454246).

Lubienski, Sarah T., Rebecca McGraw, & Marilyn Strutchens. (2004). NAEP findings regarding gender: Mathematics achievement, student affect, and learning practices. In Peter Kloosterman & Frank K. Lester Jr. (Eds.), *Results and interpretations of the 1990 through 2000 mathematics assessments of the National Assessment of Educational Progress* (pp. 305–336). Reston, VA: National Council of Teachers of Mathematics.

Mead, Sara. (2006, June). *The truth about boys and girls.* Washington, DC: Education Sector.

Mishel, Lawrence, & Joydeep Roy. (2006, April). *Rethinking high school graduation rates and trends.* Washington, DC: Economic Policy Institute.

U.S. Department of Education, National Center for Education Statistics. (2001). *The Nation's Report Card: Mathematics 2000,* by J. S. Braswell, A. D. Lutkus, W. S. Grigg, S. L. Santapau, B. Tay-Lim, & M. Johnson (NCES 2001-517). Washington, DC: U.S. Government Printing Office.

———. (2002). *National education longitudinal study 1988: Fourth follow-up* (NELS:1988/2000).

Washington, DC: Author. Data analysis system available from http://nces.ed.gov/dasolv2/tables/mainPage.asp?mode=NEW&filenumber=2.

———. (2004). *Trends in educational equity of girls & women: 2004,* by Catherine Freeman (NCES 2005-016). Washington, DC: U.S. Government Printing Office. Retrieved October 17, 2007, from http://nces.ed.gov/pubs2005/2005016.pdf.

———. (2005a). *NAEP 2004 trends in academic progress: Three decades of student performance in reading and mathematics,* by Marianne Perie, Rebecca Moran, & Anthony D. Lutkus (NCES 2005-464). Washington, DC: U.S. Government Printing Office. Retrieved October 17, 2007, from http://nces.ed.gov/nationsreportcard/pdf/main2005/2005464.pdf.

———. (2005b). *The Nation's Report Card long-term trend: Trends in average mathematics scale scores by gender.* Washington, DC: Author. Retrieved October 26, 2007, from http://nces.ed.gov/nationsreportcard/ltt/results2004/sub-math-gender.asp.

———. (2005c). *The Nation's Report Card long-term trend: Trends in average reading scale scores by gender.* Washington, DC: Author. Retrieved October 26, 2007, from http://nces.ed.gov/nationsreportcard/ltt/results2004/sub-reading-gender.asp.

———. (2005d). *The Nation's Report Card: Mathematics 2005,* by Marianne Perie, Wendy S. Grigg, & Gloria S. Dion (NCES 2006-453). Washington, DC: U.S. Government Printing Office. Retrieved October 17, 2007, from http://nces.ed.gov/nationsreportcard/pdf/main2005/2006453.pdf.

———. (2006a). *Dropout rates in the United States: 2002 and 2003,* by Jennifer Laird, Stephen Lew, Matthew DeBell, & Chris Chapman (NCES 2006-062). Washington, DC: Author. Retrieved October 17, 2007, from http://nces.ed.gov/pubs2006/2006-062.pdf.

———. (2006b). *Placing college graduation rates in context. How 4-year college graduation rates vary with selectivity and the size of low-income enrollment,* by L. Horn (NCES 2007-161). Washington, DC: Author. Retrieved October 16, 2007, from http://nces.ed.gov/pubs2007/2007161.pdf.

———. (2007a). *The condition of education 2007* (NCES 2007-064). Washington, DC: Author. Retrieved October 18, 2007, from http://nces.ed.gov/pubs2007/2007064.pdf.

———. (2007b). *Digest of education statistics 2006,* by Thomas D. Snyder, Sally A. Dillow, & Charlene M. Hoffman (NCES 2007-017). Washington, DC: U.S. Government Printing Office. Retrieved October 18, 2007, from http://nces.ed.gov/pubs2007/2007017.pdf.

———. (2007c). *Mapping 2005 state proficiency standards onto the NAEP scales* (NCES 2007-482). Washington, DC: Author. Retrieved October 18, 2007, from http://nces.ed.gov/nationsreportcard/pdf/studies/2007482.pdf.

———. (2007d). NAEP data explorer. Washington, DC: Author. Data analysis system available from http://nces.ed.gov/nationsreportcard/naepdata.

———. (2007e). *The Nation's Report Card.* Washington, DC: Author. Retrieved October 16, 2007, from http://nces.ed.gov/nationsreportcard/.

———. (2007f). *The Nations Report Card: America's high school graduates: Results from the 2005 NAEP high school transcript study,* by C. Shettle, S. Roey, J. Mordica, R. Perkins, C. Nord, J. Teodorovic, et al. (NCES 2007-467). Washington, DC: U.S. Government Printing Office. Retrieved October 18, 2007, from http://nces.ed.gov/nationsreportcard/pdf/studies/2007467.pdf.

———. (2007g). *The Nation's Report Card Mathematics 2007,* by Jihyun Lee, Wendy S. Grigg, & Gloria S. Dion (NCES 2007-494). Washington, DC: Author. Retrieved October 17, 2007, from http://nces.ed.gov/nationsreportcard/pdf/main2007/2007494.pdf.

———. (2007h). *The Nation's Report Car: National Assessment of Educational Progress* website. Washington, DC: Author. Retrieved October 16, 2007, from http://nces.ed.gov/nationsreportcard/about/ltt_main_diff.asp.

———. (2007i). *The Nation's Report Card: Reading 2007,* by Jihyun Lee, Wendy S. Grigg, & Patricia L. Donahue (NCES 2007-496). Washington, DC: Author. Retrieved October 17, 2007, from http://nces.ed.gov/nationsreportcard/pdf/main2007/2007496.pdf.

———. (2007j). *The Nation's Report Card: 12th-grade reading and mathematics 2005,* by Wendy Grigg, Patricia L. Donahue, & Gloria Dion (NCES 2007-468). Washington, DC: Author. Retrieved October 17, 2007, from http://nces.ed.gov/nationsreportcard/pubs/main2005/2007468.asp#pdflist.

———. (2007k). *Postsecondary institutions in the United States: Fall 2006 and degrees and other awards conferred: 2005–06,* by Laura G. Knapp, Janice E. Kelly-Reid, Scott A. Ginder, & Elise Miller (NCES 2007-166). Washington, DC: Author.

Retrieved October 17, 2007, from http://nces.ed
.gov/pubs2007/2007166.pdf.

———. (20071). *Preschool: First findings from the
preschool follow-up of the early childhood longitudinal study, birth cohort (ECLS-B),* by Jodi Jacobson Chernoff, Kristin Denton Flanagan, Cameron
McPhee, &Jennifer Park (NCES 2008-025).
Washington, DC: Author. Retrieved December 2,

2007, from http://nces.ed.gov/pubs2008/2008025
.pdf.

———. (2007m). *Status and trends in the education
of racial and ethnic minorities,* by Angelina
KewalRamani, Lauren Gilbertson, Mary Ann Fox, &
Stephen Provasnik (NCES 2007-039). Washington,
DC: Author. Retrieved October 16, 2007, from
http://nces.ed.gov/pubs2007/2007039.pdf.

Christianne Corbett is a research associate at AAUW. She has a master's degree in cultural
anthropology from the University of Colorado and bachelor's degrees in government
and aerospace engineering from the University of Notre Dame. *Catherine Hill* is director
of research at AAUW, where she focuses on higher education and women's economic
security. She has a bachelor's and a master's degree from Cornell University and a
doctorate in public policy from Rutgers University. *Andresse St. Rose* is a graduate
research assistant at AAUW and a doctoral candidate in education policy at George
Washington University. She has a bachelor's degree in biology from Hamilton College
and a master's degree in higher education administration from Boston College.

QUESTIONS FOR REFLECTION

1. Why do you think it is that "many people remain uncomfortable with the educational and professional advances of girls and women, especially when they threaten
   to outdistance their male peers"?
2. What are the three overarching conclusions the authors of the AAUW report present, and do they reflect the world you see in your own educational setting?
3. After reading "How Boys Learn" by Gurian and Stevens and this report by the
   AAUW, how should educators treat gender differences in schools? Is there a "boy
   crisis" or a "girl crisis" in our educational system and, if so, what should be done?

Probing More Deeply into the Theory of Multiple Intelligences

HOWARD GARDNER

*ABSTRACT: The originator of multiple intelligences theory discusses
several misconceptions educators have about how to apply the theory to the
teaching–learning process. The seven intelligences are based on explicit criteria
and "come into being" when they interact with specific real-world content.
While educators can assess proficiency at using intelligences for different tasks,
they cannot assess intelligences per se.*

No one has been more surprised than I by the continuing interest among educators in the theory of
multiple intelligences ("MI," as it has become

known). Almost 15 years after the manuscript of
Frames of Mind (1983; 1993a) was completed, I
continue on a nearly daily basis to hear about

schools that are carrying out experiments in implementing MI. And, on occasion, I encounter a series of thoughtful essays such as the set assembled here.

As a result of the almost constant interaction with the "field," I have come to expect certain understandings and misunderstandings of MI. I began to respond to these interpretations, first through correspondence and then through "replies" to reviews and critiques. In 1995, after 10 years of relative silence, I issued a more formal response, in the form of reflections on seven "myths about multiple intelligences" (Gardner, 1995). This article gave me an opportunity to address directly some of the most common misconceptions about the theory and, as best I could, to set the record straight.

Since publishing these reflections, I have begun to think about the theory from a different perspective. Like any new formulation, "MI theory" is prone to be apprehended initially in certain ways. Sometimes the initial apprehensions (and misapprehensions) endure; more commonly, they alter over time in various, often in predictable, ways.

It may surprise readers to know that I have observed this process even in myself; I have held some of the common misconceptions about MI theory, even as I have come over time to understand aspects of the theory more deeply. In these notes, I identify a series of steps that seem to me to reflect increasingly deep readings of the theory.

Judging the book by its title. Anyone who has published a book of non-fiction will recognize symptoms of the most superficial readings of the book (or, more likely, examination of its cover). Such individuals show no evidence of having even cracked the binding. I have read and heard individuals talk about "multiple intelligence" (sic) as if there were a single intelligence, composed of many parts—in direct contradiction to my claim that there exist a number of relatively autonomous human intellectual capacities. Displaying the ability to read the table of contents but not further, many have written about the "six intelligences," though I have never asserted that there were fewer than seven intelligences. The apparent reason for this misstep:

in *Frames of Mind* I devote a single chapter to the two personal intelligences, thus suggesting to the skimmer that I consider these two as if they are one. Finally, I cannot enumerate how often I have been said to posit a "spiritual intelligence" though I have never done so, and have in fact explicitly rejected that possibility both orally and in writings (Gardner, 1995; 1999).

"MI-Lite" based on a skim or a cocktail party conversation. Those who have made at least a half-hearted effort to understand what the author had in mind usually recognize that "multiple intelligence" (sic) is plural, that there are at least seven separate intelligences, and that the only newly accepted intelligence is that of the Naturalist. Of equal importance, they appreciate that my theory constitutes a critique of the hegemony of one or two intelligences—usually the linguistic and logical varieties that are (over-) valued in school. And they infer that I am not fond of tests of the standard psychometric variety. Indeed, such readers are often attracted more by what they think I oppose (IQ tests, the SAT, a one-dimensional approach to students) than by the actual claims of the theory.

Still, these individuals prove most susceptible to the misconceptions to which I earlier referred. It is from them that I am likely to hear that:

1. One ought to have seven tests. (Alas, you can't get from MI to psychometrics-as-usual.)
2. An intelligence is the same as a domain, discipline, or craft. (Actually, any domain can use several intelligences, and any intelligence can be drawn upon in numerous domains.)
3. An intelligence is indistinguishable from a "learning style." (In fact "style" turns out to be a slippery concept, one quite different from an intelligence.)
4. There is an official Gardner or "MI approach" to schools. (There is not such an approach, and I hope there never will be.)

My psychologist colleagues are more likely to succumb to three other myths:

5. MI theory is not based on empirical data. (This nonsensical view could not be held by anyone

who has ever spent more than five minutes skimming through the book.)

6. MI theory is incompatible with hereditarian or environmental accounts. (In fact, the theory takes no position on the sources of different intellectual profiles.)

7. Gardner's notion of intelligence is too broad. (Actually, it is the psychometric view that is too narrow, substituting one form of scholasticism for the rich set of capacities that comprise the human mind.)

One further misconception unites many skimmers with those who do not even bother to skim. That is a belief that I favor an un-rigorous curriculum, one that spurns the standard disciplines, hard work, and regular assessment.

Nothing could be further from the truth. I am actually a proponent of teaching the classical disciplines and I attempt to adhere to the highest standards, both for others and for myself. Unlike many readers, I see no incompatibility whatsoever between a belief in MI and pursuit of a rigorous education. Rather, I feel that only if we recognize multiple intelligences can we reach more students, and give those students the opportunity to demonstrate what they have understood.

TOWARD A DEEPER GRASP OF THE THEORY

Those who have studied key writings and have engaged in reflection and dialogue about the theory have come to appreciate a number of important insights. In what follows, I state these insights and suggest their possible educational implications.

The Intelligences Are Based on Explicit Criteria.

What makes MI theory more than a parade of personal preferences is a set of eight criteria that were laid out explicitly in Chapter 4 of *Frames of Mind*. These range from the existence of populations that feature an unusual amount of a certain intelligence (e.g., prodigies); to localization of an intelligence in particular regions of the brain; to susceptibility to encoding in a symbolic system. Of the many candidate intelligences proposed and reviewed so far (e.g., auditory or visual; humor or cooking; intuitive or moral), only eight have qualified in terms of these criteria. Those who would posit additional intelligences have the obligation to assess candidates on these criteria, and to make available the results of this evaluation (Gardner, 1999).

The intelligences reflect a specific scientific wager. As I envision them, the intelligences have emerged over the millennia as a response to the environments in which humans have lived. They constitute, as it were, a cognitive record of the evolutionary past. If my list of intelligences is close to the mark, it will mean that my colleagues and I have succeeded in figuring out what the brain has evolved to do—to use a current phrase, that we have carved nature at its proper joints.

To be sure, culture has not evolved simply to fit nature, but the kinds of skills that we expect individuals to achieve do reflect the capacities that individuals actually possess. The challenge confronting educators is to figure out how to help individuals employ their distinctive intellectual profiles to help master the tasks and disciplines needed to thrive in the society.

The Intelligences Respond to Specific Content in the World.

Scientifically, an intelligence is best thought of as a "biopsychological construct": that is, if we understood much more than we do about the genetic and neural aspects of the human mind, we could delineate the various psychological skills and capacities that humans are capable of exhibiting. Despite the convenient existence of the word, however, it makes little sense to think of intelligences in the abstract. Intelligences only come into being because the world in which we live features various contents—among them, the sounds and syntax of language, the sounds and rhythms of music, the species of nature, the other persons in our environment, and so on.

These facts lead to the most challenging implication of MI theory. If our minds respond to the actual varied contents of the world, then it does not make sense to posit the existence of "all-purpose" faculties. There is, in the last analysis, no *generalized* memory: There is memory for language, memory for music, memory for spatial environments, and so on. Nor, despite current buzzwords, can we speak about critical or creative thinking in an unmodified way. Rather, there is critical thinking using one or more intelligences, and there is creativity in one, or in more than one, domain.

Powerful educational implications lurk here. We must be leery about claiming to enhance general abilities like thinking or problem solving or memory; it is important to examine *which* problem is being solved, *which* kind of information is being memorized. Even more important, the teacher must be wary of claims about transfer. Though transfer of skill is a proper goal for any educator, such transfer cannot be taken for granted—and especially not when such transfer is alleged to occur across intelligences. The cautious educator assumes that particular intelligences can be enhanced, but remains skeptical of the notion that use of one set of intellectual skills will necessarily enhance others.

Despite the Seductive Terminology, We Cannot Assess Intelligences: We Can at Most Assess Proficiency in Different Tasks.

Given the positing of multiple intelligences, there is an almost inevitable slippage toward the idea that we could assess an individual's intelligences, or profile of intelligences. And even those who recognize the limits (or inappropriateness) of standard measures are still tempted to create some kind of a battery or milieu that "takes the temperature" of different intelligences. I know: I have more than once succumbed to this temptation myself.

But because intelligences are the kinds of constructs that they are, it is simply not possible to

assess an individual intelligence or an individual's intelligences with any degree of reliability. All that one can ever assess in psychology is performance on some kind of task. And so, if an individual does well in learning a melody and in recognizing when that melody has been embedded in harmony, we do not have the right to proclaim her "musically intelligent"; the most that we can infer is that the individual has presumptively exhibited musical intelligence on this single measure.

The greater the number of tasks sampled, the more likely it is that a statement about "strength" or "weakness" in an intelligence will acquire some validity. Even here, however, one must be careful. For just because it *appears* that a task was solved by the use of a particular intelligence, we cannot be certain this is so. A person is free to solve a task in whichever manner he likes. Inferences about mind or brain mechanisms can only be made as a result of carefully designed experiments, ones that most educators (and, truth to tell, most researchers) are in no position to conduct.

For informal purposes, it is certainly acceptable to speculate that a person is relying on certain intelligences rather than others, or that she exhibits a strength in one but not another intelligence. Because actual inference about intelligences is problematic, however, educators should be cautious about characterizing the intellectual profiles of students. While seven or eight labels may be preferable to one (smart or stupid), labeling can still be pernicious, and particularly so when there is little empirical warrant for it.

The Road between Theory and Practice Runs in Two Directions.

Many individuals, practitioners as well as researchers, adopt a jaundiced view of the relation between theory and practice. On this "conduit" view, researchers collect data and then develop theories about a topic (say, the nature of human intelligence); the implications of the theories are reasonably straightforward (e.g., let's train all intelligences equally); and practitioners consume the material and attempt to apply the theory as faithfully as possible (Voilà—behold a multiple intelligences classroom!).

This description is wrong in every respect. Within the research world, the relations among theory, data, and inference are complex and ever-changing. Any theoretical statement or conclusion can lead to an indefinite number of possible practical implications. Only actual testing "in the real world" will indicate which, if any, of the implications holds water. And most important, those who theorize about the human world have as much to learn from practitioners as vice versa.

Continuing the confessional mode of this essay, I freely admit that I once held a version of this mental model. While I was not initially bent on applying my theory in practical settings, I assumed that the theory would be revised in the light of further research and nothing else.

Here the events of the past decade have been most auspicious—and most enlightening. My colleagues and I have learned an enormous amount from the various practical projects that have been inspired by MI theory—those that we designed ourselves (Gardner, 1993b) and equally, those generated by ingenious practitioners . . . (cf., Krechevsky, Hoerr, and Gardner, 1995). . . .

Developmental psychology and cognitive psychology confirm an important lesson: It is not possible to short-circuit the learning process. Even those with more than a nodding acquaintance with "MI theory" need to work out their understandings in their own way and at their own pace. And if my own understanding of the theory continues to change, I can hardly expect anyone else to accept any "reading" as conclusive—even that of the founding theorist. Still, I hope that these reflections may help to frame readers' encounters with MI theory and efforts to draw on these ideas in ways that are helpful to students.

REFERENCES

Gardner, H. *Frames of Mind: The Theory of Multiple Intelligences.* New York: Basic Books, 1983. (A tenth anniversary edition with a new introduction was published in 1993.)

———. *Multiple Intelligences. The Theory in Practice.* New York: Basic Books, 1993b.

———. "Reflections on Multiple Intelligences: Myths and Messages." *Phi Delta Kappan,* November 1995.

———. "Are There Additional Intelligences?" In *Education, Information, and Transformation: Essays on Learning and Thinking,* edited by J. Kane. Englewood Cliffs, NJ.: Prentice-Hall, 1999.

Krechevsky, M.; Hoerr, T.; and Gardner, H. "Complementary Energies: Implementing MI Theory from the Laboratory and the Field." In *Creating New Educational Communities,* 94th Yearbook of the National Society for the Study of Education (Part 1), edited by J. Oakes and K. H. Quartz. Chicago: University of Chicago Press, 1995.

Howard Gardner is professor of education and codirector of Project Zero at the Harvard Graduate School of Education and an adjunct professor of neurology at the Boston University School of Medicine.

QUESTIONS FOR REFLECTION

1. Why does Gardner believe "we must be leery about claiming to enhance general abilities like thinking or problem solving or memory"? What are the implications of this statement for curriculum planners?

2. Why should educators be cautious about characterizing the intellectual profiles of students?

3. What does Gardner mean when he states that the "road between theory and practice runs in two directions"? What professional experiences have you had that confirm Gardner's view?

Culturally Relevant Pedagogy: Ingredients for Critical Reflection

TYRONE C. HOWARD

ABSTRACT: Teacher reflection continues to be part of the teacher educa-tion literature and, as Howard discusses here, critical reflection has more re-cently been recommended as a means of incorporating issues of equity and social justice into teaching, thinking, and practice. This article offers critical reflection as a prelude to creating culturally relevant teaching strategies. Howard outlines theoretical and practical considerations for critical reflection and culturally relevant teaching for teacher education. The author argues that the development of culturally relevant teaching strategies is contingent upon critical reflection about race and culture of teachers and their students.

As the United States endures its largest influx of immigrants, along with the increasing number of U.S.-born ethnic minorities, the nation must be prepared to make the necessary adjustments to face the changing ethnic texture of its citizens (Banks, 2001). The shift in ethnic demographics has important implications for schools and, more importantly, classroom teachers. While students of color currently comprise approximately one third of the U.S. school population, the U.S. De-partment of Commerce (1996) projects that by the year 2050 African American, Asian American, and Latino students will constitute close to 57% of all U.S. students.

As educators address the demographic divide (Gay & Howard, 2001), teachers must face the re-ality that they will continue to come into contact with students whose cultural, ethnic, linguistic, racial, and social class backgrounds differ from their own. In short, U.S. schools will continue to become learning spaces where an increasingly ho-mogeneous teaching population (mostly White, fe-male, and middle class) will come into contact with an increasingly heterogeneous student population (primarily students of color, and from low-income backgrounds). Thus, teacher educators must reconceptualize the manner in which new teachers are prepared, and provide them with the skills and knowledge that will be best suited for effectively educating today's diverse student population.

In order to provide more meaningful knowl-edge and skills for teaching in today's cultural context, teacher educators must be able to help preservice teachers critically analyze important is-sues such as race, ethnicity, and culture, and rec-ognize how these important concepts shape the learning experience for many students. More specifically, teachers must be able to construct pedagogical practices that have relevance and meaning to students' social and cultural realities. The purpose of this article is to highlight the im-portance of critical teacher reflection as a tool for creating culturally relevant teaching practices.

Culturally relevant pedagogy has been de-scribed by a number of researchers as an effective means of meeting the academic and social needs of culturally diverse students (Gay, 2000; Howard, 2001; Ladson-Billings, 1994; Shade, Kelly, & Oberg, 1997). Gay (2000) asserts that culturally relevant pedagogy uses "the cultural knowledge, prior experiences, frames of reference, and per-formance styles of ethnically diverse students to make learning more relevant to and effective [for students]. . . . It teaches to and through strengths of these students. It is culturally validating and af-firming" (p. 29). An additional, and some would argue the most important, goal of culturally relevant pedagogy is to increase the academic achievement of culturally diverse students.

This article is concerned with ways that teacher educators can equip preservice teachers with the necessary skills to critically reflect on their own racial and cultural identities and to recognize how these identities coexist with the cultural compositions of their students. Three central ideas will be examined in the article. In the first section, I will examine why race and culture are important concepts in teaching and learning. The increasing degree of racial homogeneity among teachers and heterogeneity among students carries important implications for all educators. The second section will detail why critical teacher reflection is important in developing culturally relevant pedagogy. The racial and cultural incongruence between teachers and students merits ongoing discussion, reflection, and analysis of racial identities on behalf of teachers, and is critical in developing a culturally relevant pedagogy for diverse learners. The finial section offers solutions and skills that can be utilized by teachers and teacher educators to conduct the critical type of reflection that may help teachers effectively develop and use culturally relevant pedagogical practices with students from culturally diverse backgrounds.

WHY DOES RACE MATTER? AND WHAT DOES IT HAVE TO DO WITH TEACHING?

Race has been, and remains, one of the more intriguing paradoxes of U.S. society. As a nation, the United States has explicitly and implicitly subscribed to racial hierarchies for the past four centuries (Horsman, 1981; Omi & Winant, 1986). DuBois' (1903) notion that the preeminent problem of the 20th century would be the color line continues to ring true even louder in the 21st century. An examination of school achievement along racial lines underscores clear racial divisions about who is benefiting from school and who is not. Take for example the case of African American and Latino students. The two groups constitute the largest ethnic minority groups in U.S. schools. Yet the academic underachievement of many African American and Latino students has been abysmal for decades. Academically, a majority of African American students lag behind grade-level competence in core subject areas such as reading, math, science, and social studies (NCES, 1998, 2000). Latino students fare slightly better than African American students, but they have an unacceptable dropout rate that has remained near 30% over the past three decades and shows no sign of improving (NCES, 1998, 2000).

Socially and emotionally, African American and Latino students have struggled to adjust in U.S. schools. These students are grossly overrepresented in special needs categories (Ford & Harris, 1999). Currently, African American and Latino students constitute approximately 28% of the nation's public school enrollment. However, during the 1998–99 school year they represented close to 50% of all students labeled as mentally retarded, nearly 40% of all students identified as developmentally delayed, and approximately 37% of all students classified as emotionally disturbed (U.S. Department of Education, 1999). In many school districts the percentage of African American and Latino students labeled at-risk, ineducable, or in need of special or remedial education services is twice that of their overall percentage in schools (U.S. Department of Education, 1998).

The disturbing educational trends of African American and Latino students has led to reified images of students who appear to be more suited for special education and remedial schooling, and less suited for gifted education and advance placement. The persistent school failure of an increasing number of racially diverse students should prompt educators to ask the difficult, yet obvious question: What, if anything, does race and culture have to do with the widespread underachievement of nonmainstream students? Thus, the need to rethink pedagogical practices is critical if underachieving student populations are to have improved chances for school success.

Teachers need to understand that racially diverse students frequently bring cultural capital to the classroom that is oftentimes drastically different from mainstream norms and worldviews. Bourdieu (1973) discusses cultural capital as a form of cultural transmission that individuals acquire from their given social structure. Cultural capital embodies the norms, social practices, ideologies, language, and behavior that are part of a given context. Thus, if students come from a home or social structure in which the cultural capital places a high value on their non-English, native language, they may be at an extreme disadvantage in many U.S. schools that frequently give considerable privilege to students whose primary language is English. Bourdieu argues that many times education systems institute "pedagogic action," which requires a familiarization with the dominant culture and all its beliefs, behaviors, and ideals. The schism that exists between students who are familiar with dominant or mainstream cultural capital and those who are not may explain some of the academic discrepancy among students from diverse backgrounds.

The racial and cultural incongruence between students and teachers may be another factor that explains school failure of students of color. Teacher practice and thought must be reconceptualized in a manner that recognizes and respects the intricacies of cultural and racial difference. Teachers must construct pedagogical practices in ways that are culturally relevant, racially affirming, and socially meaningful for their students. In summary, it should be clear that race has always and continues to matter in an increasingly racially diverse society. More importantly, many of the patterns of success and failure in U.S. schools have obvious racial ramifications, that cannot be ignored. Thus, it is crucial that teachers begin critical discussions about their perceptions of racially diverse students.

CRITICAL REFLECTION AND CULTURALLY RELEVANT PEDAGOGY

Over the past decade the teacher education literature has seen an increase in works concerning reflection for preservice teachers (Gore, 1987; Gore & Zeichner, 1991; Schön, 1983; Sparkes, 1991). Central to much of this work has been the idea that reflection gives attention to one's experiences and behaviors, and meanings are made and interpreted from them to inform future decision-making. Dewey (1933) was one of the early theorists who talked about the value of reflection in education. He viewed reflection as a special form of problem solving steeped in scaffolding of experiences and events that should be viewed as an active and deliberate cognitive process. Much of Dewey's philosophical framework still guides the thinking on reflection in education. The term *critical reflection* attempts to look at reflection within moral, political, and ethical contexts of teaching. Issues pertaining to equity, access, and social justice are typically ascribed to critical reflection (Calderhead, 1989; Gore, 1987). Critical reflection is the type of processing that is crucial to the concept of culturally relevant pedagogy. More importantly, it is the notion of "reflective action" that Dewey referred to as the active component of behavioral intervention. Thus, once cognitive processing is complete, reflective action can be a more useful tool for addressing social and emotional issues, namely those issues pertaining to race and culture.

One of the central tenets of culturally relevant teaching is a rejection of deficit-based thinking about culturally diverse students. Ladson-Billings (1994) has argued that one of the central principles of culturally relevant pedagogy is an authentic belief that students from culturally diverse and low-income backgrounds are capable learners. She maintains that if students are treated competently they will ultimately demonstrate high degrees of competence. To become culturally relevant, teachers need to engage in honest, critical reflection that challenges them to see how their positionality influences their students in either positive or negative ways. Critical reflection should include an examination of how race, culture, and social class shape students' thinking, learning, and various understandings of the world.

In adding further clarity to the concept of critical reflection, there are three areas that should be essential components toward the development of culturally relevant teaching practices. First, teachers must acknowledge how deficit-based notions of diverse students continue to permeate traditional school thinking, practices, and placement, and critique their own thoughts and practices to ensure they do not reinforce prejudiced behavior. Second, culturally relevant pedagogy recognizes the explicit connection between culture and learning, and sees students' cultural capital as an asset and not a detriment to their school success. Third, culturally relevant teaching is mindful of how traditional teaching practices reflect middle-class, European American cultural values, and thus seeks to incorporate a wider range of dynamic and fluid teaching practices.

Effective reflection of race within a diverse cultural context requires teachers to engage in one of the more difficult processes for all individuals—honest self-reflection and critique of their own thoughts and behaviors. Critical reflection requires one to seek deeper levels of self-knowledge, and to acknowledge how one's own worldview can shape students' conceptions of self. Palmer (1998) contends that "we teach who we are," and that for teachers, separating one's own lived experiences from the act of teaching is an arduous, yet necessary task. Palmer (1998) maintains the following:

> Teaching, like any truly human activity, emerges from one's inwardness, for better or worse. As I teach, I project the condition of my soul onto my students, my subject, and our way of being together. The entanglements I experience in the classroom are often no more or less than the convolutions of my inner life. Viewed from this angle, teaching holds a mirror to the soul. If I am willing to look in that mirror and not run from what I see, I have a chance to gain self knowledge—and knowing myself is as crucial to good teaching as knowing my students and my subject. . . . In fact, knowing my students and my subject depends heavily on self-knowledge. When I do not know myself, I cannot know who my students are. I will see them through a glass darkly, in the shadows of my own unexamined

life—and when I cannot see them clearly, I cannot teach them well. (p. 2)

Palmer's notion of "we teach who we are" has significant implications for teachers of today's learners. What is important, within a culturally relevant pedagogical framework, is for teachers to ask themselves the important question of whether "who we are" contributes to the underachievement of students who are not like us. Critical reflection can be useful in helping teachers recognize if they consciously or subconsciously subscribe to deficit-based notions of culturally diverse students.

The Difficulty of Critical Reflection

The formation of a culturally relevant teaching paradigm becomes extremely difficult, if not impossible, without critical reflection. The nature of critical reflection can be an arduous task because it forces the individual to ask challenging questions that pertain to one's construction of individuals from diverse racial, ethnic, and cultural backgrounds. While posing these questions proves difficult, honest answering of such questions becomes the bigger and more difficult hurdle to clear. Yet, the stakes for teachers are too high not to engage in this process. As the teaching profession becomes increasingly homogeneous, given the task of educating an increasingly heterogeneous student population, reflections on racial and cultural differences are essential. In order to become a culturally relevant pedagogue, teachers must be prepared to engage in a rigorous and oftentimes painful reflection process about what it means to teach students who come from different racial and cultural backgrounds than their own. Some of the questions that teachers should consider in this reflective process could include the following:

1. How frequently and what types of interactions did I have with individuals from racial backgrounds different from my own growing up?
2. Who were the primary persons that helped to shape my perspectives of individuals from

different racial groups? How were their opinions formed?

3. Have I ever harbored prejudiced thoughts towards people from different racial backgrounds?

4. If I do harbor prejudiced thoughts, what effects do such thoughts have on students who come from those backgrounds?

5. Do I create negative profiles of individuals who come from different racial backgrounds?

An honest and thoughtful reflection on these types of questions often becomes painful because it may result in individuals recognizing that close family members harbored racist and prejudiced notions of racially diverse groups that were passed down from generation to generation. Coming to grips with such unfortunate realities is critical in developing an antiracist pedagogy.

An antiracist pedagogy requires teachers to adopt a commitment to thinking, feeling, and acting in ways that combat racial discrimination in schools. Derman-Sparks and Brunson-Phillips (1997) maintain that there are four key steps in developing an antiracist pedagogy: (a) develop deeper self-knowledge about one's racial and cultural identity, and how racism has shaped this identity; (b) acquire a new information base about the role that race and racism play in various educational policies and practices; (c) de-center and extend empathy to increase one's knowledge base about racially and culturally diverse groups; and (d) become activists to develop skills and competence to combat racial inequities in work, school, and community settings.

It is critical for teacher educators to provide spaces for preservice teachers to express their uncertainties, frustrations, and regrets over prejudiced notions. Milner (2003) suggests that teacher educators should guide the reflection on race with preservice teachers by using "race reflective journaling." He describes race reflective journaling as a process wherein teachers are able to process issues of racial differences in a more private manner through writing, as opposed to sharing ideas of racial and cultural differences in a more open and public forum that might become uncomfortable and difficult for some. Milner presents a critical

reflective questionnaire about race that can serve as an excellent guide for teacher educators to facilitate sensitive discussions about race.

Critical teacher reflection is essential to culturally relevant pedagogy because it can ultimately measure teachers' levels of concern and care for their students. A teacher's willingness to ask tough questions about his or her own attitudes toward diverse students can reflect a true commitment that the individual has toward students' academic success and emotional well-being. A number of scholars have included the concept of care as a critical component of effective teaching (Gay, 2000; Howard, 2001; Valenzuela, 1999). Gay (2000) maintains that one of the most fundamental features of culturally responsive teaching is the power of caring. She states that caring is frequently manifested through teacher attitudes, expectations and behaviors. Nieto (1999) posits that "the way students are thought about and treated by society and consequently by the schools they attend and the educators who teach them is fundamental in creating academic success or failure" (p. 167).

A CASE STUDY OF CRITICAL REFLECTION: TEACHING TEACHERS TO REFLECT

As an instructor in a teacher education program that prepares teachers to teach in urban school settings, I have been part of a team of faculty members who have created a new course titled "Identity and Teaching." The purpose of this mandatory course is for preservice teachers to interrogate various notions of their multiple identities. The students wrestle with questions such as, Who am I? What do I believe? Does who I am and what I believe have ramifications for the students I teach? As part of the course, students engage in readings and activities that pertain to their own racial, ethnic, social class, and gender identities. The reflections and revelations that emanate from the course are invaluable, and the emotional outpouring is a testament to how difficult it is for many individuals to come to grips with their own notions of privilege. Many of the students, though, have come to realize the value in critical reflection and the correlation it can have for them teaching in culturally diverse school settings.

A number of types of identity are explored in the course. However, grappling with race has been the most challenging for the preservice teachers. Many of the students in the course explain how their discomfort is a result of race being a taboo topic, and they express concerns such as not wanting their comments to appear racially insensitive, racist, prejudiced, or politically incorrect. Yet, I have found that part of guiding race-related discussions is to not allow individuals' discomfort or ignorance about race to become an escape for not addressing and analyzing their own beliefs.

To assist the reflective process in the identity course each of the instructors went through a 3-day workshop before teaching the course. The instructors engaged in a series of activities identical to the ones they take their own students through that asks them to come to grips with their own identities around race, ethnicity, social class, and gender. The willingness on the part of teacher educators to share their own lived experiences, expose their own human frailties, and reflect on their ever-evolving identities within a community of diverse individuals is important. The practice of reflecting on race in teacher education becomes superficial at best if facilitators of such discussions are not clear and comfortable with their own identity and, more importantly, the identity of others.

Being able to effectively initiate and facilitate critical reflection about race and race-related issues requires the ability to critically examine one's own personal beliefs, opinions, and values about racial identity, and the race of others; and the ramifications of these intersecting and colliding values and beliefs. Therefore, whatever reflective mechanisms are put in place in teacher education programs must go beyond reflection just for the sake of thinking about issues in teaching. Critical reflection should inform all facets of teaching and become culturally relevant for the students being taught. In order for these measures to possess optimum effect, a number of suggestions are offered to aid teacher educators, preservice teachers, inservice teachers, and school administrators on how to translate critical reflection into culturally relevant teaching.

1. Ensure that teacher education faculty members are able to sufficiently address the complex nature of race, ethnicity, and culture.

This task can prove to be difficult if there are not faculty members willing to engage in critical reflection. However, clinical educators, lecturers, or mentor teachers can be equally helpful in facilitating this process with preservice teachers. In many ways, if the teacher education program as a whole is not concerned with issues of equity and access, and does not address the role of race and ethnicity in education, critical reflection will become a fruitless endeavor.

2. Be aware that reflection is a never-ending process.

Schön (1987) describes reflection as a process that is tied to action, and talks about the need for "reflection-in-action." He conceptualizes reflection-in-action as an ongoing process that is predicated on continually thinking about one's actions and then modifying them accordingly. For teacher educators engaging preservice teachers in critical reflection, it is important to stress that one never completely arrives at a place of completion with their reflection. The very nature of teaching is built on revisiting curriculum, pedagogy, and assessment. Preservice teachers should be mindful of the fact that even the most seasoned teachers who use culturally relevant forms of teaching are prone to mistakes, lapses in judgment, or other forms of missteps. However, they acknowledge their errors and improve their teaching accordingly.

3. Be explicit about what to reflect about.

There are a number of considerations teachers must keep in mind in a critical reflection process. Teachers should examine class data on an ongoing basis and ask deep-seated questions about equity in the classroom. For example, questions that could be used to guide reflection could include:

- What is the racial breakdown of students who are referred for special needs services?
- What is the racial breakdown for students referred for gifted education or AP courses?

- How frequently do I differentiate instruction?
- Do scoring rubrics give inherent advantages for certain ways of knowing and expression?
- Do I allow culturally based differences in language, speech, reading, and writing to shape my perceptions about students' cognitive ability?
- Do I create a multitude of ways to evaluate students? Or do I rely solely on paper, pencil, and oral responses? How often do I allow nontraditional means of assessment, such as role-playing, skits, poetry, rap, self-evaluations, Socratic seminars, journaling, student-led conferences, or cooperative group projects, to be a part of my class?

4. Recognize that teaching is not a neutral act. Ladson-Billings (1994) contends that culturally relevant teaching seeks to instill political consciousness in students. Thus, teachers should be mindful of how their actions can contribute to the development of a consciousness that is emancipatory and has social and cultural relevance. Conversely, teachers who refuse to monitor their own beliefs and classroom ethos can contribute to resistance on the part of students. Recognizing that all facets of teaching carry explicit and implicit political implications should result in ongoing reflection to clarify the educational agenda that is being promoted within a classroom setting.

5. Avoid reductive notions of culture.

Culturally relevant pedagogy is based on the inclusion of cultural referents that students bring from home. Teachers must be careful to not allow racial classifications of students to be used as rigid and reductive cultural characteristics. A critical reflection process enables teachers to recognize the vast array of differences that can exist within groups. Thus, not all African American students work well in groups, not all Latino students are second language learners, and all Asian American students are not high achievers. Teachers must avoid creating stereotypical profiles of students that may only do more harm than good. While there may be central tendencies shown within groups, teachers should develop individual profiles of students based on students' own thoughts and behaviors.

CONCLUSION

The need for critical reflection can be an important tool for all teachers. Yet, teachers of students from diverse backgrounds stand to gain immeasurable benefits from a process that requires them to put the needs of their students ahead of all other considerations. The call for a culturally relevant pedagogy is situated on the belief that many of the current educational practices and philosophies that permeate schools have failed miserably when it comes to educating students from culturally diverse and low-income backgrounds. Culturally relevant teaching offers an intervention for reversing the perennial underachievement that has become commonplace for an increasing number of students. However, the assistance of teacher educators in this process cannot be understated. Critical reflection is a personal and challenging look at one's identity as an individual person and as an active professional. Facilitation of this process must be sensitive and considerate to the lived experiences that people bring to their current time and space. The purpose of critical reflection should not be to indict teachers for what they believe and why it does not work for students. It is a process of improving practice, rethinking philosophies, and becoming effective teachers for today's ever-changing student population. Given the current cultural and racial demographics of our schools and society, the stakes we face as a profession and as a nation are too high to fail in this endeavor.

REFERENCES

Banks, J. A. (2001). *Cultural diversity and education: Foundations, curriculum, and teaching.* Boston: Allyn & Bacon.

Bourdieu, P. (1973). Cultural reproduction and social reproduction. In R. Brown (Ed.), *Knowledge, education and cultural changes* (pp. 56–69). London: Tavistock.

Calderhead, J. (1989). Reflective teaching and teacher education. *Teaching and Teacher Education, 5*(1), 43–51.

Derman-Sparks, L., & Brunson-Phillips, C. (1997). *Teaching/learning anti-racism.* New York: Teachers College Press.

Dewey, J. (1933). *How we think: A restatement of the relation of reflective thinking to the educative process.* Boston: D.C. Heath.

DuBois, W. E. B. (1903). *The souls of Black folk.* New York: Penguin Books.

Ford, D. Y., & Harris, J. J. (1999). *Gifted multicultural education.* New York: Teachers College Press.

Gay, G. (2000). *Culturally responsive teaching.* New York: Teachers College Press.

Gay, G., & Howard, T. C. (2001). Multicultural education for the 21st century. *The Teacher Educator, 36*(1), 1–16.

Gore, J. (1987, March–April). Reflecting on reflective teaching. *Journal of Teacher Education,* 33–39.

Gore, J., & Zeichner, K. (1991). Action research and reflective teaching in preservice teacher education: A case study from the United States. *Teaching and Teacher Education, 7*(2), 119–136.

Horsman, R. (1981). *Race and manifest destiny.* Cambridge, MA: Harvard University Press.

Howard, T. C. (2001). Powerful pedagogy for African American students: Conceptions of culturally relevant pedagogy. *Urban Education, 36*(2), 179–202.

Ladson-Billings, G. (1994). *The dreamkeepers.* San Francisco: Jossey-Bass.

Milner, H. R. (2003). Reflection, racial competence, and critical pedagogy: How do we prepare preser-

vice teachers to pose tough questions? *Race, Ethnicity, and Education, 6*(2), 193–208.

Nieto, S. (1999). *Affirming diversity* (3rd ed.). New York: Longman Press.

Omi, M., & Winant, H. (1986). *Racial formation in the United States: From the 1960's to the 1980's.* New York: Routledge.

Palmer, P. J. (1998). *The courage to teach.* San Francisco: Jossey-Bass.

Schön, D. (1983). *The reflective practitioner: How professionals think in action.* New York: Basic Books.

Schön, D. (1987). *Educating the reflective practitioner: Toward a new design for teaching and learning in the professions.* San Francisco: Jossey Bass.

Shade, B. J., Kelly, C., & Oberg, M. (1997). *Creating culturally responsive classrooms.* Washington, DC: American Psychological Association.

Sparkes, A. (1991). The culture of teaching, critical reflection and change: Possibilities and problems. *Educational Management and Administration, 19*(1), 4–19.

U.S. Department of Commerce. (1996). *Current population reports: Populations projects of the United States by age, sex, race and Hispanic origin: 1995 to 2050.*

United States Department of Education, National Center for Education Statistics. (1998). *Digest of Education Statistics, 1998.*

United States Department of Education, National Center for Education Statistics. (1999). *Digest of Education Statistics, 1999.*

Valenzuela, S. (1999). *Subtractive schooling.* New York: SUNY Press.

Tyrone Howard is an associate professor of urban schooling at the University of Washington, Seattle.

QUESTIONS FOR REFLECTION

1. Howard sees critical teacher reflection as an important tool for creating culturally relevant teaching practices. What is culturally relevant teaching and how does it affect student learning?

2. What guidelines does Howard offer to infuse critical reflection about race and culture into the modern curriculum, both for teachers and for students?

3. How might you bring the concept of culturally relevant pedagogy to your current educational setting? What would be the major obstacles to getting people to be more critically reflective in their practice and how would you overcome resistance?

Authentic Assessment and Student Performance in Inclusive Secondary Schools

M. BRUCE KING
JENNIFER SCHROEDER
DAVID CHAWSZCZEWSKI

ABSTRACT: *This article outlines the model of Authentic Intellectual Work and presents initial findings from a study of inclusion and reform in four secondary schools across the United States. Generally, teachers were able to adapt assessments for special education students while maintaining intellectual challenge. Consistent with other research, there was a significant relationship between the authenticity of task demands and the authenticity of the work that students produced. With more authentic and challenging tasks, students with disabilities performed better than both students with and students without disabilities who received less authentic tasks.*

In the current context of school reform, teaching and learning of high intellectual quality (e.g., Newmann & Wehlage, 1995) and teaching for understanding (e.g., Cohen, McLaughlin, & Talbert, 1993) offer compelling alternatives to more traditional forms of instruction focused on basic skills and content. In schools that restructure around a vision of authentic pedagogy and student achievement, students learn more and learning occurs more equitably across student groups (Newmann, Marks, & Gamoran, 1996). At the same time, calls for reform in special education focus on the inclusion of students with disabilities in general education classes (e.g., Lipsky & Gartner, 1996).

In this brief, we investigate the intersection of these reform movements. Specifically, we address two questions:

1. In secondary schools with inclusionary practices, to what extent are teacher-designed assessments authentic?
2. How do students with and without disabilities perform on these assessments?

Data comes from high schools that are participating in a 5-year national study conducted by the Research Institute on Secondary Education Reform (RISER) for Youth with Disabilities at the University of Wisconsin–Madison.

AUTHENTIC AND INCLUSIVE REFORM

Most recent education reforms have been generated with limited research on or consideration of the implications of the reforms for students with disabilities. But changes in special education do not evolve in isolation from broader national policy interests and issues. Thus, RISER is focused on schools engaged in reform efforts that include students with disabilities and seeks to identify educational practices that benefit *all* students.

RISER is grounded in the model of authentic intellectual work. Developed as part of a national study of school restructuring (Newmann & Wehlage, 1995), authentic teaching and learning provide the framework for the study of classroom practices that include both students with and students without disabilities. Authentic intellectual work is consistent with the recent emphasis on constructivist teaching, which has been advocated as a productive alternative to traditional instructional approaches in special education. These traditional approaches have been criticized for operating from a deficit model in which learning expectations for students with disabilities are significantly lowered (Trent, Artiles, & Englert, 1998).

AUTHENTIC INTELLECTUAL WORK

- *Construction of Knowledge*
- *Disciplined Inquiry*
- *Value Beyond School*

Authentic intellectual work is defined by three general characteristics (Newmann & Wehlage, 1995). The first characteristic is *construction of knowledge*. In the conventional curriculum, students largely identify the knowledge that others have produced (e.g., by recognizing the difference between verbs and nouns, labeling parts of a plant, or matching historical events to their dates). In authentic work, however, students go beyond memorizing and repeating facts, information, definitions, or formulas to produce new knowledge or meaning. This kind of work involves higher order thinking in which students analyze, interpret, or evaluate information in a novel way. The mere reproduction of knowledge does not constitute authentic academic achievement.

A second defining feature of authentic achievement is its reliance on a particular type of cognitive work called *disciplined inquiry*. Disciplined inquiry consists of (a) using a knowledge base, (b) striving for in-depth understanding of relevant knowledge and concepts, and (c) expressing conclusions through elaborated communication. By contrast, much of the traditional pedagogy in schools asks students to show only a superficial awareness of a vast number of topics and requires only brief responses from students (e.g., true–false, multiple-choice, or short answers).

A third characteristic of authentic achievement is that it has *value beyond school*—that is, it has meaning or value apart from documenting or certifying the learner's competence. In authentic work, students make connections between what they are learning and important personal or social issues. Achievements of this sort—whether a performance, exhibition, or written communication—actually influence others and thus have a value that is missing in tasks such as quizzes and standardized tests that only assess an individual student's knowledge or skills.

These three characteristics are the basis for the standards we are using to assess the intellectual quality of teaching and learning in participating schools. (See sidebar for examples of standards for scoring teachers' assignments in writing and math. For all standards and scoring criteria used in this study, see the RISER Web site, www.wcer.wisc.edu/riser.) Teachers' lessons, assignments, and student work can score high on some of these characteristics but lower on others, and one would not expect all activities to score high on all three all of the time. *Practice, memorization, and drill are necessary to build the knowledge and skills needed for more challenging tasks or to prepare for exams required for promotion or advancement. But teachers should provide as much opportunity as possible for all students, including those with disabilities, to engage in and become competent in challenging intellectual work.*

Standards for Teachers' Assignments in Writing

Standard 1: Construction of Knowledge

The assignment asks students to interpret, analyze, synthesize, or evaluate information in writing about a topic, rather than merely to reproduce information.

Standard 2: Disciplined Inquiry Through Elaborated Written Communication

The assignment asks students to draw conclusions or make generalizations or arguments and support them through extended writing.

Standard 3: Value Beyond School Through Connection to Students' Lives

The assignment asks students to connect the topic to experiences, feelings, or situations significant in their lives.

Standards for Teachers' Assignments in Math

Standard 1: Construction of Knowledge

The assignment asks students to organize and interpret information in addressing a mathematical concept, problem, or issue.

Standard 2: Disciplined Inquiry Through Elaborated Written Communication

The assignment asks students to elaborate on their understanding, explanations, or conclusions through extended writing—for example, by explaining a solution path through prose, tables, equations, or diagrams.

Standard 3: Value Beyond School Through Connection to Students' Lives

The assignment asks students to address a concept, problem, or issue that is similar to one they have encountered or are likely to encounter in daily life outside school.

Also central to the SAIL model is the inclusion of special education students in the mainstream of the general education curriculum. Critics point to potentially serious problems with inclusion (see Hanley-Maxwell et al., 1999, for a summary), however, inclusion is prominent in the national reform agenda of special education. Proponents argue that with appropriate accommodations for students' disabilities, both special and regular education students should benefit from inclusive environments. Across the United States, students with a wide range of disabilities are being educated in inclusive settings. In this study of secondary schools that practice inclusion, we explore the degree of authenticity in teacher-designed assessments and the performance of regular and special education students on these assessments.

RESEARCH METHODOLOGY AND ANALYSIS

We present findings from two sets of data collected during the 1999–2000 school year. The first data set (*whole class*) included assessment tasks and the student work on those tasks from 8 teachers in each of two schools. These 16 teachers represented the main academic subject areas of language arts, science, math, and social studies—one teacher in each area from Grades 9–10, and one in each area from Grades 11–12 at each school. The teachers submitted one assessment task that they considered to be an important indicator of what students learned in one of their classes, along with the work the students in that class completed for that task. They also submitted a checklist of accommodations they made, if any, for students with disabilities.

The second data set (*matched pairs*) came from 35 teachers in three of the schools (Schroeder, 2000). The teachers represented the main academic subject areas of language arts, science, math, and social studies (8, 7, 10, and 10 teachers, respectively) across Grades 9–12. These teachers also submitted one assessment task that they considered to be an important indicator of what students learned in one of their classes. However, this set of data differed from the first in that teachers submitted work completed by just two students in the classroom, one student with a disability and one student without a disability, allowing for comparisons between students with and without disabilities on each task. Teachers also submitted a checklist of accommodations they made, if any, for both regular and special education students.

For both data sets, each task was rated on the extent to which the intellectual work it required met each of three standards corresponding to the general characteristics of authentic achievement—construction of knowledge, in-depth understanding through elaborated written communication, and connection to students' lives. For example, a writing task that scored high on construction of knowledge would meet the following criterion: "The task's dominant expectation is for students to interpret, analyze, synthesize, or evaluate information, rather than merely to reproduce information." To score high on elaborated written communication, a mathematics task would need to ask explicitly for generalization and support in students' responses; that is, the task would require students to show through writing their solution paths and to explain the solution paths with evidence such as models or examples. To score high on the third standard—connection to students' lives—a science task would need to present students with a scientific question, issue, or problem that they would have actually encountered or would be likely to encounter in their daily lives; it would ask students to make connections between the topic and real-world situations.

Student work was also evaluated on three standards consistent with the characteristics of authentic intellectual work, but these standards varied somewhat by subject areas. The standards for student work in math, science, and social studies were analysis, disciplinary concepts, and elaborated written communication. The standards for student work in writing were construction of knowledge, forms and conventions, and elaborated written communication.

For both sets of data, scores assigned to the tasks and student work for each of the three standards of authenticity were added to yield two overall scores, one for authenticity of the task and one for authenticity of work produced by students. The scores for each of the standards and the two overall scores were then compared and statistical analyses run to determine if any differences existed between standards, between academic subjects, or between students with and without disabilities. Correlational analyses were also run on the overall scores to determine if any relationships existed between task authenticity and authenticity of work produced by students with and without disabilities. We report these results below.

FINDINGS (DATA SET 1, WHOLE CLASS)

Overall degree of authenticity of tasks. Across the 16 classes, the mean rating for task authenticity on all submitted tasks was 6.53 (*SD* = 1.33; SD stands for the standard deviation which is a measure of how much scores deviate from the mean.). Task authenticity scores can range from a low of 3 to a high of 10, which means that the mean score across all tasks fell in the middle of the range of possible scores. Despite this fact, the actual range for the scores on the assessment tasks included in this sample was from 3 to 8. Therefore, no task received the highest score possible for task authenticity, whereas one received the lowest score.

Across the 16 teachers in the four subject areas, the first two standards (construction of knowledge and elaborated written communication) received roughly equal emphasis on the tasks. Tasks in social studies, science, and writing scored consistently higher on construction of knowledge and elaborated written communication than did math tasks. Standard 3, connection to students' lives, scored consistently lower with all the tasks but one scoring a 1. This result exemplifies the persisting difficulty of developing assignments that ask students to address real-world problems and to explore the connections between topics or concepts and these problems.

Previous research has shown that student performance in math, social studies, and writing is higher in classes with higher levels of authentic pedagogy (Avery, 1999; Newmann & Associates, 1996; Newmann, Lopez, & Bryk, 1998; Newmann et al., 1996). We now explore whether this relationship holds in our study, both for regular and special education students.

Overall degree of authenticity of student work. For the 16 tasks submitted, the mean overall rating for the authenticity of work produced by students was 7.21 (*SD* = 2.41). Overall student work authenticity scores can range from a low of 3 to a high of 12, which means that the mean score across all student work fell close to the middle of the range of possible scores. The range of scores for the student work included in this sample was from 4 to 12. Therefore, some student work did receive the highest score possible for work authenticity, but none received the lowest score.

The authenticity ratings given to student work were further compared by student disability status. The scores on work produced by students *without* disabilities were compared to the scores on work produced by students *with* disabilities to determine if there were any significant differences between the work produced by the two groups. Overall, the mean rating of work authenticity for students without disabilities was 7.42 (*SD* = 2.47) and for students with disabilities was 6.54 (*SD* = 2.05). This difference was statistically significant, indicating that students with disabilities produced work lower in authenticity than that produced by their nondisabled peers.

Relationship between tasks and student achievement. Finally, we summarize findings on (a) the relationship between task authenticity and student achievement on the tasks and (b) achievement results for students with and without disabilities. The first important finding is that, consistent with previous research, there was a significant relationship between the authenticity of task demands and the authenticity of the work that students produced. That is, task demands that were rated lower in authenticity were associated with student work that was rated lower in authenticity. Conversely, task demands that were higher in authenticity were associated with student work that was also higher in authenticity. This relationship was the same for tasks and work produced by students with and without disabilities.

Categorizing tasks as below average in task authenticity (< 6.5) or above average in task authenticity (≥ 6.5) provides a further illustration of this relationship. The average authenticity score for student work when task demands were *below average* in authenticity was 6.24 (*SD* = 2.27). When task authenticity demands were *above average*, however, the average authenticity score for student work was 8.43 (*SD* = 2.01), a difference of more than two points (see Figure 1).

When task demands and student work were analyzed by student disability status, similar results

FIGURE 1

Mean Ratings for Authenticity of all Student Work When Task Demands Are Categorized as Below or Above Average (First Data Set)

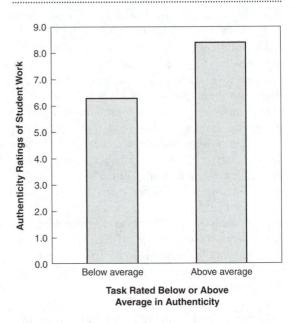

Task Rated Below or Above Average in Authenticity

were found (see Figure 2). On tasks that were below average in authenticity, students without disabilities produced work that received an average score of 6.42 (*SD* = 2.39). Students with disabilities produced work that received an average score of 5.63 (*SD* = 1.66) when given the same task demands. This score is slightly lower than that produced by their nondisabled peers, but the difference is not statistically significant.

When students were given task demands that were above average in authenticity, students without disabilities produced work that received an average score of 8.62 (*SD* = 2.00). Students with disabilities produced work that received an average score of 7.72 (*SD* = 1.92) when given the same task demands—again, a slightly lower score than that of their nondisabled peers.

Although students with disabilities did not score, on average, as well as students without

FIGURE 2

Mean Ratings for Authenticity of Student Work for Students with and without Disabilities Relative to Tasks Rated Below or Above Average in Authenticity (First Data Set)

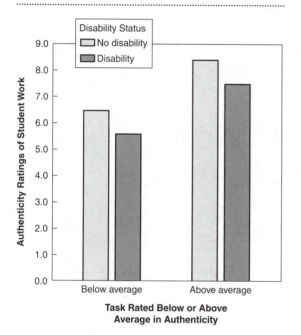

Task Rated Below or Above Average in Authenticity

disabilities, we note two important trends. First, students with disabilities who were given higher scoring (i.e., above-average) tasks performed considerably better (7.72) than students with disabilities who were given below-average tasks (5.63). That is, *special education students in these classes who received tasks with higher intellectual challenge outperformed those who received tasks with less challenge.*

Second, students with disabilities who were given higher scoring (i.e., above-average) tasks performed better (7.72) than students without disabilities who were given below-average tasks (6.42). *Special education students in these classes who received tasks with higher intellectual challenge outperformed their nondisabled peers who received tasks with less challenge.*

FINDINGS (DATA SET 2, MATCHED PAIRS)

The matching of pairs of students in the second set of data allows for much of the same information to be gathered about tasks and student work. However, differences between the two data sets allow for comparisons within pairs of students.

Overall degree of authenticity of tasks. Across the 35 teachers in the second data set, the mean rating for task authenticity on all tasks was 7.30 (*SD* = 2.09). This average fell just above the middle of the range of possible scores (slightly higher than the first data set, which had a mean of 6.53). The actual range for the scores on the assessment tasks included in this data set was from 3 to 10. Therefore, some tasks in this data set, unlike those in the first data set, did receive the highest score possible for task authenticity.

These data yield an additional comparison. Ratings of task authenticity were compared for the tasks given to students with and without disabilities to determine whether the accommodations given to students changed the intellectual demands of the tasks. To benefit from the general education setting and to be able to complete the same tasks as their peers, students with disabilities often require accommodations (McGee, Mutch, & Leyland, 1993). An accommodation that involved eliminating certain parts of a task could lower task authenticity if the parts eliminated were those requiring students to analyze information (construction of knowledge), elaborate on their explanations through extended writing (elaborated written communication), or connect the topic to their lives (connection to students' lives). Accommodations could conceivably increase the authenticity of a task, although none did so in this set of data.

Although the task was generally the same for each pair of students in the second data set, some differences were found in task authenticity. Because of accommodations, students without disabilities received tasks with an overall mean rating of 7.43 (*SD* = 2.12), whereas students with disabilities received tasks with an overall mean rating of 7.17 (*SD* = 2.06). This difference, though small, is statistically significant. Because of the evidence that indicates that task authenticity and the authenticity of student work are related, changes in task demands due to accommodations may be important in determining what students produce. We note, however, that for the vast majority of tasks (85.7%), accommodations made no difference in the degree of intellectual demands.

Overall degree of authenticity of student work. For the 35 tasks submitted, the mean overall rating for the authenticity of work produced by students was 7.47 (*SD* = 2.64). The mean score across all student work fell in the middle of the range of possible scores. The range of scores for the student work included in this sample was from 3 to 12.

The authenticity ratings given to student work in the second data set, as in the first, were compared by student disability status. The mean rating of work authenticity for students without disabilities was 8.03 (*SD* = 2.64), and for students with disabilities it was 6.91 (*SD* = 2.65). This difference was statistically significant, indicating that students with disabilities produced work lower in authenticity than that produced by their nondisabled peers. However, despite this overall difference, it is interesting to note that whereas 37% of the students with disabilities produced work that was lower in authenticity than that produced by their matched nondisabled peer, *nearly 63% produced work that was the same, or higher, in authenticity than that produced by their matched peer* (see Figure 3).

Relationship between tasks and student achievement. Consistent with previous research and the data provided by the first data set, there was a significant relationship between the authenticity of task demands and the authenticity of the work that students produced. That is, task demands that were rated lower in authenticity were associated with student work that was rated lower in authenticity. Conversely, task demands that were higher in authenticity were associated with student work that was also higher in authenticity.

FIGURE 3

Percentage of Work Produced by Students with Disabilities (SWD) Receiving Authenticity Ratings Lower or Higher Than, or the Same as, the Work Produced by Students without Disabilities (Second Data Set)

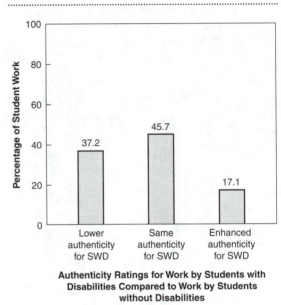

Authenticity Ratings for Work by Students with Disabilities Compared to Work by Students without Disabilities

CONCLUSIONS

Teachers who use more authentic assessments elicit more authentic work from students with and without disabilities. As these data demonstrate, teachers who design and give assessment tasks that call for higher order thinking, requiring analysis or interpretation, in-depth understanding, direct connections to the field under study, and an appeal to an audience beyond the classroom, will enable students to respond in a more sophisticated manner. Students are encouraged to demonstrate their understanding through the construction of knowledge rather than the mere reproduction of facts. Assessments that call for students to respond constructively create opportunities for them to achieve in a manner not captured through a variety of traditional assessment procedures.

These findings suggest that students with disabilities can respond well to more authentic tasks. Although students with disabilities did not score as well on more authentic tasks as their nondisabled peers, *with more challenging tasks, students with disabilities performed better than students with and without disabilities who received less challenging tasks.* Student achievement generally seems to benefit from the use of more authentic forms of assessment, and the achievement of students with disabilities, who are typically unaccounted for at the secondary level, is no exception.

Although accommodations were used extensively in Data Set 2, they altered the authenticity of only 14% of the 35 tasks. This result demonstrates that *teachers are able to adapt assessments for special education students while maintaining the level of intellectual challenge.* Significantly, teachers can sustain high expectations of students in inclusive classrooms. At the same time, the result suggests that challenging tasks can be given to mixed groups of students, including students with disabilities, with relatively minor accommodations.

That said, some explanations are needed for the continuing differences between the scores of disabled and nondisabled students, regardless of the level of a task's authenticity. For one, the assessments included here demanded a certain level of literacy, in both reading and writing, which may make tasks more difficult for certain students because of their disabilities. A broad definition of *elaborated communication* would allow students to show in-depth understanding through a variety of media, not simply through writing as was required for this study. Alternative student products such as demonstrations or exhibitions may provide a solution for this particular problem but are still atypical in schools. A second explanation arises from the pedagogical context in which the assessments are administered. Although not considered in this study, the curriculum and instruction employed before a given assessment may have an impact on disabled students' abilities to respond, given the nature of their disabilities and classroom accommodations.

Put simply, the instruction provided to students will affect their ability to access and successfully complete an assessment task.

There is more work to be done with regard to these issues. We are collecting additional assessment data (teacher tasks and student work) from all four high schools participating in the study. We are also visiting the schools to conduct observations of teachers' lessons in the four main subject areas. The lessons are rated according to criteria for authentic instruction. These data will provide further insight into the promise of authentic and inclusive reforms for students with disabilities.

REFERENCES

Avery, P. (1999). Authentic instruction and assessment. *Social Education, 63*(6), 368–373.

Cohen, D. K., McLaughlin, M. W., & Talbert, J. E. (Eds.). (1993). *Teaching for understanding: Challenges for policy and practice.* San Francisco: Jossey-Bass.

Hanley-Maxwell, C., Phelps, L. A., Braden, J., & Warren, V. W. (1999). *Schools of authentic and inclusive learning* (Brief #1). Madison, WI: Research Institute on Secondary Education Reform for Youth with Disabilities.

Lipsky, D. K., & Gartner, A. (1996). Inclusive education and school restructuring. In W. Stainback & S. Stainback (Eds.), *Controversial issues confronting special education* (pp. 3–15). Boston: Allyn & Bacon.

McGee, A. M., Mutch, L. M., & Leyland, A. (1993). Assessing children who cannot be "tested." *Educational Psychology, 13*(1), 43–48.

Newmann, F. M., & Associates. (1996). *Authentic achievement: Restructuring schools for intellectual quality.* San Francisco: Jossey-Bass.

Newmann, F. M., Lopez, G., & Bryk, A. S. (1998). *The quality of intellectual work in Chicago schools.* Chicago: Consortium on Chicago School Research.

Newmann, F. M., Marks, H. M., & Gamoran, A. (1996). Authentic pedagogy and student performance. *American Journal of Education, 104,* 280–312.

Newmann, F. M., & Wehlage, G. G. (1995). *Successful school restructuring: A report to the public and educators.* Madison, WI: University of Wisconsin, Wisconsin Center for Education Research.

Schroeder, J. L. (2000). *Authentic learning and accommodations for students with disabilities and without disabilities in restructuring secondary schools.* Unpublished master's thesis, University of Wisconsin–Madison.

Trent, S. C., Artiles, A. J., & Englert, C. S. (1998). From deficit thinking to social constructivism: A review of theory, research, and practice in special education. *Review of Research in Education, 23,* 277–307.

M. Bruce King is a research scientist with the Wisconsin Center for Education Research at the University of Wisconsin–Madison. *Jennifer Schroeder* is an assistant professor at Texas A&M University–Commerce and works as a school psychology consultant in the public schools. *David Chawszczewski* works as a teacher educator and consultant in Milwaukee, Wisconsin.

QUESTIONS FOR REFLECTION

1. What is authentic assessment and why is it important to education? Likewise, what would you say authentic *pedagogy* is?
2. How would you go about applying the lessons learned from this research to your own classroom? What features or characteristics of the initial findings would guide you as you sought to make this transition?
3. The authors conclude that teachers who use more authentic assessments elicit more authentic work from students, regardless of whether the students have or do not have disabilities. What does this tell you about the nature of the work done in schools? How might you share what you have learned from this research with your colleagues in education?

AUTHORS' NOTE: This reading is adapted from "Authentic Assessment and Student Performance in Inclusive Schools," Brief #5, Research Institute on Secondary Education Reform for Youth with Disabilities (RISER), December, 2001. See www.wcer.wisc.edu/riser/Brief%205.pdf. The brief was supported by a grant from the U.S. Department of Education, Office of Special Education and Rehabilitative Services, Office of Special Education Programs (#H158J970001) and by the Wisconsin Center for Education Research, School of Education, University of Wisconsin–Madison. Any opinions, findings, or conclusions are those of the authors and do not necessarily reflect the views of the supporting agencies.

Leaders' Voices— Putting Theory into Practice

Lifelines: An Ethnographic Study of an IEP Student

ELSA C. BRO

ABSTRACT: Teaching is a challenging job where river guides and teachers share important characteristics. Here, Elsa C. Bro relates her insightful experiences and realizations as she studies a high school sophomore with learning difficulties.

Because sometimes I live in a hurricane of words and not one of them can save me.

—Naomi Shihab Nye,
"You Know Who You Are"

Several summers ago in raft-guide school, I learned a valuable lesson that can be applied in the classroom: Have a prepared rescue plan for nearly every imaginable scenario. Anticipate. More often than not, however, this nugget of knowledge was passed down to novice guides without the opportunity to practice the skills in low-stakes situations. As a result, my only summer as a raft guide I depended on luck. Guiding by intuition may have been acceptable for pleasure payers but not for students who would be left in my trust in the classroom.

Whether teaching or guiding vacationers down rivers, there is a chance that something could go wrong. Some days are calm; others are turbulent. Before I student taught, while I had the time to observe other teachers in action, my goal was to become a knowledgeable guide who understands the nature and nebulous patterns of learning differences so that I could steer students to success.

In a Literacy and Culture class at Lewis and Clark College, I had an aha moment: If I was going to be able to recognize, anticipate, and prevent the holes that swallow students' ability to participate in a community of learners, I needed data. I became an ethnographer, collecting copious amounts of field notes in a study of one student with literacy challenges. After too many near-death experiences as a river guide, I appreciated having the time to prepare a thoughtful teaching plan for my first year. I intended to use this case study as a reference for how I could modify instruction for future students with diverse learning needs.

Teaching Journal   September 8

This week I learned that being a good observer is not easy, especially when I am grasping for any little drip of free time to get to know the sea of faces that I will be teaching in December. What's easy is accepting an offer to jump into a small group activity to get an insider's look. Solving analogies, for example, is more engaging and fun than lurking on the periphery.

However, my senses are sharper when I am left alone to observe from a distance. From my corner spot next to the student portfolios, I notice Shannon's lackadaisical nature, how his attention remains on sleep's threshold. I note the incessant tap-tap-tapping of Tyrone's feet and muse over his mind's music. The same students read and return text messages. Laticia eats sliced green-apple spears from a plastic bag. Lacrosse team?

Observation time is a privilege, a gift that many teachers aren't granted while navigating new curriculum, diverse learning needs, and growing class sizes. While in this privileged position I'm going to get to know who these students are as individuals. A prediction: cultivating and maintaining this keen awareness will be a challenging task for a first-year teacher.

READING THE LANDSCAPE

As a student intern observing Ms. Lewis's fifth-period sophomore English class, I was drawn into the landscape of ebullient faces, swirling voices, and swift minds. The energy in the room reaffirmed my commitment to teach. For ten weeks, my mission in the classroom was reconnaissance, scouting for potential obstacles that could impede the learning success of any one of thirty fifteen- and sixteen-year-olds. I looked for eddies, the mysterious cross-currents that can suck victims into their roiling vortices, spilling gear and carefully prepared plans for a smooth ride.

On my third day observing at Central High, I joined a heterogeneous group reading scenes 2 and 3 from *Antigone*. The group included two students on individual education plans (IEPs)—Courtney and Carla—and Josh and Patterson, two advanced placement students. Voices sounded out in a chorus of characters' voices from the play. Josh and Patterson claimed their parts with alacrity while Carla read without affect.

"It was not God's procla . . . proclammae. . . ."

"Proclamation," corrected Patterson, one of Central High's all-state racquetball champions.

Carla's soft voice fell off, becoming almost inaudible as she continued, "that final Justice that rules the world below makes no such laws. Your edet, edit. . . . ."

"Edict!" Patterson interjected.

"Your edict, King, was strong. But all your strength is weakness itself against the imm-oooaa-tal. . . ."

As Carla struggled to match sound and symbol, Josh and Courtney kept their eyes on the text. *Just give her time to sound it out*, I wanted to say.

At that instant Patterson sighed, shaking his head in exasperation. "Immortal!"

With her head down now, Carla's giggles hid the fact that she was drowning in embarrassment. "OK," she said at last, straightening up in her desk. She drew in a deep breath and salvaged her last line: "Immortal unrecorded laws of God."

After completing the reading, our group decided to do the summary questions individually. The volume of the other voices in the room made it difficult to concentrate. I reread the first question several times. With my years of reading and learning in various environments, I was surprised at how distracted I was. If I couldn't focus, how could the students?

My mind drifted to Carla. She kept to herself, which made the story of her mind mysterious and intriguing. Her visible lack of the usual teenage-girl behavior—giggling, whispering, and lip-reading conversations with friends while the teacher was instructing—disturbed me. How could I get to know her better without pushing her away? From my adolescence I knew that being singled out from the crowd is a bummer; generally, teens are more receptive to one-on-one talks. With only two minutes until the lunch bell, I decided to address Carla in front of her peers.

"Carla, how are you doing today?" I asked, motioning to her blank sheet of paper. "You didn't answer any questions."

"I'm tired. I didn't go to bed until 2:00 a.m." Her body drooped in her desk.

"Why?"

"Because I got in a fight with my mother and had to go to my brother's."

"What happened?"

"Well, my mom's an alcoholic, and we've never gotten along," she continued. "I used to live with my dad, but I won't go there to live again."

I did not know what to say. What does one say when confronted with the realization that some teens do not have a home to go to? "I'm sorry to hear that. Do you have enough people to talk to about this?"

"Yes," she said definitively. The lunch bell buzzed. All students surged for the hall except Carla, who sauntered slowly to the door, alone.

Teaching Journal   September 14

Imagine reading two whole scenes from a play out loud in front of your classmates and stumbling over words in every sentence. Patterson has made himself the authority on pronunciation, correcting Carla every time she stumbles. I wonder how this reading exercise makes her feel. What is it that makes certain words difficult for Carla to read? Is she getting the help she needs to become a better reader? Need to watch for patterns.

I am surprised at how comfortable she was opening up to me in front of her peers. She was completely unconcerned about disclosing personal info. Now her faded look in class is starting to make sense. It sounds like she has some real challenges to face at home, which could be impeding her progress on schoolwork.

SEEKING RESOURCES

The rotating block schedule went round and round. With school holidays, assemblies, and student absences, I considered myself lucky if I was able to take a half hour of field notes on my case study and squeeze in a twenty-minute conference each week. As my December start date for teaching approached, I had to seek other resources to make sense of Carla's reading difficulty so that I would know how to differentiate instruction for her and other students.

How far would I have to stretch myself as a teacher to reach her? How would I manage to prepare individualized instruction for every student? Would I have to do this alone? While searching for the answers to my questions, I became familiar with another reality of teaching: Taking work home is inevitable. To be a great teacher, one must research.

Readers and Writers with a Difference illuminates some useful clues for identifying troubled readers. Rhodes and Dudley-Marling note, "miscues . . . follow a pattern . . . and give us information about readers' thought processes during reading. . . . When good readers produce miscues they err on the side of meaning. Poor readers tend to err on the side of phonics" (42). The authors

suggest that teachers watch for students relying too heavily on one system for reading. In addition, considering whether the miscues vary as a function of the texts themselves or of the students' background experiences aids in preparing developmentally appropriate, challenging lesson plans.

I discovered that Carla's miscues while reading *Antigone* clearly demonstrated a dependence on phonics. Her focus was on making the right sounds, not on decoding the meaning of the text. The abstract language of a Greek tragedy may have been too dense for her, making word recognition spotty at best. Speaking with her ninth-grade English teacher and conducting a reading interview would help to further fill in the blanks.

Teaching Journal   October 1

During a conference with my mentor teacher this morning, we discussed her disappointment that over half of the students did not pass the Certificate of Initial Mastery (CIM) requirements on their narrative essays [Oregon requires that sophomores be assessed on specific reading and writing benchmarks]. Carla is the only student who did not turn in her essay. Even though it was due over a week ago, Ms. Lewis is willing to let Carla turn her essay in whenever she can. Overall, Carla has good attendance, which makes me further question why she is falling behind. I wonder what I can do to help her turn assignments in on time.

CONDUCTING A READING INTERVIEW

The next day I met Carla in first-period Marketing to shadow her for the day. I was curious to see if her behavior and reading patterns were consistent in her other classes. My essential questions were: How do various instructional activities interface with Carla's learning needs? Which processes aid her reading comprehension?

Carla plopped down a cell phone on her desk and began reading a memo from the color guard coach about the upcoming competition. She looked tired.

"Is it hard for you to get up for class this early?" I asked.

"Sometimes, but right now I am sick with a cold, and I can't get better."

"Did you eat breakfast?"

"No, I didn't have time," she replied quietly.

I was drawn to the scene on her desk: a white, plastic binder papered with pictures of horses. "Are you passionate about horses?"

"Yes, I go to my uncle's on the weekends to train horses to be ridden. I used to have my own horse there, too, but not anymore."

I wondered how Carla learned to ride and train horses and if this process carried over into the classroom.

Mr. Resch handed out three photocopied articles while explaining the different ways advertisers categorize target markets. He instructed us to read the articles and write down who the target market was. I watched Carla read while I read.

Carla completed the reading and supporting evidence for the target markets without any noticeable challenges. Her answers were nondescript and in incomplete sentences, although there were no spelling errors. My answers contained more details. Glancing at other students' answers, I found brevity.

Teaching Journal   October 2

Me: I saw that you are finishing your reading at the same time as your classmates. You mentioned before that you have a hard time following along with the story when you have to read it out loud. What helps you to understand the reading in Marketing class?

Carla: I don't know. These articles aren't so hard to read, and it helps that I don't have to listen to anyone else reading aloud.

Me: I see. Is it easier to read quietly or out loud?

Carla: They're both hard. I am a slower reader, and so I need more time. I usually need someone to explain to me what is going on in the book. That's why I'm so slow.

Me: What makes it difficult to get your homework done?

Carla: Well, I have color guard practice after school, and when I come home it's hard to do my homework, because my mom blames me for not giving her enough attention. When I'm in my room she bangs on my door, so it's hard to concentrate. Also, I have dyslexia.

Me: Oh. I didn't know. How does this make reading challenging?

Carla: I am a very slow reader and writer. I need more time to understand what's going on, and I feel bored in class.

Me: What do you mean you feel bored?

Carla: Well, it's hard to take notes while listening in class, so a lot of times I feel lost.

Me: Well, if it's OK with you I will talk to Ms. Lewis to see what we can do to adjust our instruction so that it serves you better.

Carla: OK.

Journal Reflection   October 5

On two separate occasions Carla has clued me in on the predicament she faces at home trapped between two difficult choices: homework or Mom. Due to the overwhelming stress and guilt accompanying the mind of a child with an alcoholic parent, Carla is starved for guidance, resources, and support. After school and color guard practice with the band, there is little quiet, uninterrupted time to complete homework. Carla has determined that isolation is the only way; she locks herself in her room to avoid her mother, who is easily angered when not given enough attention.

Concentrating on writing a narrative essay often becomes impossible, as does reading a tenth-grade text like *Antigone* or "Where Have You Gone, Charming Billy?" After rereading the same lines countless times, Carla gives up. For someone like Carla it is imperative that reading time, proofreading, and answers to questions are provided in class, due to the dearth of support at home.

RELYING ON LABELS

In third-period French I, Mr. Rainier moved to the overhead and, before I could take out my notepad, my ears were flooded with French dialogue. His arms flagged the students like a composer. While the rest of the class scribbled down conjugations, Carla just listened. The situation reminded me of Mr. Thelan, my authoritarian, incessantly perspiring high school French teacher. The recollection of relentless drills and the D that I received on the final oral exam made me shudder.

Mr. Rainier squeezed between rows to check that the day's assignment was complete. Carla's worksheet was half blank, and as Mr. Rainier swept by, she expertly hid the incomplete part underneath a messy pile of vocabulary sheets. Saved!

Mr. Rainier whisked around the class with a stack of homework to return. A worksheet fluttered onto Carla's desk; the F in the top margin seemed to leap off the page. She quickly flipped it over.

"Carla, we need to meet sometime to talk about this, OK?" he said, nodding his head.

Carla mirrored Mr. Rainier, nodding her head in compliance.

The French lesson continued, but Carla was not invited to participate. I wondered if teachers purposely did not call on students with IEPs because they were trying to avoid the possibility of humiliating a student. Had Mr. Rainier and Carla agreed on alternative ways to assess her progress? Was there a plan in place that ensured that Carla was able to set and achieve some attainable goals?

"So, what's the story on your French homework?" I asked as subtly as possible on our way to the cafeteria.

"Everything's OK," she responded, "because Mr. Rainier knows I have an IEP."

I did not see it that way.

Teaching Journal   October 26

Apparently, scrambling to copy or cover up incomplete assignments at the last minute is a way of life for students who don't have a quiet place to do homework in the evening. I am curious to learn what other unsanctioned literacies are used to beat a system that doesn't support all students equitably. I understand that Carla definitely has more challenges affecting learning success than the average teenager. Yet, I can't help but wonder if her lack of concern in the classroom is a result of her taking advantage of the flexibility her IEP grants her.

In *Between Worlds,* Freeman and Freeman warn educators about the irreversible damage of labeling students. Students who are labeled "begin to see themselves as limited" (140). Teachers who lower their expectations about students' performance give the perception that students are not capable of being challenged, taking risks, and

stretching themselves as learners. Once students learn that they are "different," they often disown and disengage from their academic experience. Consequently, lowered student performance confirms teachers' beliefs, and a "cycle of failure is established" (141).

After observing consistent performance patterns in all of Carla's classes, I came to a troubling conclusion. Instead of asking for help when she was having difficulty reading or writing, Carla relied on her IEP to bump her through her classes. Under the Accommodations and Modifications heading, her IEP required the following: partial credit for work considered late; break down long-term assignments into smaller, more manageable parts; extended time on tests, reading, and writing assignments; may take tests, quizzes, or work on assignments in the resource room as needed; preferential seating away from distractions. Under Assessment Modifications and Accommodations, it states that when taking multiple-choice tests or on-demand performance assessments and work samples, Carla may have extended time if needed. The categories Supplementary Aids and Services and Supports for School Personnel remain blank.

My mentor teacher abhors the burdensome paper trail that depersonalizes teacher-student relationships, yet she is not doing anything to change the system. At the beginning of the school year she is given IEPs, which go into a file. That is it. Throughout my observations of the fifth-period sophomore English class, none of the students with IEPs were called on during whole-class discussions until I asked Ms. Lewis what her rationale was. She admitted that she purposely does not call on students with IEPs for fear of embarrassing them. I think that teachers need to ask themselves if this practice is honoring students or allowing them to slip through the cracks.

Teaching Journal   November 3

I have found no evidence of adaptations or accommodations being exercised to help Carla become an active participant in any of her classes. Since I have been at my internship site, she has never requested, or been offered, extra time on tests or quizzes, nor have teachers broken down larger assignments into chunks for easier understanding. First action to take: create seating chart that places Carla in close proximity to teacher; this would lessen distractions.

IDENTIFYING DIFFICULTIES

Seeing that Carla may never turn in her narrative essay, Ms. Lewis employed me to offer a writing conference. I still did not understand what Carla meant when she told me that she is dyslexic. Her IEP does not state this, as dyslexia falls under the mysterious heading of "learning disabled," offering a vague understanding of how to accommodate students' needs. I was not sure how I could help her. With Carla's permission, I took a copy of her essay, hoping that together we could identify the words and letters that tripped her up in the writing process. What I found was baffling.

Teaching Journal   November 12

At first glance, Carla's handwritten narrative essay is reminiscent of a ball of barbed wire; sentences have been erased and rewritten, scratched out, and redirected with arrows going this way and that. There are significant spelling and sentence structure errors, although she's got a good lead and conclusion. Luckily, she was here on peer edit day; she got some good feedback.

Her areas of trouble included homophones, contractions, mixing up vowels, using a single consonant when there should be double consonants, and switched letters in words (see Figure 1). Based on what I knew about Carla's invented spelling, I could provide one minilesson per week that targeted a repeated spelling error. In addition, I would provide corrections on two troublesome conventions per essay until the mistake was corrected through revision and review.

Whereas my ethnographic study began with observations and a collection of literary artifacts, the lack of resources for "learning disabled" students motivated me to question school counselors and special education caseworkers. Where were they? Who were they, and why wasn't my mentor teacher familiar with them?

FIGURE 1
Patterns of Error in Spelling and Usage

Incorrect	Correct
restronts	restaurants
licycle	Lysol
Weeks	weeks
to	too
though	threw/through
deiced	decided
Over	over
druk	drunk
achool	alcohol
grams	germs
brake	break
thought	through
we're	were
but	put
tal	tall
fravorit	favorite

I went to the office of Carla's counselor to seek out who could be Carla's "school safety" when home life got rough and oversee Carla's progress to make sure she was not being left behind. In my idealistic mind I assumed that there must be a mentoring program for younger students. After all, Central had just implemented a fully staffed career center for older students.

"Unfortunately, Carla does not have priority visitations unless she is a junior, is in crisis, or is high risk," the counselor explained, handing me brochures to two off-campus counseling groups for girls. "There are scholarships for low-income students," she said with a smile.

The groups could give Carla the self-esteem and support that she lacked at home, yet I had the sinking feeling that transportation would present a challenge. For a split second I pondered the possibility of arranging rides for Carla but then realized that I had to draw the line somewhere.

Even though I wanted the best for Carla, as a new teacher it was imperative to set up appropriate boundaries from the beginning.

"Since Carla's on an IEP, she does have a case-worker who will know how to better serve her academic needs. If you go to the main office, they can tell you where to find the resource room."

I was beginning to feel resistance. "Is there *anything* I can do to help Carla be more successful in her classes?"

"Does she have a student planner? Here," the counselor said, pointing to a box of orange Central High student handbooks. "Take one for yourself and one for Carla. Usually grades improve when students learn organization and time-management skills."

I left the counseling office feeling waterlogged. I was disappointed by the lack of support for students who may depend on school to give them a sense of accomplishment. If students were not learning at school, what would they do once they were in the real world? Certainly Carla's home life and difficulty reading placed her in the high-risk category, didn't they?

Teaching Journal	November 15

Carla's classroom performance is plummeting. With two incomplete assignments today, she's standing at a 64% in Sophomore English and is failing French. No one is seriously addressing the obtuse patterns of her writing or the frequency that she does not turn in assignments. I fear that if we, the resource guides of this student, do not collaborate to get her back onboard soon, we will be looking at a case of hypothermia.

ACCOMMODATING INDIVIDUAL NEEDS

I was relieved to discover that I would not have to cross these uncharted waters alone. In the resource room, Mr. Blair, Carla's caseworker, told me how IEPs function. Once a student is assessed as being "learning disabled," a caseworker monitors the student's attendance and grades, maintaining a three-week conference schedule unless there is an obvious risk of failure or conflict to address. In between the three-week cycles, Mr. Blair assured me that he is available for writing consultations, proofreading, homework help, and goal setting for high-stakes projects. He also offered to be the "bad guy" if I needed support taking disciplinary action.

Most students on IEPs are encouraged to take at least one special education class, such as an English learning lab where they receive help on assignments. The accommodations on an IEP are designed to lighten class loads while tailoring learning objectives to meet individuals' needs. Special education classes may be appropriate for some students; however, others may benefit from being in mainstream classrooms alongside students with varying abilities. Freeman and Freeman tell us that students doing interactive activities learn more when placed in heterogeneous groups. For example, classes structured around thematic units that take an interdisciplinary approach are apt to be more relevant and inclusive to all students (197).

Unfortunately, it takes assertive parents or a proactive student to receive the support that is needed to overcome reading challenges that sabotage successful learning experiences. In fact, most students do not want to be singled out as "different" and battle it out in regular classes to save face. This seemed to be Carla's case. In Mr. Blair's opinion, she was not keeping in touch with him as she should. In the same way that instruction and assessment are inseparable, Carla's way of navigating and coping with home life spilled over into school life; she prefers to be invisible. After moving from one bad home situation with her father to another with her mother, Carla has internalized the negative relationships she has had with adults. Adults who are close to her inevitably hurt her. Adults cannot be trusted.

Rescue Kit Strategies	November 21

I am determined to reach her. First, I will make myself accountable for following through with the accommodations outlined on her IEP. I will provide large reading texts and projects in advance to give Carla adequate time. Mr. Blair will also receive copies of high-stakes assignments in order to provide support and assessment. Finally, if Carla feels comfortable I am going to offer to meet her once a week to check in. During our conferences I will offer to read texts or test questions aloud to her, dictate answers to test questions, have writing workshop, or just talk.

Throughout classroom instruction I will strategically frame students' thinking by providing visuals of essential and unit questions. Daily agendas will be posted to anchor the focus of students who have fleeting attention spans; students will know when they will be able to stretch and socialize around learning. I will offer "hurdle help" by chunking information and adjusting individual goals to meet students' varying skill levels. Groups of varying abilities will support learning while cultivating perspective and empathy.

I am as curious about Carla's home life, school literacies, and learning needs today as I was when I started my study. However, I celebrate the leap in understanding I have made around Carla's reading and writing challenges. My experiences as observer and ethnographer have been invaluable to my development as a teacher. I now feel confident that I can prevent unnecessary calamities in the classroom by providing accommodations that make learning enjoyable and accessible, and it is my hope that this ethnographic study will help other new teachers find multiple pathways to knowing their dynamic, unique, and differently abled students.

Even after this ethnographic study, I wonder how we, as teacher-researchers, are truly able to know individual students. I realize, though, that we are not alone out there. By making the time to seek out staff supports and resources within the school, being a first-year teacher does not seem as daunting. I know where to find an ally to work with, someone to toss lifelines with, in hopes that they will be caught and held onto.

WORKS CITED

Freeman, David F., and Yvonne S. Freeman. *Between Worlds: Access to Second Language Acquisition.* 2nd ed. Portsmouth: Heinemann, 2001.

Rhodes, Lynn K., and Curt Dudley-Marling. *Readers and Writers with a Difference: A Holistic Approach to Teaching Learning Disabled and Remedial Students.* Portsmouth: Heinemann, 1988.

Elsa C. Bro, originally from Iowa, teaches English as a second language at an elementary school in the French Alps.

QUESTIONS FOR REFLECTION

1. What does Bro's use of ethnography as a data collection method allow her to learn about her students? How might another form of data collection have yielded different results?
2. Would this article "lose" something if Bro had elected not to include her journal writing and the interview transcripts?
3. What characteristics of Bro's approach to Carla's learning difficulties can you imagine using in your classroom? How could they be applied to all students, not just those with obvious learning challenges?

LEARNING ACTIVITIES

Critical Thinking

1. In light of constructivist views of learning, how can teachers increase their knowledge of students' understanding? How should teachers take into account students' social, cultural, linguistic, and academic backgrounds?
2. What is your preferred learning style? Where, when, and how do you learn best?
3. In regard to multiple intelligences theory, in which intelligences are you most proficient? Least proficient? How do these areas of greatest (and least) proficiency affect your learning?
4. What are the risks of using learning styles and/or multiple intelligences theory to design learning activities for students?
5. Herbert A. Thelen has pointed out that "If we get too comfortable, we stop growing. Students can put pressure on us to work within their comfort zone. Let's be kind about that. Kind enough to help them learn to be uncomfortable" (quoted in *Models of Teaching,* 7th edition [Allyn and Bacon, 2004, p. 337]). What are the implications of Thelen's statement for curriculum leaders who develop learning activities to "fit" students' learning styles?

Application Activities

1. Examine a recent curriculum guide of interest to you or in your field of study to identify the learning theory (or theories) that is the basis for the suggested learning activities. What additional learning activities, based on other theories of learning, could be added?
2. In *Practical Intelligence for School* (HarperCollins, 1996), Howard Gardner and a team of researchers have proposed another form of intelligence—*practical intelligence,* "the ability to understand one's environment, and to use this knowledge in figuring out how best to achieve one's goals" (p. ix). They believe that practical intelligence consists of five themes that can be taught: *knowing why, knowing self, knowing differences, knowing process,* and *reworking.* In planning curricula at the level with which you are most interested, how useful is the concept of practical intelligence?
3. At the level and in the content area of greatest interest to you, identify several learning activities that address each of the seven multiple intelligences identified by Gardner.

Field Experiences

1. Interview a teacher at your level of greatest interest, K–12 through higher education, for the purpose of clarifying the learning theory (or theories) that guides the teacher. Formulate your interview questions in light of the material in this chapter.
2. At the level and in the subject area of greatest interest to you, observe a teacher to identify the learning theory (or theories) he or she uses. What differences do you note among the students' responses to their teacher? Is there evidence of different learning styles among the students?

Internet Activities

1. Conduct an Internet search on one or more of the topics listed below. Gather resources and information relevant to your current, or anticipated, curriculum leadership activities.

multiple intelligences	learning styles
learning theories	behavior modification
cognitive science	brain research
constructivism	neuroscience

2. Go to the site for Harvard Project Zero codirected by Howard Gardner. For almost 40 years Project Zero has studied how children and adults learn. At this site, gather information relevant to your current, or anticipated, curriculum planning activities.

part two # Developing, Implementing, and Evaluating the Curriculum

5

Approaches to Curriculum Development

FOCUS QUESTIONS

1. How should school leaders apply curriculum theory and research during the curriculum development process?

2. What is the nature of curriculum development at the macro and micro levels?

3. What are the differences between subject-centered and student-centered curricula?

4. What is the role of standards in the curriculum development process and how might school leaders' understanding of standards shape curriculum development?

5. What are some arguments for and against higher standards for the curriculum?

6. What are some recent trends in curriculum development?

7. What role can students play in curriculum development?

From your reading of Chapters 1 through 4, you now understand the significance of goals and values and the three bases of curriculum planning—social forces, human development, and learning and learning styles. A major aim of this chapter, then, is to move from *planning* the curriculum to *developing* (or writing) the curriculum.

The title of Franklin Bobbitt's classic work, *How to Make a Curriculum* (1924), might suggest that developing a curriculum is a straightforward process. According to Bobbitt, a curriculum should be developed "scientifically" by analyzing the daily activities of adult life and then creating behavioral objectives for those activities.

Bobbitt's approach suggests that one need only apply curriculum theory and research to the processes of curriculum development. However, curriculum theory and research do not set forth, in cookbook fashion, exactly how one should develop a curriculum. Instead, it may be helpful to think of curriculum theory and research as providing "rules of thumb" for a school leader to follow as he or she provides leadership for curriculum development.

Clearly, there is no single right way to develop a curriculum. As John Dewey points out in "The Sources of a Science of Education" in this chapter, "No conclusion of scientific research can be converted into an immediate rule of educational art. For there is no educational practice whatever which is not highly complex; that is to say, which does not contain many other conditions and factors than are included in the scientific finding." The significance of any one research study for educational practice, then, can be determined only as the results of that study are balanced with an understanding of the "conditions and factors" that influence the situation. Connections among research results and surrounding environmental influences should be made until they reciprocally confirm and illuminate one another, or until each gives the other added meaning.

When these connecting principles are understood, the curriculum leader is more likely to make the "best" decisions throughout the curriculum development process. To make such informed decisions, Dewey (1904, p. 10) maintains elsewhere that educators should acquire and develop a fundamental mental process, the ultimate aim of which is "the intellectual method and material of good workmanship." According to Dewey, this intellectual method is the criterion against which educational decisions—from curriculum development to selecting instructional strategies—should be made. Dewey also suggests several personal dispositions that characterize those who use the method: intellectual independence (p. 16) and responsibility, initiative, skill in scholarship (p. 21), willingness to be a "thoughtful and alert" student of education (p. 15), and a spirit of inquiry. In addition, Dewey stresses the need to develop the "habit of viewing the entire curriculum as a continuous growth, reflecting the growth of mind itself" (p. 26).

APPROACHES TO CURRICULUM DEVELOPMENT

The articles on goals and values and the three bases of the curriculum in the first four chapters of this book make it evident that a school leader can follow many different designs in planning a curriculum. These designs are not mutually exclusive; they can be used together or separately to address various types of curricular goals, differences among learners, and different types of knowledge.

There is no easy-to-follow set of procedures for developing a curriculum. While there are many "models" for curriculum design, none are intended to provide step-by-step procedures for developing curricula. However, Ralph Tyler's classic text, *Basic Principles of Curriculum and Instruction,* contained four salient questions, now known as the "Tyler rationale," that must be considered, in some fashion, at least, when planning a curriculum:

1. What educational purposes should the school seek to attain?
2. What educational experiences can be provided that are likely to attain these purposes?
3. How can these educational experiences be effectively organized?
4. How can we determine whether these purposes are being attained? (Tyler, 1949, p. 1)

The Tyler rationale has been used by many curriculum leaders as a set of general guidelines for developing a curriculum; however, others have criticized the rationale as being a linear, means-end model that oversimplifies the complexities of curriculum planning. They believe the Tyler rationale underestimates the complexities of curriculum development. The rationale advocates a straightforward, step-by-step process that, in reality, is difficult to follow in the "real" world of schools. Nevertheless, Tyler's classic work has been used by many school leaders to bring some degree of order and focus to the curriculum development process. Thus, as curriculum theorists Francis P.

Hunkins and Patricia A. Hammill (1994, p. 7) observe, "Despite all the criticism of Tyler, his thinking is still dominant in schools across the nation."

When first introduced, Tyler's model represented a modern view of curriculum design. Developing the curriculum, according to Tyler, required a mechanical, rational approach that could be followed systematically in any context, with any group of students. Today, however, postmodernist views of the world are leading to curriculum designs that are based on diverse voices, meanings, and points of view. As Hunkins and Hammill (1994) point out:

> we are realizing with increasing sophistication that life is organic, not mechanical; the universe is dynamic, not stable; the process of curriculum development is not passive acceptance of steps, but evolves from action within the system in particular contexts; and that goals emerge oftentimes from the very experiences in which people engage. (p. 10)

Similarly, in "Teachers, Public Life, and Curriculum Reform" in this chapter, Henry A. Giroux points out that "the language of curriculum, like other discourses, does not merely reflect a pregiven reality; on the contrary, it selectively offers depictions of the larger world through representations that people struggle over to name what counts as knowledge, what counts as communities of learning, what social relationships matter, and what visions of the future can be represented as legitimate."

The Focus of Curriculum Development

When providing leadership for curriculum development, the leader should understand two dimensions of curriculum development: the target and the time orientation (see Figure 5.1). The target of curriculum development may be at the macro or the micro level.

At the macro level, decisions about the content of the curriculum apply to large groups of students. National goals for education and state-level curriculum standards are examples of macro level curricular decisions. At the micro level, curriculum decisions are made that apply to groups of students in a particular school or classroom. To some extent, all teachers are micro-level curriculum developers—that is, they make numerous decisions about the curricular experiences they provide students in their classrooms.

Another dimension of curriculum development is the time orientation—does the curriculum focus on the present or the future? In addition to national goals and state-level curriculum standards, the semester-long, monthly, or unit plans that teachers make are examples of future-oriented curriculum development. Present-oriented curriculum development usually occurs at the classroom level and is influenced by the unique needs of specific groups of students. The daily or weekly curriculum decisions and lesson plans that teachers make are examples of present-oriented curriculum development.

Student-Centered versus Subject-Centered Curricula

A key concern in curriculum development is whether greater emphasis should be given to the requirements of the subject area or to the needs of the students. It is helpful to imagine where a school curriculum might be placed on the following continuum.

Student-Centered ← ————————→ Subject-Centered
Curriculum   Curriculum

FIGURE 5.1

Two Dimensions of Curriculum Development: The Target and Time Orientation

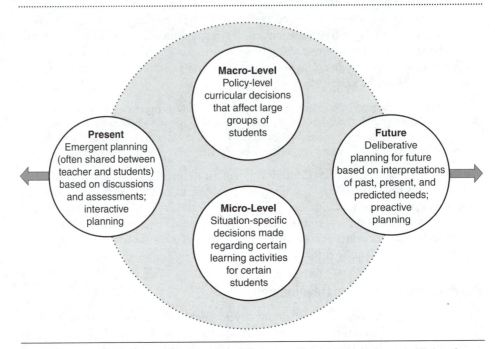

Source: Forrest W. Parkay and Beverly Stanford, *Becoming a Teacher,* 7th ed. Boston: Allyn and Bacon, 2007, p. 358.

Although no curriculum is entirely subject- or student-centered, curricula vary considerably in the degree to which they emphasize one or the other. The subject-centered curriculum places primary emphasis on the logical order of the discipline students are to study. The teacher of such a curriculum is a subject-matter expert and is primarily concerned with helping students understand the facts, laws, and principles of the discipline. Subject-centered curricula are more typical of high school education.

Some teachers develop curricula that reflect greater concern for students and their needs. Though teachers of the student-centered curriculum also teach content, they emphasize the growth and development of students. This emphasis is generally more typical of elementary school curricula.

Curriculum Leadership Strategy

A major challenge of keeping students engaged in various curricula is maintaining their interest, especially when the material is largely subject-centered. When presenting material to students, look for approaches that make the subject material relevant and timely. Strategies include examples from current events, students' personal experiences, and real-world scenarios or case studies.

THE CURRICULUM DEVELOPMENT PROCESS

The process of developing a curriculum usually begins with an examination of the knowledge, skills, attitudes, and values students should exhibit on completion of a unit of study. The following are among the factors curriculum leaders should consider at this stage of the curriculum development process:

- The desired balance between the *acquisition of content* and *mastery of processes*
- Sequencing of content
- Students' prior knowledge
- Identifying methods for assessing student learning
- Short-term versus long-term performance
- Quality versus quantity

The Appendix on page 260 presents a "generic" plan for developing a unit of study. At minimum, a plan for a unit of study should include the following six elements:

1. Introduction
2. Objectives
3. Content of Unit
4. Methods and Activities
5. Teaching Materials and/or Resources
6. Assessment of Student Learning

Standards and Curriculum Development

Since the 1990s, curriculum development has focused increasingly on higher, "world-class" standards. Standards-based education (SBE) is premised on the belief that *all* students are capable of meeting high standards.

In the past, expectations for students from poor families and students from minority groups were sometimes lower than for other students. Today, SBE is seen as a way of ensuring that excellence and equity become part of our nation's public school system. As President George W. Bush pointed out prior to his election for a second term in 2004: "The educational divide [between African Americans and Hispanic students and white students] is caused by the soft bigotry of low expectations" (Bush, 2004, 114). Similarly, in "A Principal Looks Back: Standards Matter" in this chapter, Kim Marshall reflects on 15 years as principal of an inner-city elementary school and notes that "the absence of meaningful external standards before 1998 prevented our strenuous and thoughtful efforts [at school improvement] from having much traction."

In response to the call for higher standards, state departments of education, school districts, and schools undertook numerous curricular reforms and developed more exacting, authentic methods for assessing student learning. Typically, "higher standards" was interpreted by parents, the public, and lawmakers to mean that teachers should expect more of their students. Toward this end, various macro-level mandates were made: detailed statements of the knowledge and skills students were to acquire under the more rigorous standards; higher test scores to receive passing grades or to be promoted to the next level; and more English, science, and mathematics. Since 2007, all states have adopted state standards for what students should know and be able to do. For example, here are standards in geometry from three states:

> **Colorado:** Students use geometric concepts, properties, and relationships in problem-solving situations and communicate the reasoning used in solving these problems.

> **North Dakota:** Students understand and apply geometric concepts and spatial relationships to represent and solve problems in mathematical and nonmathematical situations.

> **Wyoming:** Students apply geometric concepts, properties, and relationships in problem-solving situations. Students communicate the reasoning used in solving these problems.

Responses to SBE have been mixed. On the one hand, advocates of higher standards agreed with observers such as Diane Ravitch, educational historian and author of *National Standards in American Education: A Citizen's Guide* (1995),who points out that:

- Standards can improve achievement by clearly defining what is to be taught and what kind of performance is expected.
- Standards (national, state, and local) are necessary for equality of opportunity.
- National standards provide a valuable coordinating function.
- Standards and assessments provide consumer protection by supplying accurate information to students and parents.
- Standards and assessments serve as an important signaling device to students, parents, teachers, employers, and colleges (Ravitch, 1996, pp. 134–135).

On the other hand, numerous concerns were expressed by opponents of the effort to develop "world-class" standards for America's educational system. The following are among the arguments these critics raised:

- Higher standards further bias educational opportunities in favor of students from advantaged backgrounds, intensify the class-based structure of American society, and increase the disparities between rich and poor schools.
- Raising standards might eventually lead to the development of a national curriculum, thereby increasing the role of federal government in education.
- The push for higher standards is fueled by conservative political groups that wish to undo educational gains made by historically underrepresented groups.
- Preoccupation with raising standards diverts attention from more meaningful educational reform.
- "World-class" standards are often vague and not linked to valid assessments and scoring rubrics.

Perhaps the most controversial standards to come forth during the 1990s were those developed for U.S. and world history by the National Center for History in the

Schools. Immediately after the standards were issued in 1994, conservative groups, including the Council for Basic Education, asserted that the standards covered discrimination experienced by minority groups and women, while they omitted certain historical figures and positive features of the westward expansion and other aspects of American life. Some critics even charged that the standards were so "politically correct" that they reflected an anti-Western bias. In response to such widespread criticism, the center rewrote the standards, this time with input from the Council for Basic Education, 33 national education organizations, and more than 1,000 educators. The revised standards were issued in 1996 with endorsements from many groups that were critical of the previous standards.

Content and Performance Standards

Standards documents prepared by state education agencies, local school districts, and professional associations typically refer to two types of standards—content standards and performance standards. *Content standards,* as the term implies, refer to the agreed-on content—or knowledge and skills—students should acquire in different academic areas. A common phrase in standards documents is that content standards represent "what students should know and be able to do."

Content standards are often subdivided into benchmarks (frequently called *indicators*). Benchmarks are content standards that are presented as specific statements of what students should understand and be able to do *at specific grade levels or developmental stages.* The following is an example of a benchmark: "at the end of the eighth grade, the student understands basic properties of two- and three-dimensional figures." In addition, many standards documents refer to *performance standards.* A performance standard specifies "how good is good enough." Performance standards are used to assess the *degree to which* students have attained standards in an academic area.

Performance standards require teacher judgment about the quality of performance or level of proficiency required. Performance standards differ from content standards because performance standards reflect levels of proficiency. A performance standard for evaluating students' written essays, for example, might be as follows: 5 = outstanding, 4 = exemplary, 3 = proficient, 2 = progressing, and 1 = standard not met.

Standards Developed by Professional Associations

In addition to national, state, and local efforts to raise standards, professional associations are playing a key role in SBE by developing standards that reflect the knowledge, skills, and attitudes students should acquire in the subject-matter disciplines. In many cases, professional associations have developed specific grade-level performance standards. These standards include statements that reflect desired levels of achievement, quality of performance, or level of proficiency. In addition, professional associations have developed classroom activities related to standards.

Educational stakeholders can use standards developed by professional associations in the following ways.

- State departments of education, school districts, and schools can use the standards as a guide for developing curricula and assessments of student learning.
- Teachers can use standards to (1) develop goals and objectives for units and courses, (2) evaluate their teaching, and (3) develop ideas for instructional activities and classroom assessments.
- Parents and community members can use standards to assess the quality of education in their local schools and to monitor the achievement levels of their children.

Aligning Curricula and Textbooks with Standards

An important part of curriculum leadership involves "aligning" curricula and textbooks with national and state standards and "curriculum frameworks." Curriculum alignment may take two forms. A curriculum is *horizontally aligned* when teachers within a specific grade level coordinate instruction across disciplines and examine their school's curriculum to ensure that course content and instruction dovetail across and/or within subject areas. A curriculum is *vertically aligned* when subjects are connected across grade levels so that students experience increasingly complex instructional programs as they move through the grades.

Like school leaders and teachers, textbook publishers and authors have been influenced significantly by the development of academic standards throughout the nation. Since the "bottom line" for publishing companies is making a profit, they pay close attention to the calls of educational policymakers for more rigorous standards in our nation's schools.

Many publishers are revising their textbooks so they are in alignment with state standards and curriculum frameworks, particularly in populous states that make statewide adoptions of textbooks, such as California and Texas. In states such as these, school districts can only purchase textbooks that are on state textbook adoption lists.

Since highly populated states influence publishers more than less populated states, it has been observed that "As California and Texas go [regarding the development of state-approved textbook adoption lists], so goes the rest of the nation."

Curriculum Leadership Strategy

State and national standards are likely to change as policies and people in office change. Rather than seeing each change as "just another hoop to jump through," think of changing standards as an opportunity to reevaluate curricula and assess progress. New goals can often be drafted and existing benchmarks evaluated in a manner that makes meaning of what occurs in the school day-to-day.

To address many of the standards discussed above, LaQuanda Brown writes in "The Case for Teacher-Led Improvement" in this chapter's *Leaders' Voices* article that, "Teachers and principals must be creative, systemic thinkers and learners, and collaborative leaders. They must be willing to implement solutions that are nontraditional, speak to the needs and interests of the students, and address the summative and formative data that answer to the state and federal mandates and guidelines that outline the responsibilities of successful schools." It is through collaborative leading that standards are aligned with curricula and student learning is assessed in a meaningful way that will directly influence the curricula.

Curriculum Frameworks

A curriculum framework is a document, usually published by a state education agency, that provides guidelines, recommended instructional and assessment strategies, suggested resources, and models for school leaders and teachers to use as they develop curricula that are aligned with national and state standards. Curriculum frameworks are usually written by teams of teachers and state agency personnel, and they serve as a bridge between national and state standards and local curriculum and instructional strategies. In Alaska, for example, curriculum frameworks in digital format and "Frameworks Resource Kits" in specific subjects are given to teachers by the Department of Education and Early Development. The digital format provides state-of-the-art information in different formats, including video clips of educators explaining standards-based curricula.

Standards and No Child Left Behind (NCLB)

In 2002, President George W. Bush signed the No Child Left Behind (NCLB) legislation. High standards are a key element of NCLB. As President Bush said immediately after his election to a second term in 2004: "We must continue to work on education reform to bring high standards and accountability, not just to elementary schools, but to the high schools as well" (White House News Conference, November 4, 2004). However, prior to his election as the 44th President of the United States, Barack Obama suggested that, under his administration, NCLB might be revised: "[Teachers] feel betrayed and frustrated by No Child Left Behind. We shouldn't reauthorize it without changing it fundamentally. We left the money behind for [NCLB]. . . . We can find new ways to increase pay that are developed with teachers, not imposed on them and not based on some arbitrary test score. That's how we're going to close the achievement gap" (retrieved from www.barackobama.com/issues/education/index. php).

Rather than emphasize academic goals per se, the NCLB reform bill mandated statewide testing in reading and mathematics each year in grades 3–8, with schools held accountable for students' performance on state proficiency tests. Key features of NCLB include the following:

- States create their own standards for what a child should know and learn for all grades. Standards must be developed in math and reading immediately. Standards must also be developed for science by the 2005–06 school year.
- With standards in place, states must test every student's progress toward those standards by using tests that are aligned with the standards. Beginning in the 2002–03 school year, schools must administer tests in each of three grade spans: grades 3–5, grades 6–9, and grades 10–12 in all schools. Beginning in the

2005–06 school year, tests must be administered every year in grades 3 through 8 in math and reading. Beginning in the 2007–08 school year, science achievement must also be tested.

- Each state, school district, and school will be expected to make Adequate Yearly Progress (AYP) toward meeting state standards. This progress will be measured for all students by sorting test results for students who are economically disadvantaged, are from racial or ethnic minority groups, have disabilities, or have limited English proficiency.
- School and district performance will be publicly reported in district and state report cards. Individual school results will be on the district report cards.[*]
- If the district or school continually fails to make Adequate Yearly Progress toward the standards, then they will be held accountable (U.S. Department of Education, 2002).
- While the NCLB Act allows each of the 50 states to select the test it wishes to use, the Gallup Poll of the Public's Attitudes toward the Public Schools revealed that 68 percent of respondents favor requiring all 50 states to use a nationally standardized test (Rose and Gallup, 2002).

Students and Curriculum Development

As pointed out in Chapter 1, learners should be clearly aware of the goals being sought by their teachers and the goals embedded in the curriculum they are experiencing. In addition, though, learners formulate their own curricular goals throughout the process of instruction.

While the goals teachers use to guide their planning and those sought by the learners need not be identical, they should overlap. The teacher's and learners' goals for a learning experience must be understood by both the teacher and the learners, and the goals must be compatible or they are not likely to be achieved. An effective way to achieve this congruence is through some form of student–teacher planning. As Glen Hass states in "Who Should Plan the Curriculum?" in this chapter, the student is the "major untapped resource in curriculum planning."

To attain a variety of curricular goals and objectives, accomplished teachers have developed a broad repertoire of models of teaching that complement their student–teacher planning. They have, as David T. Gordon points out in "The Limits of Ideology: Curriculum and the Culture Wars" in this chapter, "techniques in their teaching repertoire that reflect how children learn and make sense of things." In actual practice, each model in the repertoire is eclectic—in other words, a combination of two or more models of teaching. In Chapter 6, models of teaching are described that are based on behavioral psychology, human development, cognitive processes, and social interactions.

CRITERION QUESTIONS—CURRICULUM DEVELOPMENT

The articles in this chapter present varying perspectives on the processes of curriculum development, which should reflect careful consideration of goals and values and all three of the curriculum bases. The following are among the criterion questions that can be derived from the different perspectives on curriculum development presented in this chapter:

1. Does the curriculum reflect an appropriate balance between subject-centeredness and student-centeredness?
2. Does the curriculum reflect a desired balance between acquisition of content and mastery of processes?
3. Are clear, appropriately high standards reflected in the curriculum?
4. Does the curriculum development process consider students' prior knowledge?
5. Does the curriculum include methods for assessing student learning?

REFERENCES

Bobbitt, F. *How to Make a Curriculum.* Boston: Houghton Mifflin, 1924.

Bush, G. W. "The Essential Work of Democracy." *Phi Delta Kappan* 86, no. 2 (2004): 114.

Bush, G. W. White House News Conference. Novemeber 4, 2004.

Dewey, John. "The Relation of Theory to Practice in Education." In *The Relation of Theory to Practice in Education,* the Third Yearbook of the National Society for the Scientific Study of Education, Part 1, pp. 9–30. Bloomington, IN: Public School Publishing Co., 1904.

Hunkins, Francis P., & Patricia A. Hammill. "Beyond Tyler and Taba: Reconceptualizing the Curriculum Process." *Peabody Journal of Education* 69, no. 3 (Spring 1994): 4–18.

Obama, B. A World Class Education. Retrieved November 2008 from www.barackobama.com/issues/education/index.php

Ravitch, Diane. "The Case for National Standards and Assessments." *The Clearing House* 69, no. 3 (January/February 1996): 134–135.

National Standards in American Education: A Citizen's Guide. Washington, DC: The Brookings Institution, 1995.

Rose, L. C., & A. M. Gallup. "The 34th Annual Phi Delta Kappa/Gallup Poll of the Public's Attitudes toward the Public Schools." *Phi Delta Kappan* 84, no. 1,(September 2002): 41–56.

Tyler, Ralph W. *Basic Principles of Curriculum and Instruction.* Chicago: The University of Chicago Press, 1949.

U.S. Department of Education. "Introduction." *No Child Left Behind.* Washington, DC: U.S. Department of Education, 2002. Retrieved May 2003 from www.nclb.gov/next/overview/index.html

APPENDIX

"Generic" Plan for a Unit of Study

Teacher _____ Grade Level _____ Subject _____

Unit Topic _____ Length of Time _____

1. *Introduction:* What is the nature and scope of the unit? How will the unit benefit students? Briefly, what skills, concepts, issues, and activities will the unit address?

2. *Objectives:* (expected learning outcomes—i.e., what will students be expected to be able to do? Objectives can cover the cognitive, psychomotor, and affective domains).
   a. What do I expect students to be able to do?
   b. What changes in students' behavior do I wish to see?
   c. What should each be able to do to demonstrate mastery of each objective in the unit?

3. *Content of Unit*
   a. What topics will I cover in my teaching? When will I teach those topics?
   b. Skills, topics, subtopics, concepts, issues, information, and so on, covered in unit.
   c. List of activities and time for each (e.g., 1 week, 2 class sessions).

4. *Methods and Activities*
   a. How am I going to teach the unit?
   b. What methods will I use (e.g., large-group discussions, cooperative learning groups, discovery learning, mastery learning, etc.)?
   c. In what activities will students participate (e.g., preparing oral and/or written reports, working in small committees, going on field trips, playing educational games, listening to guest speakers, etc.)?

5. *Teaching Materials and/or Resources*
   a. What materials and/or resources will I need to teach the unit?
   b. What materials will students need?
   c. What textbooks, software, or reference materials will be used?

6. *Assessment of Student Learning*
   a. How will I measure and evaluate students' progress or achievement?
   b. How will I know if I have achieved the objectives for the unit?
   c. What assessments will I use to measure students' learning (quizzes, tests, observations of classroom behavior, portfolios, projects, performances, etc.)?

The Sources of a Science of Education

JOHN DEWEY (1859–1952)

ABSTRACT: Dewey suggests that "science" can be seen as a systematic method of inquiry within an area of professional practice. Thus, educational activities such as curriculum planning, instruction, and the organization and administration of schools may be said to be "scientific" if they are done systematically, with particular attention to a rigorous intellectual technique. However, science should not be seen as providing rules that should be applied to the art of education; instead, science enriches professional judgment and provides a wider range of alternatives that can be applied to educational problems.

EDUCATION AS A SCIENCE

The title may suggest to some minds that it begs a prior question: Is there a science of education? And still more fundamentally, Can there be a science of education? Are the procedures and aims of education such that it is possible to reduce them to anything properly called a science? Similar questions exist in other fields. The issue is not unknown in history; it is raised in medicine and law. As far as education is concerned, I may confess at once that I have put the question in its apparently question-begging form in order to avoid discussion of questions that are important but that are also full of thorns and attended with controversial divisions.

It is enough for our purposes to note that the word "science" has a wide range.

There are those who would restrict the term to mathematics or to disciplines in which exact results can be determined by rigorous methods of demonstration. Such a conception limits even the claims of physics and chemistry to be sciences, for according to it the only scientific portion of these subjects is the strictly mathematical. The position of what are ordinarily termed the biological sciences is even more dubious, while social subjects and psychology would hardly rank as sciences at all, when measured by this definition. Clearly we must take the idea of science with some latitude. We must take

it with sufficient looseness to include all the subjects that are usually regarded as sciences. The important thing is to discover those traits in virtue of which various fields are called scientific. When we raise the question in this way, we are led to put emphasis upon methods of dealing with subject-matter rather than to look for uniform objective traits in subject matter. From this point of view, science signifies, I take it, the existence of systematic methods of inquiry, which, when they are brought to bear on a range of facts, enable us to understand them better and to control them more intelligently, less haphazardly and with less routine.

No one would doubt that our practices in hygiene and medicine are less casual, less results of a mixture of guess work and tradition, than they used to be, nor that this difference has been made by development of methods of investigating and testing. There is an intellectual technique by which discovery and organization of material go on cumulatively, and by means of which one inquirer can repeat the researches of another, confirm or discredit them, and add still more to the capital stock of knowledge. Moreover, the methods when they are used tend to perfect themselves, to suggest new problems, new investigations, which refine old procedures and create new and better ones.

The question as to the sources of a science of education is, then, to be taken in this sense. What are the ways by means of which the function of education in all its branches and phases—selection of material for the curriculum, methods of instruction and discipline, organization and administration of schools—can be conducted with systematic increase of intelligent control and understanding? What are the materials upon which we may—and should—draw in order that educational activities may become in a less degree products of routine, tradition, accident, and transitory accidental influences? From what sources shall we draw so that there shall be steady and cumulative growth of intelligent, communicable insight, and power of direction?

Here is the answer to those who decry pedagogical study on the ground that success in teaching and in moral direction of pupils is often not in any direct ratio to knowledge of educational principles. Here is "A" who is much more successful than "B" in teaching, awakening the enthusiasm of his students for learning, inspiring them morally by personal example and contact, and yet relatively ignorant of educational history, psychology, approved methods, etc., which "B" possesses in abundant measure. The facts are admitted. But what is overlooked by the objector is that the successes of such individuals tend to be born and to die with them: beneficial consequences extend only to those pupils who have personal contact with such gifted teachers. No one can measure the waste and loss that have come from the fact that the contributions of such men and women in the past have been thus confined, and the only way by which we can prevent such waste in the future is by methods which enable us to make an analysis of what the gifted teacher does intuitively, so that something accruing from his work can be communicated to others. Even in the things conventionally recognized as sciences, the insights of unusual persons remain important and there is no leveling down to a uniform procedure. But the existence of science gives common efficacy to the experiences of the genius; it makes it possible for the results of special power to become part of the working equipment of other inquirers, instead of perishing as they arose.

The individual capacities of the Newtons, Boyles, Joules, Darwins, Lyells, Helmholtzes, are not destroyed because of the existence of science; their differences from others and the impossibility of predicting on the basis of past science what discoveries they would make—that is, the impossibility of regulating their activities by antecedent sciences—persist. But science makes it possible for others to benefit systematically by what they achieved.

The existence of scientific method protects us also from a danger that attends the operations of men of unusual power: dangers of slavish imitation, partisanship, and such jealous devotion to them and their work as to get in the way of her progress. Anybody can notice today that the effect of an original and powerful teacher is not all to the good. Those influenced by him often show a one-sided interest; they tend to form schools, and to become impervious to other problems and truths; they incline to swear by the words of their master and to go on repeating his thoughts after him, and often without the spirit and insight that originally made them significant. Observation also shows that these results happen oftenest in those subjects in which scientific method is least developed. Where these methods are of longer standing students adopt methods rather than merely results, and employ them with flexibility rather than in literal reproduction.

This digression seems to be justified not merely because those who object to the idea of a science put personality and its unique gifts in opposition to science, but also because those who recommend science sometimes urge that uniformity of procedure will be its consequence. So it seems worthwhile to dwell on the fact that in the subjects best developed from the scientific point of view, the opposite is the case. Command of scientific methods and systematized subject-matter liberates individuals; it enables them to see new problems, devise new procedures, and, in general, makes for diversification rather than for set uniformity. But at the same time these diversifications have a cumulative effect in an advance shared by all workers in the field.

EDUCATION AS AN ART

This theme is, I think, closely connected with another point which is often urged, namely, that education is an art rather than a science. That, in concrete operation, education is an art, either a mechanical art or a fine art, is unquestionable. If there were an opposition between science and art, I should be compelled to side with those who assert that education is an art. But there is no opposition, although there is a distinction. We must not be misled by words. Engineering is, in actual practice, an art. But it is an art that progressively incorporates more and more of science into itself, more of mathematics, physics, and chemistry. It is the kind of art it is precisely because of a content of scientific subject-matter which guides it as a practical operation. There is room for the original and daring projects of exceptional individuals. But their distinction lies not in the fact that they turn their backs upon science, but in the fact that they make new integrations of scientific material and turn it to new and previously unfamiliar and unforeseen uses. When, in education, the psychologist or observer and experimentalist in any field reduces his findings to a rule which is to be uniformly adopted, then, only, is there a result which is objectionable and destructive of the free play of education as an art.

But this happens not because of scientific method but because of departure from it. It is not the capable engineer who treats scientific findings as imposing upon him a certain course which is to be rigidly adhered to: it is the third- or fourth-rate man who adopts this course. Even more, it is the unskilled day laborer who follows it. For even if the practice adopted is one that follows from science and could not have been discovered or employed except for science, when it is converted into a uniform rule of procedure it becomes an empirical rule-of-thumb procedure—just as a person may use a table of logarithms mechanically without knowing anything about mathematics.

The danger is great in the degree in which the attempt to develop scientific method is recent. Nobody would deny that education is still in a condition of transition from an empirical to a scientific status. In its empirical form the chief factors determining education are tradition, imitative reproduction, response to various external pressures wherein the strongest force wins out, and the gifts, native and acquired, of individual teachers. In this situation there is a strong tendency to identify teaching ability with the use of procedures that yield immediately successful results, success being measured by such things as order in the classroom, correct recitations by pupils in assigned lessons, passing of examinations, promotion of pupils to a higher grade, etc.

For the most part, these are the standards by which a community judges the worth of a teacher. Prospective teachers come to training schools, whether in normal schools or colleges, with such ideas implicit in their minds. They want very largely to find out how to do things with the maximum prospect of success. Put baldly, they want recipes. Now, to such persons science is of value because it puts a stamp of final approval upon this and that specific procedure. It is very easy for science to be regarded as a guarantee that goes with the sale of goods rather than as a light to the eyes and a lamp to the feet. It is prized for its prestige value rather than as an organ of personal illumination and liberation. It is prized because it is thought to give unquestionable authenticity and authority to a specific procedure to be carried out in the school room. So conceived, science is antagonistic to education as an art.

EXPERIENCE AND ABSTRACTION

The history of the more mature sciences shows two characteristics. Their original problems were set by difficulties that offered themselves in the ordinary region of practical affairs. Men obtained fire by rubbing sticks together and noted how things grew warm when they pressed on each other, long before they had any theory of heat. Such everyday experiences in their seeming inconsistency with the phenomena of flame and fire finally led to the conception of heat as a mode of molecular motion. But it led to this conception only when the ordinary phenomena were reflected upon in detachment from the conditions and uses under which they exhibit themselves in practices. There is no science without abstraction, and abstraction means fundamentally that certain occurrences are removed from the dimension of familiar practical experience into that of reflective or theoretical inquiry.

To be able to get away for the time being from entanglement in the urgencies and needs of immediate practical concerns is a condition of the origin of scientific treatment in any field. Preoccupation with attaining some direct end or practical utility, always limits scientific inquiry. For it restricts the field of attention and thought, since we note only those things that are immediately connected with what we want to do or get at the moment. Theory is in the end, as has been well said, the most practical of all things, because this widening of the range of attention beyond nearby purpose and desire eventually results in the creation of wider and farther-reaching purposes and enables us to use a much wider and deeper range of conditions and means than were expressed in the observation of primitive practical purposes. For the time being, however, the formation of theories demands a resolute turning aside from the needs of practical operations previously performed.

This detachment is peculiarly hard to secure in the case of those persons who are concerned with building up the scientific content of educational practices and arts. There is a pressure for immediate results, for demonstration of a quick, short-time span of usefulness in school. There is a tendency to convert the results of statistical inquiries and laboratory experiments into directions and rules for the conduct of school administration and instruction. Results tend to be directly grabbed, as it were, and put into operation by teachers. Then there is the leisure for that slow and gradual independent growth of theories that is a necessary condition of the formation of a true science. This danger is peculiarly imminent in a science of education because its very recentness and novelty arouse skepticism as to its possibility and its value. The human desire to prove that the scientific mode of attack is really of value brings pressure to convert scientific conclusions into rules and standards of schoolroom practice.

It would perhaps be invidious to select examples too near to current situations. Some illustration, however, is needed to give definiteness to what has been said. I select an instance which is remote in time and crude in itself. An investigator found that girls between the ages of eleven and fourteen mature more rapidly than boys of the same age. From this fact, or presumed fact, he drew the inference that during these years boys and girls should be separated for purposes of instruction. He converted an intellectual finding into an immediate rule of school practice.

That the conversion was rash, few would deny. The reason is obvious. School administration and instruction is a much more complex operation than was the factor contained in the scientific result. The significance of one factor for educational practice can be determined only as it is balanced with many other factors. Taken by itself, this illustration is so crude that to generalize from it might seem to furnish only a caricature. But the principle involved is of universal application. No conclusion of scientific research can be converted into an immediate rule of educational art. For there is no educational practice whatever which is not highly complex; that is to say, which does not contain many other conditions and factors than are included in the scientific finding.

Nevertheless, scientific findings are of practical utility, and the situation is wrongly interpreted when it is used to disparage the value of science in the art of education. What it militates against is the transformation of scientific findings into rules of action. Suppose for the moment that the finding about the different rates of maturing in boys and girls of a certain age is confirmed by continued investigation, and is to be accepted as fact. While it does not translate into a specific rule of fixed procedure, it is of some worth. The teacher who really knows this fact will have his personal attitude changed. He will be on the alert to make certain observations which would otherwise escape him; he will be enabled to interpret some facts which would otherwise be confused and misunderstood. This knowledge and understanding render his practice more intelligent, more flexible, and better adapted to deal effectively with concrete phenomena of practice.

Nor does this tell the whole story. Continued investigation reveals other relevant facts. Each investigation and conclusion is special, but the tendency of an increasing number and variety of specialized results is to create new points of view and a wider field of observation. Various special findings have a cumulative effect; they reinforce and extend one another, and in time lead to the detection of principles that bind together a number of facts that are diverse and even isolated in their *prima facie* occurrence. These connecting principles which link different phenomena together we call laws.

Facts which are so interrelated form a system, a science. The practitioner who knows the system and its laws is evidently in possession of a powerful instrument for observing and interpreting what goes on before him. This intellectual tool affects his attitudes and modes of response in what he does. Because the range of understanding is deepened and widened, he can take into account remote consequences which were originally hidden from view and hence were ignored in his actions. Greater continuity is introduced; he does not isolate situations and deal with them in separation as he was compelled to do when ignorant of connecting principles. At the same time, his practical dealings become more flexible. Seeing more relations he sees more possibilities, more opportunities. He is emancipated from the need of following tradition and special precedents. His ability to judge being enriched, he has a wider range of alternatives to select from in dealing with individual situations.

WHAT SCIENCE MEANS

If we gather up these conclusions in a summary we reach the following results. In the first place, no genuine science is formed by isolated conclusions, no matter how scientifically correct the technique by which these isolated results are reached, and no matter how exact they are. Science does not emerge until these various findings are linked together to form a relatively coherent system—that is, until they reciprocally confirm and illuminate one another, or until each gives the others added meaning. Now this development requires time, and it requires more time in the degree in which the transition from an empirical condition to a scientific one is recent and hence imperfect.

John Dewey was, at various times during his career, professor of philosophy, Columbia University; head of the Department of Philosophy and director of the School of Education at the University of Chicago; and professor of philosophy at the University of Michigan.

QUESTIONS FOR REFLECTION

1. What does Dewey mean when he says that the effect of an "original and powerful teacher is not all to the good"? What remedy is available to offset the sometimes unfavorable effects of such teachers, according to Dewey? Have you been taught by this type of teacher? If so, how did those experiences influence your learning?
2. Under what circumstances does Dewey consider science to be "antagonistic" to education as an art?
3. When, according to Dewey, is "theory the most practical of all things"? Do you agree with his argument?

Teachers, Public Life, and Curriculum Reform

HENRY A. GIROUX

ABSTRACT: *Discourse related to curriculum and teaching reflects the points of view of those involved and cannot be separated from issues of history, power, and politics. Dominant views of curriculum and teaching claim objectivity, but they fail to link schooling to complex political, economic, and cultural forces; and they see teachers as technicians, bureaucratic agents, and deskilled intellectuals. Thus, a critical theory of curriculum must consider questions of representation, justice, and power. Toward this end, teachers' roles should be restructured so they become critical agents who take risks (or "go for broke") and act as "public intellectuals" who bring issues of equity, community, and social justice to the fore.*

REASSERTING THE PRIMACY OF THE POLITICAL IN CURRICULUM THEORY

The connection between curriculum and teaching is structured by a series of issues that are not always present in the language of the current educational reform movement. This is evident, for instance, in the way mainstream educational reformers often ignore the problematic relationship between curriculum as a socially constructed narrative on the one hand, and the interface of teaching and politics on the other. Mainstream curriculum reformers often view curriculum as an objective text that merely has to be imparted to students.[1]

In opposition to this view, I want to argue that the language used by administrators, teachers, students, and others involved in either constructing, implementing, or receiving the classroom curriculum actively produces particular social identities, "imagined communities," specific competencies, and distinctive ways of life. Moreover, the language of curriculum, like other discourses, does not merely reflect a pregiven reality; on the contrary, it selectively offers depictions of the larger world through representations that people struggle over to name what counts as knowledge, what counts as communities of learning, what social relationships matter, and what visions of the future can be represented as legitimate (Aronowitz & Giroux, 1993).

Of course, if curriculum is seen as a terrain of struggle, one that is shot through with ethical considerations, it becomes reasonable to assume that talk about teaching and curriculum should not be removed from considerations of history, power, and politics. After all, the language of curriculum is both historical and contingent. Theories of curriculum have emerged from past struggles and are often heavily weighted in favor of those who have power, authority, and institutional legitimation.

Curriculum is also political in that state governments, locally elected school boards, and powerful business and publishing interests exercise enormous influence over teaching practices and curriculum policies (Apple & Christian-Smith, 1992). Moreover, the culture of the school is often representative of those features of the dominant culture that it affirms, sustains, selects, and legitimates. Thus, the distinction between high and low status academic subjects, the organization of knowledge into disciplines, and the allocation of knowledge and symbolic rewards to different groups indicates how politics work to influence the curriculum.

Within dominant versions of curriculum and teaching, there is little room theoretically to understand the dynamics of power as they work in schools, particularly around the mechanisms of tracking, racial and gender discrimination, testing, and other mechanisms of exclusion (Oaks, 1985). Mainstream educational reformers such as William Bennett, Chester Finn, Jr., and Dianne Ravitch exhibit little understanding of schooling as a site that actively produces different histories, social groups, and student identities under profound conditions of inequality. This is true, in part, because many dominant versions of curriculum and teaching legitimate themselves through unproblematized claims to objectivity and an obsession with empiricist forms of accountability. But, more importantly, many mainstream theorists of curriculum refuse to link schooling to the complex political, economic, and cultural relations that structure it as a borderland of movement and translation rather than a fixed and unitary site.

When inserted into this matrix of power, difference, and social justice, schools cannot be abstracted from the larger society where histories mix, languages and identities intermingle, values clash, and different groups struggle over how they are represented and how they might represent themselves. Questions of representation, justice, and power are central to any critical theory of curriculum. This is especially true in a society in which Afro-Americans, women, and other people of color are vastly underrepresented in both schools and other dominant cultural institutions. Of course, the issue of representation as I am using it here suggests that meaning is always political, actively involved in producing diverse social positions, and inextricably implicated in relations of power.

Educators generally exhibit a deep suspicion of politics, and this is not unwarranted when politics is reduced to a form of dogmatism. And, yet, it is impossible for teachers to become agents in the classroom without a broader understanding of politics and the emancipatory possibilities it provides for thinking about and shaping their own practices. Recognizing the politics of one's location as an educator should not imply that one's pedagogical practice is inflexible, fixed, or intolerant. To insist

that teachers recognize the political nature of their own work can be understood as part of a broader critical effort to make them self-reflective of the interests and assumptions that shape their classroom practices. Roger Simon (1992) captures this sentiment by arguing that by inserting the political back into the discourse of teaching educators can "initiate rather than close off the problem of responsibility" (p. 16) for those classroom practices generated by their claim to knowledge and authority.

In what follows, I want to offer an alternative language for defining the purpose and meaning of teacher work. While I have talked about teachers as intellectuals in another context, I want to extend this analysis by analyzing what the implications are for redefining teachers as public intellectuals.[2] In part, I want to explore this position by drawing upon my own training as a teacher and some of the problems I had to face when actually working in the public schools. I will conclude by highlighting some of the defining principles that might structure the content and context of what it means for teachers to assume the role of a public intellectual.

TRADITION AND THE PEDAGOGY OF RISK

Let me begin by saying that we are living through a very dangerous time. . . . We are in a revolutionary situation, no matter how unpopular that word has become in this country. The society in which we live is desperately menaced, not by [the cold war] but from within. So any citizen of this country who figures himself as responsible—and particularly those of you who deal with the minds and hearts of young people—must be prepared to "go for broke." Or to put it another way, you must understand that in the attempt to correct so many generations of bad faith and cruelty, when it is operating not only in the classroom but in society, you will meet the most fantastic, the most brutal, and the most determined resistance. There is no point in pretending that this won't happen. . . . [And yet] the obligation of anyone who thinks

of him or herself as responsible is to examine society and try to change it and to fight it—at no
matter what risk. This is the only hope society
has. This is the only way societies change. (Baldwin,
1988, p. 3)

I read the words of the famed African-American
novelist James Baldwin less as a prescription for
cynicism and powerlessness than I do as an
expression of hope. Baldwin's words are moving
because he confers a sense of moral and political
responsibility upon teachers by presupposing that
they are critical agents who can move between
theory and practice in order to take risks, refine
their visions, and make a difference for both their
students and the world in which they live. In order to take up Baldwin's challenge for teachers to
"go for broke," to act in the classroom and the
world with courage and dignity, it is important for
educators to recognize that the current challenge
facing public schools is one of the most serious
that any generation of existing and prospective
teachers has ever had to face. Politically, the U.S.
has lived through 12 years of reforms in which
teachers have been invited to deskill themselves,
to become technicians, or, in more ideological
terms, to accept their role as "clerks of the em-
pire." We live at a time when state legislators and
federal officials are increasingly calling for the
testing of teachers and the implementation of
standardized curriculum; at the same time, legislators and government officials are ignoring the
most important people in the reform effort, the
teachers. Within this grim scenario, the voices of
teachers have been largely absent from the debate
about education. It gets worse.

Economically, the working conditions of
teachers, especially those in the urban districts
with a low tax base, have badly deteriorated. The
story is a familiar one: overcrowded classrooms,
inadequate resources, low salaries, and a rise in
teacher-directed violence. In part, this is due to
the increased financial cutbacks to the public sector
by the Federal Government, the tax revolt of the
1970s by the middle-class that put a ceiling on the
ability of cities and states to raise revenue for public services, and the refusal by wide segments of

the society to believe that public schooling is
essential to the health of a democratic society.
Compounding these problems is a dominant
vision of schooling defined largely through the
logic of corporate values and the imperatives of
the marketplace. Schools are being treated as if
their only purpose were to train future workers,
and teachers are being viewed as corporate foot-
soldiers whose role is to provide students with the
skills necessary for the business world. In short,
part of the crisis of teaching is the result of a
vision of schooling that subordinates issues of
equity, community, and social justice to pragmatic
considerations that enshrine the marketplace and
accountability schemes that standardize the social
relations of schooling. The political and ideological climate does not look favorable for teachers at
the moment. But it does offer prospective and existing teachers the challenge to engage in dialogue and debate regarding important issues such
as the nature and purpose of teacher preparation,
the meaning of educational leadership, and the
dominant forms of classroom teaching.

I think that if existing and future teachers are
willing to "go for broke," to use Baldwin's term,
they will need to re-imagine teaching as part of a
project of critique and possibility. But there is
more at stake here than simply a change in who
controls the conditions under which teachers
work. This is important, but what is also needed
is a new language, a new way of naming, order-
ing, and representing how power works in
schools. It is precisely through a more critical language that teachers might be able to recognize
the power of their own agency in order to raise
and act upon such questions as: What range of
purposes should schools serve? What knowledge
is of most worth? What does it mean for teachers
and students to know something? In what direction should teachers and students desire? What
notions of authority should structure teaching
and learning? These questions are important because they force educators to engage in a process
of self-critique while simultaneously highlighting
the central role that teachers might play in any
viable attempt to reform the public schools.

My own journey into teaching was largely shaped by undergraduate education training and my first year of student teaching. While the content and context of these experiences shaped my initial understanding of myself as a teacher, they did not prepare me for the specific tasks and problems of what it meant to address the many problems I had to confront in my first job. In what follows, I want to speak from my own experiences in order to illuminate the shortcomings of the educational theories that both shaped my perceptions of teaching and the classroom practices I was expected to implement.

LEARNING TO BE A TECHNICIAN

During the time that I studied to be a teacher, for the most part I learned how to master classroom methods, read Bloom's taxonomy, and became adept at administering tests, but I was never asked to question how testing might be used as a sorting device to track and marginalize certain groups. Like many prospective teachers of my generation, I was taught how to master a body of knowledge defined within separate academic disciplines, but I never learned to question what the hierarchical organization of knowledge meant and how it conferred authority and power. For example, I was never taught to raise questions about what knowledge was worth knowing and why, why schools legitimated some forms of knowledge and ignored others, why English was more important than art, and why it was considered unworthy to take a course in which one worked with one's hands. I never engaged in a classroom discussion about whose interests were served through the teaching and legitimation of particular forms of school knowledge, or how knowledge served to silence and disempower particular social groups. Moreover, I was not given the opportunity to reflect upon the authoritarian principles that actually structure classroom life and how these could be understood by analyzing social, political, and economic conditions outside of schools. If a student slept in the morning at his or her desk, I was taught to approach the issue as a problem of discipline and management. I was not alerted to recognize the social conditions that may have caused such behavior. That is, to the possibility that the student may have a drug-related problem, be hungry, sick, or simply exhausted because of conditions in his or her home life. I learned quickly to separate out the problems of society from the problems of schooling and hence became illiterate in understanding the complexity of the relationship between schools and the larger social order.

My initial teaching assignment was in a school in which the teacher turnover rate exceeded 85% each year. The first day I walked into that school I was met by some students hanging out in the lobby. They greeted me with stares born of territorial rights and suspicion and one of them jokingly asked me: "Hey man, you're new, what's your name?" I remember thinking they had violated some sort of rule regarding teacher-student relationships by addressing me that way. Questions of identity, culture, and racism had not been factored into my understanding of teaching and schooling at the time. I had no idea that the questions that would be raised for me that year had less to do with the sterile language of methods I had learned as an undergraduate than they did with becoming culturally and politically literate about the context-specific histories and experiences that informed where my students came from and how they viewed themselves and others. I had no idea of how important it was to create a meaningful and safe classroom for them so that I could connect my teaching to their own languages, cultures, and lived experiences. I soon found out that giving students some sense of power and ownership over their own educational experience has more to do with developing a language that was risk taking and self-critical for me and meaningful, practical, and transformative for them. During that first year, I also learned something about the ways in which many school administrators are educated.

LEADERSHIP WITHOUT VISION

During that first year, I rented movies from the American Friends Service Committee, ignored the officially designated curriculum textbooks, and eventually put my own books and magazine articles on reserve in the school library for my students to read. Hoping to give my students some control over the conditions for producing knowledge, I encouraged them to produce their own texts through the use of school video equipment, cameras, and daily journals. Within a very short time, I came into conflict with the school principal. He was a mix between General Patton and the Encino Man. At six foot three, weighing in at 250 pounds, his presence seemed a bit overwhelming and intimidating. The first time he called me into his office, I learned something about how he was educated. He told me that in his mind students should be quiet in classrooms, teachers should stick to giving lectures and writing on the board, and that I was never to ask a student a question that he or she could not answer. He further suggested that rather than developing my own materials in class I should use the curricula packages made available through the good wishes of local businesses and companies. While clearly being a reflection, if not a parody, of the worst kind of teacher training, he adamantly believed strict management controls, rigid systems of accountability, and lock step discipline were at the heart of educational leadership. Hence, I found myself in a secular version of hell. This was a school in which teaching became reduced to the sterile logic of flow charts. Moreover, it was a school in which power was wielded largely by white, male administrators further reinforcing the isolation and despair of most of the teachers. I engaged in forms of guerrilla warfare with this administration, but in order to survive I had to enlist the help of a few other teachers and some members of the community. At the end of the school year, I was encouraged not to come back. Fortunately, I had another teaching job back east and ended up in a much better school.

In retrospect, the dominant view of educational leadership has had a resurgence during the Reagan and Bush eras. Its overall effect has been to limit teachers' control over the development and planning of curriculum, to reinforce the bureaucratic organization of the school, and to remove teachers from the process of judging and implementing classroom instruction. This is evident in the growing call for national testing, national curriculum standards, and the concerted attack on developing multicultural curricula. The ideology that guides this model and its view of pedagogy is that the behavior of teachers needs to be controlled and made consistent and predictable across different schools and student populations. The effect is not only to remove teachers from the process of deliberation and reflection, but also to routinize the nature of learning and classroom pedagogy. In this approach, it is assumed that all students can learn from the same standardized materials, instructional techniques, and modes of evaluation. The notion that students come from different histories, experiences, and cultures is strategically ignored within this approach. The notion that pedagogy should be attentive to specific contexts is ignored.

TEACHERS AS PUBLIC INTELLECTUALS

I want to challenge these views by arguing that one way to rethink and restructure the nature of teacher work is to view teachers as public intellectuals. The unease expressed about the identity and role of teachers as public intellectuals has a long tradition in the United States and has become the focus of a number of recent debates. On one level, there are conservatives who argue that teachers who address public issues from the perspective of a committed position are simply part of what they call the political correctness movement. In this case, there is a deep suspicion of any attempt to open up the possibility for educators to address pressing social issues and to connect them to their teaching. Moreover, within the broad parameters of this view schools are seen as apolitical institutions whose primary purpose is to both prepare students for the work place and to reproduce the alleged common values that define the "American" way of life.[3] At the same time, many liberals have argued that while teachers should address public issues they should do so from the perspective of a particular teaching methodology. This is evident in Gerald Graff's (1992) call for educators to teach the conflicts. In this view, the struggle over representations replaces how a politics of meaning might help students identify, engage, and transform relations of power that generate the material conditions of racism, sexism, poverty, and other oppressive conditions. Moreover, some radical feminists have argued that the call for teachers to be public intellectuals promotes leadership models that are largely patriarchal and overly rational in the forms of authority they secure. While there may be an element of truth in all of these positions, they all display enormous theoretical shortcomings. Conservatives often refuse to problematize their own version of what is legitimate intellectual knowledge and how it works to secure particular forms of authority by simply labeling as politically correct individuals, groups, or views that challenge the basic tenets of the status quo. Liberals, on the other hand, inhabit a terrain that wavers between rejecting a principled standpoint from which to teach and staunchly arguing for a pedagogy that is academically rigorous and fair. Caught between a discourse of fairness and the appeal to provocative teaching methods, liberals have no language for clarifying the moral visions that structure their views of the relationship between knowledge and authority and the practices it promotes. Moreover, they increasingly have come to believe that teaching from a particular standpoint is tantamount to imposing an ideological position upon students. This has led in some cases to a form of McCarthyism in which critical educators are summarily dismissed as being guilty of ideological indoctrination. While the feminist critique is the most interesting, it underplays the possibility for using authority in ways which allow teachers to be more self-critical while simultaneously providing the conditions for students to recognize the possibility for democratic agency in both themselves and others. Operating out of a language of binarisms, some feminist education critics essentialize the positions of their opponents and in doing so present a dehistoricized and reductionistic view of critical pedagogy. Most importantly, all of these positions share in the failure to address the possibility for teachers to become a force for democratization both within and outside of schools.

As public intellectuals, teachers must bring to bear in their classrooms and other pedagogical sites the courage, analytical tools, moral vision, time, and dedication that is necessary to return schools to their primary task: being places of critical education in the service of creating a public sphere of citizens who are able to exercise power over their own lives and especially over the conditions of knowledge acquisition. Central to any such reform effort is the recognition that democracy is not a set of formal rules of participation, but the lived experience of empowerment for the vast majority. Moreover, the call for schools as democratic public spheres should not be limited to the call for equal access to schools, equal opportunity, or other arguments defined in terms of the principles of equality. Equality is a crucial aspect of democratizing schools, but teachers should not limit their demands to the call for equality. Instead, the rallying cry of teachers should be organized around the practice of empowerment for the vast majority of students in this country who need to be educated in the spirit of a critical democracy.[4]

This suggests another dimension in defining the role of public intellectuals. Such intellectuals must combine their role as educators and citizens. This implies they must connect the practice of classroom teaching to the operation of power in the larger society. At the same time, they must be attentive to those broader social forces that influence the workings of schooling and pedagogy. What is at issue here is a commitment on the part of teachers as public intellectuals to extend the principles of social justice to all spheres of economic, political, and cultural life. Within this discourse, the experiences that constitute the production of knowledge, identities, and social values in the schools are inextricably linked to the quality of moral and political life of the wider society. Hence, the reform of schooling must be seen as a part of a wider revitalization of public life.

This should not suggest that as public intellectuals, teachers represent a vanguardist group dedicated to simply reproducing another master narrative. In fact, as public intellectuals it is important for them to link their role as critical agents to their ability to be critical of their own politics while constantly engaging in dialogue with other educators, community people, various cultural workers, and students. As public intellectuals, teachers need to be aware of the limits of their own positions, make their pedagogies context specific, challenge the current organization of knowledge into fixed disciplines, and work in solidarity with others to gain some control over the conditions of their work. At the very least, this suggests that teachers will have to struggle on many different fronts in order to transform the conditions of work and learning that go on in schools. This means not only working with community people, teachers, students, and parents to open up progressive spaces within classrooms, but also forming alliances with other cultural workers in order to debate and shape educational policy at the local, state, and federal levels of government.

As public intellectuals, teachers need to provide the conditions for students to learn that the relationship between knowledge and power can be emancipatory, that their histories and experiences matter, and that what they say and do can count as part of a wider struggle to change the world around them. More specifically, teachers need to argue for forms of pedagogy that close the gap between the school and the real world. The curriculum needs to be organized around knowledge that relates to the communities, cultures, and traditions that give students a sense of history, identity, and place. This suggests pedagogical approaches that do more than make learning context specific, it also points to the need to expand the range of cultural texts that inform what counts as knowledge. As public intellectuals, teachers need to understand and use those electronically mediated knowledge forms that constitute the terrain of popular culture. This is the world of media texts—videos, films, music, and other mechanisms of popular culture constituted outside of the technology of print and the book. Put another way, the content of the curriculum needs to affirm and critically enrich the meaning, language, and knowledge that students actually use to negotiate and inform their lives.

While it is central for teachers to expand the relevance of the curriculum to include the richness and diversity of the students they actually teach, they also need to correspondingly decenter the curriculum. That is, students should be actively involved with issues of governance, "including setting learning goals, selecting courses, and having their own, autonomous organizations, including a free press" (Aronowitz, in press). Not only does the distribution of power among teachers, students, and administrators provide the conditions for students to become agents in their learning process, it also provides the basis for collective learning, civic action, and ethical responsibility. Moreover, such agency emerges as a lived experience rather than as the mastery of an academic subject.

In addition, as public intellectuals, teachers need to make the issue of cultural difference a defining principal of curriculum development and research. In an age of shifting demographics, large scale immigration, and multiracial communities, teachers must make a firm commitment to cultural difference as central to the relationship of schooling and citizenship (Giroux, 1992). In the first instance, this means dismantling and deconstructing the legacy of nativism and racial chauvinism that has defined the rhetoric of school reform for the last decade. The Reagan and Bush era witnessed a full-fledged attack on the rights of minorities, civil rights legislation, affirmative action, and the legitimation of curriculum reforms pandering to Eurocentric interests. Teachers can affirm their commitment to democratic public life and cultural democracy by struggling in and outside of their classrooms in solidarity with others to reverse these policies in order to make schools more attentive to the cultural resources that students bring to the public schools. At one level, this means working to develop legislation that protects the civil rights of all groups. Equally important is the need for teachers to take the lead in encouraging programs that open school curricula to the narratives of cultural difference, without falling into the trap of merely romanticizing the experience of "Otherness." At stake here is the development of an educational policy that asserts public education as part of a broader ethical and political discourse, one that both challenges and transforms those curricula reforms of the last decade that are profoundly racist in context and content. In part, this suggests changing the terms of the debate regarding the relationship between schooling and national identity, moving away from an assimilationist ethic and the profoundly Eurocentric fantasies of a common culture to one which links national identity to diverse traditions and histories.

In short, as public intellectuals, teachers need to address the imperatives of citizenship. In part, this means addressing how schools can create the conditions for students to be social agents willing to struggle for expanding the critical public cultures that make a democracy viable. Consequently, any notion of pedagogy must be seen as a form of cultural politics, that is, a politic that highlights the role of education, as it takes place in a variety of public sites, to open up rather than close down the possibilities for keeping justice and hope alive at a time of shrinking possibilities.

NOTES

1. This is particularly true with respect to those mainstream reformers arguing for national standards and testing. In this discourse, students are always on the receiving end of the learning experience. It is as if the histories, experiences, and communities that shape their identities and sense of place are irrelevant to what is taught and how it is taught. See, for example, Hirsch (1987); Finn, Jr. and Ravitch (1987); for an alternative to this position, see Apple (1993); Giroux (1988a); Giroux (1993). For an examination of schools that view teachers as more than clerks and technicians, see Wood (1993).

2. I have taken up this issue more extensively in Giroux (1988b), and Aronowitz and Giroux (1993).

3. For a trenchant analysis of the political correctness movement, see Aronowitz (1993), especially Chapter 1; see also Frank (1993).

4. I take this issue up in Giroux (1988b).

REFERENCES

Apple, M. (1993). *Official knowledge*. New York: Routledge.

Apple, M., & Christian-Smith, L. K. (Eds.). (1992). *The politics of the textbook*. New York: Routledge.

Aronowitz, S. (1993). *Roll over Beethoven: The return of cultural strife*. Hanover: Wesleyan University Press.

Aronowitz, S. (in press). A different perspective on educational inequality. *The Review of Education/Pedagogy/Cultural Studies*.

Aronowitz, S., & Giroux, H. A. (1993). *Education still under siege*. Westport, CT: Bergin & Garvey.

Baldwin, J. (1988). A talk to teachers. In Simonson & Waler (Eds.), *Multicultural literacy: Opening the American mind* (pp. 3–12). Saint Paul, MN: Graywolf Press.

Finn, C., Jr., & Ravitch, D. (1987). *What our 17-year olds know*. New York: Harper & Row.

Frank, J. (1993). In the waiting room: Canons, communities, "Political Correctness." In M. Edmunson (Ed.), *Wild Orchids: Messages from American universities* (pp. 127–149). New York: Penguin.

Giroux, H. A. (1988a). *Teachers as intellectuals*. Westport, CT: Bergin & Garvey.

Giroux, H. A. (1988b). *Schooling and the struggle for public life*. Minneapolis: University of Minnesota Press.

Giroux, H. A. (1992). *Border crossings*. New York: Routledge.

Giroux, H. A. (1993). *Living dangerously: The politics of multiculturalism*. New York: Peter Lang.

Graff, G. (1992). Teaching the conflicts. In D. J. Gless & B. H. Smith (Eds.), *The politics of liberal education* (pp. 57–73). Durham: Duke University Press.

Hirsch, E. D. (1987). *Cultural literacy*. Boston: Houghton Mifflin.

Oaks, J. (1985). *Keeping track: How schools structure inequality*. New Haven: Yale University Press.

Simon, R. (1922). *Teaching against the grain*. Westport, CT: Bergin & Garvey.

Wood, G. (1933). *Schools that work*. New York: Penguin Books.

Henry A. Giroux holds the Waterbury Chair Professorship in Secondary Education, Pennsylvania State University, University Park.

QUESTIONS FOR REFLECTION

1. Why does Giroux advocate "inserting the political back into the discourse of teaching"? Do you agree? What arguments might be raised by critics of Giroux's recommendation?
2. If curriculum leaders were to become "public intellectuals," how would this influence their leadership activities? In other words, what would they do differently?
3. In regard to the educational setting with which you are most familiar, what would it mean if you were to "go for broke" in the manner that Giroux suggests? What forms of resistance might you encounter? Does Giroux exaggerate when he says that teachers and other responsible citizens who "go for broke" should realize "that in the attempt to correct so many generations of bad faith and cruelty, when it is operating not only in the classroom but in society, [they] will meet the most fantastic, the most brutal, and the most determined resistance"?
4. Do you agree with Giroux that the dominant view of educational leadership has served to limit teacher involvement in the development and planning of curricula? On the basis of your professional experiences, can you cite evidence that teacher involvement in curriculum planning is increasing?

Who Should Plan the Curriculum?

GLEN HASS (1915–1997)

ABSTRACT: Several groups have important roles to play in curriculum leadership. Scholars from the disciplines can provide input on what should be taught and how to implement the curriculum. Parents and other citizens in our pluralistic society can help to formulate goals and values to be included in the curriculum. Students, since they are well positioned to identify advantages and disadvantages of the current curriculum, can participate in seven aspects of curriculum planning, from determining what shall be studied to identifying methods for evaluating success in learning. Lastly, educators can play a key role by creating structures that facilitate the processes of collaborative curriculum leadership.

In these times of complex, often insoluble problems and rapid change, it is urgent that professionals in curriculum planning take a new look at the question, "Who Should Plan the Curriculum?" It is apparent that the curriculum planning and teaching that is needed involves many factors that go beyond the scope of any single discipline or profession. In addition, change is now so rapid in our society and world, that today's curriculum is unsuited for tomorrow's world and is as outmoded as the Model T for the world of twenty years from tomorrow—the world whose leaders are now in the classrooms.

THE CURRICULUM WE NEED

Today's curriculum planners should study conditions and trends in contemporary society and probable conditions and requirements for democratic living . . . at the beginning of the twenty-first century. Education for the future is almost useless unless it prepares learners to meet problems that are new and that neither they nor anyone else has ever encountered before. All professionals in education need an image of tomorrow as curricula are planned. All too often we now see a "good curriculum" as the present one with its problems removed.

In facing toward the future we must find ways to teach innovation, problem solving, a love of learning; students must acquire the tools of analysis, expression, and understanding. We will surely find that learners of all ages must be prepared for work that does not yet exist. We will see that we all will have numerous increasingly complex tasks as buyers, voters, parents, legislators, and cooperative planners.

All interested citizens, parents, learners, and scholars from many of the disciplines should be encouraged to work with teachers, principals, curriculum leaders, state department of education and federal education agency personnel in the planning. This involvement in planning by all interested parties should begin in the local school and school district, but it should also occur regularly on a state, national and international basis. A democratic society cannot permit uniformity and centralization. The undefined, but onrushing future requires many different autonomous, alternative efforts to cope with its challenges and problems.

In the past many curriculum writers have stated that laypersons and scholars should be encouraged to work with professional educators in planning the curriculum. They have also frequently stated that collaborative models for planning are needed. They have, however, often given inadequate attention to the particular role of each type of planner in the planning process. Lacking adequate role definition we have often, as educators, overemphasized our mission to instruct the public, and have been un-

dersensitive to, or intolerant of, suggestion and dissent. Let us try to define the particular role of each group in curriculum planning.

ROLE OF SCHOLARS

What is the role in curriculum planning of scholars from disciplines other than education? There are at least two ways in which they can help. They can often give crucial advice regarding *what* should be taught; and they can often suggest *means of implementing* curriculum decisions.

For instance, in the 1960s, scholars in biology, mathematics, and physics worked with teachers and other curriculum workers in determining what should be taught. These planners found that the textbooks in use contained almost none of the modern concepts, although greater change in knowledge had occurred in the past fifty years than in the preceding 500. They also learned that greater emphasis was needed on unifying concepts so that the total number of basic ideas to be learned might be reduced. Now the collaboration of scholars is needed to identify the concepts which are most relevant to alternative futures so that they may become the focus of the curriculum.

Sociologists can give particular assistance in determining the means by which goals of education may be achieved and in identifying the essential values and behavior patterns which must be learned as society changes. Of equal importance is the fact that sociologists, as future planners, can aid the educator in understanding some of the characteristics of the society in which his or her students will live in the future. Together they can devise a better educational program to prepare for it.

Anthropologists can shed light on the reasons for the direction of the development of various aspects of the culture. They can help the school to plan to counterbalance pressures for conformity and to attach greater emphasis to creativity and critical judgment. They can help in planning to develop in each student an understanding of his or her powers and limitations for creating and modifying society. Anthropologists can also help in developing curriculum plans for the future.

Scholars from many disciplines can aid in curriculum planning by identifying the central concepts and rules for discovering the nature of the discipline. In the terms in which they are now represented, many of the disciplines are increasingly unteachable. We need a philosophical synthesis, appropriate to our world, the future, and to the learners, that can be taught—and only the scholars working alongside educators can achieve this synthesis.

ROLE OF PARENTS AND OTHER CITIZENS

In the long run, we can only build the curriculum and use the teaching methods which the active public will accept. We must work with the public and have orderly patterns for its participation. People need to be involved in the process of planning the curriculum in order to change their beliefs, attitudes, and behavior regarding it.

A fundamental question is, whose values are to be represented in the curricula for the learners of a particular community? Curriculum planners must recognize that a monolithic curriculum is not acceptable to parents and other citizens in a pluralistic society. Curriculum leaders and teachers should work with parents and other active citizens in setting the yearly educational goals for a particular classroom, school, or district. Within the larger framework of the school system, local communities, teachers, and principals should define *together* what each school community sees as the most important focus for the coming year. Public education transmits values and beliefs as well as knowledge. Since values and beliefs are very much family and community matters, parents and other citizens must be involved in curriculum planning.

From 1960 to the present, the prevailing practice in many school districts has been to curtail opportunities for citizen participation, and, increasingly, to try to confine curriculum decision-making to the professional educators. In the late 1960s this led to the press for community control through decentralization of large, urban school districts—a prime example of our failure to involve citizens in curriculum planning. Such involvement would have helped teachers and other curriculum planners to be sensitive to the realities of life in the school community.

Many parents are concerned today about whether their children seem to be learning the "basics" needed for survival in our society. Some parents are concerned as to whether the content and operation of the school and its curriculum give students pride in their own race and ethnic background. All parents often wonder whether teachers genuinely accept and share their concern about the learning of their children. Without cooperative planning each group often sees the other as insensitive, as having unreasonable expectations, and as making unrealistic demands.

It is a matter of crucial importance that many school systems invent and use structural devices to bring about a sharing of thinking about the curriculum by the lay citizens of the community and professional staff members.

Staff members must learn to work with citizens; citizens must take part but not take over. This should begin at the level of the parents planning with the teacher about their concerns for their children and should move from there to the citizens advisory council and the systemwide curriculum committee. The profession, in each community, and the teacher, in each classroom, is responsible for establishing these channels.

ROLE OF STUDENTS

The student is the major untapped resource in curriculum planning. Students are in the best position to explain many of the advantages and deficiencies of the present curriculum. Their ideas and reactions are of very great importance. Research has shown many times that learning is significantly improved when students share in planning and evaluating the curriculum.

In the process of instruction, learners should share in setting goals and objectives. In a particular learning experience the initial objectives should be those that the student sees, at that time, as interesting and meaningful. While the objectives the teacher uses to guide his or her planning and those sought by learners need not be identical, there should be much overlapping. The teacher's and learner's goals for a learning experience certainly must be understood by both, and they must be compatible or they are not likely to be achieved.

Too little use is made of teacher-student planning. The understanding and skills of planning are among the most important outcomes of education. Perhaps more teachers would plan with their students if they realized that student-teacher planning has at least seven aspects, and that they might begin to plan with students about any one of them:

1. What is to be studied?
2. Why are we having this learning activity?
3. How shall we go about it?
4. Where might we do what needs to be done?
5. When shall we do it?
6. Who will do each part of the job?
7. How can we evaluate our success in learning?

While student participation in the choice of topics may be possible only in certain subjects, there is no reason why extensive use of the other aspects of teacher-student planning should not be used in all subjects.

ROLE OF EDUCATORS

The role of professional educators is one that will grow and develop as they work with the scholars, parents, other citizens, and students.

It is the job of the teacher, principal, and curriculum consultant to provide structure for planning with others, to inform, to offer recommendations, to bring together contributions from many sources, and to work out a recommended plan of action. In the analysis of the curriculum that is planned, professional educators must be certain that it takes account of the nature of the learner, of the society of which he or she is a part, and of the future. This part of the educator's role

is not new, but it has increasing importance as he plans with others who are not so likely to give adequate attention to the various bases for curriculum decisions.

The professional curriculum planner should be alert to the necessity for relating schools to the surrounding political, economic, and social forces so that the means and goals of the curriculum harmonize with the lives of learners in particular circumstances.

Frequently, educators need to take a stand for what they believe, sharing what they know and feel. The public relies on the vision and courage of educators to present recommendations for curriculum improvement. Such recommendations should be related to a sense of purpose, the ability to think and analyze, and a proper respect for the requirements of human response. The educator, in recommending, must carefully avoid the appearance that the curriculum is solely the professional's business. Experience over time in working together helps to solve this problem.

A most important part of the teacher's role is to communicate to students his or her own valuing of learning. Teachers often motivate learners by their own motivations. Learners learn to like to learn from teachers who exhibit the intellectual accomplishment of regularly acquiring and acting on new knowledge.

Finally, professional educators must evaluate and interrelate the contributions from other planners and evolve a curriculum plan which they implement in their own classrooms or which they submit for the approval of the curriculum council or committee.

MOVING AHEAD

If it is recognized that all public policy in education is the product of professional-lay interaction, then one of the main roadblocks to progress can be removed. Increasing the communication between scholars in various disciplines and professional educators would be a valuable step forward. A next step is to make greater use of that largely untapped resource—student contributions to curriculum planning. In each community, professional educators should move to establish the structural devices needed so that scholars, citizens, students, and professional educators may share in planning the curriculum needed. Because of the importance of education, each should be enabled to make his or her particular contribution to curriculum planning.

Who should plan the curriculum? Everyone interested in the future; everyone concerned for the quality of education being experienced by the leaders of the future who are now in our classrooms.

Glen Hass was professor of education, emeritus, University of Florida, Gainesville, and twice national president of the John Dewey Society.

QUESTIONS FOR REFLECTION

1. Do you agree that "The student is the major untapped resource in curriculum planning"? Why or why not?
2. In regard to the level and curricular area with which you are most interested, what "structures" could you create to increase the involvement of the following groups in planning the curriculum: students, parents, and community members, and other educators?
3. What guidelines should curriculum leaders follow in facilitating collaborative curriculum planning?

A Principal Looks Back: Standards Matter

KIM MARSHALL

ABSTRACT: After 15 years as the principal of Boston's Mather School, the nation's oldest public elementary school, Marshall takes a critical look at his accomplishments and his failings. With approximately 600 inner-city students—many of whom did not speak English at home—Marshall faced the challenges of countless urban principals. Given that, he credits the improvements Mather School saw in the 1990s to rigorous state standards and the high-stakes Massachusetts Comprehensive Assessment System (MCAS) test.

After fifteen years as principal of an inner-city elementary school, I am a battle-hardened veteran with his ideals still intact. I welcome this opportunity to look at how the introduction of standards affected the day-to-day struggle to bring a first-rate education to all students.

I became principal of Boston's Mather School after three experiences that neatly framed some of the challenges of school leadership. Fresh out of college in 1969, I taught sixth graders in a Boston middle school and operated pretty much as a lone wolf, writing my own curriculum and at one point actually cutting the wires of my classroom public address speaker to silence the incessant schoolwide announcements. In my nine years in the classroom, I know that students learned a lot, but I was never held accountable to any external standards.

In 1980, intrigued by the "effective schools" research (including the work of Ron Edmonds and the British study, *Fifteen Thousand Hours*), I spent a year at the Harvard Graduate School of Education and sat at the feet of Edmonds himself. I steeped myself in his research on what seemed to make some urban schools work (strong instructional leadership, high expectations, a focus on basics, effective use of test data, and a safe and humane climate) and said "Amen" to his searing comment on failing urban schools: "We can, whenever and wherever we choose, successfully teach all children whose schooling is of interest to us. We already know more than we need in order to do this. Whether we do it must finally depend on how we feel about the fact that we haven't so far." I was eager to become a school leader and put these ideas to work.

But while I was in graduate school, the voters of Massachusetts passed a tax-limiting referendum that sent Boston into a budget tailspin and closed twenty-seven schools. This nixed any chance I had of being made a principal in the near future, and I prepared to return to my classroom.

Instead, I was hired as chief architect of a new citywide curriculum by Boston's Superintendent of Schools, Robert Spillane, a forceful advocate of higher student achievement and more accountable schools. This was right around the time *A Nation at Risk* came out, and I found myself in the thick of Boston's response to the "rising tide of mediocrity." Later, under Spillane's successor, Laval Wilson, I directed an ambitious systemwide strategic planning process. My colleagues and I did some useful work, but throughout my years in the central office I felt that our efforts were often like pushing a string. Without like-minded principals pulling our initiatives into the schools, we often didn't make much of a difference.

When I finally became a principal in 1987, my experiences as a teacher, graduate student, and bureaucrat had shown me three aspects of the urban school challenge: (a) talented but often cussedly independent teachers working in isolation from their colleagues and external standards; (b) provocative research theories about the key factors associated with effective urban schools; and (c) the limited power of the central office to push change into schools that had a great deal of autonomy and very little accountability. Now that I was in the principal's office, I thought I was ideally situated to make a difference for teachers and kids. Was I right?

First, the good news. Over the last fifteen years, Mather students have made significant gains. Our student attendance went from 89 percent to 95 percent and our staff attendance went from 92 percent to 98 percent. Our test scores went from rock bottom in citywide standings to about two-thirds of the way up the pack. A recent in-depth review gave us a solid B+ based on an intensive inspection of the school and standardized test scores. And in 1999, the Mather was recognized for having the biggest gains in the MCAS (the rigorous Massachusetts statewide tests) of any large elementary school in the state. I am proud of these gains and of dramatic improvements in staff skills and training, student climate, philanthropic support, and the physical plant.

But now some more sobering news. The gains we made came in agonizingly slow increments, and were accompanied by many false starts, detours, and regressions. Graphs of our students' test scores did not show the clean, linear progress I had expected. Far too many of our students score in the bottom category on standardized tests, too few are Proficient and Advanced, and our student suspension rate is too high. Serious work remains to be done.

When judging schools, everyone is an expert. If the Mather's student achievement was extraordinary, people would attribute it to certain "obvious" factors: the principal's leadership, his 78-hour workweek, recruiting great teachers, raising money and bringing in lots of resources, using the research on effective schools, and so on. But our student achievement is not extraordinary. This means that despite a lot of hard work, some key ingredients were missing.

I have a theory. I think that the absence of meaningful external standards before 1998 prevented our strenuous and thoughtful efforts from having much traction. I would like to test this theory by examining ten notorious barriers to high student achievement, our struggle with each of them before the introduction of external standards, and what changed when Massachusetts finally mandated high-stakes tests.

1. Teacher isolation. In my first months as principal, I was struck by how cut off Mather teachers were from each other and from a sense of schoolwide purpose. I understood teachers' urge to close their classroom doors and do their own thing; I had done the same thing when I was a teacher. But my reading of the effective schools research and my experience in the central office convinced me that if Mather teachers worked in isolation, there would be pockets of excellence but schoolwide performance would continue to be abysmal.

So I struggled to get the faculty working as a team. I circulated a daily newsletter (dubbed the Mather Memo) and tried to focus staff meetings on curriculum and effective teaching strategies. I encouraged staff to share their successes, publicly praised good teaching, and successfully advocated for a record-breaking number of citywide Gold Apple awards for Mather teachers. I recruited a corporate partner whose generosity made it possible, among other things, to have occasional staff luncheons and an annual Christmas party.

But morale never seemed to get out of the sub-basement. Staff meetings gravitated to student discipline problems, and as a young principal who was seen as being too "nice" to students, I was often on the defensive. We spent very little time talking about teaching and learning, and did not develop a sense of schoolwide teamwork. The result? Teachers continued to work as private artisans, sometimes masterfully, sometimes with painful mediocrity—and the overall results continued to be very disappointing.

2. Lack of teamwork. Having failed to unite the staff as one big happy family, I decided that grade-level teams were a more manageable arena in which to work on improving collegiality. I began to schedule the school so that teachers at the same grade level had the same free periods. Teams began to meet at least once a week and held occasional after-school or weekend retreats (for which they were paid). A few years later, a scheduling consultant taught me how to create once-a-week 90-minute team meetings by scheduling Art, Computer, Library, Music, and Phys Ed classes back-to-back with lunch. This gave teams even more time to meet.

After much debate, we also introduced "looping," with the entire fourth-grade team moving up to fifth grade with the same students (fifth-grade teachers looped back to fourth). Teachers found that spending two years with the same class strengthened relationships with students and parents and within their grade-level teams, and a few years later the kindergarten and first-grade teams decided to begin looping.

But despite the amount of time that teams spent together, there was a strong tendency for the agendas to be dominated by field trips, war stories about troubled students, and other management issues, with all too little attention to sharing curriculum ideas. I urged teams to use their meetings to take a hard look at student results and use the data to plan ways to improve outcomes, and I tried to bring in training and effective coaches to work with the teams, but I had limited success shifting the agendas of these meetings. In retrospect, I probably would have been more successful if I had attended team meetings and played more of a leadership role, but I was almost always downstairs managing the cafeteria at this point in the day and reasoned that teachers needed to be empowered to run their own meetings.

3. Curriculum anarchy. During my early years as principal, I was struck by the fact that most teachers resisted using a common set of grade-level standards. In the central office, I had been involved in creating Boston's citywide curriculum goals, and I was stunned by the degree to which they were simply ignored. While teachers enjoyed their "academic freedom," it caused constant problems. While teachers in one grade emphasized multiculturalism, teachers in the next grade judged students on their knowledge of traditional history facts. While one team focused on grammar and spelling, another cared deeply about style and voice. While one encouraged students to use calculators, the next wanted students to be proficient at long multiplication and division. These ragged "hand-offs" were a frequent source of unhappiness. But teachers almost never shared their feelings with the offending colleagues in the grade just below theirs. That would have risked scary confrontations on deep pedagogical disagreements, which teachers were sure would undermine staff morale. But the absence of honest discussion—culminating in an agreed-upon grade-by-grade curriculum—doomed the Mather to a deeper morale problem stemming from suppressed anger—and lousy test scores.

I saw curriculum anarchy as a major leadership challenge, and tried again and again to get teachers to buy into a coherent K–5 sequence. At one staff retreat, I asked teachers at each grade level to talk to those at the grade just below and just above theirs and agree to better curriculum hand-offs. People listened politely to each other, but made very few changes in what they were teaching. Undaunted, I brought in newly written Massachusetts curriculum frameworks and national curriculum documents, but they did not match the tests our students were required to take and could therefore be ignored with impunity. When the Boston central office produced a cumbersome new curriculum in 1996, I "translated" it into teacher-friendly packets for each grade level—but these had little impact on the private curriculums in many classrooms.

As a result, far too many of our students moved to the next grade with uneven preparation, and our fifth graders, although better prepared than most Boston elementary graduates, entered middle school with big gaps in their knowledge and skills. It was not a pretty picture, and I was intensely frustrated that I could not find a way to change it.

4. Weak alignment. As I wrestled with the curriculum issue, I saw that tests were a vital part of getting teachers on the same page. But virtually all of the standardized tests that students took were poorly aligned with the classroom curriculum (whatever that was) and were not well respected by most teachers. Boston's attempt to write citywide curriculum tests in the 1980s was not well received, and the tests quickly fell into disuse. The tests that teachers gave every Friday and at the end of each curriculum unit were of uneven quality and covered a wide variety of topics with an even wider range of expectations and criteria for excellence. The only tests that got a modicum of respect were the Metropolitan Achievement Tests, which were given in reading and math at every grade level except kindergarten, with school-by-school results published in Boston newspapers.

Sensing that teachers cared about the Metropolitan, I thought that might be a lever for getting teachers on the same curriculum page and making predictable hand-offs of skills and knowledge to the next grade. I did a careful analysis of the Metropolitan and, without quoting specific test items, told teachers at each grade level what the test covered in reading and math. Did teachers use my pages and pages of goals? They did not. And hard as it was for me to admit it, they had a point. Teachers did not think they could improve their students' scores by teaching toward the items I had extracted from the tests—or toward Boston's curriculum, for that matter. The Metropolitans, being norm-referenced tests, were designed to spread students out on a bell-shaped curve and were not aligned to a specific set of curriculum goals or "sensitive" to good teaching (you could work hard and teach well and not have your efforts show up in improved scores). What's more, I was pushing the ethical envelope by briefing teachers on the standards that were covered by a supposedly secret test. If Mather scores had skyrocketed, there might have been a major scandal.

But I had stumbled onto an important insight. The key to turning around teachers' well-founded cynicism about the tests they were required to give and the curriculum they were supposed to teach was to make sure that tests really measured a thoughtful K–12 curriculum. We needed to find both missing elements—a clear grade-by-grade curriculum and aligned tests—at the same time. I could not persuade teachers to buy into one without the other, and without both I could not coax teachers out of the isolation of their classrooms.

5. Low expectations. Another barrier in my early years as principal was teachers' pessimism about producing significant student achievement gains. Hamstrung by the lack of aligned curriculum and tests, gun-shy about addressing their colleagues' idiosyncratic classroom goals, and discouraged by the visible results of poverty (85% of our students qualified for free and reduced-price meals and the community around the school was plagued by unemployment and violence), most teachers regarded themselves as hard-working martyrs in a hopeless cause.

Going for broke in my second month as principal, I brought in Jeff Howard, the charismatic African American social psychologist, and his "Efficacy" message hit home. Jeff spoke of combating our students' lack of achievement motivation by getting them to see that you are not just born smart—you can get smart by applying effective effort. He grabbed the faculty's attention with the notion that we could dramatically improve our results by directly confronting the downward spiral of negative beliefs about intelligence and effort. Over lunch, most of the staff buzzed with excitement.

But after lunch Jeff had to go to another school, and the consultant he left in charge was swamped by defensive and increasingly angry reactions. Was he suggesting that teachers were racist? Was he saying that teachers were making the problem worse? And what did he suggest they do on *Monday*? By late afternoon, it was clear that my gamble to unite the staff around this approach had failed.

Licking my wounds, I took a more incremental approach over the next few years, using private conversations, team meetings, the Mather Memo, and research articles to drive home the message that much higher student achievement was doable at the Mather School. I sent small groups of teachers to Efficacy training, and eventually brought in one of Jeff Howard's colleagues to train the whole staff. It was an uphill battle, but gradually Efficacy beliefs were accepted as part of the school's mission and it became taboo to express negative expectations about students' potential.

But we still did not see dramatic increases in our Metropolitan test scores. Belief was not enough. We needed something more to boost achievement in every classroom.

6. Negativism. The area in which I was least effective in my early years was dealing with some strong personalities who declared war on my goals as principal. It's been observed that inner-city schools attract and nurture strong personalities and can develop a negative culture. When a leader starts to mess around with the unspoken expectations and mores of such a culture, he is playing with fire. When I appeared on the scene preaching that "All Children Can Learn," these teachers reacted with disbelief and active resistance. A parody of the Mather Memo ridiculed my idealism: "For Sale: Rose-Colored Glasses! Buy Now! Cheap! Get that glowing feeling while all falls apart around you."

I was often aghast at the vehemence with which these teachers attacked me. Monthly confrontations with the Faculty Senate invariably got my stomach churning, and I took to quoting W. B. Yeats: "The best lack all conviction, and the worst are full of passionate intensity." I jokingly dubbed my antagonists the Gang of Six, but I could not hide my dismay when it was reported to me that on the day of the first Efficacy seminar, one of these teachers was overheard to say in the bathroom, "If I had a gun, I'd shoot Jeff Howard dead." I was continually off balance, and every mistake I made became a major crisis ("People are outraged! Morale has never been worse!"). On several occasions, I failed to set limits on outrageous and insubordinate behavior and assert my prerogatives as principal.

Over a period of years, the most negative people realized that I wasn't going anywhere and transferred out. They had understudies, and there were struggles almost every year in which I battled with them (not always very skillfully) for the hearts and minds of the silent majority, but the school gradually developed a more positive culture. However, it was only when we were confronted with a compelling external mandate that the positive folks found their voice and the remaining negative staff members fell silent.

7. A harried principal. As every busy principal knows, the hardest part of the job is making time for instructional leadership while dealing with the myriad administrative and disciplinary challenges of running a school. The limitless number of tasks that need to be done can also serve as a very plausible excuse for not dealing with the more intractable work of improving teaching and learning. After my initial setbacks with the staff, I plunged into a major campaign to raise money for a gala 350th anniversary celebration and was successful in sprucing up the aging and neglected building and garnering a great deal of publicity for the school. Although these improvements were important, I had no illusions that they were the heart of the matter.

As I got better at handling the constant stream of "over-the-transom" demands on my time, I prided myself at being able to juggle several balls at once and often quoted an intern's observation that I had two hundred separate interactions in a single day—and that did not include greeting students in the halls. I became an "intensity junkie," addicted to being frantically busy and constantly in demand. I had fallen victim to H.S.P.S.—Hyperactive Superficial Principal Syndrome—and was spending far too little time on teaching and learning.

This realization led me to devise a plan for dropping in on five teachers a day for brief, unannounced supervisory visits. These visits and my follow-up conversations with teachers gave me a much better handle what was going on in classrooms, improved my rapport with the staff, and formed the basis for much more insightful performance evaluations.

But like a recovering addict, I continued to struggle with H.S.P.S. on a daily basis. I gradually accepted that I could not (as I had naively hoped) be the school's staff developer. I began to bring in

"coaches" in literacy, math, and science to work with teachers in their classrooms and team meetings. I stopped sending teachers off to isolated workshops and invested in training within the building. These changes greatly improved the quality of staff development for teachers—but test scores were still not improving as much as we hoped.

8. Not focusing on results. I became increasingly convinced that the most important reason for our disappointing scores was that we were spending too little time actually looking at what students were learning. The teachers' contract allowed me to supervise classroom teaching and inspect teachers' lesson plans, but woe betide a principal who tries to evaluate a teacher based on student learning outcomes. Resistance to evaluating teachers on results is well-founded at one level: unsophisticated administrators might use unsuitable measures like norm-referenced tests or unfairly evaluate teachers for failing to reach grade-level standards with students who were poorly taught the year before or had significant learning deficits.

But not looking at the results of teaching during the school year is part of a broader American tendency to "teach, test, and hope for the best." The headlong rush through the curriculum (whatever that might be) is rarely interrupted by a thoughtful look at how students are doing and what needs to be fixed right now or changed next year. For a principal to ask for copies of unit tests and a breakdown of student scores is profoundly counter-cultural. These private artifacts are none of the principal's business. Teacher teams don't use them much either. They rarely pause at the end of a teaching unit to look at which teaching "moves" and materials produce the best gains, which are less successful, and which students need more help. With one notable exception, I failed to get teachers to slow down, relax about the accountability bugaboo, and talk about best practices in the light of the work students actually produced.

9. Mystery grading criteria. Looking at student work, especially writing and other open-ended products, is virtually impossible without objective grading tools. In many schools, the criteria for getting an A are a secret locked up in each teacher's brain, with top grades going to students who are good mind readers. The absence of clear, public, usable guides for scoring student work prevents students from getting helpful feedback and robs teacher teams of the data they need to improve their performance.

In 1996, the Mather made a successful foray into the world of standards-based thinking. Spurred on by a summer workshop with Grant Wiggins, the author of two books on assessment, including *Assessing Student Performance,* we wrote rubrics (scoring guides) for student writing that described in a one-pager for each grade the specific criteria for getting a score of 4, 3, 2, and 1 in Mechanics/Usage, Content/Organization, and Style/Voice. It was striking how much higher our standards were once we had written these rubrics; now we knew what proficiency looked like! We could also guarantee that the same piece of student writing would get the same scores no matter who graded it. Encouraged by our success, we began to give students a "cold prompt" writing assignment (a topic they had never seen before, no help from the teacher) in September, November, March, and June. Teachers scored the papers together and then discussed the results.

This process was a breakthrough. We had found a way to score student writing objectively; we were sharing the criteria with students and parents in advance (no surprises, no excuses); we were giving "dipstick" assessments at several points each year; teachers at each grade were working as a team to score students' work; and teachers were analyzing students' work, giving students feedback, and fine-tuning their teaching. We began to see significant improvements in our students' writing.

But after a few years of regular scoring meetings and charting of students' progress, our efforts began to flag. Finding enough time was always an issue, especially since the scoring/data analysis meetings were hard to fit into our 90-minute team meetings and many teachers had after-school family commitments. It takes very strong

leadership—or another equally powerful force—to sustain this kind of work.

10. No schoolwide plan. Over the years, we eyeballed many different programs to turn around student achievement—Effective Schools, Efficacy, Success for All, Core Knowledge, Accelerated Schools, Comer, Schools Without Failure, Multiple Intelligences, Whole Language, Multicultural, and others—but none got the buy-in needed for successful implementation. As a result, we kept trying to "grow our own"—an exhausting and frustrating process. In the late 1990s, one "whole school" reform program was mandated as part of a Boston grant program. We appreciated the help (and the money!) but felt there were crucial pieces missing and drove the program administrators crazy by constantly second-guessing their model and adding components of our own. Perhaps we were asking for too much. Perhaps we should have committed to a less-than-perfect program and given it a chance to work. But we were on a constant quest for a better mousetrap.

As we continued our search, two more narrowly focused programs had a big impact. The first was Reading Recovery, a highly effective, low-tech, data-driven program for struggling first graders. What caught the attention of the whole staff was that most of the students who appeared to be doomed to school failure got back on track after twelve weeks of hard work with the highly trained Reading Recovery teachers.

After a few years of successful implementation, there was enough support to get all primary-grade teachers to buy into the Literacy Collaborative program, which was created by Irene Fountas and Gay Sue Pinnell to align the way reading and writing are taught in regular classrooms with Reading Recovery. All of our K–3 teachers bought into the program and were trained by one of their colleagues through in-class coaching and a 40-hour after-school course in which teachers looked at student work and data (using a new scale of reading proficiency) and talked constantly about best practices in a low-stakes, collegial atmosphere. The program produced significant gains in our student achievement in the lower grades, and during the 2001–2002 school year we introduced the upper-grade version of Literacy Collaborative.

But these very effective literacy programs were not part of a coherent schoolwide change plan. And this, along with all the other factors discussed above, prevented us from getting the kinds of achievement gains we knew our students could produce. . . .

Children who enter school with middle-class home advantages tend to do well, even if they attend ineffective schools. But disadvantaged children desperately need effective schools to teach them key life skills and launch them into success. Unless there is strong leadership pushing back, the ten factors will make things much worse for these children. If teachers work in isolation, if there isn't effective teamwork, if the curriculum is undefined and weakly aligned with tests, if there are low expectations, if a negative culture prevails, if the principal is constantly distracted by non-academic matters, if the school does not measure and analyze student outcomes, and if the staff lacks a coherent overall improvement plan, then students' entering inequalities will be amplified and poor children will fall further and further behind, widening the achievement gap into a chasm.

This presents a tremendous professional—and moral—challenge to principals, because they are ideally situated to influence each of these factors. If the principal is an effective instructional leader, the forces will be pushed back (at least for the time being) and the gap will narrow. For vulnerable, school-dependent children, this is a godsend.

How did I measure up to this challenge? For more than a decade, I had limited success pushing back the powerful gap-widening forces. Mather students only began to make real progress when strong external standards were introduced, and that did not happen until Massachusetts introduced high-stakes tests (the MCAS) in 1998.

When we heard that 800-pound gorilla knocking on our door, the turnaround happened with amazing speed. As our fourth graders took the first round of MCAS tests, one of our most effective teachers (who taught fourth grade) burst into tears at a staff meeting and proclaimed, "No more Lone Ranger!" She pleaded with her colleagues in kindergarten, first grade, second grade, and third grade to prepare students with the necessary building blocks so that she would never again have to watch her students being humiliated by a test for which they were so poorly prepared.

Some of our colleagues joined the handwringing across Massachusetts about making students the victims of a forced march to high standards. But in a subsequent meeting, the staff sat down and actually took portions of the MCAS and came to these conclusions: (a) although the test is hard, it really does measure the kinds of skills and knowledge students need to be successful in the twenty-first century; (b) the MCAS is a curriculum-referenced test whose items are released every year, making it possible to align the curriculum and study for the test (we are lucky to live in Massachusetts; some states use norm-referenced tests and keep their tests secret); (c) our students have a long way to go; but (d) most of our kids *can* reach the proficient level if the whole school teaches effectively over time.

The only problem was that the Massachusetts frameworks and tests were pegged to grades four, eight, and ten, leaving some uncertainty about curriculum goals for the other grades. But the grade-four tests and accompanying "bridge" documents gave us much more information than we had before. We set up committees that worked with consultants to "tease back" the standards, and we then worked as a staff (with parent input) to create booklets with clear grade-by-grade proficiency targets accompanied by rubrics and exemplars of good student work. We also set a schoolwide achievement target four years into the future (an idea suggested by Jeff Howard), and then spelled out SMART goals (Specific, Measurable, Attainable, Relevant, and Timebound) for each grade level to act as steppingstones toward the long-range target. Each year since, we have updated the SMART goals with higher and higher expectations.

I believe that the rigorous, high-stakes MCAS tests had a dramatic impact on all of the areas with which we had struggled for so long. The grade-by-grade MCAS-aligned targets put an end to curriculum anarchy and kicked off the process of locating or writing during-the-year assessments aligned with those goals. This in turn focused the curriculum and produced data that teams could sink their teeth into, giving much more substance to their meetings. The rubrics we had developed just a year before were key tools in objectively measuring student writing and displaying data in ways that encouraged effective team discussions on improving results. As teachers gave up some "academic freedom," their isolation from each other was greatly reduced and grade-level teams had a common purpose. Our staff confronted the issue of teacher expectations when we took portions of the MCAS ourselves, and there was much less negative energy as we united in a relentless push for proficiency—a term we had never used before. My work as an administrator was much more focused on student learning results, which helped in the continuing struggle with H.S.P.S. And, finally, the perennial search for the perfect school improvement program came full circle to a very straightforward mission: preparing students with the specific proficiencies needed to be successful at the next grade level and graduate from fifth grade with the skills and knowledge to get on the honor roll in any middle school. We began to focus all our energy on continuously improving each of the components of a "power cycle": clear unit goals, pretests, effective teaching, formative assessments, data analysis, feedback to students and parents, and a safety net for students who fall through the cracks.

The elements for greatly improved achievement are falling into place, and there's help from the central office: Boston's citywide curriculum goals are being aligned with the MCAS and reframed in a compact format for each grade level, and additional coaching and professional time are being given to all schools. I believe that the Mather's student achievement will take off as the staff hones all the elements and captures big enough chunks of focused staff meeting time to process student work and data effectively. The most important work is hard to do within the school day, even in 90-minute meetings. Special afterschool retreats have to be in teachers' calendars well in advance, money has to be available to pay stipends, and teachers need some initial coaching on making these data analysis meetings really effective. With strong leadership and continuing staff buy-in, these ingredients ought to make it possible for virtually all students to reach at least the proficient level.

In closing, I want to return to the Ron Edmonds statement cited earlier. Edmonds often said that the existence of even *one* effective urban school (and he found a number of them) proved that we knew how to turn around failing schools—which meant that there was no excuse for any urban school to be ineffective. With these words, Edmonds laid a colossal guilt trip on urban educators who were not getting good results. His stinging rebuke may have jolted some educators out of fatalistic attitudes and gotten them thinking about ways to improve their schools. But was Edmonds right that we knew in 1978 how to turn around failing schools? Was he fair to thoughtful, hard-working school leaders? Was he a little glib about what it would take to close the gap?

From my experience as a principal, I can testify that Edmonds and his generation of researchers did not provide a detailed road map to help a failing school find its way out of the woods. Without that, success depended too much on extraordinary talent, great personal charisma, an impossibly heroic work ethic, a strong staff already in place, and luck—which allowed cynics to dismiss isolated urban successes as idiosyncratic and say they proved nothing about broader school change.

But Edmonds' much more basic contribution was in getting three key messages into the heads of people who cared about urban schools: 1) demographics are not destiny, and inner-city children can achieve at high levels; 2) some specific school characteristics are linked to beating the demographic odds; and 3) we therefore need to stop making excuses and get to work.

Turning around failing schools is extraordinarily difficult. My 15-year struggle to make one school effective has brought me face to face with my own personal and professional limitations and made me a student of school effectiveness and the key factors that get people and institutions to work more successfully. I have learned that the starting point has to be an almost religious belief that it can be done, and Edmonds served as high priest in that regard. A second necessity is an outline of what an effective school looks like, and the correlates of effective urban schools (which have held up remarkably well over the years) have given me a vision of the pieces that need to be in place for all children to learn at high levels. A third key piece is real expertise on turning around failing schools. Craft knowledge has increased by leaps and bounds. If I could go back to 1987 and start over again as principal with current knowledge about school improvement, progress would be made much more rapidly.

But student achievement would still not have reached its full potential without a fourth tool: strong external standards linked to high-stakes curriculum tests. I believe that the arrival of standards and tests in the late 1990s provided the traction needed for a principal to push back the powerful gap-widening forces that operate within all schools.

Building on the accumulated lessons of researchers and practitioners, today's principals are in a much better position to be successful. If they believe passionately that their students can achieve proficiency, if they have a clear vision of what makes a school effective, if they learn the lessons of school change, and if they take advantage of external assessments, principals should be able to lead a school staff to bring a first-rate education to every child. Ron Edmonds would have smiled about that. So should all of us.

Kim Marshall resigned from Boston's Mather School in 2002. He was principal there for 15 years.

QUESTIONS FOR REFLECTION

1. What does Marshall list as the ten notorious barriers to high school achievement? Looking back on your high school experience, would you say his list is accurate? What would you add or remove from the list? Why?
2. Marshall credits one single thing as the greatest contribution to improved performance at Mather School. What is it? How did this come to have such a tremendous impact on student performance?
3. What does Marshall wish he had done differently at Mather School in his tenure there? What can you learn from his experiences to help you when dealing with issues of student achievement?

The Limits of Ideology: Curriculum and the Culture Wars

DAVID T. GORDON

ABSTRACT: Gordon examines the culture wars that broke out in the wake of A Nation at Risk—*between conservatives and liberals—over what was required to best teach literacy in America's schools. He observes that ideological orthodoxy for setting educational agendas is very limited and inevitably leads to conflict and poorly served students in the classroom. Gordon stresses the need for a balanced, or integrated, approach to curricular reforms—one that makes the most of what different strategies offer in order to reach the widest range of children. Finally, policymakers and education researchers need to do a better job of clarifying the goals, means and justifications for reforms. Once those objectives have been clarified, teacher leaders need to be given comprehensive training, support, and incentive if reforms are to be taken to scale.*

Just months before she died in 1999, Jeanne Chall, a leading literacy scholar of the twentieth century, participated in a forum at the Harvard Graduate School of Education called "Beyond the Reading Wars." In the 1960s, Chall had written *Learning to Read: The Great Debate* to address the rancorous debate over whether beginning readers should learn letters and sounds before delving into books or immerse themselves in texts, picking up the sights, sounds, and meaning of words along the way. *Learning to Read* had displayed a mountain of research about the need for beginning readers to have both phonics instruction and access to interesting reading material. What more was there to say? Yet here was Chall more than thirty years later discussing a whole new round of reading debates.

In a comical exchange with the moderator, Chall was asked if a certain high-profile report issued earlier that year would settle the matter. "Well," she replied, "the basic knowledge was known for the longest time. Even the Greeks knew what kind of combination [of instruction] you needed in teaching reading. Thirty years ago I said the research showed that you do need phonics. And then you *do* need to read, you see."

"So why do we keep fighting about whole language and phonics?"

"I know many of my friends say it's a political thing," Chall replied. "The ones who like the alphabet are right-wingers, Republicans. Can you imagine? At any rate, somebody discovered along the way that you really didn't need to know all the letters. You could remember the words. That is more fun. You don't have to drill."

"And those fun people are the Democrats? The ones who don't do any work?" the moderator asked.

"Yes, the liberals," said Chall.[1]

The banter was humorous—and meant to be. But it also revealed some frustration over the tenor and substance of the disputes about reading instruction during the 1980s and 1990s. Chall, it has been said, was one to "follow the evidence fearlessly wherever it might lead."[2] Yet the curriculum debates that came after *A Nation at Risk* were often fueled not by a sober and fearless analysis of what the evidence said is best, but by ideological and political partisanship. More often than not, it led to the kind of absurd characterizations Chall was poking fun at, the oversimplifications that turned reading- and math-teaching strategies into salvos within the culture wars. Somewhere along the line phonics and arithmetic became "conservative"—the pedagogical equivalents of Reaganomics, mink coats, and Anita

Bryant—while whole language and reform math became "liberal," lumped in with the progressive income tax and *Mother Jones.*

Given the sense of urgency to improve education following *A Nation at Risk,* school reform was bound to take on the look of blood sport in certain cases, particularly regarding reading and math instruction. Bitter squabbles have broken out over science and social studies instruction, high-stakes testing, and school choice. But the reading and math wars have been generally nastier and more emotional than even those conflicts. It's not hard to understand why. Reading and math are the bedrock of children's learning, the primary subjects of elementary education. Later success in school and college depends on success in those subjects during the preK–3 years.

The broad bipartisan support for the No Child Left Behind Act (NCLB) of 2001 may prove to be something of a truce, if not a peace treaty, in the curriculum wars. Conservatives and liberals, traditionalists and progressives agreed that an emphasis on "scientific," or research-based, instruction and standards was needed so that K–12 decisionmaking would be influenced less by ideology and more by practical and proven solutions to classroom dilemmas.

If the wars really are ended, what can be learned from them? One thing they teach us is the limits of ideological orthodoxy for setting educational agendas. When ideologues impose lopsided solutions, conflict is inevitable—and children are poorly served. A related lesson is about the importance of a balanced, or integrated, approach to curricular reforms—one that makes the most of what different strategies offer in order to reach the widest range of children. Not only does that usually make the most sense, but research shows that teachers seldom incorporate new materials and reform strategies whole hog. Without some evidence that proposed changes are indeed an improvement, and without a specific plan for putting those changes into practice, teachers will take it on themselves to interpret and integrate them into the practices they already know. Which suggests a third lesson: that policymakers and

education researchers need to do a better job of clarifying the goals, means, and justifications for reforms. Finally, once those objectives have been clarified, teachers need to be given comprehensive training, support, and incentive if reforms are to be taken to scale.

THE PROBLEM OF IDEOLOGY

Educational ideologies are a useful starting point for discussion, for *describing* the ideal positions of different sides in a debate, but they are not very helpful for *prescribing* solutions. The post–*Nation at Risk* years have shown that reality trumps ideology time and again. California's reading and math reforms are good examples.

The state's 1987 English/Language Arts framework tried to overhaul reading instruction by installing a curriculum meant to convey "the magic of language" and "touch students' lives and stimulate their minds and hearts." It called for a radical change in instructional practice. Out was phonics: proponents of the new method argued that such skill-building exercises—"drill-and-kill"—bored students and stymied their natural excitement about reading. In came whole language, which would immerse students in texts and do away with direct instruction in letter-sound relationships, spelling, and so forth. Students would learn to read as they learned to speak—by jumping right in and doing it—and focus on the meaning of words, not their sounds or particular parts. Fundamental skills would be picked up along the way, in context. This dispute is an old story in American education—from the "alphabetic method" of Noah Webster's speller and McGuffey's readers to attacks by Horace Mann and John Dewey on phonics-based instruction to *Why Johnny Can't Read,* the 1955 bestseller that induced a public outcry for a return to direct phonics instruction.

That's where Jeanne Chall comes in. In 1961, the Carnegie Corporation of New York asked Chall, then at the City University of New York, to determine what the evidence said. She analyzed dozens of studies published from 1910 to 1967, reviewed the most widely used reading textbooks and their teachers manuals, talked with authors and editors of beginning reading programs, and visited hundreds of classrooms in the United States and the United Kingdom. She published her results in 1967 in *Learning to Read*.

The verdict? A combination of phonics for beginners and good literature for all was best. "To read, one needs to be able to use *both* the alphabetic principle and the meaning of words," she wrote. "What distinguished the more effective beginning reading instruction was its early emphasis on learning the code. Instruction that focused, at the beginning, on meaning tended to produce less favorable results." Early phonics instruction in which children learn letter-sound relationships by sounding out words as they read was especially beneficial to children of low socioeconomic status who did not come from language-rich or literacy-rich homes.[3]

In the 1970s and 1980s, when education research was exploring new territory in beginning reading through the lenses of psychology and neurology, evidence continued to mount showing the efficacy of early phonics instruction combined with exposure to high-quality reading material. Later editions of *Learning to Read*, published in 1983 and 1996, reported even stronger support of the advantages of "code emphasis over meaning emphasis" for beginning readers.[4]

But whole language, the latest incarnation of the whole-word method, was winning the ideological battle. It got the approval of teachers unions, schools of education, and others sympathetic to its progressive underpinnings. Its idealized view of children as self-motivated, joyful learners who, with the right encouragement, could construct meaning out of texts without having to know a bunch of rules had a highly romantic appeal.[5]

Whatever its merits, whole language was done a disservice by those adherents who presented it in increasingly strident ways, turning the reading debate into a conflict between good and evil rather than what it should have been: a difference of opinion between people of good will. In California, the discussion took on an almost "theological" character, as journalist Nicholas Lemann puts it, shaped by the crusading, absolutist fervor of its participants.[6]

California's education leaders bought into an ideology rather than a proven, research-based instructional plan. Consulting with whole-language advocates, they were presented with a "choice": (a) provide beginning readers with a humane, nurturing whole-language environment in which their natural interest and love for rich reading material would flourish, or (b) offer them mind-numbing phonics-based instruction. Bill Honig, California's superintendent of public instruction at the time, would later claim, "We thought we were pushing literature. We were neutral on phonics. Then the whole-language movement hijacked what we were doing."[7] The new framework didn't mention whole language directly, but it was full of the theory's romantic language, as its references to the "magic" of language and efforts to "stimulate hearts and minds" suggest.

A similar theological good-versus-evil hue colored the state's math reforms, which included the introduction of new frameworks in 1985 and 1992. Familiar themes emerged, pitting a child-centered ideology emphasizing "real-life" problem-solving against the boring, factory-floor experience of arithmetic drills and pencil-and-paper computation. With reform math, students would use calculators and manipulatives—objects such as beans, sticks, or blocks—to understand numeric relationships. They would read about math problems and discuss them in an effort to understand not just computational value but how such knowledge applies in life. They would work in small groups, tackling together the sorts of problems one encounters in everyday life. Basic skills would—like phonics in the reading reforms—get picked up by students along the way in an informal or indirect manner. This same departure from a basic-skills emphasis characterized the 1989 standards issued by the National Council of Teachers of Mathematics (NCTM). To reformers, traditional instruction was "mindless mimicry mathematics."[8]

Of course, ideological excess was not limited to reformers. By the early 1990s, grassroots opposition to both the math and reading frameworks in California had swelled into a statewide movement. Helped by the relatively new technologies of the World Wide Web and email, parents and mathematicians founded Mathematically Correct, an advocacy group that became a powerful opponent of what was now being called "fuzzy math" after the reform's endorsement of estimation rather than computation. Meanwhile, the media began seeking and fording extreme examples of the new methods in action. In one memorable anecdote, *Time* magazine reporter Margot Hornblower visited a fifth-grade class in Sun Valley, California, where the teacher began class by asking, "What if everybody here had to shake hands with everyone else? How many handshakes would that take?" The kids split into small groups and puzzled over the activity for some time—the reporter said for an hour, the teacher later said twenty minutes. Regardless, none of the children could arrive at an answer, and the class tried it again the next day.[9]

Such stories were often exaggerated by opponents of the reforms as representative of the depth and scope of reforms. This was unfair. But they had a potent political effect. In 1997, California revised its framework again to blend traditional instruction with reform methods, putting a greater emphasis on arithmetic, computation, and paper-and-pencil algorithms such as long division. In 2000, the NCTM did the same. But the NCTM also made a point of spelling out more clearly how the standards should be applied, especially in the elementary and middle grades. In some ways, the NCTM saw the math wars as a great misunderstanding and suggested that the revised standards were a clarification, not a correction, of the 1989 framework.[10]

A similar uprising took place over reading. Years after overseeing the 1987 reform, California's former superintendent of public instruction Bill Honig would say, "The best antidote to a zealous philosophy is reality."[11] The coup de grace for whole language in his state came with the publication of the 1994 National Assessment of Educational Progress (NAEP) reading scores. In just eight years, California had fallen from first among states to dead last, tied with Louisiana. Fifty-nine percent of fourth graders could not read at the fourth-grade level, compared to a national average of 44 percent reading below grade level. African American and Hispanic children fared worst, with 71 percent and 81 percent, respectively, lacking necessary reading skills, compared with 44 percent of white students.

Whole-language proponents cited a number of factors to explain the change, such as larger class size, a new surge of immigration, the high percentage of students from families of low socioeconomic status, and poor training of teachers in whole-language teaching. They pointed out that other states using whole language, such as New Hampshire, had improved test scores significantly.[12] But those arguments fell on deaf ears, especially the arguments about immigration and poverty, given that 49 percent of those who read below basic levels had college graduates for parents. Nowhere else in the nation did the children of college-educated parents score lower than in California.[13]

Something was clearly wrong with California reading instruction, and conservatives had a field day promoting an image of a huge state bureaucracy imposing illiteracy on its children with its politically correct theory. Even before the NAEP scores came out, Republicans had held up whole language from coast to coast in 1994, when they won their first congressional majority in half a century, as a symbol of failed "liberal" ideas. They were not above their own ideological excesses: fundamentalist Christians suggested that whole language's goal of helping students make meaning out of texts was an effort to undermine a literal, or fundamentalist, reading of anything, but especially the Bible.[14]

After the NAEP embarrassment, California amended its reading framework in 1996, calling for a "balanced, comprehensive approach" to reading instruction in its schools that would provide direct instruction in phonics, vocabulary, and spelling while acknowledging whole-language advocates' concern that, of course, "the best instruction provides a strong relationship between what children learn in phonics and what they read."[15] It was a point Jeanne Chall had made in *Learning to Read* twenty-nine years earlier.

THE NEED FOR BALANCE

Chall had warned against taking phonics to an extreme. Early phonics instruction was a necessary tool that should be replaced with reading good stories as quickly as possible. But she had also criticized education professionals for ignoring half a century of research evidence because of their ideological bias against skills-based phonics instruction—the belief that phonics was incompatible with progressive education.[16]

Even as research continued in the 1990s to demonstrate the need for a balanced reading approach, whole-language theorists attacked advocates of balance in baldly political terms. A founding theorist of whole language bizarrely accused Jeanne Chall of doing the bidding of "right-wing" groups bent on destroying public education because she had unmasked the potential harm of a radical application of his theory.[17]

At this time, the federal government did what the Carnegie Corporation had tried to do in supporting Chall's work in the 1960s: get beyond the ideological squabbles to determine what reading research actually said. The National Research Council (NRC), the research arm of the National Academy of Sciences, took up the task. Three shifts in thinking during the 1980s made the project compelling, according to Catherine Snow, the Harvard literacy expert who directed the study. First, a large body of new research increased our understanding of the importance of preschool experiences in the development of literacy—that during those years, children are not just getting ready for reading instruction but actively developing literacy skills. Second, research conducted in the previous two decades about the nature of the reading process had resolved many of the

issues phonics and whole-language advocates were fighting about, demolishing some theoretical underpinnings of what Snow calls "radical whole-language practice"—research that had yet to filter down to the trenches. Third, given this consensus on instructional matters, prevention of reading problems rather than reading instruction per se became more of a concern.

In 1998, the NRC issued its verdict: both sides in the reading wars were right—and both were wrong. "The reading wars are over," the panel declared. The findings, published in a book titled *Preventing Reading Difficulties in Young Children*, emphasized the need for reading instruction that balanced and integrated what phonics and whole-language proponents were advocating. Good readers accomplish three things, said the report: "They understand the alphabetic system of English to identify printed works; they have and use background knowledge and strategies to obtain meaning from print; and they read fluently." In other words, they understand and appreciate both the sounds and the meanings of words. The report placed special emphasis on the impact of the preschool years. What kinds of experiences do children need *before* they get to school and formal reading instruction begins?[18]

In a later edition of the book, the authors expressed concern about the use of the term *balance,* a metaphor that, they said, could imply "a little of this and a little of that" or suggest evenly dividing classroom time between phonics and comprehension activities. Instead, they clarified their findings as a call for *integrating* these strategies so that "the opportunities to learn these two aspects of skilled reading should be going on at the same time, in the context of the same activities, and that the choice of instructional activities should be part of an overall, coherent approach to supporting literacy development, not a haphazard selection from unrelated, though varied, activities."[19]

Mathematicians opposed to radical reforms made similar arguments in favor of balanced math instruction that teaches basic skills but also links them to real-life contexts. They argued that having a rich understanding of the abstract concepts and basic facts of mathematics is essential to being able to adapt that knowledge to a variety of plausible and authentic circumstances. Since there is inevitably an abstract or theoretical aspect to any principle, separating the conceptual from the actual is counterproductive and confusing.

TEACHERS TAKE MATTERS INTO THEIR OWN HANDS

While researchers and policymakers have come to the realization that balanced instruction works best, school practitioners seem to have known that all along. Their natural gravitation toward balanced instruction is typical of how school reform works, according to historians David Tyack and William Tobin: "Reformers believe their innovations will transform schools, but it is important to recognize that schools change reforms. Over and over again teachers have selectively implemented and altered reforms."[20]

For example, in one 1995 study, researchers found that children in classes identified as "whole language" made greater gains in reading comprehension than those in classes tagged "basic skills." They also became independent readers more quickly. But when the researchers took a closer look, they found that those whole-language classrooms actually provided abundant instruction in basic skills.[21]

Meanwhile, in their decade-long study of California math reform, researchers David K. Cohen and Heather C. Hill found that teachers by and large reported using a mix of methods, taking parts of the curriculum that made sense and ignoring those that didn't:

> What reformers and opponents packaged tidily, teachers disaggregated and reassembled. Their logic was different from and more complex than both the logic put forward by reformers in the frameworks, who saw what we call "conventional" and "reform" ideas about teaching and student learning as opposed to each other, and to the critics of reform, whose view of these matters was at least as black and white as that of the reformers. Though many

teachers expressed strong allegiance to the principal reform ideas, most did not discard the corresponding conventional ideas.[22]

A 1999 report by the *Harvard Education Letter* found a similar pattern among teachers in Massachusetts, where teachers and curriculum coordinators using materials based on the 1989 NCTM reform math standards began supplementing materials that focused heavily on problem-solving with paper-and-pencil, skills-building worksheets. For example, the math curriculum coordinator for public schools in Braintree, William Kendall, told education journalist Andreae Downs, "It's often good to blend curricula. Kids need practice. It's not enough just to get the big idea and move on, you need practice before you get it right."[23]

Why do practitioners take matters into their own hands? Cohen and Hill ventured a few guesses. First, school practitioners often get conflicting messages from policymakers at various levels about whether, for example, to teach basic skills or discard them. State directives may be contradicted by district-level directives or by leaders in schools—principals, teacher leaders, or the strong lobbying of local parents' groups that are at odds with state policy. So many different messages may make teachers feel that the best thing to do is keep on keeping on until the problem is sorted out.

Another explanation cited by Cohen and Hill is that "teachers learn things from experience that reformers, critics, and policymakers can never know because they lack the experience and rarely inquire of teachers." When math reforms didn't work in California, policymakers accused teachers of not committing to the framework or of implementing the reforms ineffectively by mixing innovative practices and content with traditional ones. But teachers often told researchers that their professional experience might require them to adjust on the fly to help certain students or classes build essential skills. Like lawyers, doctors, architects, or other professionals, teachers knew that what is drawn up on the board rarely translates easily into practice.

In their analysis of the California math reforms, Cohen and Hill found a great gap between what was prescribed as policy and what took place in practice.[24] This complicated the effort to try to evaluate reforms and assign blame or credit for failure or success—a point California whole-language advocates also made when trying to explain the state's miserable showing in reading in 1994. The interpretation and implementation of standards can vary in each district, school, and classroom. New standards-based curriculum materials often have errors, and the commitment of time and resources to preparing teachers to use such new materials also varies widely.

Because reform efforts often produce glass-half-full and glass-half-empty results, the conclusions we draw from those results must be carefully weighed so that, to paraphrase Bill Honig, reality maintains the upper hand over ideology. For example, researchers at Northwestern University and the University of Chicago compared international math scores to determine how fifth-grade students who had been enrolled in the K–4 reform program Everyday Mathematics matched up with their U.S. and foreign counterparts. The researchers found that the Taiwanese and Japanese fifth graders performed better than all of the American students. Students in Everyday Mathematics outperformed U.S. students from traditional math classes, scored higher than the Taiwanese in some cases, and, on average, scored only slightly lower than Japanese students. Is this good news or bad news? Do we see progress being made through the reform program and should we build on these apparent gains? Or do we just see continued failure—Americans languishing behind the world *again*—and scrap the program?

The value of education research to practice and policymaking naturally depends on the quality or the trustworthiness of the research itself. In 2000, the *Christian Science Monitor* reported that two math reform programs—Core-Plus and the Connected Math Project—got favorable reviews from the U.S. Department of Education based on research conducted by people affiliated with the curricula's developers. Core-Plus was evaluated by an education researcher from the University of Iowa who was a co-director of the program—and in line to receive royalties from sales of its textbooks. "Nobody, including research ethicists, argues that [the Core-Plus study is] invalid," wrote reporter Mark Clayton. Many observers noted that the study would probably provide useful data and analysis about the program. But without a truly independent review, the DOE's recommendation is suspect—and gives ample fodder to skeptics of reforms.[25]

Concerns about skewed research have also been raised by whole-language proponents about recent reports on reading instruction. They note, for example, that the study *Teaching Children to Read*, commissioned by the National Institute of Child Health and Human Development and published in 2000, clearly favored an increased emphasis on phonics instruction. The report, which laid the groundwork for the "Reading First" initiative passed into law as part of the No Child Left Behind Act, focused on quantitative research—that is, studies connecting teaching strategies to test scores. By ignoring qualitative research studies—such as case studies, small-group studies, and in-school observation—the report gave an incomplete picture of the role of classroom instruction in improved reading scores, critics said. In 2002, a new panel went back to the drawing board, looking at qualitative research as well.[26]

New York Times education columnist Richard Rothstein suggests that the current emphasis in federal legislation on "scientifically based research"—the language used in the Reading Excellence Act of 1998 and repeated numerous times in No Child Left Behind—may undermine the balanced approach by tilting policy in favor of phonics because "scientific study is easier for phonics than whole language." He writes: "Researchers can teach about phonemes, then test if children they know get 'car' by removing a sound from 'cart.' It is harder to design experiments to see if storytelling spurs a desire to read." Rothstein also points out that "[s]cientific studies of separate parts of a reading program exist, but there is no well-established science that precisely balances phonemic awareness, phonics, vocabulary lessons and storytelling. The balance differs for each child. Teachers fluent in both skill- and literature-based techniques are needed."[27]

HELPING TEACHERS SUPPORT REFORMS

The past twenty years of reform have also shown that getting teachers to change their practice has been more difficult than expected. The teaching profession is by nature a conservative one. For example, Cohen and Hill report that the math-reform ideas that got the most teacher approval were those that did little to challenge conventional practice and required only modest effort to implement—a little more time here, a change in activities there. Anything that appeared to subvert or challenge what they considered to be essential math teaching and learning got only reluctant attention, if any. "All of this suggests one final explanation," write Cohen and Hill. "[L]earning is often slow and painful, and even when rapid, it attaches to inherited ideas, intellectual structures, and familiar practices."[28]

A comparative study of math teaching in the United States and China demonstrates the importance of teacher knowledge. In an effort to learn why Americans did more poorly, researcher Liping Ma, senior scholar at the Carnegie Foundation for the Advancement of Teaching, found that a high percentage of U.S. teachers had a weak grasp of basic math concepts, particularly at the elementary school level. Teachers lacked a fundamental understanding of standard algorithms, as well as alternative means of problem-solving and why the standard ones have been determined most efficient. A teacher "should know these various solutions of the problem, know how and why students came up with them, know the relationship between the nonstandard ways and the standard way, and know the single conception underlying all the different ways," she writes in her influential book, *Knowing and Teaching Elementary Mathematics*. Ma suggests that to improve mathematics instruction in the United States,

more attention must be paid to fundamental math knowledge in preservice teacher training, teacher preparation time, and professional development.[29]

But knowing how to teach math involves more than simply knowing mathematics, and attention to content knowledge alone won't improve teaching and learning. According to the research of Stanford University's Linda Darling-Hammond, students learn best from teachers who have university-level courses in math education as well as a fundamentally sound math knowledge. "Sometimes very bright people who are not taught to teach are very poor teachers because they don't know what it is to struggle to learn, and haven't thought much about how people learn. Content is important, but it isn't enough," she told the *Harvard Education Letter*. Teachers' ability to adapt curricula to the needs of each student is crucial to improved instruction in any curriculum, she says.[30] Critics of education programs who say that teacher training should focus primarily on content, not pedagogy, fail to appreciate the special skills required for good teaching. Katherine K. Merseth, director of teacher education at Harvard and a former math teacher, says fundamental content knowledge is of course essential. But teachers also need techniques in their teaching repertoire that reflect how children learn and make sense of things:

> Can you explain to me why one-half divided by two-thirds is three-fourths? Don't tell me how to do it, because that's what many people will do. Give me an example. Tell me a story that represents that equation. We all know you invert and multiply. But why? Or as a kid once said, "If *x* equals five, why did you call it *x*? Why didn't you just call it five?" You need to be able to draw on the content knowledge itself. But simply having the content background will not make you an effective teacher. To be an effective teacher, you must understand your audience.[31]

In their study, Cohen and Hill found that efforts were successful "only when teachers had significant opportunities to learn how to improve mathematics teaching. When teachers had extended opportunities to study and learn the new mathematics curriculum that their students would use, they were more likely to report practices similar to the aims of the state policy. These opportunities, which often lasted for three days or more, were not typical of professional education in U.S. schools." Having the opportunity to examine student work with colleagues and discuss it in the context of what reforms were trying to achieve was crucial to making classroom improvements.[32]

That same lesson is true of reading. Both preservice and inservice training of teachers is essential to improving reading instruction. John Goodlad, a founder of the Center for Educational Renewal at the University of Washington, Seattle, has argued that the paltry preparation of most primary-grade teachers—the average teacher takes one university-level course in reading instruction—makes intervention to help poor readers almost impossible: "Diagnosis and remediation of the nonreaders lie largely outside the repertoire of teachers whose brief pedagogical preparation provided little more than an overview."[33] Meanwhile, the NRC found that "[p]rofessional development of teachers, teachers aides, and professional or volunteer tutors [was] integral to each program—there is an important relationship between the skill of the teacher and the response of the children to early intervention. Effective intervention programs pay close attention to the preparation and supervision of the teachers or tutors."[34]

At the twentieth anniversary of *A Nation at Risk,* that is a recurring theme, not only in discussions about curriculum reform but also about reform in general. Improving the work of teachers must be central; that is, proposed solutions should be practice based and not simply responses to ideological braying in the public arena. Although it often takes partisan firebrands to get the attention of policymakers, the ideas and prescriptions of ideologues are usually too simplistic and unbending to be helpful in shaping effective reform practices. They make good conversation starters but poor plans for action. The curriculum battles of the post–*Nation at Risk* period have long since demonstrated their limits.

Only a sober assessment of what works on the classroom level—which requires a complex, intensive, and ongoing discussion of the work schools and teachers do, both generally and in very specific, on-the-scene ways—can bring about the kinds of improvements and reforms the writers of *A Nation at Risk* hoped to inspire with their rhetorical alarms. In its 1998 report calling for an end to the reading wars, the NRC committee noted, "The knowledge base is now large enough that the controversies that have dominated discussions of reading development and reading instruction have given way to a widely honored *pax lectura,* the conditions of which include a shared focus on the needs and rights of all children to learn to read."[35] One can only hope that such a peace will pervade future discussions about how best to educate children, giving sobriety and reason the upper hand over the ideological excesses that Jeanne Chall laid bare in 1999. To do so, we, like Chall, must be willing to go fearlessly wherever the evidence leads.

NOTES

1. The Askwith Education Forum "Beyond the Reading Wars" was held at the Harvard Graduate School of Education on 8 April 1999.
2. The quotation is attributed to E. D. Hirsch, Jr., in "A Tribute to Jeanne Chall," *American Educator 25,* no. 1 (Spring 2001), 16.
3. See "Introduction to the Third Edition" in Jeanne S. Chall, *Learning to Read: The Great Debate,* 3rd ed. (New York: Harcourt Brace, 1996).
4. Ibid.
5. See E. D. Hirsch's critique of the Romantic underpinnings of progressivism in *The Schools We Need and Why We Don't Have Them* (New York: Doubleday, 1996).
6. See an interview with Lemann in "The President's Big Test," *Frontline,* 28 March 2002. Online at www.pbs.org/wgbh/pages/frontline/shows/schools/nochild/lemann.html
7. Honig is quoted in Nicholas Lemann, "The Reading Wars," *Atlantic Monthly 280,* no. 5 (November 1997), 128–134.
8. National Research Council, *Everybody Counts* (Washington, DC: Author, 1989).

9. Romesh Ratnesar et al., "This Is Math? Suddenly, Math Becomes Fun and Games," *Time,* 25 August 1997, pp. 66–67.

10. See Andreae Downs, "Will New Standards Quiet the Math Wars?" *Harvard Education Letter 16,* no. 6 (November/December 2000), 4–6.

11. Quoted in Barbara Matson, "Whole Language or Phonics? Teachers and Researchers Find the Middle Ground Most Fertile," *Harvard Education Letter 12,* no. 2 (March/April 1996), 3.

12. Diane Ravitch provides an overview of the debate in "It Is Time to Stop the War" in Tom Loveless, ed., *The Great Curriculum Debate* (Washington, DC: Brookings Institution Press, 2001).

13. See G. Reid Lyon's statement to the U.S. Senate's Committee on Labor and Human Resources on reading and literacy initiatives, 28 April 1998. Lyon is chief of the Child Development and Behavior for the National Institute of Child Health and Human Development.

14. See Ellen H. Brinkley, "What's Religion Got to Do with Attacks on Whole Language?" in Kenneth S. Goodman, ed., *In Defense of Good Teaching* (Portland, ME: Stenhouse, 1998).

15. California Department of Education, "Teaching Reading: A Balanced, Comprehensive Approach to Teaching Reading in Prekindergarten through Grade Three," Program Advisory (Sacramento: Author, 1996).

16. Chall, *Learning to Read,* pp. 288–300.

17. Matson, "Whole Language or Phonics?"

18. See Catherine E. Snow, "Preventing Reading Difficulties in Young Children: Precursors and Fallout" in Tom Loveless, ed., *The Great Curriculum Debate,* pp. 229–246.

19. Preface to the third edition of Catherine E. Snow, M. Susan Burns, and Peg Griffin, *Preventing Reading Difficulties in Young Children* (Washington, DC: National Academy Press, 2000). Online at www.nap.edu/readingroom/books/prdyc/

20. See David Tyack and William Tobin, "The 'Grammar' of Schooling: Why Has It Been So Hard to Change?" *American Educational Research Journal 31,* no. 3 (Fall 1994), 478.

21. Matson, "Whole Language or Phonics?"

22. David K. Cohen and Heather C. Hill, *Learning Policy. When State Education Reform Works* (New Haven, CT: Yale University Press, 2001), pp. 70–71.

23. Downs, "Will New Standards Quiet the Math Wars?"

24. Cohen and Hill, *Learning Policy,* p. 71.

25. Mark Clayton, "Flaws in the Evaluation Process," *Christian Science Monitor,* 23 May 2000.

26. National Reading Panel, *Teaching Children to Read;* Kathleen Kennedy Manzo, "New Panels to Form to Study Reading Research," *Education Week,* 30 January 2002, p. 5; Kathleen Kennedy Manzo, "Reading Panel Urges Phonies for All in K–6," *Education Week,* 19 April 2000, pp. 1, 14; also of interest is Thomas Newkirk, "Reading and the Limits of Science," *Education Week,* 24 April 2002, p. 39.

27. Richard Rothstein, "Reading Factions Should Make Amends," *New York Times,* 5 September 2001, p. B7.

28. Cohen and Hill, *Learning Policy,* pp. 71–72.

29. See Liping Ma, *Knowing and Teaching Elementary Mathematics* (Mahwah, NJ: Lawrence Erlbaum, 1999), pp. 144–153.

30. Downs, "Will New Standards Quiet the Math Wars?"

31. "Arming New Teachers with Survival Skills," *Harvard Education Letter 18,* no. 5 (September/October 2002), 8.

32. Cohen and Hill, *Learning Policy,* p. 3.

33. John I. Goodlad, "Producing Teachers Who Understand, Care, and Believe," *Education Week,* 5 February 1997, p. 36.

34. Catherine E. Snow, M. Susan Burns, and Peg Griffin, *Preventing Reading Difficulties in Young Children* (Washington, DC: National Academy Press, 1998), p. 273. Online at www.nap.edu/reading room/books/prdyc/

35. Ibid., p. vi.

David T. Gordon is editor of the *Harvard Education Letter* and a former associate editor at *Newsweek.*

QUESTIONS FOR REFLECTION

1. Gordon writes that ideological orthodoxy for setting educational agendas is very limited and inevitably leads to conflict and poorly served students in the classroom. What

does he mean by the term "ideological orthodoxy" and how does it lead to conflict and poorly served children? What evidence does he cite to support his claims?

2. Do you think politics belongs in the K–12 curriculum? Should political ideologies determine the content, even the methodology, used to teach students? If so, whose political ideas should be represented? How would you go about ensuring equal representation? Is equal representation even possible or desirable?

3. How should we end what has been labeled "the reading wars"? Is the country too culturally divided for a truce, or is some kind of compromise possible? How would we know if we have ideologically "balanced" the curriculum? What would a balanced curriculum look like?

The Muddle Machine: Confessions of a Textbook Editor

TAMIM ANSARY

ABSTRACT: Why are so many textbooks bland and unimaginative? A former editor describes the daunting combination of bureaucratic hurdles, political correctness, and self-appointed censors that stand in the way of a good educational read.

Some years ago, I signed on as an editor at a major publisher of elementary and high school textbooks, filled with the idealistic belief that I'd be working with equally idealistic authors to create books that would excite teachers and fill young minds with Big Ideas.

Not so.

I got a hint of things to come when I overheard my boss lamenting, "The books are done and we still don't have an author! I *must* sign someone today!"

Every time a friend with kids in school tells me textbooks are too generic, I think back to that moment. "Who writes these things?" people ask me. I have to tell them, without a hint of irony, "No one." It's symptomatic of the whole muddled mess that is the $4.3 billion textbook business.

Textbooks are a core part of the curriculum, as crucial to the teacher as a blueprint is to a carpenter, so one might assume they are conceived, researched, written, and published as unique contributions to advancing knowledge. In fact, most of these books fall far short of their important role in the educational scheme of things. They are processed into existence using the pulp of what already exists, rising like swamp things from the compost of the past. The mulch is turned and tended by many layers of editors who scrub it of anything possibly objectionable before it is fed into a government-run "adoption" system that provides mediocre material to students of all ages.

WELCOME TO THE MACHINE

The first product I helped create was a basal language arts program. The word *basal* refers to a comprehensive package that includes students' textbooks for a sequence of grades, plus associated teachers' manuals and endless workbooks, tests, answer keys, transparencies, and other "ancillaries." My company had dominated this market for years, but the brass felt that our flagship program was dated. They wanted something new, built from scratch.

Publisher (A) decides to create a new high school textbook from scratch. Idea lightbulb heats compost heap of similar textbooks (B), causing them to break down into sludge, which is simmered into master list of topics (C). Redundancies are boiled off (D) and philosophy (E) is mixed in. Elixir of topics drains into brain of editor, who starts worrying (F) about conservatives in Texas and liberal zealots in California. Editor transforms topics into outline (G), which flows to writers (H), causing them to begin scribbling. Editor begins worrying about finding name author (I). Text from writers is forced into mold of key curriculum guidelines (J). State frameworks for most states (K) are ignored. Tail (L) of key adoption state of Texas wags dog, which responds by taking textbook-size bites (M) from bales of compressed text. Name author (N) is signed to book. Book is reviewed (O). Too much evolution? Conservatives shoot it down. Not multiracial enough? Liberals shoot it down. Editor patches up holes and end-runs objections (P). Books finally make it to students (Q).

Sounds like a mandate for innovation, right? It wasn't. We got all the language arts textbooks in use and went through them carefully, jotting down every topic, subtopic, skill, and subskill we could find at each grade level. We compiled these into a master list, eliminated the redundancies, and came up with the core content of our new textbook. Or, as I like to call it, the "chum."

But wait. If every publisher was going through this same process (and they were), how was ours to stand out? Time to stir in a philosophy.

By *philosophy*, I mean a pedagogical idea. These conceptual enthusiasms surge through the education universe in waves. Textbook editors try to see the next one coming and shape their program to embody it.

The new ideas are born at universities and wash down to publishers through research papers and conferences. Textbook editors swarm to events like the five-day International Reading Association conference to pick up the buzz. They all run around wondering, What's the coming thing? Is it critical thinking? Metacognition? Constructivism? Project-based learning?

At those same conferences, senior editors look for up-and-coming academics and influential educational consultants to sign as "authors" of the textbooks that the worker bees are already putting together back at the shop.

CONTENT LITE

Once a philosophy has been fixed on and added, we shape the pulp to fit key curriculum guidelines. Every state has a prescribed compendium of what kids should learn—tedious lists of buffeted objectives consisting mostly of sentences like this:

> The student shall be provided content necessary to formulate, discuss, critique, and review hypotheses, theories, laws, and principles and their strengths and weaknesses.

If you should meet a textbook editor and he or she seems eccentric (odd hair, facial tics, et cetera), it's because this is a person who has spent hundreds of hours scrutinizing countless pages filled with such action items, trying to determine if the textbook can arguably be said to support each objective.

Of course, no one looks at all the state frameworks. Arizona's guidelines? Frankly, my dear, we don't give a damn. Rhode Island's? Pardon me while I die laughing. Some states are definitely more important than others. More on this later.

Eventually, at each grade level, the editors distill their notes into detailed outlines, a task roughly comparable to what sixth-century jurists in Byzantium must have faced when they carved Justinian's Code out of the jungle of Roman law. Finally, they divide the outline into theoretically manageable parts and assign these to writers to flesh into sentences.

What comes back isn't even close to being the book. The first project I worked on was at this stage when I arrived. My assignment was to reduce a stack of pages 17 inches high, supplied by 40 writers, to a 3-inch stack that would sound as if it had all come from one source. The original text was just ore. A few of the original words survived, I suppose, but no whole sentences.

To avoid the unwelcome appearance of originality at this stage, editors send their writers *voluminous* guidelines. I am one of these writers, and this summer I wrote a 10-page story for a reading program. The guideline for the assignment, delivered to me in a three-ring binder, was 300 pages long.

BON APPÉTIT

With so much at stake, how did we get into this turgid mess? In the '80s and '90s, a feeding frenzy broke out among publishing houses as they all fought to swallow their competitors. Harcourt Brace Jovanovich bought Holt, Rinehart and Winston. Houghton Mifflin bought D.C. Heath and Co. McGraw-Hill bought Macmillan. Silver Burdett bought Ginn—or was it Ginn that bought Silver? It doesn't matter, because soon enough both were devoured by

Prentice Hall, which in turn was gobbled up by Simon & Schuster.

Then, in the late '90s, even bigger corporations began circling. Almost all the familiar textbook brands of yore vanished or ended up in the bellies of just four big sharks: Pearson, a British company; Vivendi Universal, a French firm; Reed Elsevier, a British-Dutch concern; and McGraw-Hill, the lone American-owned textbook conglomerate.

This concentration of money and power caused dramatic changes. In 1974, there were 22 major basal reading programs; now there are 5 or 6. As the number of basals (in all subject areas) shrank, so did editorial staffs. Many downsized editors floated off and started "development houses," private firms that contract with educational publishers to deliver chunks of programs. They hire freelance managers to manage freelance editors to manage teams of freelance writers to produce text that skeleton crews of development-house executives send on to publishing-house executives, who then pass it on to various committees for massaging.

A few years ago, I got an assignment from a development house to write a lesson on a particular reading skill. The freelance editor sent me the corresponding lessons from our client's three major competitors. "Here's what the other companies are doing," she told me. "Cover everything they do, only better." I had to laugh: I had written (for other development houses) all three of the lessons I was competing with.

THE CRUELEST MONTH

In textbook publishing, April is the cruelest month. That's when certain states announce which textbooks they're adopting. When it comes to setting the agenda for textbook publishing, only the 22 states that have a formal adoption process count. The other 28 are irrelevant—even though they include populous giants like New York, Pennsylvania, and Ohio—because they allow all publishers to come in and market programs directly to local school districts.

Adoption states, by contrast, buy new textbooks on a regular cycle, usually every six years, and they allow only certain programs to be sold in their state. They draw up the list at the beginning of each cycle, and woe to publishers that fail to make that list, because for the next 72 months they will have zero sales in that state.

Among the adoption states, Texas, California, and Florida have unrivaled clout. Yes, size does matter. Together, these three have roughly 13 million students in K–12 public schools. The next 18 adoption states put together have about 12.7 million. Though the Big Three have different total numbers of students, they each spend about the same amount of money on textbooks. For the current school year, they budgeted more than $900 million for instructional materials, more than a quarter of all the money that will be spent on textbooks in the nation.

Obviously, publishers create products specifically for the adoptions in those three key states. They then sell the same product to everybody else, because basals are very expensive to produce—a K–8 reading program can cost as much as $60 million. Publishers hope to recoup the costs of a big program from the sudden gush of money in a big adoption state, then turn a profit on the subsequent trickle from the "open territories." Those that fail to make the list in Texas, California, or Florida are stuck recouping costs for the next six years. Strapped for money to spend on projects for the next adoption period, they're likely to fail again. As the cycle grows vicious, they turn into lunch meat.

DON'T MESS WITH TEXAS

The big three adoption states are not equal, however. In that elite trio, Texas rules. California has more students (more than 6 million versus just over 4 million in Texas), but Texas spends just as much money (approximately $42 billion) on its public schools. More important, Texas allocates a dedicated chunk of funds specifically for textbooks. That money can't be used for anything else, and all of it *must* be spent in the adoption year. Furthermore, Texas has particular power when it comes to high school textbooks, since California adopts statewide only for textbooks from kindergarten though 8th grade, while the Lone Star State's adoption process applies to textbooks from kindergarten through 12th grade.

If you're creating a new textbook, therefore, you start by scrutinizing *Texas Essential Knowledge and Skills* (TEKS). This document is drawn up by a group of curriculum experts, teachers, and political insiders appointed by the 15 members of the Texas Board of Education, currently 5 Democrats and 10 Republicans, about half of whom have a background in education. TEKS describes what Texas wants and what the entire nation will therefore get.

Texas is truly the tail that wags the dog. There is, however, a tail that wags this mighty tail. Every adoption state allows private citizens to review textbooks and raise objections. Publishers must respond to these objections at open hearings.

In the late '60s a Texas couple, Mel and Norma Gabler, figured out how to use their state's adoption hearings to put pressure on textbook publishers. The Gablers had no academic credentials or teaching background, but they knew what they wanted taught—phonics, sexual abstinence, free enterprise, creationism, and the primacy of Judeo-Christian values—and considered themselves in a battle against a "politically correct degradation of academics." Expert organizers, the Gablers possessed a flair for constructing arguments out of the language of official curriculum guidelines. The Longview, Texas-based nonprofit corporation they founded 43 years ago, Educational Research Analysts, continues to review textbooks and lobby against liberal content in textbooks.

The Gablers no longer appear in person at adoption hearings, but through workshops, books, and how-to manuals, they trained a whole generation of conservative Christian activists to carry on their work.

Citizens also pressure textbook companies at California adoption hearings. These objections come mostly from such liberal organizations as Norman Lear's People for the American Way, or from individual citizens who look at proposed textbooks when they are on display before adoption in 30 centers around the state. Concern in California is normally of the politically correct sort—objections, for example, to such perceived gaffes as using the word *Indian* instead of *Native American*. To make the list in California, books must be scrupulously stereotype free: No textbook can show African Americans playing sports, Asians using computers, or women taking care of children. Anyone who stays in textbook publishing long enough develops radar for what will and won't get past the blanding process of both the conservative and liberal watchdogs.

Responding to citizens' objections in adoption hearings is a delicate art. Publishers learn never to confront the assumptions behind an objection. That just causes deeper criticism. For example, a health textbook I worked on had a picture of a girl on a windy beach. One concerned citizen believed he could detect the outlines of the girl's underwear through her dress. Our response: She's at the beach, so that's her bathing suit. It worked.

A social studies textbook was attacked because a full-page photograph showed a large family gathered around a dinner table. The objection? They looked like Arabs. Did we rise up indignantly at this un-American display of bias? We did not. Instead, we said that the family was Armenian. It worked.

Of course, publishers prefer to face no objections at all. That's why going through a major adoption, especially a Texas adoption, is like earning a professional certificate in textbook editing. Survivors just *know* things.

What do they know?

Mainly, they know how to censor themselves. Once, I remember an editorial group was discussing literary selections to include in a reading anthology. We were about to agree on one selection when someone mentioned that the author of this piece had drawn a protest at a Texas adoption because he had allegedly belonged to an organization called One World Council, rumored to be a "Communist front."

At that moment, someone pointed out another story that fit our criteria. Without further conversation, we chose that one and moved on. Only in retrospect did I realize we had censored the first story based on rumors of allegations. Our unspoken thinking seemed to be, If even the most unlikely taint existed, the Gablers would find it, so why take a chance?

Self-censorship like this goes unreported because we the censors hardly notice ourselves doing it. In that room, none of us said no to any story. We just converged around a different story. The dangerous author, incidentally, was celebrated best-selling science fiction writer Isaac Asimov.

TURN THE PAGE

There's no quick, simple fix for the blanding of American textbooks, but several steps are key to reform.

- Revamp our funding mechanisms to let teachers assemble their own curricula from numerous individual sources instead of forcing them to rely on single comprehensive packages from national textbook factories. We can't have a different curriculum in every classroom, of course, but surely there's a way to achieve coherence without stultification.

- Reduce basals to reference books—slim core texts that set forth as clearly as a dictionary the essential skills and information to be learned at each grade level in each subject. In content areas like history and science, the core texts would be like mini-encyclopedias, fact-checked by experts in the field and then reviewed by master teachers for scope and sequence.

Dull? No, because these cores would not be the actual instructional material students would use. They would be analogous to operating systems in the world of software. If there are only a few of these and they're pretty similar, it's OK. Local districts and classroom teachers would receive funds enabling them to assemble their own constellations of lessons and supporting materials around the core texts, purchased not from a few behemoths but from hundreds of smaller publishing houses such as those that currently supply the supplementary-textbook industry.

- Just as software developers create applications for particular operating systems, textbook developers should develop materials that plug into the core texts. Small companies and even individuals who see a niche could produce a module to fill it. None would need $60 million to break even. Imagine, for example, a world-history core. One publisher might produce a series of historical novellas by a writer and a historian working together to go with various places and periods in history. Another might create a map of the world, software that animates at the click of a mouse to show political boundaries swelling, shrinking, and shifting over hundreds of years. Another might produce a board game that dramatizes the connections between trade and cultural diffusion. Hundreds of publishers could compete to produce lessons that fulfill some aspect of the core text, the point of reference.

The intellect, dedication, and inventiveness of textbook editors, abundant throughout the industry but often stifled and underappreciated, would be unleashed with—I predict—extraordinary results for teachers and students.

Bundling selections from this forest of material to create curriculum packages might itself emerge as a job description in educational publishing.

The possibilities are endless. And shouldn't endless possibility be the point?

Tamim Ansary, a columnist for Encarta.com and author of *West of Kabul and East of New York,* has written 38 nonfiction books for children. He was an editor at Harcourt Brace Jovanovich for nine years and has written for Houghton Mifflin, McDougall Littell, Prentice Hall, and many other textbook publishers.

QUESTIONS FOR REFLECTION

1. What should be the content of textbooks in today's classrooms? Should there be a common textbook curriculum, or should there be local control over what teachers use to teach with?
2. What does Ansary point to as the biggest problem in today's textbook market? What are some possible solutions? Can the problem be fixed or is it too late?
3. Certain states, namely Texas and California, dominate control of the textbooks many other states adopt for their own curriculum. What are the consequences of this kind of centralized control?
4. What do the Gablers teach us about influence and control within the curriculum? Should so few people ever have this kind of power within the curriculum? Who should be responsible for addressing small interest groups like the Gablers and their nonprofit corporation?

Leaders' Voices—
Putting Theory into Practice

The Case for Teacher-Led School Improvement

LAQUANDA BROWN

ABSTRACT: One of the new buzz phrases in education is "teachers as leaders." While this term intrigues educational professionals, it is not a term that should be used loosely. In this article, Brown argues that principals must take the lead in transforming teachers into leaders and increasing the instructional capacity of schools by building consensus, creating a leadership team, and grooming teacher leaders. Retaining effective teachers and developing them into leaders is essential for school improvement, which will ultimately lead to school success. And given the expanded roles and responsibilities of principals, it is crucial that district and school administrators cultivate teachers to successfully share leadership responsibilities.

Leithwood (1994) identifies the four I's of school leadership—individual consideration, intellectual stimulation, inspirational motivation, and idealized influence—that are essential for schools to be successful in the 21st century. Leithwood's four I's are what he refers to as the elements of transformational leadership. In a school where the principal is focused on building the leadership influence of teachers, the principal must teach, exhibit, and train teachers on the intellectual stimulation of school leadership. Through the intellectual-stimulation approach, the principal helps the school staff to have vision and foresight in looking at old problems in new ways by working together to create, identify, and implement innovative, workable solutions.

BUILD CAPACITY AND CONSENSUS

Administrators must build instructional capacity and instructional consensus among school staff. However, many administrators are still at a loss on how to accomplish this daunting task. The principal has to fulfill many complex administrative responsibilities each day. Some decisions must be made immediately, while other decisions may allow the principal to include input from teachers and other stakeholders. Gabriel (2005) writes that it is useful to let someone else propose the change and that the principal should not be the only person in the school to offer solutions.

For example, there may be a concept that the principal truly believes in, such as building time into the school day during which every student and teacher is involved in independent reading. However, before the principal brings this proposal to the faculty, he or she should find out if other members of the school staff share this same philosophy. If other staff members share the principal's philosophy, then the issue should be introduced to the staff as a capacity-building activity. In addition to teachers, custodians and other staff members may also agree with the proposal. If this is the case, staff members (other than the principal and teachers) may introduce the initiative to the faculty to begin critical conversations on implementing the instructional practice into the daily school program. Administrators must be cognizant of the fact that true school improvement involves everyone on the school staff, and must therefore incorporate every member of the staff in the decision-making process.

DEVELOP A LEADERSHIP TEAM

An additional component of creating an atmosphere of shared leadership, where teachers work collectively with administrators to implement research-based instructional practices and methodologies, is to create an effective school leadership team. A strong and purposeful leadership team is able to adequately sustain the responsibilities and challenges of becoming an effective school. To create a strong leadership team, the principal must create an atmosphere of shared data collection and analysis, shared decision-making, and shared respect among the team. For example, the principal must create an environment where teachers feel comfortable offering suggestions, asking questions, and providing feedback. In addition, the atmosphere must be conducive to teachers sharing the responsibility of identifying problems, offering viable solutions, and working collaboratively to create a plan to implement agreed upon solutions.

DuFour, DuFour, Eaker, and Karhanck (2004) write about the power of collective intelligence, or the practice of professionals working collaboratively to solve problems within an organization, as well as the practice of "harnessing the power of collective intelligence that already resides in the school to solve problems." Similarly, Marzano, Waters, and McNulty (2004) describe the concept of agreed-upon processes that "enhance communication among community members, provide for efficient reconciliation of disagreements, and keep the members attuned to the current status of the community." This research reflects the well-known fact that successful schools have a culture of collaborative, sound, research-based decision-making practices that focus on the needs of the school. DuFour, DuFour, Eaker, and Karhanek (2004) note that "these schools made astonishing progress with existing amounts of time and funding. They did not wait for someone from the outside to give them the magic formula, the perfect program, or more resources." Part of the culture of change and excellence involves a great deal of teacher collaboration and faculty ownership of the identified issues and possible solutions.

GROOM TEACHER LEADERS

School principals must create a cadre of teacher leaders for each grade level and for each content area. The teacher-leader selection process must be based on a variety of leadership traits and instructional qualities and must be equitable, nonbiased, and honest.

More important, the teacher leaders and the members of the school's leadership teams should have an innate desire to serve, should have a high level of commitment to the total functioning of the school, and should have a spirit of dedicated volunteerism.

The principal should not be the only person choosing the teacher leaders. A principal may choose to have the school staff nominate teacher leaders, or perhaps there may be a teacher-leader nomination committee. Teachers should also have the option to decline the opportunity to become a teacher leader without fear of consequence. Furthermore, the teacher-leader selection process should result in teacher leaders wanting to serve the school by taking part in the school-improvement group. Essentially, this practice gives teachers the opportunity to operate as joint and collaborative leaders.

In order to build capacity for instructional knowledge and delivery, which ultimately will positively affect student achievement, there must be a system in place for ongoing training of effective, standards-based instructional planning, standards-based delivery, and standards-based assessment. In addition, teacher leaders should be trained by a variety of experts, including the principal, assistant principal, instructional coach, district- or state-level content expert, district- or state-level instructional coordinator, and district- or state-level master teacher.

The teacher leaders must also be provided the opportunity to train teachers within the school day. Trainings must be nonthreatening, collaborative, and data-driven. Teachers should also be given opportunities to provide open and honest feedback on trainings. For instance, summative assessments may indicate that teachers need training on differentiated instruction or on delivering best instructional practices to students. The teachers, however, may voice concerns on needing training that focuses on delivering quality, collaborative instruction or on the use of standards-based assessments and standards-based grading practices.

Therefore, in order to build quality consensus, teachers must have a voice in the types of training offered by teacher leaders. Thus, teacher leaders should provide and implement quality training systems that offer a balance for classroom teachers and that answer to the data as well as to the teachers' requests.

Teacher-led leadership includes the process of teachers analyzing, disaggregating, and conversing about students' achievement, attendance, and discipline data. In addition, a part of the data conversation must address cause, or the "why" questions. The "why" questions must be qualitative, substantial, and correlated to the ongoing data-collection process. This is a practice that is also not easy to master and may call for training. For instance, if the school-achievement data indicates high literacy and low math scores, it is not enough for teachers and administrators to know this fact. The team must work together to figure out why this is the case and what plan can be collaboratively created and implemented that speaks to the causes.

For example, a "Needs Improvement" school that may also be involved in restructuring will require the school staff to have a central, daily focus on data collection and data analysis. Due to the status of the school's progress, focusing on student-achievement data is a critical step to increasing student performance. Listed below are examples of some of the "why" questions that the school might use to help guide and inform instruction:

- Why are the male students scoring higher than the female students in science?
- Why are the female students not interested in the science curriculum?
- Why are the female students outperforming the male students in reading?
- Why are the majority of the students at performance level 3 in science male?
- Why are the male students only interested in certain types of writing, such as writing poetry?
- Why are the students that are scoring the lowest on summative and formative assessments also the students who miss the most school days during the course of the school year?

- Why is less than 10 percent of the total school population performing in the highest category of student achievement?
- Why are more of the fiscal resources being used to address the areas of low student performance?

These are examples of the types of questions that must be asked and seriously considered by teachers and administrators to ensure that a school begins to focus and move into a large-scale school-improvement planning and implementation phase.

Teachers and school leaders can achieve amazing feats of school improvement when everyone works together. In some of the most challenging schools in the nation, teachers and students are thriving because teachers feel comfortable identifying problems, conversing together about solutions, and carrying out solutions that speak to those challenges.

Teachers and principals must be creative, systemic thinkers and learners, and collaborative leaders. They must be willing to implement solutions that are nontraditional, speak to the needs and interests of the students, and address the summative and formative data that answer to the state and federal mandates and guidelines that outline the responsibilities of successful schools. Gabriel (2005) writes that teacher leadership "can transform schools from houses of detention to houses of attention—for both student and teacher." To allow this process to fully develop, administrators must maintain an open, responsive, and receptive attitude to new ideas, realizing that often the most effective strategies and suggestions come from sources within the school building.

REFERENCES

DuFour, R., DuFour, R., Eaker, R., & Karhanek, G. (2004). *Whatever it takes: How professional learning communities respond when kids don't learn.* Bloomington, IN: Solution Tree.

Gabriel, J. (2005). *How to thrive as a teacher leader.* Alexandria, VA: Association for Supervision and Curriculum Development.

Leithwood, K. (1994). Leadership for school restructuring. *Educational Administration Quarterly, 30*(4), 498–518.

Marzano, R., Waters, T., & McNulty, B. (2005). *School leadership that works: From research to results.* Alexandria, VA: Association for Supervision and Curriculum Development.

LaQuanda Brown is principal of King-Danforth Elementary School in Macon, Georgia.

QUESTIONS FOR REFLECTION

1. Do you think teacher leaders are critical to school improvement efforts? Why or why not?
2. What is the instructional capacity and instructional consensus that Brown writes about? She offers strategies to build capacity and consensus. What are her strategies and do you think they are feasible?
3. Does the term "teacher leader" resonate for you in your current educational setting? Is it authentically applied and recognized or does it feel like "just a new buzz word"? What evidence can you cite to support your response?

LEARNING ACTIVITIES

Critical Thinking

1. Review the four questions in the Tyler rationale for curriculum development. What additional questions would need to be asked when developing a curriculum? Give reasons for your choices.
2. Testing is obviously an important part of the effort to raise standards. To what extent do you think the current emphasis on standardized tests encourages teachers to "teach to the test"?
3. If teachers "teach to the test," is this an effective or ineffective way to promote student learning?

Application Activities

1. Reflect on your experiences taking standardized tests. What factors increased your anxiety about taking such tests? What factors reduced that anxiety? Based on your own experiences, how might you help your students reduce their anxiety about taking tests?
2. Is it fair to hold teachers accountable for student learning? Should teachers of students whose home backgrounds are less supportive of education be held as accountable as teachers of students whose backgrounds are highly supportive?
3. Ask your instructor to arrange for a curriculum coordinator from the local school district to visit your class. In addition to finding out about this coordinator's work, ask him or her to describe how the effort to raise standards and No Child Left Behind legislation have influenced curriculum development in the district.
4. Using the "'Generic' Lesson Plan for a Unit of Study" presented in this chapter, prepare a lesson plan at the grade level and in the subject area which you teach (or are preparing to teach). Include at least one authentic classroom assessment of students' learning in your plan.

Field Experiences

1. Spend a half-day at a school at the level with which you are most familiar. Take note of your impressions regarding the extent to which the curricula you observe are student-centered or subject-centered. Share your observations with others in your curriculum class.
2. Interview a few students outside of the classroom during a school day. Ask them to comment on the degree of "fit" between their teachers' curriculum goals and the curriculum goals they have for themselves. Share your findings with others in your class.

Internet Activities

1. Go online to your state's department of education homepage and find the link to the state's standards. Then compare your state's standards with the standards from

another state. How are the two sets of standards similar? Different? Is one set of standards clearer than the other?

2. Visit the homepage of a professional association in the subject area which you are preparing to teach. Locate the curriculum standards developed by the association and compare them with the curriculum standards developed by your state. How are the two sets of standards similar? Different? Is one set of standards clearer than the other?

Curriculum Implementation, Instruction, and Technology

FOCUS QUESTIONS

1. What are the interrelationships between curriculum implementation and instruction?

2. What role can technology play in curriculum implementation?

3. What are the characteristics of learning tasks that students find meaningful and authentic?

4. What are some models of teaching that are based on behavioral psychology, human development, cognitive processes, and social interactions?

5. What can school leaders do to integrate technology into the curriculum?

6. What expectations does today's tech-savvy student bring to school? How might the curriculum be adapted to address the changing needs and demands of a new generation of learners?

This chapter focuses on the interrelationships between curriculum implementation and instruction and the mediating role and function of technology in the modern classroom. The articles in this chapter illustrate, in varying ways, that *what* teachers teach (the content of the curriculum) is as important as *how* they teach (the instructional methods used). The role of technology to change teaching and learning is also discussed in the chapter and in the articles. As technology changes the world we live in, so, too, does it change education. Curriculum decisions are now influenced by technology in ways unimaginable fifty years ago, and the next fifty years promise changes equally dramatic.

Within the curriculum field, some theorists consider curriculum and instruction as separate, yet related, dimensions of education (see Beauchamp's *Curriculum Theory* [1981], for example). Others see the distinction between the two as an artificial construct (see Dewey's *Democracy and Education* [1916], for example). Regardless of how one views the relationship between curriculum and instruction, both are vital elements of the educative process. As the following comments by a teacher suggest, teaching requires expertise at developing the curriculum—*and* expertise at using instructional methods to reach curriculum goals:

> Before becoming a teacher, I imagined that I would teach my students, they would take a test, and I would evaluate my teaching based on their test scores. Actually, that cycle happens very little. It is a part of teaching, but relating to kids, being able to encourage them, being able to laugh with them matters more and more as I develop my teaching style. Encouragement, respect, and trust—those things really make a difference. I am really interested in my subject, mathematics, but I am learning that what matters most to students and to me is becoming excited about learning. When I feel that excitement from the kids . . . that's what makes teaching great.

Curriculum and instruction are not separate, mutually exclusive elements of teaching; they are connected, as the figure below suggests. They are both part of teaching; each influences the other. When a teacher decides to include certain content in the curriculum, that decision means that some methods of instruction will be better suited than others to teach that content to students. On the other hand, a particular instructional method (cooperative learning, for example) is more effective at presenting certain types of content than others. Effective teachers know that they must develop knowledge and skills in both areas—from planning the *what* of the curriculum to planning the *how* of instruction.

Curriculum   **Instruction**
(What)   (How)

INSTRUCTIONAL METHODS

Curriculum leaders understand that appropriate instructional methods, as well as a meaningful curriculum, are key elements of an effective learning environment. They understand that what the teacher does and what students do have powerful influences on learning and on the quality of classroom life.

After developing a curriculum, a teacher must answer the question "What instructional methods will enable me to achieve my curricular goals?" Teachers also must realize that instructional activities should meet *students'* goals. The activities must be meaningful and authentic for students. As Dewey points out in "Progressive Organization of Subject Matter" in this chapter, knowledge should be viewed as progressing out of the learner's experiences rather than as something outside of those experiences. Developing appropriate learning activities, therefore, requires thoughtfulness, insight into the motivations of students, and good judgment.

Authentic learning tasks enable students to see the connections between the curriculum and the world beyond the classroom—both now and in the future. To understand how authentic learning tasks can motivate students to learn, the reader may wish to reflect on his or her own school experiences. Do you recall memorizing facts only because they would appear on a test? Did you ever wonder why a teacher asked you to complete a learning task? Did you ever feel that a teacher asked you to do "busywork"? What kinds of learning tasks motivated you the most?

Herbert A. Thelen (1981, p. 86) contends that authenticity represents "the first criterion all educational activity must meet." According to Thelen, an activity is authentic for a person if he or she "feels emotionally 'involved' and mentally stimulated . . . is aware of choices and enjoys the challenge of making decisions," and feels he or she "has something to bring to the activity and that its outcome will be important" (Thelen, 1981, p. 86).

A comprehensive nationwide study of successfully restructured schools reported that "authentic pedagogy" helps students to (1) "construct knowledge" through the use of higher-order thinking, (2) acquire "deep knowledge" (relatively complex understandings of subject matter), (3) engage in "substantive conversations" with teachers and peers, and (4) make connections between substantive knowledge and the world beyond the classroom (Newmann & Wehlage, 1995; Newmann et al., 1996). In addition, as Figure 6.1 shows, the use of highly authentic pedagogy in classes boosts achievement for students at all grade levels.

FIGURE 6.1

Level of Authentic Student Performance for Students Who Experienced Low, Average, and High Authentic Pedagogy in Restructuring Elementary, Middle, and High Schools

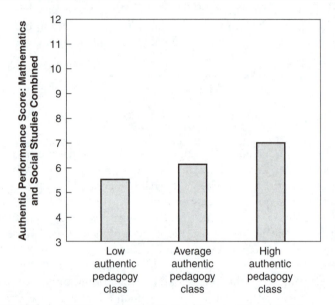

Note: The analysis included 2,100 students in 125 classrooms in 23 schools. Most students had either a mathematics or social studies score, and the two subjects were scored on the same 12-point scale. There were no major differences in the effect of authentic pedagogy on achievement between the two subjects.

Source: Fred M. Newmann and Gary G. Wehlage, *Successful School Restructuring: A Report to the Public and Educators by the Center on Organization and Restructuring of Schools.* University of Wisconsin-Madison: Center on Organization and Restructuring of Schools, 1995, pp. 21, 55. Reprinted by permission.

A REPERTOIRE OF MODELS OF TEACHING

As just stated, the curriculum goals to be attained significantly influence the instructional methods (or "models" of teaching) a teacher uses. In addition, variables such as the teacher's style, learners' characteristics, the culture of the school and surrounding community, and the resources available influence the selection of instructional methods. Together, these variables contribute to the repertoire of models of teaching a teacher develops to reach curriculum goals.

A model of teaching provides the teacher with a "blueprint" of sorts for attaining curriculum goals. In addition, "models of teaching are really models of *learning*. As we help students acquire information, ideas, skills, values, ways of thinking, and means of expressing themselves, we are also teaching them how to learn" (Joyce, Weil, & Calhoun, 2004, p. 7). Table 6.1 presents brief descriptions of five widely used

TABLE 6.1

Five Models of Teaching

	Goals and Rationale	Methods
Mastery Learning	Virtually all students can learn material if given enough time and taught in the appropriate manner. Students learn best when they participate in a structured, systematic program of learning that enables them to progress in small sequenced steps.	• Set objectives and standards for mastery. • Teach content directly to students. • Provide corrective feedback to students on their learning. • Provide additional time and help in correcting errors. • Follow cycle of teaching, testing, reteaching, and retesting.
Cooperative Learning	Students can be motivated to learn by working cooperatively in small groups if rewards are made available to the group as a whole and to individual members of the group.	• Small groups (4–6 students) work together on learning activities. • Assignments require that students help one another while working on a group project. • In competitive arrangements, groups may compete against one another. • Group members contribute to group goals according to their talents, interests, and abilities.
Theory into Practice	Teachers make decisions in three primary areas: content to be taught, how students will learn, and the behaviors the teacher will use in the classroom. The effectiveness of teaching is related to the quality of decisions the teacher makes in these areas.	The teacher follows seven steps in the classroom: 1. Orients students to material to be learned. 2. Tells students what they will learn and why it is important. 3. Presents new material that consists of knowledge, skills, or processes students are to learn. 4. Models what students are expected to do. 5. Checks for student understanding. 6. Gives students opportunity for practice under the teacher's guidance. 7. Makes assignments that give students opportunity to practice what they have learned on their own.
Behavior Modification	Teachers can "shape" student learning by using various forms of reinforcement. Human behavior is learned, and behaviors that are positively reinforced (rewarded) tend to increase while those that are not reinforced tend to decrease.	• Teacher begins by presenting stimulus in the form of new material. • The behavior of students is observed by the teacher. • Appropriate behaviors are reinforced by the teacher as quickly as possible.
Nondirective Teaching	Learning can be facilitated if teachers focus on personal development of students and create opportunities for students to increase their self-understanding and self-concepts. The key to effective teaching is the teachers' ability to understand students and to involve them in a teaching-learning partnership.	• Teacher acts as a facilitator of learning. • Teacher creates learning environments that support personal growth and development. • Teacher acts in the role of a counselor who helps students to understand themselves, clarify their goals, and accept responsibility for their behavior.

models of teaching: mastery learning, cooperative learning, theory into practice, behavior modification, and nondirective teaching.

To attain a variety of curricular goals and objectives, accomplished teachers have developed a broad repertoire of models of teaching. In actual practice, each model in the repertoire is eclectic—in other words, a combination of two or more models of teaching. The following sections describe models of teaching that are based on behavioral psychology, human development, cognitive processes, and social interactions.

Models Based on Behavioral Psychology

Many teachers use models of teaching that have emerged from our greater understanding of how people acquire or change their behaviors. Direct instruction, for example, is a systematic instructional method that focuses on the transmission of knowledge and skills from the teacher (and the curriculum) to the student. Direct instruction is organized on the basis of observable learning behaviors and the actual products of learning. Generally, direct instruction is most appropriate for step-by-step knowledge acquisition and basic skills development but not appropriate for teaching less structured higher-order skills such as writing, the analysis of social issues, and problem solving.

Extensive research was conducted in the 1970s and 1980s on the effectiveness of direct instruction (Gagne, 1974, 1977; Good & Grouws, 1979; Rosenshine, 1988; Rosenshine & Stevens, 1986). The following eight steps are a synthesis of research on direct instruction and may be used with students ranging in age from elementary to senior high school.

1. Orient students to the lesson by telling them what they will learn.
2. Review previously learned skills and concepts related to the new material.
3. Present new material, using examples and demonstrations.
4. Assess students' understanding by asking questions; correct misunderstandings.
5. Allow students to practice new skills or apply new information.
6. Provide feedback and corrections as students practice.
7. Include newly learned material in homework.
8. Review material periodically.

A direct instruction method called *mastery learning* is based on two assumptions about learning: (1) virtually all students can learn material if given enough time and taught appropriately and (2) students learn best when they participate in a structured, systematic program of learning that enables them to progress in small, sequenced steps (Bloom, 1981; Carroll, 1963). The following five steps present the mastery learning cycle:

1. Set objectives and standards for mastery.
2. Teach content directly to students.
3. Provide corrective feedback to students on their learning.
4. Provide additional time and help in correcting errors.
5. Follow a cycle of teaching, testing, reteaching, and retesting.

In mastery learning, students take diagnostic tests and then are guided to do corrective exercises or activities to improve their learning. These may take the form of programmed instruction, workbooks, computer drill and practice, or educational games. After the corrective lessons, students are given another test and are more likely to achieve mastery.

Models Based on Human Development

As pointed out in Chapter 3, human development is a significant basis of the curriculum. Similarly, effective instructional methods are developmentally appropriate, meet students' diverse learning needs, and recognize the importance of learning that occurs in social contexts. For example, one way that students reach higher levels of development is to observe and then imitate their parents, teachers, and peers, who act as models. As Woolfolk (2001, p. 327) points out:

> Modeling has long been used, of course, to teach dance, sports, and crafts, as well as skills in subjects such as home economics, chemistry, and shop. Modeling can also be applied deliberately in the classroom to teach mental skills and to broaden horizons—to teach new ways of thinking. Teachers serve as models for a vast range of behaviors, from pronouncing vocabulary words, to reacting to the seizure of an epileptic student, to being enthusiastic about learning.

Effective teachers also use modeling by "thinking out loud" and following three basic steps of "mental modeling" (Duffy & Roehler, 1989):

1. Show students the reasoning involved.
2. Make students conscious of the reasoning involved.
3. Focus students on applying the reasoning.

In this way, teachers can help students become aware of their learning processes and enhance their ability to learn.

Since the mid-1980s, several educational researchers have examined how learners *construct* understanding of new material. As pointed out in Chapter 4, constructivist views of learning focus on how learners make sense of new information—how they construct meaning based on what they already know. Teachers with this constructivist view of learning focus on students' thinking about the material being learned and, through carefully orchestrated cues, prompts, and questions, help students arrive at a deeper understanding of the material. The common elements of constructivist teaching include the following:

- The teacher elicits students' prior knowledge of the material and uses this as the starting point for instruction.
- The teacher not only presents material to students, but he or she also responds to students' efforts to learn the material. While teaching, the teacher must *learn about students' learning.*
- Students not only absorb information, but they also actively use that information to construct meaning.
- The teacher creates a social milieu within the classroom, a community of learners that allows students to reflect and talk with one another as they construct meaning and solve problems.

Constructivist teachers provide students with support, or "scaffolding," as they learn new material. By observing the child and listening carefully to what he or she says, the teacher provides scaffolding in the form of clues, encouragement, suggestions, or other assistance to guide students' learning efforts. The teacher varies the amount of support given on the basis of the student's understanding. If the student understands little, the teacher gives more support. On the other hand, the teacher gives progressively less support as the student's understanding becomes more evident. Overall, the teacher provides just enough scaffolding to enable the student to "discover" the material on his or her own.

Models Based on Cognitive Processes

Some models of teaching are derived from the mental processes involved in learning—thinking, remembering, problem solving, and creativity. Information processing, for example, is a branch of cognitive science concerned with how people use their long- and short-term memory to access information and solve problems. The computer is often used as an analogy for information-processing views of learning:

> Like the computer, the human mind takes in information, performs operations on it to change its form and content, stores the information, retrieves it when needed, and generates responses to it. Thus, processing involves gathering and representing information, or encoding; holding information, or storage; and getting at the information when needed, or retrieval. The whole system is guided by control processes that determine how and when information will flow through the system. (Woolfolk, 2001, p. 243)

Although several systematic approaches to instruction are based on information processing—teaching students how to memorize, think inductively or deductively, acquire concepts, or use the scientific method, for example—they all focus on how people acquire and use information. Inquiry learning (often called *discovery learning*) is one example of a widely used model of teaching that develops students' abilities to acquire and use information. Students are given opportunities to inquire into subjects so that they "discover" knowledge for themselves. In "Structures in Learning" in this chapter, Jerome Bruner points out that discovery learning also enables students to see that knowledge has a structure, an internal connectedness and meaningfulness.

When teachers ask students to go beyond information in a text to make inferences, draw conclusions, or form generalizations; and when teachers do not answer students' questions, preferring instead to have students develop their own answers, they are using methods based on inquiry and discovery learning. These methods are best suited for teaching concepts, relationships, and theoretical abstractions, and for having students formulate and test hypotheses.

Inquiry learning and discovery learning approaches frequently use a *research-share-perform* cycle. During the *research* phase, students generate their own questions and hypotheses about a topic. They reflect on their prior experiences and knowledge and formulate a main question for inquiry. Research is carried out in small groups that focus on specific parts of the larger research question. During the *share* phase, knowledge is developed during a dialogue between students and teacher and among students themselves. The usefulness of the knowledge is evaluated by the group which, ideally, functions as a *learning community*. During the *perform* phase, students integrate and synthesize their shared knowledge by making presentations to the public.

The following example shows how inquiry and discovery learning in a first-grade classroom fostered a high level of student involvement and thinking.

> The children are gathered around a table on which a candle and jar have been placed. The teacher, Jackie Wiseman, lights the candle and, after it has burned brightly for a minute or two, covers it carefully with the jar. The candle grows dim, flickers, and goes out. Then she produces another candle and a larger jar, and the exercise is repeated. The candle goes out, but more slowly. Jackie produces two more candles and jars of different sizes, and the children light the candles, place the jars over them, and the flames slowly go out. "Now we're going to develop some ideas about what has just happened," she says. "I want you to ask me questions about those candles and jars and what you just observed." (Joyce, Weil, & Calhoun, 2004, p. 3)

Another form of inquiry learning is known as contextual teaching and learning (CTL). CTL is an approach to teaching based on the theory that students learn best in a concrete manner. They learn best when they are involved in hands-on activities and have opportunities for personal discovery within the context of relationships that are familiar to them. In a CTL environment, students construct, apply, and demonstrate knowledge in relevant contexts. They learn material that is meaningful, relevant, and vital to their futures. Students construct, apply, and demonstrate knowledge in relevant contexts.

Actually, contextual teaching and learning is not new. CTL is derived from the ideas of John Dewey. In *Democracy and Education* (1916), Dewey observed that "the great waste in school comes from . . . the isolation of the school—its isolation from life." During the 1970s, contextual teaching and learning was referred to as *experiential learning* or *applied learning*. In contextual teaching and learning classrooms, "it is the major task of the teacher to broaden students' perceptions so that meaning becomes visible and the purpose of learning immediately understandable. This is not an add-on or something nice to do. It is fundamental if students are to be able to connect knowing with doing" (Parnell, 2000).

Curriculum Leadership Strategy

School leaders should provide professional development that prepares teachers to use new models of teaching to implement new curricula. The best approach is to anticipate instructional needs and address them early; minimizing anxiety goes a long way toward managing change.

Models Based on Social Interactions

As every teacher knows, student peer groups can be a deterrent to academic performance; however, they can also motivate students to excel. Because school learning occurs in a social setting, models of teaching based on social interactions—cooperative learning, for example—can provide teachers with options for increasing students' learning.

A powerful model of teaching based on social interactions is group investigation, in which the teacher's role is to create an environment that allows students to determine what they will study and how. Students are presented with a situation to which they "react and discover basic conflicts among their attitudes, ideas, and modes of perception. On the basis of this information, they identify the problem to be investigated, analyze the roles required to solve it, organize themselves to take these roles, act, report, and evaluate these results" (Thelen, 1960, p. 82).

The teacher's role in group investigation is multifaceted; he or she is an organizer, guide, resource person, counselor, and evaluator. The method is very effective in increasing student achievement (Sharan & Sharan, 1989/90), positive attitudes toward learning, and the cohesiveness of the classroom group. The model also allows students to inquire into problems that interest them and enables each student to make a meaningful, authentic contribution to the group's effort based on his or her experiences, interests, knowledge, and skills.

Another model of teaching based on social interactions is project-based learning (PBL). In PBL classrooms, students work in teams to explore real-world problems and create presentations to share what they have learned. Compared with learning solely from textbooks, this approach has many benefits for students, including deeper knowledge of subject matter, increased self-direction and motivation, and improved research and problem-solving skills. However, the benefits of project-based learning are not always assured, as Kathleen Vail cautions in "Nurturing the Life of the Mind" in this chapter: "Project-based learning always has the potential to be based on fun rather than content."

A three-year 1997 study of two British secondary schools—one that used open-ended projects and one that used more traditional, direct instruction—found striking differences between the two schools in measures of student understanding as well as standardized achievement data in mathematics. Students at the project-based school did better than those at the more traditional school both on math problems requiring analytical or conceptual thought and on those requiring memory of a rule or formula. Three times as many students at the project-based school received the top grade achievable on the national examination in math (George Lucas Educational Foundation, 2001).

Project-based learning, which transforms teaching from *teachers telling* to *students doing,* includes five key elements:

1. Engaging learning experiences that involve students in complex, real-world projects through which they develop and apply skills and knowledge
2. Recognizing that significant learning taps students' inherent drive to learn, their capability to do important work, and need to be taken seriously
3. Learning for which general curricular outcomes can be identified up front, while specific outcomes of the students' learning are neither predetermined nor fully predictable
4. Learning that requires students to draw from many information sources and disciplines in order to solve problems
5. Experiences through which students learn to manage and allocate resources such as time and materials (Oaks, Grantman, & Pedras, 2001, p. 443)

BASIC PRINCIPLES OF CURRICULUM IMPLEMENTATION AND INSTRUCTION

In *Basic Principles of Curriculum and Instruction* (1949), Ralph Tyler stressed the importance of analyzing educational purposes, learning experiences, organization of those experiences, and evaluation of outcomes. Tyler's paradigm for the interrelationships between curriculum and instruction is viewed by many as "the perennial paradigm of curriculum studies that dominates the field to this day" (Schubert, 1986, p. 82).

Clearly, the "educational purposes" discussed in Tyler's seminal book are realized by a curriculum if it results in the following three outcomes for learners: (1) they acquire an understanding of the subject at hand; (2) they can apply what they have learned to new situations; and (3) they have a desire to continue learning. However, identification of these outcomes does not tell us exactly *how* to attain them. Tyler's book notwithstanding, we are still confronted with the question: What *are* the basic principles of curriculum and instruction? What do effective teachers do when they are teaching? How do they communicate with students? How do they manage classroom activities? What models of teaching do they use? As Carol Lupton points out in this chapter's *Leaders' Voices* section ("Ideals vs. Reality in the Classroom"), "today's educators are encouraged to provide a variety of teaching experiences—linguistic, logical-mathematical, musical, spatial, bodily kinesthetic, interpersonal, and intrapersonal—to increase opportunities for success for all students. Easy to say, hard to do."

In addition to providing a variety of teaching experiences inside the classroom, Charlotte Danielson writes in "The Many Faces of Leadership" that teacher leaders can find a wealth of opportunities to extend their influence beyond their own classrooms to their teaching teams, schools, and districts. No longer is teaching and learning confined to the classroom as teacher leaders are transforming the notion of learning and where it occurs.

As the previous chapters of this book suggest, answers to questions such as the preceding are not easy to formulate. The interrelationships between curriculum and instruction are reciprocal and complex. Ultimately, our quest to identify *the* principles of curriculum and instruction yields results similar to the "Principles of Effective Teaching" presented in an International Academy of Education publication titled, simply, *Teaching*. We close this section by presenting these 12 principles, retitled "Basic Principles of Curriculum and Instruction," in Table 6.2. The principles, based on extensive research on teaching and learning, illustrate the complex interrelationships between curriculum and instruction. While the principles may appear deceptively simple, they require a high degree of skill and understanding to put into practice in actual classrooms.

TECHNOLOGY AND CURRICULUM DEVELOPMENT

One need not look far to see how technology is impacting schools across the country. The proliferation of cell phones and digital music players alone demonstrates how much has changed in the past ten years. Cell phones are now fashion accessories that are practically available to everyone, and mp3 music players such as the iPod are as ubiquitous as the Walkmans and portable CD players of a generation ago. Students

TABLE 6.2
Basic Principles of Curriculum and Instruction

1. **Supportive Classroom Environment:** Students learn best within cohesive and caring learning communities.
2. **Opportunity to Learn:** Students learn more when most of the available time is allocated to curriculum-related activities and the classroom management system emphasizes maintaining their engagement in those activities.
3. **Curriculum Alignment:** All components of the curriculum are aligned to create a cohesive program for accomplishing instructional purposes and goals.
4. **Establishing Learning Opportunities:** Teachers can prepare students for learning by providing an initial structure to clarify intended outcomes and cue desired learning strategies.
5. **Coherent Content:** To facilitate meaningful learning and retention, content is explained clearly and developed with emphasis on its structure and connections.
6. **Thoughtful Discourse:** Questions are planned to engage students in sustained discourse structured around powerful ideas.
7. **Practice and Application Activities:** Students need sufficient opportunities to practice and apply what they are learning and to receive improvement-oriented feedback.
8. **Scaffolding Students' Task Engagement:** The teacher provides whatever assistance students need to enable them to engage in learning activities productively.
9. **Strategic Teaching:** The teacher models and instructs students in learning and self-regulation activities.
10. **Cooperative Learning:** Students often benefit from working in pairs or small groups to construct understandings or help one another master skills.
11. **Goal-Oriented Assessment:** The teacher uses a variety of formal and informal assessment methods to monitor progress toward learning goals.
12. **Achievement Expectations:** The teacher establishes and follows through on appropriate expectations for learning outcomes.

Source: Adapted from Brophy, J. *Teaching—Educational Practice Series–1.* Brussels, Belgium: International Academy of Education, 1999, pp. 366–367.

can be seen carrying iPods, cell phones, video cameras, laptops, and digital cameras with them everywhere they go—and often these multiple capabilities are housed within the same device. Websites such as Facebook and MySpace are changing the way students communicate, socialize, and network, and other sites such as YouTube and iTunes bring media to students seamlessly, whether at home, on campus, or on the move. Media content comes onto campus every minute of the school day through cell phones, the Internet, email, text messages, and general entertainment (music, video, blogs, etc.).

To keep up with the media and technology environment today's students inhabit outside of school, educators must incorporate technology into the modern curriculum. Unfortunately, as Marc Prensky writes in "Adopt and Adapt: Twenty-First-Century Schools Need Twenty-First-Century Technology" in this chapter, schools "famously resist change." But, he cautions, resisting today's digital technology "will be truly lethal to our children's education. They live in an incredibly fast-moving world significantly different" than any before it, and they will demand things faster than "their teachers are used to providing them" as well as presenting "other new learning needs." In addition to meeting student expectations, technology use by teachers is also a requirement of the No Child Left Behind Act, which requires that all students will be technologically literate by the end of the eighth grade. The definition of "technologically literate" is left up to the states, and there is no requirement for states to report their progress on this goal. However, NCLB requires states to show how they will ensure that technology is integrated throughout all of their curriculum and instruction.

According to the editor of *Technological Horizons in Education (T.H.E.) Journal,* technology should be reflected in the curriculum development process:

> We [must] revisit our state and national core content standards for students and teachers. Can we have science standards with no mention of technology when scientists rely so heavily on technology to do science? Can we have English/Language Arts standards with no mention of technology when most anyone who writes a sentence in his or her job uses word processing, and anyone in the business world doing research goes to the Internet for information? We need to bring our curriculum up to 21st century reality. We need to assess our students' knowledge and skills in a way that is consistent with how that knowledge and those skills are used in the real world. This is the context in which we should be integrating technology throughout all of curriculum and instruction. (Fletcher 2004, p. 6)

A New Generation of Students

To provide effective leadership for curriculum development, school leaders should understand today's tech-savvy students. With few exceptions, students are more "wired" than their teachers. Generations ago, students came to school with notebooks, pencils, and pens; today, they come to school with cell phones, laptops, and iPods. As the George Lucas Educational Foundation points out, "for this digital generation, electronic media is increasingly seductive, influential, and pervasive, yet most schools treat the written word as the only means of communication worthy of study" (George Lucas Educational Foundation, February 9, 2008).

Today's students have grown up in "a techno-drenched atmosphere that has trained them to absorb and process information in fundamentally different ways" (McHugh, 2005). For example, students in grades 3–12 spend an average of six hours and twenty-one minutes each day using some type of media. Since today's students are skilled at multitasking, the figure jumps to about eight-and-a-half hours and includes almost four hours watching TV and fifty minutes of video game play. Homework, however, receives only fifty minutes of their time (Rideout, Roberts, & Foehr, 2005).

As the following data about online learning indicate, technology has transformed curriculum development, teaching, and learning:

- Twenty-six states offer full-time schooling programs for grades K–12, up from five states in 2007.
- In 2007, Michigan became the first state to require high school students to have online learning experience before they graduate.
- An estimated 92,000 students are registered at more than 190 charter schools (George Lucas Educational Foundation, January 12, 2008).

In the following excerpt from his introduction to the U.S. Department of Commerce's report titled *Visions 2020: Transforming Education and Training through*

Advanced Technologies, Bill Gates, former chairman of the Microsoft Corporation, describes the impact of technology on the curriculum:

> The Internet has brought an unprecedented level of great educational content to a wide audience, encouraging teachers to share curriculums and resources worldwide. E-mail has facilitated improved communication among administrators, teachers, students, parents and educational researchers, and emerging Web services technologies will create further opportunities for collaborative learning. Increased industry and government funding in learning science promises to vastly improve the ways technology is applied to learning. And in the years ahead, a whole generation of kids will leave college and enter the workforce with a broad understanding of the ways they can use technology effectively in their jobs.

Many state departments of education have developed technology competency guidelines that curriculum leaders can use in designing staff development programs for classroom teachers. For example, California teachers participate in the Technology Proficiency for California Teachers (CTAP) project. CTAP has prepared the "Professional Profiles" and "Performance Indicators" shown in Table 6.3 to guide teachers' professional development as they learn to use technology "to further classroom management, communication, lesson design and student performance."

TECHNOLOGY AND TRANSFORMATION OF THE CURRICULUM

Since the early 1980s, curriculum leaders have used computers as an instructional delivery system to present information to students. Today, these leaders use computers not only for highly structured drill-and-practice exercises, but as a catalyst for group investigation and inquiry. They incorporate up-to-date technology to stimulate students' higher-order thinking, creativity, and problem solving. Tech-savvy curriculum leaders understand that technology is a tool to create a rich, stimulating environment that fosters collaboration, inquiry, and decision making.

Technology has transformed teaching and learning in our nation's schools. Each day, students communicate via the Internet with other students around the world. They use child-oriented search engines such as Yahooligans! and KIDLINK to search the World Wide Web for information about whales, the Brazilian rain forest, or the planet Mars. They go to chat rooms or newsgroups for children, where they can chat with children in other countries or participate in global networking projects for children.

Moreover, the influence of technology on the curriculum shows no signs of letting up—as Bill Gates stated: "In the next few years—a time I call the 'digital decade'—we'll see computing become a much more significant and indispensable part of all our lives."

Curriculum Leadership Strategy

Today's school librarians are quickly becoming media specialists who can prove to be invaluable to a school leader. Given rapid changes in technology, meeting with the school media specialist on a regular basis can provide a school leader with up-to-date information about the latest technologies and media.

TABLE 6.3
Technology Proficiency for Teachers

Professional Profile	Performance Indicators
• Identifies, selects and uses digital communication tools appropriately • Uses digital tools to communicate with students, parents, and community members to enhance management and learning	• Evidence of the use of a variety of communication tools based on resources available, (i.e., telephone, email, fax, listserv, or web page) • Evidence of the management of information using technology to increase communication, (i.e., web pages, voice mail, homework hotlines, etc.)
• Supports student learning through collaboration with parents, subject matter experts, educators, and others using digital tools • Participates in professional growth activities that utilize digital communication tools	• Evidence of sustained communication with parents, students, and/or colleagues (i.e., mailing lists, video conferencing, online staff development, shared network folders, etc.) • Student projects that utilize digital tools to interact with subject matter experts • Lesson/activity plans designed collaboratively using appropriate communication tools as a medium (i.e., email, listserv, shared network folders, mailing lists, videoconferences, etc.)
• Uses digital communication tools to work with educators and subject matter experts to design classroom activities to support student learning • Seeks out and draws upon the expertise of others to support the learning process and technology enhanced curriculum	• Student work that exemplifies evidence of active collaboration with outside experts • Interdisciplinary lessons and cross grade level projects
• Provides leadership by participating in school-wide decision making and learning activities that support learning through the use of technology • Actively contributes to the development or updating of site- or district-based technology plans • Explores new technologies and recommends innovative educational applications appropriate to the curricular needs of the students and site	• Participation in grade level or department activities to develop a school site technology plan • Pursues continuing education (i.e., educational technology, conference attendance, curriculum integration, online courses workshops) • Evidence of active participation in the site or district decision making process regarding the use and acquisition of technology (i.e., grade level, technology committee, technology planning, etc.)

Source: California Department of Education, Technology Proficiency for California Teachers (CTAP). (Retrieved August 14, 2004, from www.fcoe.k12.ca.us/techprof/professional_profiles.htm#Communication%20and%20Collaboration).

The CEO Forum on Education and Technology (2001) has called on teachers to use technologies to help students develop the following "21st century skills" they will need for life and work in the digital age:

Digital Age Literacy
1. Basic, scientific, and technological literacy
2. Visual and information literacy
3. Cultural literacy and global awareness

Inventive Thinking

1. Adaptability/managing complexity
2. Curiosity, creativity, and risk taking
3. Higher-order thinking and sound reasoning

Effective Communication

1. Teaming, collaboration, and interpersonal skills
2. Personal and social responsibility
3. Interactive communication

High Productivity

1. Prioritizing, planning, and managing for results
2. Effective use of real-world tools
3. Relevant, high-quality products

Although the array of currently available technology for the classroom is dazzling, Ted McCain and Ian Jukes, authors of *Windows on the Future: Education in the Age of Technology,* predict even more dazzling technologies in the future: "Electronics have increased in power more than 1,000,000 times since the development of ENIRC [electronic numerical integrator and calculator, an early computer introduced in 1946], but the greatest changes still lie ahead. Fasten your seat belts!" (2001).

In addition to transforming how much and how quickly information can be processed, technology is changing the very nature of schooling and classrooms themselves. As John K. Waters discusses in his article "A Movable Feast" in this chapter, classrooms of the future will likely look very different from those of today with furniture on wheels, wireless islands, and work spaces designed to enable collaborative classroom interaction. By challenging traditional ideas about where and how learning takes place in the classroom, educators and technology specialists are at work designing K–12 classrooms with digitally inspired and technologically purposeful architecture, all intended to support sound pedagogical practice.

Just as new technological skills are needed in the workplace, a high degree of technological literacy is needed for curriculum development, implementation, and evaluation. Thus, acquiring proficiency in the ever-evolving array of technologies should be an important part of professional development for curriculum leaders. However, educators frequently complain of a lack of training in how to use technology to reach their curriculum goals. Only 20 percent of teachers believe they are well prepared to integrate educational technology into the curriculum, and among the teachers who seek training in technology, 50 percent pay for their training with their own money (CEO Forum on Education and Technology, 1999).

Today's curriculum leaders, along with others who have an interest in education, are becoming more sophisticated in understanding the strengths and limitations of technology as a tool to enhance the curriculum. They know full well that like another educational tool—the book—the computer can be a powerful, almost unlimited medium for instruction and learning, if they carefully reflect on how it will further the attainment of curriculum goals.

CRITERION QUESTIONS—CURRICULUM IMPLEMENTATION AND TECHNOLOGY

The articles in this chapter examine the interrelationships among curriculum implementation, instruction, and technology. The criterion questions for this chapter are as follows:

1. Does the teacher leader play a role in planning and implementing the curriculum as well as assessing how technology might be used in both instruction and assessment?
2. Are appropriate instructional methods (or models of teaching) used to attain the purposes and goals of the curriculum?
3. Are the instructional activities meaningful and authentic for students?
4. Does the curriculum focus on technological literacy for all students?

REFERENCES

Beauchamp, G. A. *Curriculum Theory.* Itasca, IL: F. E. Peacock, 1981.

Black, P., Harrison, C., Lee, C., Marshall, B., & Wiliam, D. "Working inside the Black Box: Assessment for Learning in the Classroom." *Phi Delta Kappan* (September 2004): 9–21.

Bloom, B. S. *All Our Children Learning: A Primer for Parents, Teachers, and Other Educators.* New York: McGraw-Hill, 1981.

Carroll, J. "A Model of School Learning." *Teachers College Record* 64 (1963): 723–733.

CEO Forum on Education and Technology. *School Technology and Readiness Report.* Washington, DC: Author, 1999.

Dewey, J. *Democracy and Education.* New York: Macmillan, 1916.

Duffy, G., and Roehler, L. "The Tension between Information-Giving and Mediation: Perspectives on Instructional Explanation and Teacher Change." In J. Brophy (ed.), *Advances in Research on Teaching,* vol. 1. Greenwich, CT: JAI Press, 1989.

Fletcher, G. H. "Integrating Technology throughout Education." *Technological Horizons in Education (T.H.E.) Journal* 32, no. 3 (2004): 4, 6.

Gagne, R. M. *Essentials of Learning for Instruction.* Hinsdale, IL: Dryden, 1974.

Gagne, R. M. *The Conditions of Learning,* 3rd Ed. New York: Holt, Rinehart and Winston, 1977.

Gates, B. "Introduction." In R. Hinrichs, *A Vision for Lifelong Learning—Year 2020, 2020 Visions: Transforming Education and Training through Advanced Technologies,* pp. 1–12. Washington, DC: U.S. Department of Commerce, 2002.

George Lucas Educational Foundation. *Project-Based Learning Research.* Retrieved November 2001 from www.glef.org./index.html.

———. "By the Numbers: Online Learning." Retrieved January 12, 2008, from www.edutopia.org/stat-online-learning.

———. "Edutopia's Greatest Hits!: A Short List of Your Favorites." Retreived February 9, 2008, from www.edutopia.org/edutopias-greatest-hits.

Good, T. E., and Grouws, D. "The Missouri Mathematics Effectiveness Project: An Experimental Study in Fourth-Grade Classrooms." *Journal of Educational Psychology* 71 (1979): 355–362.

Guenemoen, R. F., Thompson, S. J., Thurlow, M. L., and Lehr, C. A. *A Self-Study Guide to Implementation of Inclusive Assessment and Accountability Systems: A Best Practice*

Approach. Minneapolis: University of Minnesota, National Center on Educational Outcomes, 2001.

Joyce, B., Weil, M., and Calhoun, E. *Models of Teaching* (7th ed.). Boston: Allyn and Bacon, 2004.

Jonassen, D. H., and Howland, J. *Learning to Solve Problems with Technology: A Constructivist Perspective*. Upper Saddle River, NJ: Merrill Prentice Hall, 2003.

McCain, T., and Jukes, I. *Classroom Assessment: Principles and Practice for Effective Instruction* (2nd ed.). Boston: Allyn and Bacon, 2001.

McHugh, J. Synching Up with the iKid: Connecting to the Twenty-First-Century Student. *Edutopia* 1, no. 7, 2005: 33–35.

Newmann, F. M., and Wehlage, G. G. *Successful School Restructuring: A Report to the Public and Educators by the Center on Organization and Restructuring of Schools*. Madison: University of Wisconsin, Center on Organization and Restructuring of Schools, 1995.

Newmann, F. M., et al., (Eds.). *Authentic Achievement: Restructuring Schools for Intellectual Quality*. San Francisco: Jossey-Bass, 1996.

Oaks, M. M., Grantman, R., and Pedras, M. "Technological Literacy: A Twenty-First Century Imperative." In F. W Parkay and G. Hass (Eds.), *Curriculum Planning: A Contemporary Approach* (7th ed.), pp. 439–445. Boston: Allyn and Bacon, 2001.

Oosterhof, A. *Developing and Using Classroom Assessments*. Upper Saddle River, NJ: Merrill Prentice Hall, 2003.

Parnell, D. *Contextual Teaching Works*. Waco, TX: Center for Occupational Research and Development, 2000.

Rideout, V., Roberts, D. F., and Foehr, U. G. *Generation M: Media in the Lives of 8–18-Year Olds*. Menlo Park, CA: The Kaiser Family Foundation, 2005.

Rosenshine, B. "Explicit Teaching." In D. Berliner and B. Rosenshine (Eds.), *Talks to Teachers*. New York: Random House, 1988.

Rosenshine, B., and Stevens, R. "Teaching Functions." In M. C. Wittrock (Ed.), *Handbook of Research on Teaching* (3rd ed.). New York: Macmillan, 1986.

Schubert, W. H. *Curriculum: Perspective, Paradigm, and Possibility*. New York: Macmillan, 1986.

Sharan, Y., and Sharan, S. "Group Investigation Expands Cooperative Learning." *Educational Leadership* (December/January 1989/90): 17–21.

Stiggins, R. "New Assessment Beliefs for a New School Mission." *Phi Delta Kappan* (September 2004): 22–27.

Thelen, H. A. *Education and the Human Quest*. New York: Harper and Row, 1960.

———. *The Classroom Society: The Construction of Educational Experience*. New York: Wiley, 1981.

Tileston, D. W. *What Every Teacher Should Know about Student Assessment*. Thousand Oaks, CA: Corwin Press, 2004.

Tombari, M. L., and Borich, G. D. *Authentic Assessment in the Classroom: Applications and Practice*. Upper Saddle River, NJ: Merrill, 1999.

Tyler, R. *Basic Principles of Curriculum and Instruction*. Chicago: University of Chicago Press, 1949.

Vygotsky, L. S. *Mind in Society: The Development of Higher Mental Process*. Cambridge, MA: Harvard University Press, 1978.

———. *Thought and Language*. Cambridge, MA: MIT Press, 1986.

Woolfolk, A. E. *Educational Psychology* (8th ed.). Boston: Allyn and Bacon, 2001.

Progressive Organization of Subject Matter

JOHN DEWEY (1859–1952)

ABSTRACT: *In the following, Dewey explains a key principle of progressive education—the continuity of educative experience. Instead of presenting subject matter that is* beyond *the life experiences of learners, the curriculum should begin with material that falls* within *those experiences. Once this connection has been established, the subject can be developed progressively into a fuller, richer, and more organized form; and this new knowledge becomes an "instrumentality" for further learning.*

One consideration stands out clearly when education is conceived in terms of experience. Anything which can be called a study, whether arithmetic, history, geography, or one of the natural sciences, must be derived from materials which at the outset fall within the scope of ordinary life-experience. In this respect the newer education contrasts sharply with procedures which start with facts and truths that are outside the range of the experience of those taught, and which, therefore, have the problem of discovering ways and means of bringing them within experience. Undoubtedly one chief cause for the great success of newer methods in early elementary education has been its observance of the contrary principle.

But finding the material for learning within experience is only the first step. The next step is the progressive development of what is already experienced into a fuller and richer and also more organized form, a form that gradually approximates that in which subject-matter is presented to the skilled, mature person. That this change is possible without departing from the organic connection of education with experience is shown by the fact that this change takes place outside of the school and apart from formal education. The infant, for example, begins with an environment of objects that is very restricted in space and time. That environment steadily expands by the momentum inherent in experience itself without aid from scholastic instruction. As the infant learns to reach, creep, walk, and talk, the intrinsic subject-matter of its experience widens and deepens. It comes into connection with new objects and events which call out new powers, while the exercise of these powers refines and enlarges the content of its experience. Life-space and life-durations are expanded. The environment, the world of experience, constantly grows larger and, so to speak, thicker. The educator who receives the child at the end of this period has to find ways for doing consciously and deliberately what "nature" accomplishes in the earlier years.

It is hardly necessary to insist upon the first of the two conditions which have been specified. It is a cardinal precept of the newer school of education that the beginning of instruction shall be made with the experience learners already have; that this experience and the capacities that have been developed during its course provide the starting point for all further learning. I am not so sure that the other condition, that of orderly development toward expansion and organization of subject-matter through growth of experience, receives as much attention. Yet the principle of continuity of educative experience requires that equal thought and attention be given to solution of this aspect of the educational problem. Undoubtedly this phase of the problem is more difficult than the other. Those who deal with the preschool child, with the kindergarten child, and with the boy and girl of the early primary years do not have much difficulty in determining the range of past experience or in finding activities that connect in vital ways with it. With older children both factors of the problem offer increased difficulties to the educator. It is harder to find out the background of the experience of individuals and harder to find out just how the subject-matters already contained in that experience shall be directed so as to lead out to larger and better organized fields.

It is a mistake to suppose that the principle of the leading on of experience to something different is adequately satisfied simply by giving pupils some new experiences any more than it is by seeing to it that they have greater skill and ease in dealing with things with which they are already familiar. It is also essential that the new objects and events be related intellectually to those of earlier experiences, and this means that there be some advance made in conscious articulation of facts and ideas. It thus becomes the office of the educator to select those things within the range of existing experience that have the promise and potentiality of presenting new problems which by stimulating new ways of observation and judgment will expand the area of further experience. He must constantly regard what is already won not as a fixed possession but as an agency and instrumentality for opening new fields which make new demands upon existing powers of observation and of intelligent use of memory. Connectedness in growth must be his constant watchword.

The educator more than the member of any other profession is concerned to have a long look ahead. The physician may feel his job done when he has restored a patient to health. He has undoubtedly the obligation of advising him how to live so as to avoid similar troubles in the future. But, after all, the conduct of his life is his own affair, not the physician's; and what is more important for the present point is that as far as the physician does occupy himself with instruction and advice as to the future of his patient he takes upon himself the function of an educator. The lawyer is occupied with winning a suit for his client or getting the latter out of some complication into which he has got himself. If it goes beyond the case presented to him he too becomes an educator. The educator by the very nature of

his work is obliged to see his present work in terms of what it accomplishes, or fails to accomplish, for a future whose objects are linked with those of the present.

Here, again, the problem for the progressive educator is more difficult than for the teacher in the traditional school. The latter had indeed to look ahead. But unless his personality and enthusiasm took him beyond the limits that hedged in the traditional school, he could content himself with thinking of the next examination period or the promotion to the next class. He could envisage the future in terms of factors that lay within the requirements of the school system as that conventionally existed. There is incumbent upon the teacher who links education and actual experience together a more serious and a harder business. He must be aware of the potentialities for leading students into new fields which belong to experiences already had, and must use this knowledge as his criterion for selection and arrangement of the conditions that influence their present experience.

Because the studies of the traditional school consisted of subject-matter that was selected and arranged on the basis of the judgment of adults as to what would be useful for the young sometime in the future, the material to be learned was settled upon outside the present life-experience of the learner. In consequence, it had to do with the past; it was such as had proved useful to men in past ages. By reaction to an opposite extreme, as unfortunate as it was probably natural under the circumstances, the sound idea that education should derive its materials from present experience and should enable the learner to cope with the problems of the present and future has often been converted into the idea that progressive schools can to a very large extent ignore the past. If the present could be cut off from the past, this conclusion would be sound. But the achievements of the past provide the only means at command for understanding the present. Just as the individual has to draw in memory upon his own past to understand the conditions in which he individually finds himself, so the issues and problems of present *social* life are in such intimate and direct connection with the past that students cannot be prepared to understand either these problems or the best way of dealing with them without delving into their roots in the past. In other words, the sound principle that the objectives of learning are in the future and its immediate materials are in present experience can be carried into effect only in the degree that present experience is stretched, as it were, backward. It can expand into the future only as it is also enlarged to take in the past.

John Dewey was, at various times during his career, professor of philosophy, Columbia University; head of the Department of Philosophy and director of the School of Education at the University of Chicago; and professor of philosophy at the University of Michigan.

QUESTIONS FOR REFLECTION

1. How does a curriculum that is organized according to Dewey's ideas incorporate the past, present, and future?
2. What criticisms might be made regarding Dewey's position that "the beginning of instruction [should] be made with the experience learners already have"? How would Dewey respond to these criticisms?
3. What techniques can curriculum planners and teachers use to determine the learners' "range of past experiences"?

Structures in Learning

JEROME S. BRUNER

ABSTRACT: Each discipline of knowledge has a structure, and students should be provided with learning experiences that enable them to "discover" that structure. The aim of learning, therefore, is to acquire the processes of inquiry that characterize the discipline, rather than to merely learn "about" the discipline.

Every subject has a structure, a rightness, a beauty. It is this structure that provides the underlying simplicity of things, and it is by learning its nature that we come to appreciate the intrinsic meaning of a subject.

Let me illustrate by reference to geography. Children in the fifth grade of a suburban school were about to study the geography of the Central states as part of a social studies unit. Previous units on the Southeastern states, taught by rote, had proved a bore. Could geography be taught as a rational discipline? Determined to find out, the teachers devised a unit in which students would have to figure out not only where things are located, but why they are there. This involves a sense of the structure of geography.

The children were given a map of the Central states in which only rivers, large bodies of water, agricultural products, and natural resources were shown. They were not allowed to consult their books. Their task was to find Chicago, "the largest city in the North Central states."

The argument got under way immediately. One child came up with the idea that Chicago must be on the junction of the three large lakes. No matter that at this point he did not know the names of the lakes—Huron, Superior, and Michigan—his theory was well reasoned. A big city produced a lot of products, and the easiest and most logical way to ship these products is by water.

But a second child rose immediately to the opposition. A big city needed lots of food, and he placed Chicago where there are corn and hogs—right in the middle of Iowa.

A third child saw the issue more broadly—recognizing virtues in both previous arguments. He pointed out that large quantities of food can be grown in river valleys. Whether he had learned this from a previous social studies unit or from raising carrot seeds, we shall never know. If you had a river, he reasoned, you had not only food but transportation. He pointed to a spot on the map not far from St. Louis. "There is where Chicago *ought* to be." Would that graduate students would always do so well!

Not all the answers were so closely reasoned, though even the wild ones had about them a sense of the necessity involved in a city's location.

One argued, for example, that all American cities have skyscrapers, which require steel, so he placed Chicago in the middle of the Mesabi Range. At least he was thinking on his own, with a sense of the constraints imposed on the location of cities.

After forty-five minutes, the children were told they could pull down the "real" wall map (the one with names) and see where Chicago really is. After the map was down, each of the contending parties pointed out how close they had come to being right. Chicago had not been located. But the location of cities was no longer a matter of unthinking chance for this group of children.

What had the children learned? A way of thinking about geography, a way of dealing with its raw data.

They had learned that there is some relationship between the requirements of living and man's habitat. If that is all they got out of their geography lesson, that is plenty. Did they remember which is Lake Huron? Lake Superior? Lake Michigan? Do you?

Teachers have asked me about "the new curricula" as though they were some special magic potion. They are nothing of the sort. The new curricula, like our little exercise in geography, are based on the fact that knowledge has an internal connectedness, a meaningfulness, and that for facts to be appreciated and understood and remembered, they must be fitted into that internal meaningful context.

The set of prime numbers is not some arbitrary nonsense. What can be said about quantities that cannot be arranged into multiple columns and rows? Discussing that will get you on to the structure of primes and factorability.

It often takes the deepest minds to discern the simplest structure in knowledge. For this reason if for no other, the great scholar and the great scientist and the greatly compassionate person are needed in the building of new curricula.

There is one other point. Our geographical example made much of discovery. What difference does discovery make in the learning of the young? First, let it be clear what the act of discovery entails. It is only rarely on the frontier of knowledge that new facts are "discovered" in the sense of being encountered, as Newton suggested, as "islands of truth in an uncharted sea of ignorance." Discovery, whether by a schoolboy going it on his own or by a scientist, is most often a matter of rearranging or transforming evidence in such a way that one is not enabled to go beyond the evidence to new insights. Discovery involves the finding of the right structure, the meaningfulness.

Consider now what benefits the child might derive from the experience of learning through his own discoveries. These benefits can be discussed in terms of increased intellectual potency, intrinsic rewards, useful learning techniques, and better memory processes.

For the child to develop *intellectual potency*, he must be encouraged to search out and find regularities and relationships in his environment. To do this, he needs to be armed with the expectancy that there is something for him to find and, once aroused by this expectancy, he must devise his own ways of searching and finding.

Emphasis on discovery in learning has the effect upon the learner of leading him to be a constructionist—to organize what he encounters in such a manner that he not only discovers regularity and relatedness, but also avoids the kind of information drift that fails to keep account of how the information will be used.

In speaking of *intrinsic motives* for learning (as opposed to extrinsic motives), it must be recognized that much of the problem in leading a child to effective cognitive activity is to free him from the immediate control of environmental punishments and rewards.

For example, studies show that children who seem to be early over-achievers in school are likely to be seekers after the "right way to do it" and that their capacity for transforming their learning into useful thought structures tends to be less than that of children merely achieving at levels predicted by intelligence tests.

The hypothesis drawn from these studies is that if a child is able to approach learning as a task of discovering something rather than "learning about it" he will tend to find a more personally meaningful reward in his own competency and self-achievement in the subject than he will find in the approval of others.

There are many ways of coming to the *techniques of inquiry*, or the heuristics of discovery. One of them is by careful study of the formalization of these techniques in logic, statistics, mathematics, and the like. If a child is going to pursue inquiry as an eventual way of life, particularly in the sciences, formal study is essential. Yet, whoever has taught kindergarten and the early primary grades (periods of intense inquiry) knows that an understanding of the formal aspect of inquiry is not sufficient or always possible.

Children appear to have a series of attitudes and activities they associate with inquiry. Rather than a formal approach to the relevance of variables in their search, they depend on their sense of what things among an ensemble of things "smell right" as being of the proper order of magnitude or scope of severity.

It is evident then that if children are to learn the working techniques of discovery, they must be afforded the opportunities of problem solving. The more they practice problem solving, the more likely they are to generalize what they learn into a style of inquiry that serves for any kind of task they may encounter. It is doubtful that anyone ever improves in the art and technique of inquiry by any other means than engaging in inquiry, or problem solving.

The first premise in a theory concerning the *improvement of memory processes* is that the principal problem of human memory is not storage, but retrieval. The premise may be inferred from the fact that recognition (i.e., recall with the aid of maximum prompts) is extraordinarily good in human beings—particularly in comparison to spontaneous recall when information must be recalled without external aids or prompts. The key to retrieval is organization.

There are myriad findings to indicate that any organization of information that reduces the collective complexity of material by embedding it into a mental structure the child has constructed will make that material more accessible for retrieval. In sum, the child's very attitudes and activities that characterize "figuring out" or "discovering" things for himself also seem to have the effect of making material easier to remember.

If man's intellectual excellence is the most important among his perfections (as Maimonides, the great Hispanic-Judaic philosopher once said), then it is also the case that the most uniquely personal of all that man knows is that which he discovers for himself. What difference does it make when we encourage discovery in the young? It creates, as Maimonides would put it, a special and unique relation between knowledge possessed and the possessor.

After a career as professor of psychology and director, Center for Cognitive Studies, Harvard University, *Jerome Bruner* was Watts Chair of Experimental Psychology, Oxford University, England, 1972–1979.

QUESTIONS FOR REFLECTION

1. What does Bruner mean when he states: "It often takes the deepest minds to discern the simplest structure in knowledge"? Can you give an example?
2. What is "intellectual potency," and how can it be developed within students?
3. What is "information drift," and what curricular experiences help students avoid it?
4. In recommending the development of "new" curricula, why does Bruner call for the involvement of the "greatly compassionate person" as well as "the great scholar and the great scientist"?

Nurturing the Life of the Mind

KATHLEEN VAIL

ABSTRACT: *Although anti-intellectualism is part of the history and culture of the United States, it does not have to define the nation's schools. Schools must rid themselves of anti-intellectualism and make sure that true intellect has the chance to flourish by taking a critical look at their curriculum, what their teachers are reading, and the way in which they treat academically gifted students. In fact, a reintroduction of the liberal arts—literature, history, poetry, philosophy, and art—might be the best way to rid schools of anti-intellectualism.*

You don't need to look far for evidence that we Americans don't place a very high value on intellect. Our heroes are athletes, entertainers, and entrepreneurs, not scholars. But our schools, with their high academic standards, high-stakes tests, and performance bonuses for improved achievement scores—surely our schools are bastions of intellectualism?

Not necessarily.

Your parents and community, even your teachers and administrators, perhaps even you, might unwittingly be holding back your schools from cultivating intellect in your students and exposing them to the joys of the life of the mind.

Why? Because as a nation, we just don't trust brainy people. The stereotype of the muddle-headed professor—the one who can recite passages of Dante's *Inferno* in the original Italian but doesn't realize his pants are on backwards—is alive and well. We'd rather our children were sociable than scholarly. The results of a 1995 Public Agenda survey clearly point out our distrust of scholars and academics. Seven out of 10 Americans agreed that "people who are highly educated often turn out to be book smart but lack the common sense and understanding of regular folk." Seven out of 10 respondents said they would be very or somewhat concerned if their child earned excellent grades but had only a few close friends and seldom participated in social activities. In focus groups, a New Jersey parent said, "If you focus on the brain, it becomes too tedious." A Cincinnati woman avowed, "If everyone were a genius, it would be a dull world."

Schools are places where we send our children to get a practical education—not to pursue knowledge for knowledge's sake. Symptoms of pervasive anti-intellectualism in our schools aren't difficult to find:

- A former school board member in Armonk, N.Y., pulled her son and daughter out of the public schools and placed them in a private school. She'd become increasingly frustrated trying to get more challenging classes for her son. Some staff members resisted creating a gifted program because the other students "would feel bad about not being selected," she said.

- A Columbiana, Ala., school board member asked administrators to investigate middle school English teacher Pam Cooper, who was teaching Shakespeare and Chaucer to eighth-graders. The board member worried that students shouldn't be reading books they'd later encounter in high school literature classes, books that seemed to be beyond their ability level.

- School boards around the country are questioning the merit of homework. The Piscataway, NJ., school board, for example, recently limited the amount of homework teachers could assign, discouraged weekend and holiday assignments, and prohibited teachers from grading work done at home. Parents complained that homework was interfering with their children's extracurricular activities.

"Schools have always been in a society where practical is more important than intellectual," says education historian and writer Diane Ravitch. "Schools could be a counterbalance." Ravitch's latest book, *Left Back: A Century of Failed School Reforms,* traces what she considers the roots of anti-intellectualism in our schools. Schools, she concludes, are anything but a counterbalance to American's distaste for intellectual pursuits.

But they could and should be. When we encourage our children to reject the life of the mind, we leave them vulnerable to exploitation and control. Without the ability to think critically, to defend their ideas and understand the ideas of others, they cannot fully participate in our democracy. If we continue along this path, says writer Earl Shorris, our nation will suffer. "We will become a second-rate country," he says. "We will have a less civil society."

AN AMERICAN TRADITION

"Intellect is resented as a form of power or privilege," wrote historian and professor Richard Hofstadter in *Anti-Intellectualism in American Life,* a Pulitzer-Prize winning book tracing the roots of anti-intellectualism in U.S. politics, religion, and education. Published in 1963, it is considered a watershed book on the subject and rings as true today as it did 30 years ago.

Animosity toward intellectuals is in our country's DNA. From the beginning of our nation's history, according to Hofstadter, our democratic and populist urges have driven us to reject anything that smacks of elitism. Practicality, common sense, and native intelligence have been considered more noble qualities than anything you could learn from a book. Ralph Waldo Emerson and other Transcendentalist philosophers of the 19th century thought schooling and rigorous book learning put unnatural restraints on children. Emerson wrote in his journal: "We are shut up in schools and college recitation rooms for ten or fifteen years and come out at last with a bellyful of words and do not know a thing."

Mark Twain's *Huckleberry Finn* exemplified American anti-intellectualism. The novel's hero avoids being civilized—going to school and learning to read—so he can preserve his innate goodness.

Intellect, according to Hofstadter, is different from native intelligence, a quality we grudgingly admire. Intellect is the critical, creative, and contemplative side of the mind. Intelligence seeks to grasp, manipulate, re-order, and adjust, while intellect examines, ponders, wonders, theorizes, criticizes, and imagines.

School remains a place where intellect is mistrusted. As Hofstadter put it, our country's educational system is in the grips of people who "joyfully and militantly proclaim their hostility to intellect and their eagerness to identify with children who show the least intellectual promise."

Anti-intellectualism is part of our history and our culture, but it doesn't have to define our schools. Many ideas exist on how to make school a place where the life of the mind is valued as much as high test scores or athletic prowess or social status. Some of those ideas contradict each other, and some of the people who espouse them have distinct political agendas or leanings. But true intellect is nonpartisan. The best way to make sure it can flower in your schools is to start by taking a critical look at your curriculum, your teachers, and your school culture.

WHAT ARE YOU TEACHING?

The idea that children must be entertained and feel good while they learn has been embraced by many well-meaning educators. In many classrooms, as a result, students are watching movies, working on multimedia presentations, surfing the Internet, putting on plays, and dissecting popular song lyrics. The idea is to motivate students, but the emphasis on enjoyment as a facile substitute for engagement creates a culture in which students are not likely to challenge themselves or stretch their abilities. After all, if students are not shown the intrinsic rewards that come from working hard to understand a concept, they won't do it on their own. The probable result? A life spent shying away from books, poetry, art, music, public policy discussions—anything that takes an effort to understand or appreciate and has no immediate or obvious payoff.

Project-based learning always has the potential to be based on fun rather than content, says former teacher and administrator Elaine McEwan, who wrote *Angry Parents, Failing Schools: What's Wrong with Public Schools and What You Can Do*

About It. She uses the example of a class of academically struggling elementary school students in Arizona that spent 37 hours—more than a school week—building a papier-mache dinosaur. The local newspaper even ran a photo of the students and their handiwork. "Those kids couldn't read well, and they spent all that time messing with chicken wire and wheat paste," says McEwan.

The trend toward teaching skills rather than content has become especially popular with the advent of the Internet. Because information is changing so quickly, the argument goes, it makes more sense to teach students how to find information than to impart it to them. But if students are deprived of content and context, their forays into the Internet might not go beyond looking up the Backstreet Boys web site.

One of the most prominent proponents of imparting knowledge to children along with the skills to probe more deeply is E. D. Hirsch, the founder of the Core Knowledge curriculum approach and author of *Cultural Literacy: What Every American Needs to Know*. The University of Virginia English professor once gave a reading comprehension test to a community college class in Richmond, Va. The students were tested on a passage comparing Robert E. Lee to Ulysses S. Grant. Hirsch was astounded to discover that most of the students, living in an area rich with Civil War history, had no idea who either man was. This experience gave Hirsch the idea for compiling his dictionary of cultural literacy—a basic body of knowledge that educated people should have at their command to be successful in school and in life.

The idea of a core body of knowledge appeals to educators such as McEwan, who worry that many teachers value process over content. Project-based learning is popular with parents, she says, because they want their children to have fun.

The quality of content concerns Santa Monica, Calif., English teacher Carol Jago, who directs the California Reading and Literature Project at the University of California Los Angeles. Jago resists assigning popular novels in her English classes, believing that students at all grade levels should read the classics.

"In the interests of being more inclusive, we've backed away from making demands on students," says Jago. "We should expand and challenge them." Teachers should help students enter into intelligent discourse about what is enduring about a particular piece of literature, she says, but it's hard for teachers to provide the necessary connections for their students and help them develop critical thinking skills. In some classrooms, Jago says, the teachers have a pact with their students: "I won't work too hard; you won't work too hard."

Jago worries that the well-publicized trend toward school boards limiting homework could have repercussions in districts all over the country. If English teachers can't assign homework, she asks, how will they teach novels to their students? The fastest way to create two classes of students is to do away with homework, she says. The Advanced Placement kids will do the reading anyway. The kids who need the extra help the most will fall by the wayside.

Diane Ravitch points to the no-homework trend as a symptom of anti-intellectualism in the schools. "Homework is more time for students to read and write," she says. Cutting back on homework to give students more time to socialize hardly encourages them to take their schoolwork more seriously.

WHAT ARE YOUR TEACHERS READING?

"All too often . . . in the history of the United States, the school teacher has been in no position to serve as a model to the intellectual life," Hofstadter wrote. "Too often he has not only no claims to an intellectual life of his own, but not even an adequate workmanlike competence in the skills he is supposed to impart."

Harsh words, perhaps, but Hofstadter's idea makes sense: If teachers—on the front line of education—don't have an active intellectual life, they're not likely to communicate a love of learning and critical thinking to their students.

In his 1995 book, *Out of Our Minds: Anti-Intellectualism and Talent Development in American Schools,* Craig Howley cites several

studies about the education and habits of public school teachers. According to one study, prospective teachers take fewer liberal arts courses than their counterparts in other arts and science majors—and fewer upper-division courses in any subject except pedagogy. It appears, Howley writes, that prospective teachers do not often make a special effort during their college years to pursue advanced study in fields other than pedagogy.

Frequent reading of literature in academic fields is the mark of the scholar, Howley says, so it's logical to look at teachers' reading habits. Readers tend to be more reflective and more critical than nonreaders, argues Howley, who found that studies of teachers' reading showed two patterns: One is that teachers don't read very much—on average, just 3.2 books a year. (In fact, 11 percent of those surveyed said they had not read a single book during the current year.) The second pattern is that when teachers do read, they prefer popular books rather than scholarly or professional literature. Of those who were reading about education, most were reading books intended for the general public.

It's true that U.S. teachers have traditionally been poorly paid and not well respected, which means that the best and the brightest are often not attracted to teaching. But until teachers can be role models and exhibit their own love of learning and academics, the children won't get it.

"Create a culture among the adults, a community of adults who are learners, who are excited about ideas in the other disciplines," says Deborah Meier, educator and author of *The Power of Their Ideas.* "The school must represent the culture it wants to encourage. If we want kids to feel that an intellectual life belongs to them, it must belong to the teacher, too."

HOW DO YOU TREAT YOUR SMART KIDS?

"Far from conceiving the mediocre, reluctant, or incapable student as an obstacle or special problem in a school system devoted to educating the interested, the capable, and the gifted," wrote

Hofstadter, "American education entered upon a crusade to exalt the academically uninterested or ungifted child into a kind of cult-hero."

If schools were strongholds of intellect, then the most academically able students would be the stars. But take a look at any web site aimed at parents of gifted children, and you'll see they say gifted students have almost as much trouble in school as students who don't do well. Children with advanced intellectual ability often are not given the tools they need to succeed. Ridiculed by classmates, resented by teachers, unchallenged by the standard curriculum, they're often ostracized, unhappy, or just plain bored.

Carolyn Kottmeyer, a Pennsylvania mother of two gifted daughters, recounts how a resentful fifth-grade math teacher taunted the older daughter, who received individual instruction from another math teacher. More than once, the regular math teacher walked past the library where the girl was studying. Once she stopped and asked her, "What's a Box-and-Whiskers Plot?" When the girl didn't know, the teacher turned to the class of students standing in the hallway and said, "And you think you're such a genius in math."

Such stories are shockingly common. One parent on Kottmeyer's web site says a teacher told her it was good for her sixth-grade son to be bored because "it prepares him for real life." These parents have tales of teachers who say excessive reading will hurt their child's eyesight; administrators who don't want to allow a boy to skip a grade because others will be getting their driver's licenses before him; principals who don't want to advance students because other parents will ask for the same privilege. Parents tell of teachers and principals who recommend Ritalin for children who are acting up in class because they are bored, or who deny gifted kids entrance to advanced classes because they say the students have behavior problems brought on by boredom.

Smart kids question teachers and are often nonconformists. They are taunted by their peers for being too smart or knowing too much. Some children, in desperation to fit in, hide their academic gifts. "Parents see kids who are excited about going to school, then slowly getting turned off," says Peter Rosenstein, executive director of the National Association for Gifted Children, in Washington, D.C. "Parents find out that nothing the teacher taught that day was new to the child."

Lynne Bernstein, the New York school board member who took her children out of the public school, says her son had a teacher who told him to stop raising his hand and let other children answer some questions. "You get ridiculed, you stop talking," says Bernstein.

The academic reputation of the affluent Armonk school district was the reason Bernstein and her family moved to the community. Instead, she found that a culture of noncompetition was preventing the teachers and staff from pushing kids to do more. "My kids are bright students, and they weren't being challenged," she says.

After winning election to the school board three years ago, Bernstein started a committee to look at what the district was offering gifted students. There was a great deal of resistance even to studying the issue, she says—let alone establishing a program for more advanced students.

But small changes are coming to the district now, including offering additional honors classes at the high school level. Parents are growing nervous because their children aren't being accepted into top colleges, says Bernstein. These parents are pressuring the district to change.

"Learning comes with hard work. It's a struggle," says Bernstein. "We aren't pushing these kids enough, on the bottom, top, and middle."

When the smartest students aren't rewarded and sometimes even feel punished for being academically gifted, other students in a school are hardly likely to see any rewards in doing well, either.

"Schools must create a culture where learning is valued and people get excited about information," says former teacher McEwan. "You don't have to be embarrassed to use big words. We have to make learning cool."

BUT IS IT PRACTICAL?

The purpose of public schools has never been to create thinking, analyzing, intellectual citizens, charges John Taylor Gatto, a 30-year New York City public school teacher and New York State Teacher of the Year in 1991. And that's why they're not doing it now. Today's schools are products of 19th-century industrialists, whose purpose was to prepare people to be good employees—docile, productive, and addicted consumers. And if that's what the public wants, says Gatto, using the Socratic method to teach children to critique great works and question the way things are is a hazard to society.

"Intellect requires a critical mind, not a retentive mind," says Gatto. "Schools can't tolerate questioning."

Gatto is an outspoken critic of the public schools and an advocate of home schooling. He argues that our schools are modeled after factories where repetition and conformity are stressed over thought and expression. "The bell schedule is insane," says Gatto. "It's a rat-training device to make nothing mean very much." When you are interrupted over and over again, what you are doing loses importance, he says. "It creates apathy."

In fact, Gatto and others contend, most of what we consider to be education is actually training. The children at poorer schools receive vocational training. The children in middle-class and affluent schools receive training to become what [Howley] calls "intelligent careerists." In this role, he says, they are capable of responding efficiently and pragmatically to work-related problems but unable, or at least disinclined, to examine the broad social, economic, and political context in which the problems are set.

The emphasis on training over education clearly stems from Americans' love of practicality. It's easy to convince parents that their children need certain courses so they can get high-paying jobs when they graduate. But when we believe that the only reason to get an education is to make money, says Howley, "we create a society that thinks about jobs and profit making as universals."

Worse, he says, the idea that education is solely a means to earn money has made us into narcissists whose only goal in life is to make more money—not to be responsible to each other or our community.

A CASE FOR THE HUMANITIES

Propose a rigorous course of study in the humanities and liberal arts, and you'll hear protests: It's traditional. It's elitist. It's full of dead white European males. It's not inclusive. It's not relevant. It's not practical. And besides, it's too hard for our students.

Perhaps the best way to rid schools of anti-intellectualism is to reintroduce liberal arts: literature, history, poetry, philosophy, art. Through these subjects, students can learn mankind's best ideas, and they can begin constructing their own life of the mind.

When New York writer Earl Shorris started research for a book on the poor in the United States, he ended up establishing a program that brings the humanities to the inner-city poor. Students are chosen on the basis of their income, their ability to read, and their desire. Some are homeless, some never finished high school, some are in prison, some struggle with drug addiction, but they are taught by professors from elite universities.

"You've been cheated," Shorris tells his students. "Rich people learn the humanities; you didn't. The humanities are a foundation for getting along in the world, for thinking, for learning to reflect on the world instead of just reacting to whatever force is turned against you. . . . Will the humanities make you rich? Yes, absolutely. But not in terms of money. In terms of life."

Shorris sees evidence that the humanities can improve the quality of our lives. In his book, *Riches for the Poor,* he recounts a conversation with one of his students. The man called Shorris to tell him about a problem with a colleague who was making him so angry that he wanted to hit her. He restrained himself, and saved his job, he said, by asking himself, "What would Socrates do?"

After five years, with the support of private foundations and government grants, Shorris' Clemente Course in the Humanities is being taught at about two dozen sites in the United States, Canada, and Mexico. And he is working on a program that would bring the course to public school teachers who would, in turn, pass their knowledge on to their students.

Teaching the humanities is ultimately more practical than training students to perform specific jobs, says Shorris: "If you give human beings the best that human beings have produced, they are changed."

Kathleen Vail is an associate editor of the *American School Board Journal.*

QUESTIONS FOR REFLECTION

1. Do you agree with Vail that there is a spirit of anti-intellectualism in America's schools? Who does she blame for what she sees as an anti-intellectualism and what has caused this trend?
2. What are Vail's solutions to rid the schools of anti-intellectualism and does she offer a practical and realistic plan for educators? What barriers within the school might teachers and school leaders face when attempting to implement her ideas?
3. Is anti-intellectualism too culturally embedded in the American psyche for schools to make a difference regarding intellectual pursuits or can schools accomplish the task of reintroducing intellectualism into the culture by way of the curriculum?

The Many Faces of Leadership

CHARLOTTE DANIELSON

ABSTRACT: Charlotte Danielson explores the concept of teachers as leaders and discusses how teachers can find a wealth of opportunities to extend their influence beyond their own classrooms to their teaching teams, schools, and districts. Teacher leaders, she points out, are in a position to take a long view of a school's future and can carry out long-range projects that many administrators will not be at the school to see completed.

In every good school, there are teachers whose vision extends beyond their own classrooms—even beyond their own teams or departments. Such teachers recognize that students' school experiences depend not only on interaction with individual teachers, but also on the complex systems in place throughout the school and district. This awareness prompts these teachers to want to influence change. They experience professional restlessness—what some have called the "leadership itch." Sometimes on their own initiative and sometimes within a more formal structure, these professionals find a variety of ways to exercise teacher leadership.

WHY TEACHER LEADERSHIP?

Today more than ever, a number of interconnected factors argue for the necessity of teacher leadership in schools. Teaching is a flat profession. In most professions, as the practitioner gains experience, he or she has the opportunity to exercise greater responsibility and assume more significant challenges. This is not true of teaching. The 20-year veteran's responsibilities are essentially the same as those of the newly licensed novice. In many settings, the only way for a teacher to extend his or her influence is to become an administrator. Many teachers recognize that this is not the right avenue for them. The job of an administrator entails work that does not interest them, but they still have the urge to exercise wider influence in their schools and in the profession. This desire for greater responsibility, if left unfulfilled, can lead to frustration and even cynicism.

Teachers' tenure in schools is longer than that of administrators. In many settings, administrators remain in their positions for only three to four years, whereas teachers stay far longer. Teachers often hold the institutional memory; they are the custodians of the school culture. School districts that want to improve make a wise investment when they cultivate and encourage teacher leaders, because they are in a position to take the long view and carry out long-range projects.

The demands of the modern principalship are practically impossible to meet. Principals today are expected to be visionaries (instilling a sense of purpose in their staff) and competent managers (maintaining the physical plant, submitting budgets on time), as well as instructional leaders (coaching teachers in the nuances of classroom practice). In addition, the principal has become the point person for accountability requirements imposed by states and the federal government, and he or she must respond to multiple stakeholders (parents, staff members, the district central office, and the larger community). Under such pressure from a range of sources, many administrators simply cannot devote enough time and energy to school improvement.

Principals have limited expertise. Like all educators, most principals have their own areas of instructional expertise. A principal who was formerly a mathematics teacher may know a lot about research-based instructional practices in math, but not much about instruction in world languages. The school administrator cannot be an expert in everything. Individual teachers, of course, have their own particular areas of knowledge, but a group of teacher leaders can supply the variety of professional knowledge needed for sustained school improvement.

Given these factors, school improvement depends more than ever on the active involvement of teacher leaders. School administrators can't do it all.

Qualities and Skills of Teacher Leaders

Teacher leaders serve in two fundamental types of roles: formal and informal. Formal teacher leaders fill such roles as department chair, master teacher, or instructional coach. These individuals typically apply for their positions and are chosen through a selection process. Ideally, they also receive training for their new responsibilities. Formal teacher leaders play vital roles in most schools. In many cases, these teacher leaders manage curriculum projects, facilitate teacher study groups, provide workshops, and order materials. They may also evaluate other teachers, in which case their colleagues are likely to regard them as pseudoadministrators.

Informal teacher leaders, in contrast, emerge spontaneously and organically from the teacher ranks. Instead of being selected, they take the initiative to address a problem or institute a new program. They have no positional authority; their influence stems from the respect they command from their colleagues through their expertise and practice.

Whether they are selected for a formal leadership role or spontaneously assume an informal role, effective teacher leaders exhibit important skills, values, and dispositions. Teacher leaders call others to action and energize them with the aim of improving teaching and learning. As Michael Fullan writes: "The litmus test of all leadership is whether it mobilizes people's commitment to putting their energy into actions designed to improve things. It is individual commitment, but above all it is collective mobilization."[1]

[1] Fullan, M. (2007). *Leading in a culture of change* (rev. ed.). San Francisco: Jossey-Bass, p. 9.

A hallmark of leadership, therefore, is the ability to collaborate with others. Teacher leaders must enlist colleagues to support their vision, build consensus among diverse groups of educators, and convince others of the importance of what they are proposing and the feasibility of their general plan for improvement. They must be respected for their own instructional skills. They also must understand evidence and information and recognize the need to focus on those aspects of the schools program that will yield important gains in student learning.

A number of values and dispositions make certain individuals ideally suited for teacher leadership. Effective teacher leaders are open-minded and respectful of others' views. They display optimism and enthusiasm, confidence and decisiveness. They persevere and do not permit setbacks to derail an important initiative they are pursuing. On the other hand, they are flexible and willing to try a different approach if the first effort runs into roadblocks.

Many attributes of good teacher leaders are fundamentally the same as the attributes of good teachers: persuasiveness, open-mindedness, flexibility, confidence, and expertise in their fields. Despite these similarities, however, working with colleagues is profoundly different from working with students, and the skills that teachers learn in their preparation programs do not necessarily prepare them to extend their leadership beyond their own classrooms. To assume a leadership role, they may need expertise in curriculum planning, assessment design, data analysis, and the like. They may also need to develop the abilities to listen actively, facilitate meetings, keep a group discussion on track, decide on a course of action, and monitor progress. These skills are not typically taught in teacher preparation programs.

WHAT DO TEACHER LEADERS DO?

Three main areas of school life benefit from the involvement of teacher leaders (see "Where Teacher Leaders Extend Their Reach"). In each area, this involvement may take place within the teacher leader's own department or team, across the school, or beyond the school. No setting is more "advanced" than another; each has its own requirements and calls on its own particular skills and inclinations.

Within the Department or Team

Leading change within one's own department or team may require considerable interpersonal skill and tact. The success of such an effort also depends on the teacher leader's having established credibility and trust with his or her colleagues.

Leadership at this level can take many forms. Teacher leaders may coordinate a program in which students in the 6th grade read to kindergarten students during their lunch period. Or they may invite their colleagues to examine the reasons for student underperformance in writing. In many different ways, teacher leaders mobilize the efforts of their closest colleagues to enhance the school's program for the benefit of students.

For example, William, a middle school math teacher, brought a situation to his 6th grade teaching team, asking for their thoughts. He had noticed that many of the girls in his class were not participating in group activities as enthusiastically as he expected.

One of William's colleagues offered to visit his class and see whether she could help him understand the situation better. She observed several classes and took notes on what she saw and heard: the nature of the activities students were asked to do, types of questions the teacher and students asked, interactions among the students, and so on.

What she observed was stunning: William, unknown to himself, was not challenging the girls in the class as much as the boys: When a girl encountered difficulty, he supplied the answer or a significant "hint"; he called on the boys more frequently than the girls to answer challenging questions; and he was more likely to encourage the boys to challenge one another's thinking about the math problems.

William was astonished at his colleague's findings and set about changing his behavior. His approach to this situation revealed extraordinary openness and courage. He and his colleague reported their findings and William's plan for action to the rest of the team. Soon, other teachers on the 6th grade team set about systematically assisting one another with similar questions and situations, as well as bringing the results back to the team for discussion.

Across the School

Some of the most powerful opportunities for teacher leadership relate to areas that have enormous influence on the daily lives of students across the school, such as the master schedule, grading policy, or student programs. For example, many students experience the most memorable activities of their school careers through participating in the school play, being on the debate team, or taking an advanced class that enables them to engage deeply with academic content. Ensuring that students have full access to such opportunities involves a collective effort, requiring discussion and consideration of alternatives. This is the work of leadership. And although administrators play an important facilitative role, teachers—who are closer to the action—frequently put forward important ideas and can assume a leadership role.

Grading policies also have a profound effect on how students experience their learning activities. Jennifer, a high school history teacher, found herself troubled by her students' responses to tests and papers. She read their work carefully and provided thoughtful feedback. But when she returned their papers, the students seemed interested only in the grade; some never even read her careful comments. Also, she noticed that some students would decline to turn in work altogether if they knew it was going to be late, believing that it was not "worth it" to complete it.

Jennifer invited interested teachers from across the school to join her in exploring alternate approaches to grading. The teachers met for an entire school year, and each of them conducted systematic discussions with their students. Toward the end of the year, the group made a recommen-

dation to the entire faculty; as a result, the school piloted a different grading system the following year that incorporated formative assessment and student self-assessment. At the end of three years, the school's approach to grading was considerably different; the teachers were convinced that the new system resulted in greater student buy-in and commitment to high-quality work.

Beyond the School

Teacher leaders contribute beyond their own school when they participate in a districtwide teacher evaluation committee or curriculum team, make a presentation at a state or national conference, serve on a state standards board, or speak at a school board meeting as the voice of teachers in the community. Again, these teachers are doing more than teaching their own students (as brilliant as they may be in that work); they are influencing the larger education environment in their communities and perhaps their states.

For example, Maria, a high school Spanish teacher, noticed that there weren't good opportunities for her to meet with and learn from other Spanish teachers in the area. The state organization of language teachers had not recruited many members in her school or in neighboring schools.

Maria decided to begin a chapter of the American Association of Teachers of Spanish and Portuguese in her area. She sent e-mail notices to teachers in other schools and scheduled an organizational meeting. Although response was slow at first, over the course of several years the chapter became vibrant. Before long, members were scheduling visits to one another's schools and preparing presentations for the state conference.

CONDITIONS THAT PROMOTE TEACHER LEADERSHIP

Not every school is hospitable to the emergence of teacher leaders, particularly informal teacher leaders. The school administrator plays a crucial role in fostering the conditions that facilitate teacher leadership, including the following:

1. *A safe environment for risk taking.* Teachers must be confident that administrators and other teachers will not criticize them for expressing ideas that might seem unusual at first. Some of the most effective approaches to solving difficult issues in schools may not be intuitively obvious but may require that educators think creatively, which can only happen in a safe environment. School administrators should make it clear that teachers are safe to express ideas and take professional risks.

For example, a principal could raise discussion questions at a staff meeting: What would make the professional environment safe in our school? How would it be similar to the climate you create in your own classrooms? Following the establishment of these professional norms, the principal could schedule a brief, but regular, time at staff meetings for "wacko ideas," during which any teacher could propose doing something different.

2. *Administrators who encourage teacher leaders.* Administrators' commitment to cultivating teacher leaders plays an essential role in their development. Administrators must be proactive in helping teachers acquire the skills they need to take advantage of opportunities for leadership (data analysis, meeting facilitation, and so on). Unfortunately, some administrators jealously guard their turf, apparently fearing that ambitious teacher leaders will somehow undermine their own authority. In fact, one of the enduring paradoxes of leadership is that the more an administrator shares power, the more authority he or she gains.

Where Teacher Leaders Extend Their Reach

The following are just a few examples of ways in which teachers may exercise their leadership within three areas of school life.

Schoolwide Policies and Programs
- Work with colleagues to design the schedule so that students have longer periods of time in each subject.
- Serve as the building liaison to student teachers.
- Lead a school task force to overhaul the school's approach to homework.
- Represent the school in a districtwide or statewide program for drug-free schools.

Teaching and Learning
- Organize a lesson study to examine the teaching team's or department's approach to a certain topic or concept.
- Serve on a schoolwide committee to analyze student achievement data.
- Help design a teacher mentoring program for the district.
- Make a presentation at a state or local conference on alternative assessment methods.

Communication and Community Relations
- Publish a department newsletter for parents.
- Initiate a regular meeting time to confer with colleagues about individual students.
- Develop procedures for specialist and generalist teachers to share their assessments of and plans for individual students.
- Serve on the district or state parent-teacher association.
- Lead an initiative to formulate methods for students who leave the district to carry information with them about their learning.

Source: From *Teacher Leadership That Strengthens Professional Practice,* by Charlotte Danielson, 2006, Alexandria, VA: ASCD. Adapted with permission.

3. *Absence of the "tall poppy syndrome."* It's not only administrators who, on occasion, stand in the way of teacher leaders. Sometimes the teachers themselves resist taking on leadership roles, or make it difficult for their colleagues to do so. In Australia, this is called the tall poppy syndrome—those who stick their heads up risk being cut down to size. This phenomenon might take the form of teachers' reluctance to announce to their colleagues that they have been recognized by the National Board for Professional Teaching Standards. To counteract this syndrome, the school administrator needs to create a culture that honors teachers who step outside their traditional roles and take on leadership projects.

4. *Opportunities to learn leadership skills.* As noted earlier, the skills required for teacher leadership are not part of the preparation program for most teachers. If teacher leaders are to emerge and make their full contribution, they need opportunities to learn the necessary skills of curriculum planning, instructional improvement, assessment design, collaboration, and facilitation. Teachers can learn these skills through school-level professional development, of course, but they may also build these skills through districtwide or university-based courses and seminars. Whatever the source, the opportunities must be available and sufficiently convenient for teachers to take advantage of them.

THE NEED FOR TEACHER LEADERSHIP

Teacher leadership is an idea whose time has come. The unprecedented demands being placed on schools today require leadership at every level. Yet many schools are still organized as though all the important decisions are made by administrators and carried out by teachers.

In the most successful schools, teachers supported by administrators take initiative to improve schoolwide policies and programs, teaching and learning, and communication. By understanding the phenomenon of teacher leadership and helping teachers develop the skills required to act as leaders, we will improve schools and help teachers realize their full potential.

Charlotte Danielson is an education consultant in Princeton, New Jersey. She is the author of many books, including *Teacher Leadership That Strengthens Professional Practice* (ASCD, 2006).

QUESTIONS FOR REFLECTION

1. How does Danielson's vision of teacher leadership and the impact on the curriculum and learning differ from what Richard Ackerman and Sarah Mackenzie wrote about in Chapter 1? How are their positions similar?
2. What qualities and skills distinguish teacher leaders from other teachers? Do you see those qualities exhibited by teachers or other educators you work with?
3. How can teacher leaders extend their reach to be most effective in the promotion of student learning and achievement? Are there ideas not covered by the article that you think are critical to teacher leadership? Explain.

Adopt and Adapt: Twenty-First-Century Schools Need Twenty-First-Century Technology

MARC PRENSKY

ABSTRACT: Speaking as a technological insider, Prensky sizes up the current technology landscape in the modern school and finds it wanting—disjointed, scattered, and underutilized. Prensky envisions the field of education overcoming many of the barriers that keep true technological integration from occurring and writes of a future environment that will meet students' needs and expectations.

The biggest question about technology and schools in the twenty-first century is not so much "What can it do?" but, rather, "When will it get to do it?" We all know life will be much different by 2100. Will school? First, it helps to look at the typical process of technology adoption (keeping in mind, of course, that schools are not typical of anything). It's typically a four-step process:

1. Dabbling.
2. Doing old things in old ways.
3. Doing old things in new ways.
4. Doing new things in new ways.

Until recently, we have mostly been dabbling with technology in our schools: A few Apples here. A PC there. Random creation of software by teachers and other individuals—some very good, much bad. A few edutainment disks. Dabbling.

OLD THINGS IN OLD WAYS

When a new technology appears, our first instinct is always to continue doing things within the technology the way we've always done it. People still illuminated the first printed Gutenberg Bibles by hand. Television pioneers set up single cameras in "great" theater seats. The result was pretty much like what came before; some elements may have been lost, but the results were certainly cheaper, and far more efficient.

That is almost exclusively what we now do with educational technology. We use it mostly to pass documents around, but now in electronic form, and the result is not very different from what we have always known.

People certainly are putting courses, curricula, and lesson plans online. This trend is important, but it's hardly new—it will be new only when those courses, curricula, and lesson plans are very different and technology influenced, when they are set up so they can be found and mixed and matched easily, when they are continually iterated and updated, and when the kids have a big say in their creation. Certainly, systems for maintaining records and assessment online, such as PowerSchool, a Web-based student-information system from Apple (and similar products from Pearson School Systems and Chancery Software), have emerged, but the records and assessments we ask for and keep, for the most part, haven't changed.

I would even include writing, creating, submitting, and sharing work digitally on the computer via email or instant messaging in the category of doing old things (communicating and exchanging) in old ways (passing stuff around). Is there educational progress, though? It appears that students who write on a computer turn in longer and higher-quality assignments than those who compose by hand, even though it's still writing. A middle school principal in Maine (where all middle schoolers are supplied with computers) proclaims that the debate over handwriting is finally over—all assignments must be keyboarded. You can mourn the passing of handwriting if you must; the kids certainly won't. If they are writing better and more detailed papers, yes, there has been progress.

But new technology still faces a great deal of resistance. Today, even in many schools with computers, Luddite administrators (and even Luddite technology administrators) lock down the machines, refusing to allow students to access email. Many also block instant messaging, cell phones, cell-phone cameras, unfiltered Internet access, Wikipedia, and other potentially highly effective educational tools and technologies, to our kids' tremendous frustration. Even where technology has not been blocked, much of the digitized educational materials and records are just examples of using computers to collect old stuff (such as data or lesson plans) in old ways (by filing). There are some educational benefits, though, including allowing teachers to access data more easily and parents to do so more extensively.

OLD THINGS IN NEW WAYS

Recently, a number of our schools (a very small number) have entered the stage of doing other old things in new ways. Now, it begins to get a little more interesting. "I used to have to tell my students about phenomena, or have them read; now I can show them," says Jim Doane, a science teacher at Scarborough Middle School, in Scarborough, Maine. When we begin adding digital demonstrations through video and Flash animation, we are giving students new, better ways to get information.

In a growing number of simulations, ranging from the off-the-shelf *SimCity* and *Civilization III* to Muzzy Lane's *Making History* to MIT's experimental *Revolution* and *Supercharged,* students—even elementary school children—can now manipulate whole virtual systems, from cities to countries to refineries, rather than just handling manipulatives.

In Education Simulations' *Real Lives,* children take on the persona of a peasant farmer in Bangladesh, a Brazilian factory worker, a police officer in Nigeria, a Polish computer operator, or a lawyer in the United States, among others, experiencing those lives based on real-world statistical data. Riverdeep's *School Tycoon* enables kids to build a school to their liking. With these tools, students act like scientists and innovators, rather than serve as empty vessels. They arrive at their own conclusions through controlled experimentation and what scientists call "enlightened trial and error."

Still, our best teachers have always used interactive models for demonstrations, and students, like scientists and military planners, have been conducting simulations in sand, on paper, and in their heads for thousands of years. So, though some observers trumpet these uses of technology as great innovations, they are really still examples of doing old things in new ways.

But there are many more old things children are doing in new ways—innovations they have invented or adopted as their preferred method of behavior—that have not yet made their way into our schools. These include buying school materials (clothes, supplies, and even homework) on eBay and the Internet; exchanging music on P2P sites; building games with modding (modifying) tools; setting up meetings and dates online; posting personal information and creations for others to check out; meeting people through cell phones; building libraries of music and movies; working together in self-formed teams in multiplayer online role-playing games; creating and using online reputation systems; peer rating of comments; online gaming; screen saver analysis; photoblogging; programming; exploring; and even transgressing and testing social norms.

An important question is, how many of these new ways will ever be integrated into our instruction—or even understood by educators? If we want to move the useful adoption of technology forward, it is crucial for educators to learn to listen, to observe, to ask, and to try all the new methods their students have already figured out, and do so regularly.

Two big factors stand in the way of our making more and faster progress in technology adoption in our schools. One of these is technological, the other social.

The Big Tech Barrier: One-to-One

The missing technological element is true one-to-one computing, in which each student has a device he or she can work on, keep, customize, and take home. For true technological advance to occur, the computers must be personal to each learner. When used properly and well for education, these computers become extensions of the students' personal self and brain. They must have each student's stuff and each student's style all over them (in case you haven't noticed, kids love to customize and make technology personal), and that is something sharing just doesn't allow. Any ratio that involves sharing computers—even two kids to a computer—will delay the technology revolution from happening.

Many groups are working on solutions to the one-to-one problem, and this approach is being implemented in several places, including Maine; Vail, Arizona; Florida's Broward County Schools; and the Lemon Grove School District, in Lemon Grove, California. Those who cite cost as a barrier to implementing one-to-one computing should know that the prices of these devices, as with all technology, are falling dramatically. Although the expense is often estimated at $500 to $1,000 per unit, this year, according to longtime computer visionary Nicholas Negroponte, we will see a basic, laptop computer for roughly $100.

The Social Barrier: Digital Immigrants

A second key barrier to technological adoption is more challenging. Schools (which really means the teachers and administrators) famously resist change. Though some observers, including multiple-intelligences guru Howard Gardner, point to schools as the "conservators" of our culture, and therefore instinctively conservative in what they do, the resistance comes more from the fact that our public school system has evolved an extremely delicate balance between many sets of pressures—political, parental, social, organizational, supervisory, and financial—that any technological change is bound to disrupt. For example, such shifting certainly initially means more work and pressure on educators, who already feel overburdened.

In the past, the pressure against disruption has always been stronger than the pressure for change. So, as new technologies—from radio to television, from telephones to cell phones, from cameras to video cams, or even Wikipedia—have come down the pike, American public schools have fearfully stood ready to exclude them. Change hasn't happened.

But resisting today's digital technology will be truly lethal to our children's education. They live in an incredibly fast-moving world significantly different than the one we grew up in. The number-one technology request of today's students is to have email and instant messaging always available and part of school. They not only need things faster than their teachers are used to providing them, they also have many other new learning needs as well, such as random access to information and multiple data streams.

These "digital natives" are born into digital technology. Conversely, their teachers (and all older adults) are "digital immigrants." Having learned about digital technology later in life, digital immigrants retain their predigital "accents"—such as, thinking that virtual relationships (those that exist only online) are somehow less real or important than face-to-face ones. Such outmoded perspectives are serious barriers to our students' twenty-first-century progress.

Many schools still ban new digital technologies, such as cell phones and Wikipedia. Even when schools do try to move forward, they often face anti-technology pressure from parents demanding that schools go "back to basics." Many teachers, under pressure from all sides, are often so afraid to experiment and to trust their kids with technology that they demand extensive "training" before they will try anything new. All these factors impede even the many schools trying to change.

NEW PROBLEMS, NEW SOLUTIONS

With very few exceptions, our schools have not been physically designed for computers. Much time in our schools' forty-five-minute instructional periods is often wasted in computer setup and shutdown. Teachers are often unsure about how to integrate technology in their lesson plans and, often, administrators have little, if any, guidance to give them. In many places where technology could liberate teachers most, such as automatic grading of homework and tests, automation has been neglected. Adding digital technology is generally disruptive to what schools and teachers do, and the pressure of high-stakes testing only exacerbates this problem.

How, then, do we move forward?

First, consult the students. They are far ahead of their educators in terms of taking advantage of digital technology and using it to their advantage. We cannot, no matter how hard we try or how smart we are (or think we are), invent the future education of our children for them. The only way to move forward effectively is to combine what they know about technology with what we know and require about education. Sadly, in most cases, no one asks for their opinion. I go to conference after conference on school technology, and nary a student is in sight. I do hope that, after having pointed this situation out a hundred times or so, I will find that it is starting to change. Students will have to help, and we will have to think harder about how to make this happen.

NEW THINGS IN NEW WAYS

For the digital age, we need new curricula, new organization, new architecture, new teaching, new student assessments, new parental connections, new administration procedures, and many other elements. Some people suggest using emerging models from business—but these, for the most part, don't apply. Others suggest trying to change school size—but this will not help much if we are still doing the wrong things, only in smaller spaces.

What we're talking about is invention—new things in new ways. Change is the order of the day in our kids' twenty-first-century lives. It ought to be the order of the day in their schools as well. Not only would students welcome it, they will soon demand it. Angus King, the former governor of Maine who pushed for one-to-one computing in that state's schools, recently suggested our kids "should sue us" for better education. I suggest that every lesson plan, every class, every school, every school district, and every state ought to try something new and then report to all of us what works and what doesn't; after all, we do have the Internet.

Some people will no doubt worry that, with all this experimentation, our children's education will be hurt. "When will we have time for the curriculum," they will ask, "and for all the standardized testing being mandated?" If we really offered our children some great future-oriented content (such as, for example, that they could learn about nanotechnology, bioethics, genetic medicine, and neuroscience in neat interactive ways from real experts), and they could develop their skills in programming, knowledge filtering, using their connectivity, and maximizing their hardware, and that they could do so with cutting-edge, powerful, miniaturized, customizable, and one-to-one technology, I bet they would complete the "standard" curriculum in half the time it now takes, with high test scores all around. To get everyone to the good stuff, the faster kids would work with and pull up the ones who were behind.

In other words, if we truly offer our kids an Edutopia worth having, I believe our students will work as hard as they can to get there. So, let's not just adopt technology into our schools. Let's adapt it, push it, pull it, iterate with it, experiment with it, test it, and redo it, until we reach the point where we and our kids truly feel we've done our very best. Then, let's push it and pull it some more. And let's do it quickly, so the twenty-second century doesn't catch us by surprise with too much of our work undone.

A big effort? Absolutely. But our kids deserve no less.

Marc Prensky, founder and CEO of Games2train, is a speaker, writer, consultant, and game designer. He is the author of *Digital Game-Based Learning* (McGraw-Hill, 2001) and *Don't Bother Me, Mom, I'm Learning* (Paragon, 2005).

QUESTIONS FOR REFLECTION

1. What is the current educational technology landscape that Prensky describes? Does this description match your experiences with technology in education today?
2. How does Prensky envision education overcoming the many barriers that keep true technological integration from occurring in schools? What does he say specifically needs to happen for schools to realize their technological potential?
3. What does Prensky's idealized future environment look like and do you think we will ever get there? Or will education always be playing catch up to the real world when it comes to technology?

A Movable Feast

JOHN K. WATERS

ABSTRACT: Imagine a classroom with furniture on wheels, wireless islands, and work spaces designed to enable collaborative classroom interaction. Waters profiles educators who are challenging traditional ideas about where and how learning takes place as they design cutting-edge K–12 classrooms with digitally inspired and technologically purposeful architecture, all intended to support sound pedagogical practice.

Back when Menko Johnson was teaching sixth-, seventh-, and eighth-graders about computers at Crestview Middle School in Columbus, OH, he spent most of his time in a gymnasium that had been converted into a computer lab. The students' desks were arranged along the walls, and when they worked on the computers, they faced those walls.

"It was a classic computer lab environment," Johnson recalls. "It meant that 80 percent of my students had their backs to me most of the time. The room was arranged that way, not because it would be a good teaching setup, but to accommodate the wiring."

It is also a classic example of a learning space made less effective by technology.

Today, Johnson is an instructional technologist at San Jose State University in California, where he focuses his time on the effective integration of technology and learning spaces, with an emphasis on collaboration and flexibility. Johnson is part of a team supporting SJSU's state-of-the-art, 10,000-square-foot Academic Success Center. At the heart of the project is an incubator classroom that combines movable furniture with an array of audiovisual technologies designed to enable collaborative classroom interaction.

"In the old days, we let the technology dictate the configuration of the learning space," he says. "Now what we talk about is a flexible classroom that can be arranged any way you like into a teaching environment that suits you. In our case, that means that we use tables and chairs instead of desks. And just about every piece of furniture is on wheels so that the space can be easily reconfigured. Think of the classroom as a grid on which you can move the tables and chairs anywhere you want."

Johnson believes that the lessons learned at SJSU can help K–12 districts design more effective, tech-enabled classrooms. In elementary classes, for example, where the younger students stay in one room all day, movable furniture and wireless computer stations could allow the teacher to reconfigure the space on the fly to support different activities. The SJSU incubator classroom features three projection screens: a large one in front and two on the sides. This configuration would allow, say, a high school teacher to display multiple pieces of information to different work groups collaborating within the same classroom in what Johnson calls "micro-environments." A central server, like the one housed in the incubator space, could facilitate collaboration in any classroom by connecting wireless laptops.

Though the focus of Johnson's work is the impact of technology on instruction and student learning, he insists that a successful synchronizing of technology and classroom puts the teaching before the gadgetry.

"Whenever we talk about technology in education, we have to start with the pedagogy," he says. "What are your teaching goals? What are you trying to achieve? What types of learning do you want to happen? It is true that we are surrounded by, and even immersed in, technology, but we still have to leverage it in a way that is educationally useful, in a way that's better than what we don't do digitally. Just because it's digital doesn't mean it's better for learning."

The key is to think about how the technology will support your teaching goals, Johnson says, but you also want a physical space that supports the technology. That includes things like flexible furniture and easy access to power and networking outlets. The pedagogy, technology, and architecture revolve around each other, he says, but always with the educational issues at the center.

"Let's assume that you are trying to create K–12 learners that are problem solvers," Johnson explains. "You want them to be able to take in information, assess it, digest it, and assemble it to solve problems as a team. If your students are sitting at tiny desks in rows facing the front of a rectangular classroom, it's going to be difficult to achieve that goal."

BEYOND BORDERS

But even with the teaching mission front and center in the classroom design process, in some ways the technology is still defining the learning space, observes Diana Oblinger, vice president of Educause, a Raleigh, NC-based nonprofit association that promotes the intelligent use of information technology. The good news is, Oblinger adds, rather than forcing students to face the walls, technology is knocking those walls down.

"Now that you have wireless connectivity, any place can become a learning space," she says. "We're no longer thinking about learning as something that is contained in a traditional classroom. Consequently, the design emphasis is shifting to focus on what you want students to do, rather than what the space is all about. Schools can, and in many cases will, evolve into spaces that resemble learning complexes, where some students are in classes, some are in groups in the library, and others are gathered outdoors."

Oblinger is responsible for Educause's teaching and learning activities and is director of the group's Learning Initiative. She also serves as an adjunct professor of adult and higher education at North Carolina State University. And she is the co-editor of six books, including *The Learning Revolution: The Challenge of Information Technology in the Academy* (Anker Publishing, 1987) and *Educating the Net Generation* (Educause, 2005). Educause focuses on colleges and universities, but Oblinger says that much of her work on the design of the modern classroom is applicable to K–12 learning environments.

"It's important to remember that the pedagogy and the people come first," Oblinger says. "It's not about the technology; it's not about the design. These are spaces designed for learning. That said, you want to look at the activities the technology might enable in a classroom setting. You want to provide students with direct access to resources, so that if you are asking them to work on a problem they can go to the web to look things up. You want to make all the things that people might need to do in class—from accessing information to collaborating with other students, drafting documents to doing calculations—available through the integration of the technology."

While classroom designers are rearranging the desks and moving the power outlets in real space, the phenomenon known as Web 2.0 is transforming cyberspace, and in the process, Oblinger says, challenging long-held notions of how students study. As the web evolves from a collection of HTML web pages into a multimedia computing platform, it is fast becoming a world rife with collaborative technologies—wikis, blogs, social networking sites—all of which are widely used by students to share an enormous range of information and experiences. Oblinger says this revolution has to be accounted for in a classroom layout.

"What you're seeing all over the world is that people are using wireless networks, and a variety of collaboration tools have emerged to take advantage of that technology. Consequently, tools that allow people to come together physically and virtually must be part of any classroom design."

CHALLENGING EXPECTATIONS

One of the biggest roadblocks to achieving integration of the physical and the virtual in K–12 classrooms is a set of time-honored presumptions of what a classroom should look like such as, it should be rectangular, and have a front and a back.

"Right now, most school districts have what are called 'educational specifications,'" explains Henry Sanoff, distinguished professor in the School of Architecture at North Carolina State University's College of Design. "This is a laundry list of specs for every room that goes into a school, including the size of the rooms. It's like a straitjacket. Some districts are more flexible, but by and large, the ed specs have dominated the production of schools for decades. That's why all schools tend to look alike. And the advent of computers hasn't changed that."

Oblinger says that shaking up expectations of what a classroom is supposed to look like is a good way to get teachers thinking in new ways about what they are doing. "The environment sends a lot of subtle and not-so-subtle cues about what's going to happen in the space," she says. "The concept is called built pedagogy. It suggests that the way a room is designed dictates the teaching approach, or sends teachers into certain mental defaults.

"I walked into a lecture theater a few days ago that had 500 seats, all facing forward, all in rows. The lights were pointed at the stage. There was a lectern up there with a screen behind it. When you walk into a space like that, whether you are a learner or an instructor, your mental default is that the audience will sit there silently while the teacher lectures at them. If I had walked into a room with no central focal point, filled with round tables with free-standing chairs, and everyone was facing each other, and there were screens on all four walls, I would assume, as would the students, that this would be a much more collaborative environment."

Grant Strobel has learned firsthand how different classroom architecture can change an instructor's teaching style. Strobel is the tech ed teacher at Lake Geneva Middle School in Wisconsin. He works in the school's 2,600-square-foot Technology Center, an open classroom—no dividers, no cubicles—designed for a modular education program covering 18 different areas of technology. Built in 1999, the classroom is furnished with free-standing islands equipped with computers and a range of tools for hands-on projects and group problem solving. Each learning module covers a different technology, from radios to rockets, lasers to IT. Students work at the islands in pairs, Strobel explains, but the classroom also has three work tables where they can gather in greater numbers.

The wide-open design of the Lake Geneva Tech Center keeps Strobel "constantly cruising," as he puts it. The design has changed his ideas about what constitutes effective teaching. "I'll never go back into a traditional classroom," Strobel says. "The kids are so much more engaged in here. For one thing, it's completely hands-on. I'm not going to stand up in front of the classroom today and tell you how robots are used in the world or how rockets work. It's a completely different style of teaching."

WINDOW SHOPPING

One way to get past the bias toward traditional models is by doing a bit of window shopping. If you want to know what constitutes an effective integration of technology and classroom design, Johnson advises, take a look at what is working in another school district. "I think exposure to other classrooms is critical—even at colleges and universities, which tend to be ahead of K–12 in this area," he says. "At some level, a classroom is a classroom. When you are in an environment for a long time, you forget—or you've never had an opportunity to see—what it's like to do something really differently. If you don't see other sites, you may never be exposed to some radically different approaches that could inspire you. The worst thing you can do is to think that you're going to have all the answers."

And take your information technology people with you. "You definitely want to involve IT in your planning," Johnson says. "The disconnect we see so often is that the IT people don't understand how to teach with technology. Remember, these are the guys who put the computers on the wall. The input from the instructor here is critical. Where are you going to stand and actually teach? How are you going to be able to see these screens, get to those students? These are things that teachers will understand instinctively, but the tech guys will need to be told." Perhaps the most imposing obstacle to a truly tech-optimized K–12 classroom, says Johnson, is the existing physical infrastructure. "In K–12, you have to contend with legacy architecture, and in many—maybe most—cases, you just have to work with what you've got."

Sanoff actually sees a fixation on technology as another potential obstacle. "We haven't yet come to grips with getting the conventional classroom to work effectively," he says, "and it's unlikely that the technology is going to make a radical difference if we don't use what we understand about the diverse ways in which children learn to create teaching settings that encourage exploration, creativity, and innovation. We're not at that level yet—and the technology is not going to help if the objectives aren't very clear. The truth is, we probably spend too much time and energy looking at new toys as a substitute for addressing some of the most critical issues in education."

Differing with Sanoff, Oblinger insists that technology is now an inextricable part of the classroom design equation, but she agrees that we haven't yet figured out how to optimize it. "We understand now that this is the most connected generation," she says. "What we're just starting to figure out is how that translates into more effective classroom design. The technology is changing, and our notions about what people are comfortable with, technologically, must too shift with it."

John K. Waters is a freelance writer based in Palo Alto, CA.

QUESTIONS FOR REFLECTION

1. What do the "cutting-edge" classrooms of tomorrow look like and what is required to get schools to that idealized future?
2. Waters writes about place and calls for educators to completely revise their expectations of what a classroom should look like. What does he mean by these statements and how could teachers be supported to better prepare them for the new design and function of their learning spaces?
3. What are the potential drawbacks of a cutting-edge classroom like Waters describes in his article and how should educators balance technology and its benefits with curriculum needs that often exist apart from technology?

Leaders' Voices—
Putting Theory into Practice

Ideals vs. Reality in the Classroom

CAROL LUPTON

ABSTRACT: Lupton describes how the ideals of her pre-service teacher preparation program were given a "reality check" when she found herself working in a real school with real kids. Ultimately, she asks how teachers can engage children when there are so many competing distractions for their attention. She concludes that taking pleasure in the little accomplishments her students make tells her she is reaching them.

Years ago, as a student at Mary Washington College, I was assigned to write my philosophy of teaching as an exit paper in a class called Foundations of Teaching. I not only wrote it, I believed it. I would be a phenomenal teacher, a leader of students engaged in a lifelong journey in our quest for knowledge. I would guide my students as they searched for deeper meanings. I would encourage them to appreciate insights that increased self-awareness. I would applaud them when they recognized universal truths about mankind. My students would accomplish all of this simply by learning to read and write. I would do the rest. I would be the inspiration, I would be the motivation, I would be Everything for Everybody. I would be *it*.

I smile now when I reminisce about my idealistic theorizing. What was I thinking?! My imaginary classroom was obviously occupied by humanoids from an unknown planet. I had left out the most important factor of all—Today's Kids.

I entered this profession armed with a philosophy that I thought was "profound." Unfortunately, my college didn't provide a course called introduction to Middle School Mentality 101: "Hold on to your hats and prepare for one wild ride." I used to work at a middle school that had a 53 percent minority population, an irony when you think about it. Our majority was called "the minority." Thirty-four percent of our 1200 students received free or reduced lunch. That's a polite way of saying one-third of our students lived below poverty level. Our mobility rate was 30.4 percent. They came, they went. Sometimes they left because of heartbreaking circumstances. Those were the times when they cried, and so did I. In addition to this recitation of statistics, let me share some of the reality stories from my students' lives—weapons charges, drug violations, Social Services interventions, run-ins with the police, teen pregnancy. You name it, we had it.

Once I became a full-time teacher, I had to reexamine my philosophy. It was a little "unrealistic"—not to mention it focused strictly on me, me, me. Remember? "All my students had to do was learn to read and write. I would do the rest." Now educational research indicates that there are multiple basic learning styles. As a result, today's educators are encouraged to provide students with a variety of teaching experiences—linguistic, logical-mathematical, musical, spatial, bodily kinesthetic, interpersonal, and intrapersonal. This plan increases opportunities for success for all students. Easy to say, hard to do. Teachers must be armed with an arsenal of Attention-Grabbing-Lesson-Plans if they intend to survive. Today's students are not easily impressed. I know *mine* aren't. For example, try pulling out workbooks to do reinforcement exercises. You'll hear students protest loudly, "Busy work!" They expect stimulation. New gimmicks are required to maintain their interest, every day.

The educator's litany of expectations goes something like this, "Be creative, provide variety, cover the curriculum, maintain discipline, and don't forget, students must master reading and writing in the process." Therein lies the rub. How do we engage their interest long enough for them to attain the skills we teach? I grapple with this question every day.

We live in a symbol-based society. People must be able to read and write to attain their full potential in today's job market. When I tell my students this, they respond, "Says who? You?" But look at the facts, I tell them: From first grade through the remainder of school, classes are taught using textbooks. The "I-hate-to-read" student is an unsuccessful student. Will this unsuccessful student all of a sudden become a successful adult? I don't think so. My students love to point out the exceptions, but I believe they accept the logic in my argument.

I truly believe students must participate actively as players, not spectators, in the educational process in order to succeed. However, before I get too carried away with theory, it's time for a reality check. Wouldn't it be grand if a lofty philosophy could accomplish so much? Unfortunately, I work in the real world. Come with me and take a peek into my classroom on a typical day: Do you see the student who twists and turns like a pretzel and absolutely cannot sit still? How about the ones who come late and leave early? Then there are the few who never open their books . . . if they bring a book at all, or a pencil, or paper. Listen to those pleas for one-on-one attention that are too numerous to count. My classes as a whole are never entirely quiet. I always know if I am holding their attention. The minute interest starts to wane, they let me know (with brutal blows to my ego at times). Demanding too rigid an environment frustrates them. However, certain ground rules must be maintained. For example, I draw the line at comments such as: "This story sucks" "The main character must be LD" "This is boring" "You're boring" "I'm bored" or any variety on the "too bored for words" theme.

Remember, in today's world we teachers are in constant competition with the world of entertainment. Our students have access to TVs, computers, compact disc players and the list goes on and on. They have zero tolerance for boredom. All they need to do is press a button and change the channel. It's not that easy for students to change *me*. However, I do believe that teaching requires the personality of an entertainer to even attempt to compete. The teacher must be the producer, writer and star of the production each and every day.

Recently, I felt brave enough to ask my students for their evaluation of my teaching techniques this school year. We started with something relatively safe, I thought. I asked them for their definition of reading. The answers included "awesome." Listen to this one: "Books make a path for me. When I'm feeling down and alone, I pick up my book and read. Then my real world disappears and my book takes me on journeys and wild adventures. My book is my world, it's my friend." Wow, right? Remarkable is more like it. A student who spent last summer in a juvenile detention center wrote that response. Here's another one: "I like when words leap out and play basketball with my mind." I was so impressed! Maybe I am doing something right. Maybe I don't have to give up on my cerebral philosophy after all. Of course, not all the responses were complimentary. I got the flip side too. For example, one of my students wrote, "Reading is like putting me in jail and not giving me food." Oh well, I consoled myself—he did use a simile. And then, my nemesis this year, the dreaded "boring" word: "I only read for an assignment or if I am bored and there is absolutely positively with no shadow of a doubt *nothing* to do." But, I remind myself, this comment came from a student who would have written one word (boring) at the beginning of the year. He is now up to 24 words to tell me the same thing. I see growth in this response. Have you ever noticed that teachers are eternal optimists? We have to be. Otherwise, we couldn't keep coming back day after day.

Actually, I haven't given up my idealistic philosophy about teaching. I am a leader of students engaged in a lifelong journey in our quest for knowledge. There are days when I trudge rather than cavort, as I would have liked. There are days when I lose sight of the path and I have to rely on my students to lead the way. I am battle weary I admit, but I still have the energy to keep repeating the message, "Learn to read; learn to write. Education is the key to success." My philosophy may be tattered, but it's still intact. It's just undergoing the revision process at this time.

Carol Lupton is a seventh-grade language arts teacher at E. H. Marsteller Middle School in Manassas, VA.

QUESTIONS FOR REFLECTION

1. What were the author's unrealistic expectations of teaching when she was in her preservice program? Do you think this kind of idealism is common amongst soon-to-be teachers?
2. What was the most sobering part of Lupton's "reality check" when she finally got out into the "real world" of teaching? What was Lupton dealing with on a day-to-day basis that her philosophy of teaching statement did not address?
3. Do you think many beginning teachers go through a kind of "reality check" when they begin teaching on their own? How do you think they respond to the experience? How might you expect yourself to respond?

LEARNING ACTIVITIES

Critical Thinking

1. How can school leaders create an environment that supports sound curriculum implementation and instruction?

2. What are the biggest barriers to student engagement with the curriculum? How might educational leaders address these barriers and facilitate teaching and learning for all students?

3. In addition to the content and processes students learn through the use of educational technology, what "lessons" might they learn through the "hidden curriculum" created by educational technology?

4. In regard to the subject area and grade level with which you are most familiar, what are the advantages and disadvantages of teaching concepts with and without educational technology?

5. Based on your experiences, is the classroom use of educational technology educationally sound? To what extent does educational technology merely entertain students?

Application Activities

1. In the area and at the level with which you are most familiar, examine a set of curriculum materials (a textbook, curriculum guide, etc.) to determine how the curriculum is taught. Based on the information presented in this chapter, what suggestions do you have for how the materials might be better implemented and improved?

2. Design a workshop for teachers at the level and in the subject area with which you are most familiar. The aim of the workshop should be to expand teachers' repertoire of knowledge and skills related to instruction.

3. Prepare a catalog of interactive multimedia resources and materials in a curricular area of interest. For each entry, include an annotation that briefly describes the resource materials, how teachers might use them, and where they may be obtained. As with the selection of any curriculum materials, try to find evidence of effectiveness, such as results of field tests, published reviews of educational software, awards, or testimonials from educators.

Field Experiences

1. Interview one or more teachers to find out how they implement new curriculum into an existing curriculum. To what extent do they use the models of teaching discussed in this chapter?

2. Interview a group of students in the subject area and at the grade level you teach (or plan to teach) to find out how they use technology as part of their educational experience. What surprises you about what they say? How might their "insider" use of technology influence the way you teach and lead?

3. Survey a local school district to determine the educational technologies used by teachers. How and how often are these technologies used for instruction? What is the availability of computers and software for student use?

Internet Activities

1. Find an online chat room frequented by school leaders and/or teachers and enter (or initiate) a discussion on educational technology. What are their views of integrating

technology into the classroom? What technologies, software, and instructional activities have they found most effective?

2. Survey the Internet to begin locating and creating bookmarks or favorites for websites and teacher discussion groups that focus on implementing technology into the curriculum. Visit three or more home pages from the following list of research publications on the Internet. These journals frequently have articles that focus on the effectiveness of different teaching methods. Read an article that focuses on a teaching method of interest to you. What does the article say about the effectiveness of that method? What are the implications for the methods you use (or will use) as a teacher?

American Educational Research Journal
Contemporary Educational Psychology
Educational Psychology Review
Journal of Educational Psychology
Journal of Teaching and Teacher Education

Cognition and Instruction
Educational Psychologist
Educational Researcher
Review of Research in Education
Review of Educational Research

7

FOCUS QUESTIONS

1. What is curriculum evaluation?
2. What is the educational leader's role in curriculum evaluation and assessment of learning?
3. How can classroom assessments enhance student learning?
4. What are some "alternative assessments" teachers can use to assess student learning?

Curriculum Evaluation and Assessment of Learning

As pointed out in Chapter 5, the fourth question of Ralph Tyler's rationale stresses the importance of evaluating the curriculum—that is, determining whether the educational purposes of a curriculum have been attained. The "educational purposes" discussed in Tyler's seminal book, *Basic Principles of Curriculum and Instruction,* are realized if curriculum implementation results in the following three outcomes for learners: (1) they acquire an understanding of the subject at hand; (2) they can apply what they have learned to new situations; and (3) they have a desire to continue learning. This chapter focuses on the educational leader's key role in curriculum evaluation and assessment of student learning.

CURRICULUM EVALUATION

Curriculum evaluation involves making systematic judgments about the quality, or value, of educational programs in a school or district and developing strategies for improving those programs. The individual in the best position to monitor the processes of curriculum evaluation is, of course, a building principal, superintendent, or curriculum director. As Cremin (1965, p. 58) noted more than four decades ago, "Someone must look at the curriculum whole and raise insistent questions of priority and relationship." To answer such "questions of priority and relationship," the educational leader must understand the distinction between formative and summative evaluation of the curriculum.

Curriculum Leadership Strategy

When evaluating a curriculum, remember to gather data that represent not just the written, taught, and learned curriculum, but also the hidden and experienced curriculum.

FORMATIVE AND SUMMATIVE EVALUATION

When teachers measure students' attainment of knowledge and skills for the purpose of making decisions about their teaching, they are engaging in *formative evaluation*. Teachers use the results of formative evaluations to make decisions about what curricular experiences are appropriate for students. For example, as an aid to planning a new curriculum unit, a teacher may assess students' understanding of the new material by having them take a short diagnostic test or quiz, complete homework or seatwork assignments, or participate in a group project.

School administrators should also encourage teachers to conduct informal formative evaluations while they are teaching. For instance, teachers may pay close attention to what students say; they may use probing questions to gauge students' understanding of the subject; and they will note students' facial expressions and behavior. During these informal formative evaluations, teachers not only assess students' understanding; they also assess students' attitudes toward learning the subject. For example, in the following, a teacher makes some candid comments about his informal formative evaluations while teaching:

> I'd become dissatisfied with the closed Q & A style that my unthinking teaching had fallen into, and I would frequently be lazy in my acceptance of right answers and sometimes even tacit complicity with a class to make sure none of us had to work too hard. . . . They and I knew that if the Q & A wasn't going smoothly, I'd change the question, answer it myself, or only seek answers from the "brighter students." There must have been times (still are?) where an outside observer would see my lessons as a small discussion group surrounded by many sleepy onlookers. (Black, Harrison, Lee, Marshall, & Wiliam, 2004, p. 11)

When teachers use measurements of student learning to determine grades at the end of a unit, semester, or year, and to decide whether students are ready to proceed to the next phase of their education, they are engaging in *summative evaluation*. Summative evaluations provide educational leaders and teachers with an overview of student learning across a broad range of knowledge and skills. Formative evaluations, on the other hand, are usually more focused and cover a narrower range of knowledge and skills. Superintendents, building principals, and curriculum directors use the results of summative evaluations to guide their decisions related to curriculum leadership and to foster continuous improvement of the curriculum.

As Carol Ann Tomlinson writes in "Learning to Love Assessment," informative assessment plays a critical role in judging performances, guiding student learning, and shaping instruction. The critical role of informative assessment is essential for both formative and summative assessment.

ASSESSMENT OF LEARNING

A key element of curriculum evaluation involves assessing the extent to which students have acquired the knowledge and skills that comprise the goals and outcomes of a curriculum. For most people, the term *assessment* brings to mind a four-step process: (1) the teacher prepares a test (or selects a preexisting test) to cover material that has been taught, (2) students take the test, (3) the teacher corrects the test, and (4) the teacher assigns grades based on how well students performed on the test. Classroom assessment, however, "is more than accurate recall," as Jay McTighe, Elliott Seif, and Grant Wiggins point out in "You *Can* Teach for Meaning" in this chapter. Assessment provides information educational leaders use to determine the degree to which curriculum goals are being attained in a school or district and to develop strategies for curriculum reform and improvement.

School administrators must remember that there is no single "right way" to assess student learning. They understand the importance of providing students with multiple opportunities to demonstrate what they know and are able to do. If students know that they have different ways to demonstrate their success, they develop more positive views of themselves as learners. They find learning to be an enjoyable experience.

Students who previously might have disliked one area of a school's curriculum because they associated assessments of learning in that area with failure, can develop positive views about the curriculum if they know they have different ways to demonstrate their learning. They know that they have multiple opportunities to be successful. As a specialist in assessment puts it, "We [now] understand how to use classroom assessment to keep students confident that the achievement target is within reach. . . . We must build classroom environments in which students use assessments to understand what success looks like and how to do better next time. . . . If teachers assess accurately and use the results effectively, then students prosper" (Stiggins, 2004, pp. 24–26).

Standardized Assessments

Standardized assessments (or standardized tests) are pencil-and-paper tests that are taken by large groups of students and scored in a uniform manner. The test items, conditions under which students take the test, how the tests are scored, and how the scores are interpreted are "standardized" for all who take the test. This standardization enables educational leaders to compare scores for different groups of students within a school or among different schools within a district. Standardized assessments are administered at the district, state, and national levels.

The first standardized test in the United States was administered by Horace Mann, secretary of the Massachusetts State Board of Education, in the mid-1800s. Mann, who eventually came to be known as the "father of the common school," wanted to classify students by ability and gather evidence for the effectiveness of the state school system. He hoped to use the results of the state test to further his educational reform efforts. Prior to the use of this standardized test, teachers conducted their own assessments at the individual classroom level.

Current examples of standardized tests are the Iowa Test of Basic Skills, California Achievement Test, Metropolitan Achievement Tests, the Stanford Achievement Test, the Scholastic Assessment Test (SAT), and the American College Test Assessment (ACT). In addition, the federal government funds the National Assessment of Educational Progress (NAEP). Periodically, NAEP is used to sample student achievement around the country. On a biannual basis, the performance of national samples of 9, 13, and 17 year olds is assessed. Educational policymakers then use the results—reported by geographic region, gender, and ethnic background—to guide their decision making. First administered in 1969, NAEP has assessed student learning in all areas of the curriculum.

Norm-Referenced Assessments. Some standardized assessments are norm-referenced—that is, students' scores are compared with scores of other students who are similar. The comparison group of students, called the *norm group,* is usually from the same age group and grade level. An individual student's score is then compared to the average, or mean, score for the total group. Norm-referenced tests are used to determine where a student is compared to the "typical" performance of other students at the same age and grade level. Thus, norm-referenced assessments enable school administrators and teachers to rank students in terms of their achievement.

To understand the meaning of scores on a norm-referenced assessment, imagine that a student received a total of 75 points on a 100-point norm-referenced assessment. If the mean, or average, score for the comparison group of students was also 75, the student would be at the 50th percentile. That is, 50 percent of the students in the comparison group scored higher, and 50 percent scored lower. However, if the mean score for the comparison group was 90, the student might be in the 30th percentile. That is, 70 percent of students in the comparison group scored higher, and 30 percent scored lower.

The preceding example can also be used to illustrate how scores on norm-referenced tests should be interpreted carefully. Norm-referenced test scores can be misused. If the student scored in the 30th percentile, it would be a mistake to assume that score is evidence that the student is doing poorly. The student might not have done well on the material covered by the norm-referenced assessment; however, the student might be doing quite well in other areas not included in the test.

Criterion-Referenced Assessments. Other standardized assessments are criterion-referenced—that is, students' learning is compared with clearly defined criteria or standards, rather than the performance of other students. Criterion-referenced assessments do not indicate what is "average" or "typical" for students from the same age group and grade level. Criterion-referenced assessments indicate what students know and can do within a specific area of the curriculum. Students' scores are not compared with the scores of other groups of students.

Educational leaders might use the results of criterion-referenced assessments to determine the percentage of students at a school who can calculate the square root of numbers, write well-organized paragraphs, or type 60 words per minute on a computer keyboard. In other words, assessments are made with reference to specific curriculum goals rather than the performance of other students on the assessments.

Curriculum Leadership Strategy

During the initial implementation stage of a new curriculum, assessment data should be used for formative purposes rather than to judge the success or failure of the curriculum.

EMERGING TRENDS IN ASSESSMENT OF LEARNING

Declining test scores, international comparisons of student achievement, and calls to hold teachers more accountable have fueled a movement to assess student learning with an ever-increasing number of standardized tests. Test scores are frequently used to make "high-stakes" decisions about school administrator and teacher accountability and promotion of students to the next grade level.

The majority of the public supports testing in schools. According to the 2004 Phi Delta Kappa/Gallup Poll, 40 percent believe there is "about the right amount" of testing, while 22 percent believe there is "not enough" (Rose & Gallup, 2004). However, the percentage believing there is "too much" testing increased from 20 percent in 1997 to 32 percent in 2004. According to the 2004 poll, the public is almost evenly divided regarding the use of standardized test scores to judge the quality of teachers (49 percent favor, 47 percent oppose, and 4 percent "don't know") and to determine whether a student should receive a high school diploma (51 percent favor, 47 percent oppose, and 2 percent "don't know").

The drive for more testing has, in some cases, led to a lowering of curriculum standards. For example, some states have changed their assessment criteria to avoid the penalties that the federal No Child Left Behind act (NCLB) imposes on schools whose students score low on standardized tests. According to NCLB, states that fail to comply risk losing federal education money. Schools deemed failing several years in a row must offer tutoring to low-achieving students and, eventually, can be forced into complete reorganization. But the law leaves it up to the states to establish their own standards of success. The following states are among those that have modified their assessment criteria:

• Texas reduced the number of questions that students must answer correctly to pass the third-grade reading exam from 24 out of 36 to 20.

• Michigan lowered the percentage of students who must pass statewide tests to certify a school as making adequate progress. For example, the percentage of high school students that must pass English tests has been reduced from 75 to 42 percent.

• Colorado changed the grading system used on its tests, combining students previously characterized on the basis of test scores as "partially proficient" with those called "proficient."

Given these modifications, some experts believe radical change is required in the area of student accountability to avoid simply changing the rules to be compliant with federal laws. Real change is necessary to make accountability a function of student learning. Ken Jones writes in "A Balanced School Accountability Model: An Alternative to High-Stakes Testing" that the very health of our public school system depends on defining a new model of accountability that is more than just test scores. Similarly, Lisa H. Meyers writes ("Time for a Tune-Up: Comprehensive Curriculum Evaluation," *Leaders' Voices,* this chapter) that educators must go far beyond aligning curricula with state standards and implement a more systematic approach to evaluating both curricula and student learning.

State-Level Performance-Based Assessments. Many states have developed statewide performance-based curriculum goals. Washington State, for example, developed the Essential Academic Learning Requirements (EALRs), which includes mandatory assessments of students' performance at the elementary, middle, and high school levels. The EALRs are based on the following four goals, each of which includes several outcomes and essential learning requirements:

Goal 1: *Read* with comprehension, *write* with skill, and *communicate* effectively and responsibly in a variety of ways and settings.

Goal 2: *Know* and *apply* the core concepts and principles of mathematics; social, physical, and life sciences; civics; history and geography; arts; and health and fitness.

Goal 3: *Think* analytically, logically, and creatively, and *integrate* experiences and knowledge to form reasoned judgments and solve problems.

Goal 4: *Understand* the importance of work and how performance, effort, and decisions directly affect future career and educational opportunities.

The EALRs are intended to improve student achievement and raise academic standards. Instruments for measuring student achievement were developed for the fourth-, seventh-, and tenth-grade levels. "Benchmarks"—points in time used to measure students' progress—were developed for the three grade levels, predicated on the assumption that students would have mastered certain skills and knowledge upon completion of those grades. Participation in the fourth-grade assessment became mandatory for all schools in Washington as of spring 1998 and mandatory for seventh-grade and tenth-grade students as of spring 2001.

Washington's assessment system has four major components that school leaders can use to guide curriculum reform efforts: state-level assessments, classroom-based assessments, professional staff development, and a "context indicator" system. The state-level assessments require students to select and/or create responses to demonstrate their skills, knowledge, and understanding for each of the EALRs. Unlike traditional norm-referenced assessments, none of the state assessments are timed, so students feel little pressure to rush through their work.

The second component of the system is classroom-based assessment. These assessments address learning requirements not easily measured by the state assessment (e.g., oral presentations or group discussion); offer administrators and teachers opportunities to gather evidence of learning that best fit the needs of individual students; and assist administrators and teachers in gathering valid evidence of student learning (Ensign, 1998).

The third component of the new assessment system is professional development. Ongoing, comprehensive training and support for administrators and teachers improves their understanding of the EALRs, the elements of sound assessment, and effective instructional techniques that enable students to achieve the state standards. Learning and Assessment Centers have been established in several locations across the state to further facilitate use of the assessment system (Ensign, 1998).

The last component is the "context indicator" system. The context indicators provide administrators with insight into why some students might not achieve to the desired level and identify factors that both inhibit and support students' learning. Context indicators include such information as faculty experience and training, instructional strategies employed, condition of facilities and equipment, availability of appropriate instructional materials and technology, relevant characteristics of the students and the community, and school dropout and graduation rates (Ensign, 1998).

Performance-based assessment focuses on students' ability to apply knowledge, skills, and work habits through the performance of tasks they find meaningful and engaging. While traditional testing helps administrators and teachers answer the question, "Do students *know* content?" performance-based assessment helps answer the question, "How well can students *use* what they know?"

Students should find that performance tasks are interesting and relevant to the knowledge, skills, and work habits emphasized in the curriculum. If appropriate, students can help teachers construct performance-based assessments. For example, elementary-level and high-school-level students helped their teachers construct the following two performance-based assessments, each of which required students to create graphs.

Example 1—Elementary Level

At various times during the school day, students observe and count, at fifteen-minute intervals, the number of cars and trucks that crossed an unlit intersection near their school. Students also gather the same information for a lit intersection near the school. Using data for both intersections, students construct graphs to illustrate the results. If the data suggest the need for a light at the unlit intersection, the graphs will be sent to the local police department.

As students work on various parts of this performance task, the teacher would observe students and make judgments about the quality of their work. Do the counts of cars and trucks appear to be accurate? Do the graphs illustrate the results clearly? Is the students' decision about the need for a traffic light supported by the data they have gathered?

Example 2—High School Level

Students go online to find data on traffic accidents in their state. Based on the data they locate, students prepare graphs that show, by driver's age, various types of accidents, fatalities, speed at the time of accident, and so on. Exemplary graphs will be displayed in the driver education classroom.

As with the elementary-level example, the teacher would make judgments about the quality of the high school students' work. Naturally, these judgments would reflect the teacher's beliefs about the characteristics of exemplary student work at the high school level. Did students visit online sites that have extensive, accurate data on traffic accidents? Were students exhaustive in their online search? Do their graphs show a high degree of technical accuracy? Do the graphs "look professional"?

While the push to assess student learning more frequently has led to some modifications in assessment criteria, new forms of assessment are being used more widely. Innovations in assessment are partly in response to criticisms of the fairness and objectivity of standardized tests, such as the Iowa Test of Basic Skills, the Scholastic Assessment Test (SAT), and the American College Test (ACT). Educators and the public have criticized these tests not only for class and gender bias in their content but also for failing to measure accurately students' true knowledge, skills, and levels of achievement. For all these reasons, today's educational leaders encourage teachers to go beyond traditional pencil-and-paper tests, oral questioning, and formal and informal observations. In addition, they encourage teachers to use an array of new assessment tools—individual and small-group projects, portfolios of work, exhibitions, videotaped demonstrations of skills, and community-based activities, to name a few.

Increasingly, educational leaders are urging teachers to use alternative assessments—that is, "forms of assessment that require the active construction of meaning rather than the passive regurgitation of isolated facts" (McMillan, 2001, p. 14). If assessments are limited to "regurgitation of isolated facts" they can foster "TestThink," as Nelson Maylone explains in this chapter. Likewise, James D. Allen encourages educators to take a critical look at how summative assessment is ultimately communicated to students in "What Is the Purpose of Grades?" Allen provides suggestions for ways educators can authentically and validly assess students' learning of academic content as he challenges conventional practice in teacher preparation programs.

The following sections examine several forms of alternative assessments: authentic assessments, portfolio assessments, peer assessments, self-assessments, performance-based assessments, alternate assessments, and project-based learning.

Authentic Assessment

Authentic assessment (sometimes called *alternative assessment*) requires students to use higher-level thinking skills to perform, create, or solve a real-life problem, not just choose one of several designated responses as on a multiple-choice test item. A teacher might use authentic assessment to evaluate the quality of individual and small-group projects, videotaped demonstrations of skills, or participation in community-based activities. In science, for example, students might design and conduct an experiment to solve a problem and then explain in writing how they solved the problem.

Authentic assessments require students to solve problems or to work on tasks that approximate as much as possible those they will encounter beyond the classroom. For example, authentic assessment might allow students to select projects on which they will be evaluated, such as writing a brochure, making a map, creating a recipe, writing and directing a play, critiquing a performance, inventing something useful, producing a video, creating a model, writing a children's book, and so on. In addition, authentic assessment encourages students to develop their own responses to problem situations by allowing them to decide what information is relevant and how that information should be organized and used.

When teachers use authentic assessment to determine what students have learned—and the depth to which they have learned it—student achievement and attitudes toward learning improve. For example, a study of eleven pairs of K–12 science and math teachers found that when teachers assess student learning in real-life problem-solving situations, learning and attitudes toward school improve (Appalachia Educational Laboratory, 1993).

Portfolio Assessment

Professionals in the fine arts, architecture, photography, and advertising routinely compile portfolios to document their best work. They show their portfolios to prospective clients or employers. Periodically, the professional will update the portfolio contents to reflect his or her latest, and best, accomplishments.

Similarly, portfolio assessment in education is based on a collection of student work that "tell[s] a story of a learner's growth in proficiency, long-term achievement, and significant accomplishments in a given academic area" (Tombari & Borich 1999, p. 164). In short, a portfolio provides examples of important work undertaken by a student, and it represents that student's best work. For example, a high school physics student might include in a portfolio (1) a written report of a physics lab experiment illustrating how vector principles and Newton's laws explain the motion of objects in two dimensions, (2) photographs of that experiment in progress, (3) a certificate of merit received at a local science fair, and (4) an annotated list of Internet sites related to vector principles and Newton's laws.

For students, an important part of portfolio assessment is clarifying the criteria used to select work to be included in the portfolio, and then selecting, organizing, and presenting that work for the teacher to assess. The following purposes have been suggested for student portfolios:

- Growth monitoring, in which portfolio content is used to document student progress toward goals or improvement in proficiency.
- Skill certification, in which the portfolio is used to establish which instructional goals the student has adequately accomplished.
- Evidence of best work, in which the portfolio contains a student's exemplary work and presents the highest level of proficiency the student has achieved with each goal.
- External assessment, in which the portfolio is used to establish student proficiency by agencies outside the classroom, such as the school, school district, or a state agency.
- Communication with parents, in which a portfolio is taken home or maintained at home to convey how the child is performing at school (Oosterhof, 2003, p. 186).

Three general guidelines should be followed to maximize the learning that results from students' involvement in portfolio development:

1. Students should individualize their portfolios—that is, portfolios should focus on the attainment of instructional goals that are important and meaningful for the students.
2. Portfolios should focus on students' accomplishments, their best work—not on their mistakes or limitations.
3. Portfolios should be collaboratively evaluated by teacher and students.

Peer Assessment

Peer assessment occurs when students assess one another's work. Typically, peer assessment is done informally during a class session. At times, a student may be more open to accepting critical feedback from a peer than from the teacher. A peer may use a manner of speaking typical of that age level (word choice, for example), and it may be easier for another student to understand the feedback. Moreover, as the following teacher indicates, peer assessment frees the teacher to observe the peer assessment process and to provide input when necessary:

> We regularly do peer marking—I find this very helpful indeed. A lot of misconceptions come to the fore, and we then discuss these as we are going over the homework. I then go over the peer marking and talk to pupils individually as I go round the room. (Black et al., 2004, p. 14)

Self-Assessment

Self-assessment occurs when students assess their own work and their thought processes while completing that work. It has been suggested that self-assessment "is the most underused form of classroom assessment but has the most flexibility and power as a combined assessment and learning tool" (Tileston, 2004, p. 99). When students assess their own work they become more aware of the factors that promote, or hinder, their learning. Students may, for example, ask assessment questions such as the following: What have I learned as a result of this activity? What problems did I encounter during my learning? How will I overcome these problems in the future?

Performance-Based Assessment

Put simply, performance-based assessment is based on observation and judgment (Stiggins, 2001). In some cases, the teacher observes and then evaluates an actual performance or application of a skill; in others, the teacher evaluates a product created by the student. For example, a teacher might observe a student perform a task or review a student-produced product and then judge its quality. Or a teacher might observe a student's science experiment and judge the quality of the thinking involved, or read a student's research report in history and judge the quality of argumentation and writing. In sum, performance assessment is used to determine what students can *do* as well as what they *know*.

Alternate Assessments

Alternate assessments are designed to measure the performance of students who are unable to participate in traditional large-scale assessments used by school districts and state departments of education. This approach to assessment emerged as a result of the reference to "alternate assessment" in the 1997 reauthorization of the Individuals with Disabilities Education Act (IDEA), which called for states to have alternate assessments in place by the year 2000. An alternate assessment is an alternative way of gathering data about what a student, regardless of the severity of his or her disability, knows and can do. Alternate strategies for collecting data might consist of observing the student during the school day, asking the student to perform a task and noting the level of performance, or interviewing parents or guardians about the student's activities outside of school. For students with disabilities, alternate assessments can be administered to students who have a unique array of educational goals and experiences and who differ greatly in their ability to respond to stimuli, solve problems, and provide responses.

Most states are in the process of developing alternate assessments for students with severe disabilities. The National Center on Educational Outcomes at the University of Minnesota suggests six principles for developing inclusive assessment and accountability systems:

Principle 1. All students with disabilities are included in the assessment system.

Principle 2. Decisions about how students with disabilities participate in the assessment system are the result of clearly articulated participation, accommodation, and alternate assessment decision-making processes.

Principle 3. All students with disabilities are included when student scores are publicly reported, in the same frequency and format as all other students, whether they participate with or without accommodations, or in an alternate assessment.

Principle 4. The assessment performance of students with disabilities has the same impact on the final accountability index as the performance of other students, regardless of how the students participate in the assessment system (i.e., with or without accommodation, or in an alternate assessment).

Principle 5. There is improvement of both the assessment system and the accountability system over time, through the processes of formal monitoring, ongoing evaluation, and systematic training in the context of emerging research and best practice.

Principle 6. Every policy and practice reflects the belief that *all students* must be included in state and district assessment and accountability systems (Guenemoen, Thompson, Thurlow, & Lehr, 2001).

The U.S. Department of Education decided in 2003 that the achievement of students with severe learning problems could be compared to the achievement of students without learning problems. The new ruling would enable more schools to demonstrate that they had made adequate yearly progress (AYP), a key requirement of the No Child Left Behind act.

Prior to the Department of Education ruling, students who took alternate assessments could not be considered "proficient." In addition, many schools failed to make adequate yearly progress (AYP) because their students with disabilities scored low on "regular" assessments or did not take the assessments. Thus, schools were "penalized" when they reported their yearly achievement scores for all students. Furthermore, schools that received federal aid for the poor but failed to make adequate yearly progress could face increasing sanctions from the government.

According to the new ruling, states could develop their own criteria to identify students with "significant cognitive disabilities." The federal government required that standards for students with disabilities be tied to state academic standards, however. Identified students would be tested against standards appropriate for their intellectual development, and their scores counted as part of their school's overall academic performance.

Regardless of which methods of assessment are used, Kathryn Parker Boudett, Richard J. Murnane, Elizabeth City, and Liane Moody write in "Using Student Assessment Data to Improve Instruction" (this chapter) that it is the use of student assessment data to improve instruction that is key to educational reform efforts. Data-driven decision making is critical for teachers and leaders who seek to transform assessment data into improved student assessment.

CRITERION QUESTIONS—CURRICULUM EVALUATION AND ASSESSMENT OF LEARNING

The articles in this chapter examine the educational leader's key role in curriculum evaluation and assessment of learning. The criterion questions for this chapter are as follows:

1. Are both formative and summative evaluation used to make judgments about the quality of the curriculum?
2. Are appropriate assessments used to determine if the purposes and goals of the curriculum have been attained?
3. Are assessments of learning meaningful and authentic for students?
4. Are multiple, diverse forms of assessment used to determine what students know and are able to do?
5. Do assessments of student learning require the active construction of meaning, not just recall of information?

REFERENCES

Appalachia Educational Laboratory. *Alternative Assessment in Math and Science: Moving Toward a Moving Target.* Charleston, WV: Author, 1993.

Black, P., Harrison, C., Lee, C., Marshall, B., & Wiliam, D. "Working Inside the Black Box: Assessment for Learning in the Classroom." *Phi Delta Kappan,* (September, 2004): 9–21.

Cremin, L. *The Genius of American Education.* New York: Vintage, 1965.

Ensign, G. *The Washington Assessment of Student Learning: An Update—May 1998.* Olympia: Washington Commission on Student Learning, 1998.

Guenemoen, R. F., Thompson, S. J., Thurlow, M. L., & Lehr, C. A. *A Self-Study Guide to Implementation of Inclusive Assessment and Accountability Systems: A Best Practice Approach.* Minneapolis: University of Minnesota, National Center on Educational Outcomes, 2001.

McMillan, J. H. *Classroom Assessment: Principles and Practice for Effective Instruction,* 2nd Ed. Boston: Allyn and Bacon, 2006.

Oosterhof, A. *Developing and Using Classroom Assessments.* Upper Saddle River, NJ: Merrill Prentice Hall, 2003.

Rose, L. C., & Gallup, A. M. "The 36th Phi Delta Kappa/Gallup Poll of the Public's Attitudes toward the Public Schools." *Phi Delta Kappan* (September, 2004): 41–56.

Stiggins, R. *Student-Involved Classroom Assessment,* 3rd Ed. Upper Saddle River, NJ: Merrill Prentice Hall, 2001.

Stiggins, R. "New Assessment Beliefs for a New School Mission." *Phi Delta Kappan* (September, 2004): 22–27.

Tileston, D. W. *What Every Teacher Should Know about Student Assessment.* Thousand Oaks, CA: Corwin Press, 2004.

Tombari, M. L., & G. D. Borich. *Authentic Assessment in the classroom: Applications and Practice.* New York: Pearson Education, 1998.

TestThink

NELSON MAYLONE

ABSTRACT: For all the debate in America over the state of its public schools, those on the political Left and Right agree that the achievement gaps are real. According to Maylone, the skills that standardized tests truly measure may be useful in only one context: taking tests. In this article, Maylone also examines the notion of student testing behaviors, which he calls TestThink, and questions what students really learn from all these tests.

For all the fractious debate in America over the state of our public schools, those on the political Left and Right agree that the "achievement gaps" are real. But what do most people mean when they say *achievement gaps*? Gaps in standardized test scores, of course. The gaps consist of the differences between test scores of students of color and those of white students and between scores of poor children and those of their wealthier peers.

Referring to those test score gaps as achievement gaps naturally implies acceptance of the tests as valid measures of student knowledge and skills. But the perceived academic achievement gaps might actually reflect differences in students' abilities (or willingness) to behave in idiosyncratic ways while taking standardized tests—ways which are unconnected to content knowledge or to "general aptitude." I call such student testing behaviors TestThink. In the context of the current "No Child Left Untested" environment, I think it's appropriate to reexamine this notion.

Let's assume that TestThink is real. Is it possible to articulate how a student with well-developed TestThink skills behaves while taking a standardized or other traditional objective test? From my own experience, including years of interviewing students and educators, I believe we can do so.

Perhaps more than anything else, TestThinkers are fast. Not only can they spot correct multiple-choice answers, they can do it *quickly*. TestThinkers know they don't generally have time to ponder or to thoughtfully analyze or to thoroughly consider ways in which alternative answer

choices might reasonably be considered correct. Furthermore, TestThinkers understand that collaboration with others is out of the question and that the use of external resources and experts is forbidden. After all, standardized tests aren't assessing students' resourcefulness.

TestThinkers are in full command of helpful test-taking techniques that exist independent of knowledge and mastery of skills. They recognize the process of elimination as a good method for increasing their chances of guessing correct multiple-choice answers when they are otherwise clueless (thus generating false-positive test scores). TestThinkers are on the lookout for implausible answers and syntactic clues. They spend time—but not too much!—thinking about which answers the makers of the test might want them to choose.

That's a tough challenge, even for skilled Test-Thinkers. And they clearly meet their match in dubiously worded test questions, where dumb luck rules. What is all but a theme of standardized tests is that the test writers knew what *they* meant but didn't notice that there was at least one other logical way to interpret the question or task.

NOT FUNNY

This is a common phenomenon in everyday conversation. We're always asking others to clarify their statements or their questions. Think of the anxious kindergartner being dropped off for her first day of school. She asks her mother, "When will I be through?" The mother answers, "At lunch-time." "No," the child responds, "I mean, how old will I be when I don't have to go to school any more?"

TestThinkers always simply focus on *what the test-makers want,* even though, without a stretch, more than one of the choices which are offered for a given test question might make sense.

One good way to ensure that the issue of item ambiguity would get a proper public airing would be to have all education policy makers—legislators, in particular—take the tests they're foisting on children. My experience, though, is that elected state and federal officials are loath to undertake such an enterprise. I believe they have an intuitive understanding, developed during their own school days, that the tests aren't fair and their scores might be embarrassingly low.

In the area of mathematics, which is where I spent most of my K–12 teaching career, TestThinkers use crystalline, no-nonsense, analytic, strictly linear thinking. They know that a sharp-edged, coldly logical, "adult" model of problem solving is preferred by test writers and scorers (ignoring for a moment the fact that test-makers always *want* some students to do poorly). An attitude of "crack the conundrum" is effective.

FORGET IT

TestThinkers know that peripheral factors that might truly determine the correct answer in real life are to be disregarded. Students whose comments reveal practical thinking are clearly *not* TestThinkers. There's no time for musing. TestThinkers speedily distill math problems down to their computational essentials. They know that they must ignore otherwise-important contextual realities.

If asked to round $443 to the nearest hundred, TestThinkers know not to ask if that amount is someone's Internal Revenue Service tax bill, in which case rounding down is ill advised. In fact, they know that they shouldn't be asking any questions at all.

If a test item begins by noting, "Thomas, an eighth-grader, ran the second mile of a three-mile cross-country race in four minutes and 50 seconds," TestThinkers know to discount the fact that a middle-schooler couldn't run a solo mile that quickly, let alone the second mile of a three-mile run. TestThinkers don't look for real-world constraints; they just *solve the problem.*

If Tania read five books in March, 10 in April, and 15 in May, TestThinkers know that she will surely read 20 in June. No matter that school will be out and that the pizza-party rewards for reading books will have ended. TestThinkers know that trends are always constant.

If a test item asks how many square feet of carpeting one should buy to cover the floor of a room that measures 10 ft. by 11 ft., TestThinkers know to simply multiply to get an answer of 110 sq.-ft., even though carpet rolls are typically 12 ft. wide, meaning that buying only 110 sq.-ft. would leave you with either lots of bare wood floor or unnecessary seams.

For TestThinkers, there is great clarity regarding the high stakes associated with standardized tests, even at early ages. Knowing that scores affect college admission, scholarships, and labels of success or failure, TestThinkers with money (or those with moneyed parents) take advantage of test-preparation courses that can make them even better TestThinkers.

Students blessed with a flair for TestThink have at least a vague awareness that policy makers and—even more important—their parents generally view standardized test scores as reliable indicators of . . . *something.* Intelligence? Accumulated knowledge? Aptitude? Inherent reasoning ability? It depends on whom one asks.

TestThinkers may even discern parents' and legislators' attitudes: "I survived standardized tests, and, by God, it built character. It'll do the same for today's kids!" To quote President Bush on the apparent increase in student test anxiety today, "Too bad."

Society in general and employers in particular are telling educators that we should prepare students to be resourceful and innovative team members.

TestThinkers know, however, that they must think "*inside* the box" in order to do well on standardized tests and that problems must be solved alone—collaboration would obviously be cheating.

Let us ignore for the moment the clear test-taking advantages that TestThinkers possess. Are the skills associated with TestThinking useless? I don't think so. Speedy, Mr. Spock-style logical thinking can be an important skill. Computer programmers must think analytically, and airline pilots need to make good decisions instantly (although in both cases informed intuition may be just as important).

Working quickly can sometimes be good, but speed *can* also equal impulsiveness, thoughtlessness, and haste. This raises a nasty question: Are students who do well on standardized tests (i.e., good TestThinkers) less likely to be collaborative, creative adults? Even nastier, might the current pressures on educators and children to produce high standardized test scores be inadvertently promoting *undesirable* social characteristics?

NASTIER STILL

If so, that runs counter to the statements of those who produce and administer the big tests. In my state, these advocates of the tests claim that "competitive scholastic experience" provides students with excellent preparation for the real world that awaits them after high school graduation.

In Michigan, a school's designation of success or failure under new accreditation rules will be based primarily on students' scores on the state test. In other words, schools with high percentages of TestThinkers will do very well. (Give Tom Watkins, state superintendent of public instruction, credit for capping the tests' impact on accreditation at only 67%.)

If that's true, I'm not sure that it's fair. All sorts of questions come to mind. First, if Test-Think is real, how many children are skilled at TestThink? Which ones? Is being a TestThinker normal? Is doing well on tests the only thing Test-Think is good for? What percentage of children at

each stage of development are capable of good TestThinking?

Then, too, TestThinkers may be especially adept at choosing correct responses on selected-response items as opposed to producing them on constructed response items. How is *choosing* the correct answer from a list cognitively different from *producing* an answer from scratch and then having to defend that response?

NO BUZZ

To illustrate the importance of the issue, try to answer this question: Who was the first American to travel into space? Maybe you answered it correctly, maybe you didn't. If you didn't, the odds are that you'll get it right anyway when it's posed in a multiple-choice format: Who was the first American to travel into space? A. Neil Armstrong; B. Buzz Aldrin; C. Alan Shepard; D. Christa McAuliffe.

Let's see. I have no idea who it was, but . . . it can't be Armstrong or Aldrin. I think they were the first guys to land on the moon. And wasn't Christa McAuliffe the teacher on the *Challenger*? Must be Shepard.

Still more questions are lurking in the shadowy world of TestThinking. Are alternative, non-TestThink approaches to demonstrations of knowledge and problem solving legitimate? If so, are standardized tests biased against *non-*TestThinkers who have otherwise mastered the curriculum? Does high socioeconomic status tend to promote good TestThinking?

And more provocatively, we might ask if some subgroups in America intuitively recognize Test-Think as inconsistent with their definitions of healthy ways of thinking. Are the shrillest cynics correct when they claim that standardized testing is more about sorting and maintaining the status quo than it is about legitimate assessment? Are standardized tests closely aligned with white, middle-, and upper-class culture?

I honestly don't know the answers to these questions, but I believe that, now more than ever, it's important for educators, parents, and policy makers to wrestle with them. Maybe TestThink is a cynical construct. Maybe it's perfectly appropriate to ask kids to don their specialized testing hats at times and to expect them to draw on a narrow (and teachable) set of skills for obtaining high scores.

Still, if we are going to attach immensely high stakes to standardized test scores, shouldn't we be sure that the real subject matter isn't the tests themselves?

Nelson Maylone is assistant professor of educational psychology, College of Education, Eastern Michigan University, Ypsilanti.

QUESTIONS FOR REFLECTION

1. What is "TestThink" and is there any value for students to be good at it? Besides school, what are situations in life when being able to take a test well matters? Make a list and compare it with others.
2. What do you think should be the role of tests in the current curriculum? Are there subjects which more easily lend themselves to testing as a measure of competence? In which subjects do tests provide little, if any, value? In which subjects are they quite valuable?
3. Make a list of the advantages and disadvantages of using tests to measure learning. Do the advantages outweigh the disadvantages? Explain.
4. If you were able to abolish all tests, but had to find some other mechanism to measure student learning, what would you use? How would you use it to measure learning? Like tests, what would be the limitations? What would be the advantages? Finally, how would you know if your measurement worked at measuring what students have learned?

You *Can* Teach for Meaning

JAY MCTIGHE
ELLIOTT SEIF
GRANT WIGGINS

ABSTRACT: Is teaching for meaning impractical in the real world of content standards and high-stakes testing? Teachers seem to think so as they devote greater amounts of time to practicing for the test and covering large amounts of facts and figures that hold out a promise of proficiency. The authors debunk two prevailing misconceptions: that covering tested items and test format is the only way to safeguard or raise test scores; and, that breadth of coverage is preferable to a deeper and more focused approach to content.

Teaching is more than covering content, learning is more than merely taking in, and assessment is more than accurate recall. Meaning must be made, and understanding must be earned. Students are more likely to make meaning and gain understanding when they link new information to prior knowledge, relate facts to "big ideas," explore essential questions, and apply their learning in new contexts.

Consider the following classroom scenarios (Tharp, Estrada, & Yamauchi, 2000). A 6th grade teacher asks students to collect data from home on the height and weight of various family members. Students discuss the following questions in groups: How could we represent these data? What is the most effective way? Students decide on specific approaches and share them with the class. A spirited discussion takes place on the best approach.

A 4th grade teacher asks students to explore the Eskimo culture through research and discussion. Using the textbook and multiple resources, the class tackles the following question: What makes Eskimo life similar to and different from your life? Students define and describe ideas about Eskimo life, using a graphic organizer to make connections between concepts and facts. In small groups, they develop a project on an aspect of Eskimo life, conduct research, organize data, and draw conclusions that compare Eskimo life with their own lives. The teacher has shared a rubric identifying the key features of successful project work. She regularly collects samples of student work to provide feedback and offer suggestions for improvement.

These two examples illustrate a curricular and instructional approach that we call *teaching for meaning and understanding*. This approach embodies five key principles:

- Understanding big ideas in content is central to the work of students.
- Students can only find and make meaning when they are asked to inquire, think at high levels, and solve problems.
- Students should be expected to apply knowledge and skills in meaningful tasks within authentic contexts.
- Teachers should regularly use thought-provoking, engaging, and interactive instructional strategies.
- Students need opportunities to revise their assignments using clear examples of successful work, known criteria, and timely feedback.

Teachers who regularly use this approach center their planning on three recurring questions that should be at the heart of any serious education reform: What are the big ideas and core processes that students should come to understand? What will teachers look for as evidence that students truly understand the big ideas and can apply their knowledge and skills in meaningful and effective ways? What teaching strategies will help students make meaning of curriculum content while avoiding the problems of aimless coverage and activity-oriented instruction?

Such an approach to teaching and learning is more apt to engage the learner and yield meaningful, lasting learning than traditional fact-based and procedure-based lecture, recitation, or textbook instruction. Yet when well-intentioned teachers and administrators are asked to put these ideas into practice, it is not uncommon to hear a chorus of *Yes, but*'s. The message? Teaching for meaning is fine in the abstract, but such ideas are impractical in the real world of content standards and high-stakes testing. The current focus on state and local content standards, related testing programs, No Child Left Behind, and accountability have strengthened the view that we must use more traditional teaching approaches to produce high levels of achievement.

Ironically, a key lever in the standards-based reform strategy—the use of high-stakes external tests—has unwittingly provided teachers with a rationalization for avoiding or minimizing the need to teach for meaning and in-depth understanding. Teachers are more likely to spend time practicing for the test, covering many facts and procedures and using traditional lecture and recitation methods in the hope that more students will become proficient.

Two key *Yes, but*'s interfere with the promise of teaching for meaning: Yes, but . . . we have to teach to the state or national test. Yes, but . . . we have too much content to cover. Both are misconceptions.

MISCONCEPTION NUMBER 1: WE HAVE TO TEACH TO THE TEST

Many educators believe that instructing and assessing for understanding are incompatible with state mandates and standardized tests. Although they rarely offer research to support this claim, these educators imply that teachers are stuck teaching to the test against their will. They would teach for meaning, if they could. The implicit assumption is that teachers can only safeguard or raise test scores by covering tested items and practicing the test format. By implication, there is no time for the kind of in-depth and engaging instruction that helps students make meaning and deepens their understanding of big ideas.

We contend that teachers can best raise test scores over the long haul by teaching the key ideas and processes contained in content standards in rich and engaging ways; by collecting evidence of student understanding of that content through robust local assessments rather than one-shot standardized testing; and by using engaging and effective instructional strategies that help students explore core concepts through inquiry and problem solving.

What evidence supports these contentions? A summary of the last 30 years of research on learning and cognition shows that learning for meaning leads to greater retention and use of information and ideas (Bransford, Brown, & Cocking, 2000). One avenue of this research explored the differences between novices and experts in various fields. Psychologists learned that experts have more than just a lot of facts in their heads: They actually *think* differently than novices do. According to the researchers, "expertise requires something else: a well-organized knowledge of concepts, principles, and procedures of inquiry"(p. 239). This finding suggests that students, to become knowledgeable and competent in a field of study, should develop not only a solid foundation of factual knowledge but also a conceptual framework that facilitates meaningful learning.

Data from the Trends in International Mathematics and Science Study (TIMSS) also challenge the premise that teaching to the test is the best way to achieve higher scores. TIMSS tested the mathematics and science achievement of students in 42 countries at three grade levels (4, 8, and 12). Although the outcomes of TIMSS are well

known—U.S. students do not perform as well as students in most other industrialized countries (Martin, Mullis, Gregory, Hoyle, & Shen, 2000)—the results of its less publicized teaching studies offer additional insights. In an exhaustive analysis of mathematics instruction in Japan, Germany, and the United States, Stigler and Hiebert (1999) present striking evidence of the benefits of teaching for meaning and understanding. In Japan, a high-achieving country, mathematics teachers state that their primary aim is to develop conceptual understanding in their students. Compared with teachers in the United States, they cover less ground in terms of discrete topics, skills, or pages in a textbook, but they emphasize problem-based learning in which students derive and explain rules and theorems, thus leading to deeper understanding. A recent TIMSS analysis of data from seven countries indicates that all high-achieving countries use a percentage of their mathematics problems to help students explore concepts and make connections, whereas U.S. teachers tend to emphasize algorithmic plug-in of procedures instead of genuine reasoning and problem solving (Hiebert et al., 2003; Stigler & Hiebert, 2004).

Compatible findings emerged in an ambitious study of 24 restructured schools—eight elementary, eight middle, and eight high schools—in 16 states (Newmann & Associates, 1996). The research showed that students improved their performance in mathematics and social studies and that inequalities among high- and low-performing students diminished when the curriculum included sustained examination of a few important topics rather than superficial coverage of many topics; when teachers framed instruction around challenging and relevant questions; and when students were required to provide oral and written explanations for their responses.

Two additional studies of factors influencing student achievement were conducted in Chicago Public Schools. Smith, Lee, and Newmann (2001) examined test scores from more than 100,000 students in grades 2–8 and surveys from more than 5,000 teachers in 384 Chicago elementary schools. The study compared teachers who used interactive teaching methods with those who used noninteractive teaching methods. The researchers then looked at subsequent achievement in reading and mathematics.

The researchers described interactive instruction methods as follows:

> Teachers . . . create situations in which students . . . ask questions, develop strategies for solving problems, and communicate with one another. Students are often expected to explain their answers and discuss how they arrived at their conclusions. These teachers usually assess students' mastery of knowledge through discussions, projects, or tests that demand explanation and extended writing. Students work on applications or interpretations of the material to develop new or deeper understandings of a given topic. Such assignments may take several days to complete. Students in interactive classrooms are often encouraged to choose the questions or topics they wish to study within an instructional unit designed by the teacher. Different students may be working on different tasks during the same class period. (p. 12)

The study found clear and consistent correlations between interactive teaching methods and higher levels of learning and achievement.

In a related study (Newmann, Bryk, & Nagaoka, 2001), researchers in Chicago systematically collected and analyzed classroom writing and mathematics assignments given in grades 3, 6, and 8 by randomly selected schools and control schools for a three-year period. Researchers rated assignments according to the degree to which the work required authentic intellectual activity, which the researchers defined as "construction of knowledge, through the use of disciplined inquiry, to produce discourse, products, or performances that have value beyond school" (pp. 14–15). The study concluded that students who received assignments requiring more challenging intellectual work also achieved greater-than-average gains on the Iowa Tests of Basic Skills in reading and mathematics and demonstrated higher performance in reading, mathematics, and writing on the Illinois Goals Assessment Program.

MISCONCEPTION NUMBER 2: WE HAVE TOO MUCH CONTENT TO COVER

Teachers from kindergarten to graduate school wrestle with the realities of the information age and the knowledge explosion: There is simply too much information to cover. In theory, the standards movement promised a solution to the problem of information overload by identifying curricular priorities. Content standards were intended to specify what is most important for students to know and be able to do, thus providing a much-needed focus and set of priorities for curriculum, instruction, and assessment. In practice, however, content standards committees at the national, state, and district levels often worked in isolation to produce overly ambitious lists of "essentials" for their disciplines. Rather than streamlining the curriculum, the plethora of standards added to the coverage problem, especially at the elementary level, where teachers must teach standards and benchmarks in multiple subjects (Marzano & [Kendell], 1998). The matter is further complicated by teachers' propensity to focus on overloaded textbooks as the primary resource for addressing their obligations to the content standards. U.S. textbook publishers try to cover the waterfront to appease state textbook adoption committees, national subject-area organizations, and various special-interest groups. Project 2061's study of mathematics and science textbooks (Kesidou & Roseman, 2002; Kulm, 1999) found few commercial texts that were not "a mile wide and an inch deep."

Teachers confronted with thick textbooks and long lists of content standards may understandably come to the erroneous conclusion that they must cover huge amounts of content. They feel that "if it is in my book, it has to be taught." The perceived need to "cover" is typically based on two implicit assumptions that we think are unfounded. The first assumption is that if a teacher covers specific material—that is, talks about it and assigns some work—students will adequately learn it for tests. The second is that teachers should typically address standards one at a time in lesson planning.

We know of no research that supports the idea that a coverage mode of instruction increases achievement on external tests. In fact, current research suggests that "uncoverage"—focusing on fewer topics and core understandings—is more likely to increase student achievement. The TIMSS research that demonstrated lower achievement scores for U.S. students found that U.S. mathematics and science curriculums were unfocused and included too many topics (Schmidt, McKnight, & Raizen, 1997). In contrast, high-achieving countries offered fewer topics at each level, coupled with more coherent and focused content. This concentrated focus enabled teachers and students to gradually build more complex understandings in mathematics, to delve deeply into subject matter, and to attain higher levels of achievement (Schmidt, 2004; Schmidt, Houang, & Cogan, 2002).

Recent studies on mathematics reform curriculums described by Senk and Thompson (2003) also support using an "uncoverage" approach to improve student achievement. All the mathematics reform curriculums that Senk and Thompson studied were designed to help students understand fundamental mathematical concepts and ideas. Longitudinal data from middle schools show that students using understanding-based mathematics curriculums demonstrated superior performance in both nonroutine problem solving and mathematical skills. Other studies on high school mathematics reform programs showed that students in these programs developed additional skills and understandings while not falling behind on traditional content.

The second misconception—that content standards and benchmarks should be addressed one at a time through targeted lessons—is often reinforced by state and national standardized tests that typically sample the standards and benchmarks one at a time through decontextualized items. Thus, the presentation of both tests and standards documents often misleadingly suggests that teachers should teach to standards one bit at a time. From this point of view, teachers certainly do not have enough time to address all standards.

We suggest clustering discrete standards under an umbrella of big ideas. This approach renders teaching more efficient while applying a principle of effective learning derived from research. Bransford and colleagues suggest that

> Experts' knowledge is not simply a list of facts and formulas that are relevant to the domain; instead, their knowledge is organized around core concepts or "big ideas" that guide their thinking about the domain. (2000, p. 24)

Similarly, the use of complex performance assessments enables students to apply facts, concepts, and skills contained in multiple standards in a more meaningful way while enabling educators to assess for true understanding, not just for recall or recognition.

IMPLICATIONS

Teaching for meaning and understanding leads to more lasting and significant student learning. Although we have made a strong case against two widely held objections to this approach, we realize that educators must test, debate, and explore these claims in their respective settings.

We therefore encourage you to conduct ongoing action research at the school and district levels that compares the kind of curriculum, assessment, and instruction described here with teaching that focuses on covering content or practicing for standardized accountability tests. Are students more engaged when you frame content in provocative essential questions? Do students show increased understanding when they have some choice in the manner in which they demonstrate their knowledge? Is performance on traditional assessments compromised when learners have the opportunity to apply their knowledge in authentic situations? Do inquiry-based and problem-based instruction energize teachers?

Let the results speak for themselves. We hope that by "uncovering" some of these unfounded claims, we will encourage educators and district leaders to take a more proactive stance and focus on what they *can* do to improve learning in today's standards-based world.

REFERENCES

Bransford, J., Brown, A., & Cocking, R. (Eds.). (2000). *How people learn: Brain, mind, experience, and school.* Washington, DC: National Research Council.

Hiebert, J., Gallimore, R., Garnier, H., Givvin, K. B., Hollingsworth, H., Jacobs, J., et al. (2003). *Teaching mathematics in seven countries: Results from the TIMSS 1999 video study* (NCES 2003–013). Washington, DC: U.S. Department of Education.

Kesidou, S., & Roseman, J. E. (2002). How well do middle school science programs measure up? *Journal of Research in Science Teaching, 39*(6), 522–549.

Kulm, G. (1999). Evaluating mathematics textbooks. *Basic Education, 43*(9), 6–8.

Martin, M., Mullis, I., Gregory, K., Hoyle, C., & Shen, C. (2000). *Effective schools in science and mathematics: IEA's Third International Mathematics and Science Study.* Boston: International Study Center, Lynch School of Education, Boston College.

Marzano, R. J., & Kendell, J. S. (1998). *Awash in a sea of standards.* Aurora, CO: Mid-continent Research for Education and Learning.

Newmann, F., & Associates. (1996). *Authentic achievement: Restructuring schools for intellectual quality.* San Francisco: Jossey-Bass.

Newmann, F., Bryk, A., & Nagaoka, J. (2001). *Authentic intellectual work and standardized tests: Conflict or coexistence?* Chicago: Consortium on Chicago School Research.

Schmidt, W. (2004). A vision for mathematics. *Educational Leadership, 61*(5), 6–11.

Schmidt, W., Houang, R., & Cogan, L. (2002). A coherent curriculum: The case for mathematics. *American Educator, 26*(2), 10–26, 47–48.

Schmidt, W., McKnight, C., & Raizen, S. (1997). *A splintered vision: An investigation of U.S. science and mathematics education.* Norwell, MA: Kluwer Academic Publishers.

Senk, S., & Thompson, D. (2003). *Standards-based school mathematics curricula: What are they? What do students learn?* Mahwah, NJ: Erlbaum.

Smith, J., Lee, V., & Newmann, F. (2001). *Instruction and achievement in Chicago elementary schools.* Chicago: Consortium on Chicago School Research.

Stigler, J., & Hiebert, J. (1999). *The teaching gap.* New York: Free Press.

Stigler, J., & Hiebert, J. (2004). Improving mathematics teaching. *Educational Leadership, 61*(5), 12–16.

Tharp, R., Estrada, S., & Yamauchi, L. (2000). *Teaching transformed: Achieving excellence, fairness, inclusion, and harmony.* Boulder, CO: Westview Press.

Jay McTighe and *Grant Wiggins* are coauthors of *Understanding by Design* (Association for Supervision and Curriculum Development [ASCD], 1998) and *The Understanding by Design Handbook* (ASCD, 1999). *Elliott Seif* is a member of the ASCD Understanding by Design cadre.

QUESTIONS FOR REFLECTION

1. The authors debunk two common myths regarding testing in this article. What are they? Do you think that the authors' conclusions are accurate?
2. What does it mean to "teach for meaning" and do you know anyone who *wouldn't* want to teach for meaning? Given that, what do the authors mean by the phrase?
3. How does the notion of action research factor into the major themes covered by the authors? What is action research and how would you go about using it in your own classroom to measure whether or not you have successfully taught the subject material?

Learning to Love Assessment

CAROL ANN TOMLINSON

ABSTRACT: Tomlinson discusses her "insightful journey" as she comes to grips with informative assessment and begins to see the critical role it plays in judging performance, guiding students, and shaping instruction. In the author's mind, informative assessment is not an end in itself, but the beginning of better instruction. Tomlinson offers ten understandings about classroom assessment that sometimes gradually and sometimes suddenly illuminate her work.

When I was a young teacher—young both in years and in understanding of the profession I had entered—I nonetheless went about my work as though I comprehended its various elements. I immediately set out to arrange furniture, put up bulletin boards, make lesson plans, assign homework, give tests, compute grades, and distribute report cards as though I knew what I was doing.

I had not set out to be a teacher, and so I had not really studied education in any meaningful way. I had not student taught. Had I done those things, however, I am not convinced that my evolution as a teacher would have been remarkably different. In either case, my long apprenticeship as a student (Lortie, 1975) would likely have dominated any more recent knowledge I might have acquired about what it means to be a teacher. I simply "played school" in the same way that young children "play house"—by mimicking what we think the adults around us do.

The one element I knew I was unprepared to confront was classroom management. Consequently that's the element that garnered most of my attention during my early teaching years. The element to which I gave least attention was assessment. In truth, I didn't even know the word *assessment* for a good number of years. I simply knew I was supposed to give tests and grades. I didn't much like tests in those years. It was difficult for me to move beyond their judgmental aspect. They made kids nervous. They made me nervous. With no understanding of the role of assessment in a dynamic and success-oriented classroom, I initially ignored assessment when I could and did it when I had to.

Now, more than three decades into the teaching career I never intended to have, it's difficult for me to remember exactly when I had the legion of insights that have contributed to my growth as an educator. I do know, however, that those insights are the milestones that mark my evolution from seeing teaching as a job to seeing teaching as a science-informed art that has become a passion.

Following are 10 understandings about classroom assessment that sometimes gradually and sometimes suddenly illuminated my work. I am not finished with the insights yet because I am not finished with my work as a teacher or learner. I present the understandings in something like the order they unfolded in my thinking.

The formulation of one insight generally prepared the way for the next. Now, of course, they are seamless, interconnected, and interdependent. But they did not come to me that way. Over time and taken together, the understandings make me an advocate of informative assessment— a concept that initially played no conscious role in my work as a teacher.

UNDERSTANDING 1: INFORMATIVE ASSESSMENT ISN'T JUST ABOUT TESTS

Initially I thought about assessment as test giving. Over time, I became aware of students who did poorly on tests but who showed other evidence of learning. They solved problems well, contributed to discussions, generated rich ideas, drew sketches to illustrate, and role-played. When they wanted to communicate, they always found a way. I began to realize that when I gave students multiple ways to express learning or gave them a say in how they could show what they knew, more students were engaged. More to the point, more students were learning.

Although I still had a shallow sense of the possibilities of assessment, I did at least begin to try in multiple ways to let kids show what they knew. I used more authentic products as well as tests to gain a sense of student understanding. I began to realize that when one form of assessment was ineffective for a student, it did not necessarily indicate a lack of student success but could, in fact, represent a poor fit between the student and the method through which I was trying to make the student communicate, I studied students to see what forms of assessment worked for them and to be sure I never settled for a single assessment as an adequate representation of what a student knew.

UNDERSTANDING 2: INFORMATIVE ASSESSMENT REALLY ISN'T ABOUT THE GRADE BOOK

At about the same time that Understanding 1 emerged in my thinking, I began to sense that filling a grade book was both less interesting and less useful than trying to figure out what individual students knew, understood, or could do. My thinking was shifting from assessment as judging students to assessment as guiding students. I was beginning to think about student accomplishment more than about student ranking (Wiggins, 1993).

Giving students feedback seemed to be more productive than giving them grades. If I carefully and consistently gave them feedback about their work, I felt more like a teacher than a warden. I felt more respectful of the students and their possibilities (Wiggins, 1993). I began to understand the difference between teaching for success and "gotcha" teaching and to sense the crucial role of informative assessment in the former.

UNDERSTANDING 3: INFORMATIVE ASSESSMENT ISN'T ALWAYS FORMAL

I also became conscious of the fact that some of the most valuable insights I gleaned about students came from moments or events that I'd never associated with assessment. When I read in a student's journal that his parents were divorcing, I understood why he was disengaged in class. I got a clear picture of one student's misunderstanding when I walked around as students worked and saw a diagram she made to represent how she understood the concept we were discussing. I could figure out how to help a student be more successful in small groups when I took the time to study systematically, but from a distance, what he did to make groups grow impatient with him.

Assessment, then, was more than "tests plus other formats." Informative assessment could occur any time I went in search of information about a student. In fact, it could occur when I was not actively searching but was merely conscious of what was happening around me.

I began to talk in more purposeful ways with students as they entered and left the classroom. I began to carry around a clipboard on which I took notes about students. I developed a filing system that enabled me to easily store and retrieve information about students as individuals and learners. I was more focused in moving around the room to spot-check student work in progress for particular proficiencies. I began to sense that virtually all student products and interactions can serve as informative assessment because I, as a teacher, have the power to use them that way.

UNDERSTANDING 4: INFORMATIVE ASSESSMENT ISN'T SEPARATE FROM THE CURRICULUM

Early in my teaching, I made lesson plans. Later on, I made unit plans. In neither time frame did I see assessment as a part of the curriculum design process. As is the case with many teachers, I planned what I would teach, taught it, and then created assessments. The assessments were largely derived from what had transpired during a segment of lessons and ultimately what had transpired during a unit of study. It was a while before I understood what Wiggins and McTighe (1998) call backward design.

That evolution came in three stages for me. First, I began to understand the imperative of laying out precisely what mattered most for students to know and be able to do—but also what they should understand—as a result of our work together. Then I began to discover that many of my lessons had been only loosely coupled to learning goals. I'd sometimes (often?) been teaching in response to what my students liked rather than in response to crucial learning goals. I understood the need to make certain that my teaching was a consistent match for what students needed to know, understand, and be able to do at the end of a unit. Finally, I began to realize that if I wanted to teach for success, my assessments had to be absolutely aligned with the knowledge, understanding, and skill I'd designated as essential learning outcomes. There was a glimmer of recognition in my work that assessment was a part of—not apart from—curriculum design.

UNDERSTANDING 5: INFORMATIVE ASSESSMENT ISN'T ABOUT "AFTER"

I came to understand that assessments that came at the end of a unit—although important manifestations of student knowledge, understanding, and skill—were less useful to me as a teacher than were assessments that occurred during a unit of study. By the time I gave and graded a final assessment, we were already moving on to a new topic or unit. There was only a limited amount I could do at that stage with information that revealed to me that some students fell short of mastering essential outcomes—or that others had likely been bored senseless by instruction that focused on outcomes they had mastered long before the unit had begun. When I studied student work in the course of a unit, however, I could do many things to support or

extend student learning. I began to be a devotee of formative assessment, although I did not know that term for many years.

It took time before I understood the crucial role of preassessment or diagnostic assessment in teaching. Likely the insight was the product of the embarrassment of realizing that a student had no idea what I was talking about because he or she lacked vocabulary I assumed every 7th grader knew or of having a student answer a question in class early in a unit that made it clear he already knew more about the topic at hand than I was planning to teach. At that point, I began to check early in the year to see whether students could read the textbook, how well they could produce expository writing, what their spelling level was, and so on. I began systematically to use preassessments before a unit started to see where students stood in regard to prerequisite and upcoming knowledge, understanding, and skills.

UNDERSTANDING 6: INFORMATIVE ASSESSMENT ISN'T AN END IN ITSELF

I slowly came to realize that the most useful assessment practices would shape how I taught. I began to explore and appreciate two potent principles of informative assessment. First, the greatest power of assessment information lies in its capacity to help me see how to be a better teacher. If I know what students are and are not grasping at a given moment in a sequence of study, I know how to plan our time better. I know when to reteach, when to move ahead, and when to explain or demonstrate something in another way. Informative assessment is not an end in itself, but the beginning of better instruction.

UNDERSTANDING 7: INFORMATIVE ASSESSMENT ISN'T SEPARATE FROM INSTRUCTION

A second and related understanding hovered around my sense that assessment should teach me how to be a better teacher. Whether I liked it or not, informative assessment always demonstrated to me that my students' knowledge, understanding, and skill were emerging along different time continuums and at different depths. It became excruciatingly clear that my brilliant teaching was not equally brilliant for everyone in my classes. In other words, informative assessment helped me solidify a need for differentiation. As Lorna Earl (2003) notes, if teachers know a precise learning destination and consistently check to see where students are relative to that destination, differentiation isn't just an option; it's the logical next step in teaching. Informative assessment made it clear—at first, painfully so—that if I meant for every student to succeed, I was going to have to teach with both singular and group needs in mind.

UNDERSTANDING 8: INFORMATIVE ASSESSMENT ISN'T JUST ABOUT STUDENT READINESS

Initially, my emergent sense of the power of assessment to improve my teaching focused on student readiness. At the time, I was teaching in a school with a bimodal population—lots of students were three or more years behind grade level or three or more years above grade level, with almost no students in between. Addressing that expansive gap in student readiness was a daily challenge. I was coming to realize the role of informative assessment in ensuring that students worked as often as possible at appropriate levels of challenge (Earl, 2003).

Only later was I aware of the potential role of assessment in determining what students cared about and how they learned. When I could attach what I was teaching to what students cared about, they learned more readily and more durably. When I could give them options about how to learn and express what they knew, learning improved. I realized I could pursue insights about student interests and preferred modes of learning, just as I had about their readiness needs.

I began to use surveys to determine student interests, hunt for clues about their individual and shared passions, and take notes on who learned better alone and who learned better in small groups. I began to ask students to write to me about which instructional approaches were working for them and which were not. I was coming to understand that learning is multidimensional and that assessment could help me understand learners as multidimensional as well.

UNDERSTANDING 9: INFORMATIVE ASSESSMENT ISN'T JUST ABOUT FINDING WEAKNESSES

As my sense of the elasticity of assessment developed, so did my sense of the wisdom of using assessment to accentuate student positives rather than negatives. With readiness-based assessments, I had most often been on the hunt for what students didn't know, couldn't do, or didn't understand. Using assessment to focus on student interests and learning preferences illustrated for me the power of emphasizing what works for students.

When I saw "positive space" in students and reflected that to them, the results were stunningly different from when I reported on their "negative space." It gave students something to build on—a sense of possibility. I began to spend at least as much time gathering assessment information on what students could do as on what they couldn't. That, in turn, helped me develop a conviction that each student in my classes brought strengths to our work and that it was my job to bring those strengths to the surface so that all of us could benefit.

UNDERSTANDING 10: INFORMATIVE ASSESSMENT ISN'T JUST FOR THE TEACHER

Up to this point, much of my thinking was about the teacher—about me, my class, my work, my growth. The first nine understandings about assessment were, in fact, crucial to my development. But it was the 10th understanding that revolutionized what happened in the classrooms I shared with my students. I finally began to grasp that teaching requires a plural pronoun. The best teaching is never so much about me as about us. I began to see my students as full partners in their success.

My sense of the role of assessment necessarily shifted. I was a better teacher—but more to the point, my students were better learners when assessment helped all of us push learning forward (Earl, 2003). When students clearly understood our learning objectives, knew precisely what success would look like, understood how each assignment contributed to their success, could articulate the role of assessment in ensuring their success, and understood that their work correlated with their needs, they developed a sense of self-efficacy that was powerful in their lives as learners. Over time, as I developed, my students got better at self-monitoring, self-managing, and self-modifying (Costa & Kallick, 2004). They developed an internal locus of control that caused them to work hard rather than to rely on luck or the teacher's good will (Stiggins, 2000).

ASSESSING WISELY

Lorna Earl (2003) distinguishes between assessment of learning, assessment for learning, and assessment as learning. In many ways, my growth as a teacher slowly and imperfectly followed that progression. I began by seeing assessment as judging performance, then as informing teaching, and finally as informing learning. In reality, all those perspectives play a role in effective teaching. The key is where we place the emphasis.

Certainly a teacher and his or her students need to know who reaches (and exceeds) important learning targets—thus summative assessment, or assessment of learning, has a place in teaching. Robust learning generally requires robust teaching, and both diagnostic and formative assessments, or assessments for learning, are catalysts for better teaching. In the end, however, when assessment is seen as learning—for students as well as for teachers—it becomes most informative and generative for students and teachers alike.

REFERENCES

Costa, A., & Kallick, B. (2004). *Assessment strategies for self-directed learning.* Thousand Oaks, CA: Corwin.

Earl, L. (2003). *Assessment as learning: Using classroom assessment to maximize student learning.* Thousand Oaks, CA: Corwin.

Lortie, D. (1975). *Schoolteacher: A sociological study.* Chicago: University of Chicago Press.

Stiggins, R. (2000). *Student-involved classroom assessment* (3rd ed.). Upper Saddle River, NJ: Prentice-Hall.

Wiggins, G. (1993). *Assessing student performance: Exploring the purpose and limits of testing.* San Francisco: Jossey-Bass.

Wiggins, G., & McTighe, J. (1998). *Understanding by design.* Alexandria, VA: Association for Supervision and Curriculum Development.

Carol Ann Tomlinson is professor of Educational Leadership, Foundation, and Policy at the University of Virginia in Charlottesville.

QUESTIONS FOR REFLECTION

1. What strategies can help educators and students move beyond the judgmental aspects of tests and other forms of assessment?
2. Which of Tomlinson's ten understandings about classroom assessment stood out most for you? What made those resonate?
3. Lorna Earl (2003) is cited in the article for her writing that distinguishes between assessment *of* learning, assessment *for* learning, and assessment *as* learning. What are the distinctions she is referring to and how might a teacher or other educator help students see the distinctions between each kind of assessment?

A Balanced School Accountability Model: An Alternative to High-Stakes Testing

KEN JONES

ABSTRACT: The health of our public schools, Jones argues, depends on defining a new model of accountability—one that is balanced and comprehensive and involves much more than test scores. Jones proposes a way of evaluating schools in the United States which could serve as an alternative to the system of using high-stakes testing for school accountability. Four core areas comprise his model: improving student learning; creating opportunities for learning; ability to be responsive to students, parents, and community; and ensuring schools have the proper organizational capacity.

For some time now, it has been apparent to many in the education community that state and federal policies intended to develop greater school accountability for the learning of all students have been terribly counterproductive. The use of high-stakes testing of students has been fraught with flawed assumptions, oversimplified understandings of school realities, undemocratic concentration of power, undermining of the teaching profession, and predictably disastrous consequences for our most vulnerable students. Far from the noble ideal of leaving no child behind, current policies, if continued, are bound to increase existing inequities, trivialize schooling, and mislead the public about the quality and promise of public education.

What is needed is a better means for evaluating schools, an alternative to the present system of using high-stakes testing for school accountability. A new model, based on a different set of assumptions and understandings about school realities and approaches to power, is required. It must be focused on the needs of learners and on the goals of having high expectations for all rather than on the prerequisites of a bureaucratic measurement system.

PREMISES

In the realm of student learning, the question of outcomes has often been considered primary: what do we want students to know and be able to do as a result of schooling? Once the desired outcomes have been specified, school reform efforts have proceeded to address the thorny questions of how to attain them. Starting from desired outcomes is an important shift in how to think about what does or does not make sense in classroom instruction.

In the realm of school accountability, however, little attention has been paid to corresponding outcome-related questions. It has simply been assumed that schools should be accountable for improved student learning, as measured by external test scores. It has been largely assumed by policy makers that external tests do, in fact, adequately measure student learning. These and other assumptions about school accountability must be questioned if we are to develop a more successful accountability model. It would be well to start from basic questions about the purposes and audiences of schools. For what, to whom, and by what means should schools be held accountable? The following answers to these questions provide a set of premises on which a new school accountability system can be based.

For What Should Schools Be Accountable? Schools should be held accountable for at least the following:

• *The physical and emotional well-being of students.* The caring aspect of school is essential to high-quality education. Parents expect that their children will be safe in schools and that adults in schools will tend to their affective as well as cognitive needs. In addition, we know that learning depends on a caring school climate that nurtures positive relationships.

• *Student learning.* Student learning is complex and multifaceted. It includes acquiring not only knowledge of disciplinary subject matter but also the thinking skills and dispositions needed in a modern democratic society.

• *Teacher learning.* Having a knowledgeable and skilled teacher is the most significant factor in student learning and should be fostered in multiple ways, compatible with the principles of adult learning. Schools must have sufficient time and funding to enable teachers to improve their own performance, according to professional teaching standards.

• *Equity and access.* Given the history of inequity with respect to minority and underserved student populations, schools must be accountable for placing a special emphasis on improving equity and access, providing fair opportunities for all to learn to high standards. Our press for excellence must include a press for fairness.

• *Improvement.* Schools should be expected to function as learning organizations, continuously engaged in self-assessment and adjustment in an effort to meet the needs of their students. The capacity to do so must be ensured and nurtured.

To Whom Should Schools Be Accountable? Schools should be held accountable to their primary clients: students, parents, and the local community. Current accountability systems make the state and federal governments the locus of power and decision making. But the primary clients of schools should be empowered to make decisions about the ends of education, not just the means, provided there are checks to ensure equity and access and adherence to professional standards for teaching.

By What Means Should Schools Be Held Accountable? To determine how well schools are fulfilling their responsibilities, multiple measures should be used. Measures of school accountability should include both qualitative and quantitative approaches, taking into account local contexts, responsiveness to student and community needs, and professional practices and standards. Because schools are complex and unique institutions that address multiple societal needs, there should also be allowances for local measures, customized to meet local needs and concerns. A standardized approach toward school accountability cannot work in a nation as diverse as the U.S.

Given these premises, what are the proper roles of a government-developed and publicly funded school accountability system?

• It should serve to improve student learning and school practices and to ensure equity and access, not to reward or punish schools.
• It should provide guidance and information for local decision making, not classify schools as successes or failures.
• It should reflect a democratic approach, including a balance of responsibility and power among different levels of government.

A BALANCED MODEL

An accountability framework called the "balanced scorecard" is currently employed in the business world and provides a useful perspective for schools.[1] This framework consists of four areas that must be evaluated to give a comprehensive view of the health of an organization. The premise is that both outcomes and operations must be measured if the feedback system is to be used to improve the organization, not just monitor it. In the business context, the four components of the framework are: 1) financial, 2) internal business, 3) customer, and 4) innovation and learning.

Applying this four-part approach to education, we can use the following aspects of school performance as the components of a balanced school accountability model: 1) student learning; 2) opportunity to learn; 3) responsiveness to students, parents, and community; and 4) organizational capacity for improvement. Each of these aspects must be attended to and fostered by an evaluation system that has a sufficiently high resolution to take into account the full complexity and scope of modern-day schools.

1. Student Learning. Principles of high-quality assessment have been well articulated by various organizations and should be followed.[2] What is needed is a system that

- is primarily intended to improve student learning;
- aligns with local curricula;
- emphasizes applied learning and thinking skills, not just declarative knowledge and basic skills;
- embodies the principle of multiple measures, including a variety of formats such as writing, open-response questions, and performance-based tasks; and
- is accessible to students with diverse learning styles, intelligence profiles, exceptionalities, and cultural backgrounds.

Currently, there is a mismatch between what cognitive science and brain research have shown about human learning and how schools and educational bureaucracies continue to measure learning.[3] We now know that human intellectual abilities are malleable and that people learn through a social and cultural process of constructing knowledge and understandings in given contexts. And yet we continue to conduct schooling and assessment guided by the outdated beliefs that intelligence is fixed, that knowledge exists apart from culture and context, and that learning is best induced through the behaviorist model of stimulus/response.

Scientific measurement cannot truly "objectify" learning and rate it hierarchically. Accurate decisions about the quality and depth of an individual's learning must be based on human judgment. While test scores and other assessment data are useful and necessary sources of information, a fair assessment of a person's learning can be made only by other people, preferably by those who know the person best in his or her own context. A reasonable process for determining the measure of student learning could involve local panels of teachers, parents, and community members, who review data about student performance and make decisions about promotion, placement, graduation, and so on.

What is missing in most current accountability systems is not just a human adjudication system, but also a local assessment component that addresses local curricula, contexts, and cultures. A large-scale external test is not sufficient to determine a student's achievement. District, school, and classroom assessments must also be developed as part of a comprehensive means of collecting data on student learning. The states of Maine and Nebraska are currently developing just such systems.[4]

Most important, locally developed assessments depend on the knowledge and "assessment literacy" of teachers.[5] Most teachers have not been adequately trained in assessment and need substantial and ongoing professional development to create valid and reliable tasks and build effective classroom assessment repertoires. This means that an investment must be made in teacher learning about assessment. The value of such an investment is not only in the promise of improved classroom instruction and measurement. Research also shows that improved classroom assessment results in improved student achievement on external tests.[6]

Last, the need to determine the effectiveness of the larger state school system can either support or undermine such local efforts. If state or federal agencies require data to be aggregated from local to state levels, local decision making is necessarily weakened, and an undue emphasis is placed on standardized methods. If, however, the state and federal agencies do not rely on local assessment systems to gauge the health of the larger system, much may be gained. In New Zealand, for example, a system of educational monitoring is in place that uses matrix sampling on tasks that include one-to-one videotaped interviews, team tasks, and independent tasks.[7] No stakes are entailed for schools or students. The data are profiled and shared with schools for the purpose of teacher professional development and as a means of developing model tasks for local assessments. Such a system supports rather than undermines local assessment efforts.

2. Opportunity to Learn. How can students be expected to meet high standards if they are not given a fair opportunity to learn? This question has yet to be answered with respect to school accountability. Schools should be accountable for providing equitable opportunities for all students to learn, and we must develop ways to determine how well they do so.

At the heart of the matter is that the responsibility for opportunity to learn must be shared by the district and state. The inequitable funding of public schools, particularly the disparity between the schools of the haves and those of the have-nots, places the schools of disadvantaged students in unjust and often horrifying circumstances. Over the past decade, there have been lawsuits in various states attempting to redress this imbalance, which is largely a result of dependence on property taxes for school funding. Yet not a great deal of progress has been made.

How should we define and put into practice our understanding of opportunity to learn? How will we measure it? How can an accountability system foster it?

At a minimum, one might expect that schools and school systems will provide qualified teachers, adequate instructional materials, and sound facilities. This is the contention in a recent lawsuit, *Williams* v. *State of California*, in which the plaintiffs argued for an accountability system that is reciprocal—that is, while schools are held accountable for performance, the state is held accountable for ensuring adequate resources.[8]

But there is more to this issue than just funding. Jeannie Oakes describes a framework that includes opportunity-to-learn indicators for access to knowledge, professional teaching conditions,

and "press for achievement."[9] Linda Darling-Hammond stresses the "fair and humane treatment" of students in a set of standards for professional practice.[10]

As such standards for opportunity to learn are articulated, the question arises as to how to monitor and report on them. Clearly, the degree of adherence to these standards cannot be determined through the proxy of testing. It is necessary to conduct observations in schools and classrooms and to evaluate the quality both of individual teachers and of the school as a whole. Teacher evaluation has received a great deal of criticism for being ineffective. The hit-and-run observations that principals typically conduct do little to determine whether teachers are meeting established professional teaching standards. Unions have been described as more interested in protecting their membership than in ensuring high-quality teaching. A promising development that has potential for breaking through this impasse is the recent initiation of peer-review processes by a number of teacher unions. Adam Urbanski, president of the Rochester Teachers Association and director of the Teacher Union Reform Network (TURN), has been a leader in advocating for and implementing such teacher evaluation processes. In a recent unpublished manuscript, he describes how the process should work:

- Some classroom observation by peers and supervisors, structured by a narrative instrument (not a checklist) based on professional standards such as those of the National Board for Professional Teaching Standards (NBPTS) and framed by the teacher's goals for the lesson/unit;
- Information from previous evaluations and feedback, such as structured references from colleagues and other supervisors;
- Portfolios that might include examples of teaching syllabi, assignments made, feedback given to students and samples of student work, feedback received from parents and students as well as colleagues, data on student progress, teaching exhibitions such as videotaped teaching

samples, professional development initiatives taken, and structured self-evaluation. All summative evaluation decisions about promotions or continued employment should be made by a specially established committee of teachers and administrators.

Urbanski goes on to describe safeguards for due process and for preventing malpractice. He also describes how such a process could be used in conjunction with professional development for improving teaching and school practice.[11]

In order to evaluate the performance of a school as a whole, a school review process will be necessary. Variations of inspectorates and school-quality reviews have been developed in New York, Rhode Island, Maine, and other states, as well as in Britain, New Zealand, Australia, and other countries.[12] In order for such reviews to serve the purpose of school improvement, the data should be collected in a "critical friend" manner, through a combination of school self-assessment and collegial visitations. Findings from such a process should not be employed in a bureaucratic and judgmental way but rather should be given as descriptions to local councils charged with evaluating school accountability. As with all aspects of any school renewal initiative, the quality and effectiveness of a review system will depend on the time, resources, and institutional support given to it.

Who will ensure that adequate opportunities to learn are present in schools? As described below, a system of reciprocal accountability must be set up so that both local accountability councils and the state itself serve to "mind the store" for all students. The issue of equitable funding will undoubtedly be resolved through the courts.

3. Responsiveness to Students, Parents, and Community. Current accountability systems move power and decision making away from the primary clients of the education system and more and more toward state and federal agencies. As high-stakes testing dictates the curriculum, less and less choice is available for students. Parent or community concerns about what is happening in the classroom and to the students have become less important to schools than meeting state mandates.

As the primary stakeholders in the schools, parents and communities must be made part of the effort to hold schools accountable. There are many examples of local community organizations, especially in urban areas, that have taken on the task of insisting that schools are responsive to the needs of children.[13]

To demonstrate responsiveness to students, parents, and the community, schools must go beyond sponsoring parent/teacher organizations or encouraging parent involvement as a means to gain support for existing school practices. They must also do more than gather survey information about stakeholders' satisfaction. True accountability to the primary clients for schools entails shifting power relationships.

Local school-based councils must be created that have real power to effect school change. These councils would review accountability information from state and local assessments as well as from school-quality review processes and make recommendations to school boards about school policies and priorities. They would hold school boards accountable for the development and implementation of school improvement plans. Phillip Schlechty discusses how such councils might work:

> Community leaders who are concerned about the futures of their communities and their schools should join together to create a nonprofit corporation intended to support efforts of school leaders to focus on the future and to ensure that lasting values as well as immediate interests are included in the education decision-making process. It would also be the function of this group to establish a small subgroup of the community's most trusted leaders who would annually evaluate the performance of the school board as stewards of the common good and would make these evaluations known to the community. . . .
>
> In a sense, the relationship between the school district and the monitoring function of the new corporation should be something akin to the relationship between the quality assurance division

of a corporation and the operating units in the corporation. . . .

When the data indicate that goals are not being met, the president of the corporation, working with the superintendent and the board of education, would seek to discover why this was the case, and would seek as well to create new approaches that might enhance the prospect of achieving the stated goals and the intended ends. It is not intended that the new corporation simply identify problems and weaknesses, it is intended that the leaders of this organization also participate in the creation of solutions and participate in creating support for solutions once they have been identified or created.[14]

Communities must determine how to sustain such councils and ensure that they do not pursue narrow agendas. The composition of councils in urban settings will probably be different from those in rural or suburban settings. Standards and acceptable variations for councils will be important topics for public discussion.

4. Organizational Capacity. If schools are going to be held accountable to high levels of performance, the question arises: Do schools have the internal capacity to rise to those levels? To what degree are the resources of schools "organized into a collective enterprise, with shared commitment and collaboration among staff to achieve a clear purpose for student learning"?[15] The issue of meaningful and ongoing teacher professional development is especially pertinent to whether or not schools are capable of enabling all students to meet higher standards of performance. A great deal of research has shed light on what kind of professional development is most effective in promoting school improvement.[16]

Schools must also attend to the issue of teacher empowerment. Teachers are increasingly controlled and disempowered in various ways. This leads to a declining sense of efficacy and professionalism and a heightened sense of job dissatisfaction and has become a factor in the attrition that is contributing to the growing teaching shortage.[17] Principals must share leadership with teachers and others as a means of sustaining capacity.

To be an effective collective enterprise, a school must develop an internal accountability system. That is, it must take responsibility for developing goals and priorities based on the ongoing collection and analysis of data, it must monitor its performance, and it must report its findings and actions to its public. Many schools have not moved past the stage of accepting individual teacher responsibility rather than collective responsibility as the norm.[18] States and districts must cooperate with schools to nurture and insist upon the development of such collective internal norms.

THE NEW ROLE OF THE STATE

For a balanced model of school accountability to succeed, there must be a system in which states and districts are jointly responsible with schools and communities for student learning. Reciprocal accountability is needed: one level of the system is responsible to the others, and all are responsible to the public.

The role of state and federal agencies with respect to school accountability is much in need of redefinition. Agencies at these levels should not serve primarily in an enforcement role. Rather, their roles should be to establish standards for local accountability systems, to provide resources and guidance, and to set in place processes for quality review of such systems. Certainly there should be no high-stakes testing from the state and federal levels, no mandatory curricula, and no manipulation through funding. Where there are clear cases of faulty local accountability systems—those lacking any of the four elements discussed above (appropriate assessment systems; adequate opportunities to learn; responsiveness to students, parents, and community; or organizational capacity)—supportive efforts from the state and federal levels should be undertaken.

Are there any circumstances in which a state should intervene forcibly in a school or district? If an accountability system is to work toward school improvement for all schools, does that system not need such "teeth"? This question must be addressed in a way that acknowledges the multi-level nature of this school accountability model. One might envision at least three cases in which the state would take on a more assertive role: 1) to investigate claims or appeals from students, parents, or the community that the local accountability system is not meeting the standards set for such systems; 2) to require local schools and districts to respond to findings in the data that show significant student learning deficiencies, inequity in the opportunities to learn for all students, or lack of responsiveness to students, parents, or communities; and 3) to provide additional resources and guidance to improve the organizational capacity of the local school or district. Is it conceivable that a state might take over a local school or district in this model? Yes, but only after the most comprehensive evaluation of the local accountability system has shown that there is no alternative—and then only on a temporary basis.

It is of great importance to the health of our public schools that we begin as soon as possible to define a new model for school accountability, one that is balanced and comprehensive. Schools can and should be held accountable to their primary clients for much more than test scores, in a way that supports improvement rather than punishes deficiencies. The current model of using high-stakes testing is a recipe for public school failure, putting our democratic nation at risk.

NOTES

1. Robert S. Kaplan and David P. Norton, "The Balanced Scorecard—Measures That Drive Performance," *Harvard Business Review,* January/February 1992, pp. 71–79.

2. National Forum on Assessment, *Principles and Indicators for Student Assessment Systems* (Boston: FairTest, 1993), available at www.fairtest.org/k-12.htm.

3. Lorrie A. Shepard, "The Role of Assessment in a Learning Culture," *Educational Researcher,* October 2000, pp. 4–14.

4. Debra Smith and Lynne Miller, *Comprehensive Local Assessment Systems (CLASs) Primer: A Guide to Assessment System Design and Use* (Gorham: Southern Maine Partnership, University of Southern Maine, 2003), available at www.usm.maine.edu/smp/tools/primer.htm; and "Nebraska School-Based, Teacher-Led Assessment Reporting System (STARS)," available at www.nde.state.ne.us/stars/index.html.

5. Richard J. Stiggins, *Student-Centered Classroom Assessment* (Columbus, Ohio: Merrill, 1997).

6. Paul Black and Dylan Wiliam, "Inside the Black Box: Raising Standards through Classroom Assessment," *Phi Delta Kappan,* October 1998, pp. 139–48; and Paul Black et al., *Working Inside the Black Box: Assessment for Learning in the Classroom* (London, U.K.: Department of Educational and Professional Studies, King's College, 2002).

7. Terry Crooks, "Design and Implementation of a National Assessment Programme: New Zealand's National Education Monitoring Project (NEMP)," paper presented at the annual meeting of the Canadian Society for the Study of Education, Toronto, May 2002.

8. Jeannie Oakes, "Education Inadequacy, Inequality, and Failed State Policy: A Synthesis of Expert Reports Prepared for *Williams* v. *State of California,*" 2003, available at www.decentschools.org/experts.php.

9. Jeannie Oakes, "What Educational Indicators? The Case for Assessing the School Context," *Educational Evaluation and Policy Analysis,* Summer 1989, pp. 181–99.

10. Linda Darling-Hammond, *Standards of Practice for Learning Centered Schools* (New York: National Center for Restructuring Education, Schools, and Teaching, Teachers College, 1992).

11. Adam Urbanski, "Teacher Professionalism and Teacher Accountability: Toward a More Genuine Teaching Profession," unpublished manuscript, 1998.

12. Jacqueline Ancess, *Outside/Inside, Inside/Outside: Developing and Implementing the School Quality Review* (New York: National Center for Restructuring Education, Schools, and Teaching, Teachers College, 1996); New Zealand Education Review Office, *Frameworks for Reviews in Schools,* available at www.ero.govt.nz/EdRevInfo/Schedrevs/SchoolFramework.htm; Debra R. Smith and David J. Ruff, "Building a Culture of Inquiry:

The School Quality Review Initiative," in David Allen, ed., *Assessing Student Learning: From Grading to Understanding* (New York: Teachers College Press, 1998), pp. 164–82.

13. Kavitha Mediratte, Norm Fruchter, and Anne C. Lewis, *Organizing for School Reform: How Communities Are Finding Their Voice and Reclaiming Their Public Schools* (New York: Institute for Education and Social Policy, Steinhardt School of Education, New York University, October 2002).

14. Phillip Schlechty, *Systemic Change and the Revitalization of Public Education* (San Francisco: Jossey-Bass, forthcoming).

15. Fred M. Newmann, M. Bruce King, and Mark Rigdon, "Accountability and School Performance: Implications from Restructuring Schools," *Harvard Educational Review,* Spring 1997, p. 47.

16. Judith Warren Little, "Teachers' Professional Development in a Climate of Educational Reform," *Educational Evaluation and Policy Analysis,* vol. 15, 1993, pp. 129–51; and Milbrey W. McLaughlin and Joan Talbert, *Professional Communities and the Work of High School Teaching* (Chicago: University of Chicago Press, 2001).

17. Richard M. Ingersoll, *Who Controls Teachers' Work? Power and Accountability in America's Schools* (Cambridge, Mass.: Harvard University Press, 2003).

18. Charles Abelman et al., *When Accountability Knocks, Will Anyone Answer?* (Philadelphia: Consortium for Policy Research in Education, University of Pennsylvania, CPRE Research Report Series RR-42, 1999).

Ken Jones is the director of teacher education, University of Southern Maine, Gorham.

QUESTIONS FOR REFLECTION

1. Jones argues that the health of our public schools depends on defining a new model of accountability. Do you agree with this statement and the argument he develops in this article? Explain.

2. The model that is presented in this article is based on an accountability framework called the "balanced scorecard" that is currently employed in the business world. Is it realistic to expect something that works well in business to also work well in education? How are business and education different? How are they similar?

3. How might you bring Jones' balanced school accountability model to your educational setting? Who do you think would be supportive of a new model such as this one? Where do you think resistance would come from? How would you confront that resistance?

Using Student Assessment Data to Improve Instruction

KATHRYN PARKER
BOUDETT
RICHARD J. MURNANE
ELIZABETH CITY
LIANE MOODY

ABSTRACT: *The authors describe an innovative course at the Harvard Graduate School of Education that places graduate students and public school teachers on school-based teams and asks them to solve real problems using real student data. Key features and goals of the workshop are outlined as well as the various methods that were used to address educational improvement, which included an emphasis on the complexity of school reform. Workshop participants were taught to interpret and use data in effective reform initiatives which highlights the importance of pursuing educational change in the context of school-based teams.*

State accountability systems that are based on test data and the No Child Left Behind Act have put educators under great pressure to improve their students' scores on standardized tests. Much has been written about the possibility that school faculties will resort to "drill and kill," a response that will reduce the quality of children's education. Much less has been written about what it takes for teachers and administrators to be able to use student assessment results to learn about children's skills and about the effectiveness of instruction—and then to use that learning to guide instructional improvements.

We report here on a yearlong workshop for teachers and administrators from the Boston Public Schools (BPS) and for students from the Harvard Graduate School of Education (HGSE). There are four key elements of our course design: 1) organizing around a clear process, 2) teaching about three kinds of tools, 3) assigning projects that use real school data, and 4) supporting collaborative work. While we by no means claim that our approach is the only way to teach educators to make constructive use of student assessment results, we believe that our experiences provide useful lessons to school and district leaders who want to help educators learn to do this work.

WORKSHOP OVERVIEW

While the workshop described here is a graduate course, it is very different from other courses that teach students how to understand basic statistics, make inferences from data, and use statistical software. What makes it different is its focus on placing data analysis in the greater context of school improvement. Participants are assigned to school-based teams consisting of both BPS faculty members and Harvard graduate students and spend the bulk of the course working with real school data to solve problems. The aim is for participating schools to benefit from a structured and supported opportunity to make progress on work they need to do and for HGSE students to benefit from a truly authentic learning experience.

In the last academic year, workshop participants included 16 teachers and administrators from nine Boston schools and 10 HGSE students, who were matched with the schools to form school-based teams. The schools included four high schools, two middle schools, and three elementary schools (one K–8 and two K–5). Most HGSE students also served as principal or teacher-leader interns at the participating schools, and all of the HGSE students had at least three years of teaching experience. Course participants received one semester of Harvard credit for successfully completing the course, which met for 13 sessions of 2½ hours each over the course of the school year.

Throughout the workshop, those of us who taught the course collected data to inform the evolving course design and to provide evidence for our research. Sources included online surveys conducted at the beginning, middle, and end of the course; assignments produced by school teams and individuals; and notes from group debriefing sessions, focus groups, and observations during classes and from school site visits. From these varied sources, we came to understand that the main impact of the course was a change in participants' attitudes toward using data. In short, they developed the *conviction* that using data to reflect upon practice could have a powerful effect on teaching and learning, as well as the *confidence* that they had gained the skills and knowledge needed to lead this kind of work. Now for some specifics about the four elements of our course design.

Design Element 1. Organizing around a Clear Process. Our teaching team designed the course syllabus around an improvement cycle that we adapted from the literature on school improvement (Figure 1). The cycle we developed consisted of the following steps: 1) identify patterns in data, 2) choose pattern to explore, 3) dig deeper, 4) agree on problem, 5) ask why, 6) examine current practices, 7) develop action plan, 8) implement action plan, and 9) assess action plan. We focused each class on a particular step in the cycle, and a typical lesson plan included instruction about the step itself and relevant tools for carrying it out, time for teams to practice using the tools in completing a group assignment pertaining to the step, and instructor consultations with school teams to discuss progress.

Using a cycle to structure our course allowed us to address all of the stages of school improvement while providing individualized support to school teams that were in very different places with their

FIGURE 1

Improvement Cycle

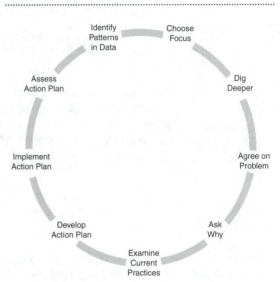

work. With a clear and understandable cycle in place, the school teams were able to approach the task of using data as a process of manageable steps. We offer the following recommendations about how to use an improvement process in professional development focused on data use.

1. *Emphasize that the real process is more complicated than any schematic model may suggest.* We knew that the process our teaching team created was in some sense arbitrary. In practice, educators would not work through the steps of the cycle one at a time. Instead, they would double back and revisit the various parts of the process as reality demanded. To help participants understand this, we began the course by giving teams an envelope containing squares of paper, each with the text of one cycle step. We asked the teams to use poster paper, markers, and tape to work together to create a visual representation of how their school could work through these steps. We invited groups to add, change, duplicate, or delete any of the steps we had offered.

When it came time for the groups to share their visual representations, there was great variety in the processes designed. One group made a kind of staircase; another created a wheel-like design with data analysis at the center. Almost all groups made use of arrows going in many directions between the various steps of the process. In the discussion that followed, we shared our version of the improvement cycle, the one around which we had organized the course. We explained that the process of improvement needs structure and that this structure would help us support the progress of all the different school teams. We emphasized, however, that the cycle itself should remain flexible and meet the needs of the schools' ongoing inquiry into their practice.

2. *Create assignments that allow participants to engage in the steps of the cycle one at a time in order to meet school objectives.* We required each school team to complete two major projects by the end of the course, both of which involved applying the cycle to their own school's data. The first was to create a PowerPoint presentation summarizing their school's progress on each step of the improvement cycle. We asked the teams to begin working on these presentations early in the course, to add slides after each class, and to revisit and revise the slides they had done for previous assignments. We chose this project format so that we could allow teams to experience data-based work as an iterative process in which knowledge is adapted as new information becomes available.

The second assignment was to develop an action plan for implementing the team's proposed solution to the problem that it had identified and examined. The action plan showed who would be responsible for doing what, when it was to be done, what intermediate outcomes one would expect to see if the plan were implemented correctly, and how the school would collect data to evaluate these outcomes. In creating an action plan, we encouraged each team to consult frequently with colleagues who were not involved in the course. The purpose was twofold: to elicit ideas for improving the plan and to build buy-in for incorporating the team's

action plan into the Whole School Improvement Plan, which the central office requires of all schools in the BPS.

3. *Conduct the course over a long enough period to allow the work to sink in.* Our course met for 13 sessions, beginning in September and ending in May. This meant that enough calendar time elapsed between classes to allow the teams to make meaningful progress on their projects. If we had tried to condense the work into one or two intensive weekends, the teams would not have been able to apply their learning to their day-to-day work. In our beginning-of-year survey, many participants described the amount of available data as "overwhelming" and identified lack of time as the biggest barrier to using data to inform instruction. In our end-of-year survey, participants reported that organizing the course around the improvement cycle provided a structure that made their work more manageable. Twenty-three out of 24 survey respondents reported that they would use the cycle in the future, either in their own work or when guiding others in instructional improvement. One principal intern echoed the sentiments of many respondents when she described the cycle as "a comprehensive step-by-step process to examine data and understand it. It helps those who have not done this kind of work before to see where they are going all along the way."

Design Element 2. Teaching How to Use Tools for Each Cycle Step. We discovered that educators need to learn how to use three distinct kinds of tools in order to employ data effectively and that the lack of any one of them hampers progress. Software tools—such as Excel and PowerPoint—help participants negotiate the technical challenges of producing meaningful analyses. Data analysis tools—such as item analysis, disaggregation, and the use of flow charts—help participants to think about data in structured ways. Process tools—such as the Question Formulation Technique and the Tuning Protocol—help participants in discussing data and making collaborative decisions based on what they see in the data.

We began most class sessions with a demonstration of specific tools and then allowed time for teams to practice using them to complete that day's featured cycle step. We selected many of our tools from our two required texts: *Data Analysis for Continuous Schoolwide Improvement,* by Victoria Bernhardt, and *The Power of Protocols: An Educator's Guide to Better Practice,* by Joseph P. McDonald et al. Below we offer our recommendations for teaching educators how to use the various types of tools.

1. *Provide step-by-step guidance for software tools.* As part of our midyear survey we asked participants open-response questions about what they still needed from the course. The most common response was that the course did not focus enough on teaching participants how to use technology to analyze data.

In working with the Boston Public Schools, we encountered some valuable software tools. The BPS central office and its external partner, the Boston Plan for Excellence, had recently designed and created intranet software called MyBPS to assist schools and individual teachers in analyzing assessment data. This software gives schools access to assessment data for their own school and performs basic data analyses. For example, a teacher who wanted to analyze how his students performed on the multiple-choice math items on the Massachusetts Comprehensive Assessment System (MCAS) could use MyBPS software to display a bar chart showing the percentage of eighth-graders in his school who answered each of the multiple-choice items correctly. Then, by clicking on the item number below each percentage bar, he could display how many students selected each of the possible responses, along with the text of the question and the state standard to which it pertains. Such data analysis would have been much more difficult without the use of MyBPS.

In the original design of the technical training for the course, we mistakenly believed that a simple demonstration of the capacities of MyBPS would be enough to launch groups in their work.

The survey feedback we received at midyear demonstrated that workshop participants needed more hands-on work with the technology, so we created in-class tutorials on how to use specific components of the software to do the kinds of data analysis and presentation tasks required by the course assignments. Since our class met in a computer lab, the instructor could walk participants through each of the tutorials on a projection screen, while the participants worked through the tasks on individual computers. These in-class tutorials allowed workshop participants to practice using the technology for real school purposes, while receiving in-depth support.

Similarly, the participants needed real facility with Excel and PowerPoint in order to use multiple sources of data and create effective presentations. Again, we found that hands-on tutorials were necessary. No progress could be made on our goal of teaching participants to make data analysis a part of their school improvement planning until we had helped them with the technical challenges of summing a column of numbers in Excel or copying into PowerPoint a graph created with the district's MyBPS software.

2. *Offer hands-on experiences.* Using software wasn't the only occasion when hands-on experience proved to be important. One of our first assignments was to ask participants to complete all sections of the English language and mathematics portions of the MCAS test for the grade level relevant to their school. This sparked some lively discussions about the depth and breadth of the test content, about the variety of question types (multiple-choice, short-answer, open-response, long-composition), and about the importance of stamina in doing well on the MCAS exams. This firsthand knowledge proved important when participants brainstormed about possible explanations for the patterns they found in the test data for the students in their schools.

Hands-on experience also facilitated the participants' understanding of another data collection tool: surveys. We required participants to take three online surveys during the course of the year.

Class discussions of the experience of *taking* the surveys helped participants understand aspects of survey design that they could then apply when conducting surveys as part of their own data-collection efforts. We also used the survey data we collected for the course to model for participants how to make effective visual representations of responses to different types of questions. Finally, we discussed with participants the ways in which insights from the survey responses led us to change our lesson plans for what to teach and how to teach it. Given that the goal of the course was to show people how to use data to inform instruction, frequent modeling of this skill in our own teaching was an important aspect of our pedagogy.

3. *Practice using process tools.* More than half of the steps in the improvement cycle require groups to make choices, form hypotheses, and plan actions. The extent to which group work is central to effective decision making led us to teach the use of process tools: strategies for helping groups to build consensus, make decisions, and provide constructive feedback. Many participants told us that they were surprised at how much they valued learning about the process tools. Although they might not have explored these kinds of tools on their own, they felt they benefited from being "forced" to use them in the workshop.

When asked what aspects of the course they might use in their future work, the participants frequently cited the process tools as highly portable, flexible strategies that they could see themselves using in a number of contexts in their future work. Participants particularly appreciated the Question Formulation Technique (described at www.rightquestion.org) and the Tuning Protocol (described at www.essentialschools.org/cs/ resources/view/ces_res/54). As one principal intern explained, "The protocols will be helpful in many situations—running meetings, beginning difficult conversations, and looking at data."

Design Element 3. Assigning Projects That Use Real School Data. It would have been much easier to teach many of the technical topics if, instead of having participants work in school-based teams

using their own data, we had asked them to read a case study and work on dummy data that we had constructed to illustrate key points. However, how people understand the meaning of data has a lot to do with the extent to which they understand the context from which the data are taken. Once people in schools realize how important their specialized knowledge is to the process of data analysis, they become energized to learn the more technical aspects of working with data. Participants are more invested in sifting through patterns in the data when they are trying to understand the performance of their own students.

This benefit was not obtained without cost, however. Since schools participating in the course were so different from one another—in terms of size, grade levels, previous experience using data, and level of administrative support—allowing schools to use their own data challenged us to find ways to differentiate instruction to support teams with widely differing needs. We offer the following suggestions for dealing with these challenges.

1. *Learn the context for each school.* For each assignment, we asked teams to submit a one-page "reflective memo" describing the challenges they faced in working on the tasks for that session, what they learned, and what they thought the teaching team should know about their progress in general. These memos showed us which of the tools we offered were most valuable and also helped us understand the unique context for each school's work.

While school teams were working on their own during the last hour of class time, we made sure that at least one member of the teaching team approached each group for a private consultation These informal meetings (five to 25 minutes) were the primary means through which the teaching team provided feedback to school teams about their assignments. They also provided an important opportunity for participants and the teaching staff to get to know one another.

Outside of class we offered two other types of support for group work. Teaching fellows made as many as two visits to schools to work with teams on shaping their projects. All three members of the teaching team were also available by e-mail and phone; individuals tended to use this avenue for requesting support in managing interpersonal dynamics in their groups.

2. *Offer guidelines for what high-quality work looks like.* For the first couple of assignments, members of the teaching team were a bit surprised at how often we found ourselves saying, "That's not what we were asking for." To provide clearer guidance about expectations, we began distributing templates showing the kinds of slides participants were expected to create and checklists describing what high-quality work would look like for each slide. Participants reported that these templates helped them make progress on their group assignments, and we found that the quality of the teams' work improved.

3. *Prioritize the kinds of data analyses to support.* Sources of student performance data include formative assessments, classroom assignments and portfolios, surveys of students and teachers, and observations of and conversations with students. Clarifying that all of these data sources can contribute to understanding student achievement patterns was critical in obtaining buy-in from participants.

However, supporting teams in learning *how to use* these multiple sources was particularly challenging. Some teams in our course proposed conducting faculty surveys; others planned structured interviews with students as they worked through particular test questions; others conducted observations within their schools or at best-practice sites. Although in many cases teams seemed to enjoy the process of collecting these different, potentially valuable types of data, finding the time and will to work on organizing and analyzing them was a different story. Teams routinely missed their own targets for when they would get this work done. We attempted to support the teams in their efforts, but the variety of initiatives made it difficult to know what kinds of in-class tutorials would be useful to all.

Because there are so many different potential data sources, those who would teach a course such as this need to make choices about which ones to support most fully. Given Boston's recent commitment to supporting online analysis of formative assessments (low-stakes assessments aligned with state standards that can be scored quickly), next year we plan to provide greater emphasis on how to use these data to explore the teams' hypothesized root causes of student learning difficulties. We envision that this will encourage more systematic analysis of this kind of information.

4. *Understand that many factors will influence whether action plans are actually implemented.* In our end-of-year survey we asked participants whether they believed that the action plans they developed for their schools would be implemented. At least one person from six of the nine teams responded that it was "very likely" that the work would be used. However, on only two of the nine teams did *all teammates* agree that the results would be used.

When we asked participants to explain their responses in their own words, they cited many factors favoring implementation, including: 1) the action plan is practical, aligned with work that the school is already doing, and designed to use structures that are already in place; 2) the action plan is specific, easy to understand, and "doable"; 3) the school is in state-imposed "corrective action," so there is not much choice about making changes; and 4) a member of the team will be at the school site next year to encourage and facilitate implementation.

The most common factors reported as inhibiting implementation were: 1) the lack of a person from the team to take charge of the work, 2) a failure to appreciate the need to engage the school faculty in the planning process and achieve "buy-in," and 3) an inability to engage the school faculty because of protracted labor negotiations that led to "Work to Fairness" action among union members. This action sharply curtailed the out-of-class time that union members could spend on meetings. (Although course participants persevered with their work for the class, the work action made it very difficult for them to arrange meetings with other key players at their schools who could help them make authentic progress on their course assignments.)

Asking participants to use data from their own schools to solve real problems opens up the possibility that issues not directly related to the course will affect the learning experience. However, even when circumstances create a low likelihood that a team's plans will be implemented, individuals can learn a great deal about the process.

Design Element 4. Supporting Collaborative Work. No one was allowed to enroll in our course without becoming part of a school-based team. This is because we believe that the greatest potential of student assessment data lies in their ability to inspire groups of people to engage in instructionally important conversations, and the best way for individuals to become comfortable using data to inform school improvement is to practice doing it with colleagues. In our course, combining HGSE students and BPS educators had benefits for all. In our midyear survey, respondents indicated strong support for having both Harvard graduate students and Boston Public Schools teachers taking the same course and working as teammates. Respondents noted that Harvard students often brought academic knowledge, idealism, and commitment to getting the work done. They credited BPS teachers with keeping the work real and grounded.

Readers might be asking themselves how much our workshop model depends on having teams that contain both school district personnel and graduate students. We believe that this aspect of our course is not essential, as long as the instructors follow some specific guidelines.

1. *Pay attention to team size.* In end-of-year focus groups, participants talked at length about the importance of group size in determining productivity. Every person on the two five-person teams agreed that five was too many; some people on the two-person teams felt that two was not

enough. The ideal team size for a course of this kind seems to be three or four people.

2. *Plan for how participants will make time to get the work done.* Participants told us that a major contribution of the course was the time and space it gave them to do work that they had wanted to do for years but that had always been pushed aside by more pressing demands. Providing class time for teams to make progress on their work is essential; it is not realistic to assume that participants will be able to find large chunks of time to do all of the necessary work outside of class. Nonetheless, it is essential that teams find some time outside of class to get the work done. The participants gave us consistent feedback that they found it extremely hard to coordinate meetings outside of class because of their differing schedules and locations. Next year, we plan to require participants to meet during "off weeks" at specified times. We will also provide assignment templates and suggest protocols to ensure that these meetings are productive.

Harvard graduate students provided many hours of work for their teams. In the absence of such students, an administrator, coach, or teacher leader could contribute that time if he or she were released from some responsibilities during the school week in order to pursue this work.

3. *Be clear about course expectations.* Some participants found it frustrating that members of their teams often brought differing goals, expectations, and time commitments to the work, and a couple of teams experienced personality conflicts. As a result, in the end-of-year survey, there was no team in which all members reported that their team functioned "very well," and five of nine teams had at least one member report that the team functioned "not so well." It is important at the outset to be clear with participants about how much time is required to complete the course successfully.

4. *Require that at least one team member be in a position to support the implementation of the team's action plan.* There should be someone on each team who can serve as a liaison between the team and the rest of the school and who is positioned to help implement the action plan once the course is over. We make this recommendation after having seen talented school-based teams identify an important instructional problem and devise a thoughtful plan for addressing it—only to have the action plan die a quiet death because the school principal does not see it as an important activity.

5. *Provide motivation for meeting deadlines and persevering through the cycle.* All participants in the course are busy people with many demands on their time. Because those taking our course received graduate credit for it, there was a built-in incentive to complete the work. Other courses of this type could build in incentives by providing "professional development points" for the work or by incorporating the course content into the regularly scheduled professional development hours at a school. In addition, linking the products of the course to central office requirements, such as creating yearly plans for whole school improvement, would allow participants to use the coursework to help meet district requirements. Coordinating course deadlines with meaningful district deadlines

for producing an accountability document can help create the requisite sense of urgency.

A FINAL WORD: PRACTICE WHAT YOU PREACH

Our experience indicates that educators can benefit from structured training on how to use student assessment data to improve instruction. In designing our course on this topic, our teaching team made every attempt to follow the same guidance we give participants about working together to use data to change instruction.

Our final advice, then, is: 1) create and teach the course as a collaborative effort, 2) collect and analyze data throughout the course to provide regular feedback about how much participants are learning, and 3) don't hesitate to use this information to modify instructional plans to meet demonstrated student needs. Modeling collaborative work and the revision of lesson plans based on data has allowed the teaching team to "practice what we preach" and to stay connected with the challenges of using data wisely.

Kathryn Parker Boudett is a lecturer on education; *Richard J. Murnane* is Thompson Professor of Education and Society; and *Elizabeth City* and *Liane Moody* are doctoral students in the Harvard Graduate School of Education, Cambridge, Massachusetts. All four authors have served as instructors or teaching fellows of the graduate courses they describe here.

QUESTIONS FOR REFLECTION

1. What makes the workshop described in this article so different from other courses that teach students how to understand basic statistics, make inferences from data, and understand basic statistical software?
2. Explain the three kinds of tools that are presented as part of the Harvard curriculum. What makes these tools essential components of effective data analysis?
3. A highlight of the workshop is the school teams that were created and the collaborative work that occurred. What makes collaboration such an essential component of the workshop experience? How might an educator bring that spirit of collaboration to other educational settings?

What Is the Purpose of Grades?

JAMES D. ALLEN

ABSTRACT: Allen takes a critical look at the purpose of grades and argues for ways in which educators can accurately assess student performance. He argues that preservice teachers are often inadequately prepared in practices of assessment and suggests that instruction on the assessment principle of validity is one way for better preparing future educators. Moreover, he argues that university faculty and K–12 teachers also model poor grading practices that perpetuate the practices of preservice teachers, and he provides suggestions for ways educators can authentically and validly assess students' learning of academic content.

What is the purpose of grades? In this article I present one answer to this question from a perspective that many educators might see as somewhat radical or extreme. The perspective that I take is based on the fundamental educational psychology assessment principle of validity—the validity of what learning is being assessed and the validity of the communication of that assessment to others. I believe most teachers fail to give grades to students that are as valid as they should be. Because grading is something that has been done to each of us during our many years as students, it is hard to change the invalid "grading" schema that has become embedded in our minds. Now, as educators often required to grade students, and because of this embedded schema, we often grade students in invalid ways similar to how we were graded. Inadequate education in valid assessment and grading principles and practices is a reason many teachers continue to perpetuate invalid grading practices with students. Since educational testing and assessment is a major content knowledge area in educational psychology, the issues regarding assessment and grading that I address in this article could well be addressed in an educational psychology course. If our preservice and in-service teachers are going to learn appropriate assessment and grading practices then educational psychologists need to provide the relevant information in their classes.

The most fundamental measurement principle related to meaningful assessment and grading is the principle of validity (Gallagher 1998; Gredler 1999; Linn and Gronlund 2000; Stiggins 2001). Although there are many validity issues involved in classroom assessment that classroom teachers should consider, such as making sure the way they assess students corresponds to the type of academic learning behaviors being assessed (Ormrod 2000), the focus here is on the valid assessment and communication of final class grades as summaries of students' academic achievement of content knowledge of a subject. Validity addresses the accuracy of the assessment and grading procedures used by teachers (Gallagher 1998; Gredler 1999; Linn and Gronlund 2000). Do the assessment procedures and assignment of grades accurately reflect and communicate the academic achievement of the student? Validity is important because the sole purpose of grades is to accurately communicate to others the level of academic achievement that a student has obtained (Snowman and Biehler 2003). If the grades are not accurate measures of the student's achievement, then they do not communicate the truth about the level of the student's academic achievement. Unfortunately, as stated by Cizek, even as "grades continue to be relied upon to communicate important information about [academic] performance and progress . . . they probably don't" (1996, 104).

Assigning grades to students is such a complex (and sometimes controversial) issue that some educators have proposed their abolition (Kohn 1999;

Marzano 2000). Although I find this an interesting proposal, especially if one is trying to establish a classroom learning environment that is student-centered and encourages self-regulation and self-evaluation, the current reality for most teachers is that they are required to assign grades indicating students' academic achievement in the subjects they teach. Therefore, grading should be as valid as possible. Not only is grading a major responsibility of classroom teachers, but it is also a practice with which they are often uncomfortable and that they find difficult (Barnes 1985; Lomax 1996; Thorndike 1997). The sources of the discomfort and difficulty for teachers regarding the grading of students seem to be threefold. First, the student activities that teachers think should constitute "academic achievement" and how to handle ancillary features of achievement such as students' efforts varies tremendously from teacher to teacher. Although ancillary information such as effort and attitude could be part of an overall student report, they should not be part of a grade that represents academic achievement (Tombari and Borich 1999). Second, teachers often seem to be unsettled regarding the communication function of grades, and they often try to communicate multiple pieces of information about students that can not possibly be contained within a single academic mark. This is an issue of making sure the grade is accurate as a valid communication to others. Third, because of the first two issues, many teachers assign grades that are invalid and not built on a solid principle of measurement (Cizek 1996; Marzano 2000). In addition, partially due to their long career as students experiencing invalid grading practices, as well as inadequate preservice and in-service education on assessment and grading, teachers continue to perpetuate invalid grading practices. Let us consider each of these points in greater depth.

MISCOMMUNICATION AND CONFUSING PURPOSES OF GRADES

Although students learn many things in the classroom, the primary objective is for students to learn academic content knowledge of a particular subject. In order for teachers to know if students are achieving this academic knowledge, they generally are required to not only assess students' knowledge in some way, but eventually summarize that assessment into a letter or numerical grade. This is known as "summative" evaluation. Hopefully, teachers are also gathering nongraded "formative" assessments of students to provide feedback to students as they learn, as well as considering how to motivate students to learn and encouraging them to be self-regulated learners. However, generally, teachers have to eventually place a grade on a grade sheet indicating what level of content knowledge a student has achieved in the subject listed. But why do we place a grade on a grade sheet, report card, or transcript? Why do we create a permanent written record of the grade? And why is the grade listed next to a name of an academic course such as English, U.S. History, Algebra, or Educational Psychology?

As illustrated by the title of the 1996 Yearbook of the Association for Supervision and Curriculum Development, Communicating Student Learning to interested parties is an important function of schools and teachers (Guskey 1996). Although there are various means to communicate student learning, currently a single report card grade for each academic subject is the most common and generally accepted system in middle and secondary schools (Bailey and McTighe 1996; Lake and Kafka 1996). Bailey and McTighe argue that as a communication system, "the primary purpose of secondary level grades and reports [is] to communicate student achievement" so that informed decisions can be made about the student's future (1996, 120). Similarly, authors of major texts devoted to classroom assessment suggest that the major reason for assigning grades is to create a public record of a students academic achievement that can accurately and effectively communicate to others the level of mastery of a subject a student has demonstrated (Airasian 2000; Gallagher 1998; Gredler 1999; Linn and Gronlund 2000; Nitko 2001; Oosterhof 2001; Stiggins 2001). Nitko points out that:

"Grades . . . are used by students, parents, other teachers, guidance counselors, school officials, postsecondary educational institutions, and employers. Therefore [teachers] must assign grades with utmost care and maintain their validity" (2001, 365). However, according to Marzano, in contrast to teachers', students', parents', and community members' assumption that grades are valid "measures of student achievement . . . grades are so imprecise that they are almost meaningless" (2000, 1). Due to the wide variability in the criteria used in grading practices from teacher to teacher, the validity of student grades is unknown and they have limited value as guides for planning the academic and career futures of students (Thorndike 1997). Thus, if a single grade on a report card or transcript is to effectively communicate information to all these varied parties, then that single grade has to have some shared and accurate meaning (O'Connor 1995).

This lack of shared meaning seems to be found throughout our education system. A study by Baron (2000) shows that there is lack of coherence in the beliefs about grades held by parents and students and those held by the education community. Even in the same school, teachers often hold very different views about the purpose of grades and fail to communicate with their colleagues about their grading practices (Kain 1996). Grading practices by teachers rarely follow the measurement principles and grading practices recommended in measurement textbooks (Cross and Frary 1996; Frary, Cross, and Weber 1993). New teachers often work independently and are left to figure out their own grading policies, gradually adhering to the school's norms. There is a similar lack of coherence and communication among college teachers (Barnes, Bull, Campbell, and Perry 1998). Friedman and Frisbie (1995, 2000) make a particularly strong argument for making sure that report card grades accurately report information to parents about a student's academic progress and that teachers and administrators share a common understanding of what information a grade should communicate. They suggest that since grades become part of a stu-

dents' permanent record, the purpose of these grades must be to communicate a valid summary of a student's academic achievement in the subject that is listed next to the grade on the record.

Grading systems used by teachers vary widely and unpredictably and often have low levels of validity due to the inclusion of nonacademic criteria used in the calculation of grades (Allen and Lambating 2001; Brookhart 1994; 2004; Frary, Cross, and Weber 1993; Olson 1989). Teachers have been found to make decisions about grades related to student effort in attempts to be "fair" in their grading practices (Barnes 1985). Studies have found that two out of three teachers believe that effort, student conduct, and attitude should influence final grades of students (Cross and Frary 1996; Frary, Cross, and Weber 1993). It has also been shown that grades are used as a motivational tool as well as to develop good study habits (Oosterhof 2001) and desirable classroom management behaviors (Allen 1983). Grades should not be a hodgepodge of factors such as student's level of effort, innate aptitude, compliance to rules, attendance, social behaviors, attitudes, or other nonachievement measures (Friedman and Frisbie 2000; Ornstein 1994). Although these factors may indirectly influence students' achievement of content knowledge, subjective—and often unknown to the teacher—factors such as these complicate the ability to interpret a grade since these factors may directly conflict with each other and distort the meaning of a grade measuring academic achievement (Cross and Frary 1996; Guskey 1994; Linn and Gronlund 2000; Nitko 2001; Stiggins 2001; Stumpo 1997). Nonacademic factors are often used as criteria for assigning grades because some teachers consider the consequences of grades more important than the value of clear communication of information and the interpretability of the grades (Brookhart 1993). It follows then that instead of the grade being a function of what a student has learned it has become a function of many variables. Simply put, it would appear that grades are often measures of how well a student lives up to the teacher's expectation of what a good student is rather than measuring the student's academic achievement in the subject matter objectives.

A grade can not be a teacher's "merged judgment"[1] of these factors, since as a single letter or numeric mark, the reported grade must communicate a single fact about the student if it is to be a valid or accurate source of information coherently shared between the reporter of the grade and the grade report's audience. How is the reader of a student's single grade on a transcript to know which factors are included and how much each unknown factor was weighed by the grade giver to determine the grade? Also, since many of these factors such as effort, motivation, and student attitude are subjective measures made by a teacher, their inclusion in a grade related to academic achievement increases the chance for the grade to be biased or unreliable, and thus invalid. The purpose of an academic report is to communicate the level of academic achievement that a student has developed over a course of study. Therefore, the sole purpose of a grade on an academic report, if it is to be a valid source of information, is to communicate the academic achievement of the student. If other factors about the student are deemed important, such as a student's attitude, level of effort, or social behavior, then other appropriate forms of reporting these factors must be made available and used. If a multidimensional view of the student is desired, then a multidimensional system of reporting is required. Using a single grade as a summary of a teacher's "merged judgment" of a student leads to miscommunication, confusion, and a continuation of the lack of coherence among stakeholders about what a grade represents.

Since important decisions are often based on a student's grade, invalid grades may result in dire consequences for the student. Grades can open up or close down important learning opportunities for students (Jasmine 1999). With high grades, students get admitted to colleges and universities of their choice and receive scholarships and tuition assistance, since grades are a major selection criterion in the college admission

process. The reverse is also true. It is very difficult for students to get admitted to some schools if their grades are not sufficiently high. Invalid grades that understate the student's knowledge may prevent a student with ability to pursue certain educational or career opportunities. Also, based on principles of attribution and social cognitive theories, if students receive grades lower than ones that accurately depict their true level of academic knowledge, it may lead students to believe they lack the ability to succeed academically and lower their sense of self-efficacy as well as their motivation to learn (Pintrich and Schunk 2002).

GRADING AND LACK OF PROFESSIONAL TRAINING

Cizek argues that the "lack of knowledge and interest in grading translates into a serious information breakdown in education" and that "reforming classroom assessment and grading practices will require educators' commitment to professional development, [and] classroom-relevant training programs" (1996, 103). Cizek's statement implies that an important area that needs to be addressed is the training of teachers in grading practices based on sound measurement principles relevant to their classroom lives.

This lack of knowledge about measurement theory and application to grading practices is a pervasive problem with preservice teacher training at the college level (Goodwin 2001; Schafer 1991; Stiggins 1991, 1999). One of the goals of a teacher education program should be to prepare preservice and in-service teachers to develop effective methods to assess students and to communicate clearly and accurately through their grading practices that assessment to others. However, very few teacher education programs include measurement or assessment courses. Allen and Lambating (2001) found in a random sample of teacher education programs that less than one-third required an assessment course, and many of those that did were courses focused on "informal" assessments, or standardized assessment of students with special needs and not focused on classroom assessment and grading. Fewer than half of the fifty states require specific coursework on assessment for their initial certification of teachers (Lomax 1996; O'Sullivan and Chalnick 1991; Stiggins 1999).

Although assigning grades is probably the most important measurement decision that classroom teachers make, the coverage of grading in assessment textbooks is often not as fully developed as other measurement topics that are less relevant to teachers' day-to-day assessment practices (Airasian 1991; Lomax 1996). According to Stiggins (1999), how the concepts of "reliability" and "validity" are related to classroom grading practices is not addressed in the courses which introduce these terms to our preservice teachers. It is important to look at this issue because validity and reliability are considered the most fundamental principles related to measurement and therefore important to classroom assessment and grading (Gallagher 1998; Gredler 1999; Linn and Gronlund 2000).

Some argue that even when teachers are provided with some measurement instruction, they still use subjective value judgements when assigning grades (Brookhart 1993). Undergraduate teacher education majors, when asked about the criteria that should be used for their own grades, believe that "effort" is more important than amount of academic content learned (Placier 1995). One contributing factor may be that after sixteen years of obtaining grades based on factors other than academic achievement, teachers-in-training have a difficult time accepting theoretical principles that do not match with their personal experience. Many beliefs about school practices are well established before students enter college and often are resistant to change (Britzman 1986, 1991; [Ginsburg] and Clift 1990; Holt-Reynolds 1992; Pajares 1992; Richardson 1996). They form many of their perspectives about teaching from their years of observing teachers and their teaching practices (Lortie 1975). They have been recipients of hundreds of grades from their K–12 teachers

and college professors before taking on the responsibility of assigning grades to their own students. Their perception regarding grades comes from their own long experience as students.

Brookhart (1998) suggests that classroom assessment and grading practices are at the center of effective management of classroom instruction and learning. Through the use of real classroom scenarios, preservice teachers need to be taught assessment strategies in relationship to instruction and not as decontextualized measurement principles. As the past president of the American Educational Research Association, Lorrie Shepard has stated: "The transformation of assessment practices cannot be accomplished in separate tests and measurement courses, but rather should be a central concern in teaching methods courses" (2000, 4). In addition to instruction on how to assess and grade using sound principles of measurement, research suggests that preservice teachers need hands-on experience in grading students and how to work with cooperating teachers who assess and grade in ways different than those learned by the preservice teachers (Barnes 1985; Lomax 1996).

What the literature suggests is that educators at all levels make decisions when assigning grades that are not based on sound principles of validity that ensure the grade is a meaningful communication of a student's level of academic achievement. The literature also suggests that students in teacher education programs may be more influenced by the grading practices they have experienced as students in the past, as well as in their current courses taught by their education professors, than by what they learn about assessment and grading in their courses. Additionally, teachers in the field, as products of teacher education programs, seem to exhibit grading practices that confirm that they have not been influenced by measurement courses (Lambating and Allen 2002). This may be because they did not take any assessment courses, or because their long-held beliefs about grading were left unchallenged and the courses did not focus on assessment and grading issues related to measuring classroom learning.

EDUCATIONAL IMPLICATIONS AND CONCLUSION

Concerns about the validity and reliability of grades for communicating meaningful information about students' academic progress have been raised for a long time (see Starch and Elliot 1912, 1913a, 1913b; Adams 1932). In addition, trying to help teachers to understand the purpose and effective functions of grades in the overall evaluation system has been addressed repeatedly in the literature (Airasian 2000; Brookhart 1993; Cross and Frary 1996; Gredler 1999; Guskey 1996; Linn and Gronlund 2000; Marzano 2000; O'Connor 1995; Stiggins 2001). However, there seems to be little progress being made in this area in actual classroom practice.

Two major thrusts need to occur in reforming grading practices. First, if factors such as effort, attitude, compliance, and behavior are to be noted about a student on a report card, then they should be reported with a separate mark and not figured in as part of a grade for academic achievement of content knowledge. However, as in most situations, if a teacher must summarize and communicate a student's classroom progress in an academic subject through a single report card grade, then there must be a consensus that the grade represents the most accurate statement of the student's academic achievement, and only academic achievement. This is the essence of valid assessment. To include nonacademic criteria, such as the student's effort, compliance, attitude, or behavior, makes the grade impossible to interpret in any meaningful way. Perhaps, a simple way to reach this consensus is to teach ourselves and those we prepare to be teachers to reflect on the following question: "If I was given a student's transcript with a single letter grade listed next to the subject I teach, what would be the most logical interpretation I could make about what the grade represents about the student's knowledge of that academic subject?" Therefore, that is what I should try to have my grades communicate to whomever will read and interpret them in the future.

In order for teachers to act consistently in assigning valid grades based only on appropriate achievement criteria, a second major initiative needs to be undertaken to help teachers understand how to make good grading decisions. This initiative is best addressed through teacher education programs taking on the challenge to improve the assessment training of their students and improve their own grading practices. This entails several dimensions.

First, students' long-held beliefs about the purpose and use of grades need to be challenged by teacher educators. Students' beliefs and value systems related to grades need to be exposed and examined to help them understand the unscientific basis of their grading beliefs. Second, once these beliefs are exposed, instructors must provide students with the theoretical base for good assessment and grading practices as explicated by measurement experts that would replace students' naive notions of assessment and grading. This could be either through self-contained measurement courses taught in a relevant manner by educational psychologists, or integrated into methods courses through collaboration between educational psychology and teacher-education specialists. It would help if more teacher-education programs required adequate instruction on classroom assessment and grading practices. There also needs to be more effective and meaningful grading practices addressed in-depth in measurement textbooks. Third, teacher education students need to be provided with opportunities to encounter grading activities before they are placed into student teaching, in order to practice applying assessment principles and theory to classroom grading issues. Finally, during student teaching experiences, education majors must be given the opportunity, in conjunction with their cooperating teachers and the support of their college supervisors, to actually develop and implement a valid evaluation and grading plan. Schools of education need to work with school district teachers to help improve the communication system for which grades function. Providing in-service "assessment and grading" workshops for practicing teachers, especially those operating as cooperating teachers, might help to establish a consensus of what is appropriate criteria to use for determining and assigning valid grades to indicate academic achievement.

One way to accomplish many of the above steps is through the use of case studies that focus on assessment and grading dilemmas often faced by real teachers. Discussion of case studies can help students to reflect on and expose their belief systems about grades and grading, and analyze them in relationship to educational psychology assessment principles such as validity. One example is the Sarah Hanover case which focuses on a grading dilemma a teacher must deal with when the question of the validity of a student's grade is raised by the student's parent (Silverman, Welty, and Lyon 1996).

However, the area that may be the most difficult to address is the change in the grading practices that teacher educators use in evaluating students. As long as preservice and in-service teachers take classes from education professors who base grading decisions on more than academic achievement, they will have little reason to either believe what we say or practice what we preach about assessment and grading. As teacher educators, we need to model sound grading practices in our own courses in which grades accurately communicate students' achievement of content knowledge learned in our courses, and not how hard they work or how often they attend our classes.

My intention in this article has been to suggest that by giving serious reflection to the meaning of the educational psychology measurement principle of validity, grading practices can improve and the grades we assign to students as teachers can be more accurate and educationally meaningful. We need to begin to break the cycle of invalid grading practices that prevail throughout the education system, and the only behaviors we as teachers can truly control are our own.

NOTE

1. The author has borrowed this phrase from an anonymous reviewer.

REFERENCES

Adams, W. L. 1932. Why teachers say they fail pupils. *Educational Administration and Supervision* 18: 594–600.

Airasian, P. W. 1991. Perspectives on measurement instruction. *Educational Measurement Issues and Practice* 10 (1): 13–16, 26.

———. 2000. *Assessment in the classroom: A concise approach.* 2nd ed. Boston: McGraw-Hill.

Allen, J. D. 1983. Classroom management: Students' perspectives, goals and strategies. Paper presented at the annual meeting of the American Educational Research Association, Montreal, Canada, April.

Allen, J. D., and J. Lambating. 2001. Validity and reliability in assessment and grading: Perspectives of preservice and inservice teachers and teacher education professors. Paper presented at the annual meeting of the American Educational Research Association, Seattle, April.

Bailey, J., and J. McTighe. 1996. Reporting achievement at the secondary level: What and how. In Guskey 1996, 119–40.

Barnes, L. B., K. S. Bull, N. J. Campbell, and K. M. Perry. 1998. Discipline-related differences in teaching and grading philosophies among undergraduate teaching faculty. Paper presented at the annual meeting of the American Educational Research Association, San Diego, April.

Barnes, S. 1985. A study of classroom pupil evaluation: The missing link in teacher education. *Journal of Teacher Education* 36 (4): 46–49.

Baron, P. A. B. 2000. Consequential validity for high school grades: What is the meaning of grades for senders and receivers? Paper presented at the annual meeting of the American Educational Research Association, New Orleans, April.

Britzman, D. P. 1986. Cultural myths in the making of a teacher: Biography and social structure in teacher education. *Harvard Educational Review* 56 (4): 442–56.

———. 1991. *Practice makes practice: A critical study of learning to teach.* New York: State University of New York Press.

Brookhatt, S. M. 1993. Teachers' grading practices: Meaning and values. *Journal of Educational Measurement* 30 (2): 123–42.

———. 1994, Teachers' grading: Practice and theory. *Applied Measurement in Education* 7 (4): 279–301.

———. 1998. Teaching about grading and communicating assessment results. Paper presented at the annual meeting of the National Council on Measurement in Education, San Diego, April, 1998.

———. 2004. *Grading.* Upper Saddle River, NJ: Pearson/Merrill/Prentice Hall.

Cizek, G. J. 1996. Grades: The final frontier in assessment reform. *NASSP Bulletin* 80 (584): 103–10.

Cross, L. H., and R. B. Frary. 1996. Hodgepodge grading: Endorsed by students and teachers alike. Paper presented at the annual meeting of the National Council on Measurement in Education, New York, April.

Frary, R. B., L. H. Cross, and L. J. Weber. 1993. Testing and grading practices and opinions of secondary teachers of academic subjects: Implications for instruction in measurement. *Educational Measurement: Issues and Practice* 12 (3): 2330.

Friedman, S. J., and D. A. Frisbie. 1995. The influence of report cards on the validity of grades reported to parents. *Educational and Psychological Measurement* 55 (1): 5–26.

———. 2000. Making report cards measure up. *Education Digest* 65 (5): 45–50.

Gallagher, J. D. 1998. *Classroom assessment for teachers.* Upper Saddle River, NJ: Merrill/Prentice Hall.

Ginsburg, M. B., and R. T. Clift. 1990. The hidden curriculum of preservice teacher education. In *Handbook of research on teacher education,* ed. W. R. Houston, 450–65. New York: Macmillan.

Goodwin, A. L. 2001. The case of one child: Making the shift from personal knowledge to informed practice. Paper presented at the annual meeting of the American Educational Research Association, Seattle, April.

Gredler, M. E. 1999. *Classroom assessment and learning.* New York: Longman.

Guskey, T. R. 1994. Making the grade: What benefits students? *Educational Leadership* 52 (2): 14–20.

———. 1996. *ASCD Yearbook, 1996: Communicating student learning.* Alexandria, VA: Association for Supervision and Curriculum Development.

Holt-Reynolds, D. 1992. Personal history-based beliefs as relevant prior knowledge in coursework: Can we practice what we preach? *American Educational Research Journal* 29(2): 325–49.

Jasmine, T. 1999. Grade distributions, grading procedures, and students' evaluations of instructors: A justice perspective. *Journal of Psychology* 133 (3): 263–71.

Kain, D. L. 1996. Looking beneath the surface: Teacher collaboration through the lens of grading practices. *Teachers College Record* 97 (4): 569–87.

Kohn, A. 1999. Grading is degrading. *Education Digest* 65 (1): 59–64.

Lake, K., and K. Kafka. 1996. Reporting methods in grades 1–8. In Guskey 1996, 90–118.

Lambating, J., and J. D. Allen. 2002. How the multiple functions of grades influence their validity and value as measures of academic achievement. Paper presented at the annual meeting of the American Educational Research Association, New Orleans, April.

Linn, R. L., and N. E. Gronlund. 2000. *Measurement and assessment in teaching.* 8th ed. Englewood Cliffs, NJ: Merrill/Prentice Hall.

Lomax, R. G. 1996. On becoming assessment literate: An initial look at preservice teachers' beliefs and practices. *Teacher Educator* 31 (4): 292–303.

Lortie, D. 1975. *Schoolteacher: A sociological study.* Chicago: University of Chicago Press.

Marzano, R. J. 2000. *Transforming classroom grading.* Alexandria, VA: Association for Supervision and Curriculum Development.

Nitko, A. J. 2001. *Educational assessment of students.* 3rd ed. Upper Saddle River, NJ: Merrill/Prentice Hall.

O'Connor, K. 1995. Guidelines for grading that support learning and student success. *NASSP Bulletin* 79 (571): 91–101.

Olson, C. H. 1989. On the validity of performance grades: The relationship between teacher-assigned grades and standard measures of subject matter acquisition. Paper presented at the annual meeting of the National Council on Measurement in Education, San Francisco, March.

Oosterhof, A. 2001. *Classroom application of educational measurement.* Upper Saddle River, NJ: Prentice Hall.

Ormrod, J. E. 2000. *Educational psychology: Developing learners.* 3rd ed. Upper Saddle River, NJ: Merrill/Prentice Hall.

Ornstein, A. C. 1994. Grading practices and policies: An overview and some suggestions. *NASSP Bulletin* 78 (561): 55–64.

O'Sullivan, R. G., and M. K. Chalnick. 1991. Measurement-related course work requirements for teacher certification and recertification. *Educational Measurement Issues and Practice* 10 (1): 17–19, 23.

Pajares, M. F. 1992. Teachers' beliefs and educational research: Cleaning up a messy construct. *Review of Educational Research* 62 (3): 307–32.

Pintrich, P. R., and D. H. Schunk 2002. *Motivation in education*. 2nd ed. Upper Saddle River; NJ: Merrill/Prentice Hall.

Placier, M. 1995. "But I have to have an A": Probing the cultural meanings and ethical dilemmas of grades in teacher education. *Teacher Education Quarterly* 22 (1): 45–63.

Richardson, V. 1996. The role of attitudes and beliefs in learning to teach. In *Handbook of research on teacher education*, 2nd ed., ed. J. Sikula, T. Buttery, and E. Guyton, 102–19. New York: Macmillan.

Schafer, W. D. 1991. Essential assessment skills in professional education of teachers. *Educational Measurement: Issues and Practice* 10 (1): 3–6, 12.

Shepard, L. A. 2000. The role of assessment in a learning culture. *Educational Researcher* 29 (7): 4–14.

Silverman, R., W. M. Welty, and S. Lyon. 1996. *Case studies for teacher problem solving*. 2nd ed. New York: McGraw-Hill.

Snowman, J., and R. F. Biehler. 2003. *Psychology applied to teaching*. 10th ed. Boston: Houghton Mifflin.

Starch, D., and E. C. Elliot. 1912. Reliability of grading of high-school work in English. *School Review* 20: 442–57.

———. 1913a. Reliability of grading work in mathematics. *School Review* 21: 254–59.

———. 1913b. Reliability of grading work in history. *School Review* 20: 676–81.

Stiggins, R. J. 1991. Relevant classroom assessment training for teachers. *Educational Measurement: Issues and Practice* 10 (1): 7–12.

———. 1999. Evaluating classroom assessment training in teacher education programs. *Educational Measurement: Issues and Practice* 18 (1): 23–27.

———. 2001. *Student-involved classroom assessment*. 3rd ed. Upper Saddle River, NJ: Merrill/Prentice Hall.

Stumpo, V. M. 1997. 3-tier grading sharpens student assessment. *Education Digest* 63 (4): 51–54.

Thorndike, R. M. 1997. *Measurement and Evaluation*. 6th ed. Upper Saddle River, NJ: Merrill/Prentice Hall.

Tombari, M., and G. Borich. 1999. *Authentic assessment in the classroom*. Upper Saddle River, NJ: Merrill/Prentice Hall.

James D. Allen is a professor of educational psychology in the Department of Educational and School Psychology at the College of Saint Rose in Albany, New York.

QUESTIONS FOR REFLECTION

1. Allen presents alternative ways that educators can accurately assess student performance. What are the central arguments he presents and how does he see his strategies as better tools for assessment?
2. What is the principle of validity Allen writes about and how does he suggest it be used to better prepare future educators?
3. What strategies does Allen propose for training educators to use grading differently? Are they realistic? How might these strategies be implemented in your educational setting?

Leaders' Voices—
Putting Theory into Practice

Time for a Tune-Up:
Comprehensive Curriculum Evaluation

LISA H. MEYERS

ABSTRACT: Comprehensive curriculum evaluation goes far beyond align-ing curricula with state standards. Meyers explains how a systematic look at the validity, implementation, and effectiveness of the curriculum yields far more beneficial results at Valley Lutheran High School in Saginaw, Michigan. Moreover, she writes that all stakeholders should have a chance to contribute to the development of a high-quality curriculum.

How important is a high-quality curriculum? A school without a quality curriculum is like a car without an engine—neither goes anywhere. One responsibility of a school administrator is to ensure that quality curriculum is designed, adopted, and implemented. However, a worthy curriculum is more than a list of subjects or top-ics covered in a school and it is certainly more than a set of objectives for any particular course. It encompasses a number of interdependent fac-tors including what students learn and how, what teaching strategies are most effective, and how the structure of the school supports both student achievement and teacher effectiveness (Rogers, 1997).

The No Child Left Behind act (NCLB) has focused attention of an entire nation on the curriculum of an individual district, and educa-tors are keenly aware of this external scrutiny. If curriculum is the engine that drives teaching and learning, then the curriculum improvement process becomes the tune-up for that engine through planning, developing, implementing, and evaluating the curriculum (Jasparro, 1998).

A COMPREHENSIVE PROCESS

A typical curriculum evaluation consists of a com-mittee comparing what is currently taught to a set of standards or objectives compiled by a state department of education or a professional organi-zation. In this procedure, curriculum gaps are identified and filled by adding new topics of study to an existing list. Although there is nothing essentially wrong with this process, a more com-prehensive review model would also include an ex-amination of the curriculum's fundamental validity, implementation, and effectiveness (Jasparro, 1998). The final goal of such a procedure would be gen-eral agreement to the following:

- The curriculum meets state standards and benchmarks.
- The curriculum is relevant and sufficient, i.e., valid.
- The curriculum is effectively implemented.
- Students are achieving key objectives at an acceptable level.

Certainly the first statement is the easiest to verify; however, time spent on the last three components will heighten the power of the curriculum to impact student learning.

VALIDITY

For a curriculum to be considered valid, it must focus on objectives that are truly worthy including those that are relevant to basic living, academic continuance, career success, and responsible citizenship. Wiggins and McTighe (1998) stresses the need to first place objectives that qualify as "enduring understandings" at the very heart of the curriculum, followed by those objectives that are important to know and do and lastly those with which it is worth being familiar. Determining what exactly those enduring understandings might be is no easy task. At our high school, we have solicited outside input on that very question through a variety of methods. Parents were invited to be a part of a focus group that explored essential components of the curriculum. After several nights of work, the parents made recommendations to include curriculum material that centered on knowledge and skills they believed remained significant throughout their adult lives—skills, such as the ability to solve problems and support arguments, and knowledge, such as the vocabulary required to communicate in the various disciplines and an understanding of civil rights and responsibilities.

Making and maintaining connections with instructors at local colleges to obtain a realistic picture of what students should know and be able to do by the time they enter college has also been helpful. Local employers could surely add insight about what learning objectives truly endure beyond formal education into the workplace. We have gleaned some of the most valuable feedback on curriculum through our alumni surveys, in which former students comment on their preparedness for college classes or jobs. We have incorporated questions about particular subject areas into the survey to gain specific, helpful information about those topical areas in which students felt best prepared and those in which they felt under prepared, and summaries of their responses have been

shared with the appropriate departments. Including feedback from outside sources provides for a well-rounded curriculum without the bias that is possible in a strictly internal curriculum evaluation (Dalton and Wright, 1999). Throughout the steady unyielding pace of a school year, educators can sometimes lose sight of the relationship between the curriculum and the world outside the school walls. Allowing opportunities for students, parents, and community members to weigh in on curriculum matters goes a long way toward designing a curriculum that is relevant and sufficient and in the best interest of students.

IMPLEMENTATION

The written curriculum, no matter how high the quality, has no real power without proper implementation and that relies most heavily upon trained educators. Regular reviews of the curriculum by individual teachers and departments help to ensure that objectives are being covered completely and consistently. Administrators who are responsible for teacher supervision but have a minimal understanding of the overall curriculum can expect to see evidence during observations that the curriculum is being followed. Here again, the broader definition of curriculum becomes critical. A curriculum evaluation can look at more than what should be taught and if it is taught. An in-depth evaluation will study how it is taught. We use yearly teacher evaluations that are completed by students. These evaluations give faculty members a better understanding of the students' perception of teacher effectiveness. This information is extremely helpful because it comes directly from the individuals who are most affected by curriculum and instruction.

To encourage student input on curriculum, a group of 20 students were invited to participate in a professional development day for teachers. The students represented a wide range of abilities, interests, and academic success. Teachers had previously formed five committees and each committee was stationed in a different classroom on that day.

The students were divided into five teams that traveled from room to room in 20-minute blocks to share their ideas with the faculty committee. The students were surprisingly candid and well-spoken as they described what was working well and what they still needed from their high school education. Besides hearing about effective methods of instruction, the teachers heard again and again that the students desperately needed to be active participants in their own education. These thoughts made an impression that no in-service has ever been able to match and have influenced the methods of curriculum delivery for many teachers.

EVALUATION

The last component in a comprehensive curriculum review is to evaluate the degree to which students are achieving key objectives. Standardized testing provides one means of assessing students, and a teacher-written assessment targeting specific learning outcomes is another. The latter may be more suitable as the correlation between the selected curriculum and the assessment instrument will be tighter. Teacher collaboration in designing common assessments to use across subject areas or grade levels is another task that yields great benefits. If all of the U.S. History teachers get together and write a final exam to be administered to each U.S. History student, the probability of curriculum consistency between teachers is much higher. Comparisons between the test results and the learning objectives are more meaningful because they can be applied across the broad group of course sections. The most exciting result of writing a common assessment is the positive power that flows from teachers working closely together to improve curriculum and instruction. It is important to note that using student achievement to evaluate curriculum should not occur in isolation. It is still possible for students to perform well on poor quality objectives. A comprehensive curriculum evaluation must inspect student achievement only after the quality of the curriculum has been verified.

OUTSIDE INFLUENCES

Educators certainly play the biggest role in curriculum evaluation and revision. They must be aware, however, of the tremendous influences by several outside sources. Both federal and state government influence what is to be taught and how it will be assessed. Textbook publishers have considerable power in setting curriculum as do agencies that design standardized tests like the ACT, SAT, or state-sponsored achievement tests. Professional associations (such as the National Council for Teachers of Mathematics) and accrediting organizations (such as the North Central Association) weigh in on curriculum issues and are often referenced during evaluation. The impact of outside influences is not inherently negative; the various organizations can act as valuable resources for those responsible for curriculum evaluation and development.

Recommendations for curriculum modifications resulting from research of outside sources should be examined and appraised in light of what is best for students. Nonetheless, it is not in the best interest of students for educators to completely relinquish the power found in designing curriculum to those who do not intimately know the students.

CHALLENGES

Although the benefits of conducting regular curriculum evaluations are great, there are a number of potential challenges. Finding the right combination between state standards and benchmarks and community-based curriculum needs can be problematic. Keep an open mind about the integration of relevant curriculum into what has already been prescribed and allow experienced teachers to have flexibility in their curriculum design. Some teachers may resist curriculum changes when traditional or favorite topics are affected. Reassure those teachers that their success in the classroom is based upon how they teach and not what they teach, and encourage them to take risks that can powerfully affect students. Achieving a proper balance between breadth and depth of curriculum is difficult but crucial. A curriculum that covers everything yet lacks necessary depth does not significantly improve a student's ability to learn and therefore threatens future success in school and career.

A major hurdle for curriculum administration is solving the time dilemma. The comprehensive curriculum evaluation process takes more time than the traditional method. Setting aside regular time during the school year for departments to meet and discuss curriculum and instruction issues keeps the topic at the forefront and reduces time and effort later when a full curriculum review is scheduled. An additional challenge for educational leaders is the hesitancy and uncertainty that comes from lack of familiarity with the existing curriculum and with current trends. Use the curriculum evaluation process as a means to become acquainted with the learning outcomes for the school and to talk with teachers about what is going on in their subject areas. Challenges notwithstanding, the benefits of a quality curriculum evaluation far outweigh any possible difficulties or obstacles.

The keys to successful curriculum evaluation are having an established plan that cycles through each of the curriculum areas at least once every four to five years and charging responsible staff members to both oversee the process and hold other participants accountable. Keeping curriculum up-to-date is a continual process that demands focused time and attention. New curriculum is being developed and promoted to educators all the time; however, without an evaluation plan to study the quality, implementation, student achievement, and effectiveness, the chances of true comprehensive curriculum improvement are slim (Jasparro, 1998). To keep the curriculum engine running smoothly, regular tune-ups must be performed by highly-trained personnel who can diagnose engine problems before they lead to an actual breakdown. With careful attention, quality curriculum can motivate teachers, inspire students, and contribute to the highly effective education desired by all.

REFERENCES

Dalton, B., & Wright, L. (1999). Using community input for the curriculum review process. *Journal of Social Work Education, 35*(2), 275–88.

Jasparro, R. J. (1998). Applying systems thinking to curriculum evaluation. *NASSP Bulletin, 82*(598), 80–86.

Rogers, B. (1997). Informing the shape of the curriculum: New views of knowledge and its representation in schooling. *Journal of Curriculum Studies, 29*(6), 683–710.

Wiggins, G., & McTighe, J. (1998). *Understanding by design*. Alexandria, VA: Association for Supervision and Curriculum Development.

Lisa H. Meyers, a math teacher for 18 years, is academic dean of Valley Lutheran High School in Saginaw, Michigan.

QUESTIONS FOR REFLECTION

1. Meyers claims that a comprehensive curriculum evaluation goes beyond aligning curricula with state standards. What did Valley Lutheran do that made for a more comprehensive curriculum evaluation and went beyond simply aligning curricula with state standards?

2. How might other schools learn from Valley Lutheran's approach to curriculum evaluation? What made their approach more effective than other approaches that are often used?

3. What are the challenges of conducting regular curriculum evaluations and what does Meyers recommend educators do to confront and overcome these challenges?

LEARNING ACTIVITIES

Critical Thinking

1. Reflect on your K–12 school experiences. To what extent did you practice self-assessment of your own learning? What effect(s) did this have on your motivation to succeed?
2. How much emphasis do you think educational leaders should place on using alternative assessments in the classroom?
3. What are the advantages of peer assessment? Disadvantages? To what extent do you plan to encourage teachers to use peer assessment in their classrooms?

Application Activities

1. In the area and at the level with which you are most familiar, examine a set of curriculum materials (a textbook, curriculum guide, etc.) to determine how student learning is assessed. Based on the information presented in this chapter, what suggestions do you have for how the assessment of student learning might be improved?
2. Design a workshop for teachers at the level and in the subject area with which you are most familiar. The aim of the workshop should be to expand teachers' repertoire of knowledge and skills related to assessing student learning.

Field Experiences

1. Interview one or more school leaders to find out how they evaluate the curriculum at the building and/or district level. To what extent do they encourage teachers to use the alternative forms of assessment discussed in this chapter?
2. Interview a group of students in the subject area and at the grade level with which you are most familiar to find out how they assess their own learning. What are the effects of self-assessment on their motivation to succeed?

Internet Activities

1. Survey the Internet to begin locating and creating bookmarks or favorites for websites and administrator discussion groups that focus on different approaches to assessing student learning.
2. Visit the Internet home pages of three or more of the research publications in the following list. These journals frequently have articles that focus on curriculum evaluation and assessment of learning. Read one of these articles that interests you. What does the article say about approaches to curriculum evaluation and assessment of learning? What are the implications for your approach to educational leadership?

American Educational Research Journal   *Cognition and Instruction*
Contemporary Educational Psychology   *Educational Psychologist*
Educational Psychology Review   *Educational Researcher*
Journal of Educational Psychology   *Review of Research in Education*
Journal of Teaching and Teacher Education   *Review of Educational Research*

8

Early Childhood and Elementary Curricula

FOCUS QUESTIONS

1. Why should curriculum leaders be familiar with educational programs at levels other than the one at which they work?

2. How can preschool and elementary-level education contribute to the long-range growth and development of students?

3. In light of the three curriculum bases, and other relevant curriculum criteria, describe several goals for childhood educational programs.

In keeping with the definition of *curriculum* presented in Chapter 1, the chapters in Part III of this book focus on *programs of education* in schools. The chapters are organized according to the institutional, grade-level structure of education in the United States. For the purposes of this chapter, *education for children* refers to early childhood programs for children between the ages of three and five, and elementary-level programs for children between the ages of six and eleven or twelve. Chapter 9, "Middle-Level Curricula," discusses junior high and middle-level education programs and Chapter 10, "High School Curricula," discusses secondary-level programs.

To help you understand some of the "real world" challenges associated with curriculum leadership at each level, the chapters in Part III of this book, like those in Parts I and II, include a *Leaders' Voices* section that presents first-person accounts of leadership in curriculum planning. In addition, each chapter includes a *Case Study in Curriculum Implementation* designed to illustrate some of the complexities of providing leadership for curriculum implementation at the institutional or systemwide level.

Curriculum leaders should be acquainted with educational programs at all levels, regardless of the level at which they work. For instance, you should know about goals and trends in childhood education even if your primary interest is at another level. Familiarity with your students' prior educational experiences, or those they will have in the future, will better equip you to meet their needs in the present. Knowledge of educational programs at other levels will also enable you to address important curriculum criteria such as continuity in learning, balance in the curriculum, and provision for individual differences.

Curriculum Leadership Strategy

To enhance their continuity and scope, develop your curriculum plans in light of the curricula students have experienced *prior to* enrolling in your educational program and the curricula they will experience *after* completing your program.

ELEMENTARY-LEVEL PROGRAMS

Graded elementary schools as we know them today were established in the nineteenth century when educators had little knowledge of the nature and extent of individual differences or of the stages of human development. Prior to the nineteenth century, elementary-level education was primarily for boys from the middle and upper classes; however, boys from the lower classes and girls were often taught basic literacy skills so they could read the Bible and recite religious catechisms.

Elementary schools were developed in conformity with the then prevalent ideas of child development and education. For the most part, it was believed that individual differences in education were undesirable and that the government had an obligation to educate citizens in the new republic. Horace Mann (1796–1859), Massachusetts senator and the first secretary of a state board of education, championed the *common school movement* which led to the free public, locally controlled elementary schools of today. Mann was a passionate advocate of a system of universal free schools for all children—as he wrote in one of his *Annual Reports on Education:*

> It [a system of free common schools] knows no distinction of rich and poor, of bond and free, or between those, who, in the imperfect light of this world, are seeking, through different avenues, to reach the gate of heaven. Without money and without price, it throws open its doors, and spreads the table of its bounty, for all the children of the State. (Mann, 1968, p. 754)

Today's elementary school typically consists of self-contained classrooms in which one teacher teaches all or nearly all subjects to a group of about twenty-five children. The curriculum is often integrated, with one activity and subject area flowing into another. Teacher and students usually spend most of the day in the same classroom, with students often going to other rooms for instruction in art, music, and physical education. Individual students may also attend special classes for remedial or enriched instruction, speech therapy, choir, and band.

Some elementary schools are organized around team teaching arrangements, in which two teachers are responsible for two groups of students. One teacher might present lessons in mathematics, science, and health, while another teaches reading, language arts, and history. A variation on this arrangement is for teacher responsibilities to be made according to students' ability levels. For example, one teacher might teach reading to lower-ability students and all remaining subjects to middle- and higher-ability students; while the other teaches reading to middle- and higher-ability students and all remaining subjects to lower-ability students.

The Importance of Elementary-Level Programs

"The early years are transcendentally the most important, and if this nation wishes ultimately to achieve excellence, we will give greater priority and attention to the early years and start affirming elementary teachers instead of college professors as the center-piece of learning." This statement by the late Ernest L. Boyer, President of the Carnegie Foundation for the Advancement of Teaching, reminds us that the experiences children have in elementary school provide the foundation upon which their education through adulthood is built. Clearly, the elementary school has an intense influence on children; the year the child spends in the first grade is one-sixth of his or her entire life to that point. Therefore, the lack of adequate provision for individual differences in the elementary-level curriculum can result in intense feelings of failure and rejection for some children. Failure to acquire sufficient knowledge and skills at the elementary level can exact a high price at other levels where the resulting deficiencies are very difficult to overcome.

Social changes are placing enormous new pressures on the elementary school. All of the social forces discussed in Chapter 2 are having a major impact on education for children. In addition, a major challenge for elementary schools in the twenty-first century is to establish meaningful contact with children from diverse backgrounds. The scope of this challenge is captured well in the following excerpt from Ernest Boyer's last book, *The Basic School: A Community for Learning:*

> Last fall, more than three million kindergarten children enrolled in over fifty thousand public and private schools from Bangor, Maine, to the islands of Hawaii. Most of these young students arrived at school anxious, but also eager. Some were cheerful, others troubled. Some skipped and ran, others could not walk. This new generation of students came from countless neighborhoods, from a great diversity of cultures, speaking more languages than most of us could name. And the challenge we now face is to ensure that every child will become a confident, resourceful learner. (Boyer, 1995, p. 3)

Provision for individual differences, and flexibility and continuity in learning, are thus curriculum criteria of major significance.

EARLY CHILDHOOD PROGRAMS

During the last few decades, early childhood programs have received increasing attention and support, and the thrust toward education at this level will continue to be a significant educational trend in the future. United States Census Bureau data, for example, revealed that 65 percent of all five year olds attended kindergarten in 1965; by 1980, this figure had risen to almost 96 percent; and in 2004, virtually all five year olds attended (National Center for Education Statistics, 2004a). The preprimary enrollment rates for three and four year olds have also continued to rise steadily. In 1991, 31 percent of three year olds and 52 percent of four year olds were enrolled in preprimary educational programs, including Head Start, nursery school, and prekindergarten; by 1996, these percentages had risen to 37 percent and 90 percent, respectively (National Center for Education Statistics, 1999). In 1982, about 3.2 million children attended kindergarten; by 2007, it was estimated that almost 4 million children would attend (National Center for Education Statistics, 2004a).

Educational programs for preschool-age children are provided by public and private schools, churches, and for-profit and not-for-profit day care centers; in addition, a growing number of preschool educational programs are being offered to employees in business and industry. Early childhood education may be a half-day nursery school program organized around play and socialization, or it may be a full-day academic program that focuses on teaching reading and math readiness skills to children.

Unfortunately, there is no institutionalized system of early childhood education that guarantees preschool experiences for all children, and resources to support preschool education programs have been inconsistent. Chapter 1 programs such as Head Start, Follow Through, and Success for All have continually been in jeopardy of being phased out and have never served all eligible students. It has been estimated that Head Start and similar programs serve fewer than half of the nation's three and four year olds living in poverty (Elam, Rose, & Gallup, 1992). While some research studies concluded that the benefits of Head Start tend to disappear as children move through elementary school, others concluded that the program was effective and provided a $3 return for every dollar invested (Elam, Rose, & Gallup, 1993, p. 143).

Throughout the country, the number of prekindergarten and full-day kindergarten programs is increasing, mainly as a result of studies confirming the value of early childhood education, especially for "disadvantaged" children (Karweit, 1993, 1987; McKey et al., 1985; Nieman & Gastright, 1981). A few states—Pennsylvania, Alabama, and Virginia—have modified their certification policies to include a birth through third-grade certificate, and some states are seeking to create formal public school programs for four year olds.

Curriculum Leadership Strategy

To guide your curriculum planning for early childhood programs, compile a directory of various public (government-sponsored) and private programs that serve preschool children in your local community.

The growth of early childhood education is also due to theories of human development and learning that emphasize the need for early stimulation and encouragement of curiosity in infants and young children if their intellectual potential is to be developed. Since research indicates that much of a child's intellectual development has taken place by the age of six (Woolfolk, 2005; Slavin, 2003), instruction at the preschool level helps to increase a child's interest in learning at a critical period in his or her development. Two of the most successful early childhood education programs are the federally funded Head Start and Follow Through programs.

Head Start

Since 1965, Head Start has served almost 16 million three to five year old children from low-income families. Head Start services, many of which are delivered by parents and volunteers, focus on education, socioemotional development, physical and mental health, and nutrition. In 2003, $6.6 billion was allocated to Head Start, and almost 909,600 children were enrolled in 47,000 Head Start Classrooms (Administration for Children and Families, 2004).

The educational component of Head Start provides children with curricular experiences designed to foster their intellectual, social, and emotional growth. In addition, Head Start curricula reflect the community being served, its ethnic and cultural characteristics. Research on the effectiveness of Head Start indicates that participating children show immediate gains in cognitive test scores, socioemotional test scores, and health status (McKey et al., 1985; Love, Mechstroth, & Sprachman, 1997). Over time, however, cognitive and socioemotional gains dissolve, and former Head Start students tend not to score above nonparticipants. Nevertheless, some studies have shown that former Head Start students are more likely to be promoted to the next grade level and less likely to be assigned to special education classes than their peers (McKey et al., 1985).

A unique feature of Head Start is the staff development and training provided by the program. Head Start operates the Child Development Associate (CDA) program that gives professional and nonprofessional employees an opportunity to pursue academic degrees or certification in early childhood education. Almost 80,000 persons held a CDA credential in 1998 (Administration for Children and Families, 1998).

Follow Through

The purpose of Follow Through is to sustain and augment, in kindergarten and the primary grades, the gains children from low-income families make in Head Start and similar preschool programs. Follow Through meets the educational, physical, and psychological needs of children, including supplementary or specialized instruction in regular classrooms. The program's impact was greatest in the 1970s when hundreds of thousands of children were served and the annual budget was more than $55 million; by 1998, funding had fallen to less than $10 million per year. The Follow Through program is a good example of how the curriculum criterion of individual differences can be used to develop appropriate learning experiences for students. By developing a variety of innovative educational programs for children and then evaluating those approaches over time, Follow Through has produced knowledge about programs that best facilitate the growth and development of children (Wang & Ramp, 1987; Wang & Walberg, 1988).

In the past, parents and guardians may have felt that they were to bring their children to the elementary school door and then leave. But evidence from programs such as Head Start and Follow Through indicate that parents can play an important role in the early development of their children. As a result, parents should have a more active role in developing and delivering education programs for young children. One novel way to induct parents and their children into the life of the school was suggested by John I. Goodlad (1984) in *A Place Called School,* one of the more influential educational reform reports to be released in the early 1980s. Goodlad proposed that children enter school during the month of their fourth birthday. The proposed practice would make possible a warm welcome for each child since school could begin with a birthday party. The child would then participate in subsequent birthday parties for children who followed. Needless to say, the challenge of socializing twenty or more beginning students each fall would be greatly minimized, and schooling could take on a highly individualized character. Teachers could become acquainted with just a few new children and their families each month at the time of admission, and the children would enter a stable classroom environment.

GOALS FOR CHILDHOOD EDUCATION

What goals should educational programs for children pursue? Many might be suggested—some derived, of course, from the three curriculum bases: social forces, theories of human development, and the nature of learning and learning styles. A list of goals would surely include many of the following:

1. Helping learners develop a sense of trust, autonomy, and initiative.
2. Introducing structure and organization without curbing self-expression and creativity.
3. Developing social skills through large-group, small-group, and individualized activities. (In "Why Is Kindergarten an Endangered Species?" in this chapter, Linda H. Plevyak and Kathy Morris suggest that today's kindergarten programs should place more emphasis on developing children's social skills.)
4. Providing adequate and appropriate physical and health education.
5. Teaching the fundamental skills of communication and computation.
6. Establishing a desire to learn and an appreciation for education by providing experiences that enhance interest and curiosity.
7. Developing interests in many subject areas through exposure to diverse fields of knowledge.
8. Developing feelings of self-worth and security by providing opportunities for each child to build on his or her successes.
9. Providing many opportunities for children to experience the satisfaction of achievement. Several selections in this chapter discuss how to improve children's reading programs. (In the *Case Study in Curriculum Implementation* section, "Learning to Read in Kindergarten: Has Curriculum Development Bypassed the Controversies?" by Bruce Joyce, Marilyn Hrycauk, and Emily Calhoun describe a formal reading curriculum developed by district staff members and teachers in the Northern Lights School Division of Alberta that enables students to experience "joy" and "delight" while learning to read. In "Making Instructional Decisions Based on Data: What, How, and Why," Kouider Mokhtari, Catherine A. Rosemary, and Patricia A. Edwards explain how to use three categories of data to improve reading and writing instruction programs for children. Last, in "Implementing a Schoolwide Literacy Framework to Improve Student Achievement," Douglas Fisher and Nancy Frey explain how to develop a "literacy framework" that significantly enhances children's reading, writing, and thinking abilities.)
10. Developing appreciation for the worth and differences of others. In addition, as E. H. Mike Robinson III and Jennifer R. Curry point out in their article, "Promoting Altruism in the Classroom," the early years are an opportune time to teach children to have caring, empathetic, and compassionate attitudes toward others.
11. Developing the processes of conceptualizing, problem solving, self-direction, and creating. (In this chapter's *Leaders' Voices* section, "Building a Community in Our Classroom: The Story of Bat Town, U.S.A.," Andrea McGann Keech describes how her third- and fourth-grade students conceptualized and then created a model community of their own.)
12. Developing a concern for the environment, the local and global communities, the future, and the welfare of others.

13. Helping learners to examine and develop moral values.

What additions or changes would you propose for this list of goals? Review William H. Schubert's "Perspectives on Four Curriculum Traditions" in Chapter 1; what goals would an intellectual traditionalist suggest for childhood education programs? Similarly, what goals would a social behaviorist, experientialist, and critical reconstructionist suggest?

REFERENCES

Administration for Children and Families. *Fact Sheet.* Washington, DC: The Administration for Children and Families, 2004.

Boyer, Ernest L. *The Basic School: A Community for Learning.* Princeton, NJ: The Carnegie Foundation for the Advancement of Teaching, 1995.

Elam, Stanley M., Rose, Lowell C., and Gallup, Alex M. "The 25th Annual Phi Delta Kappa Gallup Poll of the Public's Attitudes toward the Public Schools." *Phi Delta Kappan* (September 1993).

———. "The 24th Annual Phi Delta Kappa Gallup Poll of the Public's Attitudes toward the Public Schools." *Phi Delta Kappan* (September, 1992).

Goodlad, John I. *A Place Called School.* New York: Highstown, 1984.

Karweit, Nancy. "Effective Preschool and Kindergarten Programs for Students at Risk." In Bernard Spodek, ed., *Handbook of Research on the Education of Young Children.* New York: Macmillan, 1993, pp. 385–411.

———. "Full Day or Half Day Kindergarten: Does It Matter?" (Report No. 11). Baltimore, MD: The Johns Hopkins University, Center for Research on Elementary and Middle Schools, 1987.

Love, John M., Mechstroth, Alicia, and Sprachman, Susan. *Measuring the Quality of Program Environments in Head Start and Other Early Childhood Programs: A Review and Recommendations for Future Research: Working Paper Series.* Washington, DC: National Center for Education Statistics, 1997.

Mann, Horace. *Annual Reports on Education.* In Mary Mann, ed., *The Life and Works of Horace Mann,* vol. 3. Boston: Horace B. Fuller, 1968.

McKey, Ruth Hubbell, et al. *The Impact of Head Start on Children, Families, and Communities. Final Report of the Head Start Evaluation, Synthesis and Utilization Project, Executive Summary.* ERIC Documents No. ED 263 984, 1985.

National Center for Education Statistics. *The Condition of Education 2004.* Washington, DC: National Center for Education Statistics, 2004a.

———. *Projection of Education Statistics to 2013.* Washington, DC: National Center for Education Statistics, 2004b.

Nieman, R., and Gastright, Joseph F. "The Long-Term Effects of Title I Preschool and All-Day Kindergarten," *Phi Delta Kappan* 63 (November, 1981): 184–185.

Slavin, Robert E. *Educational Psychology: Theory and Practice* (7th ed). Boston: Allyn and Bacon, 2003.

Wang, Margaret C., and Ramp, Eugene A. *The National Follow Through Program: Design, Implementation, and Effects.* Philadelphia: Temple University Press, 1987.

Wang, Margaret C., and Walberg, Herbert J. *The National Follow Through Program: Lessons from Two Decades of Research Practice in School Improvement.* ERIC Document No. ED 336 191, 1988.

Woolfolk, Anita E. *Educational Psychology* (9th ed). Boston: Allyn and Bacon, 2005.

Promoting Altruism in the Classroom

E. H. MIKE ROBINSON III
JENNIFER R. CURRY

ABSTRACT: Altruism is the purest form of caring—selfless and not contingent on reward—and thus the predecessor of prosocial cognitions and behaviors. In this article, the authors explore social learning theory, which posits that children learn to be altruistic through multiple social interactions, including adult role modeling of ideal behaviors, dialectic conversations that stimulate cognitive formation and development of altruistic ideas, and role playing and instruction that increase children's perceptions of their own competencies for helping others. Research suggests that children have a greater response to adults who behave altruistically (through role modeling) versus adults who merely make statements in favor of altruism. Consequently, teachers can be great role models for caring and altruistic behavior; they can demonstrate caring, empathy, and compassion towards others in their day-to-day interactions with students.

Pro-social behavior is described as "behavior intended to benefit another" (Eisenberg et al., 1999, p. 1360). Such behaviors may include comforting, sharing, working or playing cooperatively, and displaying empathy for others (Simmons & Sands-Dudelczyk, 1983), all of which have an element of altruism. Altruism is defined by Eisenberg et al. (1999) as "behavior motivated by concern for others or by internalized values, goals, and self-rewards rather than by the expectation of concrete or social rewards, or the desire to avoid punishment or sanctions" (p. 1360). Therefore, it is our contention that altruism is the purest form of caring—selfless and non-contingent upon reward—and thus the predecessor of pro-social cognitions and behaviors (Smith, 1976). While many character education programs focus on promoting pro-social behavior, the literature holds very few suggestions for specifically promoting altruism. This article will outline some hypotheses about the need to develop altruism as a base for pro-social behavior, describe how altruism develops, and propose strategies educators can use to foster altruism in the classroom.

Many hypotheses have been proposed regarding the origination and nature of altruism; it is also debated whether an altruistic personality type

exists and, if so, whether such a characteristic is stable over time and across situations (Eisenberg et al., 1999). Historically, research has centered on the reasons why a person is either a bystander or a helper in situations involving a stranger in need. Interest in altruism heightened after the fatal stabbing of Kitty Genovese, when 38 people either saw or heard her being attacked yet did not intervene (Dovidio, 1991). This phenomenon of not intervening became known as the bystander effect, wherein the diffusion of responsibility, brought on by being in a group, negates individual action to respond to a person in crisis.

Since the 1960s, the research conducted on altruism and acts of selfless giving has helped researchers develop multiple theories about why people choose to perform altruistic acts. One theory is that altruistic tendencies are biological, in that self-sacrificing behavior may be performed with the unconscious idea that this behavior will be reciprocated in the future. Evidence supporting this hypothesis comes from monozygotic and dizygotic twin studies (Eisenberg et al., 1999), and through observations of infants, responses that reflect signs of distress exhibited by their caregivers (Zahn-Waxler, Radke-Yarrow, Wagner, & Chapman, 1992). However, the biology hypothesis does not explain why a person would help a stranger who may never have the occasion to reciprocate.

Another hypothesis comes from social learning theory, which posits that children learn to be altruistic through multiple social interactions, including adult role modeling of ideal behaviors, dialectic conversations that stimulate cognitive formation and development of altruistic ideas, and role playing and instruction that increase children's perceptions of their own competencies for helping others (Konecni & Ebbesen, 1975). In addition, Eisenberg and Fabes (1998) found that parenting style and social context may affect the development of pro-social behaviors that have an altruistic base.

Researchers have found that the type of help children offer is directly related to the repertoire of behaviors they have gleaned from their school environment. Specifically, children who attended a transactional analysis school were most likely to offer spontaneous help, children from a Montessori school were most likely to wait for a specific request for help before giving assistance, and students from a traditional school were most likely to try finding an adult to help another child rather than directly assisting the child themselves. The researchers believe that differences in helping behavior are correlated with the socialization of children in their respective education environments (Simmons & Sands-Dudelczyk, 1983).

Further evidence supporting the social learning theory of altruism comes from research by Konecni and Ebbesen (1975), who found that children have a greater response to adults who behave altruistically (through role modeling) versus adults who merely make statements in favor of altruism. Similarly, Bryan and Walbek (1970) found that children learn more and respond more positively to role modeling than to didactic instruction on altruism. They also concluded that parents and adult role models can help train children to recognize situational cues for assistance (e.g., signs of distress in another person) and also may prescribe norms for helping others (Konecni & Ebbesen, 1975). This socialization into the helping process may be the key for understanding how children discern who needs help, based on such factors as age, race, gender, and ethnicity.

One last connection of social learning theory and altruism comes from research on gender and altruistic behavior. It appears that males and females differ in the type of assistance they are likely to give, and that this qualitative difference may be based on beliefs and social norms about appropriate helping behaviors for each gender. For example, females may be more likely to attend to others empathically and verbally—giving support, empathy, and encouragement. Conversely, males are more likely to offer physically oriented altruism, with few verbally altruistic behaviors (Monk-Turner et al., 2002; Zeldin, Savin-Williams, & Small, 1984). Bihm, Gaudet, and Sale (1979) found that the amount of help offered did not differ between males and females. Furthermore, the greatest determinant of helping behavior appears to be the same in both genders: an empathic orientation toward others, characterized by cognitive and affective perspective taking and the ability to empathize accurately (Fry, 1976; Oswald, 1996).

Another hypothesis about altruism addresses cognition and internalized beliefs about helping others from a cognitive development theory basis. Cognitive schemas for altruism appear to change as children mature. Children who are high in empathic orientation or social sensitivity may internalize the helping concept and integrate these behaviors into self-concepts by incorporating the helping orientation into their belief systems (Fry, 1976). In addition, McGuire (2003) found that persons high in empathic orientation cognitively downplayed the self-cost for helping others and increased their perception of benefit to the recipient of help. This cognitive bias, which McGuire labeled a "modesty bias," serves to perpetuate and reinforce helping behavior in persons displaying altruistic tendencies.

Support exists in the literature for the cognitive schema hypothesis of altruism. Specifically, a general consensus indicates that with age, and the development of cognitive ability to take others' perspectives, comes a concomitant increase in altruistic behaviors (Eisenberg, Miller, Shell, McNalley, & Shea, 1991). However, this relationship is not linear. The relationship between age and altruistic behaviors actually appears to be curvilinear—there is an increase from birth to about 6 years of age, and then a decrease in altruistic behavior around age 7, followed by a subsequent sustained increase throughout late childhood and adolescence (Grunberg, Maycock, & Anthony, 1985).

Whether altruism has a biological basis, is socially learned, or is a cognitive schema that produces internalized beliefs that foster altruistic behaviors is a fascinating topic for consideration. According to Cushman (1990), society expanded and changed drastically with the post-modern era of industrialization and automation. These changes, in effect, produced massive social changes; however, the infrastructure did not exist to create the bonds of caring, kinship, and connectivity that were lost due to urbanization and isolation in the modern-day systems. Therefore, in order to fill the gap in the absence of these connections, our culture has become one of self-focus and consumerism—driven by the need to pursue tangibles to replace social cohesion and support networks (Cushman, 1990).

If caring is a natural, biological process, then how do we develop the innate propensity to care for others in a culture that largely promotes self-preservation and the enhancement of individuality? Children's truly innate altruistic tendencies may be discouraged through the climate of self-promotion and self-care that cultures often promote. Noddings (1992) suggests that educators must create opportunities for natural caring in the classroom if children are to develop their own instinctive caring, while simultaneously promoting ethical, intentional caring to develop those tendencies under the influence of cognition and social learning (Noddings, 1992).

While ethical caring may develop a sense of connection and community—along with notions of service and civic mindedness—natural caring also should be fostered in order to develop the individual's unique competencies and constructive

ways of knowing about caring. The benefit would be a caring classroom community. In classrooms where caring is promoted, children may be more likely to offer assistance to other children and to connect with other students and teachers. These connections may, in turn, increase the child's school success (Noddings, 1995a). But should educators be teaching values? According to Noddings (1991), values already are implicit in schools through the rules established by teachers and administrators and through messages conveyed by the behavior of adults in the school building. Values are inherently present in schools and communities; we can be intentional and *choose* the values that we pass on to the children in our care (Noddings, 1995b).

So, how can educators increase students' altruistic behaviors? There are multiple means for achieving this goal. Teachers can be great role models for caring and altruistic behavior; they can demonstrate caring, empathy, and compassion toward others in their day-to-day interactions with students. Teachers are also in a position to structure the classroom so that opportunities exist for the expression of altruism, and to recognize and acknowledge children's altruistic acts of kindness to others. An additional way that teachers can promote altruism is by infusing altruism into the curriculum in the classroom. Kohn (1993) writes that teachers may increase caring opportunities by modeling caring, using caring to problem solve, utilizing art that illustrates caring, and by teaching it directly. Here are some suggestions of ways to increase altruistic behavior, accompanied by explanations of how to execute the suggestions in the classroom.

INCREASING STUDENT AWARENESS OF ALTRUISM AND GREED

In order to foster altruistic behaviors, we have to make children aware of what constitutes altruism and the opposite of altruism—greed. We will examine ways to increase student awareness of altruism and greed-related acts through different subjects.

Young children may be exposed to the concepts of greed and altruism through literature (children's stories are rich with these ideas), commercials on television, and children's movies. After watching movies or reading stories, discuss the actions of characters that showed kindness and caring versus those that did not. Discuss with children how acts of caring and acts of greed affected the outcomes of the story for different characters. History and social studies also provide great avenues for discussion about greed and altruism. The concept of greed may be expanded to nonmaterial things, such as social status (greed may be about more than money—it might concern power and control). Let students be artistic, and have them create collages from magazines that represent acts of greed and/or altruism. Tap into kids' love of music by encouraging them to discuss themes of greed and altruism in songs. Teachers may want to create writing assignments about these concepts; for example, students could write about the kindest thing anyone ever did for them.

Older students can do research on altruistic activities. For example, what is involved in being a blood donor? What is volunteerism? Another activity may be to put students in groups and have each group research a different charitable organization (such as the YMCA, The Leukemia/Lymphoma Society, March of Dimes, Muscular Dystrophy Association, The American Cancer Society, The Humane Society, United Way, etc.). Have each group complete a research project outlining the mission of their assigned organization; how the organization is funded (such as private and corporate sponsorship, government grants, etc.); what services the organization provides and who benefits from those services; volunteer opportunities with the organization; etc. If you don't want to assign, you could let students choose from a list—we recommend that you ensure that every group has a different organization so as to increase student exposure to different organizations. After they have completed their research, teams can present their information to the entire class. You can make this creative by letting them develop commercials for their organization, as well as brochures, fliers, newspaper articles, posters, and much more!

INCREASING EMPATHIC ORIENTATION

Making students aware of their feelings and other people's feelings increases their empathic orientation. This, in turn, allows them to recognize signs of distress in other people and to empathize with others. Consequently, this type of affective response can increase their propensity for aiding and comforting others.

Literature provides a platform from which to explore a myriad of emotions. It is important to move young children beyond identifying emotions as "mad" and "sad." Have discussions about the differences between mad, frustrated, angry, furious, disappointed, etc. After reading stories, allow for a discussion of how the characters emotionally reacted to events. Encourage children to examine how a character's body language or voice let the child know what the character was feeling. Here is an example:

> "Big Bear shouted, 'I want some honey right now!' He slammed his paw on the table and growled."

If you were discussing this example with students, you would want to have them tell you how Big Bear is feeling. What things did Big Bear do that let the students know how he felt?

Have students discuss a time they experienced similar emotions to that of characters in literature. Have them discuss how they know when others are: sad, angry, confused, excited, happy, tired, etc. In order to have students understand the physical cues of emotions, you can have them act out different emotions with a partner or in groups. Tell students they are not allowed to talk; they can only show emotions through body language. Read them a statement and have them act out an emotion to go with the statement. (You may have to model this process for younger students.) For example, you state:

> "Greta realized she was all alone in the forest. She did not know her way home. How do you think she was feeling?"

Students then would act out the body language for being scared. Discuss with students what fearful or scared looks like (nail biting, turning pale, increased heart rate, widened eyes, etc.).

Another way to utilize literature is to have students recognize altruistic acts in books they are reading; conversely, you also can have children identify greedy acts. This dichotomy often exists in children's literature. Students may recount multiple altruistic acts or acts of greed performed by various characters, and then analyze and document the impact these behaviors had on other characters. Table 1 provides a sample list of authors and books that may be used for this purpose.

DEVELOPING PERSONAL VALUES ABOUT HELPING

Developing the classroom as a community is essential in promoting children's internalization of values about helping and altruism. Creating community classrooms can be done in a variety of ways. Teachers can establish tasks that each individual performs for the good of the classroom community.

Instead of making children responsible for cleaning up their own desk areas, make them responsible for one task that affects the whole classroom. For instance, make one student the chair monitor each day, and that student can be responsible for ensuring that chairs are pushed in and that no coats or backpacks are left on chairs. That same child may be in charge of erasing the boards in the classroom on the next day, and be

assigned on a following day to ensuring that all of the textbooks are shelved correctly. It is important that every child be given a task each day (this could be done on a rotating basis and assignments could be given at the beginning of the day), and that the tasks are manageable and easy enough to be done quickly. One other way to facilitate the feeling of community in the classroom is by designating the classroom supplies as community property. Instead of each child needing a pencil box, one box of pencils can be shared by the entire class.

Another way to develop personal values and beliefs about helping others is to use group discussion about moral dilemmas. Many books and stories focus on characters with a moral dilemma. Students can brainstorm ways that characters in the stories could have responded and what different outcomes would have resulted. Also, allowing students to explore their own personal values regarding helping others can contribute to the internalization of helping as a belief system. Children can write stories in which they perform an act of kindness for another person. Because children enjoy being creative, you also can have them write and perform skits or puppet shows about kindness, caring, and helping.

During the holiday season, you could discuss as a class why it is important to help others in the community. Perhaps instead of throwing a traditional school holiday party, students could benefit others in the community by hosting a holiday party for residents from a local nursing home. Students also could throw a party in honor of the school volunteers, such as parents

TABLE 1
Sample Books Containing Altruistic Acts

Author	Title	Appropriate Age Group
Shel Silverstein	*The Giving Tree*	5–8 years old
E. B. White	*Charlotte's Web*	7–10 years old
Harper Lee	*To Kill a Mockingbird*	12–14 years old

and community members. Students may want to create expressive works, such as poems, short stories, pictures, paintings, etc., of ways that they have benefited from volunteers' contributions and present these expressions at the party. This allows students to connect their own appreciation with the acts of others, thereby creating a mental schema for helping others and the benefits of helping behaviors.

INCREASING SELF-PERCEIVED COMPETENCIES FOR HELPING

Teachers can give students opportunities to increase their knowledge of the skills they possess that they can use to help others. Increasing children's self-perceived competencies for helping will aid them in recognizing skills they already have that allow them to be helpful to others.

Peer helper programs are a great way to encourage students to help others. An example of a peer helping program is Peer Tutoring, which trains students to help other students with math or reading assignments. Another type of peer helping, one that is especially useful with transient populations, such as urban or military schools, is Peer Buddies for new students. A Peer Buddy shows the new child around the classroom and acclimates him or her to the daily schedule; explains the routine of lunch and bathroom breaks; helps the student locate the library, lunchroom, lockers, and other key areas around the building; and introduces the new student to other students and teachers.

Another way to promote self-perceived competencies is to give students increased opportunities for creative problem solving. Ask the students, for example, how the class can show their appreciation and respect to the janitors. Students may come up with ideas that the teacher never would have conceived of. Allowing students to be creative and problem solve also increases their commitment to the resolution of an action plan. In the above example, the students might be more likely to follow through with the work of setting up a day to honor the workers if they are allowed to help plan the event and can create a vision for how the day will proceed.

Teachers also can help students become aware of helping opportunities by incorporating altruism into everyday activities. For example, if you are studying plant life in science, you could plan a small garden for the schoolyard that your class can maintain throughout the year. This does not have to require large amounts of time or money. Depending on the children's age, projects could include developing and implementing a school-wide recycling plan, organizing a canned food drive, or petitioning the school to adopt a nonprofit organization. These types of projects require research, planning, marketing, and a proposal for action. All of these requirements help students develop public speaking skills, writing skills, and organization, which exercises their creativity. Mathematics is infused in the agenda if you require students to calculate project costs, count donations, and track expenditures over time.

CONCLUSION

Altruism is evidenced in society through volunteerism, philanthropic support, and random acts of kindness performed every day. If our students are going to behave in altruistic ways, we first must help them recognize what altruism is, increase their awareness of others, feelings, develop their own personal values and style for helping, and increase their knowledge of their own helping competencies. Teachers are invaluable in this process. Altruism will continue to play a part in increasing the cohesion and connectivity of individuals and groups, both locally and globally. Teachers train students for life success by encouraging students to be lifelong learners and contributing members of society. They can utilize the classroom as a source of socialization to influence the moral development of children, creating opportunities for interpersonal success and engaging students to participate responsibly in the communities in which they reside.

REFERENCES

Bihm, E., Gaudet, I., & Sale, O. (1979). Altruistic responses under conditions of anonymity. *The Journal of Social Psychology, 109*, 25–30.

Bryan, J. H., & Walbek, N. H. (1970). The impact of words and deeds concerning altruism upon children. *Child Development, 41*, 747–757.

Cushman, P. (1990). Why the self is empty. *American Psychologist, 45*(5), 599–611.

Dovidio, J. (1991). The empathy-altruism hypothesis: Paradigm and promise. *Psychological Inquiry, 2*(2), 126–128.

Eisenberg, N., & Fabes, R. A. (1998). Shyness and children's emotionality, regulation, and coping: Contemporaneous, longitudinal, and across context relations. *Child Development, 69*(3), 767–790.

Eisenberg, N., Guthrie, I. K., Murphy, B. C., Shepard, S. A., Cumberland, A., & Carlo, G. (1999). Consistency and development of prosocial dispositions: A longitudinal study. *Child Development, 70*(6), 1360–1372.

Eisenberg, N., Miller, P. A., Shell, R., McNalley, S., & Shea, C. (1991). Prosocial development in adolescence: A longitudinal study. *Developmental Psychology, 27*(5), 849–858.

Fry, P. S. (1976). Children's social sensitivity, altruism, and self-gratification. *The Journal of Social Psychology, 98*, 77–88.

Grunberg, N. E., Maycock, V. A., & Anthony, B. J. (1985). Material altruism in children. *Basic and Applied Social Psychology, 6*(1), 1–11.

Kohn, A. (1993). *Punished by rewards*. Boston: Houghton Mifflin.

Konecni, V. J., & Ebbesen, E. B. (1975). Effects of the presence of children on adults' helping behavior and compliance: Two field studies. *The Journal of Social Psychology, 97*, 181–193.

McGuire, A. M. (2003). "It was nothing"—Extending evolutionary models of altruism by two social cognitive biases in judgments of the costs and benefits of helping, *Social Cognition, 21*(5), 363–394.

Monk-Turner, E., Blake, V., Chniel, F., Forbes, S., Lensey, L., & Madzuma, J. (2002). Helping hands: A study of altruistic behavior. *Gender Issues, 20*(4), 70–76.

Noddings, N. (1991). Values by deliberation of default. *Clearing House, 64*(5), 320–323.

Noddings, N. (1992). *The challenge to care in schools: An alternative approach to education*. New York: Teachers College Press.

Noddings, N. (1995a). Teaching themes of care. *Phi Delta Kappan, 76*(9), 24–29.

Noddings, N. (1995b). A morally defensible mission for schools in the 21st century. *Phi Delta Kappan, 76*(5), 365–369.

Oswald, P. A. (1996). The effects of cognitive and affective perspective taking on empathic concern and altruistic helping. *Journal of Social Psychology, 136*(5), 613–623.

Simmons, C. H., & Sands-Dudelczyk, K. (1983). Children helping peers: Altruism and preschool environment. *The Journal of Psychology, 115*, 203–207.

Smith, A. (1976). *The theory of moral sentiments* (D. D. Raphael & A. L. Macfie, Eds.). Indianapolis, IN: Liberty Fund.

Zahn-Waxler, C., Radke-Yarrow, M., Wagner, E., & Chapman, M. (1992). Development of concern for others. *Developmental Psychology, 28*(1), 126–137.

Zeldin, R. S., Savin-Williams, R. C., & Small, S. A. (1984). Dimensions of prosocial behavior in adolescent males. *The Journal of Social Psychology, 123*, 159–168.

E. H. Mike Robinson III is the Robert N. Heintzelman Eminent Scholar Chair for the study of greed and promotion of altruism at the University of Central Florida, Orlando. *Jennifer R. Curry* is a doctoral research assistant at the University of Central Florida, Orlando.

QUESTIONS FOR REFLECTION

1. Can a person be "made" to be altruistic or are some people just more selfish than others? What kind of person are you?

2. How do the authors believe educators can increase students' altruistic behaviors? What specific strategies do they suggest and what do you think of their suggestions?
3. According to the research cited in the article, children have a greater response to adults who behave altruistically (through role modeling) versus adults who merely make statements in favor of altruism. How might a teacher or other educator create an environment in which altruism is a more natural function of the curriculum and the school day?

Making Instructional Decisions Based on Data: What, How, and Why

KOUIDER MOKHTARI
CATHERINE A. ROSEMARY
PATRICIA A. EDWARDS

ABSTRACT: This article offers information on the Data Analysis Framework for Instructional Decision Making, a student assessment tool that uses guiding questions to assist school literacy team members in analyzing data, discussing the patterns and relationships within those data, and constructing interpretations that they can then translate into goals and action steps to improve reading and writing achievement. The authors discuss the three major categories of data that are considered for improving reading and writing instruction: reading performance data, professional development data, and classroom data.

One of my weaknesses, has always been documenting a student's progress, because I always found it such an overwhelming task. I would assess students, hand in the scores to an administrator, and then file them away. I literally would assess here and there, never use the results and concentrate on whole-group instruction. Individual needs based on assessment were never taken into consideration. (Calderon [a kindergarten teacher], cited in Reilly, 2007, p. 770)

If you can relate to Calderon's sense of disenchantment with respect to documenting students' progress in your classroom or school and then not using the information, you are not alone. In our teaching experiences over more than two decades, we have often heard comments such as these from many of the, PreK–12 teachers, literacy specialists, and principals in classroom and school settings with whom we have worked. We often found and continue to find that although these educators spend significant amount of time collecting assessment data, they do not take time or perhaps know how to organize and use data consistently and efficiently in instructional decision making. When asked, most teachers often admit, like Calderon, that documentation of student literacy progress is one of their weaknesses because it can be an overwhelming and time-consuming task. Other teachers say that they simply lack the knowledge and skills to develop a system for assessing and documenting students' progress.

The challenges that go along with data-based decision making are even more apparent in the current context of increased accountability as seen in local, state, and federal policies. At a time when teachers and administrators are pressed to demonstrate students' literacy growth, collecting, organizing, analyzing, and using data for instructional and curriculum improvement is a new way of working for many educators. How should assessment data be examined to improve instruction and curriculum and thereby advance students' reading and writing performance? In this column, we offer a promising framework that can support school teams (i.e., teachers, literacy coaches, data managers, and principals) in making sense of various types of data for instructional planning. Instruction that is data based and goal driven sets the stage for continuous reading and writing improvement.

RESEARCH ON THE INTERSECTION OF LITERACY ASSESSMENT AND INSTRUCTION

Literature on the influence of literacy assessment on instruction focuses on the relationship between assessment and instruction rather than on whether one does or should drive the other. In one extensive study aimed at determining how assessment influences instruction within four particular schools, Stephens and her colleagues (Stephens et al., 1995) found that "the salient relationship was not between assessment and instruction per se. Granted, the two were related, but their relationship was moderated by the decision-making model of the district" (p. 494). The implication here is that assessment and instruction issues are embedded within broader power structures within particular schools, and that both are influenced greatly by the decision-making model operating within those schools.

Shea, Murray, and Harlin (2005) noted that school-wide committees or teams typically have a wide-angle view of student achievement: The information they examine often comes from various sources and diverse perspectives. They suggested that schoolwide teams analyze aggregated or disaggregated assessment data focused on curriculum and instruction for whole classrooms, small groups, or individual learners. After reporting

students' current level of achievement, they then can make recommendations pertaining to school-wide, grade-level, or individualized instruction. However, it is important to keep in mind that "as important as these recommendations are, they should not mark the end of a committee's work. At future meetings, members must review progress made as a result of their recommendations and modify them when appropriate" (p. 148). In other words, the systematic use of data to make instructional decisions requires leadership, training, and the development of a culture of data-driven decision making and accountability.

The analytical framework described in the following section was inspired by the *Standards for the Assessment of Reading and Writing* developed and published collaboratively by The National Council of Teachers of English and the International Reading Association Joint Task Force on Assessment (1994). This valuable report provides a set of 11 standards aimed at guiding the decisions schools make about assessing the teaching of reading and writing. These standards express the conviction Joint Task Force members had that involving the entire school community is essential if assessment is truly to foster student and teacher learning. The report offers guidelines for assessment strategies that reflect the complex interactions among teachers, learners, and communities; that ensure fair and equitable treatment of all students; and that foster thoughtful literacy learning and teaching.

INTRODUCING THE DATA ANALYSIS FRAMEWORK FOR INSTRUCTIONAL DECISION MAKING

The Data Analysis Framework for Instructional Decision Making is a practical tool that provides school teams with a structure and process for organizing, analyzing, and using multiple sources and types of data for instructional decision making. Three major categories of data that are considered for improving reading and writing instruction include (1) professional development data, (2) classroom data, and (3) reading performance data.

1. Professional development data may consist of evaluation or feedback surveys and coaches' logs of how they spend their time and the types of activities they engage in to assist classroom teachers.

2. Classroom data may consist of teacher surveys of instructional practices, such as U.S. Elementary Reading Instruction ([Baumann], Hoffman, Duffy-Hester, & Moon Ro, 2000), and The Language Arts Curriculum Survey (Center for Policy Research, n.d.), which surveys teachers on the time they spend on reading components and the cognitive demand of learning tasks. Informal data on reading instruction may consist of teachers' daily lesson plans or weekly schedules that include instructional time frames, content taught, and organizational grouping (i.e., individual, small-group, or whole-group instruction). Working together, literacy coaches and teachers may use observational data collected from tools such as the Early Language and Literacy Classroom Observation Toolkit (Smith & Dickinson, 2002) and Classroom Environment Profile (Wolfersberger, Reutzel, Sudweeks, & Fawson, 2004). Coaches' documentation of informal observations conducted systematically and regularly (e.g., Bean, 2004, pp. 106–111) may also provide valuable sources of classroom data.

3. Reading performance data, arguably the most important aspect of instructional decision making, may include standardized tests, criterion-referenced tests, informal classroom assessments, and student-work samples.

Taken together, these sources provide a rich data set for school teams to use in setting goals and devising action steps to improve literacy instruction within classrooms, across grade levels, and throughout schools.

USING THE FRAMEWORK

The Data Analysis Framework for Instructional Decision Making consists of guiding questions to assist school literacy team members in analyzing data, discussing the patterns and relationships within those data, and constructing interpretations that they can then translate into goals' and action steps to improve reading and writing achievement (see Figure 1).

General procedures that may guide implementation of the Data Analysis Framework for Instructional Decision Making consist of the following five steps:

1. Organize the data set so that members of the literacy team can partner in analyzing different portions of the data set. Partnering allows for more than one set of eyes on the same data and provokes substantive discussion of individual observations.
2. Select a recorder for the team. The recorder takes notes on the team's discussion of the observations during step 4.
3. Partners analyze their data and each person jots down observations on his or her worksheet.
4. After sufficient time for partners to carefully analyze their data, the team "puts it all together" in a discussion of their findings (patterns in data) and interpretations (what the patterns show in terms of strengths and needs) and then devises professional development and school improvement goals and action steps.
5. The team plans when and how they will communicate the formative plan to other school personnel and stakeholders and monitors the implementation of their plan.

The example provided in Figure 2 illustrates the results of a school literacy team's use of the Data Analysis Framework for Instructional Decision Making. The school team example of a Put It All Together is a composite created from authentic samples of a literacy team's work. The literacy team members included the school-based literacy coach, principal, data manager, and grade-level teacher representatives in an elementary school.

FIGURE 1

Worksheet for School Teams Using Data Analysis Framework for Instructional Decision Making

Professional development data
1. What patterns do you observe in the professional development data?
2. How do you explain the patterns you see in the data?

Classroom data
1. What are some instructional strengths?
2. What aspects of instruction show a need for improvement?
3. What content and strategies are emphasized in the instruction?
4. What content and strategies are not emphasized?
5. How do you explain the patterns you see in the data?

Student data
1. What patterns do you observe in the student data at the school level, grade level, and classroom level?
   a. Where is growth demonstrated?
   b. Is the growth equal across grades?
   c. Is the growth equal for all students?
   d. What are specific areas of strength?
   e. What are specific areas that need improvement?
2. How do you explain the patterns you see in the data?

Put It All Together
1. What connections can you make between professional development data, classroom data, and student data?
2. What are the strengths and needs?
3. What do the patterns mean for you in your role (e.g., literacy coach, principal, data manager, teacher)?
4. What are the implications for change as you see them in your role?
5. Overall, based on the analysis and findings, what are the professional development and school improvement goals?
6. What action steps will you take to meet the goals?
7. How will you communicate the improvement plan to other school personnel and stakeholders?

APPLICATIONS

The Data Analysis Framework for Instructional Decision Making may be applied in a variety of preK–12 educational settings. It can be easily modified to include other types of data collected outside of literacy including mathematics, science, or other subject areas. Its team approach allows for different educator groups to collaborate—teachers within and across grade levels and district-wide school improvement teams. The Data Analysis Framework for Instructional Decision Making is easily adapted to small or large teams who may modify the questions to suit local purposes and contexts. As with other collaborative processes, the utility of the framework is best judged by those who use it for its intended purpose—to support a systematic and thorough analysis of multiple sources of data to improve student learning and achievement.

REFERENCES

Baumann, J. F., Hoffman J. V., Duffy-Hester, A. M., & Ro, J. M. (2000). The First R yesterday and today: U.S. elementary reading instruction practices reported by teachers and administrators. *Reading Research Quarterly, 35,* 338–577.

FIGURE 2

Example of a School Literacy Team's "Put It All Together" from the Data Analysis Framework for instructional Decision Making

....

Put It All Together

What connections can you make between professional development data, classroom data, and student data?

Our data overall show that professional development has helped to improve classroom instructional practices, and the student data shows stronger achievement. Coaching logs showed that the coaches are spending a large amount of time providing professional development in five areas (fluency, phonics, phonemic awareness, comprehension, and vocabulary) and not as much time on individual coaching. The teacher surveys showed strong use of research-based strategies presented at professional development which may be related to higher Early Language and Literacy Classroom Observation (ELLCO) scores in approaches to curriculum integration, reading instruction, and presence of books. ELLCO scores for oral language facilitation are lower than other areas, and students scoring at or above grade level are not making good gains. This suggests a need for differentiated instruction. Our student data showed improvement over two years, and TerraNova results showed growth in two of three grade levels.

What are the strengths and needs?

Strengths:

Better alignment of curriculum to state indicators (based on Language Arts Curriculum Survey). The disaggregated data show growth for students scoring in the at-risk and some-risk categories. Teachers are using data.

Needs:

Improve instruction for students scoring at or above grade level. First-grade scores dropped at third benchmark so we need to look more closely at first-grade instruction.

What do the patterns mean for you in your role (e.g., literacy coach, principal, teacher, data manager)?

Literacy coach:

Based on my coaching log data, I need to spend more time in classrooms, work more with teachers on differentiating instruction, and follow up with teachers after progress monitoring.

Principal:

I need to more frequently observe classroom instruction and provide feedback.

First-grade teacher:

I should identify specific areas of need for students reading below grade-level expectations and work with the coach to differentiate instruction in areas of need.

Data manager:

I need to stress progress monitoring for students reading at or above grade level more often.

(*continued*)

FIGURE 2 (Continued)

What are the implications for change as you see them in your role?

We need to utilize our data to better plan instruction. We need to streamline interventions and make sure to address needs of students reading at or above grade level. Coaches need to spend more time in classrooms and conduct teaching demonstrations.

Overall, based on the analysis and findings, what are the professional development and school improvement goals?

Professional development goals:

1. Continue to analyze and use data
   - include data at beginning of professional development
   - take time to analyze data
2. Increase differentiated instruction
   - work with teachers to plan for small groups and target needs for instruction
   - continue to examine the content of reading instruction using data and identify specifics within the five areas to target—what we want students to know and be able to do
   - assist teachers with ways to monitor student performance and analyze student work

School goals:

1. Improve data use at classroom and school levels
   - schedule grade-level meetings for teachers to analyze data regularly
   - principal follows up with literacy coach on classroom instructional needs
   - principal schedules regular observations of instruction and provides feedback to teachers
2. Align curriculum, instructional resources, and instruction with student needs
   - use intervention specialists more with first grade
   - examine what's working in our intervention model and make changes as needed
   - examine the core reading program to see how it addresses what we need to teach more effectively

How will you communicate the plan to other school personnel and stakeholders?

At the opening-of-school meeting—principal, literacy coaches, and teachers share in a presentation of findings from the data analysis and communicate broad, school goals. Teachers on the school literacy team meet with grade-level colleagues to refine goals and develop two action steps. The grade-level facilitator records specific goals and action steps.

At the follow-up meeting of the school literacy team, the grade-level facilitators share plans and post them in the professional development classroom. All teachers post respective grade-level goals in classrooms in student-centered language. At regular meetings throughout the year, the school literacy team assesses progress in meeting the goals and monitors or adjusts the action steps accordingly.

Bean, R. (2004). *The reading specialist: Leadership for the classroom, school, and community.* New York: Guilford.

Center for Policy Research. (n.d.). *The language arts curriculum survey* (Unpublished document). Madison, WI: University of Wisconsin.

International Reading Association & National Council of Teachers of English. (1994). *Standards for the assessment of reading and writing.* Newark, DE; Urbana, IL: Authors.

Reilly, M. A. (2007). Choice of action: Using data to make instructional decisions in kindergarten, *The Reading Teacher, 60,* 770–776.

Shea, M., Murray, R., & Harlin, R. (2005). *Drowning in data? How to collect, organize, and document student performance*: Portsmouth, NH: Heinemann.

Smith, M., & Dickinson, D. (2002), *Early language and literacy classroom observation toolkit*. Baltimore: Brookes.

Stephens, D., Pearson, P. D., Gilrane, C., Roe, M., Stallman, A., Shelton, J., et al. (1995). Assessment and decision making in schools: A cross-site analysis. *Reading Research Quarterly, 30,* 448–499,

Wolfersberger, M. E., Reutzel, D. R., Sudweeks, R., & Fawson, P. C. (2004). Developing and validating the classroom literacy environment profile (CLEP): A tool for examining, the "print richness" of early childhood and elementary classrooms. *Journal of Literacy Research, 36,* 211–272.

Kouider Mokhtari teaches at Miami University, Oxford, Ohio; *Catherine A. Rosemary* teaches at John Carroll University, University Heights, Ohio; & *Patricia A. Edwards* teaches at Michigan State University, East Lansing.

QUESTIONS FOR REFLECTION

1. According to the literature cited by the authors, what does the research tell us about the intersection between literacy assessment and instruction?
2. How important is authentic assessment for improved student learning? How does one go from being "overwhelmed" by the task to making it more manageable?
3. Is the Data Analysis Framework for Instructional Decision Making truly practical? What obstacles might a teacher confront in trying to successfully implement this in the classroom?

Implementing a Schoolwide Literacy Framework to Improve Student Achievement

DOUGLAS FISHER
NANCY FREY

ABSTRACT: *According to the authors, a literacy framework that is implemented schoolwide can provide teachers with an opportunity to focus their teaching rather than script it, resulting in students who read, write, and think at impressive levels. This article focuses on the teachers at Rosa Parks Elementary School and their discussions about their core beliefs regarding literacy, the literacy instructional framework developed with and for the teachers, and the professional development that was provided to all members of the learning community which have played a critical role in continued growth.*

As a profession, in the United States we have learned a great deal about quality literacy instruction. We have learned from expert teachers (e.g., Allington & Johnston, 2002; Pressley, Allington, Wharton-McDonald, Block, & Morrow, 2001) and from strategies that work (e.g., Harvey & Goudvis, 2000). We have learned to differentiate instruction (e.g., Tomlinson, 1999) and plan backward with diverse learners in mind (e.g., Wiggins & McTighe, 1998). The National Reading

Panel (National Institute of Child Health and Human Development, 2000) focused our attention on the components of reading—phonemic awareness, phonics, fluency, vocabulary, and comprehension—and the RAND study on reading comprehension (RAND Reading Study Group, 2002) reminded us of the goals for teaching reading.

Yes, we are flush with information about teaching students to read and write well. The challenge, it seems, is putting all of this information into practice at the whole-school level. While there are exceptional and highly skilled teachers at every school, we are less sure about what it takes to ensure that all teachers have the knowledge, skills, and dispositions necessary to ensure that their students develop increasingly sophisticated understandings of literacy.

In other words, our profession seems stuck with the age-old problem of going to scale. Innovations are everywhere, but few are implemented consistently across grades and teachers. The risk in making this comment is that someone will attempt to legislate, mandate, or prescribe curriculum and instruction in an attempt to ensure that evidence-based instructional practices reach every classroom. But, as Fullan, Hill, and Crevola (2006) noted, we do not need more prescriptive, scripted curriculum or instruction. Instead, we need precision in our teaching. This precision comes when teachers have an extensive knowledge base and make expert decisions, based on data, about the instructional needs of their students. The question is, how to ensure this happens.

This article profiles an underperforming school that beat the odds. Over several years, the teachers at this school clarified their understandings of, and core beliefs about, literacy. They developed an instructional framework from which to teach students to read and write, and they focused their professional development, via learning communities, to ensure that together they had a deep understanding of literacy teaching and learning.

ROSA PARKS COMMUNITY SCHOOL

In the midcity area of San Diego, California, Rosa Parks Elementary School educates between 1,450–1,500 students per year. All of these children (100%) qualify for free lunch. During the 2005–2006 school year, 78% of the students were Hispanic, 11% were Asian-Pacific Islander, 8% were African American, and 3% were white or other. Rosa Parks is situated in a community that is recognized as the highest crime area of San Diego, the poorest, and the area most in need of health and social services.

In 1999, the California Department of Education calculated an Academic Performance Index (API) for each school in the state. The API is a scale score of 200 to 1,000 that annually measures the academic performance and progress of individual schools. The state has set 800 as the API score that schools should strive to meet. As noted in Table 1, Rosa Parks was the lowest performing school in the area. The schools listed in Table 1 are in the same geographic area and constitute a feeder pattern for the same high school. While every school in this geographic area of San Diego made progress, Rosa Parks's change was

TABLE 1

Changes in Academic Performance Index (API) Achievement in Elementary Schools

School	1999	2005	Growth
Adams Elementary	543	688	+145
Central Elementary	611	686	+75
Edison Elementary	489	672	+183
Euclid Elementary	496	681	+185
Franklin Elementary	643	749	+106
Hamilton Elementary	529	696	+167
Rosa Parks Elementary	455	746	+291

Note: From the California Department of Education (www.cde.ca.gov). These seven schools are in the same geographic area of San Diego.

TABLE 2

Percentage of Students Proficient or Advanced
on the California Standards Test

Grade	2000	2005	Growth
2	9%	32%	+23%
3	12%	18%	+6%
4	15%	36%	+21%
5	10%	36%	+26%

Note: From the California Department of Education
(www.cde.ca.gov).

exceptional and noteworthy. While educating nearly 1,500 students, 72% of whom were English-language learners, Rosa Parks climbed within reach of the state target of 800 and posted an impressive 291-point gain. What was most important was that Rosa Parks exceeded the state API growth targets for each subgroup and the whole school each year between 1999 and 2005.

Table 2 contains a listing of the percentage of students who scored proficient or advanced on the English language arts California Standards Test in 2000 compared with 2005. The third-grade scores were depressed across the region, which may have to do with specific test items or a need within the school. Regardless, the achievement changes at Rosa Parks Elementary School are worth noting. At Rosa Parks, the teachers' discussions about their core beliefs about literacy, the literacy instructional framework developed with and for the teachers, and the professional development provided to all members of the learning community have played a critical role in continued growth.

CORE BELIEFS ABOUT LITERACY

When the 1999 API scores were released, the Rosa Parks principal challenged the school to respond. She asked the governance committee (an elected site-based management team) to allocate funds so that a task force could create a multiyear

schoolwide literacy plan. The governance committee supported this recommendation and charged the literacy task force with "developing a plan that can be implemented across grades, program types, and philosophical ideologies." During the first meetings, the elected literacy task force clarified their beliefs about literacy instruction. Over several meetings that started in the spring and lasted through the summer of 2000, the group of teachers, parents, and administrators agreed on the following:

- *Learning is social.* As one of the teachers noted, "Learning takes place when humans interact with one another. That means kids with kids, kids with teachers, teachers with teachers, teachers with parents, parents with kids—everything related to learning is social." The task force easily agreed with this foundational belief and engaged in discussions about the implications this had on literacy learning, including the recognition of culture and family experiences on learning. The group also noted that learning occurs through participation in a group and as such our classrooms needed to provide significant amounts of time for students to meet in groups with their peers. As Driscoll (2000) noted, learning is "a persisting change in human performance or performance potential . . . [that] must come about as a result of the learner's experience and interaction with the world" (p. 11).

- *Conversations are critical for learning.* Consistent with the core belief that learning is social, the committee focused on the role that conversations play in learning. At the most basic level, it acknowledged that teaching can be seen as an extended conversation between children and their teacher. As one member said, "If we aren't in conversations all day long, they'll never learn to read or write. The oral language of conversation builds their understanding and need for print." The task force also noted that consideration of the Zone of Proximal Development (Vygotsky, 1962/1986) in peer talk was an effective instructional element, in part, because of the conversations the "more knowledgeable other" has with the learner. Therefore, this school with so many English-language learners would commit to prioritizing opportunities for peer talk across language proficiencies, academic knowledge, and even grade level. Beyond that, the discussion focused on the conversations that children have with one another as part of their social interactions. With instruction and practice, students should develop more sophisticated conversations and question the world around them. The idea of creating conversations is consistent with the ideas of accountable talk (e.g., www.instituteforlearning.org/develop.html) and critical literacy (McLaughlin & DeVoogd, 2004), both of which were important considerations for the task force. As a peer coach noted, "It's not just talk about anything, it's talk that is focused and based on an agreed upon purpose. We have to help our students understand that."

• *Reading, writing, and oral language instruction must be integrated.* The third core belief agreed upon by the task force focused on the need to integrate the language arts. As one of the team members commented, "Enough already. Reading, writing, speaking, listening—they're all connected. We teach them like they're separate and then wonder why our kids aren't learning. You have to wonder why we would have a readers' workshop with no writing." The research on the relationship between reading and writing suggests that these two processes are complementary but that each has unique qualities (e.g., Eisterhold, 1990; Shanahan, 1984). As the discussion on this core belief continued, one of the task force members commented, "Our kids need more than [reading]. Our English learners especially need oral language. And writing is the power to share your voice with the world. We have to make sure that we focus on all three."

• *Learners require a gradual increase in responsibility.* "I'm sick to death of all of the 'independent work' that's really just a pile of worksheets. Kids don't learn from that. We need to really teach them through modeling and scaffolding." These comments from an administrator

resulted in several hours of debate about teaching and learning and the best ways to accomplish it. The issue of modeling and scaffolding could not be resolved, and the task force agreed to meet for a day and focus on this topic alone. As a follow-up to the conversation, a copy of an article on a gradual release of responsibility model for teaching comprehension (Pearson & Gallagher, 1983) was provided to each committee member. The gradual release of responsibility model posits that the teacher moves from assuming "all the responsibility for performing a task . . . to a situation in which the students assume all of the responsibility" (Duke & Pearson, 2002, p. 211).

DEVELOPING AN INSTRUCTIONAL FRAMEWORK

In addition to identifying core beliefs, the literacy task force decided to develop an instructional framework that could guide teachers' instructional decisions. As a peer coach noted, "It's all about strategies here. Teachers go to conferences or staff development sessions and come back with another strategy to add to their list. There isn't a cohesive plan for literacy development." A literacy resource teacher explained that it was like going to a buffet: "Your plate's already full, but you get another plate and pile more stuff on. There's no organization or system, just a bunch of strategies. That makes conversations between teachers hard as they don't have a common language." The development of the instructional framework found in Table 3 required three years of work and included extensive teacher input to the task force as well as professional development for the entire faculty. A summary of the development process of the literacy framework is presented here.

The literacy task force decided to focus first on teacher modeling. They knew that teachers needed to provide systematic, purposeful, and direct instruction in skills and strategies if students were to make progress. As noted by Pearson (2002),

TABLE 3

Literacy Framework

	Reading	Writing	Oral language
Components and instructional categories	• Phonemic awareness • Phonics • Cueing systems (graphophonic, semantic, syntactic, pragmatic) • Concepts about print • Fluency • Reading vocabulary • Text structure (fiction and nonfiction) • Comprehension • Metacognitive strategies	• Writing processes • Genres • Conventions • Craft • Sentencing • Paragraphing • Spelling • Fluency • Writing vocabulary	• Speaking vocabulary • Accountable talk (e.g., questioning, elaborating, extending) • Language registers • Habits of talk (speaking and listening) • Prosody
Direct instruction/ modeling (focus lessons)	• Shared reading • Read-alouds • Think-alouds	• Shared writing • Language Experience • Approach • Write-alouds • Interactive writing • Power writing	• Storytelling • Think-pair-share • K-W-L charts • Language charts
Guided instruction	• Guided reading • Responding to text • Comprehension strategy instruction • Conferences	• Guided writing • Generative writing • Writing models • Conferences	• Language modeling • Presentation skills (i.e., formal oral language) • Discussion groups • Oral cloze
Collaborative learning	• Literature circles • Book clubs • Reciprocal teaching • Partner reading • Collaborative strategic reading • Word study center • Content reading center	• Progressive writing • Paired writing • Group composition • Peer response to writing • Author's chair • Content writing center	• Discussion webs • ReQuest • Table topics • Listening stations • Oral composition • Group retellings • Cooperative learning • Readers Theatre
Independent practice with conferring	• Reading for pleasure and lifelong learning • Independent reading • Sustained silent reading • Note-making • Participating in reading conferences	• Daily writing (e.g., journals, essays, short stories, poetry) • RAFT writing • Participating in writing conferences	• Following directions • Extemporaneous and prepared speeches • Note-taking
Assessment	• Informal reading inventories • Phonemic awareness • Letter identification • Sight word lists • Running records • Vocabulary • Attitude measures • Comprehension measures • Cloze procedure • Timed reading • Metacognitive strategy index • Self-assessments	• Rubrics (holistic, analytic, diagnostic) • Spelling inventories • Attitude measures • Dictation measures • Fluency graphs • Self-assessments	• Teacher listening and monitoring • Student oral language • Student oral language observation matrix (SOLOM) • Speaking checklists • Interviews • Retelling • Self assessments

Strategy instruction was another casualty [of whole language]. . . . Direct advice from teachers about how to summarize what one has read, how to use text structure to infer relations among ideas, how to distinguish fact from opinion, how to determine the central thread of a story . . . were virtually nonexistent in the [whole language/literature-based] basals. (p. 455)

The task force recognized that many teachers were already doing read-alouds and agreed that this could be expanded to include think-alouds, shared reading, and writing instruction (Davey, 1983; Fearn & Farnan, 2001; Holdaway, 1979). Consistent with the gradual release of responsibility, the task force identified specific instructional strategies that allowed the teacher to model and provide direct instruction in writing as well. These strategies included Language Experience Approach, interactive writing, and write-alouds (Dixon & Nessel, 1983; McCarrier, Pinnell, & Fountas, 2000). Given the number of English-language learners at the school, the task force also added an instructional focus on oral language and provided teachers with information about storytelling, think-pair-share, and language charts such as K-W-L (Dillingham, 2005; Ogle, 1986; Palmer, Harshbarger, & Koch, 2001).

The discussion of teacher modeling led to a discussion of content: What should be taught? The task force struggled with this and debated a developmental approach versus a skills-based approach versus a standards-based approach. Over numerous hours and meetings, the task force agreed that grade-level content standards should guide teachers' curricular decisions. While this may seem obvious in 2007, it was not common in 2000 when these conversations first began. These discussions were powerful for task force members who were parents. One parent later remarked, "At first I was confused about what standards really meant. After a while, we figured that if we found it confusing, so did other [parents]. I started working with the parent center to do workshops for families on standards."

Focusing on grade-level content standards as the de facto curriculum did several things. First, it

changed expectations. The task force had essentially decided that every student should, and could, meet grade-level expectations. Second, it allowed teachers to focus on more than reading instruction. The content standards include writing and oral language development. Unfortunately, in many places these other language arts are neglected in an effort to increase reading scores. Third, it allowed for common assessment measures to be created. If every teacher at a specific grade level were focused on specific content standards, then students could be assessed and interventions could be developed. And, finally, a focus on grade-level standards allowed for the related services staff (e.g., speech language therapist), literacy resource teachers, special education teachers, paraprofessionals, and the parent volunteers to gain an understanding of the curriculum and expectations for students.

The second area that the task force members focused on was independent learning. They noted that teacher modeling needed to transfer to students' independent reading, writing, speaking, and listening. As such, the task force members identified a number of instructional approaches and classroom structures that would facilitate students' independent learning, such as silent sustained reading, independent reading, journal writing, note-taking, public speaking, and so on (Ivey, 2002; Laframboise & Klesius, 1993; Pilgreen, 2000). However, they recognized that independent learning was also insufficient to dramatically change student achievement.

The task force then set out to close the gap between teacher modeling and independent learning. The most obvious place to start was small-group guided instruction (Fountas & Pinnell, 1996). There is a significant body of evidence suggesting that whole-class reading instruction is insufficient and that students need to participate in small, needs-based groups (Cunningham & Cunningham, 1985; Foorman & Torgesen, 2001; Tyner, 2004). The combination of small-group and effective classroom instruction results in higher levels of achievement for students who struggle with literacy (Mathes et al., 2005). However, the task force was concerned that permanent ability grouping would harm students' self-esteem and lower their motivation to read (Allington, 1980; Flood, Lapp, Flood, & Nagel, 1992; Vaughn, Hughes, Moody, & Elbaum, 2001). As Paratore and Indrisano (2003) noted, "students placed in low-achieving [small] groups often experience low self-esteem and negative attitudes toward reading and learning" (p. 566). Pressley et al. (2001) explained,

> [Exemplary first-grade] teachers did not report using grouping by achievement. . . . Likewise, these teachers did not report relying on whole-class basal reader lessons but, instead, reported using a mixture of large- and small-group instructional plans as well as side-by-side reading and writing opportunities. . . . Instead of round-robin reading . . . these teachers reported flexible use of grouping and variety in the kinds of reading done by students." (p. 39)

This resonated with some parent task force members as well, who recounted past experiences with their own children who were in the "low" reading group year after year. As one parent said, "My boy talks always about him not being able to read. He says he is in low group, but he never gets better at his reading."

As a result, the task force focused on flexible grouping patterns and recommended that students work in mixed-ability groups when they were not with the teacher in guided instruction. The Center Activity Rotation System (Lapp, Flood, & Goss, 2000) is one example of flexible grouping. With this approach, heterogeneously grouped learners worked together in literacy centers while the teacher called four or five children from different centers to participate in homogeneously grouped teacher-directed instruction. This allowed teachers to implement the task force's recommendation that guided reading and writing groups be based on student need, noting that individual students may have needs consistent with more than one group. This modification to the most traditional implementation of guided reading ensures that students see themselves as developing readers and writers and that

the teacher has several opportunities to provide "just right" instruction based on identified needs.

The final component of the literacy framework centered on what to do with the students while they were not with the teacher for guided instruction. In most classrooms at Rosa Parks in 1999, students were engaged in independent work while the teacher met with small groups. The committee was well aware of the work of Rosenshine (1983) who reviewed the evidence on independent work and concluded that the larger the proportion of time students spend working alone, the less they learn. While some independent work is necessary and helpful in the gradual release of responsibility model, students were spending too much time working alone. In addition to the potentially harmful effects noted by Rosenshine, this was inconsistent with one of the core beliefs agreed to by the school—namely, that learning is social. In response, the task force began work on a component of the literacy framework called "collaborative learning." This started with literacy learning centers (Diller, 2003) and was soon expanded to include a number of interactive classroom structures such as reciprocal teaching, literature circles, peer-response groups, partner reading, Readers Theatre, and discussion groups (Bomer & Laman, 2004; Daniels, 2001; Martinez, Roser, & Strecker, 1998/1999; Palincsar & Brown, 1984; Paratore & McCormack, 1997; Roser & Martinez, 1995).

GOING TO SCALE: A WHOLE-SCHOOL COMMITMENT

While the schoolwide literacy plan evolved over several years, equal attention was paid to gaining support among the staff and providing responsive professional development that would move beyond the practices of individual teachers. Elected task force members from each grade level were responsible for keeping their colleagues informed of progress and frequently sought feedback from them regarding aspects of literacy instruction. This feedback loop promoted buy-in among the staff as the plan was being developed.

As we have noted, professional development was designed and delivered to ensure that every teacher in the school understood the core beliefs about literacy and the instructional framework. Again, the goal was precision teaching rather than prescriptive curriculum and instruction. The principal made an interesting comment about expectations during a school walkthrough. She said,

> If the teacher is up front and all of the students are in a large group, I expect to see one of the instructional strategies from the framework being used—shared reading, interactive writing, Language Experience Approach, storytelling, or one of those. If I walk in during guided instruction, I expect to see guided reading or writing—a small group with the teacher—and the other students in the class in group work collaborating with one another on literacy tasks such as book clubs, centers, and such. If I don't see that, I ask to see the teacher in my office so we can discuss what was happening. I don't need all of the teachers to be "on the same page," but I do expect that they'll implement the framework as we have agreed upon it.

In addition to this level of administrative support for the literacy framework, Rosa Parks teachers have had access to quality professional development. Unlike some professional development experiences known in San Diego as "seagull consulting" (they fly in, drop something off, and fly away), teachers at Rosa Parks were engaged in focused professional development, learning communities, and peer coaching.

Focused Professional Development

In many schools, professional development is episodic, uncoordinated, and lacks focus. Teachers in these schools often do not know what to expect from a professional development session and do know that little will be expected of them as a result of the inservice. This is counter to the evidence on the important link between professional development and student achievement (Joyce & Showers, 2002).

At Rosa Parks, there is a professional development committee that plans the professional

development experiences for the school a year in advance. Members draft a plan that includes specific dates and topics. In their presentation of the plan to the school governance committee (site-based leadership), they discuss the ways in which the plan for the upcoming school year aligns with the literacy beliefs and framework. Each year, as the framework is updated, revised, and completed, the professional development plan addresses those areas. The professional development committee provides whole-school seminars on specific aspects of the literacy framework (e.g., modeling comprehension, small-group phonics lessons, using book clubs), grade-level sessions in which teachers examine student work, and small-group sessions in which teachers share examples of their instruction aligned with the framework with their peers. This framework for professional development is applied to other initiatives as well. For example, a successful multiyear mathematics plan was developed and implemented in a similar fashion. It is important to note that math achievement also rose significantly during this same time period (see Table 4). The schoolwide focus on literacy did not detract from math achievement. In a similar manner, science, social studies, and schoolwide plans for English-language learners have been created at Rosa Parks.

The important points here are that the professional development plan is carefully linked—purposefully—with the literacy framework; that teachers design, develop, and implement the professional development plan; and that the plan is a public document developed a year in advance of implementation. Together, this means

TABLE 4

Changes in Math Achievement All Grades 2–5

School year	Percentage proficient/advanced
2001–2002	25.8%
2002–2003	31.8%
2003–2004	43.1%
2004–2005	56.3%

that teachers create and own their learning. As a result, more and more people implement what they learn in professional development sessions.

Learning Communities

As a significant component of the professional development plan, the staff development committee allocates two sessions per month to learning communities. For a list of frequently asked questions (FAQs) and the responses from Rosa Parks, see Table 5. The learning communities at Rosa Parks were based on professional learning communities (e.g., [DuFour] & Eaker, 1998; [DuFour], Eaker, & [DuFour], 2005) and communities of practice (e.g., Wenger, McDermott, & Snyder, 2002). At Rosa

TABLE 5
Frequently Asked Questions on Learning Communities

1. What is a learning community?

Learning communities are groups of people who meet together to discuss their own professional development and focus on improving teaching and learning in their classrooms. It is rare to have formal presentations during learning community meetings, although members are encouraged to share what they're doing in their classrooms. At Rosa Parks, teachers will select the learning community they wish to join and will cocreate the agenda for the learning community. It is important to note that the learning community time is not grade-level time—several Mondays are reserved for grade-level meetings. A wise grade level will have its members attend different learning communities and then share what they're learning during grade-level time.

2. Who's in charge of a learning community?

In learning communities, members of the group are responsible for their own learning. Having said that, most learning communities also have facilitators. For the Rosa Parks learning communities, consistent with the City Heights Educational Collaborative, the groups will be cofacilitated by someone from San Diego State University/City Heights Collaborative and a teacher from the school.

3. How do the groups get started?

During the first learning community meeting, the group will agree on the professional readings they will do during the term and how they will use their time. This plan must be submitted to the principal no later than the Friday of the first meeting.

4. When are the learning communities meeting?

The first meeting is September 24, 1:30–3:30 p.m. After that, the meetings will occur on October 8 (1:30–3:30 p.m.), November 5 (1:30–3:30 p.m.), November 10 (1:00–3:00 p.m.), November 19 (1:30–3:30 p.m.), and December 3 (1:30–3:30 p.m.). After winter break, new learning communities will be formed and dates scheduled.

5. What is the accountability for learning communities?

Overall, group members will hold themselves accountable for their own learning. In terms of administrative accountability, there will be attendance sheets submitted for each learning community meeting. In addition, the cofacilitators will summarize the session by the Friday following the meeting and submit the notes to all members of the learning community and the principal. The final meeting for the term also serves as an accountability measure of sorts. During this final meeting, each learning community will present a synopsis of their learnings to the entire faculty.

Parks, teachers identify topics from the literacy framework and form their learning communities. The communities set an agenda, identify professional readings, meet to discuss the readings and their instructional practices, share student work, and plan for change. They also invite one another into their classrooms to observe instruction and students' responses to changes in instruction.

Peer Coaching

The final component of the professional development plan at Rosa Parks is peer coaching. Rosa Parks employs five full-time peer coach/literacy resource teachers. As has been described elsewhere (Lapp, Fisher, Flood, & Frey, 2003), they supervise student teachers, provide induction support to new teachers, peer-coach veteran teachers, and facilitate professional development sessions. Consistent with the role described by Bean (2004), these five professionals ensure that teachers have the information, resources, and knowledge they need to be successful with students. At Rosa Parks, this role includes organizing literacy volunteers, parent literacy nights, and intersession and after-school reading interventions.

LESSONS LEARNED FROM IMPLEMENTING A SCHOOLWIDE LITERACY FRAMEWORK

Between 1999 and 2006, a number of changes occurred at Rosa Parks elementary school, it is clear that students read better than ever before. The faculty and administration at this school established that students living in poverty and learning English can achieve at increasingly proficient levels. They also demonstrated that focused professional development, aligned with a literacy framework, raises student achievement, even in the absence of a scripted reading program. The question remains, why did this work?

We held a small focus-group meeting, or member check, with four teachers, a peer coach, and the administrator to discuss the reasons for the

significant improvements in literacy experienced at Rosa Parks. We wanted to know if there were lessons learned that might be used by other schools to improve their students' performance. From the beginning it was clear that the literacy framework changed teachers. As the principal said, "We can have conversations now because we have a common language. We know what we're talking about when we say interactive writing or reciprocal teaching. These conversations allow teachers to share ideas and materials with one another." The peer coach added,

> It's like our teachers have internalized an instructional framework. They don't just get up there and do strategies. They know why they're doing something and how it fits into their overall goals for instruction. They understand what their students know and don't know and how to close that gap.

A fifth-grade teacher added,

> It's about purpose. I understand my purpose more than I ever have before. I also know that my students know the purpose for everything we do. I model something in whole class, and we apply it throughout the day or week. My purpose is clear, and I share that purpose with my students.

In addition to the focus on the literacy framework, three themes emerged from the conversation. The group explained the changes in achievement, in part, as the result of increased instructional time or time on task. They also noted the change in students' literacy habits as a result of common language being used both horizontally (across the grades) and vertically (K–5). Finally, they attributed part of the achievement to the investment in their professional learning and the trust the administration gave them in "doing right by kids" and not forcing a "one-size-fits-all reading program on them."

Increased Instructional Time/ Time on Task

It should not come as a surprise that teachers would notice that increased instructional time and time on task are related to high achievement. This has been documented time and again (Castle, Deniz, & Tortora, 2005; Gest & Gest, 2005). The interesting point made during the member-check conversation focused on the role that the literacy framework played in increasing instructional time and time on task. As one of the teachers noted,

> I think we see more instruction because of the framework. Teachers have a much better sense of how to use instructional time and get to it. Students know what is expected and don't waste time in transitions, wondering what's going to happen, or what they need to do to be successful.

The peer coach added,

> We've talked a lot about the framework and how teachers internalized it. But I think that it's so important, I'll talk about it again. Having an internalized framework ensures that instructional moves are purposeful—that the focus lessons are linked to guided instruction, collaborative learning, and independent learning. As a result, students spend more time actually engaged in literacy learning. And we know that getting students actively engaged changes their performance.

Schoolwide Implementation Results in Student Habits

A second theme to emerge from the member-check conversation centered on the habits that students develop after years of experience with instruction based on a framework. One teacher said,

> I can walk in classrooms at the beginning of the year and tell which students are new to us based on the way that they act during the literacy block. If they're not quite sure what's happening or what to do during collaborative learning, they're new.

A third-grade teacher added,

> My students have a bunch of habits, and we share a common language. When I say "interactive writing" or "listening stations," they know what to do. That's procedural knowledge. They also have content knowledge. When I talk about visualizing or making connections or summarizing, they know what I'm talking about. I have a head start because I know something about the experiences my students have had in previous years of schooling at Rosa Parks.

Professional Learning

Finally, the group of teachers in the member check noted the importance of focused professional development and teacher-led workshops and learning communities. They commented on their past experiences and the differences in the current professional development model at Rosa Parks. As one of them noted,

> I used to go to a bunch of "sit-and-get" trainings, and I'd take things to do because I knew that I wasn't going to use the information. I had my way, and it worked for me. Here [at Rosa Parks] the professional development is focused on our plans to improve reading and writing, and it's done by other teachers at the school. I've done some seminars, too. It's real here, and I can use the stuff we do.

The group also noted that they didn't change course throughout the years and instead remained focused on the implementation of their literacy framework. One member said,

> I know people at other schools, and they tell me about their inservices. They're always changing their topics—what they're doing in staff development. We don't do that. We update the framework, but we focus on that to get better and better every year. I'm embarrassed to see the framework we first developed, but it was a start and nobody else had one. Our framework is our best thinking today, but I'm sure it will change as we learn more and more. You see, the framework and the professional development efforts have to be linking—one to the other. When we change the framework, we have to provide teachers with professional development. When we learn things in professional development, we have to update the framework.

In addition, the group was well aware of the risk that the administration took in investing in a literacy task force, core beliefs, and a literacy framework. As a kindergarten teacher commented,

> I knew we were taking a risk not going with the [scripted reading] program. We were trusted as professionals. We were treated like professionals. And we were expected to perform as such. There's not a person at the school who didn't know that our students' achievement was directly linked to our freedom to operate the way we wanted. The trade was to implement a schoolwide framework. The alternative was a cookie-cutter program for everyone. I, for one, really appreciate our principal taking the risk and letting us try.

FINAL THOUGHTS

The development of a literacy framework, with its common set of vocabulary, and a schoolwide plan for implementation, with its common set of values, has served Rosa Parks Elementary School well. It is important to note that these results cannot be simply transplanted from one school to another without the hard work that went into the development and implementation of the plan. These approaches may not perfectly fit the context and experiences of students, teachers, and families at another school. For example, this school chose to use a guided reading approach (e.g., Fountas & Pinnell, 1996). In a comparative study of philosophically different small-group reading instruction approaches, Mathes et al. (2005) found positive results for both. What made a difference was well-developed, small-group instruction coupled with effective, whole-group literacy teaching. We believe that Rosa Parks's results stem from the schoolwide agreements, the willingness of the faculty to continually revisit and refine practices, and the link to professional development that included learning communities and peer coaching. In addition, the support and participation of families in the school community strengthened home–school connections. The participatory nature of the planning, implementation, and refinement of this school's multiyear approach to schoolwide literacy practices takes time, lots of meetings, many disagreements, and the shared epiphanies that come from working shoulder to shoulder. That's where the buy-in comes from as well. As school leaders know, shared agreements don't simply happen. They must be built, often incrementally, across months and years.

The experiences at Rosa Parks Elementary School add to the evidence presented by Fullan et al. (2006), namely the "overriding importance of just three factors in explaining student achievement: (1) motivation to learn and high expectations, (2) time on task and opportunity to learn, and focused teaching" (p. 32).

The literacy framework and professional development plan resulted in higher expectations for students and increased time on task for both teachers and students, which in turn resulted in improved opportunities to learn. The literacy framework provided teachers with an opportunity to focus their teaching rather than script their teaching. The final result is a group of students who read, write, and think at impressive levels.

REFERENCES

Allington, R. L. (1980). Poor readers don't get to read much in reading groups. *Language Arts, 57,* 873–875.

Allington, R. L., & Johnston, P. H. (2002). *Reading to learn: Lessons from exemplary fourth-grade classrooms.* New York: Guilford.

Bean, R. (2004). *The reading specialist: Leadership for the class room, school, and community.* New York: Guilford.

Bomer, R., & Laman, T. (2004). Positioning in a primary writing workshop: Joint action in the discursive production of writing subjects. *Research in the Teaching of English, 38,* 420–466.

Castle, S., Deniz, C. B., & Tortora, M. (2005). Flexible grouping and student learning in a high-needs school. *Education and Urban Society, 37,* 139–150.

Cunningham, P. M., & Cunningham, J. W. (1985). Does research support whole-class reading instruction? *Educational Leadership, 43,* 88–89.

Daniels, H. (2001). *Literature circles: Voice and choice in book clubs and reading groups* (2nd ed.). Portland, ME: Stenhouse.

Davey, B. (1983). Think aloud: Modeling the cognitive processes of reading comprehension. *Journal of Reading, 27,* 44–47.

Diller, D. (2003). *Literacy work stations: Making centers work.* Portland, ME: Stenhouse.

Dillingham, B. (2005). Performance literacy. *The Reading Teacher, 59,* 72–75.

Dixon, C., & Nessel, D. (1983). *Language experience approach to reading (and writing): Language-experience reading for second language learners.* Hayward, CA: Alemany Press.

Driscoll, M. P. (2000). *Psychology of learning for instruction* (2nd ed.). Boston: Allyn & Bacon.

DuFour, R., & Eaker, R. (1998). *Professional learning communities at work: Best practices for enhancing student achievement,* Bloomington, IN: National Education Service.

DuFour, R., Eaker, R., & DuFour, R. (2005). *On common ground: The power of professional learning communities.* Bloomington, IN: National Education Service.

Duke, N. K., & Pearson, P. D. (2002). Effective practices for developing reading comprehension. In A. E. Farstrup & S. J. Samuels (Eds.), *What research has to say about reading instruction* (3rd ed., pp. 205–242). Newark, DE: International Reading Association.

Eisterhold, J. C. (1990). Reading–writing connections: Toward a description for second language learners. In B. Kroll (Ed.), *Second language writing: Research insights for the classroom* (pp. 88–101). Cambridge, England: Cambridge University Press.

Fearn, L., & Farnan, N. (2001). *Interactions: Teaching writing and the language arts.* Boston: Houghton Mifflin.

Flood, J., Lapp, D., Flood, S., & Nagel, G. (1992). Am I allowed to group? Using flexible patterns for effective instruction. *The Reading Teacher, 45,* 608–616.

Foorman, B. R., & Torgesen, J. (2001). Critical elements of classroom and small-group instruction promote reading success in all children. *Learning Disabilities: Research & Practice, 16,* 203–212.

Fountas, I. C., & Pinnell, G. S. (1996). *Guided reading: Good first teaching for all children.* Portsmouth, NH: Heinemann.

Fullan, M., Hill, P., & Crévola, C. (2006). *Breakthrough.* Thousand Oaks, CA: Corwin Press.

Gest, S. D., & Gest, J. M. (2005). Reading tutoring for students at academic and behavioral risk: Effects on time-on-task in the classroom. *Education and Treatment of Children, 28,* 25–47.

Harvey, S., & Goudvis, A. (2000). *Strategies that work: Teaching comprehension to enhance understanding.* York, ME: Stenhouse.

Holdaway, D. (1979). *The foundations of literacy.* Portsmouth, NH: Heinemann.

Ivey, G. (2002). Getting started: Manageable literacy practices. *Educational Leadership, 60*(3), 20–23.

Joyce, B., & Showers, B. (2002). *Student achievement through staff development* (3rd ed.). Alexandria, VA: Association for Supervision and Curriculum Development.

Laframboise, K. L., & Klesius, J. (1993). A survey of writing instruction in elementary language arts classrooms. *Reading Psychology, 14,* 265–284.

Lapp, D., Fisher, D., Flood, J., & Frey, N. (2003). Dual role of the urban reading specialist. *Journal of Staff Development, 24*(2), 33–36.

Lapp, D., Flood, J., & Goss, K. (2000). Desks don't move—students do: In effective classroom environments. *The Reading Teacher, 54,* 31–36.

Martinez, M., Poser, N. L, & Strecker, S. (1998/1999). I never thought I could be a star: A Readers Theatre ticket to fluency. *The Reading Teacher, 52,* 326–334.

Mathes, P. G., Denton, C. A., Fletcher, J. M., Anthony, J. L., Francis, D. J., & Schatschneider, C. (2005). The effects of theoretically different instruction and student characteristics on the skills of straggling readers. *Reading Research Quarterly, 40,* 148–182.

McCarrier, A., Pinnelli, G. S., & Fountas, I. C. (2000). *Interactive writing: How language and literacy come together K–2.* Portsmouth, NH: Heinemann.

McLaughlin, M., & DeVoogd, G. (2004). *Critical literacy: Enhancing students' comprehension of text.* New York: Scholastic.

National Institute of Child Health and Human Development. (2000). *Report of the National Reading Panel. Teaching children to read: An evidence-based assessment of the scientific research literature on reading and its implications for reading instruction* (NIH Publication No. 00–4769). Washington, DC: U.S. Government Printing Office.

Ogle, D. M. (1986). K-W-L: A teaching model that develops active reading of expository text. *The Reading Teacher, 39,* 564–570.

Palincsar, A. S., & Brown, A. L. (1984). Reciprocal teaching of comprehension-fostering and comprehension-monitoring activities. *Cognition and Instruction, 2,* 117–175.

Palmer, B. C., Harshbarger, S. J., & Koch, C. A. (2001). Storytelling as a constructivist model for developing language and litera*cy. Journal of Poetry Therapy, 14,* 199–212.

Paratore, J. R, & Indrisano, R. (2003). Grouping for instruction in literacy. In J. Flood, D. Lapp, J. R. Squire, & J. M. Jensen (Eds.), *Handbook of research on teaching the English language arts* (2nd ed., pp. 566–572). Mahwah, NJ: Erlbaum.

Paratore, J. R., & McCormack, R. L. (Eds.). (1997). *Peer talk in the classroom: Framing from research.* Newark, DE: International Reading Association.

Pearson, P. D. (2002). American reading instruction since 1967. In N. B. Smith (Ed.), *American reading instruction* (pp. 419–486). Newark, DE: International Reading Association.

Pearson, P. D., & Gallagher, M. C. (1983). The instruction of reading comprehension. *Contemporary Educational Psychology, 8,* 317–344.

Pilgreen, J. L. (2000). *The SSR handbook: How to organize and manage a sustained silent reading program.* Portsmouth, NH: Boynton/Cook.

Pressley, M., Allington, R. L., Wharton-McDonald, R., Block, C. C., & Morrow, L. M. (2001). *Learning to read: Lessons from exemplary first-grade classrooms.* New York: Guilford.

RAND Reading Study Group. (2002). *Reading for understanding: Toward an R & D program in reading comprehension.* Santa Monica, CA: RAND.

Rosenshine, B. (1983). Teaching functions in instructional programs. *The Elementary School Journal, 83,* 335–351.

Roser, N. L., & Martinez, M. G. (1995). *Book talk and beyond: Children and teachers respond to literature.* Newark, DE: International Reading Association.

Shanahan, T. (1984). Nature of the reading–writing relation: An exploratory multivariate analysis. *Journal of Educational Psychology, 76,* 466–477.

Tomlinson, C.A. (1999). *The differentiated classroom: Responding to the needs of all learners.* Alexandria, VA: Association for Supervision and Curriculum Development.

Tyner, B. (2004). *Small-group reading instruction: A differentiated teaching model for beginning and struggling readers.* Newark, DE: International Reading Association.

Vaughn, S., Hughes, M. T., Moody, S. W., & Erlbaum, B. (2001). Instructional grouping for reading for students with LD: Implications for practice. *Intervention in School and Clinic, 36,* 131–137.

Vygotsky, L. S. (1986). *Thought and language* (A. Kozalin, Trans.). Cambridge, MA: The MIT Press. (Original work published 1962).

Wenger, E., McDermott, R., & Snyder, W. M. (2002). *Cultivating communities of practice: A guide to managing knowledge.* Boston: Harvard Business School Press.

Wiggins, G., & McTighe, J. (1998). *Understanding by design.* Alexandria, VA: Association for Supervision and Curriculum Development.

Douglas Fisher is codirector for the Center for the Advancement of Reading and a professor at San Diego State University; *Nancy Frey* teaches at San Diego State University.

QUESTIONS FOR REFLECTION

1. What do the authors mean when they talk about teachers "focusing" their teaching rather than "scripting" it? How does this result in students who read, write, and think at higher levels?
2. What were the keys to success for Rosa Parks Elementary School? What makes the progress the teachers and students experienced unique? Likewise, what are some generalizable lessons one could take from their success?
3. Do you think the literacy framework that was used at Rosa Parks Elementary School would be as effective at the institution with which you are most familiar? Why or why not?

Why Is Kindergarten an Endangered Species?

LINDA H. PLEVYAK
KATHY MORRIS

ABSTRACT: The pressure to perform on standardized tests in the upper primary grades is having an impact on the curriculum in both kindergarten and preschool programs. The push for including more academics in the kindergarten classroom requires children to already have specific skills prior to entering kindergarten. Standardized testing and the desire to incorporate academics earlier are challenging developmentally appropriate practice in both kindergarten and preschool.

All I ever needed to know I learned in kindergarten, or so the saying goes. But kindergartens today, with their focus on academic skills instead of social skills are very different from the kindergartens of a couple of generations ago. Too many children are learning in kindergarten that they are not smart enough or are lacking, somehow. They can't sit still long enough, they can't go outside and play, they have homework to do, or they didn't get recess because their teacher couldn't spare the "educational time." One concern parents, teachers, and school administrators are grappling with is what children need to know *before* entering kindergarten.

THE TRICKLE-DOWN EFFECT

When standardized testing began to be used to measure absolute academic standards that all children had to meet before moving on to the next grade, a "backward domino effect" occurred. According to research conducted by the University of Colorado, first and second grade teachers began to feel the pressure to cover higher level content and to retain students who were likely to score poorly on the third grade standardized test (Shepard, 2000). A philosophy of buying a year (retaining or starting late) to ensure future success was born. Eventually kindergarten teachers began to feel the pressure to turn out kindergartner children with sight word recognition, phonics and math skills that used to be covered in first grade (Gubernick, 2000).

Parents began to feel the academic pressure as well. When observing kindergarten programs, speaking with other parents, or from personal experience, many parents realized that their child was "not ready" for this kind of academic program. Instead of questioning the program, they either bought another year for their child, and/or enrolled their child in an "academic" preschool that would get them ready for kindergarten. Too often, however, they sent their mature pre-kindergartner to kindergarten the next year and found that their child was older, taller, heavier, more socially mature—and bored!

May (1994) found that by third grade there is very little evidence to suggest that the extra year had any benefit on cognitive skills and abilities. More importantly, those children who are older than the majority of their peers are more likely to engage in dangerous sexual behaviors and use alcohol and cigarettes (Byrd & Weitzman, 1997). These studies may be startling for parents and teachers who just want the best for children. An important question that needs to be answered is what signs should parents and educators consider to be evidence of kindergarten readiness?

KINDERGARTEN READINESS SKILLS

There are many different readiness tests and evaluations that school districts currently use to determine kindergarten readiness. A study presented at the Annual Meeting of the American Educational Research Association in 1996 found that parents, childcare givers and kindergarten teachers all ranked the same three categories as being the most indicative of kindergarten readiness (Harradine & Clifford, 1996). The three categories include: (1) being healthy, well-fed, and well rested; (2) being able to express their needs, wants, and thoughts; and (3) being enthusiastic and curious about new activities.

Another study that looked at teacher and parent expectations for kindergarten readiness found that there were statistical differences between both groups' expectations (Welch & White, 1999). Parents were more likely than teachers to rate academic skills, i.e., counting, writing, and alphabet recognition as necessary pre-kindergarten skills. The teachers' responses mirrored Harradine and Clifford's (1996) study that ranked physical health, effective communication systems, curiosity and enthusiasm as better indicators of readiness. It may be that in the five years since this study was done more kindergarten teachers mirror the parents ranking of pre-academic skills as more necessary. An assumption for this possible change may be that kindergarten teachers feel the pressure to include academic skills in the curriculum even though their beliefs may say otherwise.

PRESCHOOL BENEFITS CHILDREN

Preschool experience offers children many benefits. One documented benefit is that children who attend preschool score higher on kindergarten screening tests. For early childhood educators this is only a minimum benefit and not a primary goal of preschool. Perry conducted a study in 1999 that looked at two groups of children age four to six. Forty children attended a quality preschool and forty children did not attend any preschool program. The study found that preschool experience had a positive effect in regards to being ready for kindergarten. The experimental group scored higher on the Slosson Kindergarten Readiness Test than those children who did not attend preschool.

This finding was consistent with a statement from a Public Policy Report which also showed that programs such as Head Start, and other center-based programs were statistically linked to higher literacy and math skills than for those children who received no preschool (Zill, Collins, West, & Hausken, 1995). It is important to note that quality preschool programming, as it was defined in these studies, is based upon a constructivist philosophy. Children in these studies had many opportunities to play with a wide range of materials, engage in new activities frequently, and were immersed in language, literacy, and math skills daily.

These types of preschools are not mini-versions of kindergarten with an emphasis on the alphabet, number and writing skills. While there are some programs that are based on skill development and report improvement on tests and reading readiness as positive outcomes, studies consistently report that by grade three, these gains have leveled out among students (Shepard, 1996). A distinction needs to be made between a child's cognitive and school performance gains. Sawhill (1999) shows that attending preschool has greater positive outcomes on raising overall school performance rather than just the initial cognitive gains, which again, level off by third grade. School performance continues to remain higher for those students who attended preschool as well.

WHERE DO WE GO FROM HERE?

The pressures facing kindergarten teachers in schools today are enormous. Administrative pressure for academic achievements and emphasis on academic time at the expense of art, gym, music and recess time is a reality facing all kindergarten teachers. There are increasing numbers of students who are coming to school lacking adequate health practices, language skills, and positive emotional skills and are ill equipped to deal with the rigorous demands and pace of our kindergartens today. Kindergarten teachers need to promote their philosophy of how children learn, and document their students' development in creative ways. Studies have shown that teachers' perceptions of how students learn affect what materials they select, the placement of those materials, and the use of classroom space that are found in a kindergarten room.

Teachers' perceptions of literacy achievement affect how children move around the room and interact with materials and each other. It is imperative that kindergarten teachers be reflective of themselves and their practices in order to face the challenge of heavy academic and skill development proponents. Administrators of elementary schools also need to be educated on the development and learning styles of young children. Children at kindergarten age do not learn in the same manner as other school-age children. Elementary school administrators typically do not have course work or a background in early childhood education. The early childhood programs and schools that are successful in terms of standardized testing scores and other external measurements should be used as models to evaluate programs. Finally, schools should be competing with themselves to continuously improve the academic and social/ emotional lives of its students.

Schools are faced with populations of children who have real emotional and family needs. While schools like to say that they exist to educate children, the reality that must be faced is that children are, in a real sense, only as healthy as their families. Schools must be more of a community-based outreach for families and should not be forced to take on increased academic skills at the kindergarten level to make up for lacking test scores in the higher grades.

On a personal note, Kathy Morris, one of the authors, is a preschool teacher who has struggled, along with many parents, with the question of when to send children on to kindergarten. Last year, Kathy had three students she recommended not move on to kindergarten, despite being age ready, because they demonstrated difficulty with regulating their emotions, struggled with peer relationships and had a difficult time using their language skills to express themselves.

She attributes her conclusions to the research that placed a great deal of emphasis on these three skills for success in kindergarten and upper grades. Kathy believes in standing firm in the wake of the academic pressure to run a more "academic" preschool, and will encourage kindergarten teachers to find ways to bring play into their programs.

Early childhood educators must find their own way to be heard in their schools. There are numerous resources and a good deal of research that supports play-based preschools and kindergartens as the best practice for young children.

REFERENCES

Byrd, R., & Weitzman, M. (1994). Predictors of early grade retention among children in the United States. *Pediatrics, 93*(3), 481–487.

Gubernick, L. (2000). Holding back the years. *Offspring* (April/May), 57–60.

Harradine, C., & Clifford, R. (1996). *When are children ready for kindergarten? Views of families, kindergarten teachers, and child care providers.* Raleigh: North Carolina State Department of Human Resources. ERIC Document Reproduction Service No. ED 399 044.

May, D. (1994). School readiness: An obstacle to intervention and inclusion. *Journal of Early Intervention, 18*(3), 290–301.

Perry, D. (1999). *A study to determine the effects of pre-kindergarten on kindergarten readiness and achievement in mathematics.* ERIC Document Reproduction Service No. ED 430 701.

Sawhill, I. (1999). Kids need an early start. *Blueprint* (Fall), 137–140.

Shepard, L. (1996). Effects of introducing classroom performance assessments on student learning. *Educational Measurement: Issues and Practice, 15*(3), 7–18.

Welch, M., & White, B. (1999). *Teacher and parent expectations for kindergarten readiness.* ERIC Document Reproduction Service No. ED 437 225.

Zill, N., Collins, M., West, J., & Hausken, E. (1995). Approaching kindergarten: A look at preschoolers in the United States. *Young Children, 51*(1), 35–38.

Linda H. Plevyak is associate professor of early childhood education, University of Cincinnati. *Kathy Morris* is a preschool teacher, Brantner Elementary School.

QUESTIONS FOR REFLECTION

1. Why do the authors say that kindergarten is becoming an endangered species? What has changed in the curriculum to make such a transformation?
2. What do you think is the appropriate balance of academic skills and social skills for kindergartners? Why? What is it that kids of this age really need to learn?
3. What kinds of external pressures do kindergarten teachers face when developing a developmentally appropriate curriculum? Is there too much unnecessary pressure on today's kindergartners and their teachers? What might the consequences be of this kind of pressure and where is it coming from?

Case Study in Curriculum Implementation

Learning to Read in Kindergarten: Has Curriculum Development Bypassed the Controversies?

BRUCE JOYCE
MARILYN HRYCAUK
EMILY CALHOUN
WITH THE NORTHERN
LIGHTS KINDERGARTEN
TEACHERS

ABSTRACT: The prevailing assumption has been that a formal reading curriculum is inappropriate for kindergartners. However, district staff members and teachers in the Northern Lights School Division of Alberta were convinced that a "nurturing" approach to teaching reading would not endanger the children and might in fact prevent some of them from encountering academic difficulties in the primary grades and beyond.

We'll begin with a simple proposition: Let's teach our kindergarten students to read. We already know how to do it, so why don't we?

Within schools and school districts, decisions about curriculum and instruction in literacy have to be made on the basis of present knowledge and judgment. Such decisions can't wait until all controversies have been resolved and all the evidence is in with regard to available options. In the case of kindergarten, decisions about curriculum are complicated by debates about whether there should be a formal curriculum in reading or whether the components of the kindergarten program should be designed to develop the dimensions of emergent literacy only. But research on how to teach beginning readers grows apace, and we believe that we should take advantage of it.

In the Northern Lights School Division in Alberta, Canada—a district of 20 schools and about 6,500 students—we decided to design a formal reading curriculum for kindergarten, prepare the teachers to implement it, and conduct an action research study of student learning. Our decision stemmed from the judgment that research on beginning reading had reached the point where an effective, engaging, and multidimensional curriculum could be designed and implemented without placing our students at risk in the process. And if such a curriculum proved successful, it seemed likely that the much-publicized "learning gap" would be reduced.

Over the past five years in Northern Lights, we ("we" includes the superintendent, Ed Wittchen; the trustees; and representative teachers and administrators) had concentrated on the development of "safety nets" for low-achieving students at the second-grade level and in grades 4 through 12.[1] We based the two curriculum designs on strands of research on beginning literacy for young children and for older struggling readers and writers.[2] Currently, in both safety net curricula, about three-fourths of the students are progressing well and narrowing the distance between themselves and the district's average students. The others are holding their own.

The need for the safety net programs and our observation of the frustration and hopelessness experienced by students who needed help caused us to consider the K–3 literacy curricula and to explore whether we could strengthen them and so reduce the need for the later safety nets. We take seriously the statement by Connie Juel, who, in reacting to the National Research Council report *Preventing Reading Difficulties in Young Children*, wrote that "children who struggle in vain with reading in the first grade soon decide that they neither like nor want to read."[3] Our teachers who work in the safety net programs confirm that their job is half instruction and half therapy.

For some decades, because of the concerns about not generating demands beyond the capabilities of the students or introducing students to reading in unpleasant ways, there has been a dearth of studies on formal reading programs for kindergarten. A few studies did suggest that formal reading programs in kindergarten could have positive effects that lasted throughout schooling.

For kindergarten interventions as such, though, we had to go back to Delores Durkin's work of 30 years ago. In building a kindergarten curriculum, we were not able to draw on a body of recent research on, say, alternative kindergarten reading programs or dimensions of learning to read at age 5. We drew on the literature relevant to learning to read in grades 1 through 3 and above. Building greater literacy is a matter of considerable importance, and not damaging our students is of even greater importance. But it may be that the concerns about hurting students are based on images of brutal and primitive curricula rather than on humane and sophisticated approaches. Certainly those concerns are not based on reports of failed attempts.[4]

We made the decision that there would be no danger to the students if we proceeded deliberately and, particularly, if the teachers tracked the responses of the children carefully and were prepared to back off or change their approach if a student appeared to be stressed. Not to challenge students cognitively might be an even larger mistake than challenging them. In addition, we wanted the early experience to be not only effective but joyful—learning to read should be a delightful experience.

Our view of a nurturing curriculum appears to differ widely from the image that many people have of a reading curriculum for young children, and we believe it is that image that causes them to shy away from formal literacy instruction for kindergartners. We did not imagine students with workbooks, alphabet flash cards, or letter-by-letter phonics drills. Instead, we imagined an environment in which students would progress from their developed listening/speaking vocabularies to the reading of words, sentences, and longer text that they had created, where they would examine simple books in a relaxed atmosphere, where they would begin to write with scribbling and simple illustrations, where they would be read to regularly, and where comprehension strategies would be modeled for them through the reading and study of charming fiction and nonfiction books. If the work of childhood is play, we imagined the students playfully working their way into literacy.

PATHWAYS TO LITERACY: DESIGNING THE CURRICULUM

Our idea for a nurturing curriculum came from developments in the field of curriculum having to do with several of the emergent literacy processes. Most of the literature in this area presents ideas about and studies of students in grades 1 through 6. We saw this literature as defining dimensions for early literacy that could be incorporated into components of a kindergarten curriculum. Essentially, we categorized dozens of studies around the several dimensions:

• The development of sight vocabulary from the students listening/speaking vocabulary and the study of words encountered through wide reading.[5] Words are recognized in terms of their spelling, and, once a hundred or so are learned, the phonetic and structural categories are available to the students.

• The need for wide reading at the developed level. At the beginning, students can engage at the picture level and, gradually, can deal with books at the caption level as they learn how meaning is conveyed by the authors.[6]

• The regular study of word patterns, including spelling. The students need to learn to classify words, seeking the phonetic and structural characteristics of words and seeing the language as comprehensible. For example, as the students study the beginnings and endings of words ("onsets" and "rimes"), they build concepts, such as "Words that begin with xxxx sounds often begin with xxxx letters," and they apply those concepts when they encounter unfamiliar words: "If it begins with xxxx letter(s), then it might sound like xxxx usually does."[7]

• The need for regular (several times daily) writing and the study of writing.[8] Writing involves expressing ideas through the learned words and patterns—the essential connection between reading and writing. The attempt to write consolidates what is being learned through reading.

• The study of comprehension strategies. Although most of the research on comprehension has been done with older students, the search for meaning begins early, and the modeling of comprehension strategies is important from the beginning.[9]

• The study, by both teacher and students, of weekly and monthly progress, including the levels of books the students can read, sight words learned, phonetic and structural analysis skills, information learned, and fluency in writing.[10] For example, students can build their own files of words and can see what they are learning. Or students can record their classifications of words, can see that they have developed categories of words (e.g., these begin with . . .), and can add to them. Knowing what you know enables you to assess progress and to celebrate growth.

For our early literacy curriculum, we found that the Picture Word Inductive Model—derived from the tradition of "language experience" with the addition of concept formation and attainment models of teaching—was very important. The core of the language experience approach is the use of the students' developed listening/speaking vocabulary.[11] The students study topics and discuss them and dictate to the teacher. The dictated material becomes the source of their first sight words, and their first efforts to master the alphabetic principle come from their study of the structures of those words.

The Picture Word Inductive Model, as the name suggests, begins with photographs of scenes whose content is within the ability of the students to describe. For example, the photographs might show aspects of the local community. The students take turns identifying objects and actions in the picture. The teacher spells the words, drawing lines from the words to the elements in the picture to which they refer and so creates a picture dictionary. The students are given copies of the words, and they identify them using the picture dictionary. They proceed to classify the words, noting their similarities and differences. The teacher then selects some of the categories for extended study. Both phonetic features and structural characteristics are studied. The teacher models the creation of titles and sentences, and the students create some of their own by dictating them and learning to read the dictations. In the same fashion, the teacher creates paragraphs, and the students gradually learn to assemble titles and sentences into paragraphs about the content of the picture. The picture word cycles (inquiries into the pictures) generally take from three to five weeks.

A major assumption underpinning this view of the curriculum is that students need to become inquirers into language, seeking to build their sight vocabularies and studying the characteristics of those words as they build generalizations about phonetic and structural characteristics.

The curriculum was designed to facilitate growth through each of its strands—building vocabulary, classifying, creating sentences and paragraphs, and reading—in an integrated fashion so that each strand will support the others. As indicated above, as sight words are learned, phonetic and structural concepts will be developed through the analysis of those words. Similarly, the construction of sentences and paragraphs will be related to the sight vocabularies that are being developed. As the children read, they will identify known words and attack new ones through the phonetic, structural, and comprehension skills they are developing.

PROVIDING STAFF DEVELOPMENT TO SUPPORT IMPLEMENTATION

Once we decided that such a curriculum was feasible, designing staff development was the next step. We needed a program that was oriented to help the teachers both implement the curriculum and become a positive learning community that would study student learning and take pleasure in colleagueship and inquiry. Eight teachers in three schools in the Grand Centre/Cold Lake area were involved in the initial effort. The school faculties had agreed formally to participate, and all eight kindergarten teachers had agreed as well. Two had taught reading in the primary grades in the past, but none had attempted a formal literacy curriculum in the kindergarten. Two were first-year teachers. The superintendent, cabinet, and board of trustees were supportive, and meetings explaining the curriculum were held with parents in the spring and early fall.

The staff development included demonstrations, the study of early literacy, the analysis of practice, and the study of student learning, following the format developed by Bruce Joyce and Beverly Showers.[12] Peer coaching was embedded in the workplaces of the teachers.

THE ACTION RESEARCH INQUIRY

For the action research component of the initiative, the eight teachers and the district staff members were asked to focus on two questions: Did the multidimensional curriculum work? Did the students learn to read and to what degree, including the extent of their comfort with the process and their feelings about reading?

Informal observation was important, but the teachers were also provided with tools for the formal study of the students' learning of the alphabet, acquisition of vocabulary, general language development (including phonemic awareness), books studied or read, and development of the competence to manage unfamiliar books, including extended text, using the procedure developed by Thomas Gunning.[13] A team made up of district staff members and consultants administered the Gunning procedure in June in order to ensure standardization of the tricky process of measuring the reading competence of very young children.

To what extent is the variance in achievement explained by gender, by developed language competence as students entered kindergarten, and by class group—variables that occur repeatedly in the literature and are reported as factors in many studies? In the first year, all 141 kindergarten-age students in the three schools were enrolled and were included in the study. In all three schools, students came from a considerable variety of socioeconomic levels, and some 15 students came from First Nations reservations. Teacher judgment indicated that just one of the children entered kindergarten reading at any level. Just one student could recognize all the letters of the alphabet (tested outside the context of words).

Throughout the year the data were collected, summarized, and interpreted with respect to the response of the students. Here we concentrate on the most salient aspects of the students' learning. All eight kindergarten classes followed similar patterns. Differences between the classes were small by comparison to the general effects. For us, this was very important. Had it been that only half of the teachers had been able to implement the curriculum successfully, we would have had to do some heavy thinking.

Recognition of Letters of the Alphabet

In early October, the mean number of letters recognized (out of 52 upper- and lower-case letters) was 31. In January, the mean was 46. In March, it reached 52. That is, all the students could recognize all the letters out of context. Letter recognition was associated with the acquisition of sight vocabulary, but one was not necessarily a function of the other. The learning of sight vocabulary appeared to pull letter recognition as much as the learning of the letters facilitated the acquisition of sight vocabulary.

Acquisition of Sight Vocabulary

Our inquiry focused both on how many words were being learned and on the students' ability to learn new words. The learning of words was studied in terms of the Picture Word cycles, which ranged from about four to six weeks in length. Both the number of words learned in the cycles and the increased efficiency developed by the students were of interest here. The data below are taken from one of the classes.

Cycle 1. Twenty-two words were "shaken out" of the picture. At the end of the first week, the average number of words identified in an out-of-context assessment was five. By the end of the fourth week, the average was 16, and one student knew all 22.

Cycle 2. Twenty-two words were shaken out. At the end of the first week, the average number that the students could identify out of context was 12, and by the end of the third week, the average number identified was 20.

Cycle 3. Twenty-eight words were shaken out. At the end of the first week, the mean number of words recognized out of context was 20, and at the end of the second week, the mean was 26, with just three students recognizing 24 and none recognizing fewer than 24.

All the students appeared to increase in efficiency so that, by the end of January, they were able to add to their sight vocabularies, within the first week or two, just about all the words shaken out of the picture. For all sections, the mean percentage of words recognized after two weeks of the first cycle was 30%. By the third cycle, the mean for two weeks had risen to 90%.

Retention of Words

In May, random samples of six students in each class were tested with respect to out-of-context recognition of the words that had been shaken out through the year—for example, about 120 words in the class cited above. Mean retention was 110. In addition, words added through the generation of titles, sentences, and paragraphs were learned, many of them in the high-frequency "useful little words" category. In the class used as an example, those additional words added up to over 100.

Had the students had difficulty developing a sight vocabulary or retaining it, we would have had a serious warning signal. But such a signal did not develop, and, more important, the increase in capability was a positive signal. By midwinter, the students were mastering words within two weeks that had taken them four or five weeks in the first cycle.

Classification of Words

Once the words were shaken out, they were entered into the computer, and sets of words were given to each student. (The students could examine them and, if they did not recognize one, could use the picture dictionary to identify it.) Classifying the words was an important activity. The students were asked to sort their word cards according to the characteristics of the words. The teachers modeled classifications of various types throughout the year. In the first cycles, most students built categories on the presence of one or more letters. Later, more complex categories emerged. The teachers selected categories for instructional emphasis and led the students to develop new words and unlock unfamiliar words by using the categories. For example, having dealt with *work, works, worked, worker*, and *working*, the students could hunt for other words from which derivatives could be made. Or, knowing work and encountering working in their reading, they could try to unlock it as they learned how the *-ing* suffix operates.

The teachers studied the categories that students were developing, keeping an eye on the phonetic and structural principles that were emerging. The results are too complex to summarize briefly, but, on the whole, about 30 phonetic and about 20 structural concepts were explored intensively.

Transition to Reading Books

Throughout the year, a profusion of books was available to the students. Books were carried home for "reading to and with," and little books generated from the Picture Word activities went home to be read to parents. As the students began to learn to read independently, books at their levels accompanied them home. Our records show that 80% of the students encountered 50 or more books in this fashion, in addition to any books from home or libraries.

The assessment of independent reading levels was built around the Gunning framework, in which the students attempt to read unfamiliar books at the following levels:

- Picture Level: single words on a page are illustrated.
- Caption Level: phrases or sentences, most but not all illustrated.
- Easy Sight Level: longer and more complex, mostly high-frequency words.
- Beginning Reading: four levels, progressively longer passages, and less repetition and predictability.
- Grade 2A: requires good-sized sight vocabulary and well-developed word-attack skills.

When an assessment is administered, students read aloud books at each level, beginning with the simplest, and their deviations from print are noted. They are asked comprehension questions after the book has been read. Reaching fluency with total comprehension places a student at a particular level.

In the December assessment, all the students were able to deal with books at the Picture Level, and about one-fourth could manage Caption Level books comfortably. By February, about one-fourth had progressed to the Easy Sight Level, and a handful could manage books at a higher level.

Once again, had the students not been able to approach any level of text competently, we would have had a warning that our curriculum was failing. However, the children were progressing beyond the reading of the sentences and paragraphs developed in each Picture Word cycle and were beginning to be able to manage simple books "almost independently."

In June, the independent test team administered the assessment using a specially assembled set of books from United Kingdom publishers to reduce the likelihood that the books would be familiar to the students. The aggregated results for the eight classes were indeed encouraging.

All eight classes apparently succeeded in bringing all the students to some level of print literacy. About 40% of the students appeared to be able to read extended text, and another 30% manifested emergent ability to read extended text. Indeed, 20% reached the Grade 2A level, which includes long and complex passages and requires the exercise of complex skills both to decode and to infer word meanings. All the students could manage at least the simplest level of books.

We felt it was very important that there were no students who had experienced abject failure. Even the student who enters first grade reading independently at the picture level is armed with skills in alphabet recognition, possesses a substantial storehouse of sight words, and owns an array of phonetic and structural concepts. However, a half dozen students will need to be watched closely because, even if they were able to handle books at the caption level, they labored at the task, manifesting difficulty either in recognizing relationships between text and graphics or in using their phonetic or structural generalizations to attack unfamiliar words.

We studied the data to determine whether gender or socioeconomic status influenced levels of success, and they did not. The distributions of levels for boys and girls were almost identical, as were the distributions for students having or not having subsidized lunches.

Typically, in our district, about 20 kindergarten students would have been referred as having special needs in those eight schools. At the end of this year, just two students were referred, both for speech problems.

Comfort and Satisfaction

During the year, parents voiced their opinions regularly, and in May we prepared simple questionnaires for both the parents and the children.

We asked the parents a series of questions about the progress of their children and whether they and the children believed they were developing satisfactorily. The children were asked only whether they were learning to read and how they felt about their progress. We were trying to determine whether there was any discomfort that we were not detecting. But in response to our survey, no student or parent manifested discomfort or dissatisfaction related to the curriculum. However, some parents were anxious at the beginning and remained worried at the end of the year. Some were concerned that we had not taken a "letter by letter" synthetic phonics approach and worried that future problems might develop as a consequence. But even these parents appeared to believe that their children were progressing well "so far."

A YEAR LATER: LEAVING FIRST GRADE

Throughout first grade, we followed the students, and, at the end of the year, we gave them the Gray Oral Reading Test,[14] administered by a team of external testers. The mean Grade Level Equivalent (GLE) was 3.5 (the average for students at the end of grade 1 is 2.0). Five percent of the students were below 2.0, which is quite a distance from the 50% typical in our district in previous years.

In June 2003, 47 students, a randomly selected half of the 94 students still enrolled in the district, were administered the Gray Oral as they exited grade 2. Their average GLE was 5.0 (the national average of exiting grade-4 students). The distributions of male and female scores were almost identical. Five students (10%) scored below the average of exiting second-grade students. Typically, 30% of the students in this district or nationally in the U.S. and Canada do so.

In subsequent years, we will continue to monitor the progress of the students from each year, and we will follow the lowest-achieving students most intensively.

INTERPRETATION

The problem that faced us was whether research on beginning literacy had reached the point that we could design multidimensional curricula to introduce young children to reading with comfort and satisfaction. In our efforts to learn how much an initiative in kindergarten curriculum might improve literacy learning, reduce the likelihood of failure by students thought to be at risk, and also benefit students not thought to be at risk, our first experience must be described as positive. We will follow the students through the grades, and we will continue to scrutinize the curriculum.

The teachers were all new to a formal kindergarten reading curriculum. In the first year, they were scrambling to master a considerable number of unfamiliar instructional models, particularly the Picture Word Inductive Model, and they spent considerable energy tracking the progress of the students and trying to figure out whether they were proceeding optimally and whether the tasks were well matched to them. With greater experience, they will no doubt provide many ideas for improvement.

The issues of "developmental readiness" become moot if the knowledge base permits us to design effective and humane kindergarten curricula in reading. The progress of the students in these eight classes equals the progress of students in average first-grade classrooms and surpasses it in one very important way: no children failed, whereas one-third of the students in average first grades usually do. The half-dozen students who gained the least nonetheless arrived at first grade with substantial knowledge and skill.

In the next few years, we'll learn how these students do in the upper elementary grades, where similar efforts to change the curriculum are under way. Thus far, our results have been encouraging, but there are 400 students to follow now. We certainly want to continue the outstanding achievement we have seen so far, but we also hope to close the door on poor achievement and eliminate the need for the safety net programs. We'll see. Right now, our hypothesis is that a strong, multidimensional, formal reading program for kindergarten students can change the picture of achievement in the primary grades. Moreover, 5-year-old children, given a strong and humane curriculum, can learn to read at least as well as first-graders usually do, but without the high failure rates of so many first-grade classrooms.

We hope that our Northern Lights teachers, and all others in every venue, will set high standards and also treat their students affirmatively. We are bothered when states, provinces, and districts set goals at such a low level that they expect that 2% or 3% of the students will creep up to the next level of achievement in any given year. Ninety-five percent is a better goal. Nearly all of our little second-grade graduates can now read with the best of upper-elementary-grade students. So could nearly all of the students in all school systems.

NOTES

1. See Marilyn Hrycauk, "A Safety Net for Second-Grade Students," *Journal of Staff Development*, vol. 23, 2002, pp. 55–58; and Bruce Joyce, Marilyn Hrycauk, and Emily Calhoun, "A Second Chance for Struggling Readers," *Educational Leadership*, March 2001, pp. 42–47.
2. Emily Calhoun, *Literacy for the Primary Grades* (Saint Simons Island, Ga.: Phoenix Alliance, 1998).
3. See Connie Juel, "Learning to Read and Write," *Journal of Educational Psychology*, vol. 80, 1988, pp. 437–47.
4. In a long-term study of students who had experienced formal reading instruction in kindergarten, Ralph Hanson and Donna Farrell followed them through their high school years and found that the effects could be detected even as they graduated. See Ralph Hanson and Donna Farrell, "The Long-Term Effects on High School Seniors of Learning to Read in Kindergarten," *Reading Research Quarterly*, vol. 30, 1995, pp. 908–33. Delores Durkin's work on the positive effects of learning to read early is well known but has not changed the minds of the large number of experts on early childhood education who are more worried about

damage than about benefits. See Delores Durkin, *Children Who Read Early* (New York: Teachers College Press, 1966).

5. See, for example, William Nagy, Patricia Herman, and Richard Anderson, "Learning Words from Context," *Reading Research Quarterly*, vol. 19, 1985, pp. 304–30.

6. A crisp general review can be found in Nell Duke and P. David Pearson, "Effective Practices for Developing Reading Comprehension," in Alan Farstrup and Jay Samuels, eds., *What Research Has to Say About Reading Instruction*, 3rd ed. (Newark, Del.: International Reading Association, 2002), pp. 205–42.

7. Students need to learn to inquire into word patterns and build word-identification skills around concepts about word structures. A fine summary is provided by Linnea Ehri, "Phases of Acquisition in Learning to Read Words and Instructional Implications," paper presented at the annual meeting of the American Educational Research Association, Montreal, 1999.

8. The connection of early writing to beginning reading is growing clearer. See Carol Englart et al., "Making Strategies and Self-Talk Visible," *American Educational Research Journal*, vol. 28, 1991, pp. 337–72.

9. Several lines of research are gradually discovering a great deal about comprehension strategies and how to develop them. See Ruth Garner, *Metacognition and Reading Comprehension* (Norwood, N.J.: Ablex, 1987); and Michael Pressley et al., *Cognitive Strategy Instruction That Really Improves Student Performance* (Cambridge, Mass.: Brookline, 1995).

10. The Picture Word Inductive Model provides a set of ways to track student progress. Some variables (such as vocabulary development) are tracked weekly or more often. Others are tracked a little less frequently. See Emily Calhoun, *Teaching Beginning Reading and Writing with the Picture Word Inductive Model* (Alexandria, Va.: Association for Supervision and Curriculum Development, 1999); and Bruce Joyce and Beverly Showers, *Student Achievement Through Staff Development* (Alexandria, Va.: Association for Supervision and Curriculum Development, 2002).

11. Russell Stauffer, *The Language-Experience Approach to the Teaching of Reading* (New York: Harper & Row, 1970).

12. Joyce and Showers, op. cit.

13. Thomas Gunning, *Best Books for Beginning Readers* (Boston: Allyn and Bacon, 1998).

14. J. Lee Wiederholt and Brian Bryant, *Gray Oral Reading Tests* (Austin, Tex.: Pro-Ed, 2001).

Bruce Joyce is director of Booksend Laboratories, St. Simons Island, Georgia; *Marilyn Hrycauk* is director of instruction in the Northern Lights School Division #69, Alberta; *Emily Calhoun* is director of the Phoenix Alliance, St. Simons Island, Georgia; The Northern Lights Kindergarten Teachers are *Bev Gariepy, Christine Reynolds, Melanie Malayney, Carol Kruger, Jennifer Lawton-Codziuk, Elaine Blades, Christine Cairns, Andrea Fama,* and *Gloria Lane.*

QUESTIONS FOR REFLECTION

1. What did the authors learn by their experiment to present the kindergarteners in the Northern Lights School District with a "nurturing" curriculum? How can what they learned inform practice within other districts?

2. What were the "safety nets" the authors referred to as having been used for certain students in the district? How does the research used by the authors address the use of these safety nets?

3. What conclusions can you draw from this article regarding the use of action-based research in schools? What does research tell us about the day-to-day activities of our students, teachers, and administrators?

Leaders' Voices—
Putting Theory into Practice

Building a Community in Our Classroom:
The Story of Bat Town, U.S.A.

ANDREA MCGANN KEECH

ABSTRACT: As the passing of time and the changing of the landscape became familiar concepts to them, children in one combined third- and fourth-grade class at Roosevelt Elementary School in Iowa City, Iowa, used their growing knowledge of their town's past as the starting point for creating a model community of their own. Keech profiles the class and their project community, "Bat Town, U.S.A."

"I've got a problem" said one of my students with a thoughtful frown, "and I'd like to call a city council meeting about it. I'm not getting enough help from my business partner, and I need some advice."

"Fine," I told him, acting in my official capacity as city manager. "We can do that this afternoon right after recess."

"Then I'll need to reschedule my Resource Room time," a girl sitting near us chimed in. "I'll check with my teacher and get back to you."

"Okay," the boy replied with a nod. "This problem needs our attention now!"

I couldn't help smiling at this very serious conversation in my third and fourth grade combination class. With just a few changes in wording, the interchange could have been taking place between the actual members of our town's city council members. Instead, it was occurring in a classroom of students who were participating in a social studies simulation exercise known as *Classroom City*.[1] We had certainly come a great distance from that first day several weeks ago when we held our ribbon cutting ceremony and

officially opened the simulated city fondly known as Bat Town, U.S.A.

In our combination classes, the curriculum rotates between topics every other year. This year in social studies our focus was on communities. We had already studied communities in Japan and China. As participants in the national Kid's Voting USA project, we had followed developments in the local election. Finally, we were ready to take a long look at changes in the community of our own school, Roosevelt Elementary in Iowa City, Iowa, and to begin work on creating a thriving model classroom community of our own in room 116.

Today, Roosevelt Elementary is a school with international connections. Our proximity to the University of Iowa and programs there which attract scholars and their children from around the world makes our school fortunate enough to have an extremely rich diversity of learners. In our classroom alone there were recent arrivals from China, Japan, Sudan, Indonesia and Korea. Children representing many ethnicities come together here and learn together about their world and about themselves. Finding common ground to study the meaning of "community" presents my group with a challenge.

We focused our study of the community on the school itself, using the social studies standards themes of **PEOPLE, PLACES AND ENVIRONMENTS,** and **TIME, CONTINUITY AND CHANGE.**[2] To mark our school's sixtieth birthday a few years ago, a wonderful book called *Reflections of Theodore Roosevelt Elementary School* had been created by Dr. Nora Steinbrech, principal of the school for more than eighteen years. It tells the stories, sometimes moving, sometimes gently humorous, of students, teachers, principals, parents and friends who walked these halls before us.

We read this book together and reflected on our own stories, experiences that we'd like to pass along to future generations about our days at Roosevelt. These were recorded in memory books to keep and to share. Ideas came easily. We included a visit from Echo, the bat, and a trip to a real bat colony in an old schoolhouse; our Chinese New Year feast when we sampled all of those new and delicious foods, and the staging of our very own original drama, *The Terrible Tragedy of the Titanic.*

Next, we made an effort to begin really observing those little details of our school's architecture and design around us, the things we'd always hurried by and taken for granted without a second thought before now. Our appreciation for the passing of time heightened. "Look," someone would say as we walked past the old original facade of the building, "that's the 1931 entrance. Isn't it beautiful? Look at the carved stone!" On our way to P.E. one day, another student pointed out the place where large Palladian windows once brought in the western sunlight. "Why did they brick them in?" several children wanted to know. Well, think about the problems that could result by having enormous glass windows in a building now used as a gymnasium. "Why can't we sled down 'Suicide Hill' in the Ravine anymore?" That question had a fairly obvious answer!

We noticed the additions to our school over the years, variations in building materials, hidden "secret" passages, the signs small and large of changes which had taken place over the decades. Along with the *Reflections* book of "old" Roosevelt, we read several other excellent stories which provided us with a real sense of the passing of time and what that means in the life of a child and a community.

Who Came Down that Road? by George Ella Lyon is a book of few words and many beautiful images.[3] We used it to heighten our awareness of Time, Continuity and Change. As a young boy and his mother walk down a well-traveled path, they imagine all of those long-ago footsteps falling upon the very same path. Mastodon and woolly mammoth, buffalo and elk, Native Americans, settlers, soldiers in blue and gray, and finally a mother and her child. "Who will come next," they wonder—and we wondered, too. We composed our own original pages filled with writing and illustrations to add to the book. Each of us provided a new page, suggestions for the "next" entry, about who or what might follow the young boy and his mother down the path. Some students suggested the boy's own child might one day pass that way. An understanding of our past can provide us with a better preparation for the future.

Another book with lovely illustrations and a haunting tale of time's passing is Dyan Sheldon's *Under the Moon.*[4] Finding an arrowhead in her backyard, a young girl tries to picture a world without automobiles, airplanes, and cities. What did this place look like with open fields and clear streams? Who lived here? Who made this arrowhead she holds today? She begins to imagine what life might have been like when the "land was as open as the sky." Cultures have maintained their traditions and customs over time. We wanted to learn more about the culture that had produced the arrowhead.

Inspired by this book, I brought in a number of arrowheads turned up by the blade of my grandfather's mule-pulled plow on his farm in the 1920s for the children to examine firsthand. We then took a class trip to the natural history museum at Iowa Hall on the University of Iowa campus, where knowledgeable tour guides helped us to understand the history and uses of a wonderful variety of Native American cultural artifacts, such as arrowheads, axes, spearheads, pottery, beadwork, and clothing. We viewed and discussed several life-sized historical dioramas depicting the Meskwaki people who have lived here on the banks of our Iowa River for thousands of years. Our trip to the museum helped us to understand continuity and change in the culture of the Meskwaki, early residents of our community.

In *The House on Maple Street* by Bonnie Pryor, we read another story of an arrowhead and a small porcelain cup, how they were lost by children long ago and how they came to be found many years later by two sisters digging in their garden.[5] We wrote about treasures we might leave behind in our Roosevelt Ravine for others to find one day. What would our special things tell future "diggers" about us? Would those archeologists really appreciate the significance of beloved Beanie Babies? Taking a walk around the neighborhood, we even found an old house like the house on Maple Street. We talked about the many changes the people in the house must have seen from those windows.

We also used a series of seven amazing posters called "The Changing American Cityscape."[6] The fictional town of New Providence as depicted in the posters is actually a composite of many buildings from real cities throughout the United States at various time periods. As we looked at the first poster showing 1875, we saw horses and buggies, muddy streets, and a town just getting started. Over the weeks we added the subsequent posters in the series to the wall. "That's how our town might have looked when Roosevelt Elementary School was built," I told the children as we hung the poster from the 1930s. "There's even an airship!" a sharp-eyed boy who was then engrossed in a study of the Hindenburg pointed out. The posters range from 1885 to the 1990s. The incredible detail in this beautiful series sparks lively discussion and comparisons among the various attributes of the many decades.

We used the posters as models, and working in cooperative learning groups students did research and made our own posters of our changing Roosevelt "schoolscape" through the decades. They showed teachers' and students' clothing and hair styles, games played on the playground, popular music selections, and an outline of the school building's dimensions during a particular period of time. It became a common sight to see small clusters of students around the sets of posters throughout the day, happily discussing history and its changes—what teacher of social studies can ask for more than that?

Finally, we read Alice McLerran's story of the little community known a *Roxaboxen* set in the 1930s "on a hill on the southeast corner of Second Avenue and Eighth Street, in Yuma, Arizona."[7] The children in the story, one the author's mother, built their own town with rocks and boxes, bits of jewel-colored glass and sticks. There was a mayor and a town hall, a bakery, and *two* ice cream parlors, because in Roxaboxen "you can eat all the ice cream you want." It's just the sort of town any child would love. Everyone always had "plenty of money" because there were "plenty of shops." The story in the book took place during the Great Depression, just when our own Roosevelt School was being built. The availability of money and the ice cream were only real in the imaginations of the citizens of Roxaboxen.

Through our readings, discussions, and reflections, we learned many things about communities and the reasons which bring people together. The passing of time and the changing of the landscape became familiar concepts to us. Traditions, conventions, and common goals all played a part in our studies. Now we were ready at last to create our very own model of a community, right in the classroom. This simulation would be a more structured way of making our small community run smoothly and successfully.

To help us organize our own town, we used many elements from a unit available through

Interaction Publishers called *Classroom City*. We didn't follow the sequence of the lessons precisely, nor did we feel bound to do every aspect of the simulation. My students would have had some difficulty computing "financial interest on accounts" or figuring up their "income tax." Even adults, after all, can experience difficulty with those! We used the basic organizational guidelines and general format provided by the *Classroom City* lesson plans.

Persuasive speeches were written and delivered as children ran for public office. The election of officials followed. City council meetings were held to get things organized. Everyone submitted a flag design to represent our city and one with a prominent flying fox bat, designed by a talented girl who would eventually open The Artistic Bat Store, was chosen by popular vote. Students brainstormed together about what kinds of businesses they might like to have in Bat Town, U.S.A. and what products or services they could offer for sale to other residents and visitors. This simulation expanded our study to incorporate the social studies standards themes of **POWER, AUTHORITY AND GOVERNANCE** as well as **PRODUCTION, DISTRIBUTION AND CONSUMPTION.** A detailed listing of everyone's job duties, citizen roles and responsibilities, goals, and activities are provided in the *Classroom City* teacher's guide. Our own special touches like the classroom museum, the cookie shop, and the play station were suggested by the students themselves as our simulation progressed.

A ribbon-cutting ceremony opened the town, which the children had decided to call Bat Town, U.S.A. In science we studied bats as a part of our Physics of Sound unit, and their fascination with the world's only flying mammal continued unabated throughout the year, contributing to their interest in naming the model city for these important animals.

As teacher, I held the title of city manager to keep things smoothly on track. **CIVIC IDEAS AND PRACTICES** are an integral aspect of our model city. Thanks to a helpful and informative booklet called "The Children's Guide to Local Government" published by the Iowa City city manager's office, we were able to compare the organization of our model community, Bat Town, U.S.A., with that of our own Iowa City. A mayor and vice mayor were elected by the students. The mayor greets all visitors to the city, is the ribbon cutter at the town's opening, and conducts city council meetings. The vice mayor is second in command. S/he votes on the city council and can remove from office any public officials who fail to perform their duties.

Our city council members were elected as well. Only members of the council and the vice mayor could start a motion or vote on a motion during meetings, but anyone could approach a member with a concern and have it brought before the council. Our class meetings were lively affairs filled with spirited debates and a free exchange of ideas. The council members reviewed all citations issued by health, fire and police departments and assigned fines. They also reviewed and voted on all student applications to open a business. Potential business owners wrote a description of the purpose of their store or service, and the application needed to win the approval of three-fourths of the council before "construction" could proceed.

In addition to the elected officials, there were a myriad of positions to fill, such as police officers to enforce "speeding" violations in the hallways and "noise" ordinances; bankers to distribute income paid weekly; an editor of our illustrious newspaper, appropriately called the *Night Times;* and a fire marshal to monitor litter in desks, keep our "streets" clear of clutter, and hold fire drills as necessary. There were lots and lots of storekeepers, those entrepreneurial types who quickly learned how to make their money grow.

Busy afternoons were spent learning and practicing Robert's Rules of Order, holding city council meetings to approve or disapprove of permits for businesses, making a map of the town for visitors, designing a town logo and flag to fly, writing columns for the *Night Times* ("Dear Batty" proved a popular favorite), and preparing our town for the coming "tourist season" when younger guests would come to visit Bat Town and patronize our stores with "bat dollars" distributed by our bankers.

All students had jobs and were paid a weekly wage, according to principles suggested in the *Classroom City* teacher's guide. Money could also be earned by taking on a duty like editing or contributing features to the newspaper, assessing and collecting fines for violations of city codes, operating a popular business where students could spend their wages, or holding elected office. Fate cards that were drawn weekly either awarded money ("You specialize in decorating book covers for your friends and make $12") or deducted it ("A lost book costs you $9 to replace"). Students came up with many creative ideas for earning those sought-after "bat dollars."

We used cardboard boxes and construction paper to make store-fronts. Among the many options Bat Town shoppers could choose from were homemade cookies or Girl Scout cookies with free ice water, books for rent, origami paper cranes, samurai hats folded from newspaper, pen and ink drawings from a girl with artistic gifts in abundance, stuffed toy rentals, small erasers, stickers, handmade book markers, and a play station offering games of skill. Once the town was up and running, the excitement was tremendous. My students used some of the "bat dollars" they had earned as wages in the earlier weeks of the simulation to spend in the various shops run by their friends. There were two shifts on successive days so that everyone had turns both to sell and shop. They bought items from the businesses run by fellow students, munched cookies from the cookie shop, and visited the play station to try their luck at games like "Ghost Toss" and the tricky "Balancing Bears." They insisted on trying out everything themselves before the "tourists" arrived! Who could blame them?

As the younger children came to visit, they were welcomed by the mayor, vice-mayor, and members of the council. They were given maps of the town and the latest edition of *Night Times,* hot off the presses. Our guests were learning to count money, so each was given twenty "bat dollars" to spend and twenty minutes to spend them. One kindergartner remarked to his teacher as he departed Bat Town, "I can't believe they were only third and fourth graders!"

Seeing those happy young tourists and my even happier Bat Town citizens, so proud of their hard work and efforts, I thought to myself that this experience was truly a Roosevelt memory worth making, something the children will remember long after they've left these hallways for wider roads which beckon them to futures yet unknown. The efforts of all, and the small community we built together in room 116, will live in our memories, just as sweet old Roxaboxen lingered in the memories of those long ago children of the 1930s even "as the seasons changed and the years went by."

NOTES

1. Rod Stark, *Classroom City: A Simulation for Young Persons of Economics and Government in a Small American City, Grades 4–9* (El Cajon, CA: Interaction Publishers, 1995).
2. National Council for the Social Studies, *Expectations of Excellence: Curriculum Standards for Social Studies* (Washington, DC: Author, 1994). Time, Continuity, and Change is the second of the ten standards themes, and People, Places, and Environments is the third.
3. George Ella Lyon, *Who Came Down that Road?* (New York: Orchard Paperbacks, 1996).
4. Dyan Sheldon, *Under the Moon* (New York: Dial Books for Young Readers, 1994).
5. Bonnie Pryor, *The House on Maple Street* (New York: Mulberry Books, 1987).
6. Renata Von Tscharner, Ronald Lee Fleming and the Townscape Institute, "The Changing American Cityscape Poster Set," seven posters, portfolio, 32-page teaching guide (Palo Alto, CA: Dale Seymour Publications, 1996).
7. Alice McLerran, *Roxaboxen* (New York: Puffin Books, 1992).

Andrea McGann Keech teaches at Roosevelt Elementary School, Iowa City, Iowa.

QUESTIONS FOR REFLECTION

1. How does Keech use the concept of "community" to affect the community within her own classroom?
2. What kinds of media and artifacts did Keech use in her classroom to raise awareness of the community around the students at Roosevelt Elementary? What kinds of media or artifacts are around you that you could use to teach about the community in which you are located?
3. What kind of town was Bat Town, U.S.A.? How close was it to a *real* town and what kinds of lessons can the students in Keech's class take from their experience in Bat Town and apply to their real community?

LEARNING ACTIVITIES

Critical Thinking

1. What are the characteristics of learning experiences in the elementary curriculum that help children master the challenges that come with each stage of their development as human beings?
2. What are some of the challenges that children face today that were unknown or little known to their parents or grandparents? To what extent can (or should) these challenges be addressed in childhood education?
3. Reflect on your experiences as an elementary student. What curricular experiences enhanced your growth and development? Impeded your growth and development? What implications do your reflections have for your curriculum planning activities, regardless of the level of education which interests you most?

Application Activities

1. Invite a group of elementary-level teachers to your class and ask them to describe the steps they take in planning curricula for their students. What do they see as the most important curriculum criteria to use in planning?
2. Obtain a statement of philosophy (or mission statement) from a nearby elementary school. Analyze the statement in regard to the thirteen goals for childhood education presented in this chapter. How many of the goals are reflected in the statement?
3. Conduct a comparative survey, at ten-year intervals, of an education journal that addresses childhood education. Have there been any significant changes over the years in regard to curriculum-related issues and trends discussed in the journal? Among the journals to consider are *Child Development, Child Study Journal, Childhood Education, Children Today, Early Childhood Research Quarterly, Elementary*

School Journal, Exceptional Children, Gifted Child Quarterly, Gifted Child Today, International Journal of Early Childhood, Journal of Early Intervention, Journal of Research in Childhood Education, New Directions for Child Development, Teaching Exceptional Children, and *Young Children*.

Field Experiences

1. Interview a school psychologist, mental health worker, child protective services (CPS) worker, or similar individual to find out about the sources, signs, and treatment of psychosocial problems that can interfere with children's learning. Ask him or her to suggest ways that teachers can help students overcome these problems.
2. Visit a nearby elementary school and obtain permission to interview a few students about their curricular experiences. Take field notes based on these interviews. The following questions might serve as a guide for beginning your interviews: Do the students like school? What about it do they like and dislike? What are their favorite subjects? What about those subjects do they like? Then analyze your field notes; what themes or concerns emerge that would be useful to curriculum planners at this level?
3. Visit an agency in your community that offers services to children and their families. Ask a staff member to explain the services that are offered. Report your findings to the rest of your class.

Internet Activities

1. Go to the home page for the National Clearinghouse for Bilingual Education (NCBE) and gather information and resources on effective elementary-level programs for limited English proficiency (LEP) students. Also visit NCBE's page titled "School Reform and Student Diversity: Case Studies of Exemplary Practices for LEP Students"; from this location, "visit" several exemplary elementary schools and gather additional information and resources.
2. Go to the George Lucas Educational Foundation and gather curriculum resources and ideas relevant to your subject area and level of interest. For example, you may wish to examine the *Learn & Live* kit which contains a documentary film, hosted by Robin Williams, and a resource book that showcases innovative K–12 schools.
3. Go to one or more of the following professional organization websites dedicated to the education of young children and gather information, fact sheets, research results, resources, and publications of interest.

   Association for Childhood Education International (ACEI)
   Early Childhood Care and Development (ECCD)
   National Association for the Education of Young Children (NAEYC)
   Professional Association for Childhood Education (PACE)

9

1. What important developmental tasks confront students at the middle level?

2. How do middle-level students differ in their physical, social, psychological, and cognitive maturation?

3. What factors can threaten the healthy development of middle-level students?

4. What are some appropriate curricular goals for middle-level students?

5. How do educational programs organized around middle school concepts address the unique needs of students at the middle level?

Middle-Level Curricula

Middle-level students are *transescents*—that is, they are passing from childhood to early adolescence. In our society, transescence and early adolescence is a period from about age ten to age fifteen. Young people at this age must cope with a wide range of life stresses because they mature physically more quickly than they mature cognitively or socially. For example, the average age of menarche has dropped from sixteen years of age 150 years ago to twelve and one-half today; similarly, boys reach reproductive maturity at an earlier age. As a result, young people often do not have the social and emotional maturity to handle the freedoms and stressors that characterize our modern society.

MAJOR TRANSITIONS AND CRITICAL TURNING POINTS

Individual differences among students are greater during transescence and early adolescence than at other stages of life. There is a four-year range within each sex group from the time that the first significant fraction of the group attains puberty to the time that the last member of that sex reaches it. Generally, by the time they are twenty, both boys and girls have reached full physical growth and biological maturity. But social, psychological, and cognitive maturation are usually not in step with physical maturation. Many pressures in modern society tend to force the social, psychological, and cognitive changes of this period on the young person ahead of the biological.

As with any age group, it is important to consider the three bases of curriculum—social forces, human development, and learning and learning styles—when planning curricula for transescents and early adolescents. Toward this end, it may be helpful to review the perspectives on human development covered in Chapter 3's articles, which identify cultural, psychological, cognitive, and social factors that influence students' learning during this period. In "Teaming for Better School Climate and Improved Achievement" in this chapter, Luanne L. Kokolis explains how one junior high school reduced the "fear factor" for incoming seventh-grade students by using a teaming approach to make the environment more "school friendly" and "student focused."

Transescence and early adolescence are characterized by rapid physical growth, which is frequently uneven, with some parts of the body growing faster than others. As these physical developments occur, self-concepts must often be adjusted. Both boys and girls may go through periods where they are clumsy and awkward, only to become graceful and athletic as they become older. Since rapid growth requires a great deal of physical energy, children need plenty of food and sleep to maintain good health during this period. On many occasions, though, they may have excess energy that needs to be discharged through vigorous physical activity.

The physical changes that take place during this period are not the only changes that are occurring. In regard to Erik Erikson's eight-stage model for the human life cycle, identity versus identity confusion is the salient psychosocial crisis for early adolescents. During this time, early adolescents use new, more complex thinking abilities and begin to shape a sense of personal identity. Identity confusion can result, however, when the early adolescent is confronted with the variety of roles available to him or her.

Erikson's theory suggests that when early adolescents identify with a peer group, with their school, or with a cause beyond themselves, their sense of *fidelity*—the "virtue" of this stage—can be the "cornerstone of identity." During this stage, early adolescents are loyal and committed—in fortunate instances, they are motivated by growth-enhancing goals, aspirations, and dreams; in unfortunate instances, by people, causes, and lifestyles that alarm parents, teachers, and other adults in their lives.

Curriculum Leadership Strategy

Prior to developing curricula for middle-level students, conduct a series of focus-group interviews with students to identify their psychosocial concerns—what are their goals, aspirations, and dreams? In what ways can curricula address these concerns?

The transescent child who has looked to his or her family for care, affection, and guidance must begin to find independence in order to fulfill the developmental tasks of this period and to prepare for adulthood. They must learn to make decisions on their own and to accept the consequences of those decisions. Parents and teachers can facilitate the growth of early adolescents by praising their accomplishments and not over-dwelling on shortcomings, encouraging independence with appropriate limitations, and giving affection without expecting too much in return. In "Building Developmental Assets to Promote Success in School and in Life" in this chapter, Peter C. Scales and Judy Taccogna describe forty "developmental assets" that promote the growth and development of middle- and high-school level students. *External assets* "are the relationships and opportunities that surround young people with the support and situations that guide them to behave in healthy ways and make wise choices. *Internal assets* are those commitments, values, competencies, and self-perceptions that, when nurtured, provide the 'internal compass' that guides a young person's behavior and choices so that he or she becomes self-regulating."

Indeed, education can be a "turning point" in the lives of early adolescents: "early adolescence is the phase when young people begin to adopt behavior patterns in education . . . that can have lifelong consequences. At the same time, it is an age when, much like younger children, individuals still need special nurturing and adult guidance. For these reasons, early adolescence offers a unique window of opportunity to shape enduring patterns of healthy behavior" (Carnegie Council on Adolescent Development, 1995, p. 1). The same point, perhaps more compelling because it is in the language of her peers, is made by a sixteen-year-old named Sarah:

> I think that being a kid is the most important stage of your life. It's a time when you start to develop a personality. It's when you start to learn about who you are, and what you want to do with yourself. And it's a time when you develop trust. It's a time when you learn how to be a person in society. Unfortunately a lot of kids don't have that. If you don't grow up learning how to be a productive person, then you're going to have a problem once you grow up. (Carnegie Council on Adolescent Development, 1995, p. 2)

CURRICULAR GOALS FOR MIDDLE-LEVEL STUDENTS

The Carnegie Council on Adolescent Development asserts that there is a "volatile mismatch . . . between the organization and curriculum of middle grade schools and the intellectual and emotional needs of young adolescents" (Carnegie Council on Adolescent Development, 1989, p. 2). The "mismatch" is reflected in the number of today's parents who are "revolting" against the increasing amounts of homework assigned their children (see David Skinner's "The Homework Wars" in this chapter). Pressure to achieve academically, these parents maintain, increases the likelihood that children's emotional and social needs will be overlooked. Similarly, in this chapter's *Case Study in Curriculum Implementation* section, Donald E. Larsen and Tariq T. Akmal suggest that academic achievement in schools can be overemphasized. In "Intentional Curriculum Planning in an Age of Accountability: Explorer Middle School's Approach," they present a case study of a school that, while it has yet to meet the academic requirements of No Child Left Behind, is nonetheless a "rich, vibrant school" that is improving students' lives.

What, then, should be the goals of educational programs for middle-level students? Many goals might be suggested—some derived from social forces, some from theories of human development, and some from theories of learning and learning styles. The list would surely include helping learners to:

1. Build self-esteem and a strong sense of identity, competence, and responsibility
2. Understand and adjust to the physical changes they are experiencing
3. Deal with wider social experiences and new social arrangements
4. Explore different areas of knowledge and skill to help determine potential interests
5. Make the transition between childhood education and education for middle adolescents and prepare for the eventual transition to senior high school

6. Deal with value questions that arise because of their developing cognitive abilities, their growing need for independence, and rapid changes in society

7. Cope with social pressures from some of their peers to engage in risk-taking behaviors

8. Develop concern for the environment, the local and global communities, and the welfare of others

In addition to these eight goals, "This We Believe: Successful Schools for Young Adolescents" in this chapter presents the cultural, curricular, and instructional elements the National Middle School Association has identified as characteristic of effective middle schools.

Curriculum Leadership Strategy

Review with teachers the National Middle School Association's position paper on successful schools for young adolescents. Create a team of teacher leaders to develop and implement a series of in-service activities for teachers based on the association's recommendations.

DEVELOPMENT OF THE MIDDLE SCHOOL

A major issue for transescents and early adolescents is whether their education is best provided in a junior high school, a middle school, or some other form of school organization. During the 1950s and 1960s, dissatisfaction with junior high schools became evident as many people pointed out that junior high schools were "scaled-down" versions of high schools, complete with departmentalization, extensive athletic programs, and age-inappropriate social activities. Junior high schools, it was felt, were not providing students with a satisfactory transition into the high school, nor were they meeting the unique needs of early adolescents.

During the early 1960s, an organizational framework for a "school in the middle" was introduced. The new middle school arrangement called for moving the ninth grade into the high school, placing grades 5–8 in the middle school, and developing curricula to meet the needs of 10 to 14 year olds. By 1970, almost 2,500 middle schools had been created, and by 1990 this number had increased to almost 15,000 (George, 1993).

At first, middle schools were quite different from junior high schools—often, middle schools had more interdisciplinary, exploratory curricula; team teaching; teacher/advisor programs; flexible scheduling; smaller athletic programs; and less ability grouping. Today, the distinctions between junior high schools and middle schools have become somewhat blurred, and many innovative practices initially developed to meet the needs of students in middle schools have been incorporated in junior high schools as well.

Evidence to support the effectiveness of middle school concepts—whether they were part of middle-level or junior high programs—accumulated as the middle school movement expanded during the 1970s and 1980s. The August 1985 issue of *Middle*

School Journal presented the results of a major study of "schools in the middle" (grades 5–9), which found that most of the "effective schools" in the study were organized in 6–7–8 or 5–6–7–8 grade patterns. Moreover, principals of these schools were knowledgeable about middle-level programs and research, and they evidenced familiarity with block scheduling, interdisciplinary teaming, cocurricula programs, learning styles, teacher/advisor programs, and developmental age grouping.

Currently, the well-documented effectiveness of educational programs organized around middle school concepts is having a positive influence on schooling at other levels. For example, in this chapter's *Case Study in Curriculum Implementation* article, "Intentional Curriculum Planning in an Age of Accountability: Explorer Middle School's Approach," Donald E. Larsen and Tariq T. Akmal identify three critical elements of school effectiveness at all grade levels: "school-wide leadership whose moral purpose is manifested in a vision for intentional improvement, a web of caring and personal relationships, and ongoing planning guided by relevant data." Nevertheless, the debate about the appropriateness of schools in the middle continues—as evidenced by two contrasting articles in this chapter: "Mayhem in the Middle: Why We Should Shift to K–8," by Cheri Pierson Yecke, and "Guess Again: Will Changing the Grades Save Middle-Level Education?" by James Beane and Richard Lipka.

REFERENCES

Carnegie Council on Adolescent Development. *Great Transitions: Preparing Adolescents for a New Century,* abridged version. New York: Carnegie Council on Adolescent Development, Carnegie Corporation of New York, 1995.

Carnegie Council on Adolescent Development. *Turning Points: Preparing American Youth for the 21st Century.* Carnegie Council on Adolescent Development, Carnegie Corporation of New York, 1989.

George, Paul. "The Middle School Movement: A State-of-the-Art Report and a Glimpse Into the Future." In Glen Hass and Forrest W. Parkay, eds., *Curriculum Planning: A New Approach* (6th ed.). Boston: Allyn and Bacon, 1993, pp. 446–455.

This We Believe: Successful Schools for Young Adolescents

**NATIONAL MIDDLE
SCHOOL ASSOCIATION**

ABSTRACT: Since its inception in 1973, the National Middle School Association (NMSA) has been a voice for those committed to the educational and developmental needs of young adolescents. NMSA is the only national education association dedicated exclusively to those in the middle-level grades. This article, adapted from the NMSA executive summary "This We Believe: Successful Schools for Young Adolescents" and "NMSA's Position Statement on Curriculum, Instruction, and Assessment," presents the central features of those two landmark position papers in which the association's vision for successful schools for 10 to 15 year olds is delineated. The most profound and enduring lesson learned in thirty years of active middle school advocacy is that the fourteen characteristics are interdependent and must be implemented in concert. Research and cumulative empirical evidence have confirmed that these characteristics when present over time lead to higher levels of student achievement and overall development.

Every day, twenty million diverse, rapidly changing 10- to 15-year-olds enrolled in our nation's middle level schools are making critical and complex life choices. They are forming the attitudes, values, and habits of mind that will largely direct their behavior as adults. They deserve schools that support them fully during this key phase of life.

For middle schools to be successful, their students must be successful; for students to be successful, the school's organization, curriculum, pedagogy, and programs must be based upon the developmental readiness, needs, and interests of young adolescents. This concept is at the heart of middle level education.

The association's vision for a successful middle school is primarily delineated in 14 characteristics. Eight are facets of the culture of such schools, while six are programmatic characteristics that can evolve in such a culture. While presented as a list, the most profound and enduring lesson learned in 30 years of active middle school advocacy is that the characteristics are interdependent and must be implemented in concert. Research and cumulative, empirical evidence have confirmed that these characteristics when present over time lead to higher levels of student achievement and overall development.

National Middle School Association believes successful schools for young adolescents are characterized by a culture that includes

- **Educators who value working with this age group and are prepared to do so.** Effective middle level educators understand the developmental uniqueness of the age group, the curriculum they teach, and effective learning and assessment strategies. They need specific teacher preparation before entering the classroom and continuous professional development as they pursue their careers.

- **Courageous, collaborative leadership.** Middle level leaders understand adolescents, the society, and the theory and practice of middle level education. As the prime determiner of the school culture, the principal influences student achievement and teacher effectiveness by advocating, nurturing, and sustaining an effective instructional program.

- **A shared vision that guides decisions.** All decisions made about the school should be guided by a shared vision and the mission statement derived from it.

- **An inviting, supportive, and safe environment.** A successful school is an inviting, supportive, and safe place, a joyful community that promotes in-depth learning and enhances students' physical and emotional well-being. In such a school, human relationships are paramount.

- **High expectations for every member of the learning community.** Educators and students hold themselves and each other to high expectations. Such confidence promotes positive attitudes and behaviors and motivates students to tackle challenging learning activities. Successful schools recognize that young adolescents are capable of far more than adults often assume.

- **Students and teachers engaged in active learning.** The most successful learning strategies are ones that involve each student personally. When students routinely assume the role of teacher, and teachers demonstrate that they are still learners, a genuine learning community is present.

- **An adult advocate for every student.** Academic success and personal growth increase markedly when voting adolescents' affective needs are met. All adults in successful middle level schools are advocates, advisors, and mentors.

- **School-initiated family and community partnerships.** Successful middle schools promote family involvement and take the initiative to develop needed home-school bonds. The involvement of family is linked to higher levels of student achievement and improved student behavior.

Therefore, successful schools for young adolescents provide

- **Curriculum that is relevant, challenging, integrative, and exploratory.** An effective curriculum is based on criteria of high quality and includes learning activities that create opportunities for students to pose and answer questions that are important to them. Such a curriculum provides direction for what young adolescents should know and be able to do and helps them achieve the attitudes and behaviors needed for a full, productive, and satisfying life.

- **Multiple learning and teaching approaches that respond to their diversity.** Since young adolescents learn best through engagement and interaction, learning strategies involve students in dialogue with teachers and with one another. Teaching approaches should enhance and accommodate the diverse skills, abilities, and prior knowledge of young adolescents, and draw upon students' individual learning styles.

- **Assessment and evaluation programs that promote quality learning.** Continuous, authentic, and appropriate assessment and evaluation measures provide evidence about every student's learning progress. Grades alone are inadequate expressions for assessing the many goals of middle level education.

- **Organizational structures that support meaningful relationships and learning.** The interdisciplinary team of two to four teachers working with a common group of students is the building block for a strong learning community with its sense of family, where students and teachers know one another well, feel safe and supported, and are encouraged to take intellectual risks.

- **School-wide efforts and policies that foster health, wellness, and safety.** A school that fosters physical and psychological safety strives to build resiliency in young people by maintaining an environment in which peaceful and safe interactions are expected and supported by written policies, scheduled professional development, and student-focused activities.

- **Multifaceted guidance and support services.** Developmentally responsive middle level schools provide both teachers and specialized professionals who are readily available to offer the assistance many students need in negotiating their lives both in and out of school.

National Middle School Association fully recognizes the challenges inherent in attempts to develop curriculum, instruction, and assessment that respect and meet the distinct learning and developmental needs of young adolescents. Like elementary and high schools, middle schools must respond to local, state, and federal standards; manage growing diversity among students in a complex society; and balance effective learning practices with high-stakes accountability. In addition to these demands, designing learning activities for middle school students requires tailoring curriculum, instruction, and assessment to the variable characteristics of 10- to 15-year-old learners who are actively involved in maturing as well as in learning.

Meeting the challenges of designing engaging learning opportunities for young adolescent students does not mean and has never meant that middle schools shy away from challenging content in favor of making students feel good about themselves. Nor does it mean that classroom activities are all "fun" and devoid of any real learning. Instead, it means that middle school curriculum must be relevant, challenging, integrative, and exploratory in a climate of high expectations. Instruction has to embrace multiple teaching approaches and assessment measures.

Middle Level Curriculum

A *relevant* curriculum enables "students to pursue answers to questions they have about themselves, content, and the world." Relevant learning opportunities

- Immerse students in rich and significant content knowledge.
- Lead students to demonstrate higher levels of learning and understanding.
- Include students' questions, ideas, and concerns.
- Expand the learning community beyond the school.
- Allow young adolescents to study concepts and skills in areas of interest.

A *challenging* curriculum targets state and national standards, actively engages young adolescents in substantive issues, "and increasingly enables students to assume control of their own learning." Challenging learning opportunities

- Move beyond covering content and rote learning activities.

- Help students become skilled writers, thinkers, and researchers.
- Engage students in demanding problem solving activities.
- Explore how and why things happen.
- Examine assumptions, principles, and alternative points of view.

An *integrative* curriculum focuses on coherent ideas and concepts irrespective of arbitrary subject boundaries and enables students to see connections and real-world applications. Integrative learning opportunities

- Engage students in rigorous, in-depth study.
- Address reading, writing, and other fundamental skills within all subject areas.
- Enhance critical thinking, decision-making, and creativity.
- Require students to reflect on their learning experiences.
- Enable students to apply content and skills to their daily lives.

An *exploratory* curriculum directly reflects the curious, adventuresome nature of young adolescents. Exploration is not a classification of content; rather, it is an attitude and approach to all curriculum and instruction. Exploratory learning opportunities

- Broaden students' views of themselves and the world.
- Help students discover their interests and aptitudes.
- Assist students with career exploration and decisions about their futures.
- Contribute to the development of well-rounded, self-sufficient citizens.
- Open doors to new ideas and areas to investigate.

Middle Level Instruction

Instruction brings curriculum to life. The distinct learning characteristics of young adolescents provide the foundation for selecting learning and teaching strategies, just as they do for designing curriculum. Learning approaches in middle schools should

- Augment the skills, abilities, and prior knowledge of young adolescents.
- Cultivate multiple intelligences and students' individual learning styles.
- Offer students choices in how best to learn.
- Involve students in establishing and assessing personal goals.
- Help students acquire various ways of posing and answering questions.
- Include both student-centered and teacher-directed strategies.
- Emphasize collaboration among teachers.
- Utilize varying forms of group work and cooperative activities.
- Involve families and utilize community resources.
- Incorporate technology in the learning process.

Middle Level Assessment

A continuous, authentic, and appropriate assessment program provides many evidences of students' progress in meeting their curricular goals or objectives. Assessment strategies should honor the learning characteristics of young adolescents and increasingly de-emphasize competitive comparisons with other students. Such programs

- Document students' mastery of both essential knowledge and skills.
- Assess critical thinking, independence, responsibility, and related behavioral traits.
- Offer students' choices in how best to demonstrate their learning specify assessment criteria in advance and incorporate examples of quality work as models.
- Include a variety of formats such as journals, portfolios, demonstrations, publications, and multimedia presentations so student learnings can be shared with others.
- Inform and involve families in the assessment program.
- Provide teachers with data for planning instruction.

Moving Middle Level Curriculum, Instruction, and Assessment Forward

Some elements of effective middle grades education, such as organizing teams, have taken hold in schools across the country. Making changes in curriculum, instruction, and assessment, however, has been more difficult. Despite expanding research and improved understanding of how best to educate 10- to 15-year-olds, curricular and instructional aspects of middle schools have tended to follow traditional secondary practices. Teachers and school leaders, with the support of parents and families, must implement non-traditional practices to adequately address the learning needs of middle level students.

Classroom teachers should

1. Establish learner-centered classrooms that encourage and honor student voice.
2. Develop standards-based curricula that integrate subject area disciplines along with students' concerns and questions.
3. Design instruction to meet the diverse needs of every student.
4. Measure student progress and development with a variety of authentic assessments.
5. Guide students in discovering their aptitudes and interests.

School leaders should

1. Lead in creating a shared vision focused on the needs of young adolescent students.
2. Establish ongoing, school-based professional development that deals with teachers' identified needs.
3. Provide organizational structures that enable teachers and students to develop collaboratively relevant, challenging, integrative, and exploratory curricula.
4. Expect teachers to use a variety of student-centered instructional approaches that meet the individual needs of students.
5. Hold teachers accountable for using multiple and varied assessments that measure continuous student progress.

Parents and families should

1. Understand their child's individual strengths, weaknesses, interests, aptitudes, and talents.
2. Insist that schools and teachers address the learning needs of their 10- to 15-year-old.
3. Work with schools and teachers to establish appropriate learning outcomes for their child.
4. Expect teachers to use a variety of instructional strategies and assessment methods in their classrooms.
5. Engage in the learning process by attending classroom events, conferences, and other school activities.

Conclusion

The middle level curriculum needed for today's young adolescents is complex. Criteria of high quality call for both depth and breadth as well as the inculcation of habits of mind that will equip youth to be productive citizens and lifelong learners. Instructional and assessment practices used in implementing such a curriculum must be imaginative, varied, and involve the students in all phases. Strong leadership that understands fully the challenges middle schools face in fulfilling their heavy and distinctive responsibilities is essential all the way from the central office to the classroom.

Since its inception in 1973, the *National Middle School Association* (NMSA) has been a voice for those committed to the educational and developmental needs of young adolescents. NMSA is the only national education association dedicated exclusively to those in the middle level grades. With over 30,000 members representing principals, teachers, central office personnel, professors, college students, parents, community leaders, and educational consultants across the United States, Canada, and 46 other countries, NMSA (nmsa.org) welcomes and provides support to anyone interested in the health and education of young adolescents.

QUESTIONS FOR REFLECTION

1. What does the National Middle School Association believe is at the heart of successful middle-level education in the US? How are their recommendations different than what you might expect to read from associations that represent other grade levels?
2. In what ways could you imagine taking the general principles outlined in this article and apply them in the educational setting most familiar to you? What challenges might you confront?
3. NMSA calls for a middle school curriculum that is "relevant, challenging, integrative, and exploratory in a climate of high expectations." How does a teacher leader or other educational leader ensure this is happening in today's middle schools? What strategies might a leader employ to cover these four features of the middle-level curriculum?

Mayhem in the Middle: Why We Should Shift to K–8

CHERI PIERSON YECKE

ABSTRACT: Middle schools are increasingly switching to the K–8 model to improve student achievement. In this article, Yecke discusses the merits of such a change and the evidence that such change works. She also presents ten strategies that can help ease the transition, including her belief that adding higher grades, rather than lower, is critical as is ensuring grade-level balance, involving parents, and modifying facilities to smooth the transition.

In early 2005, the National Governors Association convened an education summit to address the dismal state of U.S. high schools. Nearly one-third of students eventually drop out, which annually costs the U.S. economy an estimated $16 billion in lost productivity. Although well intended, the solutions that many governors offered at the summit misidentified the cause of "high school" problems. Abundant evidence indicates that the seeds that produce high school failure are sown in grades 5–8 (National Center for Education Statistics, 2000). In far too many cases, U.S. middle schools are where student academic achievement goes to die.

As measured by international comparisons, such as the Trends in International Mathematics and Science Study (TIMSS), the achievement of U.S. students begins to plummet in middle school. And, as countless teachers and parents will attest, contemporary middle schools have become places where discipline is often lax and intermittent. Too many educators view middle school as an environment in which little is expected of students, either academically or behaviorally, on the assumption that students must place self-discipline and high academic expectations on hold until the hormone-driven storms of early adolescence have passed.

But if surging hormones truly drive middle school students' supposed lack of capacity to focus on academics, why does this phenomenon strike only in the United States? Other countries don't experience a similar decline in achievement at these grades. Something else is driving this precipitous drop in achievement. I propose that it is the anti-intellectualism inherent to the middle school concept.

To understand, we need to differentiate between *middle schools* and the *middle school concept*. Middle schools are simply organizational groupings, generally containing grades 6, 7, and 8. The middle school concept, on the other hand, is the belief that the purpose of these schools is to create students who are imbued with egalitarian principles; who are in touch with their political, social, and psychological selves; and who eschew competition and individual achievement to focus on identity development and perceived societal needs (Gallagher, 1991; Sicola, 1990; Toepfer, 1992). Although many U.S. middle schools are flourishing with strong and rigorous academic programs, the middle school concept—the notion that middle schools should be havens of socialization and not academies of knowledge—has wrought havoc on the intellectual development of many middle school students.

As any reform-minded superintendent or courageous middle school principal may tell you, reclaiming middle-grades schools from the clutches of the middle school concept has not been an easy task. In fact, this goal has been so elusive in some districts that the only alternative has been to eliminate the middle school grade configuration altogether, returning instead to the K–8 model.

Several urban school districts, such as Baltimore, Maryland, and Philadelphia, Pennsylvania, are now abandoning both the middle school concept and middle schools. By 2008, the number of K–8 schools in Philadelphia will have increased from 61 to 130. Baltimore has opened 30 K–8 schools in the last few years. Districts like Brookline, Massachusetts, and Cincinnati, Ohio, are now exclusively K–8. The goal for these districts is the same: to increase academic achievement and create an atmosphere more conducive to learning (Chaker, 2005).

WHY K–8?

Although many U.S. educators embraced the middle school concept during the 1970s, 1980s, and 1990s, some educators refused to jump on the bandwagon. As a result, parents, teachers, and administrators at many schools that remained K–8 discovered anecdotally that their students demonstrated fewer behavioral problems and higher academic achievement than many students enrolled in middle schools.

School district leaders in Milwaukee, Wisconsin, Baltimore, and Philadelphia wanted to determine whether they could verify these anecdotal observations through research. The studies they undertook convinced them to accelerate a shift to the K–8 model in their districts.

The Milwaukee Study

Researchers in Milwaukee conducted a longitudinal analysis of 924 Milwaukee students who either attended K–8 schools or attended K–6 elementary schools and then proceeded to a middle school for 7th and 8th grade (Simmons & Blyth, 1987). The study controlled for race, ethnicity, teacher-student ratios, and levels of teacher education.

The researchers found that the students in the K–8 schools had higher academic achievement as measured by both grade point averages and standardized test scores, especially in math. These students also participated more in extracurricular activities, demonstrated greater leadership skills, and were less likely to be bullied than those

following the elementary/middle school track. The authors concluded that the intimacy of the K–8 environment and the delay of the transition to a new school until students were more mature may have accounted for the discrepancy.

The Baltimore Study

In Baltimore, researchers undertook a longitudinal study of two cohorts of students: 2,464 students who attended K–5 schools and then went on to middle schools, and 407 students who attended K–8 schools (Baltimore City Schools, 2001). After controlling for baseline achievement, the researchers found that the students in the K–8 schools scored much higher than their middle school counterparts on standardized achievement measures in reading, language arts, and math. The students in the K–8 schools were also more likely to pass the required state tests in math. Further, more than 70 percent of the K–8 students were admitted into Baltimore's most competitive high schools, compared with only 54 percent of students from the middle schools (Baltimore City Schools, 2001).

The Philadelphia Study

Philadelphia carried its examination of the achievement of students progressing through either K–8 or middle schools into high school to determine whether academic gains or losses from either model were sustained over time. After controlling for student background, researchers analyzed achievement data from approximately 40 K–8 schools and 40 middle schools.

The analysis showed that the students in the K–8 schools had higher academic achievement than those in the middle schools and that their academic gains surpassed those of the middle school students in reading and science, with statistically higher gains in math (Offenberg, 2001).

Eleven percent more students from the K–8 schools were accepted into the most challenging high schools. Moreover, once in high school, the grade point averages of students who had attended K–8 schools were higher than those of former middle school students. Offenberg concluded, "As a group, K–8 schools are more effective than middle-grades schools serving similar communities" (2001, p. 28).

The study noted that one factor possibly contributing to these differences is the number of students at a specific grade level. Although a K–8 school and a middle school might have the same total number of students, they are spread over more grades in the K–8 school, reducing the number of students in each grade. Offenberg's report suggests that as the number of students in a given grade increases, performance gains decrease.

TEN STRATEGIES FOR TRANSITION

I conducted site visits in all three school districts—Milwaukee, Baltimore, and Philadelphia—to see how the K–8 model was working and to gather advice for those interested in making the transition to the K–8 model. I selected one school in each district to visit on the basis of the school's ethnic diversity. The schools serve low-income urban students; each school faces its own demographic challenges. All three schools came to the K–8 model by a different route.

Humboldt Park K–8 School in Milwaukee shifted from K–5 to K–8 a few years ago. Its student population is notably diverse. Approximately 35 percent of students are Hmong, 30 percent are white, 15 percent are Hispanic, and 15 percent are black. Hamilton Elementary/Middle School in Baltimore has been a K–8 school for more than 20 years; its student body is 75 percent black. The Julia de Burgos School in Philadelphia, originally a 6–8 middle school, expanded downward to add grades K–5; its student body is 89 percent Hispanic.

In all three schools, staff and administrators were commuted to meeting the needs of underprivileged students and believed that they could best accomplish this in a K–8 setting. Their advice, along with feedback from students and parents, suggests 10 strategies that can ease the transition to a K–8 model.

Strategy 1: Include parents in the process.

To ensure the success of the K–8 model, parents should participate in all aspects of the planning process. Policy decisions concerning such varied issues as curriculum, dress code, and behavioral expectations call for parental input. The most academically successful school that I visited, Humboldt Park K–8 School in Milwaukee, also has the most active and organized parents. Parents initiated the move to transition Humboldt Park into a charter school because they were concerned that district policies might undermine the school's academic program. This high level of engagement was not a reflection of higher socioeconomic status: 70 percent of students at Humboldt Park come from low-income homes.

Strategy 2: Add higher rather than lower grades.

Incrementally adding higher grades to shift an elementary school to a K–8 school appears to be a smoother process than adding lower grades to a middle school. This approach seems to minimize grade-level imbalances and necessitate fewer building modifications. Faculty members at Humboldt Park unanimously agreed that when adding grades 6, 7, and 8, schools should add only one grade each year. This gives time for students, faculty, support staff, and administration to adjust.

Strategy 3: Ensure grade-level balance.

Attaining demographic balance among the various grade levels should be a priority. Having too many older or younger students means that the needs of the dominant group can drive school policies and set the school tone. For example, one schoolwide policy limited bathroom passes because some of the middle-grades students used them to roam the halls. However, because younger students tend to use the bathroom more frequently than older students do, lower-grades teachers challenged this policy.

If transition logistics require a temporary imbalance, schools should ensure that staff members are aware of the undue weight that the overrepresented grades might bring to a school and remind them that the imbalance is only temporary.

Strategy 4: Make 6th grade a transition year.

Moving from the elementary to the upper-grades section of the school requires students to become familiar with a different location and learn rules that often give them greater freedom. Because this change usually occurs in 6th grade, it would be helpful to provide flexibility as students make the transition. Retaining some elements of the elementary school—such as recess, classroom learning centers, or walking in lines during classroom changes—may help 6th grade function as a bridge between the elementary and middle grades.

Strategy 5: Establish a strict transfer policy.

District officials need to acknowledge the challenges that transfer students bring to schools. Involuntary transfers are harder for schools to deal with and typically occur when the district administration decides to relocate students who have had difficulties elsewhere. Philadelphia wisely handles this issue through an alternative program that accommodates students with the most serious discipline problems. Baltimore has no such program in place, leaving staff members and faculty frustrated as they struggle to balance teaching students who do not have serious behavior problems with rehabilitating those who do.

Voluntary transfers present other challenges. Students who arrive from schools that have less structure and lower academic standards might find the transition to a challenging K–8 setting difficult. Humboldt Park addresses this issue by requiring mandatory after-school lessons to help transfer students catch up. Schools can also provide an opportunity for students to receive remediation in the summer before the school year starts. Either way, schools should establish a policy that helps transfer students adjust to the level of work required.

Strategy 6: Modify facilities.

A school transitioning into a K–8 structure may need to make certain physical modifications to adapt its facility to students of various ages. For example, elementary schools adding middle grades will need to add computers in the library and include books appropriate for middle-grades students. If the library has limited space, the school may need to create a separate computer lab. The school might also consider adding lockers for older students or building a more advanced science lab. For any newly K–8 school, the cafeteria will most likely require scheduling changes and menu revisions to adapt to an influx of older or younger students. Moreover, making the transition from a middle school to a K–8 school entails creating centers and "nooks" in primary classrooms and modifying restrooms by lowering toilets and sinks.

In addition, designating a separate building wing for the upper grades provides older students with some time on their own and reduces unsupervised interactions with younger students. Humboldt Park in Milwaukee does a good job of this. In contrast, Philadelphia's Julia de Burgos School, which of the three schools observed had the least separation among its students, reported the most challenges with interactions between older and younger students.

Strategy 7: Have high expectations for both academics and behavior.

High academic achievement rarely happens in an undisciplined environment. Of the schools I visited, Baltimore's Hamilton had the most behavior problems. This was also the only school in which student achievement declined in the upper grades. In contrast, Milwaukee's Humboldt Park had the strictest discipline policy. There, 75 percent of students leave kindergarten reading at the 2nd grade level.

Policies establishing academic and behavioral norms—such as consistent expectations regarding homework or dress code—will set the K–8 school's tone for years to come, and parents should be involved in drafting them. Behavioral expectations don't need to be uniform throughout the school. Schools should provide some flexibility for upper-grades students, giving them greater freedom and responsibility as they prepare to transition to high school. For example, most K–8 schools allow upper-grades students to change classes independently as opposed to walking in lines.

Strategy 8: Decide on the academic approach.

The schools that I visited in Baltimore and Milwaukee organize their upper-grades teachers by academic department. The teachers at Julia de Burgos School in Philadelphia initially sought that structure but now prefer the self-contained approach.

The self-contained model, in which students stay with the same teacher for the core subjects of reading, math, science, and social studies, appears to foster better teacher-student relationships and a more nurturing environment. But it also means that teachers must prepare for four subjects instead of one, and it may force them into unfamiliar fields in which they have received no specialized training. The departmentalized setting, in which each teacher is a specialist in one or more areas, is more likely to produce higher academic achievement but provides fewer opportunities to counsel and mentor students.

It is fairly well established that strong subject-area knowledge in teachers correlates with higher student achievement (Whitehurst, 2002). It is therefore unfortunate that in 2004, half of Philadelphia's middle-level teachers failed exams assessing their content knowledge (Snyder & Mezzacappa, 2004). Although colleges of education might bear some of the blame, these gaps might also reflect a shift away from academics that has characterized much of the middle school movement's troubled history.

U.S. middle-level teachers with subject-specific certificates appear to be a dying breed. In 1980, 80 percent of middle-level teachers held subject-specific certificates, but that number had dropped to 52 percent by 2000 (Clark, Petzko, Lucas, & Valentine, 2001). One study shows that during the 1999–2000 school year, alarming percentages of middle-grades teachers lacked a college major or certification in the areas in which they taught: 58 percent lacked a major or certification in English, 57 percent in science, 69 percent in math, 71 percent in history, and 93 percent in physical science (National Center for Education Statistics, 2002). Another recent study found that only 22 percent of middle school math teachers surveyed indicated that they had majored in math, and fewer than half had a teaching certificate in that subject (Loveless, 2004).

K–8 planners need to find the right balance. A truly compassionate education cannot allow the desire for a nurturing environment to trump access to a rigorous, well-taught curriculum.

Strategy 9: Provide greater access to advanced courses and electives.

Because the upper grades have fewer students, K–8 schools have difficulty offering advanced subjects—such as foreign language classes or advanced math—that can enrich a curriculum. However, schools should not deny challenging academic opportunities to their students because of their particular grade configuration. One solution is to work collaboratively with other K–8 schools in the district, or even with the local high school, to have itinerant teachers come to the school to offer such classes. This may require some flexibility in scheduling. Another option might involve distance learning.

Above all, students need access to higher levels of math. A study from the U.S. Department of Education found that the academic intensity and quality of a student's high school curriculum were the most important factors in determining whether students completed a bachelor degree (Adelman, 1999). Students cannot take rigorous courses in high school—especially advanced math courses—if they have not prepared themselves for this challenging work in their middle grades.

Strategy 10: Provide greater access to extracurricular opportunities.

With a larger student body in a given age group, middle schools can offer band, choir, and sports activities to a degree that K–8 schools cannot. However, several K–8 schools working together might field a team or create a band or choir. Schools could also coordinate extracurricular activities after school for all students in grades 6, 7, and 8, regardless of whether they attend a K–8 school or a middle school.

A number of districts—even those on the cutting edge of the K–8 movement—are guilty of lumping K–8 schools with elementary schools in various administrative funding classifications. This practice often rules out funding for extracurricular activities.

MOVING FORWARD

The K–8 model is no silver bullet for middle school reform, but it deserves consideration. In this era of flexible education options, K–8 schools and middle schools can coexist—provided that middle schools embrace standards and accountability.

C. S. Lewis once wrote.

> If you are on the wrong road, progress means doing an about-turn and walking back to the right road; and in that case, the man who turns back soonest is the most progressive man. Going back is the quickest way on. (1943)

This summarizes the key strategy for undoing the damage that the middle school concept has done to U.S. education: We must *go back* to find scientifically based research that reveals the strengths or weaknesses of specific education practices, *go back* to proven methodologies, and *go back* to parents and empathetically listen to their concerns.

The key to renewing middle-grades education in the United States is to treat it as education rather than as personal adjustment. That means having high academic standards, a coherent curriculum, effective instruction, strong leadership, results-based accountability, and sound discipline. That formula has begun to pay off in the primary grades. It can pay off in the middle grades as well.

REFERENCES

Adelman, C. (1999). *Answers in the toolbox: Academic intensity, attendance patterns, and bachelor's degree attainment*. Washington, DC: U.S. Department of Education.

Baltimore City Schools, Division of Research, Evaluation, and Accountability. (2001). *An examination of K–5, 6–8 versus K–8 grade configurations*. Baltimore: Author.

Chaker, A. M. (2005, April 6). Middle school goes out of fashion. *The Wall Street Journal*.

Clark, D., Petzko, V., Lucas, S., & Valentine, J. (2001, Nov. 1). *Research findings from the 2000 National Study of Leadership in Middle Level Schools*. Paper presented at the National Middle School Association annual conference, Washington, DC.

Gallagher, J. J. (1991). Education reform, values, and gifted students. *Gifted Child Quarterly, 35*(1).

Lewis, C. S. (2001). *Mere Christianity* (Book One, Chapter Five) (rev. ed.). New York: HarperCollins.

Loveless, T. (2004, November). *The 2004 Brown Center Report on American Education: How well are American students learning?* Washington, DC: The Brookings Institution.

National Center for Education Statistics. (2000). *Mathematics and science education in the eighth grade: Findings from the Third International Mathematics and Science Study*. Washington, DC: Author.

National Center for Education Statistics. (2002). *Qualifications of the public school teacher workforce: Prevalence of out-of-field teaching 1937–88 to 1999–2000*. Washington, DC: Author.

Offenberg, R. M. (2001). The efficacy of Philadelphia's K-to-8 schools compared to middle grades schools. *Middle School Journal, 32*(4), 23–29.

Sicola, P. K. (1990). Where do gifted students fit? *Journal for the Education of the Gifted, 14*(1).

Simmons, R., & Blyth, D. (1987). *Moving into adolescence: The impact of pubertal change and school context*. New York: Aldine de Gruyter.

Snyder, S., & Mezzacappa, D. (2004, March 23). Teachers come up short in testing. *Philadelphia Inquirer.*

Toepfer, C. F. (1992). Middle level school curriculum: Defining the elusive. In J. L. Irvin (Ed.), *Transforming middle-level education: Perspectives and possibilities.* Needham Heights, MA: Allyn and Bacon.

Whitehurst, G. J. (2002, March 5). *Research on teacher preparation and professional development.* Speech presented at the White House Conference on Preparing Tomorrow's Teachers. Available: www.ed.gov/admins/tchrqual/learn/preparingteachers conference/whitehurst.html

Cheri Pierson Yecke is chancellor of K–12 Public Schools for the Florida Department of Education and the author of two studies on the need for middle school reform: *The War Against Excellence: The Rising Tide of Mediocrity in America's Middle Schools* and *Mayhem in the Middle: How Middle Schools Have Failed America—And How to Make Them Work.*

QUESTIONS FOR REFLECTION

1. Do you think the current middle school model is broken? Should districts consider shifting from K–5 and 6–8 grade-level groupings to K–8 models? Why or why not?
2. What are the advantages and disadvantages of eliminating the middle school levels? How might the disadvantages be overcome in shifting to K–8 schooling?
3. Imagine that you are a member of a middle-level teaching team that would like to see your district shift from a K–5 and 6–8 model to a K–8 model. How would you proceed?

Guess Again: Will Changing the Grades Save Middle-Level Education?

JAMES BEANE
RICHARD LIPKA

ABSTRACT: *Blaming unsatisfactory student achievement on the middle school concept, argue Beane and Lipka, is a case of mistaken identity. Too many middle schools have failed to fully implement the middle school concept and educators need to look beyond grade configuration to the real problems plaguing middle schools. Although many large school districts in the country are thinking of returning grades 6–8 to the elementary school, the authors maintain that the solution to unsatisfactory school performance lies in creating a challenging curriculum, pushing for structures that support high-quality relationships, finding ways to reach out to families and communities, and addressing the systemic issue of poverty.*

Judging by some recent newspaper headlines, middle schools in the United States are once again under attack: "Mayhem in the Middle," "Are Middle Schools Bad for Kids?" and "Muddle in the Middle," we read. Middle schools have been accused of everything from stunting students' academic growth to ruining their self esteem. What's going on here?

Policymakers and the public have always had an uneasy relationship with middle schools, just as they have had with young adolescents themselves. No one seems to know quite what to do with either one. No wonder, then, that the history of middle schools has been a roller coaster of reform, in the latest dip, school officials in several large urban areas, such as Baltimore, Maryland, and Philadelphia, Pennsylvania, beleaguered by poor test scores and unmanageable student behavior, have decided to abandon 5–8 and 6–8 grade arrangements and return to K–8 schools. As a result, the media and middle school critics have gleefully declared middle schools a failure. That obituary comes as something of a surprise to many middle-level educators who thought their work was headed in a healthier direction. Could they have been so wrong?

THE MIDDLE SCHOOL CONCEPT

In the midst of all these ups and downs, middle-level education has been the subject of considerable research. Between 1991 and 2003, more than 3,700 studies related to middle schools were published (Hough, 2003). Out of these and earlier studies, a set of principles and practices generally known as the *middle school concept* emerged. Most middle-level advocates turn to two sources for a definition of the concept: the Carnegie Council on Adolescent Development's *Turning Points: Preparing American Youth for the 21st Century* (1989) and the National Middle School Association's recently updated policy statement. *This We Believe: Successful Schools for Young Adolescents* (2003). According to these two sources, high-quality middle-level schools should

- Improve academic achievement for all students.
- Understand young adolescence.
- Provide a challenging and integrative curriculum.
- Create supportive and safe environments through such structures as small teaching teams.
- Ensure better teacher preparation for the middle grades.

- Improve relationships with families and communities.

Interestingly, virtually all iterations of the middle school concept recognize that high-quality schools for young adolescents exist within a variety of grade configurations, including 5–8, 6–8, 7–8, K–8, 7–12, and K–12. And obviously, most of the components of the middle school concept are appropriate for any grade level. Why, then, would advocates of the concept specifically tie it to the middle grades? Quite simply, because they intended to implement it as an alternative to the impersonal, inequitable, and irrelevant structures and curriculums that characterized many junior high schools (and still, today, many middle schools).

Advocates of the middle school concept usually argue their case on the grounds that this approach is developmentally responsive to young adolescents. For example, they link small teaching teams to young adolescents' need for a sense of belonging and security; improved family relationships to their need for a support system through puberty's ups and downs; an integrative curriculum to their need for meaningful contexts for learning; and more appropriate teacher preparation to the many ways in which young adolescents differ from younger children and older adolescents.

Meanwhile, some studies have looked at what happens when schools actually implement the components of the middle school concept as a complete set, over time and with high fidelity (Anfara & Lipka, 2003; DePascale, 1997; Felner et al., 1997). The results? Increases in academic achievement and decreases in behavior problems, including among students who typically struggle with both. Moreover, various practices promoted by the middle school concept have independently shown considerable promise for improving achievement, engagement, and relationships: small teaching teams, authentic instruction, integrative curriculum, service learning, and affective mentorship (Beane & Brodhagen, 2001; Juvonen, Le, Kaganoff, Augustine, & Constant, 2004; National Middle School Association Research Committee, 2003).

But therein lies the real problem with the middle school concept: On the whole, its components have *not* been well implemented over time and rarely as a complete set of principles and practices. Most often, the title of "middle school" has had less to do with implementing the concept and more to do with changing the name on the front of the building.

In the unlikely event that the media and critics retract their obituary for the middle school concept, they might well title their correction "Sorry, Mistaken Identity." For they have indeed mistaken the practices found in too many middle schools for the middle school concept itself. But then, so have many middle-level educators, who thought that simply putting grades 5–8 or 6–8 together without implementing the middle school concept would ensure a better education for young adolescents. Both groups were wrong.

WHAT RESEARCH REALLY SHOWS

The 5–8 and 6–8 grade configurations most widely associated with middle schools emerged mainly as a result of two trends that took place in the 1960s and 1970s. First, as baby boomers poured into elementary schools, school districts found that moving the 5th and/or 6th grades to a "middle school" was more cost-efficient than building extra elementary schools. Second, in many northern cities and southern states, the new configuration helped move students out of segregated neighborhood K–8 schools into more integrated middle or intermediate schools (George, 1988). Advocates of reform at the middle level argued for aspects of the middle school concept from the start, but those arguments would not have produced the large-scale move to middle schools without the presence of such factors as overcrowding and desegregation.

Given the relatively poor record of full implementation of the middle school concept and the enormous difficulties facing urban schools, it is not surprising that urban school officials would envision returning grades 6–8 to the elementary school. Moreover, some evidence seems to support the K–8 model with regard to enhancing

academic achievement, encouraging parental involvement, and reducing affective difficulties for students in this age group (Abella, 2005; Baltimore City Schools, 2001; Juvonen et al., 2004; Offenberg, 2001; Simmons & Blyth, 1987).

At the same time, however, the research comparing K–8 and middle school configurations includes important caveats. First, although achievement test results for students in large urban districts may favor K–8 arrangements, such scores still fall short of state and national averages (Balfanz, Spiridakis, & Neild, 2002), and the K–8 advantage seems to disappear in the 9th grade (Abella, 2005). Second, the key difference between K–8 schools and middle schools seems to be the smaller size of the former, enabling teachers, students, and families to build better relationships. Third, virtually all of the studies caution that the middle schools involved have *not* done a good job of implementing aspects of the middle school concept. Fourth, K–8 schools do not necessarily outperform middle schools when both serve high-poverty students (Balfanz et al., 2002).

We are left with two key points. First, the advantages of K–8 schools over middle schools in urban areas reside largely to smaller class and school size, which enable these schools to support better relationships with all of their constituencies. K–8 schools remove the transition from elementary to middle school, which for unexplained reasons seems to coincide with decreasing parental involvement both in school and in the lives of their children. Second, however much improved achievement test scores appear in urban K–8 schools, such scores still do not rise to state and national averages for this age group. This is not difficult to understand when we remember that a school's poverty index is the strongest correlate and best predictor of achievement test scores (Bracey, 1997). And no matter how much the media and middle school critics want us to believe otherwise, school grade configuration is not a remedy for the rising tide of poverty in our nation's urban centers.

THE FUSS OVER GRADE LEVELS

Proponents of the middle school concept have long cautioned against equaling the concept with grade configurations. Almost 20 years ago, Paul George (1988) suggested that

> slavish adherence to one grade configuration or another continues to obscure the need for substantive change and draws our attention away from potentially viable alternatives, such as K–8 and K–12. (p. 17)

In the early 1990s, Lounsbury and Clark (1991), two widely known middle school advocates, reported that 8th graders in K–8 schools reported more favorable experiences than their counterparts in 6–8 schools. *Middle School Journal* published Offenberg's Philadelphia study showing higher achievement in K–8 schools than in middle schools (2001). And the September 2005 issue of that journal focused almost entirely on research and policy questions related to K–8 schools.

No matter which grade configuration school districts choose, the most important decision is what kind of education they will offer young adolescents. Research on both middle schools and K–8 schools clearly suggests the importance of creating small learning communities, high-quality relationships, and strong transition supports. It may well be that attaching grades 6–8 to the elementary side of schooling proves more effective in implementing these principles and practices than does treating these grades as a junior version of high school. In this case, moving to K–8 schools might actually save the middle school concept from the more dangerous trend toward inflicting on middle schools the kind of structures more usually associated with junior high school setups, such as tracking and strict subject departmentalization.

Those considering K–8 schools must understand, however, that this configuration comes with its own set of potential problems. For example, resource reductions accompanying smaller middle-grades enrollments would likely reduce the number of specialized electives, services, accelerated courses, and extracurricular activities that some parents want for their children. And

creating neighborhood K–8 schools may actually add to the resegregation of urban schools already in progress. Finally, there is certainly no guarantee that the middle grades placed within a K–8 school will implement all or any aspects of the middle school concept shown to work well with young adolescents ([McEwan], Dickinson, & Jacobson, 2005).

LOOKING BEYOND CONFIGURATION

The large urban school districts at the center of the move toward K–8 schools are complicated systems. Their sheer size may well work against creating the smaller school communities that the middle school concept promotes. Moreover, diminishing state and federal resources make school success more difficult for urban students, many of whom already suffer the injustice of having to live in poverty (Kozol, 2005). And the moves to punish struggling schools and students, sterilize the curriculum, and demand unattainable test results come down especially hard on large urban districts.

It is misleading for middle school critics to suggest that poor achievement and difficult conditions in our urban schools result from a particular school configuration. This sleight-of-hand rhetoric does a disservice to young adolescents and their schools by diverting attention from the powerful effects of poverty and the unsavory resegregation of our nation's communities and schools (Kozol, 2005).

Rather than debate which grade configuration is best for the middle grades, we would be better off expending our energy creating a curriculum that intellectually engages and inspires young adolescents, pushing for organizing structures that support high-quality relationships, and finding better ways to reach out to families and communities. If we really want to do something worthwhile for young adolescents, we should work to overcome the poverty and prejudice that relentlessly work against many of these students' chances for success inside school and for a decent life outside it.

REFERENCES

Abella, R. (2005). The effects of small K–8 centers compared to large 6–8 schools on student performance, *Middle School Journal, 37*(1), 29–35.

Anfara, V., & Lipka, R. (2003). Relating the middle school concept to school achievement. *Middle School Journal, 35*(1), 24–32.

Balfanz, R., Spiridaks, K., & Neild, R. (2002). *Will converting high-poverty middle schools facilitate achievement gains?* Philadelphia: Philadelphia Education Fund.

Baltimore City Schools, Division of Research, Evaluation, and Accountability. (2001). *An examination of K–5, 6–8 versus K–8 grade configurations.* Baltimore: Author.

Beane, J., & Brodhagen, B. (2001). Teaching in middle school. In V. Henderson (Ed.), *Handbook of research on teaching* (4th ed.), (pp. 1157–1174). Washington, DC: American Educational Research Association.

Bracey, G. (1997). *Setting the record straight: Responses to misconceptions about public education in the United States.* Alexandria, VA: ASCD.

Carnegie Council on Adolescent Development. (1989). *Turning points: Preparing for the 21st century.* New York: Author.

DePascale, C. (1997). *Education reform restructuring network: Impact documentation report.* Cambridge, MA: Data Analysts and Testing Associates.

Felner, R. D., Jackson, A. W., Kasak, D., Mulhall, P., Brand, S., & Flowers, N. (1997). The impact of school reform for the middle years. *Phi Delta Kappan, 78*(7), 528–550.

George, P. (1988, September). Education 2000: Which way the middle school? *The Clearing House, 62,* 17.

Hough, D. (2003). *R3 = Research, rhetoric, and reality: A study of studies addressing NMSA's 21st Century Research Agenda and* This We Believe. Westerville, OH: National Middle School Association.

Juvonen, J., Le, Y., Kaganoff, T., Augustine, C., & Constant, L. (2004). *Focus on the wonder years: Challenges facing the American middle school.* Santa Monica, CA: RAND Corporation.

Kozol, J. (2005). *The shame of a nation: The restoration of apartheid schooling in America.* New York: Random House.

Lounsbury, J., & Clark, D. (1991). *Inside eighth grade: From apathy to excitement.* Reston, VA: National Association of Secondary School Principle.

McEwan, K., Dickinson, T., & Jacobsen, M. (2005). How effective are K–8 schools for young adolescents? *Middle School Journal, 37*(1), 24–28.

National Middle School Association (2003). *This we believe: Successful schools for young adolescents.* Westerville, OH: Author.

National Middle School Association Research Committee (2003). *Research and resources in support of* This We Believe. Westerville, OH: National Middle School Association.

Offenberg, R. M. (2001). The efficacy of Philadelphia's K-to-8 schools compared to middle grades schools. *Middle School Journal, 32*(4), 23–29.

Simmons, R., & Blyth, D. (1987). *Moving into adolescence: The impact of pubertal change and school context.* New York: Aldine de Gruyter.

James Beane is professor in the Department of Interdisciplinary Studies in Curriculum at National-Louis University, Milwaukee, Wisconsin and author of *A Reason to Teach. Richard Lipka* is professor in the Department of Special Services and Leadership Studies at Pittsburg State University, Pittsburg, Kansas.

QUESTIONS FOR REFLECTION

1. Do you agree with Beane and Lipka's central argument that the real problem with middle school achievement is that too many middle schools have failed to fully implement the middle school concept and educators need to look beyond reconfiguration to the real problems plaguing middle schools?

2. What are the real problems plaguing middle schools today? Are these problems best solved by fully implementing the middle school concept?

3. After reading the previous article by Yecke and this one by Beane and Lipka, who do you think offers the best solution to the middle school problem? Why? What evidence is most compelling to you?

The Homework Wars

DAVID SKINNER

ABSTRACT: In the current hyperproductive, overachieving setting, a curious educational debate has broken out. The parents of the younger K–12 students are revolting against the reportedly increasing amounts of homework assigned their children. A major lightning rod for this debate has been The End of Homework, *a book by Etta Kralovec and John Buell, whose argument found an appreciative audience in* Time, Newsweek, The New York Times, People *magazine, and elsewhere. Understanding the book's argument—its strengths and weaknesses—is not necessary to understanding the debate over homework, but it is helpful to understanding the overall tenor of this controversy.*

The American child, a gloomy chorus of newspapers, magazines and books tells us, is overworked. All spontaneity is being squeezed out of him by the vise-like pressures of homework, extracurricular activities, and family. "Jumping from Spanish to karate, tap dancing to tennis—with hours of homework waiting at home—the overscheduled child is as busy as a new law firm associate," reports the *New York Times.* The article goes on to describe a small counter-trend in which some parents are putting a stop to the frenzy and letting their children, for once in their little harried lives, simply hang out or, as one of the insurgent parents explains, enjoy an informal game of pickup.

What's this? A game of catch is news? And this is said to be sociologically significant? Something must be amiss in the state of childhood today. The common diagnosis is that too much work, too much ambition, and an absence of self-directedness are harming American children. In an influential 2001 article in the *Atlantic Monthly,* David Brooks, author of *Bobos in Paradise,* christened the over-achieving American child the "Organization Kid." Reporting on the character of the generation born in the early 1980s, in which he focused on those attending some of America's most prestigious colleges, Brooks found a youth demographic of career-oriented yes-men, with nary a rebel in the bunch. Called team players and rule-followers, they are best captured by a 1997 Gallup survey Brooks cites in which 96 percent of teenagers said they got along with their parents.

In this hyperproductive, overachieving setting, a curious educational debate has broken out. The parents of the younger K–12 worker-bees are revolting against the reportedly increasing amounts of homework assigned their children. A major lightning rod for this debate has been *The End of Homework,* a book by Etta Kralovec and John Buell, whose argument found an appreciative audience in *Time, Newsweek,* the *New York Times, People* magazine, and elsewhere. For a novel polemic against a long-established educational practice, such a widespread hearing suggests that the issue has struck a chord with many American families. Understanding the book's argument—its strengths and weaknesses—is not necessary to understanding the debate over homework, but it is helpful to understanding the overall tenor of this controversy.

THE END OF HOMEWORK

What makes *The End of Homework* stand out is that it was written by academics. Etta Kralovec holds a doctorate in education from the Teachers College at Columbia University and, for over 12 years, she directed teacher education at the College of the Atlantic. John Buell, too, has spent time on the faculty at the College of the Atlantic. Now a newspaper columnist, the onetime associate editor of *The Progressive* has authored two books on political economy. In an afterword, the authors say *The End of Homework* grew out of a series of interviews with high school dropouts, many of whom cited homework as a reason they discontinued their education. This snapshot of homework's dire effect, unfortunately, requires much qualification.

Kralovec and Buell show little restraint when describing the problems brought on by the reported increase in homework. Attacking the proposition that homework inculcates good adult habits, the authors cite the historical trend in psychology away from viewing children as miniature adults, but then quickly lose perspective. "In suggesting that children need to learn to deal with adult levels of pressure, we risk doing them untold damage. By this logic, the schoolyard shootings of recent years may be likened to 'disgruntled employee' rampages." Nor do Kralovec and Buell inspire confidence by quoting a report attributing a spate of suicides in Hong Kong to "distress over homework." The report they cite is from the *Harare Herald* in Zimbabwe, not exactly a widely recognized authority on life in Hong Kong.

The End of Homework's alarmist tone is best captured, however, in its uncritical acceptance of a 1999 report from the American Association of Orthopedic Surgeons (AAOS) "that thousands of kids have back, neck, and shoulder pain caused by their heavy backpacks." The book's cover photo even shows two little kids straining like packmules under the weight of their bookbags. It so happens that orthopedic professionals themselves, at the AAOS no less, dispute the report.

To pick a recent example, a study presented at the 2003 meeting of the AAOS, based on interviews with 346 school-age orthopedic patients, found only one patient who attributed his back pain to carrying a bookbag.

Kralovec and Buell's case against homework is further diminished by the book's clear political agenda. Indeed, the telltale signs of an overriding left-wing social critique are sadly abundant. Twice inside of 100 pages, the same unilluminating quotation is trotted out from "the great radical sociologist C. Wright Mills," whose influence on this book, however, pales next to that of Harvard economist Juliet B. Schor. Schor is most famous for her controversial 1992 bestseller *The Overworked American: The Unexpected Decline of Leisure,* which argued that American adults were losing their disposable time to the steady encroachments of longer work schedules. But the book's primary findings were contradicted by existing research and just about every mainstream expert asked to offer an opinion on the subject.

Nevertheless, Schor's laborite call for a new consensus on the proper number of hours and days that should be devoted to employment (approximately half of current levels) finds an echo in *The End of Homework*'s call to American families to throw off their homework shackles and reclaim the evenings for family time. Indeed, one notices in this book more than a little overwrought socialist rhetoric. For example, after bemoaning the failure of standards-based reforms to improve achievement scores, the authors comment that the continued emphasis on homework "fits the ideological requirement of those who maintain the status quo in our economy and politics" and that homework "serves the needs of powerful groups within our society."

The book's other patron saint is Jonathan Kozol, the influential left-wing author of *Savage Inequalities* who has done more than anyone to swamp mainstream education debate with radical social criticism. In the style of Kozol, whom they cite a dozen or so times, Kralovec and Buell binge on the theme of equality when they should be carefully picking over social science data, insisting that homework "pits students who can against students who can't." And when they're not raising the specter of class warfare, Kralovec and Buell are lecturing readers on their unwillingness to recognize its insidious influence: "We suspect that many Americans may be unwilling to acknowledge the existence of an entrenched class system in the United States that serves to constrain or enhance our children's life chances." Economic inequalities, the authors inveigh, fly in the face of "our most cherished values, such as democracy and freedom." Typical of their tempestuous approach to this discrete pedagogical question, Kralovec and Buell devote their final chapter to "Homework in the Global Economy."

Hidden amid the authors' polemic, however, is a persuasive and warranted case against an educational practice of limited value. Homework, in some cases, deserves to be attacked, which makes it all the more a pity that Kralovec and Buell couldn't confine themselves to their primary subject. Their opinion that "homework is almost always counterproductive for elementary schoolchildren" is not the product of some left-wing fever swamp and deserves further consideration.

HOW MUCH

Kralovec and Buell's more serious case against homework begins with a standard social-science discussion of the difference between correlation and causality. But as often happens in critical examinations, the fact that there are obvious limits to human understanding is used to argue for a radical skepticism when it comes to the methods and aims of research. One author's qualifiers and caveats become, in the hands of his opponents, arguments for the proposition that it is impossible to know anything about what condition brought about which effect. So what if students who did a lot of homework performed well on achievement exams? Maybe it was the case that they did a lot of homework because they were high-achieving students?

Down that road, many a worthy illusion comes undone, but few usable lessons can be drawn.

Down the opposite road, however fraught it may be with epistemological limitations, we can nevertheless develop a vague picture of solid educational practice.

University of Missouri professor of psychological sciences Harris Cooper, whose research on homework is widely cited by critics on both sides of the debate, including Kralovec and Buell, offers conditional support for the practice. "Is homework better than no homework at all?" he asks in a 1980s literature review. On the basis of 17 research reports examining over 3,300 students, Cooper found that 70 percent of comparisons yielded a positive answer. In terms of class grades and standardized test scores, he found that "the average student doing homework in these studies had a higher achievement score than 55 percent of students not doing homework." Break down such average findings, however, and this modest advantage gained through homework is lost through other variables.

Perhaps the most commanding factor in deciding the homework question is age or grade level. "Older students benefited the most from doing homework," writes Cooper. "The average effect of homework was twice as large for high school as for junior high school students and twice as large again for junior high school students as for elementary school students." This raises interesting questions about homework's distribution among age groups.

Much of the homework controversy is fueled by stories of very young children burdened with lengthy assignments and complicated projects that require extensive parental involvement. Searching for evidence that such work is important to their child's education and development, the parent of a fifth grader will find only cold comfort in the research examined by Cooper. "Teachers of Grades 4, 5, and 6 might expect the average student doing homework to outscore about 52 percent of equivalent no-homework students." A 2 percentile-point advantage gained by a practice that could be interrupting dinner, stealing family time, and pitting child against parent hardly seems enough to justify the intrusion.

For high school students, however, homework can do a lot of good. "If grade level is taken into account," Cooper finds, "homework's effect on the achievement of elementary school students could be described as 'very small,' but on high school students its effect would be 'large.' " If the average fourth- through sixth-grade student who does homework can expect only a 2 percentile-point advantage over one who does none, junior high school students doing homework can expect a 10 percentile-point advantage and high school students a 19 percentile-point advantage. What's more, this effect translates into high achievement not only in class grades—which more readily reflect a positive homework effect—but also on standardized tests, which are quite significant to a student's educational future.

WHAT KIND

There are other wrinkles worth attending to. For one, Cooper himself still favors homework, but possibly not the kind that is causing the most heartache and the most headaches. "Not surprisingly, homework produced larger effects if students did more assignments per week. Surprisingly, the effect of homework was negatively related to the duration of the homework treatment—treatments spanning longer periods produced less of a homework effect." Which is to say, homework comprised of short regular assignments is probably the most effective.

One underlying lesson here should cause many enemies of homework to groan. Kralovec and Buell, for example, marshall the classic complaint, usually made by children, that homework is boring, repetitive, and basically has nothing to do with the developing child's true self. Interesting homework—the fun stuff that allows a child to express himself, that supposedly promotes "creativity" and "critical thinking" and "planning skills"—does not come off well in Cooper's study. Examining broad national and state-wide studies of the relationship between time spent on homework and its effects, Cooper found that the correlations between time spent and positive effects increased "for subjects for which homework assignments are more likely to involve rote learning, practice, or rehearsal. Alternately, subjects such as science and social studies, which often involve longer-term projects, integration of multiple skills, and creative use of non-school resources show the smallest average correlations." Note the collision of opposing pedagogical trends: improving standards by increasing homework and the movement away from rote learning. Indeed, there may be nothing more unhelpful to a student than a teacher of high standards who doesn't want to bore his students.

Interestingly, no one involved in the fight over homework has argued that parents might consider encouraging their children to put in less effort on homework that is overly time-consuming and pedagogically unproductive. Which seems a pity. Why shouldn't a parent tell his overworked fifth-grader to spend less time on that big assignment on American subcultural narratives? Or occasionally have him not do his homework at all? A little civil disobedience might be a useful way of sending a message to a teacher whose assignments are overly ambitious. And if the child gets a lower grade as a result, then it's a small price to pay. It's not as if his entire educational future is on the line.

The homework critics never suggest such a course of action, needless to say, but not because it might undermine teachers' authority, a result they otherwise happily pursue. Odd as it sounds, the fight against homework is largely about achievement, specifically about setting the price of officially recognized excellence at an acceptable rate. Reading Kralovec and Buell and the many newspaper and magazine articles depicting the rebellion against homework, one comes away with an impression in keeping with David Brooks's "Organization Kid," but with an egalitarian twist. The whole movement reflects an organization culture that wants high grades to be possible for all kids, regardless of their varying levels of ability or willingness to work, regardless of what other commitments these children have made, regardless of the importance of family.

TIME AND HOMEWORK

A significant underlying question remains to be addressed. The evidence that there is a widespread homework problem—that too many students are carrying too heavy a homework load—is largely anecdotal. There are some empirical indications of a modest increase in homework over the last 20 years or so, but other indications suggest the problem is being overstated. While some parents and families may have rather serious homework problems, these would generally appear to be private problems, hardly in need of national or even local solutions.

At least there is a consensus on standard reference points. One constant in this debate are the data gathered from the University of Michigan's 1997 Child Development supplement to the Panel Study of Income Dynamics and 1981 Study of Time Use in Social and Economic Accounts, a collection of time-use studies of children. Often appearing in the press cheek-by-jowl with quotes from overstretched parents, most reporting on the study suggests its findings support the conclusion that American children lack for leisure time amid demands imposed on them by parents and school. But the study's authors, who arguably know more than anyone about how American children are actually spending their time day-in and day-out, do not see the story this way. In fact, in a *New York Times* article, the study's primary researcher, Sandra L. Hofferth, dismissed the whole notion that the American child is overworked and overoccupied. "I don't believe in the 'hurried child' for a minute. . . . There is a lot of time that can be used for other things."

On the question of homework, Hofferth and co-author John F. Sandberg reject the claim that homework has seen a significant general increase. The average amount of time spent studying for 3- to 12-year-olds has increased from 1981 to 1997, but the vast majority of those increases (studying and reading are measured separately) are concentrated among 3- to 5-year-olds (reading) and 6- to 8-year-olds (studying). "The main reason for the increase in studying among 6- to 8-

year-olds was an increase in the proportion who did some studying at all, from one-third to more than one-half. The fact that significant increases in reading occurred among 3- to 5-year-olds probably reflects parents' increasing concern with preparing children for school."

Which is to say, homework appears to be increasing most where there was no homework before, and among age groups for whom it will do the least good. Far from a situation of the straw breaking the camel's back, we see many unburdened camels taking on their first tiny handfuls of straw, and a number of others carrying little if any more than they did in the past. This is where the story of the debate over homework takes a major turn. While arguably some American children have been turned into walking delivery systems for wicked educators bent on upsetting the home life of innocent American families, this is clearly not true across the board. In fact, one might say that a good number of American children and teenagers are already deciding how much time they want to spend on homework, and the amount of work they've opted for is not exactly back-breaking.

The Brookings Institution recently weighed in on the homework debate on this very point, arguing that "almost everything in this story [of overworked students] is wrong." Like Hofferth and Sandburg, Tom Loveless, the Brookings author, points out that most of the increase noted in the University of Michigan study is concentrated among the youngest subjects who are reading earlier and being introduced to homework at a younger age. The most telling finding in the Brookings report, however, is that "the typical student, even in high school, does not spend more than an hour per day on homework." Needless to say, this picture is quite different from the homework situation described by Kralovec and Buell, to say nothing of the dire drama described over and over in newspaper and magazine stories.

The 1997 University of Michigan time-use studies do report average increases for time spent on homework against a 1981 benchmark, but analysis by the Brookings Institution shows these increases are nearly negligible. The amount of time 3- to 5-year-olds spent studying increased from 25 minutes per week in 1981 to 36 minutes per week in 1997. This translates to an increase of two minutes a night if studying takes place five nights a week. The next group, 6- to 8-year-olds, as mentioned, saw the biggest increase, from 52 minutes a week to 2 hours and 8 minutes a week, which translates to an average increase of 15 minutes a night, bringing average homework time to a grand total of 25 minutes or so a night. The oldest group, 9- to 12-year-olds, saw only an increase of 19 minutes on average per week, an increase of less than four minutes a night. Other data culled by Brookings from the University of Michigan study show that over one-third of 9- to 12-year-olds reported doing no homework. Indeed, half of all 3- to 12-year-olds said that they were doing no homework whatsoever, despite data showing a small average increase in homework for this group.

Other research supports these findings. The National Assessment of Education Progress (NAEP) reports that a significant number of 9- and 13-year-olds are assigned no homework at all. Between 1984 and 1999, at least 26 percent and as much as 36 percent of 9-year-olds reported receiving no homework assignments the day before filling out the questionnaire. Among 13-year-olds, the numbers show a relatively large and increasing number of students assigned no homework: 17 percent in 1988, increasing to 24 percent in 1999. As for older students, the 1999 National Center for Education Statistics (NCES) reports that 12 percent of high school seniors said they were doing no homework during a typical week. Of the remaining 88 percent, most said they spent less than 5 hours a week doing homework. This, remember, is in high school, where teachers assign more work, students are expected to do more work, and homework is agreed to have the most benefits. And yet, the above NCES number tells us that most high school students who do homework spend less than an hour a day, five days a week, doing it. According to the NAEP, only

about a third of 17-year-olds have more than one hour of homework a night.

What about examining the homework habits of students who go on to college, thus controlling for the downward pull of low performers in high school? In the national survey of college freshmen performed by the University of California at Los Angeles, a surprising number report having worked no more than one hour a night as high school seniors. In 1987, only 47 percent of college freshmen surveyed said they had done more than five hours of homework a week. By 2002, that number had fallen to 34 percent—meaning only about one-third of American college freshman said they'd spent more than one hour a night on homework as high school seniors. As the Brookings report comments, such a homework load makes American high schoolers look underworked compared with their peers in other developed nations.

PLEASED WITH OURSELVES

The evidence suggests that while a significant portion of students are not carrying an insupportable burden of homework, a small percentage of students work long hours indeed—and some of them not for any good reason. We are giving the wrong kind of homework and in increasing quantities to the wrong age groups. As the Brookings report notes, 5 percent of fourth graders have more than 2 hours of homework nightly. Whether such a figure is surprising or not may merely be a question of expectations, but it hardly seems reasonable to expect 9-year-olds to be capable of finishing such quantities of after-school work. Still, that a small percentage of students are unnecessarily overworked does not justify the national press coverage and research interest this story has generated.

Why the homework controversy has received the attention it has may result from our national preference for stories that make our children seem one and all to be high achievers. Also, it's no secret that many professional and upper-class parents will undertake extraordinary measures to help their children get ahead in school in order to get ahead in the real world: These children are sent to elite schools that liberally assign homework, even as they are signed up for any number of organized activities in the name of self-improvement. And, of course, this segment of the population does more than its share to direct and set the tone for press coverage of news issues of interest to families. That surely helps explain spectacular headlines like "The Homework Ate My Family" (*Time*), "Homework Doesn't Help" (*Newsweek*), and "Overbooked: Four Hours of Homework for a Third Grader" (*People*).

So, while the overworked American child exists, he is not typical. Strangely enough, he seems to be more of an American ideal—drawn from our Lake Woebegone tendency of imagining that we're so good and hard-working, we might be too good and too hard-working. Thus do we ask ourselves why Johnny is doing so much homework, when in fact he is not.

David Skinner is an assistant managing editor at *The Weekly Standard*. Before working at *The Standard* in November 1998, he was managing editor of the *Public Interest*. He has written for the *Washington Times, Salon, Philanthropy,* the *Public Interest*, and the *Wall Street Journal*.

QUESTIONS FOR REFLECTION

1. What should be the role of homework in today's curriculum? Should there be an end to homework or should homework continue much the same as it does today? If changes to homework were to be instituted, what should change and who would monitor the change?
2. Given how many distractions there are outside of school—television, video games, sports, etc.—is there a compelling argument that homework keeps students from becoming too reliant on entertainment rather than intellectual growth?
3. Do you agree with Skinner's assertion that the "overworked American child" is not typical and that most children today have more free time than people think they do? Skinner suggests that a relatively small percentage of overworked students contributed to an unnecessarily large amount of national press coverage and research interest. Why do you think this is? Is the media to blame for creating a crisis where one doesn't truly exist?

Building Developmental Assets to Promote Success in School and in Life

PETER C. SCALES
JUDY TACCOGNA

ABSTRACT: *Both a sense of belonging and a belief in one's own competency seem to be missing from the school experiences of disengaged, underachieving students. Building students' developmental assets is a promising practice for reconnecting students and supporting achievement. Looking at schools through an "assets lens" can promote concrete changes in school organization, curriculum and instruction, cocurricular programs, support services, and community partnerships that make the whole environment more conducive to great teaching and learning.*

Students live in a school environment that is increasingly dominated by accountability measures such as standardized tests. Consequently, many schools focused on teaching tightly prescribed content knowledge and related skills in order for students to meet state benchmark standards in a variety of subject areas. In Chicago, for example, 500 education standards are aligned with 18 state goals, and more than 1,500 curriculum frameworks that dictate what content is to be taught are in turn aligned with the benchmark standards (Newmann, Lopez, and Bryk 1998). Yet standardized curriculum prescriptions often work against authentic and effective instruction (Newmann, Secada, and Wehlage 1995), and against engaging students who are most in need of more solid connections to their schools.

A PROMISING PRACTICE FOR RECONNECTING YOUTH AND SUPPORTING ACHIEVEMENT

One promising approach to increasing the likelihood of student success in both school and life is to build "developmental assets"—those relationships, opportunities, values, and skills that, when present in the lives of youth, make young people less likely to become involved in risk behaviors

and more likely to be successful in school, relationships, and life in general (Benson et al. 1999). Building developmental assets is essentially about building positive, sustained relationships, not only among students and teachers but also among parents and students, parents and teachers, students and students, and among teachers and other school staff themselves (Scales 1999). What is crucial, however, is that the use of relationships as a lens through which to view school policies and practices can effect concrete changes in curriculum and instruction, school organization, cocurricular programs, community partnerships, and support services that make the entire school environment more conducive to engagement and achievement, and to great teaching and learning (Starkman, Scales, and Roberts 1999).

One of the main strengths of asset building is that it is less a scripted program and more a way of living, a way of looking at and relating differently to students as people, a way of creating a classroom and school environment that is supportive of children and adolescents. That strength means that it does not take a significant amount of time to learn new strategies and incorporate them into a discrete portion of time during the day. Rather it means rethinking what one already does in the classroom and reframing these activities in an "asset-building lens"—for example, greeting students by name, responding to student questions and concerns, providing students with differentiated assignments, and communicating with parents.

DEVELOPMENTAL ASSETS

Developmental assets are the positive relationships, opportunities, competencies, values, and self-perceptions that youth need to succeed (see Table 1). Researchers at Search Institute, a nonprofit research organization located in Minneapolis, Minn., believe that these assets make a difference in the success and health of young people. Many studies, including research being conducted at Search Institute, indicate that building students' developmental assets is related to a variety of antecedents to achievement as well as to measures of actual performance and achievement. For example, students who report experiencing 31–40 of the developmental assets are several times more likely than students reporting an average level of 11–20 assets to get mostly As in school (38 percent versus 19 percent, according to Benson et al. 1999). Studies also have found significant relationships among variables defined similarly to the 40 developmental assets and key achievement outcomes (such as level of effort, academic goal orientations, competency beliefs, beliefs about the value of education, grades, graduation rates, and test scores), as well as among the developmental assets and those outcomes that support learning (such as lessened alcohol and other drug use, greater problem-solving skills, greater social skills, and less depression). In addition to being associated with higher levels of school achievement, the assets have also been linked to lower drug use; less sexual intercourse in the teen years; fewer conduct problems; lessened use of marijuana; and increased helping of others, leadership, and ability to overcome adversity, among other desirable outcomes (Benson et al. 1999; Leffert et al. 1998; Scales et al. 2000; Scales and Leffert 1999).

The assets (see Table 1) fall into two main classes: external and internal. *External assets* (grouped into the categories of support, empowerment, boundaries and expectations, and constructive use of time) are the relationships and opportunities that surround young people with the support and situations that guide them to behave in healthy ways and make wise choices. *Internal assets* (commitment to learning, positive values, social competencies, and positive identity) are those commitments, values, competencies, and self-perceptions that, when nurtured, provide the "internal compass" that guides a young person's behavior and choices so that he or she becomes self-regulating.

Unfortunately, research at Search Institute indicates that the typical sixth to twelfth grader experiences less than half the assets overall, and too few experience those assets that are most directly related to school success. Over the past decade, Search Institute has surveyed more than one million youth in more than 1,000 cities and towns nationwide to measure their asset levels. The basic findings have remained distressingly consistent from year to year, community to community. From the perspective of teachers and administrators at the secondary level, the situation is even more troubling: the average level of developmental assets that students report drops from sixth grade through twelfth grade, with a particularly large drop across the middle-level school years (Benson et al. 1999). Following is just one statistical highlight from Search Institute research for each of the asset categories, suggesting the depth of the challenge facing educators, parents, and students.

From the external classes, in the support category, only 25 percent of students say they experience a caring school climate. In the empowerment category, only 50 percent of students say they feel safe in their schools and neighborhoods. In the boundaries and expectations category, less than 50 percent of students think their teachers and parents have high expectations for their performance. In the constructive use of time category, fewer than six in ten students spend at least three hours per week in organized clubs, sports, or other activities sponsored by schools or community organizations, even though involvement in structured activities beyond school hours is associated with lower involvement in risk behaviors, encourages the development

TABLE 1

Forty Developmental Assets for Middle and High School Youth (ages 12 to 18)

Class and Type	Name and Definition
External	
Support	1. **Family support:** Family life provides high levels of love and support.
	2. **Positive family communication:** Young person and her or his parent(s) communicate positively, and young person is willing to seek parent(s) advice and counsel.
	3. **Other adult relationships:** Young person receives support from three or more nonparent adults.
	4. **Caring neighborhood:** Young person experiences caring neighbors.
	5. **Caring school climate:** School provides a caring, encouraging environment.
	6. **Parent involvement in schooling:** Parent(s) are actively involved in helping young person succeed in school.
Empowerment	7. **Community values youth:** Young person perceives that adults in the community value youth.
	8. **Youth as resources:** Young person is given useful roles in the community.
	9. **Service to others:** Young person serves in the community one hour or more per week.
	10. **Safety:** Young person feels safe at home, school, and in the neighborhood.
Boundaries and Expectations	11. **Family boundaries:** Family has clear rules and consequences, and monitors the young person's whereabouts.
	12. **School boundaries:** School provides clear rules and consequences.
	13. **Neighborhood boundaries:** Neighbors take responsibility for monitoring young person's behavior.
	14. **Adult role models:** Parent(s) and other adults model positive, responsible behavior.
	15. **Positive peer influence:** Young person's best friends model responsible behavior.
	16. **High expectations:** Both parent(s) and teachers encourage the young person to do well.
Constructive Use of Time	17. **Creative activities:** Young person spends three or more hours of time per week in lessons or practice in music, theater, or other arts.
	18. **Youth programs:** Young person spends three or more hours per week in sports, clubs, or organizations at school and/or in community organizations.
	19. **Religious community:** Young person spends one hour or more per week in activities in a religious institution.
	20. **Time at home:** Young person is out with friends "with nothing special to do" two nights or fewer per week.
Internal	
Commitment to Learning	21. **Achievement motivation:** Young person is motivated to do well in school.
	22. **School engagement:** Young person is actively engaged in learning.
	23. **Homework:** Young person reports doing at least one hour of homework every school day.

24. Bonding to school: Young person cares about her or his school.

25. Reading for pleasure: Young person reads for pleasure three or more hours per week.

Positive Values

26. Caring: Young person places high value on helping other people.

27. Equality and social justice: Young person places high value on promoting equality and reducing hunger and poverty.

28. Integrity: Young person acts on convictions and stands up for her or his beliefs.

29. Honesty: Young person "tells the truth even when it is not easy."

30. Responsibility: Young person accepts and takes personal responsibility.

31. Restraint: Young person believes it is important not to be sexually active or to use alcohol or other drugs.

Social Competencies

32. Planning and decision-making: Young person knows how to plan ahead and make choices.

33. Interpersonal competence: Young person has empathy, sensitivity, and friendship skills.

34. Cultural competence: Young person has knowledge of and comfort with people of different cultural/racial/ethnic backgrounds.

35. Resistance skills: Young person can resist negative peer pressure and dangerous situations.

36. Peaceful conflict resolution: Young person seeks to resolve conflict nonviolently.

Positive Identity

37. Personal power: Young person feels he or she has control over "things that happen to me."

38. Self-esteem: Young person reports having high self-esteem.

39. Sense of purpose: Young person reports that "my life has a purpose."

40. Positive view of personal future: Young person is optimistic about her or his personal future.

Note: This table may be reproduced for educational, noncommercial uses only. Copyright © 1997 by Search Institute, 700 S. Third St., Suite 210, Minneapolis, Minn. 55415; 800–888–7828; www.search-institute.org.

of other positive attributes, and assists young people in developing positive social supports and skills.

For the internal classes, in the commitment to learning category, nearly 40 percent of students do not feel engaged with school or motivated to achieve. In the positive values category, nearly 40 percent of students do not take personal responsibility for their actions. In the social competencies category, more than 70 percent of students do not consider themselves good planners and decision makers. In the positive identity category, less than 50 percent of students feel they have control over the things that happen in their life.

ASSET BUILDING IN THE SCHOOLS

Schools and districts seeking to infuse their school community with the developmental assets approach should spread efforts across these five main areas of schooling: curriculum and instruction, school organization (the building and the school day), cocurricular programs (i.e., before- and after-school programs), community partnerships (i.e., with families, neighbors, and other community members, volunteers, and business people), and support services (i.e., counseling services, health care providers, and support staff).

Before looking at each of these areas in more depth, it is useful to make explicit six basic principles of asset building.

• Everyone can be an asset builder. Administrators, teachers, custodians, bus drivers, counselors, food service staff, and countless individuals contribute to the roles played by parents and other adults in the community.

• All young people need assets. These developmental assets are crucial for all students, not just at-risk students, gifted students, or students with special needs.

• Relationships are the key. Strong, nurturing relationships support youth, engage them in learning, and focus them on positive thinking and behaviors. How often do teachers receive letters from students who write with stories about how their connections with individual teachers have made a tremendous difference their lives?

• Asset building is an ongoing process. Educators add to what parents and many others have already contributed to students' development, and they help students benefit from future relationships and opportunities.

• Consistency of messages is important. When all the people in all the settings in an adolescent's life say the same things about values and expectations, and they provide similar support and challenges, his or her world is more psychologically secure and sensible, increasing the adolescent's sense of motivation.

• Redundancy is crucial. Asset building is not a one-shot program but a commitment to provide for all students repeated exposure to caring relationships and challenging opportunities that will allow them to develop their talents, interests, and values in ways that help them reach personal goals and contribute to society.

With those six principles of asset building as background, school administrators should consider how they, in partnership with other community resources, can best build all 40 developmental assets. However, in reading the following examples,

readers might keep in mind primarily the 13 assets that research (see Scales and Leffert 1999) suggests are most important to academic success: school engagement, achievement motivation, positive peer influence, youth programs, bonding to school, school boundaries, homework, interpersonal competence, other adult relationships, high expectations, parent involvement in schooling, caring school climate, and reading for pleasure (Starkman, Scales, and Roberts 1999).

Examples of how the main areas of school functioning are tied to the school-related developmental assets include the following:

Curriculum and Instruction

Cross-curricular integration, team teaching, and exploratory programs of high interest to students help keep young people engaged, help teachers coordinate and monitor homework, and provide opportunities for youth to build adult relationships beyond those with their parents. Heterogeneous grouping (versus academic tracking) and the use of authentic assessment contribute to achievement motivation. Service learning experiences not only help students meet standards in many states but also provide students with opportunities to feel valuable and to make contributions to their community. Cooperative learning strategies reinforce the skill building needed to develop the positive peer influence and interpersonal competence assets. A comprehensive health education curriculum builds both the values and social competencies asset categories. Teachers provide clear school boundaries when they state explicitly what students must know and be able to do to receive a particular grade. Many curricula already incorporate skill-building in communication, decision making and planning; thinking about those as asset-building instructional strategies makes teaching to the assets more deliberate and intentional than it otherwise might be. One of the key skills necessary for success is the ability to read; providing training in teaching and supporting reading skills for both meaning and pleasure to teachers in all content areas at middle and high schools would not only build the reading for pleasure asset, but more important, contribute to greater reading success through continual, targeted reinforcement.

Organization

Several organizational structures currently advocated in schools support more and deeper relationships between adults and students, increase motivation, and ensure consistency in boundaries and expectations. Examples include organizing schools so that there are smaller communities within large middle or high schools (houses and teams), establishing advisor/advisee systems, using flexible scheduling, and keeping students in the same teams and with the same adults over several years (known as looping). Providing ways that students can have input into the operations of the school, including decision making and development of rules and sanctions, enhances the empowerment assets and helps develop interpersonal competencies. Asking parents to participate on committees, in learning situations, or in making decisions about what is purchased for the library increases the parent involvement asset. Opening the school doors to before- and after-school programs for young people supports all of the assets in the constructive use of time category, and can provide opportunities for peer and adult tutoring as well, enhancing the positive peer influence and relationship with adult assets.

Cocurricular Programs

Before- and after-school programs provide a wide variety of opportunities through which youth can develop assets, from involvement in the creative arts, sports, and clubs, to additional academic enrichment from tutors. Many of those opportunities also help to develop social-emotional intelligence and leadership skills and provide opportunities for service learning. To reinforce asset building most successfully, active recruitment of all students in those programs is an important element, so that participation is as inclusive as possible. Cocurricular programs are also an ideal place for parents to become involved in school-related, youth-friendly activities conducted in safe environments.

Community Partnerships

Links with businesses and other community organizations create additional opportunities for youth to build assets and enhance educational programs by providing "real world" environments in which students can learn content-related knowledge and skills at the same time. Partners such as the YMCA, Boys and Girls Clubs, and parks and recreation organizations are key providers of before- and after-school programs and all typically advocate for similar positive youth outcomes. Framing the accomplishment of those outcomes in the common language of developmental assets also brings consistency and redundancy to the messages a community and school system wants to send.

Support Services

Schools typically offer counseling and health services, but there are many other support services as well that bring caring, encouragement, and resources to students. Examples of providing potentially asset-building services within school systems include establishing on-site family resource centers; creating articulation programs to ease the transitions of students from elementary to middle and from middle to high schools; making peer mediation programs a key element in the operation of the discipline system; and providing counselors to students in ratios that allow them time to talk explicitly about issues of immediate developmental importance to them, as well as about short- and long-term planning.

CHALLENGES FOR IMPLEMENTATION

Several challenges exist in introducing and incorporating such asset-building strategies into school communities. First, it may be a challenge to communicate the relevance of asset building quickly and convincingly to school audiences who sometimes feel they have little time or energy to invest in looking at or thinking about anything that does not relate to content or instructional strategy development. Yet building assets in students is something that educators throughout America are already doing, though perhaps unsystematically.

Second, it can be a challenge to help staff learn the strategies involved in asset building and identify ways in which they can intentionally build assets through (a) relationships with students, (b) the instructional program, (c) schoolwide discipline codes, (d) mission statements, and (e) policy directions. Woven through the five areas of schooling (curriculum and instruction, school organization, cocurricular programs, community partnerships, and support services) are three approaches to incorporating asset building: building relationships, creating supportive environments, and aligning programs and practices with asset-building principles. For example, one of the basic principles of asset building is that "relationships are the key." Hence, searching for ways to build relationships with young people within each of those five areas of schooling would be productive. Teachers might provide instructional activities (e.g., cooperative learning opportunities) that foster relationships between the teacher and students and among classmates at the same time that content and skills are being taught.

Teachers and principals can help create supportive environments for students by reconsidering school organization (lengthening periods, creating houses or teams), incorporating cocurricular programs (enabling clubs or theater groups to meet after school), and implementing support services (i.e., advocating for improved counselor to student ratios). Many programs and practices already in place in schools are aligned very well with asset-building principles.

A third challenge is finding the time to learn about developmental assets and to be more intentional about building them in all students. Setting aside time involves acknowledgment that change of any kind takes some amount of thinking and assimilation of new information before a change

in behavior occurs. Most school personnel advised of the concept of asset building can almost immediately identify practices they routinely use that are asset building. Nevertheless, becoming more intentional about using those practices with all students (rather than only with the preferred or at-risk students, or those labeled special education or gifted and talented) and thinking about ways to extend the approaches to building developmental assets requires deliberate planning and a focus on changing one's behavior.

The time investment is cost-effective: The amount of time needed to expand one's ability to build assets through practices already in use is presumably far less and is more easily infused into one's thinking and current practice than the time needed to receive inservice training; learn a new practice, program, or curriculum; and begin teaching that. Asset building lends itself to being embedded into programs and practices that are already part of the school culture or classroom environment and into educators' ways of relating to students.

REFERENCES

Benson, P. L., P. C. Scales, N. Leffert, and E. C. Roehlkepartain. 1999. *A fragile foundation: The state of developmental assets among American youth.* Minneapolis, Minn.: Search Institute.

Carnegie Council on Adolescent Development. 1992. *A matter of time: Risk and opportunity in the nonschool hours.* New York: Carnegie Council on Adolescent Development.

Leffert, N., P. L. Benson, P. C. Scales, A. Sharma, D. Drake, and D. A. Blyth. 1998. Developmental assets: Measurement and prediction of risk behaviors among adolescents. *Applied Developmental Science* 2: 209–30.

Newmann, F. M., G. Lopez, and A. S. Bryk. 1998. *The quality of intellectual life in Chicago schools: A baseline report.* Chicago: Consortium on Chicago School Research.

Newmann, F. M., W. G. Secada, and G. G. Wehlage. 1995. *A guide to authentic instruction and assessment: Vision, standards, and scoring.* Madison, Wisc.: Center on Organization and Restructuring of Schools.

Scales, P. C. 1999. Care and challenge: The sources of student success. *Middle Ground* 3(2): 19–21.

Scales, P. C., P. L. Benson, N. Leffert, and D. A. Blyth. 2000. Contribution of developmental assets to the prediction of thriving among adolescents. *Applied Developmental Science* 4: 27–46.

Scales, P. C., and N. Leffert. 1999. *Developmental assets: A synthesis of the scientific research on adolescent development*. Minneapolis, Minn.: Search Institute.

Starkman, N., P. C. Scales, and C. Roberts. 1999. *Great places to learn: How asset-building schools help students succeed*. Minneapolis, Minn.: Search Institute.

Peter C. Scales is senior fellow, and *Judy Taccogna,* a former district director of curriculum and instruction, school principal, counselor, and teacher, is director/education sector, both with Search Institute, Minneapolis, Minnesota.

QUESTIONS FOR REFLECTION

1. What are "developmental assets" and do you believe they have the power that Scales and Taccogna think they do? How might you help students build developmental asset lists in your school? What barriers might impede building a list such as this for students?

2. How do the authors recommend that a school use its "asset lens" to promote concrete changes in school organization, curriculum, cocurricular programs, support services, and community partnerships? What obstacles might prevent a school from carrying out such a task? What can be done to improve the chances that a school would be successful making these kinds of changes?

3. How does asset building lend itself to being embedded into programs and practices that are already part of the school culture or classroom environment and into educators' ways of relating to students? What specific characteristics can you identify that make this possible?

Case Study in Curriculum Implementation

Intentional Curriculum Planning in an Age of Accountability: Explorer Middle School's Approach

DONALD E. LARSEN
TARIQ T. AKMAL

ABSTRACT: The following case study documents the school improvement efforts at Explorer Middle School, a school where more than 90 percent of students qualify for free or reduced-priced lunches. Although the school has yet to achieve "adequate yearly progress" as mandated by No Child Left Behind, the authors explain how, through a "model of intentional curricular and instructional planning . . . Explorer's administration, teachers, staff, students, and parents are moving [the school] forward."

"It was the best of times, it was the worst of times, it was the age of wisdom, it was the age of foolishness, it was the epoch of belief, it was the epoch of incredulity, . . . it was the spring of hope, it was the winter of despair, we had everything before us, we had nothing before us, we were all going direct to Heaven, we were all going direct the other way" (Dickens, 1859, p. 1). So begins Charles Dickens' classic novel, *A Tale of Two Cities*. Although the novel's scenes and characters are rooted in the late eighteenth century, many educators might readily apply this dichotomous description to the state of American public education in the first decade of the twenty-first century.

No Child Left Behind (NCLB) sets ambitious expectations for *all* teachers and students. Even before the reauthorization of the Elementary and Secondary Education Act in 2001, most states adopted reform measures that focused on fixed standards for student achievement (Orfield & Kornhaber, 2001; Stecher & Chun, 2001). The competence of teachers and the success of students are now being gauged by "adequate yearly progress" (AYP), a composite total of students' test scores on various state-mandated exams. Schools that do not meet the AYP standard are readily and publicly identified as having fallen

short of the mark; improvement plans followed by other, more dire, sanctions are specified when a school shows a pattern of failing to meet AYP. The U.S. Secretary of Education insists that improved student achievement and a higher standard of education will result from the mandates handed down by the U.S. Department of Education.

For those who equate standards with requiring that each student reach a specified score on a state-mandated assessment, No Child Left Behind may represent a call to accountability, an antidote to "wishy-washy" educational practices—the best of times. However, many teachers believe that state tests implemented in response to the call for higher standards in education, in fact, limit their teaching effectiveness (Barksdale-Ladd & Thomas, 2000; Sacks, 1999) and even cause a *de-skilling* effect (McNeil, 2000). Furthermore, test scores may be unrealistically equated with school effectiveness and teacher quality (Reeves, 2004; Smith, Heinecke, & Noble, 1999)—the worst of times.

Teachers, particularly those who guide students in developing skills that will be assessed by the state assessment in the spring, labor under the microscope of media scrutiny and public comparison of schools and school districts. The dissection that occurs ritually each fall in the local press suggests that standardized test scores can be analyzed by the numbers and schools neatly quantified, in much the same way that an article in *Consumer Reports* might advise the potential buyer which manufacturer produces the best can opener, and which the worst. Successful schools are seen as those that post improved test scores from the previous year. The assessment report issued each year by the Office of the Superintendent of Public Instruction in State A presents the data without acknowledging that when 82 percent of the seventh graders in Affluence Valley pass the math section of the assessment, and 16 percent of their peers in Poverty Gulch meet that standard, the scores do not compare apples with apples. The report fails to mention that the seventh grade teacher in Poverty Gulch may have coaxed 16 percent of her students to proficiency despite challenges and ethical considerations more daunting than anything the Affluence Valley teacher could imagine or acknowledge.

Some may aver that high-stakes mandates such as NCLB will result in little more than external commitment (Fullan, 2001) on the part of those charged with implementing a new requirement. However, our research (Akmal & Larsen, 2004a; Akmal & Larsen, 2004b) suggests that, even in schools whose demographics would seem to justify low expectations, teachers and administrators may intentionally embrace effective teaching practices tailored to the needs of the student populations they serve.

EXPLORER MIDDLE SCHOOL: A SCHOOL INTENT ON IMPROVEMENT

Over the past five years, we have made Explorer Middle School a focus of our research. By every conventional measure, the circumstances at Explorer might give rise to despair. Of the 720 or so sixth-, seventh-, and eighth-grade students at Explorer, more than 90 percent qualify for free or reduced-priced lunch benefits. For nearly half of the students at Explorer, English is not the language of the home. Some of the students will not begin the next school year until late September,

after the last crop in the valley has been harvested; a few students will not return from Christmas vacation in Mexico until February. From 1999–2001, Explorer averaged more than a 50 percent turnover of students during the course of the school year. In 2002, the flow had slowed to 31 percent, a rate that still justifies concern for the stability of the student population. On the seventh grade benchmark state test, few of the students show proficiency in mathematics; reading scores are slightly better. Explorer is now in year three of a state-mandated "School Improvement Plan," a consequence of failing to achieve "adequate yearly progress" as defined by state standards and No Child Left Behind.

A wooden fence across Arroyo Street from the school office bears spray-painted evidence that Explorer Middle School lies in a neighborhood that rival gangs claim as home turf. A police department cruiser rests at the curb in front of the school. The local police department and the school district have collaborated to make a "school resource officer" (SRO) a daily presence on the Explorer campus to reduce external influences on some members of the student body. Estimates of the number of students who are gang members or "junior" gang members indicate that more than half of the students, some as young as 11 years of age, are affiliated with local gangs.

Given these facts, one would not be surprised to find a building in disrepair, hardened and discouraged staff members, parents eager to take advantage of the first opportunity to transfer their children to another school within the district, and administrators who have reached the point of disheartened, apathetic management. What we have found at Explorer belies any such pessimistic assumptions.

Held to the standard of adequate yearly progress as defined by NCLB, Explorer *is* a failing school. For the teacher in the classroom, the prospect of pushing 100 percent of the student population to proficiency by 2014 might daunt the most sanguine idealist. However, staff members at Explorer have adopted a purposeful plan. They distinguish between (a) the state's expectation that pedagogy and curriculum materials will align with what will be assessed in the spring and (b) the need to do much more with their population than raise test scores. This intentionality reflects a commitment to an internalized set of values (Fullan, 2001). The carefully cultivated relationships and data-guided decision making we have observed suggest that teachers and administrators are collaborating in an explicit "'making-a-difference' sense of purpose" (Fullan, 2001, p. 20), manifested in strategies aimed at improving the achievement *and* the lives of their students. To break the cycle of poverty and low student achievement, these educators are taking a holistic approach that connects students, teachers, and schools in ways that, heretofore, had not been achieved.

Two years ago, at the request of the Explorer staff, the state assigned a school improvement facilitator to guide steps that might help the school emerge from the cloud of failure. Vern Madison, a veteran K–12 educator who works with 16 other failing schools, answered the call.

The initial steps in Explorer Middle School's journey began with what Madison describes as a "readiness-to-benefit" audit. A high-functioning school, Madison says, has three important components in place: (1) staff development targeted to student learning needs, (2) a curriculum that aligns with assessments, and (3) the universal belief that "all kids can learn." Assured that the Explorer staff members held a core belief that ability to learn is not delimited by wealth, family stability, ethnicity, or primary language, Madison has helped in drafting strategies and targets aimed at improving student achievement. Explorer's teachers and administrators have written an improvement plan that focuses on intentionality. "No Child Left Behind has forced us to become more intentional," he says. "The ultimate goal is to be more intentional tomorrow than we were today."

INTERPRETING AND USING DATA TO GUIDE PLANNING

A major part of this intentionality relies on using available data to shape plans and decisions for the school. Assessment scores from the previous spring arrive in the district office in mid-July. In August, the members of the Instructional Leadership Team (ILT) meet to examine the data and develop a narrative around that information. A comparison of Explorer seventh graders' scores with those earned by students in other schools in the district or, more likely, other parts of the state, verifies Explorer's steep uphill journey to meet improvement goals. However, Madison insists that assessment information points toward opportunities as much as toward challenges.

A central function of Explorer's ILT is to make decisions based on the learning attributes and needs of students. As the ILT members examine the assessment numbers, they disaggregate the data in order to focus also on specific populations within the school. Madison says, "It becomes not just [a matter of] presenting data but also asking, 'What do the data mean for the classroom?'"

The administrators and the teachers also critically examine the data for evidence of high achievement. One seventh grade teacher observed, "When one teacher sees that another seems to be having real success with 'Four Square Writing,' the rest of us should be asking, 'What's she doing that works?'" Because the Explorer instructional plan is built around blocks of core subjects, each core team can also examine individual student achievement from subject to subject and class to class.

Jolene Zimmerman, Explorer's principal, notes that, at a comprehensive level, her role is, "to see the bigger data picture. I try to point out [positive and negative] trends that we're experiencing, but more importantly, that we ask why those trends exist." Following this self-analytical process, the ILT submits an updated school improvement plan to the district office by October.

Research suggests that standards-based initiatives tend to reduce teaching to a "one-size-fits-all" formula that prescribes how lessons will align with state-mandated assessments (Barksdale-Ladd & Thomas, 2000; Dutro, Collins, & Collins, 2002; Kohn, 2000). In a study by Barksdale-Ladd and Thomas (2000) that included interviews with 59 teachers, one teacher lamented, "All of the most powerful teaching tools I used to use every day are no good to me now because they don't help children get ready for the test, and it makes me a robot instead of a teacher" (p. 392).

At Explorer, the school improvement process has had its detractors. A district policy adopted in 2003 requires middle schools to reserve 90 minutes daily for reading. This reading initiative has displaced lessons that some teachers prized. "We have teachers who are 'mourning' the loss of autonomy," Madison says. "And they really *are* mourning the loss of autonomy." However, while a few may lament that they have lost their favorite history unit or whale unit, even the most skeptical have been gratified as the increased focus on reading has paid dividends in the classroom. "My goodness," teachers say, "My kids are reading!"

When one subject—reading, for example—is singled out to be the focus of campus-wide efforts, other subjects may suffer a proportionate de-emphasis. Madison and several teachers observed that pressure on the content areas increased as the school plan zeroed in on reading and writing. However, Madison says, the goal of school improvement is to raise student performance to a point where the intensive intervention is no longer necessary. "As [student] skills get higher," Madison says, "our hope is that teachers can bring more of the content back into the classroom."

Though cautiously optimistic about this time-consuming investment in reading improvement that in one year alone—2003–2004—paid a 100 percent dividend, teachers at Explorer worry about all the other variables in their students' lives that may adversely affect that achievement. Empathy with the day-to-day realities of their students' lives may not occur automatically to teachers who commute to Explorer each morning from comfortable homes. As one teacher reflected, it can be difficult for a teacher who was raised in—and now lives in—a middle-class setting to comprehend why one student didn't bring her textbook to class and why another offers no explanation for not completing the homework assignment.

It's difficult for us to relate to all the different *stuff*—how many of our students are actually *being* the adults in their homes and running their homes and things like that. . . . How many of our students go home and don't know if there's going to be anyone there.

One of Explorer's assistant principals added, "When you have kids who are afraid to go home at night because the gangs are after them, they're not exactly worried about reading and writing!" Still, the goal remains to help students improve their lives while also gaining the academic skills they need to leave poverty behind.

Developing and implementing the improvement plan at Explorer has been a creative process. To ensure that all teachers might benefit from team-based planning time, as well as common teaching time, the staff requested a waiver from the union's contractual agreement. The 90-minute reading block is one departure from the contractual agreement. Classes at Explorer are delayed by 90 minutes once a week so teachers can collaborate and plan together. Both principal Zimmerman and Madison note that these teacher-initiated waivers from a contract that governs all certified staff in the district are manifestations of intentionality and moral purpose. In addition, every member of the staff has a staff development calendar for the entire school year, a document developed by the Instructional Leadership Team.

RELATIONSHIPS AS KEYS TO EFFECTIVE PLANNING

"If moral purpose is job one, relationships are job two, as you can't get anywhere without them" (Fullan, 2001, p. 51). At Explorer, intentionality is accompanied by a second, equally important part of school-wide improvement: a focus on building and maintaining relationships, beginning with the unified efforts of the staff, faculty, and administration of the school and concluding with the inclusion of students and parents in the improvement process. For teachers at Explorer Middle School, creating a vision for their learning community and charting the steps needed to attain purposeful objectives for student learning have been facilitated by development of strong bonds within the staff.

The strong friendships and high levels of respect among teachers and administrators foster deeper conversations that are more grounded in student assessment data. "Sometimes we have to look at each other, eyeball-to-eyeball across the table until we come to agreement," says Principal Zimmerman, "But at the end of the day, we're still friends and colleagues." These tight bonds also permit teachers an opportunity to lay their frustrations and concerns on the table, knowing that their colleagues are not going to criticize, but instead offer empathy and solutions.

One teacher notes, "I think what this faculty does most effectively is take care of each other. It's just amazing how many personal situations have come up with our faculty and how we have always been so supportive of each other." At the heart of this behavior is the philosophy that if the faculty and staff care about and support one another, they will be in a better position to care and provide support for their students.

Relationships at Explorer are not happenstance; they, too, are intentional and part of the overall strategy of the ILT. The School Improvement Plan contains specific reference to building teams through collaborative planning times, ensuring that teachers have enough time and professional development to be proficient in their use of data and decision-making. At an informal level, all staff birthdays, individual and team achievements, and familial occurrences are celebrated or, in time of crisis, supported. During the summer vacation the staff meets—voluntarily—simply to gather and enjoy one another's company. On weekends, many of the staff socialize or do outdoor recreation, pursue home or community projects, or shop together. Invariably, school comes up. "We sometimes solve some of our toughest problems when we aren't in school," says one member of a teaching team that spends almost every other weekend together. Is the planned curriculum affected by these relationships? "Absolutely!" says Principal Zimmerman.

"We no longer see any hidden agendas at meetings. Everybody knows what I want and they feel comfortable voicing their disagreement or support for an idea. So when we talk about something, it's an honest, no-holds-barred talk."

LEADERSHIP BY DESIGN

Intentionality, moral purpose, and relationships are essential components of a culture in which internal motivation drives the organization (Fullan, 2001). But what are the characteristics of the leader of such an organization? Fullan suggests that effective leaders instill a "can-do" ethos in those around them. "They are always hopeful—conveying a sense of optimism and an attitude of never giving up in the pursuit of highly valued goals" (Fullan, 2001, p. 7).

The ideal school administrator might be described as not just a generic manager, but an instructional leader. In practice, however, few administrators live up to this lofty expectation.

> Most principals spend relatively little time in classrooms and even less time analyzing instruction with teachers. They may arrange time for teachers' meetings and professional development, but they rarely provide intellectual leadership for growth in teaching skill. (Fink & Resnick, 2001, p. 598)

At Explorer Middle School, Jolene Zimmerman may well serve as the prototypical principal whose energy, optimism, and vision set the tone for an entire learning community.

Their prior experience with a secretive, divisive, and penny-pinching administrator left the Explorer staff distrustful of administrators and each other. "There was a lot of hurt on this faculty," Zimmerman acknowledges, "a lot of people who had not been well treated and who were not willing to trust me just because I said they should or wanted them to." Zimmerman's open style of leadership that invited and accepted input from teachers, staff, students, and parents promised to align mission with practice.

What has allowed Zimmerman to connect with a staff that had developed the "duck and cover" mentality of a shell-shocked foot soldier? For one thing, Zimmerman cultivates an open communication style. "I like to put everything on the table so that everyone can see it," Zimmerman says. Her secretary agrees:

> One thing's for sure: you always know where you stand with Jolene. If she's unhappy with something you've done, you'll know it. If she's happy about it, you'll know it. But one of the things that we all know around here is that if we don't like something, we'll have the chance to say so.

Whether inspired by Zimmerman's open communication, her follow-through on promises, or her unquenchable energy and optimism, the Explorer staff has rallied to her side. Eighteen of the staff members had requested transfers to other schools before Zimmerman received the call to Explorer. They all stayed. Zimmerman empowered the ILT to dictate the school budget. Transparency became the norm in faculty meetings and core team meetings.

The process and pace of change at Explorer since the state identified it for school improvement has elevated and accelerated the expectations of the staff. Simultaneous with this acceleration has come the potential for staff members to throw up their hands in exasperation. Jeffrey Abood, a teacher who has been on the Explorer staff for 10 years, says that the unrelenting focus on intentional instructional practices might tempt a teacher to look for a school that places fewer demands on its staff. "Quite frankly, it would be easier [to leave]," he says,

> There are probably people [at Explorer] who would like to be doing something else, but we're in this together. Ms. Zimmerman has built in that sense of interdependence. I don't know . . . it's just that sense of "roll up your sleeves and get it done."

Zimmerman says the process of breaking the inertia and moving Explorer toward improvement involved more than setting goals on which everyone could agree. She was learning to be a principal while the staff members were learning to work together. "It was sort of like building the airplane while flying it."

A can-do culture has replaced the self-protective climate that Zimmerman first encountered at Explorer. Even when teachers complain, they want to do the right thing. They want to help. Brian Morales, a special education teacher, notes that he and his colleagues have learned to trust the vision that Zimmerman has brought to the school. "People get frustrated," he observed.

> Jolene knows it's the same thing like with [our students], so you have to say, "Let's give it a shot and see how it goes." It just kind of gets everybody to level out a little bit, calm down a little bit. And then people go, "Aaaah, all right, it'll be okay." I think that people, whether they are kids or adults, just want reassurance that things are going to be okay.

Today, instead of focusing on pennies spent or developing and supporting factions, the Explorer staff focuses on kids. A "whatever-it-takes" attitude prevails. The slightest upturn in student achievement or test scores is cause for celebration. All communication with parents is published in English and in Spanish. A framed and matted copy of Explorer's state assessment scores is the first thing one sees upon entering the main office. The school custodian helps coach wrestling. One of the cooks uses her computer to keep track of and celebrate students' birthdays. During vacation breaks, as part of the school's interventional academic program, the school gym and selected classes remain open. Student volunteerism is at an all-time high, and student pride in the spotless campus is evident. "I've seen it [Explorer] go from a shell to a rich, vibrant school," says Madison.

To many educators, Explorer's recipe for school improvement might represent the pinnacle—or perhaps the precipice—of innovation. However, as Abood remarks,

> If you sit down and really think about some of the changes that we've made, they're common sense. They're common sense. I think what has been most difficult for us has been change. Change. It's just something that we needed to do.

Zimmerman acknowledges that keeping a focus both on the moral purpose behind change and on the relationships required to motivate and sustain change takes a delicate balance, but she also believes Explorer is on the right track. "But if our students' reading doesn't substantially improve next year," she says, grinning, "they [the teachers] will be ready to string me up!"

WHAT LIES IN STORE FOR EXPLORER?

Explorer Middle School's effort to improve their students' learning and lives is firmly grounded on intentionality. School-wide leadership whose moral purpose is manifested in a vision for intentional improvement, a web of caring and personal relationships, and ongoing planning guided by relevant data are the hallmarks of this school.

Explorer has developed as a kind of "nested learning community" (Fink & Resnick, 2001), a metaphor drawn from the nesting dolls sold as souvenirs in places such as Russia.

> The [nesting dolls] image seems to work because the dolls are each independent, free-standing "people," but they share a common form. And you can't decide which is the most "important" doll, the tiny one in the middle that establishes the shape for them all or the big one on the outside that encloses them all. (Fink & Resnick, 2001, p. 600)

The professionals at Explorer distinguish between the state's expectation that pedagogy and curriculum materials will align with what will be assessed in the spring and the need to do much more with their population than raise test scores. In the spring of 2004, after three years under the shadow of a school improvement plan, the seventh graders' scores on the state assessment doubled. Yet no one in this learning community is ready to erect a banner that declares "Mission Accomplished." As the faculty and staff continue to focus their efforts on helping students develop basic skills for learning (reading, writing, and mathematics), test scores will continue to climb. "Even if we don't see the scores we want," Madison insists, "Explorer is still a good place for kids to be."

According to the rubric set by NCLB, Explorer is a failing middle school, but a glance beyond the numbers shows this to be anything but true. Through a model of intentional curricular and instructional planning, Explorer's administration, teachers, staff, students, and parents are moving Explorer forward, from the worst of circumstances to the best of times.

REFERENCES

Akmal, T. T., & Larsen, D. E. (2004a). Keeping History from Repeating Itself: Involving Parents about Retention Decisions to Support Student Achievement. *Research in Middle Level Education Online, 27*(2).

Akmal, T. T., & Larsen, D. E. (2004b, April). *Aligning state reform with middle school needs: Contextualizing accountability pressure for school renewal.* Paper presented at the annual meeting of the American Educational Research Association Conference, San Diego, CA.

Barksdale-Ladd, M. A., & Thomas, K. F. (2000). What's at stake in high-stakes testing: Teachers and parents speak out. *Journal of Teacher Education, 51,* 384–397.

Dickens, C. (1859). *A tale of two cities.* New York: Walter J. Black, Inc.

Dutro, E., Collins, K. M., & Collins, J. (2002, April). *Teachers' responses to the standards movement: Perspectives from literacy practitioners in three states.* Paper presented at the annual meeting of the American Educational Research Association, New Orleans, LA.

Fink, E., & Resnick, L. B. (2001, April). Developing principals as instructional leaders. *Phi Delta Kappan, 82*(8), 598–606.

Fullan, M. (2001). *Leading in a culture of change.* San Francisco: Jossey-Bass.

Kohn, A. (2000). Burnt at the high stakes. *Journal of Teacher Education, 51,* 315–327.

McNeil, L. M. (2000). *Contradictions of school reform: Educational costs of standardized testing.* New York: Routledge.

Orfield, G., & Kornhaber, M. L. (Eds.). (2001). *Raising standards or raising barriers? Inequality and high-stakes testing in public education.* New York: The Century Foundation Press.

Reeves, D. B. (2004). *Accountability for learning: How teachers and school leaders can take charge.* Alexandria, VA: Association for Supervision and Curriculum Development.

Sacks, P. (1999). *Standardized minds: The high price of America's testing culture and what we can do to change it.* Cambridge, MA: Perseus Publishing.

Smith, M. L., Heinecke, W., & Noble, A. (1999, Winter). Assessment policy and political spectacle. *Teachers College Record, 101*(2), 157–191.

Stecher, B., & Chun, T. (2001). *School and classroom practices during two years of education reform in Washington state* (National Center for Research on Evaluation, Standards, and Student Testing/ RAND). Los Angeles: University of California.

Donald E. Larsen is assistant professor of educational administration at Western Washington University. *Tariq T. Akmal* is associate professor of teaching and learning, Washington State University.

QUESTIONS FOR REFLECTION

1. What are the implications for a school that has more than 90% of its students qualifying for free or reduced lunch? How might this school be different with regards to community, outside support, and achievement than one in which no students qualify for free or reduced lunch?
2. What key features of Explorer Middle School's yearly progress have school leaders and teachers been addressing and how have they been able to move the school forward? What do you think will be necessary to bring the school to a place where it can meet NCLB's requirement for improved annual progress?
3. Does Explorer Middle School sound like a school you would like to teach in? Why or why not? What characteristics about the school influence your answer?

Leaders' Voices— Putting Theory into Practice

Teaming for Better School Climate and Improved Achievement

LUANNE L. KOKOLIS

ABSTRACT: There are those in the school community who believe that the anxious feelings and heightened sense of anxiety experienced by sixth graders as they transition from elementary to junior high school constitute a rite of passage. Teachers and school administrators in the Indiana Area Junior High School in Pennsylvania believed differently. During one school year, school administrators and a core group of seventh-grade teachers began to have discussions centered on student achievement and the junior high school environment. From those discussions, it was determined that the junior high school environment needed to be changed in a way that was more "school friendly" and "student focused" for their incoming seventh-grade students. This article discusses teaming as a viable way to improve the school climate for seventh-grade students.

THE "FEAR FACTOR" AND URBAN LEGENDS OF THE JUNIOR HIGH

What was good 20 years ago is good now, our students perform well on state assessments, why change? There were those in our school community who believed that the anxious feelings and heightened sense of anxiety experienced by sixth graders as they transitioned from elementary to junior high school was a rite of passage. Teachers and school administrators in the Indiana Area Junior High School in Pennsylvania believed differently.

During the 2002–2003 school year, school administrators and a core group of seventh grade teachers began to have discussions centered on student achievement and the junior high school environment. From those discussions, it was determined that the junior high school environment needed to be changed in a way that was more "school friendly" and "student focused" for our incoming seventh grade students. In our rural community, siblings passed down from year to year a sense of fear to sixth graders as they embarked on their new school career, transitioning from the elementary to the middle level program. This unfounded "fear factor" transcended the years with urban legends of seventh graders being lost, sent to wrong rooms, missing buses, locked in lockers, and being intimidated by the big ninth graders. As incoming seventh graders participated in the orientation at the start of the school year, the halls were filled with wide eyes and anxious faces. It was not uncommon to have the guidance counselors, teachers, and the assistant principal assist students throughout the first few days of school in finding a room, helping with locker challenges, and calming emotionally distraught students who were overwhelmed with their new environment.

THE TRADITIONAL JUNIOR HIGH PROGRAM

The junior high school operated a traditional school program,[1] in which seventh, eighth, and ninth graders had an eight-period school day where all students moved from floor to floor for classes. The student homerooms for seventh, eighth, and ninth grades were located throughout the four floors of our school building. Courses were offered for each grade level in the core subject areas, and a diversified elective program was available to all students. Included in the junior high program were accelerated course offerings, an option for students who wanted to prepare for the high school advanced placement programs. Seventh grade students taking an advanced math course may have found themselves in a class with eighth grade students. Flexibility of scheduling was very limited. Class schedules were built primarily around the availability of teachers. To begin the school day, students reported to homerooms, which were populated alphabetically by grade level. They moved through the daily schedule of eight 40-minute class periods. As the school day came to a close, students were dismissed for the day from their eighth period class.

The enrollment fluctuated between 800 and 900 students. Over the past several years, courses have been added to the elective program to remain current with technology and state standards. Computer applications, multi-media and video production, and family and consumer science were a few of the elective courses that had been revised and updated. White boards, digital flat screens, and video projection units were placed in five computer labs. Ongoing course review to incorporate benchmarks and state standards into course content occurred through central office leadership on an annual basis. Other than the curriculum modifications and elective course offerings, there had been little change in recent years to the schedule or delivery of the school program.

IMPROVING THE SCHOOL ENVIRONMENT BY INTEGRATING THE MIDDLE SCHOOL PHILOSOPHY

Ongoing discussions with the seventh grade teachers and building administrators revolved around the trepidation experienced by incoming seventh graders at the start of the school year. One of the assistant principals had taught in a middle school and was an advocate for the benefits of teaming.[2] Seeking out a viable solution that would improve school climate for seventh grade students, the building principals led the teachers through an exploration of middle school teaming.[3] Although our community was not about to abandon our traditional junior high grade configuration, parent advisory groups and seventh grade teachers were in agreement that something should be done to alleviate apprehension and anxiety for the sixth grade students transitioning to the junior high school.

Building administrators, guidance counselors, and a volunteer group of seventh grade teachers read articles on teaming, discussed the benefits of teaming in a study group, looked for intersections of the junior high program and middle school concepts, and visited middle schools in the area. Middle school site visits provided information related to the daily schedule, team planning time, block schedules, and the benefits of a student-centered focus on teaming. Conversation included "middle schools' emphasis on the characteristics and interests of students, the importance of a close-knit school community, the accommodation of diversity, and the integration of the curriculum" (Hill, 1992, pp. v–vi).

Throughout the 2002–2003 school year, information was shared in designated committee meetings where the possibility of creating a seventh grade team concept began to unfold. At the outset, the committee expressed a need to create a support system for seventh graders with a core group of teachers. During the spring of 2003, newsletters were sent out to parents to invite their students to be a part of the teaming pilot program.

This was a two-year pilot program, which began in 2003–2004 and continued in 2004–2005, and in which one seventh grade team of 100 students was instructed by a volunteer group of five core area teachers. Parents were invited to sign up for the teaming initiative by attending an evening school program outlining the daily schedule, sharing the benefits of teaming, and describing additional opportunities for parent team conferencing. The flexibility of the daily schedule included team planning time for the team teachers; a student homeroom advised by a homeroom teacher who was one of the student's core team teachers; and a counseling component, with the seventh grade counselor linked to the team planning time. Within three weeks of the parent meeting, a team of 100 students had been identified as the first junior high seventh grade team.

DATA ANALYSIS FROM THE SEVENTH GRADE TEAM PROGRAM

At the midpoint of the second year of the teaming program, team data were collected from parent, student, and teacher surveys; student discipline referral records; parent conferencing feedback; and student course failure records. Data were analyzed to determine student, parent, and teacher responses to the pilot team program. Surveys were sent to seventh grade team parents, all seventh grade teachers, and all seventh grade students. Students from seventh grade, both on and off the team, responded to questions related to school climate, student interactions, safety, and general perceptions of the school environment. Teamed student survey responses were compared to off-team student responses. Parent surveys included questions related to teacher accessibility, student adjustment to seventh grade, school safety, and overall perceptions of school climate. In addition to survey data, school archival data, such as seventh grade discipline referrals, class failures, and student performance based on grade report comparisons pre- and post-pilot team years were used to determine whether or not measurable changes had occurred.

STUDENTS, PARENTS, AND TEACHERS SAY "YES" TO TEAMING!

Survey responses from teamed students found that they felt comfortable in their environment;

they liked being at the junior high and felt a strong sense of school community. Students' off-team responses tended to be favorable as well, but to a lesser degree. Teamed students responded that teams should be created for all students in the seventh grade. Parent responses were very favorable, and parents expressed a desire to carry the team concept into the eighth grade. Parents indicated that teachers were more accessible, and parents welcomed the opportunity to meet with all teachers at one common time. Parents also indicated that they believed the team concept helped their students adjust to the transition into the middle level school environment. A parent commented, "My son is excited about school, and I thought he would be overwhelmed; his brother was when he attended the junior high."

Teacher responses to the survey were positive as they related to team planning time, student morale, and opportunities to integrate curriculum. A viable concern surfaced related to the impact on class size for special area subjects. The common team planning time, and alterations made to the daily schedule limited seventh grade team students' ability to schedule special area courses throughout the school day. The common team planning time forced the teamed students into special subject area courses at the same time, creating larger class sizes for the art, music, technology, and consumer science classes. This was a concern that needed to be addressed before full-team implementation was considered.

The guidance counselors indicated that the conferencing opportunities had a positive impact on parent communication and provided for a student-centered focus during parent conferencing. The counselors played an important role in facilitating many team meetings and acted as liaisons between the team and parents.

STUDENT DISCIPLINE AND ACHIEVEMENT DATA

Student disciplinary incidents for seventh graders decreased significantly during the two-year pilot

TABLE 1

Seventh Grade Student Discipline Referrals

Year	Incidents
2001–02	162
2002–03	118
2003–04	89
2004–05	72

of the teaming initiative. During the final pilot year of the program, the seventh grade disciplinary referrals to the office decreased 25% from the previous year, with 11 students from the team needing disciplinary interventions, as compared to 37 off-team students needing disciplinary interventions during the first year of the pilot program.

Student academic performance was reviewed by guidance counselors and by team teachers. During the first year of the pilot program, 2% of the students on the team failed a core subject, while 7% of the off-team students failed a core subject. The second year of the pilot produced similar results, with 4% of the students on the team having failed one core subject and 7% of the off-team students failing a core subject.

FULL-TEAM IMPLEMENTATION FOR ALL SEVENTH GRADERS

For the 2005–2006 school year, a schedule was built with a traditional junior high schedule in place for eighth and ninth grade students, which included a full elective program. The seventh grade class was divided into two teams of approximately 115 students each. Building administrators and guidance counselors were aware of the need to balance the schedule so that team planning time did not negatively affect special area class sizes. The seventh grade teachers participated in a summer workshop to learn the structure of the team planning time, develop an orientation for the first day of school, and provide for collaboration to review student Pennsylvania System of School Assessment (PSSA) data.

Housed on the third floor of the building, each of the two seventh grade teams was encouraged and supported by a group of five core area teachers. All of our seventh grade homerooms, lockers, and classes were housed on the third floor, where we created a "school-within-a-school." The team schedule allowed for common team planning time for all core subject teachers, along with the seventh grade guidance counselor. Special education teachers and building administrators attended team planning time as their schedules permitted. Team planning notes were documented and made available via e-mail to all teachers who instructed seventh grade students. The team teachers used the team planning time to collaborate in preparing interdisciplinary projects such as a history-based unit integrating the study of Mesopotamia, art, and storytelling. Hallways became "Halls of History" with student work displayed by themed units throughout the school year. The seventh grade classrooms were decorated by area of study, and the rooms were alive with student exhibitions and performance-based activities. It was not uncommon to visit a classroom and see a student dressed as a Pharaoh delivering a speech to his servants, or another dressed as an artisan, describing a work of art created for the marketplace. Planning time was used to invite an "artist in residence" to spend time developing the art of storytelling and weaving the story into a piece of student-created artwork. The opportunity to meet with parents in a group setting proved to be invaluable within the school community. Common team planning time served this purpose well. The team encouraged parents to schedule a conference during team planning time to maximize parents' and teachers' time. Parents commented on the seventh grade parent survey that conferencing during the common planning had been beneficial for keeping open lines of communication between teachers and parents.

OPPORTUNITIES FOR STUDENT GAINS EMERGE FROM TEAMING

As administrators, counselors, and teachers reviewed student academic performance data for the seventh grade class (targeting comparative data from their fifth grade PSSA), it became apparent that there was a need for reading and math remediation for students who received "Basic" or "Below Basic" assessment scores in the elementary school. Teachers, counselors, and school administrators collaborated during the winter and spring of 2004–2005 to determine how to best serve the needs of the students, leading to improved eighth grade state assessment test scores. By visiting middle schools in previous years, team members were aware of the "block schedule", where 80 minutes of time might be devoted to a specific subject area. A seventh grade team English teachers[4] and a seventh grade team reading teacher[5] volunteered to take on the task of developing an 80-minute block of time devoted to English and reading. Teachers collaborated during team planning time to review individual student data related to student fifth grade PSSA reading scores. The teachers determined that if they focused on specific concepts in reading comprehension and combined the reading curriculum with the English and language arts curriculum for an extended amount of time each day, the concentrated effort would benefit the students assigned to their classes. Together with building administrators, the teachers created the 80-minute block for those students who had not been successful on the PSSA. The initial mission to modify the seventh grade program to enhance the school climate had taken on the additional focus of increasing student achievement.

The result of the collaborative effort led to the incorporation of a remediation component, which weaved through the seventh grade teaming schedule. The "literacy block" was created, in which the reading and English teachers teamed together for back-to-back, 40-minute class periods. A movable center door, to permit large-group discussions and presentations, connected their classrooms. The teachers were provided with the flexibility to team teach, with time allotted to create a program that met the individual needs of each of their students.

Book studies of Danielson's *Enhancing Professional Practice, A Framework for Teaching* (1996) and *Enhancing Student Achievement, A Framework for School Improvement* (2002), along with journal articles such as: "Using Data to Differentiate Instruction" (Brimijoin, Marquissee, & Tomlinson, 2003) and "Standards-Based Thematic Units Integrate the Arts and Energize Students and Teachers" (Bolak, Bialach, & Dunphy, 2005), provided depth in identifying best practices for the newly formed reading/language arts block. Within the class time, differentiated instruction was used on a daily basis (Brimfield, Masci, & DeFiore, 2002). The teachers created authentic learning experiences as the students became active learners. Learning centers and literary circles were part of the daily active learning opportunities. Tables were used as learning centers and students rotated from station to station as they worked through parts of speech related to current passages in an assigned reading. The teachers had the flexibility to team together for the entire block or group the students for time with one teacher, allowing the other teacher to meet with individual students for one-on-one instruction.

The teachers' schedules were created to mirror each other so that the "literacy block" English was taught to one group while "literacy block" reading was taught at the same time to another group. The teachers serviced a total of approximately 29 students split between each of two 80-minute literacy blocks. An additional 20 students attended either the 40-minute reading or 40-minute English section and were not part of the entire 80-minute literacy block. Students had opportunities to learn through learning center activities, presenting oral reflections on learned concepts, or interpreting passages through group discussion. The teachers welcomed the opportunity to have extended, intensified instructional time with the seventh grade students.

Data from the 2005–2006 school year have provided positive results for the students who participated in the literacy block. Of the students who participated in the block, 59% of the students advanced at least one performance level on the 2006 PSSA in reading—21% advanced two levels, 38% advanced one level.

In addition to English and reading, the schedule for seventh grade also provided an opportunity for students to receive remediation in math. Two team math teachers were assigned to be available for 40 minutes each day for PSSA math remediation. This collaborative time was used to assess individual student math scores for those seventh grade students who scored "Basic" or "Below Basic" on the state assessment and to provide remediation based on the individual needs for each student. For the first year of this program, this class time was not set in a formal schedule for students, so they could attend a 40-minute time slot only if their schedule aligned with that of the PSSA math teacher. In addition to regular math class, seventh grade students were sent to receive additional teacher instruction time based on math teacher recommendations and student need.

TEAMING FOR STUDENT-CENTERED SCHOOL COMMUNITY

At the outset, our goals were to sustain and encourage student success, create a child-centered approach to improve student attitudes toward school, promote a strong foundation for student connection to the school community, and establish flexibility for future scheduling adaptations. An additional goal surfaced as we provided opportunities for enrichment and for remediation for students who had not reached target performance on state assessments. The teaming initiative was the catalyst that launched academic enrichment opportunities within the school day. Many students were able to experience success in English, reading, and math due to the literacy block and PSSA math remediation. The changes and modifications incorporated into the seventh grade students' school experience have produced a student-centered approach to the academic program while diffusing the anxiety related to the transition from elementary school to a middle grades environment.

The seventh grade teaming initiative was the impetus to change the school culture. The teachers and school staff have nurtured a culture of learning for all students with a strong sense of school community. The excitement level for incoming seventh graders was positive and energized as teachers and building administrators met with sixth graders and their parents during the springs of 2004 and 2005. With the introduction of teaming and a student-centered focus in the building, the "fear factor" has diminished considerably, and junior high urban legends of days gone by faded from memory within the community. The 7–9 building was poised to build additional innovative modifications to ensure future student achievement gains, not only for state assessments in reading and math, but for continued success as they continue on their journey of becoming lifelong learners.

NOTES

1. Traditional school program refers to building a schedule of classes based on the availability of teachers to cover a specified number of classes. The school day was based on an eight-period schedule of 40-minute class periods. Students in grades seven, eight, and nine followed similar schedules during the school day. The schedule was not flexible, preventing modifications.

2. Benefits of teaming include the focus on a student-centered school community, a collaborative common planning time for a core group of team teachers, integrated content area lessons and activities, flexible scheduling, and additional opportunities to team-conference with parents.

3. Middle school teaming describes the ability to bring together a core group of teachers who experience

empowerment to effect positive change in the lives of their students. In this article, teaming refers to the seventh grade teams of students who were served by five core subject teachers. The team teachers interacted with their students during homeroom, subject area class time, and throughout the instructional day on the third floor of the building. The teaming initiative created an opportunity for collegial exchange during team planning time and an opportunity to explore flexible scheduling.

4. Mrs. Carol Tanweer, seventh grade English team teacher, created integrated activities for her students in the literacy block, leading to gains in student achievement as measured on the Pennsylvania School System Assessment test.

5. Mr. John Lyons, seventh grade reading team teacher, created integrated activities for his students, leading to measurable performance gains on the Pennsylvania School System Assessment test.

REFERENCES

Bolak, K., Bialach, D., & Dunphy, M. (2005). Standards-based, thematic units integrate the arts and engage students and teachers. *Middle School Journal, 36*(5), 9–19.

Brimfield, R., Masci, F., & DeFiore, D. (2002). Differentiating instruction to teach all learners. *Middle School Journal, 33*(3), 14–18.

Brimijoin, K., Marquissee, E., & Tomlinson, C. A. (2003). Using data to differentiate instruction. *Educational Leadership, 60*(5), 70–73.

Danielson, C. (2002). *Enhancing student achievement: A framework for school improvement.* Alexandria, VA: Association for Supervision and Curriculum Development.

Danielson, C. (1996). *Enhancing professional practice: A framework for teaching.* Alexandria, VA: Association for Supervision and Curriculum Development.

Hill, C. (2002). Foreword. In P. S. George, C. Stevenson, J. Thomason, & J. Beane, (Eds.). *The middle school—and beyond* (pp. v–vi). Alexandria, VA: Association for Supervision and Curriculum Development.

Luanne L. Kokolis, a former principal of Indiana Area Junior High School in Pennsylvania, is an associate superintendent for planning and programs at Rock Hill School District, South Carolina.

QUESTIONS FOR REFLECTION

1. What is "teaming" and how was it used by the teachers and school leaders in the article to improve the school climate for incoming seventh-grade students?
2. How might you incorporate teaming into the curriculum with which you are most familiar?
3. Besides teaming, what other initiatives can you think of that can be an impetus to change school culture? What traits do they have in common? How are they different?

LEARNING ACTIVITIES

Critical Thinking

1. Which developmental changes discussed in Chapter 3 should guide curriculum leaders in designing educational programs for transescents and early adolescents?
2. What are the essential elements of effective curricula for transescents and early adolescents?
3. William M. Alexander, generally acknowledged as the "father" of the middle school, once said, "Every student should be well known as a person by at least one adult in the school who accepts responsibility for the student's guidance." What does it mean to be "known as a person"? Why is such a relationship with an adult of critical importance to middle-level students? What steps can teachers and administrators take to ensure that each student has such a relationship?

Application Activities

1. Pioneering work in developing curricula for transescents was done by Carleton W. Washburne at the Skokie Junior High School in Winnetka, Illinois, and is described in Chapter 7 of *Winnetka: The History and Significance of an Educational Experiment* by Washburne and Sidney P. Marland (Prentice-Hall, 1963). Would the activities described in that chapter be appropriate and challenging for today's transescents? Which of the four perspectives on curriculum that William H. Schubert discusses in Chapter 1 do those activities represent?
2. When you were an early adolescent, what school experiences helped you to grow and learn? What experiences hindered you? What implications do these experiences have for your current and future curriculum planning activities?
3. Drawing from the material in this chapter, develop a short questionnaire or set of interview questions that curriculum leaders could use to learn more about early adolescents.
4. Invite a group of junior high/middle school teachers to your class and ask them to describe the steps they take in planning curricula for their students. What do they see as the most important curriculum criteria to use in planning?

Field Experiences

1. Talk with a group of early adolescents about the social forces of concern to them in their school, their community, their nation, and the world. Compare your findings with those of your fellow students.
2. Visit a junior high or middle school and ask to see the school's statement of philosophy (or mission statement) and/or set of schoolwide goals. To what extent do these materials reflect the points of view expressed in this chapter?
3. Visit an agency in your community that offers services to transescents and early adolescents and their families. Ask a staff member to describe the services that are offered. Report your findings to the rest of your class.

Internet Activities

1. Go to one or more of the following locations and gather information, research results, publications, and resources on effective educational programs for transescents and early adolescents.

   Center for Adolescent Studies
   National Middle School Association
   Online Educational Resources
   Center of Education for the Young Adolescent
   Middle Level Leadership Center
   The Middle School Information Center

2. Go to Kidlink, an organization dedicated to using the Internet to link children and youth through the age of fifteen from around the world. From this location, visit areas accessible to adults to determine the educational interests, needs, and concerns of transescents and early adolescents.
3. Go to the educator-oriented part of the Kidlink site, where you will find instructional activities that integrate various areas of the curriculum. Compile a list of activities appropriate for transescents and early adolescents. From here you can "visit" school sites where students and teachers use Kidlink in the classroom.

10

High School Curricula

FOCUS QUESTIONS

1. What are the major developmental concerns of high school–level students?

2. What are some of the "internal problems" that confront today's high schools?

3. What were the reasons behind the development of the comprehensive high school in America?

4. What recommendations have been made for restructuring high schools?

5. What are some appropriate curricular goals for high school–level students?

DEVELOPMENTAL CHALLENGES OF HIGH SCHOOL–LEVEL STUDENTS

High school–level students are beginning to seek some assurance of eventual economic independence from parents and other adults. They sense their new intellectual powers and their need to develop additional cognitive skills. Their dominant motivation most often is to achieve social status within the adolescent community and to meet the expectations of their peers. Often, they feel the tension between two orientations—engaging in behavior approved by adults versus engaging in behavior approved by peers. In this chapter's *Case Study in Curriculum Implementation* section, Hugh Campbell, a high school principal, outlines how teachers at his school developed a curriculum to help students adjust to the transition between the middle school and high school (see "Going the Extra Mile to Smooth the Transition to High School"). According to Erik Erikson, students at this level seek a "sense of identity" and the development of values they can call their own. According to Bennett M. Berger, a well-known sociologist and author of *An Essay on Culture: Symbolic Structure and Social Structure* (1995), adolescence is one of the ways that culture violates nature by insisting that, for an increasing number of years, young persons postpone their claims to the privileges and responsibilities of common citizenship. At this point, you may wish to review the perspectives on human development that have been advanced by Lawrence Kohlberg, Carol Gilligan, and others by turning to Chapter 3.

The world of today's high school–level students is dramatically different from the one their parents experienced. Technological changes, a multiplicity of social options and values, the pervasiveness of crime and violence, the media's intrusiveness and influence, and the blurring of the lines separating adults and children have a tremendous impact on today's youth. Among other challenges facing high school youth, in "Becoming Citizens of the World," Vivien Stewart suggests in this chapter that today's high school students are not prepared to be citizens of a multiethnic, multicultural, and multilingual world.

Adults may have difficulty comprehending the realities that characterize the lives of many youth today—for example, results from the South Carolina Youth Risk Behavior Survey revealed that 47 percent of adolescent males and 13 percent of adolescent females carried weapons, and large numbers reported fighting; the strongest predictors of weapon carrying and fighting were alcohol and drug use and sexual intercourse (Valois and McKewon, 1998). In this chapter's *Leaders' Voices* article, "A Tale of Two Curriculums," Mira Reisberg describes an approach to curriculum development that helps students understand and transcend the harsh realities of their lives by creating "heartfelt connections among student's lives, communities, creative intelligences, bodies, and spirits."

Curriculum Leadership Strategy

Prior to developing curricula for high school students, conduct a series of focus group interviews with students to identify their psychosocial concerns—what are their goals, aspirations, and dreams? In what ways can high school curricula address these concerns?

THE QUEST FOR SELF-IDENTITY

As young people move through their high school years, they usually come to attach less importance to the reactions of their peers and more to their quest for a strong self-identity. They tend to move from relying on others to self-reliance; their own sense of what matters, rather than the reactions of peers, guides their actions. Eliot Wigginton, the originator of the Foxfire approach to the high school curriculum, says in *Sometimes a Shining Moment: The Foxfire Experience* that the needs of high school students are best met by allowing them "to do things of importance—to do real work of real consequence in the real world" (1985, p. 236). To the extent that they have these experiences they are less likely to see the school curriculum as meaningless and to turn to self-destructive activities such as drug abuse, dropping out, school absenteeism, suicide, teenage pregnancy, vandalism, criminal activity, and cultism. In "A Tale of Two Curriculums" in this chapter, Mira Reisberg explains how she uses place-based pedagogy similar to Wigginton's Foxfire approach to prepare pre-service teachers to enter the high-stakes testing environment of today's schools.

Often, though, high school–level students gain their independence and sense of identity only after going through a period of conflict with parents, teachers, and other adults. In far too many instances, they express their defiance and rebellion by turning to the self-destructive activities mentioned above. The challenge for those who plan high school curricula, then, is to provide them with appropriate ways to express their emerging sense of independence or, as Carolyn Mamchur (1990) suggests, opportunities to use their "power" to decide what and how they learn. In "Possible Selves: Identity-Based Motivation and School Success" in this chapter, Daphna Oyserman suggests that schools can assist adolescents in successful exploration of various "school-focused possible selves."

CHALLENGES TO THE AMERICAN HIGH SCHOOL

In addition to being buffeted by frequent waves of criticism and calls for reform from external sources, high schools in the United States have been coping with a myriad of internal problems during the last few decades. Many high schools are plagued by hostility, violence, despair, alienation, and drug abuse. Their expansive campuses, large enrollments, and bureaucratic organizational structures make matters worse; and students often express underlying negativity toward teachers, administrators, and staff. Some students find their school experiences unenjoyable, if not painful. Minority group students may feel that they receive differential treatment. Typically, students ask for more openness and mutual respect. Neither students themselves nor teachers see students as influential in setting school policies. Many students believe they are not learning as much as they should. The high school typically does not use the rich resources of the community.

In addition, confirmation that high school curricula are not as rigorous as they ought to be comes from the students themselves. One survey of college students for their views on what should be included in the high school curriculum indicated that students wanted more reading, literature and vocabulary, speaking and writing skills, research papers, and computer courses (Sandel, 1991). Instead, Susan Black maintains that many high school students are "disengaged" because they experience only a narrow, skills-based curriculum while at school (see "Engaging the Disengaged Student: Research Shows Why Some Are Immersed in Learning While Others Are Indifferent" in this chapter). In addition, high school students need to learn "real-world skills," as Patricia Joyce points out in "Learning the Real-World Skills of the 21st Century" in this chapter. Joyce describes the "transitions career education curriculum" that some high schools are using to prepare students to enter the workforce.

DEVELOPMENT OF THE "COMPREHENSIVE" HIGH SCHOOL

To meet the needs of middle adolescents and to catch up with the Soviet Union in the production of engineers and scientists, former Harvard University President James B. Conant and others called for the development of the "comprehensive" high school during the 1950s and 1960s. The comprehensive high school would "provide learning opportunities for all . . . adolescents within a range from barely educable to the gifted and talented. Its purpose [would be] to enable each pupil (a) to develop to his [sic] greatest potential for his [sic] own success and happiness and (b) to make a maximum contribution to the American society of which he [sic] is a part" (Gilchrist, 1962, p. 32).

Conant recommended that "every pupil who can do so effectively and rewardingly should take a minimum of eighteen academic subjects" (1962, p. 29). This course of study, which Conant estimated 15 to 20 percent of students could complete "with profit," would include four years of mathematics, four years of one foreign language, three years of science, four years of English, and three years of social studies.

Expectations for the comprehensive high school were high. As the superintendent of University City Public Schools in Missouri wrote in 1962: "America desperately needs the developed abilities of all its youth. Citizens and educators have, in the comprehensive high school, an exciting and valuable tool to fulfill America's needs for the future" (Gilchrist, 1962, p. 33).

The comprehensive high school, however, has proven inadequate for the program of education many middle adolescents need. Some observers believe that attempts to develop comprehensive high school curricula that address the needs of all middle adolescents have resulted in curricula that lack coherence. High schools tend to try to teach "too much" to students. As a result, high school curricula focus more on *covering content* than on *developing understanding,* as Fred M. Newmann points out in "Can Depth Replace Coverage in the High School Curriculum?" in this chapter.

THE GREAT DEBATE ON HIGH SCHOOL REFORM

The 1980s saw a plethora of reform-oriented reports and books on American education, most of which focused on the high school and called for raising standards, promoting excellence, and rebuilding public confidence in the schools. The 1983 report by the National Commission on Excellence in Education, *A Nation at Risk: The Imperative for Educational Reform,* launched a great national debate on how to improve high schools in the United States. With alarm, the report claimed that the nation had "been committing an act of unthinking, unilateral educational disarmament" and cited the high rate of illiteracy among seventeen-year-olds and minority youth, a drop in SAT scores, and the need for college and business to offer remedial reading, writing, and computation. In response to the perceived ineffectiveness of America's schools, *A Nation at Risk* recommended raising standards (not clearly defined), requiring "Five New Basics" (four years of English, three years of mathematics, three years of science, three years of social studies, and one-half year of computer science) for graduation, assessing students' learning more frequently, and lengthening the school day and the school year.

Another widely discussed report was Ernest Boyer's (1983) *High School: A Report on Secondary Education in America* sponsored by the Carnegie Foundation for the Advancement of Teaching. *High School* recommends first and foremost a "core of common learnings" and service-oriented activities for all, more flexibility in scheduling, a program of electives to develop individual interests, the mastery of language, and a single track for academic and vocational students.

Broad, sweeping reform of America's high schools was also called for in *Horace's Compromise: The Dilemma of the American High School* by Theodore Sizer (1984). Through his analysis of the professional dilemmas encountered by Horace Smith, a hypothetical high school English teacher, Sizer built a case for "revamping the structure" of the high school. He asserted that higher-order thinking skills should form the core of the high school curriculum and they should be learned through students' confrontations with engaging, challenging problems. Sizer also believed that high schools should have fewer and clearer goals, and should require mastery of subject matter for graduation. Interdisciplinary nongraded curricula were essential, he believed, and instruction should be adapted to students' diverse learning styles. To put his ideas into practice, Sizer began the Coalition of Essential Schools at Brown University. From a modest beginning with five schools in 1984, the coalition grew to more than one thousand schools and twenty-four regional support centers by the end of the century.

In *Horace's School: Redesigning the American High School* (1992), Sizer further described the coalition's approach to restructuring high schools. A basic premise of the coalition is that top-down, standardized solutions to school problems don't work and that teachers must play a key role in changing schools. Since no two coalition schools are alike, each is encouraged to develop an approach to restructuring that meets the needs of faculty, students, and community. However, the restructuring efforts of coalition schools are guided by ten common principles, two of which specifically address the content of the educational program:

1. The school should focus on helping young people develop the habit of using their minds well. Schools should not attempt to be comprehensive if such a claim is made at the expense of the school's central intellectual purpose. Schools should be learner centered, addressing students' social and emotional development, as well as their academic progress.

2. The school's academic goal should be simple: that each student master a limited number of essential skills and areas of knowledge. The aphorism "Less Is More" should dominate. Curricular decisions should be guided by student interest, developmentally appropriate practice, and the aim of thorough student mastery and achievement. Students of all ages should have many opportunities to discover and construct meaning from their own experiences. (Coalition of Essential Schools, 1998)

In *Horace's Hope: What Works for the American High School* (1996), Sizer describes the lessons he learned from a decade of efforts to reform America's high schools.

GOALS FOR THE EDUCATION OF HIGH SCHOOL STUDENTS

What goals should be included in educational programs for high school–level students? As we have emphasized throughout this book, curriculum goals should be derived, in large measure, from the three curriculum bases—social forces, theories of human development, and the nature of learning and learning styles. With this perspective in mind, the goals would surely include the following:

1. Encouraging the development and practice of critical thinking, what the Coalition of Essential Schools has described as "the habit of using [one's] mind well"

2. Helping learners begin the process of career development, whether through vocational guidance, vocational education, or additional academic development

3. Providing learners with experiences that enhance their citizenship skills, sense of responsibility, and understanding of and concern for the world about them

4. Helping students to become self-directed, lifelong learners

5. Assisting learners to become self-actualized and secure in their identities

6. Assisting learners in making the transition to the world of work, to participation in their communities, and to the world of the future

Currently, virtually every state has responded to the recurring calls to reform high schools in America. Teachers are playing a greater role in restructuring and curriculum change. For example, many schools participate in collaborative school reform networks, and through these networks, teachers receive training and resources for facilitating change in their schools. As the articles in this chapter confirm, more and more educational programs for high school students are being developed in light of the recommendation from the Coalition of Essential Schools that "decisions about the details of the course of study, the use of students' and teachers' time and the choice of teaching materials and specific pedagogies must be unreservedly placed in the hands of the principal and staff" (Coalition of Essential Schools, 1998).

Curriculum Leadership Strategy

Explore the possibility of developing a reform-oriented network or coalition of high schools in your area. Create a team of teacher leaders from network schools to focus on curriculum issues that are common to the schools. The team may decide to develop a series of curriculum workshops to be held, on a rotating basis, at each school that has joined the network.

REFERENCES

Berger, Bennett M. *An Essay on Culture: Symbolic Structure and Social Structure.* Berkeley: University of California Press, 1995.

Boyer, Ernest. *High School: A Report on Secondary Education in America.* New York: Harper and Row, 1983.

Coalition of Essential Schools. "Ten Common Principles." Oakland, CA: Coalition of Essential Schools, 1998.

Conant, James B. "The Comprehensive High School." *NEA Journal* LI, no. 5 (May 1962): 29–30.

Gilchrist, Robert S. "What Is a Comprehensive High School?" *NEA Journal* LI, no. 8 (November 1962): 32–33.

Mamchur, Carolyn. "But . . . the Curriculum." *Phi Delta Kappan* 71, no. 5 (April 1990): 634–637.

Sandel, Lenore. "What High School Students Need to Know in Preparation for Success in College." *The High School Journal* 74, no. 3 (February/March 1991): 160–163.

Sizer, Theodore R. *Horace's Compromise: The Dilemma of the American High School.* Boston: Houghton Mifflin, 1984.

———. *Horace's School: Redesigning the American High School.* Boston: Houghton Mifflin, 1992.

———. *Horace's Hope: What Works for the American High School.* Boston: Houghton Mifflin, 1996.

Valois, Robert F., and Robert E. McKewon. "Frequency and Correlates of Fighting and Carrying Weapons Among Public School Adolescents." *American Journal of Health Behavior* 22, no. 1 (January–February 1998): 8–17.

Wigginton, Eliot. *Sometimes a Shining Moment: The Foxfire Experience.* Garden City, NY: Anchor Press, Doubleday, 1985.

Becoming Citizens of the World

VIVIEN STEWART

ABSTRACT: *In this article, Stewart discusses what she sees as the prepared-ness of U.S. high school graduates to be citizens of a multiethnic, multi-cultural, multilingual world and presents four trends that have contributed to the globalized society: economics and the opening of Asia; changes brought about by science and technology; international health and security matters; and changing demographics due to international migrations. Stewart believes that U.S. schools are not preparing students adequately for the challenges posed by these changes. Changes such as promotion of international knowledge, teacher training in international matters, world language teaching from elementary school through graduation, and innovative use of technology are recommended.*

The world into which today's high school students will graduate is fundamentally different from the one in which many of us grew up. We're increasingly living in a globalized society that has a whole new set of challenges. Four trends have brought us here.

The first trend is economic. The globalization of economies and the rise of Asia are central facts of the early 21st century. Since 1990, 3 billion people in China, India, and the former Soviet Union have moved from closed economies into a global one. The economies of China, India, and Japan, which represented 18 percent of the world's gross domestic product (GDP) in 2004, are expected to represent 50 percent of the world's GDP within 30 years (Wilson, 2005). One in five U.S. jobs is now tied to international trade, a proportion that will continue to increase (U.S. Census Bureau, 2004). Moreover, most U.S. companies expect the majority of their growth to be in overseas markets, which means they will increasingly require a workforce with international competence. According to the Committee for Economic Development (2006),

> To compete successfully in the global market place, both U.S.-based multinational corporations as well as small businesses increasingly need employees, with knowledge of foreign languages and cultures to market products to customers around the globe and to work effectively with foreign employees and partners in other countries.

Science and technology are changing the world and represent a second trend. In *The World Is Flat*, Thomas Friedman (2005) describes how the "wiring of the world" and the digitization of production since 1998 are making it possible for people to do increasing amounts of work any-where and anytime. Global production teams are becoming commonplace in business. In addition, scientific research, a key driver of innovation, will increasingly be conducted by international teams as other countries ramp-up their scientific capacity.

The third trend involves health and security matters. Every major issue that people face—from environmental degradation and global warming, to pandemic diseases, to energy and water short-ages, to terrorism and weapons proliferation—has an international dimension. Solving these prob-lems will require international cooperation among governments, professional organizations, and corporations. Also, as the line between do-mestic and international affairs blurs, U.S. citi-zens will increasingly vote and act on issues—such as alternative energy sources or security measures linked to terrorism—that require a greater knowl-edge of the world. In response to this need, a

2006 report from the National Association of State Boards of Education recommends infusing classroom instruction with a strong global perspective and incorporating discussions of current local, national, and international issues and events.

The fourth trend is changing demographics. Globalization has accelerated international migration. New immigrants from such regions as Asia and Central and South America are generating a diversity in U.S. communities that mirrors the diversity of the world. Knowledge of other cultures will help students understand and respect classmates from different countries and will promote effective leadership abroad.

In short, U.S. high school graduates will

- Sell to the world.
- Buy from the world.
- Work for international companies.
- Manage employees from other cultures and countries.
- Collaborate with people all over the world in joint ventures.
- Compete with people on the other side of the world for jobs and markets.
- Tackle global problems, such as AIDS, avian flu, pollution, and disaster recovery (Center for International Understanding, 2005).

However, U.S. schools are not adequately preparing students for these challenges. Surveys conducted by the Asia Society (2002) and National Geographic-Roper (2002) indicated that, compared with students in nine other industrialized countries, U.S. students lack knowledge of world geography, history, and current events. And shockingly few U.S. students learn languages that large numbers of people speak, such as Chinese (1.3 billion speakers) and Arabic (246 million speakers).

Many countries in Europe and Asia are preparing their students for the global age by raising their levels of education attainment; emphasizing international knowledge, skills, and language acquisition; and fostering respect for other cultures. The United States must create its own education

response to globalization, which should include raising standards, increasing high school and college graduation rates, and modernizing and internationalizing the curriculum.

WHAT GLOBAL COMPETENCE LOOKS LIKE

The new skill set that students will need goes well beyond the United States' current focus on the basics and on math, science, and technology. These skills are necessary, of course, but to be successful global citizens, workers, and leaders, students will need to be knowledgeable about the world, be able to communicate in languages other than English, and be informed and active citizens,

World Knowledge

Teaching about the rest of the world in U.S. schools has often focused on the superficial: food, fun, and festivals. Today, we need deeper knowledge, such as understanding significant global trends in science and technology, how regions and cultures have developed and how they interconnect, and how international trade and the global economy work. For example, students might consider how increasing the supply of fresh water or changing forms of energy use in one country could have major effects on another country.

In a world in which knowledge is changing rapidly and technology is providing access to vast amounts of information, our challenge is not merely to give students more facts about geography, customs, or particular conflicts. Rather, our challenge is to hone students' critical-thinking skills and to familiarize students with key concepts that they can apply to new situations. In this way, they can make sense of the explosion of information from different sources around the world and put factual information into perspective and context. Only then can this information become meaningful.

Teaching students about the world is not a subject in itself, separate from other content areas, but should be an integral part of *all* subjects taught. We need to open global gateways and inspire students to explore beyond their national borders. Programs like iLEARN and Global Learning and Observations to Benefit the Environment (GLOBE) make it possible for students to work collaboratively with peers in other countries. School-to-school partnerships enable both real and virtual exchanges.

U.S. students are global teenagers, similar in many ways to their technology-enabled peers around the world. Adding an international dimension to subjects and encouraging students to reach out to peers in other countries are powerful ways to make the curriculum relevant and engaging to today's youth.

Language Skills

Only about one-half of U.S. high school students study a foreign language. The majority never go beyond the introductory level, and 70 percent study Spanish (Draper & Hicks, 2002). This results in a serious lack of capacity in such languages as Arabic and Chinese, both of which are crucial to the prosperity and security of the United States.

The United States should do as other industrialized countries in Europe and Asia do—start offering foreign languages in the elementary grades, where research has shown that language learning is most effective (Pufahl, Rhodes, & Christian, 2001), and continue the emphasis in secondary school to create pipelines of proficient language speakers. U.S. students need opportunities to learn a broader range of languages, as in Australia, where 25 percent of students now learn an Asian language (Asia Society, 2002). Heritage communities in the United States—communities in which a non-English language is spoken at home, such as Spanish or Navajo—provide rich sources of teachers, students, and cultural experiences (National Language Conference, 2005). Specific practices, such as immersion experiences, can greatly enhance language proficiency.

The growing interest in learning Chinese, as shown by the fact that 2,400 U.S. high schools expressed interest in offering the new advanced placement course in Mandarin, suggests that parents and teachers are realizing the importance of communication skills in a multilingual, multicultural world (see www.AskAsia.org/Chinese). Even if graduates don't use a second language at work, quite possibly they will work in cross-cultural teams and environments.

Civic Values

U.S. students need to extend traditional American values into the global arena. These include a concern for human rights and respect for cultures that differ from the United States. By learning to understand other perspectives, students can develop critical-thinking skills and enhance their creativity.

Students should focus on becoming active and engaged citizens in both their local and global environments. Schools can promote civic engagement by weaving discussions of current events throughout the school day and through participatory forms of education, such as Model UN or the Capitol Forum on America's Future, in which high school students voice their opinions on current international issues. Schools should use technology to connect students directly to peers in other parts of the world and promote service learning projects on issues that students can address at both the local and international levels, such as alleviating hunger, providing education support to students in poverty, and improving the environment.

WHAT SCHOOLS CAN DO

Across the United States, many schools already define their mission as producing students who are prepared for work, citizenship, and leadership in the global era. These schools have found that internationalizing the curriculum creates a more exciting environment for students and teachers alike (Bell-Rose & Desai, 2005). Several approaches have proven successful.

Introducing an international studies requirement for graduation. More than a decade ago, the school board of Evanston Township, Illinois, introduced an international studies requirement for graduation and asked the high school's teachers to develop the necessary courses. Now, every sophomore in this diverse Chicago suburb must complete the one-year international studies requirement. Students choose from a series of in-depth humanities courses on the history, literature, and art of Asia, Africa, Latin America, and the Middle East. Simulations and participatory projects are central to instruction, and partnerships with local universities ensure that teachers have ongoing professional development in international affairs.

Creating an elementary school immersion program. After surveying parents and local businesses about the future needs of the community—they cited skills in English, Spanish, and Japanese as important—Seattle public schools created the John Stanford International School, a public elementary bilingual immersion school. Students spend half the day studying math, science, culture, and literacy in either Japanese or Spanish; they spend the other half of the day learning reading, writing, and social studies in English. The school also offers English as a second language courses for immigrant students and after-school courses for their parents. As a result of the school's success, the city of Seattle has recently decided to open 10 more internationally oriented schools.

Developing international schools-within-schools. The Eugene International High School is a school-within-a-school on four high school campuses in Eugene, Oregon. The school is open to all interested students. The four-year sequence of courses centers thematically on culture, history, and the political, economic, and belief systems of different world regions, such as Asia, Africa, the Middle East, and Latin America. The school also emphasizes independent research courses to give students the tools to address global issues. An extended essay and a community-service requirement in 11th and 12th grade both have an international focus. For example, one student wrote a 4,000-word research essay on hydrogen cars and

their place in the world economy. Students volunteer at such places as Centro Latino Americano, University of Oregon International Education and Exchange, and Holt International Children's Services. Finally, students have the option of pursuing the International Baccalaureate.

Teaching crucial language skills to prepare for the global economy. With strong support from Mayor Richard M. Daley, whose goal is to make Chicago a hub for international trade, the city has created the largest Chinese-language program in the United States. Twenty public schools teach Mandarin, from an all-black school on the West Side to a nearly all-Hispanic school on the South Side to more diverse schools throughout the city. For many of these students, Chinese is their third language after English and Spanish. The program resulted from partnerships among political, business, school, and community leaders and the Chinese Ministry of Education, which provides Chinese teachers and organizes a summer cultural program for Chicago educators in China.

Redesigning urban secondary schools with an international focus. Using the International High School of the Americas in San Antonio, Texas, and the Metropolitan Learning Center in Hartford, Connecticut, as anchor schools, the Asia Society has created a network of small, internationally themed secondary schools across the United States (see www.internationalstudiesschools.org/). The mission of each school is to prepare low-income students for college and to promote their knowledge of world regions and international issues. Each public or charter school incorporates international content across the curriculum, offers both Asian and European languages, provides international exchange opportunities, and provides links to international of organizations and community-service opportunities. To date, 10 schools have opened in New York City; Los Angeles; Charlotte, North Carolina; Denver, Colorado; and Houston, Texas. Additional schools are slated to open in other locations, such as Mathis and Austin, Texas, and Philadelphia, Pennsylvania.

Using student-faculty exchanges to promote curriculum change. Two public high schools in Newton, Massachusetts—Newton North and Newton South—run an exchange program with the Jingshan School in Beijing, China. Created by two teachers in 1979, the exchange enables U.S. and Chinese teachers and students to spend time in one another's schools every year. The program has served as a catalyst for districtwide curriculum change, bringing the study of Asian cultures into various academic disciplines, from social studies to science, and adding Chinese to the district's broad array of language options. The leaders of this exchange now help schools around the United States develop exchange programs with China as a way to internationalize their curriculums.

Using a K–12 foreign language sequence to promote excellence. The Glastonbury School District in Connecticut has long promoted language study beginning with a K–8 language requirement. Ninety-three percent of students study at least one foreign language, and 30 percent study more than one. The foreign language curriculum is thematic and interdisciplinary, integrating both foreign language and world history standards. All high school students take a one-semester history course on a non-Western geographic/cultural region and a civics/current issues course that includes international content. The school district's reputation for languages and international studies is a major draw for families moving to the area.

These and other pioneering schools offer models that all schools can replicate. What are the lessons learned? Have a large vision of what you want to achieve, but start slowly, one course or grade level at a time. Involve parents as well as business and community leaders in planning and supporting international education and world languages. Focus on professional development for teachers, including partnerships with local colleges, so teachers can broaden and deepen their international knowledge. Include a focus on mastery of languages, including nontraditional languages, and start at the lowest grade levels possible. Use international exchanges, both real and virtual, to

enable students to gain firsthand knowledge of the culture they are studying. If it is unfeasible for students to travel, try technology-based alternatives, such as classroom-to-classroom linkages, global science projects, and videoconferences (Sachar, 2004).

WHAT POLICYMAKERS CAN DO

Recognizing that future economic development and jobs in their states will be linked to success in the global economy, many states are developing innovations to promote international knowledge and skills. Nineteen states have been working together through the Asia Society's States Network on International Education in the Schools. States have developed commissions (North Carolina, Vermont); statewide summits (Delaware, Indiana, Massachusetts, Washington); and reports to assess the status of international education in their state (North Carolina, New Jersey, Wisconsin, West Virginia). They have created mechanisms, such as International or Global Education Councils (Ohio, Indiana, Wisconsin), and appointed International Education Coordinators to develop new policies and action plans (Delaware, Indiana, Ohio, New Jersey, Wisconsin). They are revising standards (Delaware, Idaho) or high school graduation requirements (New Mexico, Virginia) to incorporate international content. Some states are offering professional development (Oklahoma); initiating new language programs (Connecticut, Delaware, Illinois, Minnesota, Wisconsin, Wyoming); engaging in school exchanges with China (Connecticut, Massachusetts); adding crucial foreign language courses to their virtual high schools (Kentucky); and adding an international dimension to science, technology, engineering, and math (STEM) schools (Ohio, Texts). Finally, some (Arizona, Massachusetts, North Carolina, Washington) have introduced state legislation to provide additional funds to incorporate a global dimension into their schools (see http://Internationaled.org/states).

In 2006, the National Governors Association held a session on International Education at its annual meeting. In addition, the Council of Chief State School Officers recently adopted a new policy statement on global education (2007). These state efforts are a good start, but the United States has yet to make international knowledge and skills a policy priority on the federal level and develop the systems and supports necessary to get high-quality international content into U.S. classrooms.

States need to pursue four policy goals to make this happen. They should

- Redesign high schools and create new graduation requirements to motivate higher achievement and promote important international knowledge and key skills.
- Expand teacher training to deliver rigorous study in world history and cultures, economics, world regions, and global challenges.
- Develop world language pipelines from primary school to college that focus on crucial languages, such as Chinese, and that address the acute shortage of language teachers.
- Use technology in innovative ways to expand the availability of international courses and ensure that every school in the United States has an ongoing virtual link to schools in other countries.

For almost 50 years, the U.S. government has played a crucial role in fostering foreign languages and international education in *higher* education. We need to extend this commitment to K–12 education and make it an urgent priority. By doing so, we can improve students' international knowledge and skills and increase both the competitive edge and security of the United States.

In his 2006 report, *The Economics of Knowledge: Why Education Is Key for Europe's Success*, Andreas Schleicher from the Organisation for Economic Cooperation and Development wrote,

> The world is indifferent to tradition and past reputations, unforgiving of frailty and ignorant of custom or practice. Success will go to those individuals and countries which are swift to adapt, slow to complain, and open to change.

Part of the great strength of the United States is its adaptability. U.S. schools adapted to the agrarian age, then to the industrial age. It's time to open to change once more and adapt to the global age.

REFERENCES

Asia Society (2002). *States institute on international education in the schools: Institute report, November 20–22, 2002.* New York: Author.

Bell-Rose, S., & Desai, V. N. (2005). *Educating leaders for a global society.* New York: Goldman Sachs Foundation.

Center for International Understanding. (2005). *North Carolina in the world: A plan to increase student knowledge and skills about the world.* Raleigh, NC: Author.

Committee for Economic Development. (2006). *Education for global leadership: The importance of international studies and foreign language education for U.S. economic and national security.* Washington, DC: Author. Available: www.ced.org/docs/report/report_foreignlanguages.pdf

Council of Chief State School Officers. (2007). *Global education policy statement.* Washington, DC: Author. Available: www.ccsso.org/projects/International_Education/Global_Education_Policy_Statement/

Draper, J. B., & Hicks, J. H. (2002). *Foreign: language enrollments in secondary schools, fall 2000.* Washington, DC: American Council on the Teaching of Foreign Languages. Available: http://actfl.org/files/public/Enroll2000.pdf

Friedman, T. L. (2005). *The world is flat: A brief history of the twenty-first century.* New York: Farrar, Straus, and Giroux.

National Association of State Boards of Education. (2006). *Citizens for the 21st century: Revitalizing the civic mission of schools.* Alexandria, VA: Author. Available: www.nasbe.org/publications/Civic_Ed/civic_ed.html

National Geographic-Roper. (2002). *2002 global geographic literacy survey.* Washington, DC: Author.

National Language Conference. (2005). *A call to action for national foreign language capabilities* Washington, DC: Author. Available: www.nlconference.org/docs/White_Paper.pdf

Pufahl, L., Rhodes, V. C., & Christian, N. (2001). *What we can learn from foreign language teaching in other countries.* Washington, DC: Center for Applied Linguistics.

Sachar, E. (2004). *Schools for the global age: Promising practice in international education.* New York: Asia Society.

Schleicher, A. (2006). *The economics of knowledge: Why education is key for Europe's success.* Brussels: Lisbon Council. Available: www.oecd.org/dataoecd/43/11/36278531.pdf

U.S. Census Bureau. (2004). Table 2. In *Exports from manufacturing establishments: 2001* (p. 8). Washington, DC: U.S. Department of Commerce.

Wilson, W. T. (2005). *The dawn of the India century: Why India is poised to challenge China and the United States for global economic hegemony in the 21st century.* Chicago: Keystone India. Available: www.keystone-india.com/pdfs/The%20India%20Century.pdf

Vivien Stewart is vice president, Education, at the Asia Society, 725 Park Ave., New York, New York.

QUESTIONS FOR REFLECTION

1. Why doesn't Stewart believe U.S. high schools are adequately preparing students for the challenges of a changing world? What evidence does she cite and is her argument compelling?

2. How does Stewart believe U.S. high schools should be preparing students to be citizens of the world? Explain how her recommendations align with the four trends that she identifies as contributing to the globalization of society.

3. How "globally competent" are you? What more could you do to cultivate your global competence? How might you bring the importance of global competence to your current educational setting?

Engaging the Disengaged Student: Research Shows Why Some Are Immersed in Learning While Others Are Indifferent

SUSAN BLACK

ABSTRACT: In this article, Susan Black explores why some kids in the classroom are immersed in learning, while others are unmotivated and indifferent about it. She offers observations and advice to help teachers engage students in the learning process.

The 10th-graders are supposed to be writing essays in their English class. But student researchers from the University of California, Irvine, observing this Orange County classroom, report that most of the kids are indifferent to the assignment, preferring to while away their time napping, daydreaming, talking, or putting on makeup.

Researchers have no trouble spotting disengaged students—the kids who lack motivation to study and learn and spend their time watching the clock and waiting to escape from what one 10th-grader called "my private prison." In fact, disengaged students are highly visible, and their numbers are disconcerting, as I discovered during a recent tour of a city high school in upstate New York.

As we made the rounds, an assistant principal and I noticed disengaged students throughout the school. Kids nonchalantly sauntered into their rooms with no concern for the tardy bell, slouched into their desks, and tuned out the lesson, preferring to stare out the window, listen to music on personal CD players, snooze, or catch up on news with their friends.

To be sure, learning sparkled in some classrooms. But why, I wondered, are some kids immersed in learning, while others are unmotivated and indifferent? And what can schools do about this problem?

TEACHERS WHO ENGAGE STUDENTS

Schools can do plenty to keep students engaged in learning, says Charlotte Danielson, of the Educational Testing Service. Students who are deeply engaged in learning are not simply spending "time on task," she says, but are intellectually involved with curriculum topics and mentally involved in what she calls "minds-on learning."

Making that happen, not surprisingly, starts with the teacher. The best teachers, according to Danielson, keep students highly engaged throughout an entire lesson and encourage students to contribute their ideas and insights as a way of enhancing their own and other students' learning.

Danielson says the mark of a distinguished classroom is a "distinguished teacher" who has mastered a number of skills in four broad domains: planning and preparation; classroom environment; instruction; and professional responsibilities. Teachers who are adept at engaging students in learning, a skill she defines as the heart of instruction, demonstrate mastery of a number of performance standards. They:

- Represent curriculum content appropriately
- Expect students to help define topics and determine how they can be studied
- Link content to students' prior knowledge and experiences

- Ensure that students are mentally engaged in all activities and assignments
- Allow students to initiate and adapt learning activities and projects
- Form instructional groups that work to achieve learning goals
- Choose suitable instructional materials for lessons and encourage students to select resources that will help them learn
- Teach highly coherent, well-planned, and well-paced lessons that include time for student reflection.

HIGH SCHOOL SLUMP

Student disengagement occurs at all levels—in fact, some first-graders I've observed have as much apathy toward learning as many 10th-graders. But, according to Cori Brewster and Jennifer Fager, researchers at the Northwest Regional Educational Laboratory, disengagement is more frequent and more pronounced in the upper grades.

Outside influences take a particular toll on susceptible high school students, Brewster and Fager say. Such factors as unsupportive families and downtrodden neighborhoods can diminish kids' motivation and engagement in learning. In the early grades, kids from such environments can be hard to reach and difficult to motivate. By middle school, their interest in schoolwork steeply declines. And by high school, these researchers say, seriously disengaged students completely lose touch with learning. Many drift out of their classrooms and drop out for good.

Linda Lumsden, a researcher with the University of Oregon's ERIC Clearinghouse on Educational Management, says younger children generally maintain their self-confidence and believe they can succeed despite repeated failures. But older students easily lose self-confidence, attributing their failures to low ability and believing that no matter how much effort they put forth they won't succeed.

Schools can counteract negative influences and other factors that contribute to student disengagement. But first, say Brewster and Fager, it's important to know what *not* to do.

For one thing, teachers should avoid using extrinsic motivators such as pizza parties or free time. Teachers might believe that token rewards motivate students, but research shows that, in the long run, they actually diminish students' desire to learn and lower their achievement. Brewster and Fager advise teachers to develop students' intrinsic motivation by making classrooms inviting, designing challenging and compelling lessons, and giving students choices. (For more information see "The Praise Problem," August 2000 *ASBJ*.)

They also advise schools to forego ranking and comparing students according to achievement scores. Competition ends up with winners and losers, and kids who lose soon give up on themselves, detach from school, and disengage from classroom learning. Students are more likely to be engaged when teachers pay close individual attention to their interests and the ways they learn. Students stay engaged when teachers create lessons centered on "big ideas" and design assignments at the correct level of difficulty—not too easy and not impossibly difficult—so students are challenged but still able to succeed.

Focusing on intrinsic motivation pays off in the long run, Brewster and Fager say. They cite a number of research studies showing that, compared with students who are motivated by rewards, students whose motivation comes from within are more likely to:

- Earn higher grades and test scores
- Adjust better to school
- Apply more effort
- Feel more confident about their ability to learn
- Use more decision-making strategies
- Persist and complete difficult assignments
- Retain information and concepts longer
- Avoid the need for remedial courses and review
- Work on more challenging tasks
- Value lifelong learning.

Teachers who are most successful in drawing students into deep and thoughtful learning develop activities that keep students' psychological and intellectual needs in mind. Brewster and Fager cite research showing that student engagement is higher when teachers give students a strong sense of competence, grant them autonomy and opportunities to work with others, and allow them to be original and creative. Teachers who keep students engaged also give them time for self-assessment and reflection about what they've learned and how.

A PLAN FOR ENGAGEMENT

District 186 in Springfield, Ill., is one district that takes engaged learning seriously. Teachers are expected to follow the school's checklist for assessing engaged learning by answering questions such as these:

- Are students able to select resources and strategies thoughtfully and apply them to unfamiliar tasks?
- Are students excited about their learning and eager to spend extra time and effort?
- Are tasks complex and designed for students to stretch conceptually and take greater responsibility for learning?
- Do students have frequent opportunities to get to know and work with all students?
- Are groups formed for specific purposes, and are they re-formed as needs require?
- Do students have time to explore "uncharted territory"?

Springfield's expectations correspond with Vito Perrone's principles for engaging students in learning. Perrone, former director of teacher education at Harvard's Graduate School of Education, says students' intellectual engagement depends on studying topics that relate to their own lives.

Students report feeling most engaged in learning, he says, when they help define the content to be studied; have time to wonder and pursue areas of most interest; are prompted to view topics in new ways; are encouraged to raise questions; have teachers who are passionate, inventive, and respectful; become "resident experts"; create original products that demonstrate their learning; and sense that their study is open-ended rather than predetermined and predictable.

Perrone says that teachers should start by defining their goals and sharing them with their students. Then, he says, teachers need to find primary sources—such as government documents, original photographs, and genuine objects and artifacts—that can help students gain entry into new topics. As part of their planning, Perrone urges teachers to "leave room for student choices, for inquiry for interpretation, for role-playing."

Perrone's hope is that teachers avoid teaching what he calls narrow, skills-based, understanding-poor lessons. He believes all students—including those assigned to remedial or low-track classes—should have opportunities to reach understanding, not just knowledge, by "making connections among and between things, about deep and not surface knowledge, and about greater complexity, not simplicity."

Imagine the world of difference teachers in your district can make in kids' learning—and in their lives—by taking these ideas to heart and engaging your most disengaged students.

REFERENCES

Brewster, Cori, and Jennifer Fager. *Increasing Student Engagement and Motivation: From Time-on-Task to Homework.* Portland, Ore.: Northwest Regional Educational Laboratory, October 2000; www.nwrel .org/request/oct00/textonly.html.

Danielson, Charlotte. *Enhancing Professional Practice: A Framework for Teaching.* Alexandria, Va.: Association for Supervision and Curriculum Development, 1996.

Lumsden, Linda. *Student Motivation: Cultivating a Love of Learning.* Portland, Ore.: ERIC Clearinghouse on Educational Management, 1999.

Lumsden, Linda. "Student Motivation to Learn." ERIC Digest Number 92, 1994. ED370200; www.ed.gov/databases/ERIC_Digests/ed370200 .html.

Perrone, Vito. "How to Engage Students in Learning." Educational Leadership. February 1994; www.ascd .org/readingroom/edlead/9402/perrone.html.

"Student Disengagement in High School: A Precious Waste of Talent and What Can Be Done About It." Report from the Spring 1996 Class of Education 150: Changing the High School Experience. University of California, Irvine; www.gse.uci.edu/doehome/ deptinfo/faculty/becker/HS-Disengagement/ IntroChaptl.html.

Susan Black is a contributing editor to the *American School Board Journal* and is an education research consultant in Hammondsport, New York.

QUESTIONS FOR REFLECTION

1. What does Black see as the main difference between kids who are immersed in learning and those who are unmotivated and indifferent about it? Are unmotivated kids "reachable" at some point, or have they become so distant from learning that many of them will never become engaged?

2. How does Black recommend teachers engage the unengaged? Is this a realistic expectation? How much responsibility do students have to engage with their own learning?

3. How can schools that wish to better engage students learn from District 186 in Springfield, Illinois? Is the school's checklist for assessing engagement easy to follow for all schools or is it specific to those in certain conditions? Should this checklist be the basis for how all schools approach learning?

Possible Selves: Identity-Based Motivation and School Success

DAPHNA OYSERMAN

ABSTRACT: Adolescent identity development plays a crucial role in better understanding and supporting student learning and achievement. The term "possible self" has been coined to describe the incorporation of future goals into self-concept; possible selves are positive and negative images of the self already in a future state—the "clever" self who passed the algebra test, the "fat" self who failed to lose weight, the "fast" self who fell in with the "wrong" crowd. In this article, Oyserman argues that sustained self-regulation is less likely when relevant possible selves do not feel congruent with important social identities. To address this challenge, Oyserman presents a model with particular attention to school-focused possible selves, drawing heavily on her research with urban, low income and minority youths and especially her preventive intervention work.

The idea that the self is temporal and that the future-oriented components of the self are critical to understanding well-being can be traced to William James (1890/1950), who proposed that the selves we strive to become focus motivational attention, guide behavior, and are an important source of positive self-regard. James proposed that the future, as represented by one's self-relevant goals for the future, is likely to exert a major influence on current behavior. In a review of the literature, Karniol & Ross (1996) note the ubiquity of this assumption as well as the idea that these future self-relevant goals matter because they shape the strategies one chooses to achieve one's goals. Following from these models, it seems reasonable to suppose that possible self-goals play a motivational and self-regulatory role in shaping future behavior.

Indeed, the term *possible self* has been coined to describe incorporation of future goals into self-concept; *possible selves* are positive and negative images of the self already in a future state—the "clever" self who passed the algebra test, the "fat" self who failed to lose weight, the "fast" self who fell in with the "wrong" crowd (Oyserman, Bybee, & Terry, 2006; Oyserman & Markus, 1990). Failure to attain possible selves may increase risk of depression (Oyserman & Fryberg,

2006; Strauman, 2002; Strauman & Higgins, 1988) and there is some evidence that well-being (King, 2001) and performance (Ruvolo & Markus, 1992) improve when positive possible selves are brought to mind. But clearly we do not always function in an "imagine it and you will be it" kind of world; possible selves do not always sustain self-regulatory action. In spite of possible selves, youth sometimes fail algebra, gain undesired weight, and engage in behaviors they themselves would prefer to avoid.

Why might it be that possible selves might fail to sustain self-regulatory action and what would a predictive model need to take into account? In this article I argue that sustained self-regulation is less likely when relevant possible selves do not feel congruent with important social identities, when these possible selves are insufficiently cued in context, when possible selves are not linked with strategies, and when effort is undermined by misinterpretation of difficulty in working toward one's possible selves. A predictive model therefore must outline both which possible selves are likely to be contextually cued (or "on-line") and, of these possible selves, which are likely to be invested in over time. I outline and provide supporting evidence for such a predictive model, with particular attention to school-focused possible selves, drawing heavily on my research with urban, low income and minority youths and especially my preventive intervention work (see Oyserman, Brickman, & Rhodes, 2007; Oyserman et al., 2006).

While school (both doing well and avoiding failure) is a common focus of youth's possible selves (Oyserman, Johnson, James, & Bybee, 2008), school underperformance is a national problem. I propose that youth have difficulty creating and sustaining school-focused possible selves when they perceive these possible selves to be incongruent with other important aspects of their self-concept (e.g., racial-ethnic identities), live in social contexts that fail to cue strategies for attaining their school-focused possible selves, and misinterpret difficulties in working on these possible selves as evidence that school success may be an unrealistic goal. Conversely, I propose that youth will commit sustained self-regulatory effort to a possible self when the possible self feels congruent with important social identities, is contextually cued, contains behavioral strategies, and when difficulty working on the possible self is construed as normative.

SCHOOL-FOCUSED POSSIBLE SELVES AND SOCIAL IDENTITIES

Self-concepts include both personal and social identities, that is, ways of defining the self in terms of personal attributes, traits and goals as well as ways of defining the self based on group memberships and the traits and goals assumed to define one's in-groups (Oyserman, 2007). These group-based identities are likely to include community expectations about the occupations and academic attainment of in-group members. For some youth these community expectations are negative images of the in-group as low achieving (Thomas, Townsend, & Belgrave, 2003). These negative stereotypes may set the stage for assuming that school-focused possible selves are not congruent with the selves that are possible for oneself and other in-group members.

Indeed, ethnographic research suggests that high school students perceive Latinos as more likely to become manual laborers, Asians to do well in school, and African Americans to do poorly in school (Kao, 2000). The same results emerge from scenario-based experimental research, whether focused on the link between minority status and low academic attainment or on the link between low social class and low academic attainment. Thus, when a failing student is described, Latino and African American students are more likely to predict that the target is Latino or African American than white (Graham, 2001). When asked to predict academic performance a target student, low income students infer worse performance of from low (vs. middle) social class peers (Régner, Huguet, & Monteil, 2002; Weinger, 2000).

When imagining what future is possible for one's self, such negative preformed group images are likely to be highly accessible, making social group membership feel like it conflicts with school-focused possible selves. Working toward one's school-focused possible selves is likely to feel harder in the presence of accessible images of in-group members engaging in behaviors that undermine chances of attaining school-focused possible selves and failing to engage in behaviors that would help attain school-focused possible selves. While there is debate as to the degree of evidence that school success is viewed as a white middle class goal (Cook & Ludwig, 1997; Ferguson, 1998), there is consistent evidence of the stereotyped link between minority status and low achievement (e.g. Steele, 1997).

The stereotype threat literature documents that simply bringing to mind category membership as minority or working class dampens academic performance (e.g. Croizet & Claire, 1998; Steele, 1997). Individuation or separation of self from in-group alleviates this effect (Ambady, Paik, Steele, Owen-Smith, & Mitchell, 2004), but the idea of intervening to disconnect youth from their racial-ethnic in-group (e.g., creating "racelessness" see Fordham & Ogbu, 1986) is unappealing and likely to have other negative consequences (Arroyo & Zigler, 1995).

SCHOOL-FOCUSED POSSIBLE SELVES AND INOCULATION FROM OVER-INTERPRETATION OF DIFFICULTY

Rather than attempting to dampen the centrality of important social identities, a more reasonable strategy to improve success in attaining school-focused possible selves may be to increase the felt congruence between school-focused possible selves and social identity. This is not easy to do. School-focused possible selves are likely to be difficult to attain and experienced difficulty implies questions ("Why is engaging in this school-focused activity so hard for me; is this possible self really the true me? Do we have school-focused possible selves?"), the answers to which that often result in misinterpreting difficulty as meaning that school-focused possible selves are not "true" possible selves. Likewise, youth must judge whether particular behavioral patterns (e.g., asking for help) are likely to work and if they contradict in-group identity (e.g., "Will asking the teacher for help actually help me succeed in school or is it just a 'white' thing to do?").

To better understand how the feelings of difficulty that are experienced as adolescents imagine and pursue their possible selves actually influence commitment to those possible selves, it is fruitful to reconsider James' (1890) original formulation of the self. James viewed the self as composed both of content—what one thinks about when one thinks about one's self, and the accompanying metacognitive process—the feeling of thinking about one's self. This implies that self-judgments about who one is or may become are based on both content (what comes to mind) and process. Considering the content of thoughts about the self separately from the feelings associated with these thoughts parallels work in social cognition (Schwarz, 1998, 2002). This work proposes that human reasoning is accompanied by metacognitive experiences of relative ease (difficulty) and fluency (dis-fluency) (Schwarz, 1998, 2002).

Following from this research in social cognition, when imagining a possible self is accompanied by a metacognitive experience of difficulty, the feeling of difficulty is interpreted with a naïve theory—things that are hard to think of are less likely to be true (Higgins, 1998; Schwarz & Bless, 1992; Schwarz & Clore, 1996). The experience of ease or difficulty when bringing to mind a possible self can provide the basis for inferring whether a possible self is a "true" self that is worth pursuing and investing effort in or a "false" self, conflicting with social identities. Metacognitive experience of ease also provides feedback as to whether the gap between the current and possible self is manageable or unmanageable and therefore whether effort should be expanded or the possible self should be abandoned.

Though the experience of metacognitive difficulty is generally interpreted as meaning "not true for me," a number of studies have documented that other interpretations are possible (Rothman & Schwarz, 1998). For example, common sports sayings and parables involve reinterpretation of the meaning of experienced difficulty (e.g., "no pain, no gain") and the need to keep trying (e.g., "you miss 100% of the shots you don't take"). In the case of attempting to attain school-focused possible selves, while the metacognitive experience of difficulty is generally interpreted as "not the true me," the experience of difficulty could be reinterpreted to mean other things. Difficulty can be viewed as a normative part of the process (e.g., "success is 1% inspiration and 99% perspiration"). Difficulty can also provide evidence of progress (e.g., "the important things in life are the ones you really have to work for"); if difficulty and failures along the way are viewed as critical to eventual success, then difficulty is evidence of striving.

These interpretations are important because attaining school success and avoiding school failure requires ongoing behavior; it is not enough to complete one homework assignment or stay after class one day. If one's metacognitive experience is that working on a possible self is difficult and if this difficulty is interpreted with a naïve theory that ease is associated with truth, then difficulties associated with working toward the possible selves will undermine it. As is detailed in the previous section, low income and minority youth are likely to have difficulty integrating school-focused possible selves and social identities. As detailed in the following sections, they are likely to live in social contexts that do not cue strategies to help attain possible self goals and may not fully appreciate the need to have possible selves that fit with the high risk context in which they are growing up.

CONTEXTUAL CUING OF POSSIBLE SELVES

Youth growing up in low socioeconomic status (SES) contexts have multiple models of adults who failed to attain their possible selves. These models make it unlikely that youth growing up in low SES contexts will recognize the normativeness of difficulties, and instead likely that they will misinterpret feelings of difficulty as a sign [of] inevitable failure. This misinterpretation is crucial because it is likely to undermine behavioral persistence in pursuit of possible self goals. Thus rather than assuming that youth are able to make sense of difficulty as normative, low SES youth are likely to need specific inoculation from over-interpreting current difficulty and failure as predictive of future possibilities. Taken together, their metacognitive experience of difficulty is likely to provide feedback that school-focused possible selves are false rather than true selves, cuing disengagement from these possible selves and the goal pursuit they imply.

Self-concept includes an enormous amount of information about the self, but not everything one knows about oneself is likely to be accessible at any point in time and only accessible self-knowledge is likely to influence judgment, decision making and behavior (Higgins, 1996b). Therefore, it is important to consider which possible selves are likely to be contextually cued in differing social contexts. Of particular interest is the effect of resource-rich versus under-resourced contexts.

Resource-rich contexts (e.g., a middle class neighborhood school) provide models of success and a developed structure to guide the process of attaining school-focused possible selves. In these contexts, strategies may be automatically cued when possible selves are cued because parents, teachers, parents of friends, and other adults all converge to emphasize homework, persistence in the face of difficulty, tutoring or staying after school if needed. Parent involvement in school also sends a number of effort-congruent messages. By spending time at school, parent involvement implies that investment in school is worthwhile, that attaining school success is possible, is congruent with other important identities, and that the way to do it is to work hard and engage with others in school (see Oyserman, Brickman, & Rhodes, 2007).

Conversely, in under-resourced contexts, school-focused possible selves and strategies to attain them are unlikely to be automatically cued; these contexts are less likely to present easily accessible models to guide success. Youth are more likely to encounter adults who are unemployed, have low academic attainment, and hold non-professional jobs (e.g., Roderick, 2003). Given lack of easily accessible models or automatically cued strategies, youth may maintain an abstract commitment to education without connecting school-focused possible selves to everyday behavior—expressing high aspirations even as their behavior reflects avoidance or even flight from school (for qualitative description, see Roderick, 2003). Evidence for these assumptions comes from three sources: correlational studies, randomized trial intervention research and other field experiments. Parent involvement with school is associated with positive academic outcomes for low income and minority children just like it is for higher income and majority children (for an overview of this literature, see Oyserman, Brickman, & Rhodes, 2007). The negative effect of low parent involvement in school on youth academic outcomes is moderated by youth participation in a possible selves-focused intervention (Oyserman, Brickman, & Rhodes, 2007). Priming studies (Destin & Oyserman, 2007a) document increased homework focus among low-income African American and Latino students after being reminded that college can be paid for by financial aid (compared with either control condition or when simply reminded of the high cost of college). Priming studies (Destin & Oyserman, 2007b) also document that students are more likely to plan on school-focused action, such as finding ways to get extra help in classes, when contextual risk and possible selves are matched. Students expended more effort to work on school-focused possible selves in two conditions—first, when reminded of high contextual risk (e.g., on average, GPAs decline) and asked about their feared possible selves and second, when reminded of low contextual risk (e.g., on average, most students do fine) and asked about their positive expected possible selves. Focusing on positive possible selves alone is not effective in the kinds of higher risk contexts experienced by youth living in low-income neighborhoods and attending under resourced schools.

EFFECTIVE POSSIBLE SELVES

Correlational research provides initial empirical support for the self-regulatory power of possible selves and their association with better academic outcomes. Adolescents who believe that positive possible selves are likely to be attained have higher self-esteem than those who do not (Knox et al., 1998). Sixth grade students with positive academic possible selves improved their GPA by seventh grade, especially when their sixth grade academic possible selves were more positive than their current academic self-concept (Anderman, Anderman, & Griesinger, 1999). Among sixth to eighth graders, positive academic possible selves predicted higher endorsement of performance goals—wanting to do schoolwork in order to prove one's competence (Anderman et al., 1999). Even in samples at high risk of academic problems clue to high poverty concentration, youth who had more school-focused possible selves and strategies to attain them had significantly improved grades, even controlling for prior GPA than did youth with fewer of these possible selves and strategies (Oyserman, Bybee, Terry, & Hart-Johnson, 2004).

Moreover, a number of studies suggest that possible selves differ in self-regulatory effectiveness. Self-regulatory effort improves when youth have both positive possible selves (goals) and negative possible selves (fears) in the same domain ("balanced" possible selves) (Oyserman & Markus, 1990) and when youth have incorporated detailed strategies into their possible selves ("plausible" possible selves) (Oyserman et al., 2004). When possible selves are balanced, individuals select strategies that both increase the likelihood of becoming like the positive possible selves and decrease the likelihood of becoming like the negative possible selves, thereby focusing self-regulation and broadening effort (Oyserman & Markus, 1990). Plausibility provides automatic cuing of predeveloped strategies (e.g., "set my alarm," "go to class even if my friends skip").

There is evidence that having school-focused possible selves that include detailed strategies results in improved grades over the course of the school year (Oyserman et al., 2004). Simply having school-focused possible selves alone, without strategies for their attainment, is not associated with improved grades (Oyserman et al., 2004). Despite the fact that most low-income youth have at least one possible self focused on school, few of these possible selves are linked with strategies (Oyserman, Johnson, et al., 2008). Many youths fail to attain even the basic school-focused possible self goal of graduating from high school. Thus, the national average for on-time graduation is 75% overall, 50% for African Americans, and 53% for Hispanics (Orfield, Losen, Wald, & Swanson, 2004). In urban centers like Detroit, graduation estimates are even lower (between 40% and 44% on time graduation) (Detroit News, May 2005).

EVIDENCE FROM EXPERIMENTAL DESIGN STUDIES

A Process Model

Figure 1 presents a process model of the connections between possible selves, self-regulatory

FIGURE 1

Process Model: Antecedents of Self-Regulatory Effectiveness of Possible Selves

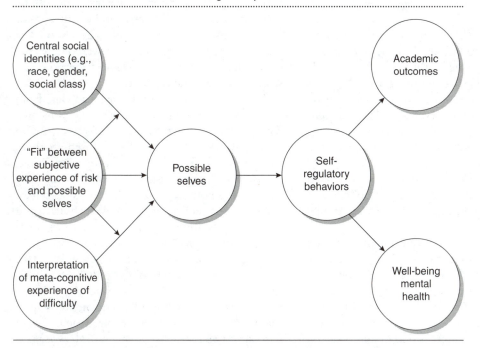

Note: Adapted with permission from Oyserman, Bybee, & Terry (2006). Possible selves and academic outcomes: When and how possible selves impel action. *Journal of Personality and Social Psychology, 91,* 188–204. Copyright 2006 American Psychological Association.

behaviors, and important outcomes for youth. The process model links social identities, fit between possible selves and social context, and metacognitive experience to possible selves and links possible selves to persistent engagement in self-regulatory behavior. In this section, I summarize results from experimental work carried out in my lab that uses this model. Demonstrating effects which move beyond correlation associations between possible selves and behavior is important because the possible selves model posits a causal process by which possible selves influence the course of important behaviors over time. Experimental designs provide stronger support for causal reasoning about possible selves. In these studies, we either cue possible selves (Brickman, Rhodes, & Oyserman, 2007) or cue both possible

selves and social contexts (Destin & Oyserman, 2007b) to provide evidence that changing possible selves leads to change in academic behavior. Based in this model, I also developed a preventive intervention and tested it with my colleagues (Oyserman et al., 2006; Oyserman, Terry, & Bybee, 2002). The intervention manual and broader conceptualization of the theory and evaluation results is available (Oyserman, 2008).

Randomized Field Trial with Two-Year Follow-Up

Goals. The goals of the intervention were to evoke possible selves and strategies to attain them, forge links between possible selves and strategies that are not otherwise automatic, inoculate youth from misinterpreting failure and setbacks in attaining these possible selves, and create a link between social identity and possible selves.

Sample and method. African American, Hispanic, and European American low-income eighth graders attending one of three targeted middle school in Detroit were randomly assigned to their regularly assigned elective or to the eleven session possible-selves based intervention. The intervention was completed by the Thanksgiving break, prior to the conclusion of the first academic quarter. To ensure that the intervention effects would be sustained over time, the intervention occurred in school, with peers, during the school day and targeted the core aspects of the process model outlined in Figure 1.

Specifically, structured group activities evoked academically focused possible selves, made clear that academic possible selves were held by peers (and therefore something that "we" aspire to), and highlighted the normativeness of difficulties and failures along the way to attaining possible self goals. Thus, the intervention operationalized the theory of how possible selves might influence self-regulatory behaviors (and through these behaviors, academic outcomes and well-being).

Data were collected with parental consent and included a baseline and three postintervention data points (spring 8th grade, fall 9th and spring 9th grade). All children were enrolled in one of three middle schools in the fall of 8th grade, tracking followed students through that year and the following transition to high school year, when students were enrolled in about 80 schools in various districts. While the income of parents was not obtained, the student body on average could be termed low-income in that 2/3 of students received free or reduced lunch and students lived in census tracts averaging 54% of households below the poverty line (U.S. Census Bureau, 2000). This rate is well above the Census Bureau's 40% cutoff for describing a tract as a high poverty area (Bishaw, 2005).

To obtain informed consent, parents were mailed home information, and this was followed up by face-to-face contact at the parent's home or via telephone to ensure that all parents had heard about the goals of the study, what data would be collected from school, teacher, and youth, and for what purpose. Given the chance to hear about the study and get their questions answered, few parents refused participation—94% of the potential sample had parental consent.

Data were collected on behavior in class from core subject teachers in middle school (first two data points) and high school (second two data points). GPA and extent of unexcused absences were obtained from school records. Youth self-reported on their possible selves, the time they spent doing homework, and their possible selves.

Youth self-report responses were based on a brief, in-class survey. In-home interviews were completed in year 1 for the 56 students suspended ($n = 11$), expelled ($n = 9$), transferred ($n = 10$), or otherwise not in school ($n = 26$). By year 2, students were enrolled in 80 schools; the at-home interview procedure was followed when in-school survey completion was not feasible. Teachers were reimbursed $5 for each assessment ($10 in year 2); students were reimbursed $5 (year 2 only).

While control condition youth attended their regularly scheduled elective, intervention condition youth received the intervention (for manual and fuller description of the model and evaluation see Oyserman, 2008). Fidelity to protocol was maintained via in vivo ratings by trained observers and weekly staff meetings (see Oyserman et al., 2006). Across the three schools, average attendance for the 11 school sessions ranged from 80% to 90% by school, with only 36 youths assigned to the intervention group failing to attend at least half the inschool sessions. In these, 13.6% of intervention group cases, the youths were not attending school (often due to suspension or move to another school).

Despite the challenges of maintaining contact with the highly mobile sample, Oyserman et al. (2006) were able to keep missing data and attrition to a minimum. Only four youth were completely lost to follow-up by the spring of 9th grade; information from at least one source (youth, teacher, or school records) was obtained at this final point for 98.5% of the intention-to-treat sample. Also, missing data rates were low. Across four measurement points, Oyserman et al. (2006) report missing 9% of youth question-naires, 11% of teacher ratings, and 12% of the by-term school records. School records and teacher ratings are of particular importance for the current study. At any point in time, almost all records (92% to 96%) and teacher ratings (83% to 97%) were obtained. Expectation maximization meth-ods were used to estimate the approximately 7.9% of data that were missing due to skipped items or unavailable information (across youth, school, and teacher data elements) incorporating the full set of preintervention variables. All results re-ported use estimated data.

While attaining and sustaining an intervention effect is notoriously difficult, Oyserman et al. (2006) documented effects that were stable and even increasing over time. This sustained effect over 2 years is particularly impressive, given the high poverty neighborhoods the youth were em-bedded in and the difficulty of improving aca-demic outcomes when prior academic attainment accounts for much of the variance to be ex-plained. They documented effects using two very different analytic strategies (structural equation modeling and longitudinal multilevel modeling) with different strengths and assumptions.

Results. Testing both direct effect and mediation effects, the authors report both moderate-sized direct effects (e.g., $d \geq .3$) on changing possible selves and linking them with strategies and, at 2-year follow-up, effects on academic outcomes ranging from large (e.g., $d \geq .7$) for time spent doing homework, change in in-class disruptive-ness and change in time spent doing homework, to moderate (e.g., $d \geq .3$) for grades, change in grades, and unexcused absences taken from school records and in-class initiative taking, change in initiative taking and disruptiveness by teacher report. The intervention also reduced 2-year follow-up risk of depression (youth reported) ($d = -.26$). Importantly, Oyserman and colleagues

(2006) also demonstrated that the 2-year follow-up effects are mediated by change in possible selves and in the possible self-to-strategy linkage. Table 1, reprinted from Oyserman et al. (2006), provides a summary of some of the main outcomes.

DISCUSSION

Although possible selves focused on school suc-cess are common, so is failure in school, suggest-ing a puzzling gap between possible selves and the sustained self-regulatory behavior needed to attain one's goals. In the current [reading], I sug-gest a process model in which self-regulation is likely when context-relevant possible selves and relevant strategies are cued, feel congruent with important social identities, and when difficulty in pursuing possible selves is understood to be nor-mative. An intervention based on this model is described as well as 1 and 2 year follow-up data. Confidence in the generalizability of results is high because a randomized design was used and participation in both the intervention and each of the four waves of data collection was over 90%. The intervention was documented to change pos-sible selves, increasing both feared off-track and school-focused possible selves and strategies to at-tain them. As hypothesized, intervention youth both had more of these possible selves and were better able to use them to improve behavioral self-regulation. The intervention produced meas-urable change in possible selves, and change in possible selves predicted change in behavioral self-regulation—going to school rather than skip-ping, behaving and participating in class, and spending time on homework; self-regulation not only improved academic outcomes but, equally importantly, reduced risk of depression.

The possible self framework assumes that mo-tivation is influenced by both positive (expected, wanted, or hoped for) possible selves and negative (feared or unwanted) possible selves. Indeed, the intervention research shows that the impact of school-focused possible selves on self-regulatory

TABLE 1

Multilevel Models: Estimated Means in Experimental and Control Conditions—Spring 8th and 9th Grade

Dependent variables[a]	Estimated condition means/percents			
	Spring of 8th grade		Spring of 9th grade	
	STL (*n* = 116)	Control (*n* = 112)	STL (*n* = 116)	Control (*n* = 112)
Change in APS balance	0.07	−0.12	—	—
Change in feared off-track PS	0.31	0.00	—	—
APS plausibility	2.36	1.96	—	—
Absences (student report)	3.49	3.95	—	—
Unexcused absences (school records)[b]	12.28	14.53	22.52	24.77
Homework time (hours/week; open ended)[b]	3.49	3.28	2.51	1.57
Homework time (hours/ week; closed ended)	4.15	3.74	—	—
Disruptive behavior (student report)	2.37	2.63	—	—
Disruptive behavior (teacher report)	1.74	1.83	1.55	1.73
In-class initiative (teacher report)	2.51	2.44	2.48	2.25
Core academic GPA (school records)	1.98	1.83	1.64	1.36
Standardized tests (school records; proportion passed)	0.83	0.77	—	—
Referral to remedial summer school	36.2%	48.2%	—	—
Retention in 8th grade	4.3%	10.7%	—	—
Depression (CESD—spring of 9th grade)[c]	—	—	10.35	12.29

Note: *N* = 228 youth in the participating sample.

STL = Treatment group.

[a]For variables with estimated means for both 8th and 9th grades, estimates were from the intercept term of a 3-level longitudinal multilevel model (time, students, homerooms); for variables with estimated means for only one grade, estimates were from cross-sectional 2-level multilevel models (students in homerooms).

[b]These positively skewed variables were log transformed for analysis; however, to facilitate interpretation, means are presented here in the original metric (i.e., in exponentiated form).

[c]Depression was measured only in the spring of 9th grade; means were estimated by a 2-level cross-sectional multilevel model.

Source: Adapted with permission from Oyserman, Bybee, & Terry (2006). Possible selves and academic outcomes: When and how possible selves impel action. *Journal of Personality and Social Psychology, 91,* 188–204. Copyright 2006 American Psychological Association.

behaviors was distinct from the impact of feared off-track possible selves on self-regulatory behaviors. Youth with balanced and plausible academically focused possible selves spent more little doing homework, were less disruptive and more

behaviorally engaged in classroom activities. Youth with feared off-track possible selves attended school more (had fewer school absences).

The distinct role of feared off-track possible selves is also congruent with a number of other self-regulatory models. For example, Carver (2004) describes self-regulation to avoid feared possible selves or anti-goals as discrepancy-enlarging self-regulation. Larsen (2004) describes the self-regulatory system as vigilant to environmental dangers; when danger is cued, individuals are more cautious about engaging in behaviors that may increase risk. Higgins (Higgins & Spiegel, 2004) describes prevention-focused self-regulation as risk averse.

Following these perspectives, youth with feared off-track possible selves can be expected to be cautious about risk increasing behaviors; they are likely to engage in action (e.g., attending school) they perceive as antithetical to their off-track selves (becoming pregnant, involved in drugs or crime). Although pregnancy and crime data were not obtained, data on absences were obtained and indeed, increased feared off-track possible selves reduced risk of school absences. While vigilant focus on anti-goals or prevention is likely to reduce risk of harm, active engagement in goal attainment (discrepancy-reducing self-regulation) is likely to increase chances of success.

In my laboratory, we followed up on the possibility that feared possible selves are more effective in risky contexts where vigilance is necessary and found this to be the case. Specifically, we examined the "fit" between perceived risk and possible selves. In a between-subjects priming design, we demonstrated that the efficacy of expected and feared possible selves in cuing school-focused motivation differed depending on how the context of school was framed. When school was described to students as a low risk context (e.g., most students do fine), then priming students to think about their expected possible selves increased their school-focused motivation. The reverse was true when school was described to students as a high risk context (e.g., most students experience declining GPAs). In this case, it was priming students to think about their feared possible selves that increased their school-focused motivation (Destin & Oyserman, 2007b).

Although self-regulatory systems theories posit roles for both discrepancy reducing (promotion)

and discrepancy increasing (prevention) systems, prevention focus, engaging in self-regulatory behavior to avoid feared possible selves, is not particularly prominent in the academic goal literature. Perhaps this is because in middle class contexts, pursuit of academic goals may more commonly involve the discrepancy reducing feedback system—engaging in self-regulatory behavior to attain positive expected possible selves. There is evidence that college students are more likely to use promotion-than prevention-focused self-regulation (e.g., Lockwood, Sadler, Fyman, & Tuck, 2004).

Prevention-focused self-regulation may become more salient in a number of circumstances. First, prevention-focused self-regulation may be more likely when social contextual risk is high, such as in circumstances of poverty. For example, first generation college students are more likely to engage in strategies to avoid feared possible selves than strategies to attain positive possible selves (Oyserman, Gant, Ager, 1995, Study 1). Ethnographic evidence from low-income high school students also highlights the salience of feared off-track possible selves—becoming unemployed, homeless and destitute (Steinitz & Solomon, 1986; see also Kaiser Foundation, 2002). Second, it is possible that culture influences choice of self-regulatory system; while Euro-Canadian college students find promotion-focused strategies compelling, Asian Canadian college students find prevention-focused strategies compelling (Lockwood, Marshall, & Sadler, 2005). Similarly, Hong Kong Chinese college students found prevention-focused reasons for action more convincing than did American college students (Lee, Aaker, & Gardner, 2000, Study 4). Prevention focus alone may not be helpful, without a framework guiding action suggesting a role for possible selves (e.g., Uskul, Keller, & Oyserman, in press).

Whether focused on positive expected or feared possible selves, self-regulation fails when individuals do not realize that a particular action is antithetical to goal achievement, when possible selves do not provide clear standards of what to attain or avoid or when possible selves are not linked with self-regulatory behaviors (e.g., Carver, 2004; Higgins, 1987). For low income teens, lapses in self-regulation may be difficult to repair—when risk of failure is high, any misstep can spell disaster. This contrasts with the situation of middle-class teens whose self-regulatory lapses can be compensated for by contextual regulation set in place by neighborhood, school, and parents. Middle class students are more likely to be provided mentoring, tutoring, monitoring, and enrichment activities whether they seek them out or not (e.g., Sampson, Morenoff, & Earls, 1999).

Low-income students are more likely to live in contexts lacking such collective efficacy resources (Sampson et al., 1999). Thus, for low-income youths, self-initiated engagement in self-regulation that focuses on attaining positive possible selves and avoiding negative possible selves is likely necessary. A number of studies have documented that when stereotype threat is activated, prevention (discrepancy enhancing) focus increases (Oyserman, Uskul, Yoder, Nesse, & Wiliams, 2007; Seibt & Förster, 2004), as do negative thoughts about one's math capacity (Cadinu, Maass, Rosabianca, & Kiesner, 2005).

These results can be construed to suggest that stereotype threat undermines academic attainment by making academic possible selves less salient and school-focused strategies less accessible as ways of avoiding off-track possible selves. While much research has focused on academic outcomes, the identity-based motivation model has also been documented in the domain of health promotion (Oyserman, Fryberg, & Yoder, 2007). Taken together, these results suggest that when possible selves feel congruent with social identity, relevant strategies are cued in context, and experienced difficulty is interpreted as part of the process, possible selves can improve goal attainment.

ACKNOWLEDGMENTS

The research reported in this [reading] was funded by NIMH grant R01 MH 58299 and by NIMH grant T32 MH63057-03, Oyserman PI.

REFERENCES

Abrams, D. (1994). Social self-regulation. *Personality and Social Psychology Bulletin, 20,* 473–483.

Abrams, D. & Hogg, M. (1990). An introduction to the social identity approach. In D. Abrams & M. Hogg (Eds.), *Social identity theory: Constructive and critical advances* (pp. 1–9). New York: Harvester Wheatsheaf and Springer-Verlag.

Altschul, I., Oyserman, D. & Bybee, D. (in press). Racial-ethnic identity in mid-adolescence: Content and change as predictors of academic attainment. *Child Development.*

Ambady, N., Paik, S., Steele, J., Owen-Smith, A., & Mitchell, J. (2004). Deflecting negative self-relevant stereotype activation: The effects of individuation. *Journal of Experimental Social Psychology, 40,* 401–408.

Arroyo, C. & Zigler, E. (1995). Racial identity, academic achievement, and the psychological well-being of economically disadvantaged adolescents. *Journal of Personality and Social Psychology, 69,* 903–914.

Belli, R. (1998). The structure of autobiographical memory and the event history calendar: Potential improvements in the quality of retrospective reports in surveys. *Memory, 6,* 383–406.

Blair, S., Blair, M., & Madamba, A. (1999). Racial/ethnic differences in high school students' academic performance: Understanding the interweave of social class and ethnicity in the family context. *Journal of Comparative Family Studies, 30,* 599–555.

Burke, P. (2003). Relationships among multiple identities. In P. Burke & T. Owens (Eds.), *Advances in identity theory and research* (pp. 195–214). New York: Kluwer Academic/Plenum.

Cadinu, M., Maass, A., Rosabianca, A., & Kiesner, J. (2005). Why do women underperform under stereotype threat? Evidence for the role of negative thinking. *Psychological Science, 16,* 572–578.

Carver, G. (2004). Self-regulation of action and affect. In R. Baumeister & K. Vohs (Eds.), *Handbook of self-regulation: Research, theory and applications* (pp. 13–39). New York: Guilford Press.

Carver, G., & Scheier, M. (1990). Principles of self-regulation: Action and emotion. In T. Higgins & R. Sorrentino (Eds.), *Handbook of Motivation and Cognition,* (Vol. 2, pp. 3–52). New York: Guilford Press.

Cohen, J. (1988). *Statistical power analysis for the behavioral sciences* (2nd ed.). Hillsdale, NJ: Erlbaum.

Cook, P., & Ludwig, J. (1997). Weighing the "burden of acting White": Are there race differences in attitudes toward education? *Journal of Policy Analysis and Management, 16,* 256–278.

Croizet, J., & Claire, T. (1998). Extending the concept of stereotype and threat to social class: The intellectual underperformance of students from low socioeconomic backgrounds. *Personality and Social Psychology Bulletin, 24,* 588–594.

Destin, M., & Oyserman, D. (2007a). Perceptions of higher education and the pursuit of current educational goals. Poster session presented at the Association for Psychological Science, Washington, DC.

Destin, M., & Oyserman, D. (2007b). *Possible selves, contextual fit, and motivation.* Manuscript under editorial review.

Detroit News. (May 29, 2005). Graduation rates. Retrieved September 15, 2005, from www.detnews.com/2005/specialreport/0505/30/A01-196697.htm

Eccles, J., & Wigfield, A. (2002). Motivational beliefs, values, and goals. *Annual Review of Psychology, 53,* 109–132.

Ellickson, P., & Hawes, J. (1989). An assessment of active versus passive methods for obtaining parental consent. *Evaluation Review, 13,* 45–55.

Ferguson, R. (1998). Comment on "The burden of acting White: Do Black adolescents disparage academic achievement?" by P. J. Cook and J. Ludwig. In G. Jencks & M. Phillips (Eds.), *The Black-White test score gap* (pp. 394–397). Washington, DC: Brookings Institution.

Finn, J., Pannozzo, G., & Voelkl, K. (1995). Disruptive and inattentive-withdrawn behavior and achievement among fourth graders. *The Elementary School Journal, 95,* 421–434.

Fordham, S., & Ogbu, J. (1986). Black students' school success: Coping with the "burden of acting white." *Urban Review, 18,* 176–206.

Graham, S. (2001). Inferences about responsibility and values: Implication for academic motivation. In F. Salili & C. Chiu (Eds.), *Student motivation: The culture and context of learning,* (pp. 31–59). Dordrecht, Netherlands: Kluwer Academic.

Higgins, T. (1987). Self-discrepancy: A theory relating self and affect. *Psychological Review, 94,* 319–340.

Higgins, T. (1996a). The "self digest": Self-knowledge serving self-regulatory functions. *Journal of Personality and Social Psychology, 71,* 1062–1083.

Higgins, T. (1996b). Knowledge activation: Accessibility, applicability, and salience. In T. Higgins & A. Kruglanski (Eds.), *Social psychology: Handbook of basic principles* (pp. 133–168). New York: Guilford Press.

Higgins, T. (1997). Beyond pleasure and pain. *American Psychologist, 52,* 1280–1300.

Higgins, T. (1998). The aboutness principle: A pervasive influence on human inference. *Social Cognition, 16,* 173–198.

Higgins, T. & Spiegel, S. (2004). Promotion and prevention strategies for self-regulation: A motivated cognition perspective. In R. Baumeister & K. Voh (Eds.), *Handbook of self-regulation: Research, theory and applications.* (pp. 171–187). New York: Guilford Press.

Hoyle, R. & Kenny, D. (1999). Sample size, reliability, and tests of statistical mediation. In R. Hoyle (Ed.), *Statistical strategies for small sample research* (pp. 195–222). Thousand Oaks, CA: Sage.

Hu, L., & Bentler, P. (1999). Cutoff criteria for fit indexes in covariance structure analysis: Conventional criteria versus new alternatives. *Structural Equation Modeling, 6,* 1–55.

James, W. (1890). *Principles of Psychology.* New York: Holt.

Joseph, J. (1996). School factors and delinquency: A study of African American youths. *Journal of Black Studies, 26,* 340–355.

Kaiser Foundation (2002). *National survey of Latinos. Summary of findings.* Retrieved September 14, 2005, from http://www.kff.org/kaiserpolls/20021217a-index.cfm

Kao, G. (2000). Group images and possible selves among adolescents: Linking stereotypes to expectations by race and ethnicity. *Sociological Forum, 15,* 407–430.

Karniol, R. & Ross, M. (1996). The motivational impact of temporal focus: Thinking about the future and the past. *Annual Review of Psychology, 47,* 593–620.

Kasen, S., Cohen, P., & Brook, J. (1998). Adolescent school experiences and drop out, adolescent pregnancy, and young adult deviant behavior. *Journal of Adolescent Research, 13,* 49–72.

Kearney, K., Hopkins, R., Mauss, A., & Weisheit, R. (1983). Sample bias resulting from a requirement for written parental consent. *Public Opinion Quarterly, 47,* 96–102.

King, L. (2001). The health benefits of writing about life goals. *Personality and Social Psychology Bulletin, 27,* 798–807.

King L., & Smith, N. (2004). Gay and straight possible selves: Goals, identity, subjective well-being, and personality development. *Journal of Personality, 72,* 967–994.

Larsen, R. (2004, November). Emotion and cognition: The case of automatic vigilance. *API Online, 18*(11). Retrieved September 14, 2005, from http://www.apa.org/science /psa/sb-larsen.html

Lee, A., Aaker, J., & Gardner, W. (2000). The pleasures and pains of distinct self-construals: The role of interdependence in regulatory focus. *Journal of Personality and Social Psychology, 78,* 1122–1134.

Lockwood, P., Sadler, P., Fyman, K., & Tuck, S. (2004). To do or not to do: Using positive and negative role models to harness motivation. *Social Cognition, 22,* 422–450.

Lockwood, P., Marshall, T., & Sadler, P. (2005). Promoting success or preventing failure: Cultural differences in motivation by positive and negative role models. *Personality and Social Psychology Bulletin, 31,* 379–392.

McDermott, P. (1995). Sex, race, class, and other demographics as explanations for children's ability and adjustment: A national appraisal. *Journal of School Psychology, 33,* 75–91.

McGuire, W., & Padawe-Singer, A. (1976). Trait salience in the spontaneous self-concept. *Journal of Personality and Social Psychology, 33,* 743–754.

Orfield, G., Losen, D., Wald, J., & Swanson, C. (2004). Losing our future: How minority youth are being left behind by the graduation rate crisis. Cambridge, MA: The Civil Rights Project at Harvard University. Retrieved September 14, 2005, from http://www.urban.org/UploadedPDF/410936_Losing OurFuture.pdf

Oyserman, D. (2001). Self-concept and identity. In A. Tesser & N. Schwarz (Eds.), *Blackwell Handbook of Social Psychology* (pp. 499–517). Malden, MA: Blackwell Press.

Oyserman, D. (2007). Social identity and self regulation. In A. Kutglanski & T. Higgins, *Social Psychology: Handbook of basic principles* (pp. 432–453). New York: Guilford Press.

Oyserman, D. (2008). *Adolescent pathways: An identity-based motivation program for school success.* Oxford University Press.

Oyserman, D., Brickman, D., & Rhodes, M. (2007). School success, possible selves and parent school-involvement. *Journal of Family Relations, 56,* 479–489.

Oyserman, D., Bybee, D., & Terry, K. (2006). Possible selves and academic outcomes: When and how possible selves impel action. *Journal of Personality and Social Psychology, 91,* 188–204.

Oyserman, D., Bybee, D., Terry, K. & Hart-Johnson, T. (2004). Possible selves as roadmaps. *Journal of Research in Personality, 38,* 130–149.

Oyserman, D., & Fryberg, S. A. (2006). The possible selves of diverse adolescents: Content and function across gender, race and national origin. In C. Dunkel & J. Kerpelman (Eds.), *Possible Selves: Theory, Research, and Application.* Huntington, NY: Nova.

Oyserman, D., Gant, L., & Ager, J. (1995). A socially contextualized model of African American identity: Possible selves and school persistence, *Journal of Personality and Social Psychology, 69,* 1216–1232.

Oyserman, D., Johnson, E., James, L., & Bybee, D. (2008). Socio-economic status, possible selves and strategies to obtain them. Under editorial review.

Oyserman, D., & Markus, H. (1990). Possible selves and delinquency. *Journal of Personality and Social Psychology, 59,* 112–125.

Oyserman, D., & Saltz, E. (1993). Competence, delinquency, and attempts to attain possible selves. *Journal of Personality and Social Psychology, 65,* 360–374.

Oyserman, D., Terry, K., & Bybee, D. (2002). A possible selves intervention to enhance school involvement. *Journal of Adolescence, 24,* 313–326.

Oyserman, D., Uskul, A., Yoder, N., Nesse, R., & Williams, D. (2007). Unfair treatment and self-regulatory focus. *Journal of Experimental Social Psychology.*

Régner, I., Huguet. P., & Monteil, J. (2002). Effects of socioeconomic status (SES) information on cognitive ability inferences: When low-SES students make use of a self-threatening stereotype. *Social Psychology of Education, 5,* 253–269.

Roderick, M. (2003). What's happening to the boys? Early high school experiences and school outcomes among African American male adolescents in Chicago. *Urban Education, 38,* 538–607.

Rothman, A., & Schwarz, N. (1998). Constructing perceptions of vulnerability: Personal relevance and the use of experiential information in health judgments. *Personality and Social Psychology Bulletin, 24,* 1053–1064.

Ruvolo, A., & Markus, H. (1992). Possible selves and performance: The power of self-relevant imagery. *Social Cognition, 10,* 95–124.

Sampson, R., Morenoff, J., & Earls, F. (1999). Beyond social capital: Spatial dynamics of collective efficacy for children. *American Sociological Review, 64,* 633–660.

Sandler, I., & Chassin, L. (2002). Training of prevention researchers: Perspectives from the Arizona State

University Prevention Research Training Program. *Prevention and Treatment, 5.* http://journals.apa .org/prevention/volume5/pre0050006a .html

Schwarz, N. (1998). Accessible content and accessibility experiences: The interplay of declarative and experiential information in judgment. *Personality and Social Psychology Review, 2,* 87–99.

Schwarz, N. (2002). Situated cognition and the wisdom of feelings: Cognitive tuning. In L. Feldman Barrett & P. Salovey (Eds.), *The Wisdom in Feelings* (pp. 144–166). New York: Guilford Press.

Schwarz, N., & Bless, H. (1992). Constructing reality and its alternatives: An inclusion/exclusion model of assimilation and contrast effects in social judgment. In L. Martin and A. Tesser (Eds.), *The construction of social judgments* (pp. 217–245). Hillsdale, NJ: Erlbaum.

Schwarz, N. & Clore, G. (1996). Feelings and phenomenal experiences. In T. Higgins and A. Kruglanski, (Eds.), *Social psychology: A handbook of basic principles,* New York: Guilford Press.

Seibt, B., & Förster, J. (2004). Stereotype threat and performance: How self-stereotypes influence processing by inducing regulatory foci. *Journal of Personality and Social Psychology, 87,* 38–56.

Settles, I. H. (2004). When multiple identities interfere: The role of identity centrality. *Personality and Social Psychology Bulletin, 30,* 487–500.

Steele, C. (1997). A threat in the air: How stereotypes shape intellectual identity and performance. *American Psychologist, 52,* 613–629.

Steinitz, V., & Soloman, E. (1986). *Starting Out: Class and Community in the Lives of Working-Class Youth.* Philadelphia: Temple University Press.

Stoep, A., Weiss, N., Kuo, E., Cheney, D., & Cohen, P. (2003). What proportion of failure to complete secondary school in the U.S. population is attributable to adolescent psychiatric disorder? *Journal of Behavioral Health Services and Research, 30,* 119–124.

Strauman, T. (2002). Self-regulation and depression. *Self & Identity, 1,* 151–157.

Strauman, T., & Higgins, T. (1988). Self-discrepancies as predictors of vulnerability to distinct syndromes of chronic emotional distress. *Journal of Personality, 56,* 685–707.

Thomas, D., Townsend, T., & Belgrave, F. (2003). The influence of cultural and racial identification on the psychosocial adjustment of inner-city African American children in school. *American Journal of Community Psychology, 32,* 217–228.

U.S. Bureau of the Census (2000). [Electronic version]. *Census 2000.*

Uskul, A. K., Keller, J., & Oyserman, D. (in press). Regulatory fit and health behavior. *Psychology & Health.*

Weinger, S. (2000). Opportunities for career success: Views of poor and middle-class children. *Children & Youth Services Review, 22,* 13–35.

Weinstein, N. (1993). Testing four competing theories of health-protective behavior. *Health Psychology, 12,* 324–333.

Daphna Oyserman is a professor in the School of Social Work and Department of Psychology at the University of Michigan and is the author of numerous research articles and book chapters.

QUESTIONS FOR REFLECTION

1. What possible selves do you have and how do they shape your perceptions of yourself, both in the present and future? How does the notion of possible selves explain your own development? How might it shape your development in the future?

2. Explain Oyserman's model and how it could contribute to improved outcomes for students, especially low income and/or ethnic minorities.

3. How might you bring Oyserman's school-focused model and her theory of possible selves to your educational setting? What outcomes might you hope for? How would you measure the efficacy of the model in action?

Learning the Real-World Skills of the 21st Century

PATRICIA JOYCE

ABSTRACT: *In this article, Joyce focuses on the development of career education programs at various high school campuses in the United States. What she reveals is that some campuses have developed programs that compound 21st century skills and academics by using the transitions career education curriculum—a complete curriculum developed by ASCL Educational Services. The curriculum includes five basic modules with lessons in every module and leads to real-life skill building for high school students as they prepare to enter the workforce.*

Students at South Houston High School learned invaluable workplace skills last summer by participating in an apprenticeship program that utilized an innovative curriculum and forged a successful partnership between school and business. The high school created a career education program that combined 21st century skills and academics. Using the Transitions career education curriculum—a comprehensive curriculum created by ASCL Educational Services to fulfill Chicago Public Schools' need for soft skills development—students learned the necessary soft skills to be successful in a career, and reinforced them in a simulated workplace which provided authentic and relevant learning.

Last spring Ed Beaudry, career and technical education instructor, began to develop a plan to combine two needs at the school. First, the administration had informed him of Siemens Building Technologies Division's interest in partnering with a school. In addition, he was aware that the school's Independent Study Center was in need of new desks. He formulated a plan to engage his students in an authentic project that addressed job skill enhancement. He approached the principal, then Deborah Aubin, who took an immediate interest, and meetings with Siemens finalized the project.

The program encompassed about 96 hours of job-skill training and construction activity. Students were selected through a hiring process, which included a basic application, group interview, attendance and discipline records, as well as letters of recommendation. Construction experience was not a prerequisite for acceptance; in fact, among the 14 girls and 11 boys in the program only one, the shop assistant, had any prior experience. Siemens Corporation provided a $600 stipend to all students who completed the four-week program. Students worked six hours a day, four days a week. This authentic applied learning experience allowed students to incorporate academics in a real-world workplace scenario.

THE TRANSITIONS CURRICULUM

The curriculum consists of five modules with twelve lessons in each module. Each lesson includes approximately two hours of activities, which are aligned to SCANS and the National Institute for Literacy's Equipped for the Future. Transitions teaches critical soft skills necessary for obtaining employment and building a lasting career. Teachers were trained on the curriculum, and then chose those lessons and activities pertinent to the project; this included interpersonal skills, career preparation, communication, self improvement and on-the-job skills. Use of these skills was woven throughout the job simulation portion of the program, and a before and after test was given to assess progress. Beaudry, Greg Arrant and Rhonda Carmody were instructors for the program. Beaudry used the On the Job module in the curriculum to help students understand that preparing for the workforce doesn't end once a job has been secured. Its purpose is to teach students to identify and navigate political systems in the workplace to establish strategic alliances and help them do their jobs, attain resources, gain more followers, and block out those who will be a detriment to them.

Workers must identify the positive political alliances to help become part of the system and avoid negative political games that will result in messy and confusing situations. Some of these situations are the basis of role-play scenarios, which will teach them how to participate in positive, ethical politics and learn to align themselves with those who can support them and help them fit into the culture of the workplace. For instance, a lesson entitled "Go with Your Gut!" helps students follow their instincts in everyday situations when a supervisor is not on hand for guidance or if the learner needs to make quick decisions. The point is that with a solid foundation of political savvy, integrity and humility, one's instinct is likely to be correct, and as a result will build confidence for future decision making. Lessons in group dynamics, such as meeting etiquette, are addressed as are multitasking and managing chaos. An extremely important topic called "How Do You Act When No One is Looking?" addresses the immense value of integrity, and students develop solutions to negative workplace temptations. The goal of this module is to teach learners how to manage themselves in groups, in ethical situations, and in times of workflow chaos so that time on the job can be productive and fulfilling.

Other modules address similar employability skills. The communication module covers interpersonal communication, perhaps the most important of all types. Researchers are finding that today's youth are less skilled in face to face communication (Simonetti, Jack L. 1999), so this module deals with anger control tools and listening, followed by appropriate actions. Practicing respectful, professional workplace communication is designed to show learners that tone of voice, vocabulary, and body language send a message. All lesson plans include vocabulary, writing exercises, videos, role-play scenarios, and assessments. Students were expected to complete all assignments and kept track of completion using Beaudry's giant grade book, which was prominently displayed in the front of the classroom.

ROLE-PLAYING

The role-playing sessions were particularly successful and popular with students. One member of each group served as the director with three or four scenarios to be presented. Students tried out for roles, learned lines, and presented frequently. They applied judgment and logic to real-life job situations. Students quickly learned to support and compliment each other on their work, making it one of the most positive experiences in the curriculum. Evidence of the success is seen in this student's feedback, "During the past four weeks I have become more confident in standing up in front of a crowd and sharing my ideas and thoughts. I've learned to work with others that I had never met, and in the end we've all become friends." Another student says, "This experience has helped me to grow so much as a person. I was able to learn how to communicate with people who at one point I thought I had nothing in common with. Getting to know my peers was an awesome experience."

ASSIGNMENTS

Written and oral assignments were presented each day, and various research assignments were also required. Using a list of the top 100 Houston companies, students selected one company which interested them either because of a hobby or career possibility. By researching both company and investor information, students grasped the overall picture of a corporation. Other research reports included informational interviewing, networking trees and corporate culture.

PUTTING THE KNOWLEDGE INTO PRACTICE

As students completed the lessons, employing those skills in the simulated workplace became seamless as the groups worked cooperatively to manufacture the individual study desks. The district purchased materials including 20 sheets of plywood for eight desks. Beaudry designed the desk to ensure that it could be created safely and successfully in the school's shop; however, students had input into the design, size and ergonomics. The desks were large and students quickly discovered cooperation was a key concept in the assembly because no student could lift or maneuver the desk alone. Students noted that the main concept they learned was how to work cooperatively. As a final touch, each group designed a corporate logo, discretely affixed to the underside of each desk. One logo included this slogan, "Heavyweight Builders: Interns United Across Texas to Achieve and Build our Way into the Future." The sense of accomplishment increased daily for each student, both academically and in the construction area, as excitement about the project grew. One student remarked, "This program has taught me how to be more confident in myself and how to rise to the occasion; it also taught me how to work together with a group. This program helped me break out of my shell."

Thursdays were set aside for fieldtrips sponsored by Siemens. Visits were made to the Museum of Natural Science and History, NASA, and the Moody Gardens. Students have already asked for a reunion, so an additional fieldtrip is planned to visit one of the local universities. A graduation luncheon was held on the last day and students gave presentations including thank-you letter and an outline of key concepts learned during the internship. Overwhelmingly, students reiterated the value of getting along and cooperative group efforts as key factors in their jobs. New principal, Steve Fullen, who eagerly embraced the internship program, expressed his pleasure at the exciting results of the program stating that "this is what schools should be about." Students also presented the project at a Board of Education meeting where they displayed the desks and the content of the program. While the new study desks were a visible end result, there was also a 10-point gain in job skill understanding and development which integrated math, writing and TEKS (Texas Essential Knowledge and Skills) standards.

One student said, "I am walking away from this program with the ability to converse with others and convey myself in a more confident and well-spoken manner, as well as many other things that will help me better myself, resulting in a brighter future."

Patricia Joyce is an education consultant with Prime Time Computer Services.

QUESTIONS FOR REFLECTION

1. Do you think high schools in the United States do an adequate job preparing students for the workforce, or does the modern high school curriculum focus too much on academic principles without enough real-world application?
2. What twenty-first–century skills that students need to be competitive in the contemporary workforce do modern high schools neglect to teach ?
3. What is the five module transition career education curriculum that Joyce writes about and how might it be used in the educational setting with which you are most familiar?

Can Depth Replace Coverage in the High School Curriculum?

FRED M. NEWMANN

ABSTRACT: The emphasis on broad content coverage is a fundamental limitation of the high school curriculum. This "addiction to coverage" allows students to develop only superficial understanding of what they study. As an alternative, the curriculum should emphasize depth. If given time to differentiate, elaborate, qualify, and integrate, students will acquire a rich understanding of content. To overcome the obstacles to depth will require cutting content from the existing curriculum, developing new approaches to assessment, and changing instructional strategies.

Debates about the high school curriculum tend to focus on two general questions. First, are students studying the proper content? In other words, are they taking the right number of courses in each content area, and do these courses provide an appropriate blend of knowledge, skills, attitudes, and values? Second, what are the best ways to organize and teach a given body of content to certain groups of students? These important questions seem likely to persist, due to a lack of definitive research and to the political nature of education policy making. Meanwhile, a more fundamental problem continues to plague our efforts. Despite an abundance of sophisticated rationales, pedagogical approaches, and curriculum designs, we usually try to teach too much.

In our research on higher-order thinking in high school social studies classes, we asked students whether they ever had the opportunity to really dig into a given topic and study it in depth for at least two weeks. John responded to our question:

> I got totally immersed in a project when the teacher forced us to do a paper on some guy. We couldn't pick him, but we had to read at least four books and write at least 100 note cards—big cards—and develop at least a 10-page paper. I got Montaigne. It ended up real interesting. As Mr. Foster pointed out, it was kind of cool that I got to be a real expert and to know more than probably five million people in America about this guy. I'm not sure what made it so interesting—whether it was Montaigne's own

works and life or just the fact that I got to know so much about him.

Asked whether he had such opportunities very often, John replied:

> Most of the time, you don't get this in school. A lot of times it's a total skim; it's very bad. The course in European history is a classic example. We covered 2,000 years. Every week we were assigned to cover a 30-page chapter. The teacher is a stickler for dates and facts. We had 50 dates a week to memorize. The pity of it all is that now I don't remember any of them. I worked so hard, and now basically all I remember is Montaigne. There's like maybe five dates I remember, when I probably learned 300 or 400 dates all year. I can't even remember a lot of the important guys we studied.
>
> I'd like to have worked where you dig in depth, but it's a double-sided sword, because if you're constantly going in-depth about each thing you come across, then you're not going to get very far. It's quantity versus quality. The only reasonable thing is you've got to find a balance. I guess there's more of a superficial quality to school now—teachers trying to cover as much as they can. They're not going into depth.

ADDICTION TO COVERAGE

We are addicted to coverage. This addiction seems endemic in high schools—where it runs rampant, especially in history—but it affects all levels of the curriculum, from kindergarten through college. We expose students to broad surveys of the disciplines and to endless sets of skills and competencies. The academic agenda includes a wide variety of topics; to cover them all, we give students time to develop only the most superficial understandings. The press for broad coverage causes many teachers to feel inadequate about leaving out so much content and apologetically mindful of the fact that much of what they teach is not fully understood by their students.

For several reasons, the addiction to coverage is destructive. First, it fosters the delusion that human beings are able to master everything worth knowing. We ought to realize that the knowledge explosion of this century has created a virtual galaxy of material worth knowing. Moreover, we ought to recognize that a crucial task of curriculum builders is to choose from this vast quantity of valuable knowledge a relatively infinitesimal portion to teach. The more we attempt to make this infinitesimal sample of knowledge representative or comprehensive, the more we delude ourselves, given the swift pace at which knowledge is accumulating. It is both arrogant and futile to assume that we can keep up with the knowledge explosion.

Furthermore, survey coverage is often a waste of time. Students learn most material in order to use it on one or two brief occasions (a quiz and a test), after which the material is quickly forgotten. When knowledge is used only rarely, it is seldom available for transfer to new situations.

Beyond simply wasting time or failing to impart knowledge of lasting value, superficial coverage has a more insidious consequence: it reinforces habits of mindlessness. Classrooms become places in which material must be learned—even though students find it nonsensical because their teachers have no time to explain. Students are denied opportunities to explore related areas that arouse their curiosity for fear of straying too far from the official list of topics to be covered. Teachers' talents for conveying subtle nuances and complexities are squelched. Not surprisingly, many students stop asking questions soon after they leave the early elementary grades. Instead, they passively allow teachers and textbooks to pour material into their heads, where they will try to store it for future use in educational exercises. However, the press to "cover" offers little opportunity to develop that material in ways that will help students meet more authentic intellectual challenges.

Most of us recognize the negative consequences of an addiction to coverage. We all want our curricula to foster fundamental understandings and complex, higher-order thinking. But despite our best intentions, we cannot break the habit.

THE ALTERNATIVE: DEPTH

The alternative to coverage, though difficult to achieve, is depth: the sustained study of a given topic that leads students beyond superficial exposure to rich, complex understanding. The topic might be "broad" (e.g., liberty, ecological balance) or "narrow" (e.g., John Winthrop's leadership in colonial America, the effect of acid rain on sugar maple trees). To gain rich understanding of a topic, students must master a great deal of information, use that information to answer a variety of questions about the topic, and generate new questions that lead to further inquiry. In demonstrating their knowledge of the topic, they should go beyond simple declarative statements to differentiation, elaboration, qualification, and integration.

Depth has been summarized as "less is more."* But *less* in this context does not mean less knowledge or information, for depth can be achieved only through the mastery of considerable information. Rather, *less* refers to less mastery of information that provides only a superficial acquaintance with a topic. In general, depth is preferable as a principle of curriculum development, because depth is more likely to facilitate lasting retention and transfer of knowledge, more likely to cultivate thoughtfulness than mindlessness, and more likely to enable us to cope in some reasonable fashion with the explosion of knowledge.

*Theodore R. Sizer, *Horace's Compromise: The Dilemma of the American High School* (Boston: Houghton Mifflin, 1984).

It is important to head off two possible misinterpretations of my advocacy of depth over coverage. First, I do not suggest that skills should replace knowledge as the focus of the curriculum. Instead, I maintain that knowledge in depth is more valuable than superficial knowledge and that, in order to achieve knowledge in depth, we must radically reduce the number of isolated bits of information that are transmitted to children.

Second, some readers may worry that emphasis on depth will produce excessive specialization and thus undermine the quest for a common core of knowledge, which is necessary for communication and social cohesion. However, there is no logical contradiction between knowledge in depth and attempts to achieve a common core. A common core can consist either of in-depth knowledge of a few topics or of superficial knowledge of many topics. What to include in the common core and what proportion of the curriculum the common core should occupy are difficult questions, but they should remain separate from the issue of superficial familiarity versus complex understanding. I am arguing here only that we should be devoting a far greater proportion of formal education to the development of complex understanding of fewer topics, whether those topics are unique to certain classes and schools or common to all of them.

OBSTACLES TO DEPTH

Why is depth so difficult to achieve? What are some of the major obstacles?

First, we must recognize that the point of education *is*, in a sense, to cover material—that is, to expose students to and make them familiar with new information. Conversely, to be unaware of information considered "basic" for productive living within a society is to be uneducated. In our society, becoming educated involves learning the meanings of thousands of words and mastering hundreds of conventions for manipulating information and communicating effectively with others.

Clearly, to master ideas and techniques, students must be exposed to information.

Unfortunately, this legitimate need for a certain degree of coverage has fostered the illusion (firmly held by professional educators and by the general public) that it is possible to teach a reasonably comprehensive sample of all the worthwhile knowledge that is currently available. We are remarkably unwilling to accept the consequences of the knowledge explosion. Instead, we cling to a conception of education more appropriate to medieval times, when formal public knowledge was relatively well-defined, finite, and manageable. Although we know that times have changed and that we can't teach everything, we apparently retain our faith in the ideal of comprehensiveness, because we continue to try to cover as much as possible.

The mounting pressure for schools to be accountable and to prove their effectiveness through students' test scores gives added impetus to an emphasis on coverage over depth. It is more convenient to test for superficial coverage, because thousands of multiple-choice test items can be constructed to tap countless bits of knowledge.

We teachers have been socialized to construe knowledge as outlines of the content of introductory textbooks. Seldom in our own undergraduate or graduate education did our professors engage us in deep inquiry, except for such special experiences as participating in an honors program or writing a graduate thesis (rare instances that are reserved for individuals who have already endured many years of ritualistic coverage). Thus many of us would hardly know what to do with students if the pressure for coverage were suddenly lifted.

Even teachers who have a commitment to depth and a vision of how to achieve it in the classroom are frustrated by the lack of suitable textbooks and other instructional materials. Literary works, journal articles, and primary sources are useful with highly motivated and able readers, but such materials are too difficult for many students, and few alternatives are available.

Another obstacle to depth is the orientation that students bring to their schoolwork. They have been rewarded primarily for completing discrete tasks that require the recognition of countless bits of knowledge. Those knowledge bits are organized into many separate subjects, and students' learning schedules are divided into small chunks of time. A variety of topics must be studied each day. Therefore, continuous and sustained study of any one topic seems virtually impossible.

Television further undermines intense and sustained concentration on a single topic. Teachers report that young people of the television generation have no patience for study in depth; they want quick, simple, unambiguous answers. Moreover, college-bound students want some assurance that they have been exposed to the range of information covered by admissions tests.

OVERCOMING THE OBSTACLES

The obstacles are formidable indeed. But teachers, administrators, and state-level policy makers who seek to overcome them may find the following recommendations helpful.

First, schools and school districts must continue to develop a rationale for study in depth. At the same time, they must focus the public's attention on the problems of addiction to coverage. In other words, they must help policy makers, academics, business leaders, and the general public to see that well-intentioned efforts to cover a broad range of material have developed into an obsession that is undermining education.

Second, instead of focusing immediately on which courses to eliminate, schools and school districts would probably find it less divisive to work first on ways of achieving depth within existing courses. Later, criteria such as the following might be used to decide which content to cut from the curriculum:

- Does the topic occupy a critical position in a hierarchy of content, so that students must master it in order to understand the important ideas that follow? Does failure to understand this particular topic put students at risk?

- If the topic is of critical importance, could it be readily learned outside of school through reading, televiewing, or some other form of independent study? Or does mastery of this topic require special guidance by a professional educator?

- Are teachers likely to spend a large amount of time developing this topic and assessing students' understanding of it, or will they simply give students a superficial exposure to the topic and then test for recognition or recall?

These criteria alone cannot resolve all the complicated issues related to the selection of curricular content. But they illustrate the kinds of educational principles (as opposed to teachers' personal preferences or faculty or school district politics) on which curriculum decisions might be based.

Third, in any individual school that tries to foster depth at the expense of coverage, the teachers will need special support as they wrestle with such issues as what content to cut from the curriculum, how to teach for depth, and how to assess new and more complex forms of mastery. Such support ought to include resources that would enable teachers to participate more fully in the development of curriculum materials and new approaches to testing and that would enable them to help one another more frequently in planning, teaching, and evaluating lessons.

At the state level, policy makers affect the coverage of content in at least five areas: assessment, textbook selection, curriculum requirements, school improvement programs, and teacher education. Let us consider the nature of state influence in each area and how the states might encourage a greater emphasis on depth.

Assessment. To the extent that state testing programs rely primarily on short-answer, multiple-choice tests that cover a broad range of subjects, the states contribute to the disease of coverage. There are two basic strategies for improving assessment. First, test developers can reduce the number of isolated bits of information covered by the tests, using instead items that allow students to demonstrate in-depth mastery of a smaller number of topics. Second, test developers can replace multiple-choice, short-answer questions with writing exercises—perhaps even speaking exercises—that require students to synthesize their ideas and to show the development of their thinking on selected topics.

Textbook Selection. States spread the disease of coverage when they adopt textbooks written primarily for survey courses aimed at comprehensive exposure. Publishers must be persuaded to prepare textbooks that take a more selective, in-depth approach; meanwhile, the states should adopt and publicize existing textbooks and other instructional materials that reflect this approach. One of the students I interviewed remarked that he had enjoyed a course in European history. "What made the course so interesting?" I asked. "Was it the teacher?" "No, the teacher was not particularly exciting," he said. "But the textbook was really terrific." He recalled neither the title of the book nor the name of its author. What he remembered was that the book did not inundate readers with dates and facts, headings, review questions, and test questions. "It was like a book you'd find in the library—a real book," he added.

State Curriculum Requirements. State legislators are pressured by every conceivable organization to insert subjects into the curriculum, and a reasonable case can be made for almost every proposed course or unit of instruction. Individually, each requirement seems legitimate; collectively, however, they often resemble a disorganized smorgasbord. Current efforts to reduce the number of electives and to return to a common core of required courses may seem to address the problem. But elective courses often enable students to inquire more deeply into specific topics than do core courses, which often become superficial surveys. We should avoid sanctifying either approach and instead support having students study fewer topics in greater depth.

School Improvement Programs. Moving away from an emphasis on coverage will be difficult.

Many teachers regard coverage as a primary educational goal. Others recognize that the pace of instruction makes thoughtful inquiry impossible, but they worry that they will do a disservice to students if they fail to cover all the territory required by state mandates and standardized tests. To resolve this complex professional dilemma, teachers need time to think, to argue, to select, and to develop new instructional materials. States should appropriate funds to help the schools pay for programs of staff development and for the production by staff members of curricula and tests that emphasize in-depth study.

Teacher Education. Colleges and universities perpetuate the addiction to coverage through survey courses and broad distribution requirements. These offerings permit many students to complete their degrees without ever having to engage in a sustained struggle to master the complexity of a field or topic. Thus higher education encourages teachers to conceive of knowledge as that which is contained on the table of contents of an introductory text. The states should counter this tendency by requiring that prospective teachers devote a greater proportion of their training to the in-depth study of an academic area.

Regardless of what we teach or how we teach it, we try to teach too much. The addiction to coverage is a futile attempt to offer students a comprehensive education; it wastes time and it undermines intellectual integrity. Instead of superficial exposure, curricula should emphasize sustained study aimed at developing complex understanding. But powerful obstacles—illusions about the nature of knowledge, pressures for accountability, patterns of socializing teachers and students, the organization of schooling, and the quality of instructional materials—stand in the way of a shift to study in depth. Moving in that direction will require action at the school, district, and state levels to cut content from the curriculum, develop new approaches to assessment, and change instructional materials and pedagogy. Most important, schools, districts, and states will have to carefully reexamine the goals of education.

Fred M. Newmann is director, National Center on Effective Secondary Schools, School of Education, University of Wisconsin, Madison.

QUESTIONS FOR REFLECTION

1. To what extent does an "addiction to coverage" characterize curricula at the elementary, junior/middle, and postsecondary levels of education? What examples can you cite?
2. In what ways does an emphasis on coverage "reinforce habits of mindlessness"?
3. What steps can curriculum planners take to help policymakers, other educators, business leaders, and the general public understand how the "addiction to coverage" undermines the educative process?

Case Study in Curriculum Implementation

Going the Extra Mile to Smooth the Transition to High School

HUGH CAMPBELL

ABSTRACT: *Although many schools have structures in place to ease the transition between middle level and high school, some students need more help. In this article, Campbell describes how Norwich Free Academy in Norwich, Connecticut, extended its freshman program into the tenth grade to help students achieve greater success.*

Many educators are concerned about ninth grade students who enter high school lacking the skills necessary for success. At the Norwich Free Academy (NFA) in Norwich, Conn., our guiding belief is that all students can learn, but several of the young people entering the NFA are one, two, or three years behind their classmates. Maybe they are missing some of the basic elements required to meet the demands of a high school curriculum. Weak study or organizational skills or gaps in their learning may have limited their success in the eighth grade, and they have to play catch-up for

four years. Perhaps they are socially immature. Or they may have rarely received the attention they needed to tackle academic challenges independently. Schools often address these issues during the ninth grade, but what happens to these students after they finish their ninth grade year?

NFA is an independent high school of 2,300 students that is the designated high school for the city of Norwich and seven surrounding towns. NFA is a large school, and students travel to and from its five classroom buildings, athletic facility, and library media center each period. Although we are confident that our ninth grade program successfully integrates students into the school community, we recognize that we have students who need extra support and attention during their second year. As both a teacher and an administrator, I saw many tenth graders struggle to complete the transition.

THE NINTH GRADE HOUSE

Ninth grade students are taught in the Cranston Building. Students are scheduled in one of five units with teacher teams from four core subject areas—English, civics, mathematics, and science—which carries over an essential component from middle level philosophy. Curriculum is often integrated to allow the students to make better connections from one subject to another. In a school our size, with students coming from eight sending communities, the teams make NFA seem smaller and more inviting.

This structure encourages a more personalized approach as the students begin their high school experience. But despite the teachers' best efforts to enhance students' skills and encourage solid study habits, not all of the students receive the messages that we are trying to send. When we researched composite GPAs over a 10-year period for each grade level, we found that our freshmen had a composite GPA of 2.35 during the first semester and 2.27 during the second semester. This was at least .4 points below any other grade. This finding reinforced our belief that not all of our ninth graders are prepared to fly independently when they leave our freshmen house. What kind of safety net could we create for our tenth graders?

THE TENTH GRADE SOLUTION

In spring 1998, a group of colleagues, including teachers from both ninth and tenth grade, guidance counselors, and the curriculum director, brainstormed ways to meet our tenth graders needs. We felt strongly that extending the unit concept for those students who needed another year of firm structure and support was a good beginning. We agreed that tenth grade might be our last chance to make any significant changes in how students approach school—before students are distracted by driver's licenses, dating, and jobs. Meanwhile, we could target one of NFA's strategic goals: Provide a private school education to a public school population.

Could a tenth grade unit fit with this strategic goal? We thought so.

First, we reviewed research on this idea. *Lessons from Privilege* provided an excellent starting point (Powell, 1996). Powell notes that "the glory of the private school is taking the third rate student and making him/her second rate." He maintains that personalizing education for each student is the answer and class size is a key component. Other research supports Powell's claims. Diana Oxley (1994) points out:

> Organizing schools by units encourages a coordinated, cross-disciplinary approach to instruction. Within a unit, teachers share a group of students in common rather than a discipline. They take collective responsibility for their students' success, and they work together to unify instruction and allow students the opportunity to exercise skills and knowledge across subjects. (P. 521–526)

Second we took a closer look at our ninth grade house to determine which practices were most effective for students. Ninth grade teams have been in existence at NFA since 1988. It was important to carefully examine which of the original concepts were still useful; what needed to be priority for change; and most important, what positive components we could replicate in a tenth grade unit. The ninth grade teachers and their house principal provided insights and experiential anecdotes on successes and failures. It was clear that the pros far out weighed the cons, and we gained a better sense of what could be done with a unit of 80 students rather than an entire class of 560 students.

Then we started to paint a picture of what we wanted the tenth grade unit to look like. We asked ourselves questions:

- What are the criteria for student selection?
- Who makes the recommendations?
- Who determines acceptance?
- Where do we set the bar for student achievement?
- How do we get the parents to buy in so there is a consistent message at home and at school?
- What kinds of interventions are we prepared to make for students who fall below expectations?
- How will teachers be selected to teach within the unit?

We decided to give the first three questions priority. We felt that we had to clearly define the types of students who would be included in the program before we could begin to recruit teachers.

We determined that the criteria for identifying students would include:

- Students who struggled freshman year, but should be doing better according to their Connecticut Mastery scores (CMT) from eighth grade and Educational Records Bureau (ERB) performance scores from ninth grade.
- Students who have an apparent weakness in one or more subject areas.
- Students with poor motivation or poor work ethics.
- Students who may have little support at home.
- Students who struggle with maturity issues connected to handling the increased responsibility of being a high school student.
- Students who were prepared to take Geometry, Biology, World History, English II, or certain electives in NFA's sequence of study. (These students took Algebra their freshman year.)

The committee decided that the unit leaders in the ninth grade house, the ninth grade guidance counselors, and the ninth grade principal would make recommendations in late January. All recommendations were forwarded to my office by the end of February. To our amazement, 160 recommendations were submitted, far exceeding our expectations.

We compiled data on each of the recommended students, including their grades, CMT scores, and ERB scores. Our director of guidance, the ninth grade house principal, and I scrutinized the data and added pertinent anecdotal information from student records and guidance counselors' observations. We whittled the list to about 90 names.

After we selected the students, we sent letters to their parents or guardians, explaining the purpose of our pilot tenth grade unit. We emphasized that the unit would provide a safety net of support for another year, and that the unit would emphasize organizational skills and good study habits. Goal setting would be an important component, so students would learn to make good long-term decisions, rather than live for the moment. Classes would have no more than 22 students. The letter also emphasized that we had high expectations for the students in the unit. We pointed out that anytime a student's performance fell below that expectation, the student's parents would be notified by a teacher. We included a postcard for the parent to return to indicate whether they were interested in having their child included in the unit.

The positive response was overwhelming. Of the 90 letters that were sent, only two parents declined. I invited each selected student to my office to discuss the unit and to encourage them to make a commitment to the program and to him- or herself. This was very important: It didn't matter so much that the parents wanted their children to be included, but how badly the students wanted it themselves. Conversations lasted anywhere between 10 to 20 minutes. It was exciting to see how many of the students were honest about their struggles in ninth grade and anxious to make a commitment to self-improvement.

The students' biggest concern about being part of the unit was being isolated. They did not want to be stuck in one building, as they were in the ninth grade, or worse, one section of one building for their core classes. I assured them that this would not be the case. Although they would share a team of teachers, these teachers would be spread out all over campus, and they would go from building to building, just like any other tenth grader. Their homerooms and guidance counselors would be assigned, like the other tenth graders and would remain the same until they were graduated.

FACULTY SELECTION

Finally, the faculty had opportunities to ask questions. The biggest concern of a few teachers was that this pilot might become the first step toward teaming the entire tenth grade. We assured them that we didn't intend to do so at present. Not all tenth grade students needed the safety net that we were planning to provide.

The committee was asked to recommend members of the faculty who had experience with the tenth grade curriculum and students. Some recommendations were made, but no one expressed overwhelming interest until I began to contact individual teachers and thoroughly explained the intent of the program. Four excellent faculty members were genuinely excited about working as a team and being part of the pilot program. These teachers were integral to the eventual success of this program.

DESIGNING CURRICULUM

The teachers and I met in spring and summer 1999 to set goals for the students and to modify our standard tenth grade curriculum to allow more integration. The teachers were excited to have this opportunity to experiment and design. We decided that they would teach four-fifths of their teaching load in the unit and teach one class outside the unit and have a common planning period. The biology and geometry teachers attended a workshop during the summer about integrating math and science curricula.

The teachers left for summer break with a complete data sheet for each student in the unit so the teachers could contact the ninth grade teachers if they had questions about a particular student.

Before the students left for the summer, we gave them two books to read. Normally, tenth grade students choose three books from the tenth grade reading list. But we required that the pilot program students read *The Seven Habits of Highly Effective Teens* by Stephen Covey (1998) and *A Separate Peace* by John

Knowles (1985). The students were also required to read a book of their choice from the tenth grade reading list. Reading *The Seven Habits* gave the students some thoughtful information about how they could fine-tune their personal lives. It was very easy to read and humorous. *A Separate Peace* was chosen by our English and history teachers for an integrated lesson. These books were common topics for class discussion after the school year began.

Scheduling the unit was a challenge. We decided that scheduling the unit in four consecutive periods would allow time for guest speakers and field trips. After announcing the schedule, we immediately lost four students who preferred to take electives that conflicted with the schedule.

ORIENTATION

Orientation sessions with both the students and the parents were held on the evening of the first day of school. We gave parents a handout titled "Back to School Tips for Parents," and we borrowed ideas from a variety of sources, including *The Complete Idiot's Guide to Parenting a Teenager* (Kelley, 1996), *Teen Tips: A Practical Survival Guide for Parents with Kids Ages 11–19* (McMahon, 1996), and a few ideas of our own. Each teacher introduced briefly discussed his or her expectations and curriculum.

The parents filled out questionnaires on how they perceived their children as students and what their hopes were for their children. Parents or guardians of 52 of the 80 students attended. The next day, we had a similar meeting with the students, and they also filled out questionnaires. The teachers received copies of the parents' and students' responses. The students were very honest in their responses, recognized their weaknesses, and seemed to welcome the opportunity to improve within the framework of the unit.

We felt that we were off to a solid start. The teachers and I met every Friday during the teachers' common prep time to compare notes, plan, and decide whether any interventions were needed. We quickly established lines of communication among the teachers, the students, and the parents or guardians. Most of our students were comfortable asking for extra help when they needed it. When a student's work fell below 80 percent in a subject, the teachers notified the student's family. The teachers divided the students into four groups and one teacher was responsible for communicating our concerns to those students' families. Individual teachers made additional calls if they felt an issue was serious enough to warrant personal contact. E-mail became the most popular means of communication for both teachers and families and allowed teachers to send assignments to students who were absent.

When the first marking period ended, we had our first bit of data to look at. We were excited that 34 percent of the students received all As or Bs in core subject areas. Only five Fs were given. It was amazing improvement for that group of students. The teachers felt that because they expected the students to meet high standards and communicated consistently with parents, the students responded. The parents did not have to wait until the end of the marking period to discover how their children were doing; they were notified regularly.

We also asked the students to fill out a first quarter review sheet. We wanted to know what differences they saw in themselves. Questions included:

- In regard to your studies, what are you doing better now as compared to last year? What do you think the reason is for your improvement?
- What do you still need to work on, and what do you intend to do about it?
- We have spoken to you a lot about how important it is to set goals and to establish relationships with people who can help you achieve those goals. What short- and long-term goals have you set?

Responses varied, but a couple of messages came through loud and clear. Students felt much more organized in their studies and they were beginning to make long-term goals. As students started to feel better about themselves and school, making long-term decisions seemed practical to them.

Prior to midyear exams, we invited parents to the school. We gave parents review sheets similar to the ones the students received. The resulting dialogue was productive, and we shared hints with parents on ways they could assist their children's study and time management.

Semester grades indicated that our efforts had been fruitful. We compared our students' grades from their first semester, ninth grade classes to their grades in their first semester, tenth grade classes. Seventy percent improved their grades in science, 65 percent improved in mathematics, 77 percent improved in English, and 77 percent improved in history. We brought the students together to applaud their efforts and encourage them to continue.

The second semester was more challenging for our teachers. The students, feeling good, naturally wanted to relax a bit. Unfortunately, there are no vacations built into our calendar at midyear. Teachers continued to keep parents apprised of student progress. Second semester results, although not as good as first semester, were still impressive. Comparing second semester grades from ninth and tenth grades: Sixty-one percent of students improved in science, 62 percent in mathematics, 61 percent in English, and 66 percent in history.

The individual success stories were many. Tina is a student of color who is extremely bright, but struggled in her freshman year. She got caught up in socializing with friends and did not pay enough attention to her studies. At the end of her freshman year, she had a GPA of 1.91. She admitted that she did not have good organizational skills and really did not know how to prepare herself for class everyday or how to study for tests.

Tina took full advantage of lessons on organizational skills and started keeping meticulous assignment books and notebooks. After a slow start, she blossomed during the second marking period and did a truly remarkable job during the second semester earning no grade lower than a B in her core subject areas. By the end of the year, she raised her GPA to 2.27.

David often clowned around in class, rarely keeping a focus on the tasks at hand. When motivated, he demonstrated that he could do excellent work, but those instances were few and far between. Because of the behavior issue, David's situation was a bit more complex than Tina's. We had a conference with his parents to obtain further insight into his patterns of behavior. We found that David had a history with attention deficit disorder and had been taken off medication when he started high school. It was quite obvious that his distractibility was getting in the way of his academic success. His parents were willing to take David back to his doctor to reassess his attention deficit issue. He was given a new prescription, and the academic dividends were almost immediate. David raised his freshman GPA of 1.16 to 1.83 at the end of tenth grade. David earned nothing lower than a B during the second semester.

There were many success stories in our tenth grade unit. Because of our teachers' dedication and the pilot program's small class sizes, teachers were able to personalize lessons for the students, which resulted in significant improvements by those students who were open to making changes in the way they studied. At the beginning of the next school year, many of the students visited their teachers to touch base. The students are anxious to share their summer activities and their new successes in school.

We will continue to monitor the students' performance in school through the eleventh and twelfth grades. We want to determine whether the lessons we taught about how to succeed in school are lasting. We will examine the students' performances on the Connecticut Academic Performance Test (CAPT), which the students took in May 2000, and their performances on the PSAT and SAT exams.

Our superintendent and our board of trustees were impressed enough by our success with this pilot program that they gave me permission to expand the program to two units during the 2000–2001 school year. A second team of teachers was recruited, and all of the teachers from last year were anxious to return. This year, each team of teachers is teaching three classes within their units. Each unit will contain approximately 65 students. The parent support and student commitment has been excellent.

Keeping students connected to school often takes extra effort and some creative thinking on the part of the school community. We feel strongly that our efforts with the tenth grade unit saved some students who might have otherwise fallen through the cracks into the sea of academic indifference.

REFERENCES

Covey, S. 1998. *The seven habits of highly effective teens.* New York: Simon and Schuster.

Kelley, K. 1996. *The complete idiot's guide to parenting a teenager.* New York: Alpha Books.

Knowles, J. 1985. *A separate peace.* New York: Bantam Books.

McMahon, T. 1996. *Teen tips: A practical survival guide for parents with kids ages 11–19.* Pocket Books.

Oxley, D. 1994. Organizing schools into small units: Alternatives to homogeneous grouping. *Phi Delta Kappan* 75(7): 521–526.

Powell, A. 1996. *Lessons from privilege.* Cambridge, Mass.: Harvard University Press.

Hugh Campbell is principal of the Tirrell Building of NFA in Norwich, Connecticut.

QUESTIONS FOR REFLECTION:

1. What is the ninth grade house and what features about it are appropriate for tenth graders' success in school?

2. Campbell's article demonstrates how collaborative work between teachers and administration can lead to system changes within a school district. How might other schools accomplish this same kind of collaboration? What are key characteristics of this collaborative effort that made it successful at Norwich Free Academy?

3. What positive outcomes can the teachers and administration point to to demonstrate that their program was a success? Is "proof" necessary to justify this kind of endeavor, or are there times when faith that a system has been improved is enough?

Leaders' Voices— Putting Theory into Practice

A Tale of Two Curriculums

MIRA REISBERG

ABSTRACT: The author, a teacher educator and illustrator of children's books, contrasts the progressive, constructivist curriculum found in most teacher education programs with the conservative, traditional curriculum that pervades today's schools. To prepare pre-service teachers for the curricular realities they will encounter in schools, the author's students experience a curriculum that incorporates a pedagogy of pleasure, place-based pedagogy, critical race theory, and social reconstructionist arts education.

Here lies a tale of two curriculums. One is a progressive, constructivist curriculum that employs strategies such as cooperative learning, inquiry-based learning, scaffolded instruction, multiple intelligences theory, and authentic assessments. The other is a conservative, traditional curriculum that, for the most part, employs teacher-delivered, top-down rote memorization activities and basic skill building techniques. These activities typically culminate in a series of high-stakes tests that determine both the child's and the school's future (McNeil, 2000). In general, teacher education programs are structured around progressive, constructivist pedagogy, while an increasingly conservative legislative body favors the traditionalist, conservative pedagogy.

Federal mandates such as No Child Left Behind (NCLB) have helped create an educational climate privileging the traditional conservative curriculum. Funding connected with NCLB is tied to "scientifically based" programs that have a traditionalist orientation of skill and drill and rote memorization (Coles, 2002; Garan, 2004). For children who struggle with issues of motivation and comprehension, focusing primarily on skill and drill programs while ignoring issues of cultural congruence and personal connection does not promote a love of learning (Delpit, 1995; Taylor, 2004).

Anyone who has learned to play a musical instrument will remember the boredom and tedium of repetitive practice and basic skills acquisition.

Without this practice they would never have been able to play. However, if the learning focused solely on technique, chances are they never connected with the heart and soul and love of music and dropped it as soon as they could. Those fortunate enough to have a teacher who taught them using culturally relevant, meaningful music and who also encouraged them to explore music in many ways frequently developed a lifelong love of music. In other words, a combination of traditional and constructivist pedagogies are needed for an effective education. Cowen (2003) has termed this a "balanced approach" to education.

This paper posits that, although basic skills and rote memorization are necessary for learning, teachers do their students a great disservice if they focus primarily on such pedagogy at the expense of meaningful experiences such as those I try to provide my students. As a teacher of pre-service elementary teachers at a major university, I have noticed the polarization between the two curriculums. However, because my future teachers will be provided with an abundance of conservative skill building materials in the field, my curriculum focuses on teaching critical, constructivist pedagogies that are vitally important. Before detailing the specifics of my curricular approach, I will provide further background information on the differences between the two curriculums.

DIFFERENCES BETWEEN THE TWO CURRICULUMS

A traditional curriculum is based on learning discrete parcels of information (or facts) that are acquired through rote memory. These facts are discipline specific and taught in a prescribed skill and drill manner within a delineated time frame. Students work alone on basal, textbook-centered problems, and their learning is assessed by tests.

A constructivist curriculum, in contrast, tends to be integrated, inter-disciplinary and inquiry-based. Learning is socially constructed, and the context of learning and students' prior knowledge are central to the educational experience. Projects are frequently student generated and group oriented, and they involve more flexibility in the use of time. In addition, authentic literature is used with portfolio and other authentic assessment models (Cambourne, 2002; Moursund, 1999).

Traditional conservatives and progressive constructionists both want children to succeed and do well. However, it appears that they have different ideas of what success means and how to go about achieving it. For many traditional conservatives, success appears to be about learning the basic cognitive and class-appropriate vocational skills that enable one to participate in the American dream. For critical, constructivist educators, the goal is less job oriented than about developing higher-order thinking skills and enabling students to become active participants in their own lives.

However, some critical pedagogues believe that constructivism simply serves to "rearrange the furniture" in an institution whose foundations are rotting. By preparing students to take tests, institutionalized constructivists have been co-opted into propping up a system that continues to colonize and dominate humans, animals, and environments (Bowers, 1997; Gruenewald, 2003a). In other words, constructivism is merely "the other side of the same coin" as traditionalism. Such arguments notwithstanding, the reality is that pre-service teachers are entering a world they cannot immediately change. Consequently, it is important to find ways to integrate pedagogies that help them teach critical thinking skills to challenge the status quo and to construct something better, while also teaching successful test-taking strategies so they can keep their jobs and students can progress to the next grade.

Meanwhile, social reproduction theorists (Kozol, 1991; Tozer, Violas, & Senese, 2002) hold that education is consciously and historically constructed to reproduce class and inequality through the different curriculums taught in economically segregated schools. One class of schooling focuses on the basics needed for low-level employment, while the other focuses on the development of creative critical thinking skills needed for positions of management and leadership. Not coincidentally, those in more privileged schools have parents who are educated to take advantage of political power by making decisions about who gets educational resources that influence test scores and opportunities (Kozol, 1991; Ladson Billings, 1998).

DEWEY OR DON'T WE?

Advocates for traditional, top-down education believe that the system of education that worked for them is best for today's children. As President George W. Bush stated in 1996:

> The building blocks of knowledge were the same yesterday and will be the same tomorrow. . . . We do not need trendy new theories or fancy experiments or feel good curriculums. The basics work. If drill gets the job done then rote is right (Coles, 2002).

However, not everyone can or did learn this way, and such approaches ignore a long history of unequal outcomes as well as the question of the purpose of education. The entire history of progressive, constructivist education tells us that students benefit from an experiential curriculum connected to their lived experiences (Dewey, 1916; Freire, 2003).

In contrast to the traditional curriculum, I propose a curriculum that centers on feeling good— about one's self, one's work, and one's place in the world. This approach strives to create heartfelt connections among student's lives, communities, creative intelligences, bodies, and spirits.

Dewey was one of the first to advocate for pleasure, connection, and integration in the curriculum. In *Interest and Effort in Education* he wrote:

> education rises or falls with our ability to make school life an interesting and absorbing experience to the child. In one sense there is no such thing as compulsory education. We can have compulsory physical attendance at school; but education comes only through willing attention to and participation in school activities. It follows that the teacher must select these activities with reference to the child's

interest, powers, and capabilities. In no other way can she guarantee that the child will be present. (Dewey, 1913, p. ix)

Although Dewey wrote these words over ninety years ago, they are still profoundly relevant and compelling for today's educators.

THE PRACTICE OF PLEASURE: TEACHING FOR SOCIAL JUSTICE AND ENVIRONMENTAL STEWARDSHIP

Engaging students is central to a curriculum based on the principle of pleasure. If learners enjoy doing something, they will do it frequently and, consequently, get good at it. If students are motivated by connections—to themselves, their communities, their environment, their classmates, and their history; if they see themselves reflected in the literature they read and as creators of literature; if they see their work as having value not only to their teachers, but also to others outside the school and in the real world—they will enjoy learning more, and participate in it with enthusiasm (Dewey, 1913, 1934; Eisner, 1995; Greene, 1978).

In brief, my course, Integrated Fine Arts, teaches pre-service teachers how to teach the various content areas using a creative integration of art and drama. These methodologies are designed to teach critical, higher-order thinking skills as well as to foster a love of learning. The curriculum consists of three conceptual threads:

1. A pedagogy of pleasure, based on the joy of sensory play while making multiple connections across content areas, personal experiences and culture (Cambourne, 2002; Dewey, 1913, 1934; Eisner, 1982, 1995, 1998; Greene, 1978).

2. A pedagogy that employs place-based education (Gruenewald, 2003b; Haas & Nachtigal, 1998; Sobel, 2004), critical race theory (Delpit, 1995; Ladson Billings, 1998, 2000; Nieto, 2000; Schwartz, 1995), and social reconstructionist arts education practices (Cahan & Kocur, 1996; Klein, 1992, 2000; Milbrandt, 2002).

3. A pedagogy that promotes democratic participation through awareness and action for social justice and environmental stewardship (Dewey, 1916; Furman & Gruenewald, 2004; Greene, 1978).

These conceptual threads are woven through a creative and critical combination of authentic, multicultural children's literature and art. What follows is a brief description of these ideas, including examples of how I encourage students to use them in their own classrooms.

Place-Based Pedagogy

In the Deweyan tradition, connection is one of the central tenets of place-based education through which students connect with their local environments as sites for situated learning experiences that benefit both themselves and their communities. Place-based educators and their students promote environmental stewardship and active participation in their "place of being." As Gruenewald (2003b) writes:

> Place-conscious education, therefore, aims to work against the isolation of schooling's discourses and practices from the living world outside the increasingly placeless institution of schooling. Furthermore, it aims to enlist teachers and students in the firsthand experience of local life and in the political process of understanding and shaping what happens there (p. 620).

Critical Race Theory

Critical race theorists advocate for understanding and shaping issues of culture and race. Among other things, they call for authenticity and critical inclusion in children's literature. Describing how the non-critical use of multicultural literature supports an ineffective liberalism that effectively maintains hegemony in the form of existing class structures and racism, they effectively ask: "Who says what and for whom," and "How culturally congruent is the curriculum with students' own cultures?" Multicultural literature that is authen-tic can truly be a valuable form of storytelling that creates agency and affirmation for all children (Ladson Billings, 2000; Nieto, 2000; Yenika Agbaw, 1997).

Social Reconstructionist Arts Education

Arts based educators taking a more holistic approach note the spiritual, emotional, and practical importance of the arts in educating the whole child while covering the content areas in fun and meaningful ways. At the same time, social reconstructionist arts educators believe that the practice of art with its sensual, reflective, and collaborative qualities can provide an excellent forum to explore and challenge official reifying discourses. As Milbrandt (2002) writes:

> Rather than accepting intellectual and moral complacency, art educators must possess the courage and the skills necessary to initiate art programs that engage students in critical inquiry, connect learning to authentic and meaningful issues in life, and inspire responsible intellectual and moral action (p. 153).

MY CURRICULUM IN ACTION

Curriculum choices strongly influence students' beliefs about race, gender, class, and environment (Parkay & Hass, 2000). Drawing on the transformational theories mentioned above, I encourage my pre-service teachers to build curriculum around a central book that is place specific, culturally authentic, and visually and linguistically aesthetic. This can jumpstart community-oriented art projects that utilize multiple intelligences (Gardner, 1983), as well as the many other forms of knowledge needed to navigate in life. I encourage inclusion of European American stories as part of the multicultural discourse to show that all students have culture and that multiculturalism does not once again marginalize people of color as separate and "other" and European Americans as cultureless (Newling, 2001).

I use quality, place-specific, multicultural literature as the starting point of a unit to model culturally congruent teaching for my pre-service students to use in their own future teaching. By starting here, they are able to find themselves and others reflected and affirmed. While exploring concepts of embedded racism, they are provided opportunities to learn about and respect the many cultures that make our world. These books also help promote environmental awareness by providing opportunities to compare and contrast place. The books also stimulate connections with students about their own communities and environments to facilitate the creation of situated learning experiences that benefit students and their communities (Gruenewald, 2003b; Haas & Nachtigal, 1998). After conducting a close reading of a book, the class compares and contrasts the embedded themes in the text and illustrations and makes connections to their own race, place and culture. From this awareness, they can then create projects that promote awareness of social and environmental issues.

For example, the book *Where Fireflies Dance* (Corpi, 1997) promoted a range of projects in my class. One was the creation of portraits and intergenerational oral histories with local senior citizens, which were exhibited and celebrated in the public library. These histories showed seniors connected to "lived history" in contrast to "official histories," while using art to address state standards of science, history, communication, reading, and writing.

A second place-based project involved creating large cut-paper murals of our local wildlife and landscape through the seasons. This project modeled how to integrate math and science with art by embedding math concepts in the numbers of animals depicted while learning about our local environment.

A third project integrated dance, drama, and science through the creation of "Science Theater": body-based interpretive dances of the life cycles of endangered and at-risk local animals with instructions on how to save them.

In a fourth example, inspired by the work of contemporary African American artist Fred Wilson, my pre-service teachers learned how to teach about embedded racism in how language is used. After creating paper-maché Halloween insect masks, students created labels for them showing how the kind of language used to exhibit African and minority art is radically different than that used to exhibit European and European American art. Their labels used demeaning vocabulary like primitive and ritual and were un-credited except for the geographic area they came from.

These examples are just some of the many projects that provide rich and meaningful ways to integrate all the content areas. They are also frequently fun and pleasure-based. These methodologies are student driven, culturally relevant, and center on collaborative learning. They incorporate time-outs for teaching content areas with more traditional methods, and the framework is there to provide connected, concrete, learning opportunities. These are valuable skills that children need to know along with the basics. What could be more important than learning how to be a multiliterate, caring, and capable member of one's community?

JUSTIFICATION AND ACCOUNTABILITY

Because teachers are frequently called upon to justify and provide accountability for their teaching methodologies, I also provide examples of research my students can cite showing that children can do well on achievement tests by doing culturally congruent, fun, and rewarding projects while also learning test-taking strategies if needed.

Teachers can also cite examples showing how all students, particularly low socioeconomic status students, do well when their learning is connected to their lives and their communities (Dillard & Blue, 2000; Ladson Billings, 2000). My future teachers can make use of arts-based research (Catterall, 1998; Cornett, 2003; Elfland, 2002; Fowler, 1996; NAEP, 1997) that describes the significantly positive outcomes of arts infused curriculums in high-stakes testing arenas as well as in other areas. As Upitis and Smithrim (2002) note, "Students, teachers, parents, artists, and administrators [can see] how the arts motivate children, referring to the emotional, physical, cognitive, and social benefits of learning in and through the arts" (p. 2). Finally, my future teachers can question why these integrated teaching methodologies are considered ineffective when wealthier schools value them so much (Kozol, 1991; Ladson Billings, 1998).

Accountability to parents and community members occurs when children and their work go out into the community, and when the community comes into the classroom. In utilizing place-based pedagogies of engaged local learning that incorporate art and literature, parents and community members can experience the delightfulness of their children's experiences, while their children learn important, real-life, integrated skills *and* how to pass mandated tests. Stakeholders can see that their children are reading, writing, performing, creating, understanding, and working with challenging math and science concepts. By enriching the traditional teacher education curriculum with these ideas, my pre-service students will be more apt to teach in ways that challenge unfairness and inequality while maintaining or exceeding mandated standards. By bridging the two curriculums and engaging and motivating students to find pleasure and meaning in their education, students will succeed academically, and, in all likelihood, they will also become lifelong learners and valuable community members.

REFERENCES

Bowers, C. A. (1997). *The culture of denial: Why the environmental movement needs a strategy for reforming universities and public schools.* Albany: State University of New York Press.

Cahan, S., & Kocur, Z. (1996). *Contemporary art and multicultural education.* New York: Routledge.

Cambourne, B. (2002). Holistic integrated approaches to reading and language arts instruction: The constructivist framework of an instructional theory. In *What research has to say about reading instruction* (pp. 25–46). Newark, NJ: International Reading Association.

Catterall, J. (1998). Does experience in the arts boost academic achievement? A response to Eisner. *Art Education, 51*(4), 6–11.

Coles, G. (2002). *Learning to read—"scientifically".* Retrieved 10/20/04, 2004, from http://www.rethinkingschools.org/special_reports/bushplan/Read154.shtml

Cornett, C. E. (2003). *Creating meaning through literature and the arts: An integration resource for classroom teachers.* Upper Saddle River, NJ: Pearson Education.

Corpi, L. (1997). *Where fireflies dance.* San Francisco, CA: Children's Book Press.

Cowen, J. E. (2003). *A balanced approach to beginning reading instruction: A synthesis of six major U.S. research studies.* Newark, NJ: International Reading Association.

Delpit, L. (1995). *Other people's children: Cultural conflict in the classroom.* New York: The New Press.

Dewey, J. (1913). *Interest and effort in education.* Boston: Houghton Mifflin.

Dewey, J. (1916). *Democracy and education: An introduction to the philosophy of education.* New York: The Macmillan Company.

Dewey, J. (1934). *Art as experience.* New York: G. P. Putnam and Sons.

Dillard, C. B., & Blue, D. A. (2000). Learning styles from a multicultural perspective: The case for culturally engaged education. In M. Gallegos & S. Hollingsworth (Eds.), *What counts as literacy: Challenging the school standards.* New York: Teachers College Press.

Eisner, E. W. (1982). *Cognition and curriculum: A basis for deciding what to teach.* New York: Longman.

Eisner, E. W. (1995). What artistically crafted research can help us understand about schools. *Educational Theory, 45*(1), n.p.

Eisner, E. W. (1998). *The kinds of schools we need: Personal essays.* Portsmouth, NH: Heinemann Educational Books.

Elfland, A. D. (2002). *Art and cognition: Integrating the visual arts in the curriculum.* New York: Teachers College Press and National Art Education Association.

Fowler, C. (1996). *Strong arts, strong schools: The promising potential and shortsighted disregard of the arts in American schooling.* New York: Oxford University Press.

Freire, P. (2003). *Pedagogy of the Oppressed* (30th Anniversary Edition ed.). New York: The Continuum International Publishing Group.

Furman, G., & Gruenewald, D. A. (2004). Expanding the landscape of social justice: A critical ecological analysis. *Educational Administration Quarterly, 40*(1), 49–78.

Garan, E. M. (2004). *In defense of our children: When politics, profit and education collide*. Portsmouth, NH: Heinemann.

Gardner, H. (1983). *Frames of mind: The theory of multiple intelligences*. New York: Basic Books.

Greene, M. (1978). *Landscapes of learning*. New York: Teachers College Press.

Gruenewald, D. A. (2003a). The best of both worlds: A critical pedagogy of place. *Educational Researcher, 32*(4), 3–12.

Gruenewald, D. A. (2003b). Foundations of place: A multidisciplinary framework for place-conscious education. *American Educational Research Journal, 40*(3), 619–654.

Guthrie, J. T. (2002). Preparing students for high-stakes test taking in reading. In A. Farstrup (Ed.), *What research has to say about reading instruction* (pp. 370–391). Newark, DE: International Reading Association.

Haas, T., & Nachtigal, P. M. (1998). *Place value: an educators' guide to good literature on rural lifeways, environments, and purposes of education*. Charleston, WV: ERIC Clearinghouse on Rural Education and Small Schools.

Klein, S. (1992). Social action and art education: A curriculum for change. *Journal of multicultural and cross-cultural research in art education, 10,* 111–125.

Klein, S. (2000). Spirituality and art education: Looking to place. *Journal of multicultural and cross-cultural research in art education, 18,* 57–66.

Kozol, J. (1991). *Savage inequalities*. New York: Crown Publishers.

Ladson Billings, G. (1998). Just what is critical race theory and what's it doing in a nice fields like education? *Qualitative studies in education, 11*(1), 7–24.

Ladson Billings, G. (2000). Reading between the lines and beyond the pages. In M. Gallegos & S. Hollingsworth (Eds.), *What counts as literacy: Challenging the school standards*. New York: Teachers College Press.

McNeil, L. M. (2000). Creating new inequalities: Contradictions of reform. *Phi Delta Kappan, 81,* 728–734.

Milbrandt, M. K. (2002). Addressing contemporary social issues in art education: A survey of public school art educators in Georgia. *Studies in art education: A journal of issues and research, 44*(1), 141–157.

Moursund, D. G. (1999). *Project-based learning using information technology*. Eugene, OR: International Society for Technology in Education.

NAEP. (1997). *The NAEP 1997 Arts Report Card: Eighth-grade findings from the National Assessment of educational progress*. Washington, DC: U.S. Department of Education, Office of Educational Research and Improvement.

Newling, M.-L. (2001). Approaches to critical literacy through literature. In L. Ramîrez & O. M. Gallardo (Eds.), *Portraits of teachers in multicultural settings: A critical literacy approach*. Boston: Allyn & Bacon.

Nieto, S. (2000). *Affirming Diversity: The Sociopolitical Context of Multicultural Education* (3rd ed.). Boston: Allyn & Bacon.

Parkay, F. W., & Hass, G. (2000). Learning and learning styles. In F. W. Parkay, & G. Hass (Eds.), *Curriculum planning: A contemporary approach* (pp. 165–171). Boston: Allyn & Bacon.

Schwartz, E. G. (1995). Crossing borders/Shifting paradigm: Multiculturalism and children's literature. *Harvard Educational Review, 65*(4), 634–649.

Sobel, D. (2004). *Place-based education: Connecting classrooms and communities*. Great Barrington, MA: The Orion Society.

Taylor, H. (2004). Education expert wonders if NCLB is too focused to accommodate children living in poverty. *School administrator's compliance hotline, 7*(2), 4–5.

Tozer, S. E., Violas, P. C., & Senese, G. (2002). *School and society: Historical and contemporary perspectives*. New York: McGraw Hill.

Yenika Agbaw, V. (1997). Taking children's literature seriously: Reading for pleasure and social change. *Language Arts 74*(6), pp. 446–453.

Mira Reisberg, a former K–6 teacher and literacy consultant for K–12 schools, is an illustrator of children's books and teaches in the School of Art at Northern Illinois University.

QUESTIONS FOR REFLECTION:

1. Reisberg suggests that "mandates such as No Child Left Behind have helped to create an educational climate privileging the traditional, conservative curriculum." Do you agree or disagree with her observation? Explain your position.
2. With respect to the subject area and grade level with which you are most familiar, how might you employ place-based pedagogy strategies such as those described by Reisberg?
3. Reisberg's article includes the following observations by President George W. Bush:

   The building blocks of knowledge were the same yesterday and will be the same tomorrow. . . . We do not need trendy new theories or fancy experiments or feel good curriculums. The basics work. If drill gets the job done then rote is right.

   To what extent do you agree or disagree with the president's view of education?

LEARNING ACTIVITIES

Critical Thinking

1. Are a common high school curriculum and uniform standards appropriate in a pluralistic society? Can a common curriculum and uniform standards be implemented with diverse groups of students? Can individual differences be accommodated? Should they be?
2. Reflect on this chapter's recommendations for changing the curriculum for high school students in light of curricular goals for this age group, the three bases of the curriculum, and curriculum criteria. Which recommendations from the articles in this chapter would you like to see implemented?
3. Which developmental changes discussed in Chapter 3 should guide curriculum planners in designing educational programs for high school students?
4. What are the essential elements of effective curricula for high school students?
5. What are some of the challenges that today's high school students face that were unknown or little known to their parents or grandparents? To what extent can (or should) these challenges be addressed in educational programs for high schoolers?

Application Activities

1. When you were a high school student, what school experiences helped you to grow and learn? What experiences hindered you? What implications do these experiences have for your current and future curriculum leadership activities?
2. Drawing from the material in this chapter, develop a short questionnaire or set of interview questions that curriculum leaders could use to learn more about high school students. Compare your questions with those of your classmates.
3. Invite a group of high school teachers to your class and ask them to describe the steps they take in planning curricula for their students. What do they see as the most important curriculum criteria to use in planning?

4. Obtain a statement of philosophy (or mission statement) from a nearby high school. Analyze the statement in regard to this chapter's six recommended goals for educational programs for high school. How many of the goals are reflected in the statement?

Field Experiences

1. Visit a nearby high school and obtain permission to interview a few students about their curricular experiences. Take field notes based on these interviews. The following questions might serve as a guide for beginning your interviews: Do the students like school? What about it do they like and dislike? What are their favorite subjects? What about those subjects do they like? What are their plans for the future? Then, analyze your field notes; what themes or concerns emerge that would be useful for curriculum leaders at this level?

2. Visit an agency in your community that offers services to high school students and their families. Ask a staff member to describe the services that are offered. Report your findings to the rest of your class.

3. Talk with a group of high school students about the social forces of concern to them in their school, their community, their nation, and the world. What implications do their concerns have for curriculum leaders at this level?

Internet Activities

1. At the Center for Research on the Education of Students Placed at Risk (CRES-PAR), gather research results and curriculum-related resources useful to those who plan educational programs for high school students placed at risk.

2. Go to the State Curriculum Frameworks and Contents Standards page maintained by the U.S. Department of Education's Office of Educational Research and Improvement (OERI) and obtain your state's secondary-level curriculum frameworks. Critique these frameworks in light of the recommendations in Chapter 10.

3. Go to OERI's Blue Ribbon Schools Program, which recognizes outstanding public and private schools. From that site, "visit" a few exemplary high schools. To what extent do they reflect the recommendations made throughout Chapter 10?

Credits

CHAPTER 1: Goals and Values

Character and Academics: What Good Schools Do by Jacques S. Benninga, Marvin W. Berkowitz, Phyllis Kuehn, & Karen Smith. From *Phi Delta Kappan* 87, no. 6 (Feb. 2006): 448–452. © 2006 Phi Delta Kappa. Used by permission of the authors and publisher.

Uncovering Teacher Leadership by Richard Ackerman & Sarah V. Mackenzie. From *Educational Leadership* 63, no. 8 (May 2006): 66–70. © 2006 Association for Supervision and Curriculum Development. Used by permission of the authors and publisher.

Perspectives on Four Curriculum Traditions by William H. Schubert. From *Educational Horizons* 74, no. 4 (Summer 1996): 169–176. © Educational Horizons. Used by permission of the author and publisher.

Democracy at Risk by William E. White, Richard van Scotter, Michael H. Haroonian, & James E. Davis. From *Social Studies* 98, no. 6 (Nov./Dec. 2007): 228–230. Reprinted with permission of the Helen Dwight Reid Educational Foundation. Published by Heldref Publications. 1319 Eighteenth St., NW, Washington, D.C. 20036-1802. Copyright © 2007.

The Organization and Subject-Matter of General Education by Robert M. Hutchins. From an address presented at the annual convention of the National Association of Secondary School Principals at Atlantic City, NJ, February 1938. Copyright 1938 National Association of Secondary School Principals. www.principals.org. Reprinted with permission.

The Case for Essentialism in Education by William C. Bagley. From *Today's Education: Journal of the National Education Association* 30, no. 7 (Oct. 1941): 201–202. Used by permission of the publisher.

The Case for Progressivism in Education by William Heard Kilpatrick. From *Today's Education: Journal of the National Education Association* 30, no. 8 (Oct. 1941): 231–232. Used by permission of the publisher.

Traditional vs. Progressive Education by John Dewey. From John Dewey, *Experience and Education,* pp. 1–10 (New York: The Macmillan Co., 1938), a Kappa Delta Pi Lecture. © 1938 Kappa Delta Pi. Used by permission.

Values: The Implicit Curriculum by Linda Inlay. From *Educational Leadership* 60, no. 6 (March 2003): 69–71. © 2003 Educational Leadership. Used by permission of the author and publisher.

CHAPTER 2: Social Forces: Present and Future

Dialogue across Cultures: Communicating with Diverse Families by Arti Joshi, Jody Eberly, & Jean Konzal. From *Multicultural Education* 13, no. 2 (Winter 2005): 11–15. © Caddo Gap Press. Used by permission of the authors and publisher.

High-Stakes Testing and Accountability as Social Constructs across Cultures by Raymond V. Padilla. From *Leaving Children Behind: How "Texas-Style" Accountability Fails Latino Youth,* Angela Valenzuela (Ed.). © 2004 State University of New York Press.

The "Three A's" of Creating an Inclusive Curriculum and Classroom by Tina M. Anctil. Article written by Tina M. Anctil for *Curriculum Planning: A Contemporary Approach,* Eighth Edition, 2006. Used by permission of the author.

The Dimensions of Multicultural Education by James A. Banks. Excerpted from *Cultural Diversity and Education: Foundation, Curriculum, and Teaching.* Boston: Pearson. © 2006 Pearson. Reprinted with the permission of the author.

A Deeper Sense of (Media) Literacy by Cynthia L. Scheibe. From *American Behavioral Scientist* 48, no. 1: 60–68. © 2004 Sage Publications. Reprinted by permission of Sage Publications.

Remembering Capital: On the Connections between French Fries and Education by Michael W. Apple. From *Journal of Curriculum Theorizing* 11, no. 1 (1995): 113–128. © 1998 Corporation for Curriculum Research. Used by permission of the author and publisher.

Teaching Media-Savvy Students about the Popular Media by Kevin Maness. From *English Journal* 93, no. 3 (Jan. 2004): 46–51. © 2004 The National Council of Teachers of English. Reprinted and used with permission.

American Education 20 Years after A Nation at Risk. Harvard Education Press, 2003, pp. 53–68. Copyright © by the President and Fellows of Harvard College. All rights reserved. Reprinted with permission. For more information, please visit www.harvardeducationpress.org.

The Limits of Ideology: Curriculum and the Culture Wars by David T. Gordon. From David T. Gordon (Ed.), *A Nation Reformed: American Education 20 Years after A Nation at Risk*. Harvard Education Press, 2003, pp. 99–113. Copyright © by the President and Fellows of Harvard College. All rights reserved. Reprinted with permission. For more information, please visit www.harvardeducationpress.org.

The Muddle Machine: Confessions of a Textbook Editor by Tamin Ansary. From *Edutopia* 1, no. 2 (Nov. 2004): 30–35. © 2004 edutopia™. Used by permission of the author and publisher.

The Case for Teacher-Led School Improvement by LaQuanda Brown. From *Principal Magazine* (Mar./Apr. 2008): 29–32. © 2008 National Association of Elementary School Principals. Used by permission of the author and publisher.

CHAPTER 6: Curriculum Implementation, Instruction, and Technology

Progressive Organization of Subject Matter by John Dewey. From John Dewey, *Experiences and Education,* pp. 86–93 (New York: The Macmillan Co., 1938), a Kappa Delta Pi Lecture. © Kappa Delta Pi. Used by permission.

Structures in Learning by Jerome S. Bruner. From *Today's Education* 52, no. 3 (March 1963): 26–27. Used by permission of the author and the publisher, the National Education Association.

Nurturing the Life of the Mind by Kathleen Vail. From *American School Board Journal* 188 (Jan. 2001): 18–23. Copyright 2001 National School Boards Association. Reprinted with permission. All rights reserved.

The Many Faces of Leadership by Charlotte Danielson. From *Educational Leadership* 65, no. 1 (2007): 14–19. © 2007 Association for Supervision and Curriculum Development. Reprinted by permission of the author.

Adopt and Adapt: Twenty-First-Century Schools Need Twenty-First-Century Technology by Marc Prensky. From *Edutopia,* Dec. 2005. © 2005 Marc Prensky.

A Movable Feast by John K. Waters. From *T.H.E. Journal* 34, no. 12 (Dec. 2007): 41–44. © 2007 1105 Media Inc. Used by permission of the author and publisher.

Ideals vs. Reality in the Classroom by Carol Lupton. From *Virginia Journal of Education* 94, no. 7 (April 2001): 18–19. Used by permission of the author and publisher.

CHAPTER 7: Curriculum Evaluation

"TestThink"? by Nelson Maylone. From *Phi Delta Kappan* 85, no. 5 (Jan. 2004): 383–386. © 2004 Phi Delta Kappa, Inc. Used by permission of the author and publisher.

You *Can* Teach for Meaning by Jay McTighe, Elliott Seif, & Grant Wiggins. From *Educational Leadership* 62, no. 1 (Sept. 2004): 26–30. © 2004 Association for Supervision and Curriculum Development. Used by permission of the authors and publisher.

Learning to Love Assessment by Carol Ann Tomlinson. From *Educational Leadership* 65, no. 4 (Dec./Jan. 2008): 8–13. © 2008 Association for Supervision and Curriculum Development. Used by permission of the author and publisher.

A Balanced School Accountability Model: An Alternative to High-Stakes Testing by Ken Jones. From *Phi Delta Kappan* 85, no. 8 (April 2004): 584–590. © 2004 Phi Delta Kappa, Inc. Used by permission of the author and publisher.

Using Student Assessment Data to Improve Instruction by Kathryn Parker Boudett, Richard J. Murnane, Elizabeth City, and Liane Moody. From *Phi Delta Kappan* 86, no. 9 (May 2005): 700–707. © 2004 Phi Delta Kappa, Inc. Used by permission of the authors and publisher.

What Is the Purpose of Grades? by James D. Allen. From *The Clearing House* 78, no. 5 (May/June 2005): 218–223. Reprinted with permission of the Helen Dwight Reid Educational Foundation. Published by Heldref Publications. 1319 Eighteenth St., NW, Washington, D.C. 20036-1802. Copyright © 2005.

Time for a Tune-Up: Comprehensive Curriculum Evaluation by Lisa H. Meyers. From *Principal Leadership* 6, no. 1 (Sept. 2005): 27–30. Copyright 2005 National Association of Secondary School Principals. www.principals.org. Reprinted with permission.

CHAPTER 8: Early Childhood and Elementary Curricula

Promoting Altruism in the Classroom by E. H. Mike Robinson III & Jennifer R. Curry. From *Childhood Education* 82, 2 (Winter 2005/2006): 68–73. © 2006 Association for Childhood Education International. Used by permission of the authors and publisher.

Making Instructional Decisions Based on Data: What, How, and Why by Kouider Mokhtari, Catherine A. Rosemary, & Patricia A. Edwards. From *The Reading Teacher* 61, no. 4: 354–359. © 2007 International Reading Association. Used by permission of the authors and publisher.

Implementing a Schoolwide Literacy Framework to Improve Student Achievement by Douglas Fisher & Nancy Frey. From *The Reading Teacher* 61, no. 1: 32–43. © 2007 International Reading Association. Used by permission of the author and publisher.

Why Is Kindergarten an Endangered Species? by Linda H. Plevyak & Kathy Morris. From *The Education Digest* 67, no. 7 (March 2002): 23–26. © 2002 The Education Digest. Used by permission of the author and publisher.

Learning to Read in Kindergarten: Has Curriculum Development Bypassed the Controversies? by Bruce Joyce, Marilyn Hrycauk, & Emily Calhoun, with the Northern Lights Kindergarten Teachers. From *Phi Delta Kappan* 85, no. 2 (Oct. 2003): 126–132. © 2003 Phi Delta Kappa, Inc. Used by permission of the author and publisher.

Building a Community in Our Classroom: The Story of Bat Town, U.S.A. by Andrea McGann Keech. From *Social Education* 65, no. 4 (May/June 2001): 232–236. © 2001 National Council for the Social Studies. Reprinted by permission.

CHAPTER 9: Middle-Level Curricula

This We Believe: Successful Schools for Young Adolescents by National Middle School Association. From *National Middle School Association Position Statement,* www.nmsa.org. © 2008 National Middle School Association. Reprinted with permission of the author and publisher.

Mayhem in the Middle: Why We Should Shift to K–8 by Cheri Pierson Yecke. From *Educational Leadership* 63, no. 7 (April 2006): 20–25. © 2006 Association for Supervision and Curriculum Development. Used by permission of the author and publisher.

Guess Again: Will Changing the Grades Save Middle-Level Education? by James Beane & Richard Lipka. From *Educational Leadership* 63, no. 7 (April 2006): 26–30. © 2006 by Association for Supervision and Curriculum Development. Used by permission of the authors.

The Homework Wars by David Skinner. Excerpted from *The Public Interest* 154 (Winter 2004): 49–60. © 2004 The Public Interest. Used by permission of the author and publisher.

Building Developmental Assets to Promote Success in School and in Life by Peter C. Scales & Judy Taccogna. Excerpted from *NASSP Bulletin* 84, no. 619 (Nov. 2000): 69–78. Copyright 2000 National Association of Secondary School Principals. Reprinted with permission.

Intentional Curriculum Planning in an Age of Accountability: Explorer Middle School's Approach by Donald E. Larsen & Tariq T. Akmal. Article written by Donald E. Larsen and Tariq T. Akmal for *Curriculum Planning: A Contemporary Approach,* Eighth Edition, 2006. Used by permission of the authors.

Teaming for Better School Climate and Improved Achievement by Luanne L. Kokolis. From *Middle School Journal* 39, no. 1 (Sept. 2007): 9–15. © 2007 by National Middle School Association. Reprinted with permission.

CHAPTER 10: High School Curricula

Becoming Citizens of the World by Vivien Stewart. From *Educational Leadership* 64, no. 7 (April 2007): 8–14. © 2007 by Association for Supervision and Curriculum Development. Used by permission of the author and publisher.

Engaging the Disengaged Student: Research Shows Why Some Are Immersed in Learning While Others Are Indifferent by Susan Black. Excerpted from the *American School Board Journal* 190, no. 12 (Dec. 2003): 58–71. Copyright 2003 National School Boards Association. Reprinted with permission. All rights reserved.

Possible Selves: Identity-Based Motivation and School Success by Daphna Oyserman. Excerpted from a chapter that appeared in *Self-Processes, Learning, and Enabling Human Potential: Dynamic Approaches (HC) (Advances in Self Research),* Herbert W. Marsh, Rhonda G. Craven, & Dennis M. McInerney (Eds.). © 2008 Information Age Publishing. Used by permission of the author and publisher.

Learning the Real-World Skills of the 21st Century by Patricia Joyce. From *Techniques* 83, no. 4 (April 2008): 25–27. © 2008 Association for Career and Technical Education. Used by permission of the author and publisher.

Can Depth Replace Coverage in the High School Curriculum? by Fred M. Newmann. From *Phi Delta Kappan* 66, no. 5 (January 1988): 345–348. © 1988 Phi Delta Kappa. Used by permission of the author and publisher.

Going the Extra Mile to Smooth the Transition to High School by Hugh Campbell. From *Principal Leadership* 1, no. 6 (Feb. 2001): 36–40. © 2001 The National Association of Secondary School Principals. Reprinted with permission.

A Tale of Two Curriculums by Mira Reisberg. Article written by Mira Reisberg for *Curriculum Planning: A Contemporary Approach,* Eighth Edition, 2006. Used by permission of the author.

Name Index

Subject Index

583

585